SHADOW & LIGHT

Literature and

the Life of Faith

SECOND EDITION

Shadow & Light

Literature and the Life of Faith

DARRYL TIPPENS · JEANNE MURRAY WALKER · STEPHEN WEATHERS ·
Pepperdine University   *University of Delaware*   *Abilene Christian University*

Second Edition

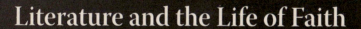

A·C·U
PRESS

SHADOW AND LIGHT:
Literature and the Life of Faith

Second Edition

A·C·U
PRESS
ACU Box 29138
Abilene, TX 79699
www.acu.edu/acupress

Source scanning, correction & preparation · Linda Childers
Cover · Fritz Miller
Book design & typesetting · William Rankin

The cover and section dividers feature *The Repentant Magdalene*, ca 1640, oil on canvas, by Georges de La Tour. Used by special permission of the Ailsa Mellon Bruce Fund. Image copyright © 2004 Board of Trustees, National Gallery of Art, Washington, DC. All other rights reserved

This book is set in Adobe® Warnock™ Pro 10/13, an OpenType® font drawn by Robert Slimbach and issued in 2000. Notes and numbering are set in Adobe® Myriad® Pro 8/9, a font designed by Slimbach and Carol Twombly which was originally issued in 1992 and issued as an OpenType font in 2000. This book was composed in Adobe® InDesign™.

ISBN 0-89112-069-6

LCCN 2004108892

❦ 10 9 8 7 6 5 4 3 2 1

Contents

Creation, fall, redemption
create gospel message

Acknowledgments

THIS EDITION OWES A GREAT DEBT to more colleagues than we can name. We are particularly grateful to the many teachers, students, and general readers who offered comments on the first edition and who inspired us to produce a more expansive second edition. We are grateful to Thom Lemmons, director of the ACU Press, who not only encouraged and supported our vision from first to last, but who took on much of the labor of securing copyright permissions. Linda Childers provided enormous support through her indefatigable scanning, correction, and preparation of the new texts for this edition. William Rankin has earned our everlasting gratitude for offering his multifaceted gifts, including book design, typesetting, glosses, and superb proofreading. We recognize the many contributions of the faculty of the English Department of Abilene Christian University who contributed to the anthology in countless ways—writing headnotes, suggesting selections, proofreading texts, and generally encouraging the project along at every turn. We are particularly grateful to George W. Walton, Gay Barton, Dana McMichael, and Steven Moore who wrote headnotes for the Second Edition. Dinora Cardoso, Associate Professor of Spanish at Pepperdine University, provided translations and editorial advice on the Spanish passages in Horton Foote's *Talking Pictures*. We must also express our appreciation to Nancy Shankle, chair of the ACU Department of English, for her generous support and constant encouragement.

We also express our great thanks to the numerous contemporary authors who have encouraged our project by offering positive comments and granting permission to include their works, including Robert Fink, Horton Foote, Al Haley, Tony Harrison, Walt McDonald, and Larry Woiwode, among others. David Bevington deserves our special praise for permitting us to include abbreviated versions of his notes to his superb edition of *Hamlet*. Jeanne wishes to thank E. Daniel Larkin III for offering his keen eye to the many hundreds of pages in this text. The three of us also applaud our loyal spouses who served by standing, waiting, and encouraging us along the way.

This anthology has had many other friends along the way; we regret that we cannot name them all here; but we trust that these splendid lovers of the written word will know who they are, will forgive our oversight, will enjoy this new edition, and will share it with friends, family, and students, just as they did the first.

Darryl Tippens
Jeanne Murray Walker
Stephen Weathers

January 2005

Preface to the Second Edition

As we put the finishing touches on the Second Edition of *Shadow and Light*, we take note of a revolution that has been occurring in universities and colleges, which we believe necessarily will affect textbooks in literature and writing courses. Elizabeth Tisdell has noted that academies and the professors who teach within them are increasingly breaking taboos of silence regarding faith and spirituality. If you type the words "spirituality and higher education" into an Internet search engine, you will discover an astounding number of websites. Books, conferences, and symposia are sprouting like mushrooms in spring. Many voices are calling for a new kind of higher education that is more holistic and spiritually focused. C. B. Dillard *et al.* have observed that "The heretofore silencing of the spiritual voice through privileging the academic voice is increasingly being drowned out by the emphatic chorus of those whose underlying visions of truth cry out, 'We are a spiritual people.'"

The current edition of *Shadow and Light* participates in this exhilarating reawakening. It includes stories, poems, essays, and plays which take seriously spiritual and ethical questions. We are convinced that the best way to restore a deep and authentic spirituality is to reconnect the awakening religious impulse of readers with the literary traditions of spiritual quest. While the Enlightenment birthed inestimably great philosophy and literature, that literature accounts for only a part of human experience. To enrich this tradition, *Shadow and Light* reaches back to some of the earliest recorded literature that deals seriously with spiritual questions and traces that literature through our own time. We hope that by giving voice to this tradition of spiritual writing, *Shadow and Light* will act as a bridge between great English literature and the all-too-often unsatisfied longing of readers. Not narrowly doctrinaire but engaged with the eternal questions of faith and doubt, human suffering, ethical behavior, and theodicy, this anthology offers a window into the ways both believers and non-believers have struggled since the Middle Ages with the big questions.

Many of the texts published here are absent from the typical anthologies available on the market. For example, when we wanted our own students to read Leo Tolstoy's masterpiece "How Much Land Does a Man Need?" we could not find it within the covers of a major anthology. Tolstoy's powerful tale of greed was not always held in such low esteem. James Joyce called it "the greatest story that the literature of the world knows." This kind of omission might be passed over as an anomaly, but we encountered the same predicament closer to home. Many of Emily Dickinson's finest poems concern her religious experience, yet they have been among her most neglected. These poems seem as artistically mature as her poems on despair and death, but again they rarely have been anthologized. The intense religious experiences of more contemporary writers like Denise Levertov, we found, were similarly under-represented in anthologies.

As we surveyed the scene, we concluded that many such works of literature, both old and new, have fallen through the cracks not because they are artistically inferior, but because for half a century they have not conformed to contemporary cultural assumptions about the meaning and purpose of life. It is not so much that these words are resented or suppressed as that they have become difficult to fathom. By the 1950s many scholars and writers had, for a variety of reasons, felt compelled to make a break with their own religious pasts. Simone Weil warned that this trend was resulting in "the growing weakness and almost disappearance, of the idea of value." Avoiding ethical zealotry, Weil was nevertheless firm: "Writers do not have to be professors of morals, but they do have to express the human condition." Now after this long period of fashionable moral ambivalence, decades after some of the works we publish here had disappeared from standard anthologies, they make particularly fresh and insightful reading.

The spiritual revolution in higher education has aided and is being aided by the recent opening of the cultural floodgates to multicultural texts. As bell hooks argues, "The spiritual awakening that is slowly taking place counterculturally will become more of a daily norm as we all willingly break mainstream cultural taboos that silence or erase our passion for spiritual practice." Tisdell has noted that the new acknowledgement of the spiritual in education has led to cultural relevance. Education becomes "emancipatory." People of color, in particular, are fueling this change. The Second Edition of *Shadow and Light* participates in this way also in the revolution of the last decade. It contains many new selections by writers of color.

Finally, in this more inclusive Second Edition we have welcomed into the fold of great spiritual literature some texts that were not included in our first edition, but which users of that edition have requested and which seem too important to leave out – that is, scripts for the theatre. Plays are recipes for the stage, and they exist most fully in performance rather than in the act of reading. However, whether experienced communally or read privately, drama in the West has maintained a steady (though often controversial) devotion to spiritual concerns. Descending from the religious rituals of the Greeks, drama has been particularly crucial in the spiritual and cultural life of people who may not have been able to read. We have included three scripts in their entirety in this Edition.

In summary, we hope this Edition of *Shadow and Light* will be useful in a number of different ways to our colleagues who teach. While its focus is on the Judeo-Christian, within that tradition many religious perspectives are represented. Including a broad spectrum of genres ranging from essays to drama, the anthology invites reflection on a wide variety of ethical issues and moral dilemmas. It might be used to complement other texts that take a more "value-neutral" approach. It can be used as the single text in either a writing or literature course. As with the First Edition, we also expect many will read this collection for personal enrichment.

With this Edition of *Shadow and Light*, then, we join many of our colleagues in a joyful celebration of works that deal with faith and spiritual questions. Through such readings we hope that students will encounter – as Jean-Paul Sartre expressed it – a moral imperative beating at the heart of the æsthetic imperative – that they will learn of the many ways people express the wonder and mystery of God in the world.

Introduction

And we must extinguish the candle, put out the light and
    relight it;
Forever must quench, forever relight the flame.
Therefore we thank Thee for our little light, that is dappled
    with shadow

✤   ✤   ✤

And we thank Thee that darkness reminds us of light.
O Light Invisible, we give Thee thanks for Thy great glory!

T. S. Eliot, "The Rock"

THE FRENCH NOVELIST Albert Camus once observed that the hallmark trait of his age was its wholesale rejection of the spiritual dimension. "We live in an unsacrosanct moment in history," the writer contends; "whole societies have wanted to discard the sacred." For many, Camus's statement has been borne out by experience. With the passing of each decade, the perception deepened that writers had less to say about faith or the possibility of the transcendent. A parallel development took place in educational institutions. The eclipse of mystery and the sacred occurred in many North American classrooms as students encountered fewer and fewer works concerned with the spiritual quest. As a result, a whole generation of readers has been dispossessed. Now, when an assigned literary text engages religious concerns, teachers are often reluctant to make explicit the spiritual themes of writers who, whatever their faith or philosophy, devoted much of their lives to exploring such subjects in their work.

Some scholars and critics still claim that literature can only be about our lives as material creatures. Literature about "the above and beyond," the transcendent, or the God of Scripture

1

is still sometimes seen as peculiar and anachronistic. The view goes something like this: Religion used to be an important element of our culture, but the writing of religious literature ended somewhere around the Renaissance (possibly with Donne or Milton); there were a few holdouts into the nineteenth century, but it's all over now. God is dead as far as significant literature is concerned.

This anthology argues otherwise. It is an attempt to restore what has been missing for fifty years in anthologies of literature. It is an attempt to right the balance and to supply to students, faculty, and general readers the tradition which began disappearing over fifty years ago

As many readers are realizing, literature about the life of faith is, in fact, richly diverse and of high quality; and, against all odds, it continues to be produced at a remarkable rate. No matter if we are living in a secular, "post-Christendom" age – stars are best seen in a dark sky. This anthology is a reminder that just as Western literature began with the quest to know the *Logos* (in Greek terms) or *Yahweh* (in biblical terms), so today a number of writers continue to seek to know God and his creation. Václav Havel, the great Czech playwright and statesman, articulated the challenge and opportunity for the person who seeks faith in our largely pessimistic age:

> There are times when we must sink to the bottom of our
> misery to understand truth, just as we must descend to
> the bottom of a well to see the stars in broad daylight.

Deep in the shadows of a secular society, we are strategically positioned to rediscover the light of the sacred. In T. S. Eliot's terms, "darkness reminds us of light."

WHAT IS THE LITERATURE OF SHADOW AND LIGHT?

FOR THE MOST PART, the readings which follow are not "spiritual classics" in the usual sense of the term. They are significant, artistically mature poems, stories, essays, and plays by recognized writers, some Jewish, some Christian, some of an uncertain or undeclared stance. What they hold in common is an attitude: they honor the spiritual quest. Whether these texts mention God directly or not – and many profoundly religious works, like the Book of Esther, do not – these works strive to present human dilemmas in their full roundness, including a significant element of mystery. Almost relentlessly, they are concerned with the search for truth, not as an exercise in futility, but as a purposeful activity of the highest order. At the same time, these authors are not afraid to ask the tough questions which people on a quest must have the courage to face. We might say these are works by writers who have gazed into the heavens for themselves. Having seen the celestial designs that others have discarded or missed, they report their findings through story, poem, meditation, and essay.

HOW SHOULD YOU APPROACH THESE READINGS?

FIRST, WELCOME THE CHALLENGES inherent in these selections. Unfortunately, many people avoid "religious" literature on the grounds that it is predictable, closed, or even propagandistic. This complaint may hold for many popular religious publications, but nothing could be further from the truth when it comes to the best works in the tradition. Mature religious art invites us to ask questions and then to move about within the space such questions open up for us. The German poet Rainer Maria Rilke's advice to a young poet seems appropriate for readers of *Shadow and Light*:

> Have patience with everything unresolved in your heart and try to love the questions themselves as if they were locked rooms or books written in a very foreign language…. And the point is, to live everything. Live the questions now.

But asking questions isn't all we are required to do. Often great works stir our moral and religious imaginations. A literary text may ultimately break its æsthetic bounds in order to interrogate the reader and demand a personal response.

Reading Tolstoy and Dickinson, Dillard and Malamud, Levertov and Singer is intellectually challenging, but it can also be potentially life-changing. "Although literature is one thing and morality a quite different one," Jean-Paul Sartre once observed, "at the heart of the æsthetic imperative we discern the moral imperative." Some narratives, like the carefully crafted parables of Jesus, demand more than æsthetic appreciation; they demand deep thought and a changed life. Stories like Dostoyevsky's "The Grand Inquisitor" and Tolstoy's "How Much Land Does a Man Need?" in the final analysis, are not about others, but about you and me. When writers aim their words at the heart, the encounter will not leave the reader indifferent or merely "entertained." Action will be the harvest of a good reading.

WHY SO MANY DOUBTS?

THE LITERATURE OF FAITH is by its very nature dialectical. Belief and doubt are as often as not near neighbors both in the Bible and in the classics. One need only think of Jeremiah, Job, or Shakespeare's King Lear to see that faith can be on speaking terms with confusion and ambiguity. In the earthly realm inhabited by such richly drawn characters, life is not a single thread, but a tapestry, as Denise Levertov describes in her poem "Web":

> Intricate and untraceable
> weaving and interweaving,
> dark strand with light...

Should we be so surprised that the literature of faith is honest about the shadows of doubt that flicker in our hearts?

Flannery O'Connor once singled out the prayer of the desperate father of an epileptic boy who cries – "I believe; help my unbelief!" (Mark 9:24) – calling it "the most natural and most human and most agonizing prayer in all the gospels, and ... the foundation prayer of faith." The literature of belief, in the same way, if it is any good at all, owns up to its doubts, even when the cracks run all the way to the bedrock of belief: Why does tragedy befall the innocent? Why do my prayers appear to go unanswered? What is justice? Who is my neighbor? Where did I come from? Where am I going?

This kind of literature also asks other questions that skeptics seldom consider: How does one account for so much beauty and goodness in the world? Why, in an age that exalts the "individual," do some people still sacrifice themselves for others? Why am I the recipient of gifts I did not earn and do not deserve? Are there blessings from beyond, or are even the most beneficial wonders of life mere accident?

Sometimes, the literature of faith asks daring questions, even to the point of laying charges at the feet of God: "Why does the way of the guilty prosper?" Jeremiah the prophet demands. "Why do all who are treacherous thrive?" To the primly pious, questions such as Jeremiah's are disturbing, even blasphemous. But being free to argue with God may be the only way back to faith. Dwelling in the House of the Lord may require a walk through the Valley of the Shadow of Death.

Elie Wiesel's works are among the best contemporary examples of the proximity of faith and doubt. Wiesel sets his masterful play, *The Trial of God*, in a Ukrainian village, the site of a terrible *pogrom* which almost completely wipes out the Jewish population in 1649. One character, Mendel, keeps protesting, "And [where is] God in all this?" Questioning God's absence or injustice can be a form of pure prayer. In *The Town Beyond the Wall*, Wiesel presents Pedro, a man who suffers unspeakable affliction. Pedro cries out:

> I want to blaspheme and I can't quite manage it. I go up against Him, I shake my fist, I froth with rage, but it's still a way of telling Him that He's there, that He exists, that He's never the same twice, that denial itself is an offering to His grandeur. The shout becomes a prayer in spite of me.

A shout of protest fading into prayer – this is the essence of shadow and light. This is the dialectic of faith.

WHY DON'T WE SEE BETTER?

HENRY JAMES'S ADVICE to writers is much quoted: "Try to be one of those on whom nothing is lost." The novelist's admonition is equally applicable to readers. To handle the literature of faith with success, one must read with extraordinary attention. "Do you have eyes, and fail to see? Do you have ears, and fail to hear?" Jesus asked those who gathered about him. These are not idle, rhetorical questions but solemn warnings that echo down to our day. Most of us "see" rather poorly. We not only fail to notice the night sky, we don't even see the important details in a story or a poem, facets of a glittering jewel just inches from us, that might change our understanding of the world. "The secret of seeing is, then, the pearl of great price," writes Annie Dillard.

Why don't we see better? We do not, in part, because frameworks of bias obscure our vision. Our formulaic assumptions may keep us from recognizing the good, the true, or the beautiful. Tennyson recognizes that our universe and its Maker are much bigger and more wondrous than our conceptual frameworks allow us to see:

> Our little systems have their day;
> They have their day and cease to be;
> They are but broken lights of thee,
> And thou, O Lord, art more than they.

Similarly, as O'Connor reminds a young man studying to become a poet, "You can't fit the Almighty into your intellectual categories." One needs a "sense of the immense sweep of creation, ... of how incomprehensible God must necessarily be to be the God of heaven and earth." Effective reading, then, requires open-mindedness. Ernst Bloch's aphorism — "Seek and ye shall wonder" — is both a rule of life and a guide for effective reading.

Of course, all readers are products of a particular age, culture, and upbringing, factors as inescapable as our genetic inheritance. Who we are and where we are in time necessarily affect the experience of literature. Still, this ought not to leave us unthinking slaves to the present age. With a spirit of adventure, imagination, and generosity, the motivated reader can enter the wonderful kingdom of literary experience, making familiar what is strange and new. C. S. Lewis says:

> To enjoy our full humanity we ought, so far as is possible, to contain within us potentially at all times, and on occasion actualize, all the modes of feeling and thinking through which [humans have] passed. You must, so far as in you lies, become an Achæan chief while reading Homer, a medieval knight while reading Malory, and an eighteenth century Londoner while reading Johnson. Only thus will you be able to judge the work "in the same spirit that its author writ"....

Because there is much in this foreign realm of literature that you might fail to understand, the challenge is to learn the idioms, the ways, "the elements" of this literary world as best you can. It is not easy to train your eyes and your heart to see deeply. Denis

Diderot declares: "Learning to see is not like learning a new language. It's like learning language for the first time." Some advice, then. Keep pen and paper handy; annotate your text; record your responses in a journal or notebook. Engage your classmates and friends in discussions of what you read. Above all, expect surprise, mystery, and wonder like a child learning to put together the first words that will be hers for a lifetime.

ARE WE HAVING FUN YET?

A FINAL TIP ON READING these works: enjoy the trip. Although literature often deals with serious and enduring questions, it was never meant to be an exercise in boredom or obscurity. Literature is a form of play, sometimes serious, sometimes amusing, often both. "Blessed are they that play, for theirs is the kingdom of heaven," exclaims Dickinson, and for good reason. In the guise of a word game we may catch a spell-binding glimpse of our lives. If this happens, literature becomes more than recreation; it becomes re-creation, touching our hearts, reshaping our moral imagination, and – sometimes – moving us to decisive action.

Unfortunately, many people assume that since religion and ethics are "serious" matters, literature concerned with faith or moral conduct must be ever earnest, ever stern. Yet the gospel by definition is always "glad tidings," and God's original intent for humanity has always been profound delight. "What is all this juice and all this joy?" Hopkins asks in his sonnet "Spring." It is, he replies, "A strain of the earth's sweet being in the beginning / In Eden garden." If these selections do not bring some pleasure, then they will have been misread.

SO WHAT HAVE WE LOST?

M OST OF US HAVE GROWN UP in the glare of the city. We are accustomed to pulsing neon, well-lit sidewalks, and cross-town freeways bathed in mercury-vapor lamps. Yet we pay dearly for these privileges. Humanity's lights obliterate the shining evidence of a vast cosmos. Beneath our artificial halo few of us have opportunity to see the marvelous constellations of Leo, Andromeda, or Pegasus. Though we may have spent years staring into a luminous electronic tube, we know far less about the heavens than did Plato, Chaucer, or Columbus.

So what have we lost? Not knowing the coordinates of Cassiopeia or Orion is perhaps no tragedy, but what if the modern environment we have constructed for ourselves, both physical and intellectual, has caused us to lose sight of other elements of our universe, of which the night sky is only one example? What happens if we lose sight of whole worlds of understanding that are basic to our humanity? What if we forget our origin and our destination? What if we forget about mystery and the experience of the sacred? Poets, writers, and artists are among those people who care deeply about such questions. Emily Dickinson once said that "mystery" is the greatest need of the human soul, yet we forget to thank God for it.

Our society is in crisis today, not because it lacks technical knowledge, tools, or skills, but because its citizens have lost touch with their origin and destination. Without a past, a future, or an "above," they do not remember where they are. Shadow and Light is an invitation to find ourselves, reorient ourselves, and to be thankful for "our little light, that is dappled with shadow." This anthology is an invitation not only to remember what it means to be human in this shadowy world, but also to imagine what creation once was and what it can be, by the grace of God. Too much has been eclipsed by the secular world. It is time for a bigger, fuller vision. As Hopkins and Vaughan knew, gazing into that deep, dazzling darkness of the Welsh night sky, there is much to behold:

> Look at the stars! look, look up at the skies!
> O look at all the fire-folk sitting in the air.
> The bright boroughs, the circle-citadels there!

✦ ✦ ✦

> I saw eternity the other night
> Like a great ring of pure and endless light,
> All calm as it was bright...

Nonfiction

John Donne

⟨ 1 5 7 2 – 1 6 3 1 ⟩

Donne, the most celebrated English clergyman of the 17th century, became seriously ill in the winter of 1623. Through a richly textured sentence structure, replete with vivid and memorable metaphors, Donne recorded his own private experience of suffering in a set of meditations entitled Devotions Upon Emergent Occasions (1624). *Louis Martz defines the central motif of the meditation as "an interior drama in which a man projects a self upon a mental stage, and there comes to understand that self in the light of the divine presence." In "Meditation 17" Donne views his illness as a form of treasure that can be used to bring the Christian soul nearer to its destination – heaven. The writer is somewhat traditional in saying that suffering is educational, teaching us that we are not self-secure, for God "is our only security." However, his colorful, dramatic figures of speech make "Meditation 17" one of the most original – and memorable – interpretations of human affliction in the English language.*

MEDITATION 17

Nunc lento sonitu dicunt, Morieris•

1 PERCHANCE HE FOR WHOM THIS BELL• tolls may be so ill, as that he knows not it tolls for him; and perchance I may think myself so much better than I am, as that they who are about me, and see my state, may have caused it to toll for me, and I know not that. The church is catholic, universal, so are all her actions; all that she does belongs to all. When she baptizes a child, that action concerns me; for that child is thereby connected to that head which is my head too, and ingrafted into that body• whereof I am a member. And when she buries a man, that action concerns me. All mankind is of one author, and is

Nunc ... Morieris •
literally, "Now, with slow sounding, they say 'you [singular] shall die'" (Latin)

this bell • passing bell, sounded for the dying

body • the church

13

one volume; when one man dies, one chapter is not torn out
of the book, but translated into a better language; and every
chapter must be so translated; God employs several translators;
some pieces are translated by age, some by sickness, some by
war, some by justice; but God's hand is in every translation,
and his hand shall bind up all our scattered leaves again, for
that library where every book shall lie open to one another.
As therefore the bell that rings to a sermon calls not upon the
preacher only, but upon the congregation to come, so this bell
calls us all; but how much more me, who am brought so near
the door by this sickness.

suit · a dispute taken to court

estimation · self-esteem

There was a contention as far as a suit* (in which piety and
dignity, religion and estimation,* were mingled) which of the
religious orders should ring to prayers first in the morning; and
it was determined, that they should ring first that rose earliest.
If we understand aright the dignity of this bell that tolls for our
evening prayer, we would be glad to make it ours by rising early,
in that application, that it might be ours as well as his, whose
indeed it is. The bell doth toll for him that thinks it doth; and

intermit · to cease temporarily or periodically

though it intermit* again, yet from that minute that that occasion
wrought upon him, he is united to God. Who casts not up his eye
to the sun when it rises? But who takes off his eye from a comet
when that breaks out? Who bends not his ear to any bell which
upon any occasion rings? But who can remove it from that bell
which is passing a piece of himself out of this world?

main · main part of the continent, mainland

● No man is an island, entire of itself; every man is a piece of
the continent, a part of the main.* If a clod be washed away by
the sea, Europe is the less, as well as if a promontory were, as
well as if a manor of thy friend's or of thine own were: any man's
death diminishes me, because I am involved in mankind, and
therefore never send to know for whom the bell tolls; it tolls for
thee. Neither can we call this a begging of misery, or a borrowing
of misery, as though we were not miserable enough of ourselves,
but must fetch in more from the next house, in taking upon us
the misery of our neighbors.

Truly it were an excusable covetousness if we did, for affliction is a treasure, and scarce any man hath enough of it. No man
hath affliction enough that is not matured and ripened by it, and
made fit for God by that affliction.

5   If a man carry treasure in bullion,* or in a wedge of gold, and have none coined into current monies, his treasure will not defray* him as he travels. Tribulation is treasure in the nature of it, but it is not current money* in the use of it, except we get nearer and nearer our home, heaven, by it. Another man may be sick too, and sick to death, and this affliction may lie in his bowels, as gold in a mine, and be of no use to him; but this bell, that tells me of his affliction, digs out and applies that gold to me, if by this consideration of another's danger I take mine own into contemplation, and so secure myself, by making my course to my God, who is our only security.

bullion · gold or silver in bulk, before it is turned into coin

defray · to pay for expenses

current money · currency, coins

John Bunyan

◀ 1 6 2 8 – 1 6 8 8 ▶

Born near Bedford, England, John Bunyan acquired a basic educa-tion while also learning his father's trade as a brazier. At age 16 he was drafted into the Puritan cause in a civil war against Charles I. Bunyan saw no actual combat. But after leaving the army at age 18, he quickly found himself in a more serious battle regarding the state of his salvation. Before the civil war, he had been a conforming member of the national Church of England; but after the war and his marriage, his sensibilities had become more Puritan. Attending the Nonconformist church in Bedford, Bunyan faced questions that led to a direct confrontation with the Word of God, an engagement compellingly described in Grace Abounding to the Chief of Sinners *(1666). Later in* The Pilgrim's Progress *(1678), he would present the warfare of the universal Christian soldier in a thicker, more involved allegorical style. But in this spiritual autobiography Bunyan provides an unadorned though powerful account of his own personal conver-sion. In the preface he writes, "I could … have stepped into a style much higher than this … and could have adorned all things more than here I have seemed to do, but I dare not. God did not play in convincing of me, the devil did not play in tempting of me, neither did I play when I sunk as into a bottomless pit …; wherefore I may not play in my relating of these experiences, but be plain and simple, and lay down the thing as it was." He did not consider spiritual warfare to be an intellectual pastime but a matter of life and death. It is not surpris-ing, then, that he wrote* Grace Abounding *from jail while serving a twelve-year term for preaching the Word without a license.*

from GRACE ABOUNDING TO THE CHIEF OF SINNERS

[126] 1   I<small>T WOULD BE TOO LONG</small> for me here to stay, to tell you in particular how God did set me down in all the things of Christ,

Bunyan's original paragraph numbers appear in brackets

17

and how he did, that he might so do, lead me into his words, 1 [126]
yea and also how he did open them unto me, make them shine
before me, and cause them to dwell with me, talk with me, and
comfort me over and over, both of his own being, and the being
of his Son, and Spirit, and Word, and Gospel.

Only this, as I said before, I will say unto you again, that in 2 [127]
general he was pleased to take this course with me, first to suffer
me to be afflicted with temptation concerning them, and then
reveal them to me; as sometimes I should lie under great guilt
for sin, even crushed to the ground therewith, and then the Lord
would show me the death of Christ, yea and so sprinkle my conscience with his blood, that I should find, and that before I was
aware, that in that conscience, where but just now did reign and
rage the law, even there would rest and abide the peace and love
of God through Christ.

Now had I an evidence, as I thought, of my salvation from 3 [128]
Heaven, with many golden seals thereon, all hanging in my sight;
now could I remember this manifestation, and the other discovery of grace with comfort; and should often long and desire that
the last day were come, that I might for ever be inflamed with the
sight, and joy, and communion of him, whose head was crowned
with thorns, whose face was spit on, and body broken, and soul
made an offering for my sins: for whereas before I lay continually
trembling at the mouth of hell; now methought I was got so far
therefrom, that I could not, when I looked back, scarce discern
it; and O thought I, that I were fourscore years old now, that I
might die quickly, that my soul might be gone to rest.

But before I had got thus far out of these my temptations, 4 [129]
I did greatly long to see some ancient godly man's experience,
who had writ some hundred of years before I was born; for, for
those who had writ in our days, I thought (but I desire them now
to pardon me) that they had writ only that which others felt, or
else had, through the strength of their wits and parts, studied to
answer such objections as they perceived others were perplexed
with, without going down themselves into the deep. Well, after
many such longings in my mind, the God in whose hands are
all our days and ways, did cast into my hand, one day, a book
of Martin Luther,˙ his comment on the Galatians,˙ so old that it
was ready to fall piece from piece, if I did but turn it over. Now

Martin Luther · German
priest (1483–1546) who
became one of the
primary voices of the
Protestant Reformation

a book … Galatians ·
an English translation of
Luther's commentary on
Galatians was published
in 1575

[129] 4 I was pleased much that such an old book had fallen into my hand; the which, when I had but a little way perused, I found my condition in his experience, so largely and profoundly handled, as if his book had been written out of my heart; this made me marvel: for thus thought I, this man could not know anything of the state of Christians now, but must needs write and speak of the experience of former days.

[130] 5 Besides, he doth most gravely also, in that book debate of the rise of these temptations, namely, blasphemy, desperation, and the like, shewing that the law of Moses,˙ as well as the devil, death, and hell, hath a very great hand therein; the which at first was very strange to me, but considering and watching, I found it so indeed. But of particulars here I intend nothing, only this methinks I must let fall before all men, I do prefer this book of Mr. Luther upon the Galatians, (excepting the Holy Bible) before all the books that ever I have seen, as most fit for a wounded conscience.

law of Moses · the law of the Old Testament, seen by Luther as emphasizing works over grace

[131] 6 And now I found, as I thought, that I loved Christ dearly. O methought my soul cleaved unto him, my affections cleaved unto him. I felt love to him as hot as fire, and now, as Job˙ said, I thought I should die in my nest; but I did quickly find, that my great love was but little, and that I, who had, as I thought, such burning love to Jesus Christ, could let him go again for a very trifle. God can tell how to abase us; and can hide pride from man. Quickly after this my love was tried to purpose.

Job · Job 29:18

[132] 7 For after the Lord had in this manner thus graciously delivered me from this great and sore temptation, and had set me down so sweetly in the faith of his holy gospel, and had given me such strong consolation and blessed evidence from heaven touching my interest in his love through Christ; the tempter came upon me again, and that with a more grievous and dreadful temptation than before.

[133] 8 And that was to sell and part with this most blessed Christ, to exchange him for the things of this life; for any thing: the temptation lay upon me for the space of a year, and did follow me so continually, that I was not rid of it one day in a month, no not sometimes one hour in many days together, unless I was asleep.

[134] 9 And though, in my judgment, I was persuaded, that those who were once effectually in Christ (as I hoped, through his grace, I had seen myself) could never lose him for ever, "for the land shall not

be sold for ever, for the land is mine," saith God (Leviticus 25:23), 9 [134]
yet it was a continual vexation to me, to think that I should have
so much as one such thought within me against a Christ, a Jesus,
that had done for me as he had done; and yet then I had almost
none others, but such blasphemous ones.

But it was neither my dislike of the thought, nor yet any desire 10 [135]
and endeavour to resist it, that in the least did shake or abate the
continuation or force and strength thereof; for it did always in
almost whatever I thought, intermix itself therewith, in such sort
that I could neither eat my food, stoop for a pin, chop a stick, or
cast mine eye to look on this or that, but still the temptation would
come, *Sell Christ for this, or sell Christ for that; sell him, sell him.*

Sometimes it would run in my thoughts not so little as a hun- 11 [136]
dred times together, sell him, sell him, sell him; against which,
I may say, for whole hours together I have been forced to stand
as continually leaning and forcing my spirit against it, lest haply
before I were aware, some wicked thought might arise in my
heart that might consent thereto; and sometimes also the tempter
would make me believe I had consented to it, then should I be

rack · a device on
which prisoners were
tied and stretched

as tortured on a rack* for whole days together.

This temptation did put me to such scares lest I should at 12 [137]
sometimes, I say, consent thereto, and be overcome therewith,

gainsay · to speak
against, contradict,
or deny

that by the very force of my mind in labouring to gainsay* and
resist this wickedness, my very body also would be put into action
or motion, by way of pushing or thrusting with my hands or
elbows; still answering, as fast as the destroyer said, *Sell him*,
I will not, I will not, I will not, I will not, no not for thousands,
thousands, thousands of worlds; thus reckoning lest I should in
the midst of these assaults, set too low a value of him, even until
I scarce well knew where I was, or how to be composed again.

At these seasons he would not let me eat my food at quiet, 13 [138]

forsooth · in truth,
indeed

but forsooth,* when I was set at the table at my meat, I must go
hence to pray, I must leave my food now, just now, so counterfeit*

counterfeit ·
fraudulently

holy would this devil be. When I was thus tempted, I should say
in myself, *Now I am at my meat, let me make an end. No*, said he,
you must do it now, or you will displease God, and despise Christ.
Wherefore I was much afflicted with these things; and because
of the sinfulness of my nature, (imagining that these things were
impulses from God) I should deny to do it as if I denied God; and

[138] 13   then should I be as guilty because I did not obey a temptation of the devil, as if I had broken the law of God indeed.

[139] 14   But to be brief, one morning as I did lie in my bed, I was, as at other times, most fiercely assaulted with this temptation, *to sell and part with Christ;* the wicked suggestion still running in my mind, *sell him, sell him, sell him,* as fast as a man could speak; against which also in my mind, as at other times I answered, no, no, not for thousands, thousands, thousands, at least twenty times together; but at last, after much striving, even until I was almost out of breath, I felt this thought pass through my heart, *Let him go if he will!* and I thought also that I felt my heart freely consent thereto. O, the diligence of Satan! O, the desperateness of man's heart!

[140] 15   Now was the battle won, and down fell I, as a bird that is shot from the top of a tree, into great guilt and fearful despair; thus getting out of my bed, I went moping into the field, but God knows with as heavy a heart as mortal man, I think, could bear; where for the space of two hours, I was like a man bereft of life, and as now past all recovery, and bound over to eternal punishment.

[141] 16   And withal, that scripture did seize upon my soul, "Or profane person, as Esau, who for one morsel of meat sold his birthright; for you know how that afterwards when he would have inherited the blessing, he was rejected, for he found no place of repentance, though he sought it carefully with tears" (Hebrews 12:16–17).

[142] 17   Now was I as one bound, I felt myself shut up unto the judgment to come; nothing now for two years together would abide with me, but damnation, and an expectation of damnation: I say, nothing now would abide with me but this, save some few moments for relief, as in the sequel you will see.

[143] 18   These words were to my soul like fetters of brass to my legs, in the continual sound of which I went for several months together. But about ten or eleven o'clock one day, as I was walking under a hedge, full of sorrow and guilt God knows, and bemoaning myself for this hard hap,* that such a thought should arise within me, suddenly this sentence bolted in upon me, The blood of Christ remits all guilt; at this I made a stand in my spirit: with that, this word took hold upon me, "The blood of Jesus Christ his Son cleanseth us from all sin" (1 John 1:7).

hap · chance, accident

Now I began to conceive peace in my soul, and methought I
saw as if the tempter did lear* and steal away from me, as being
ashamed of what he had done. At the same time also I had my
sin and the blood of Christ thus represented to me, that my sin
when compared to the blood of Christ, was no more to it, than
this little clot* or stone before me, is to this vast and wide field that
here I see: this gave me good encouragement for the space of two
or three hours, in which time also methought I saw by faith the
Son of God as suffering for my sins. But because it tarried not, I
therefore sunk in my spirit under exceeding guilt again.

But chiefly by the aforementioned scripture, concerning Esau's
selling of his birthright; for that scripture would lie all day long,
all the week long; yea, all the year long in my mind, and hold
me down, so that I could by no means lift up myself; for when
I would strive to turn me to this scripture, or that for relief, still
that sentence would be sounding in me, "For ye know, how that
afterward, when he would have inherited the blessing he found no
place of repentance, though he sought it carefully with tears."

Sometimes, indeed, I should have a touch from that in Luke
22:31, "I have prayed for thee, that thy faith fail not; but it would
not abide upon me:" neither could I indeed, when I considered
my state, find ground to conceive in the least, that there should
be the root of that grace within me, having sinned as I had done.
Now was I tore and rent in heavy case, for many days together.

Then began I with sad and careful heart, to consider of the
nature and largeness of my sin, and to search in the Word of God,
if I could in any place espy a word of promise, or any encouraging sentence by which I might take relief. Wherefore I began to
consider that third of Mark, "All manner of sins and blasphemies
shall be forgiven unto the sons of men, wherewith soever they shall
blaspheme:"* which place, methought, at a blush, did contain a large
and glorious promise for the pardon of high offences; but considering the place more fully, I thought it was rather to be understood,
as relating more chiefly to those who had, while in a natural estate,*
committed such things as there are mentioned, but not to me, who
had not only received light and mercy, but that had both after and
also contrary to that, so slighted Christ as I had done.

I feared therefore that this wicked sin of mine might be that
sin unpardonable, of which he there thus speaketh, "But he that

---

lear · slink

clot · clod

"All … blaspheme" ·
Mark 3:28

natural estate ·
ignorant of the gospel
and, thus, not born again

---

19 [144]

20 [145]

21 [146]

22 [147]

23 [148]

[148] 23   shall blaspheme against the Holy Ghost, hath never forgiveness, but is in danger of eternal damnation" (Mark 3:29): and I did the rather give credit to this, because of that sentence in the Hebrews, "For you know how that afterwards, when he would have inherited the blessing he was rejected; for he found no place of repentance, though he sought it carefully with tears."* For this stuck always with me.

"For you know ... with tears" · see Hebrews 12:17

[149] 24   And now was I both a burden and a terror to myself, nor did I ever so know, as now, what it was to be weary of my life, and yet afraid to die. O, how gladly now would I have been anybody but myself. Any thing but a man! And in any condition but mine now! For it was impossible for me to be forgiven my transgression, and to be saved from wrath to come.

[150] 25   And now began I to labour to call again time that was past, wishing a thousand times twice told, that the day was yet to come, when I should be tempted to such a sin; concluding with great indignation, both against my heart and all assaults, how I would rather have been torn in pieces, than found a consenter thereto: but alas! these thoughts and wishings, and resolvings, were now too late to help me; the thought had passed my heart, God hath let me go, and I am fallen: "O," thought I, "that it was with me as in months past, as in the days when God preserved me!" (Job 29:2).

[151] 26   Then again, being loath and unwilling to perish, I began to compare my sin with others, to see if I could find that any of those that are saved had done as I had done. So I considered David's adultery and murder,* and found them most heinous crimes, and those too committed after light and grace received: but yet by considering, I perceived that his transgressions were only such as were against the law of Moses, from which the Lord Christ could with the consent of his Word deliver him: but mine was against the gospel, yea, against the Mediator thereof; I had sold my Saviour.

David's ... murder · 2 Samuel 11

[152] 27   Now again should I be as if racked upon the wheel;* when I considered, that, besides the guilt that possessed me, I should be *so* void of grace, *so* bewitched: what, thought I, must it be no sin but this? must it needs be the *great transgression* (Psalm 19:13)? must *that* wicked one touch my soul (1 John 5:18)? O what stings did I find in all these sentences!

wheel · a device upon which prisoners were tortured

[153] 28   What? thought I, is there but one sin that is unpardonable? but one sin that layeth the soul without the reach of God's mercy,

and must I be guilty of that? must it needs be that? is there but 28 [153] one sin among so many millions of sins, for which there is no forgiveness, and must I commit this? O! unhappy sin! O unhappy man! These things would so break and confound my spirit, that I could not tell what to do, I thought at times they would have broke my wits, and still to aggravate my misery, that would run in my mind, *You know how that afterwards when he would have inherited the blessing, he was rejected.* O! none knows the terrors of those days but myself.

Peter's sin · see Matthew 26:69–75; Mark 14:66–72; Luke 22:54–62; John 18:25–27

After this, I came to consider of Peter's sin* which he com- 29 [154] mitted in denying his master; and indeed this came nighest to mine, of any that I could find; for he had denied his Saviour as I, and that after light and mercy received; yea, and that too, after warning given him: I also considered that he did it both once and twice, and that after time to consider betwixt. But though I put all these circumstances together, that if possible I might find help, yet I considered again, that his was but a denial of his master, but mine was a selling of my Saviour. Wherefore I thought with myself, that I came nearer to Judas, than either to David or Peter.

Here again, my torment would flame out, and afflict me; yea, 30 [155] it would grind me as it were to powder, to discern the preserva- tion of God towards others, while I fell into the snare: for in my thus considering of other men's sins, and comparing of them with my own, I could evidently see how God preserved them notwithstanding their wickedness, and would not let them, as he had let me, to become a son of perdition.

But O, how did my soul at this time prize the preservation that 31 [156] God did set about his people! Ah how safely did I see them walk, whom God had hedged in! They were within his care, protec- tion, and special providence: though they were full as bad as I by nature, yet because he loved them, he would not suffer them to fall without the range of mercy: but as for me, I was gone, I had done it, he would not preserve me, nor keep me, but suffered me, because I was a reprobate, to fall as I had done. Now did those

God's ... people · see, for example, Ezekiel 11:20 and Deuteronomy 28:9

blessed places, that spake of *God's keeping his people,* shine like the sun before me, though not to comfort me, but to show me the blessed state and heritage of those whom the Lord had blessed.

Now I saw, that as God had his hand in all providences and 32 [157] dispensations that overtook his elect, so he had his hand in all the

[157] 32   temptations that they had to sin against him, not to animate them unto wickedness, but to choose their temptations and troubles for them; and also to leave them, for a time, to such sins only as might not destroy, but humble them; as might not put them beyond, but lay them in the way of the renewing of his mercy. But O, what love, what care, what kindness and mercy did I now see, mixing itself with the most severe and dreadful of all God's ways to his people! He would let David, Hezekiah, Solomon, Peter, and others fall, but he would not let them fall into sin unpardonable, nor into hell for sin. O! thought I, these be the men that God hath loved; these be the men that God, though he chastised them, keeps them in safety by him, and them whom he makes to abide under the shadow of the Almighty.* But all these thoughts added sorrow, grief, and horror to me, as whatever I now thought on, it was killing to me. If I thought how God kept his own, that was killing to me; if I thought of how I was falling myself, that was killing to me. As all things wrought together for the best, and to do good to them that were the called, according to his purpose;* so I thought that all things wrought for my damage, and for my eternal overthrow.

abide … Almighty · see Psalm 91:1

all things … purpose · see Romans 8:28

[158] 33   Then again, I began to compare my sin with the sin of Judas, that if possible I might find that mine differed from that which in truth is unpardonable; and, O thought I, if it should differ from it, though but the breadth of an hair, what a happy condition is my soul in! And by considering, I found that Judas did his intentionally, but mine was against my prayer and strivings; besides, his was committed with much deliberation, but mine in a fearful hurry, on a sudden; all this while I was tossed to and fro, like the locusts,* and driven from trouble to sorrow; hearing always the sound of Esau's fall in mine ears, and of the dreadful consequences thereof.

tossed … locusts · see Psalm 109:23

[159] 34   Yet this consideration about Judas his sin, was for a while some little relief unto me: for I saw I had not, as to the circumstances, transgressed so foully as he: but this was quickly gone again, for I thought with myself there might be more ways than one to commit the unpardonable sin; and that too, there might be degrees of that, as well as of other transgressions: wherefore, for ought I yet could perceive, this iniquity of mine might be such as might never be passed by.

I was often now ashamed, that I should be like such an ugly   35 [160]
man as Judas: I thought also how loathsome I should be unto
all the saints at the day of judgment, insomuch that now I could
scarce see a good man, that I believed had a good conscience, but
I should feel my heart tremble at him, while I was in his presence.
O! now I saw a glory in walking with God, and what a mercy it
was to have a good conscience before him.

I was much about this time tempted to content myself, by   36 [161]
receiving some false opinion; as that there should be no such thing
as a day of judgment, that we should not rise again, and that sin
was no such grievous thing. The tempter suggesting thus, *For if
these things should indeed be true, yet to believe otherwise would
yield you ease for the present. If you must perish, never torment
yourself so much beforehand, drive the thoughts of damning out
of your mind, by possessing your mind with some such conclusions
that Atheists and Ranters* use to help themselves withal.*

Ranters · flourishing in
the 1600s, the Ranters
were *antinomians* – they
believed that moral law
is not binding upon
Christians, who are
forgiven and filled with
the Holy Spirit

But O! when such thoughts have passed through my heart,   37 [162]
how as it were within a step hath death and judgment been in
my view! Methought the judge stood at the door, I was as if 'twas
come already: so that such things could have no entertainment;
but methinks I see by this, that Satan will use any means to keep
the soul from Christ. He loveth not an awakened frame of spirit;
security, blindness, darkness, and error is the very kingdom and
habitation of the wicked one.

Samuel Johnson

⟨1709–1784⟩

Johnson, born into poverty and poor for most of his adulthood, became the pre-eminent literary figure in England, such that the last half of the 18th century is sometimes called The Age of Johnson. His varied output is astonishing: poetry, moralistic essays, a landmark English dictionary, a scholarly edition of Shakespeare's plays, the fable Rasselas *(1759), travel commentary, and literary criticism. His poverty was relieved when the government granted him a pension in 1762. Johnson's personal complexity elicited disdain from some and reverence from others. Prone to depression, he feared insanity. His marriage to a widow twenty years his senior seemed strange to nearly everyone. A large, hulking man with eccentric and often unpleasant habits, he was nevertheless a model of the will to succeed despite handicaps. Laziness and procrastination gave him much trouble in his professional life, and many works were written hurriedly because he had delayed too long. This habit was offset by his prodigious memory, which allowed him to compose in his head, and by his vast reading. One acquaintance said of him, "Johnson knew more books than any man alive." His Christian faith and a keen sense of his own failings kept him humble in outlook. "The Vanity of Human Wishes" (1749), Johnson's poetic meditation on human existence, ends with the idea that mankind can find peace only through religion. James Boswell struck the same note in* The Life of Samuel Johnson *(1791), saying that piety was the "ruling principle" in this writer's life.*

from PRAYERS AND MEDITATIONS

APRIL 25, 1752

1   O LORD, OUR HEAVENLY FATHER, almighty and most merciful God, in whose hands are life and death, who givest and takest away, castest down and raisest up, look with mercy on the

affliction of thy unworthy servant, turn away thine anger from me, 1
and speak peace to my troubled soul. Grant me the assistance and
comfort of thy Holy Spirit, that I may remember with thankfulness
the blessings so long enjoyed by me in the society of my departed

departed wife ·
Elizabeth "Tetty" Johnson
died March 28, 1752

wife˙; make me so to think on her precepts and example, that I
may imitate whatever was in her life acceptable in thy sight, and
avoid all by which she offended Thee. Forgive me, O merciful Lord,
all my sins, and enable me to begin and perfect that reformation
I promised her, and to persevere in that resolution, which she
implored Thee to continue, in the purposes which I recorded in
thy sight, when she lay dead before me, in obedience to thy laws,
and faith in thy word. And now, O Lord, release me from my
sorrow, fill me with just hopes, true faith, and holy consolations,
and enable me to do my duty in that state of life to which Thou
hast been pleased to call me, without disturbance from fruitless
grief, or tumultuous imaginations; that in all my thoughts, words,
and actions, I may glorify thy Holy Name, and finally obtain, what
I hope Thou hast granted to thy departed servant, everlasting joy
and felicity, through our Lord Jesus Christ. Amen.

EASTER EVE, 1761

S INCE THE COMMUNION of last Easter, I have led a life so dis- 2
sipated and useless, and my terrors and perplexities have so
much increased, that I am under great depression and discour-
agement; yet I purpose to present myself before God tomorrow,

break ... reed · see
Isaiah 42:3

with humble hope that he will not break the bruised reed.˙

Come unto me all ye that travail.˙ 2a

Come ... travail ·
Matthew 11:28

I have resolved, I hope not presumptuously, till I am afraid to
resolve again. Yet hoping in God, I steadfastly purpose to lead a
new life. O God, enable me, for Jesus Christ's sake.

WEDNESDAY, MARCH 28, 1770

T HIS IS THE DAY ON WHICH, in 1752, I was deprived of poor 3
dear Tetty. Having left off the practice of thinking on her with
some particular combinations, I have recalled her to my mind
of late less frequently; but when I recollect the time in which
we lived together, my grief for her departure is not abated; and I
have less pleasure in any good that befalls me, because she does

3   not partake it. On many occasions, I think what she would have said or done. When I saw the sea at Brighthelmstone, I wished for her to have seen it with me. But with respect to her, no rational wish is now left, but that we may meet at last where the mercy of God shall make us happy, and perhaps make us instrumental to the happiness of each other. It is now eighteen years.

AUGUST 12, 1784

4   O LORD, MY MAKER AND PROTECTOR, who hast graciously sent me into this world to work out my salvation,· enable me to drive from me all such unquiet and perplexing thoughts as may mislead or hinder me in the practice of those duties which Thou hast required. When I behold the works of thy hands, and consider the course of thy providence, give me grace always to remember that thy thoughts are not my thoughts, nor thy ways my ways.· And while it shall please Thee to continue me in this world, where much is to be done, and little to be known, teach me, by thy Holy Spirit, to withdraw my mind from unprofitable and dangerous enquiries, from difficulties vainly curious, and doubts impossible to be solved. Let me rejoice in the light which Thou hast imparted, let me serve Thee with active zeal and humble confidence, and wait with patient expectation for the time in which the soul which Thou receivest shall be satisfied with knowledge. Grant this, O Lord, for Jesus Christ's sake. Amen.

work ... salvation · see Philippians 2:12

thy thoughts ... ways · see Isaiah 55:8

John Henry Newman

◈(1 8 0 1 – 1 8 9 0)◈

*The tension between the gift of intellect and its potential dangers is
an important theme in Newman's writing. While the development of
one's God-given intellectual faculties is a natural good – a conviction
evidenced by his 1854-1858 term as rector of the newly established
Catholic University of Dublin – Newman also warns that an atheistic
inclination is the natural bent of the fallen, sin-influenced mind. The
latter conviction led him in 1845 to leave the Anglican priesthood,
as well as a position at Oxford University, and to enter the Roman
Catholic church – the only bulwark, Newman felt, that would ultimately stand against the flood of unbelief washing over western Europe.
During a brief youthful infatuation with religious liberalism, the writer
had witnessed the power of the critical faculty ("the all-corroding, all-
dissolving skepticism of the intellect") to undermine Christian doctrine.
Consequently, as he explains in* Apologia Pro Vita Sua *(1864-1865), his
spiritual autobiography, he was led in maturity to accept "the Church's
infallibility, as a provision, adapted by the mercy of the Creator, to
preserve religion in the world, and to restrain that freedom of thought,
which of course in itself is one of the greatest of our natural gifts, and to
rescue it from its own suicidal excesses." Despite his caution, Newman
was an avid champion of liberal education, producing a series of
lectures on the purpose of the college experience, later collected and
entitled* The Idea of a University *(1852). Here Newman argues, against
those who would view the university as a vocational training school,
that true education transcends narrow utilitarian ends.*

from THE IDEA OF A UNIVERSITY

KNOWLEDGE VIEWED IN RELATION TO PROFESSIONAL SKILL

1 TODAY I HAVE CONFINED MYSELF to saying that that training
of the intellect, which is best for the individual himself, best

enables him to discharge his duties to society. The Philosopher, 1
indeed, and the man of the world differ in their very notion, but
the methods, by which they are respectively formed, are pretty
much the same. The Philosopher has the same command of
matters of thought, which the true citizen and gentleman has
of matters of business and conduct. If then a practical end must
be assigned to a University course, I say it is that of training good
members of society. Its art is the art of social life, and its end is
fitness for the world. It neither confines its views to particular
professions on the one hand, nor creates heroes or inspires
genius on the other. Works indeed of genius fall under no art;
heroic minds come under no rule; a University is not a birthplace
of poets or of immortal authors, of founders of schools, leaders
of colonies, or conquerors of nations. It does not promise a generation of Aristotles or Newtons, of Napoleons or Washingtons,
of Raphaels or Shakespeares, though such miracles of nature it
has before now contained within its precincts. Nor is it content
on the other hand with forming the critic or the experimentalist,
the economist or the engineer, though such too it includes within
its scope. But a University training is the great ordinary means
to a great but ordinary end; it aims at raising the intellectual
tone of society, at cultivating the public mind, at purifying the
national taste, at supplying true principles to popular enthusiasm and fixed aims to popular aspiration, at giving enlargement
and sobriety to the ideas of the age, at facilitating the exercise
of political power, and refining the intercourse of private life. It
is the education which gives a man a clear conscious view of
his own opinions and judgments, a truth in developing them,
an eloquence in expressing them, and a force in urging them.
It teaches him to see things as they are, to go right to the point,
skein · a loose coil   to disentangle a skein* of thought, to detect what is sophistical,*
sophistical · associated   and to discard what is irrelevant. It prepares him to fill any post
with sophistry, which is   with credit, and to master any subject with facility. It shows him
characterized by the use   how to accommodate himself to others, how to throw himself
of overly subtle and often   into their state of mind, how to bring before them his own,
misleading arguments   how to influence them, how to come to an understanding with
them, how to bear with them. He is at home in any society, he
has common ground with every class; he knows when to speak
and when to be silent; he is able to converse, he is able to listen;

1 he can ask a question pertinently, and gain a lesson seasonably, when he has nothing to impart himself; he is ever ready, yet never in the way; he is a pleasant companion, and a comrade you can depend upon; he knows when to be serious and when to trifle, and he has a sure tact which enables him to trifle with gracefulness and to be serious with effect. He has the repose of a mind which lives in itself, while it lives in the world, and which has resources for its happiness at home when it cannot go abroad. He has a gift which serves him in public, and supports him in retirement, without which good fortune is but vulgar,* and with which failure and disappointment have a charm. The art which tends to make a man all this, is in the object which it pursues as useful as the art of wealth or the art of health, though it is less susceptible of method, and less tangible, less certain, less complete in its result.

vulgar · unrefined, deficient in taste

from KNOWLEDGE VIEWED IN RELATION TO RELIGION

2 Now, ON OPENING THE SUBJECT, we see at once a momentous benefit which the philosopher is likely to confer on the pastors of the Church. It is obvious that the first step which they have to effect in the conversion of man and the renovation of his nature, is his rescue from that fearful subjection to sense* which is his ordinary state. To be able to break through the meshes of that thraldom,* and to disentangle and to disengage its ten thousand holds upon the heart, is to bring it, I might almost say, halfway to Heaven. Here, even divine grace, to speak of things according to their appearances, is ordinarily baffled, and retires, without expedient or resource, before this giant fascination. Religion seems too high and unearthly to be able to exert a continued influence upon us: its effort to rouse the soul, and the soul's effort to cooperate, are too violent to last. It is like holding out the arm at full length, or supporting some great weight, which we manage to do for a time, but soon are exhausted and succumb. Nothing can act beyond its own nature; when then we are called to what is supernatural, though those extraordinary aids from Heaven are given us, with which obedience becomes possible, yet even with them it is of transcendent difficulty. We are drawn down to earth every moment with the ease and certainty of a natural gravitation, and it is only by sudden impulses and, as it were, forc-

sense · sensuality

thraldom · slavery, bondage

ible plunges that we attempt to mount upwards. Religion indeed 2
enlightens, terrifies, subdues; it gives faith, it inflicts remorse, it
inspires resolutions, it draws tears, it inflames devotion, but only
for the occasion. I repeat, it imparts an inward power which ought
to effect more than this; I am not forgetting either the real suf-
ficiency of its aids, nor the responsibility of those in whom they
fail. I am not discussing theological questions at all, I am looking
at phenomena as they lie before me, and I say that, in matter of
fact, the sinful spirit repents, and protests it will never sin again,
and for a while is protected by disgust and abhorrence from the
malice of its foe. But that foe knows too well that such seasons
of repentance are wont to have their end: he patiently waits, till
nature faints with the effort of resistance, and lies passive and
hopeless under the next access of temptation. What we need
then is some expedient or instrument, which at least will obstruct
and stave off the approach of our spiritual enemy, and which is
sufficiently congenial and level with our nature to maintain as
firm a hold upon us as the inducements of sensual gratification.
It will be our wisdom to employ nature against itself. Thus sorrow,
sickness, and care are providential antagonists to our inward dis-
orders; they come upon us as years pass on, and generally produce
their natural effects upon us, in proportion as we are subjected
to their influence. These, however, are God's instruments, not
ours; we need a similar remedy, which we can make our own,
the object of some legitimate faculty, or the aim of some natural
affection, which is capable of resting on the mind, and taking up
its familiar lodging with it, and engrossing it, and which thus
becomes a match for the besetting power of sensuality, and a sort

homeopathic of homeopathic medicine* for the disease. Here then I think is
medicine · medical the important aid which intellectual cultivation furnishes to us
treatment using minute in rescuing the victims of passion and self-will. It does not supply
quantities of substances religious motives; it is not the cause or proper antecedent of any
that in massive doses thing supernatural; it is not meritorious of heavenly aid or reward;
produce effects similar but it does a work, at least *materially* good (as theologians speak),
to those of the disease whatever be its real and formal character. It expels the excitements
being treated of sense by the introduction of those of the intellect.

prima facie · "at first This then is the *prima facie** advantage of the pursuit of 3
sight" (Latin), before Knowledge; it is the drawing the mind off from things which will
thorough analysis harm it to subjects which are worthy a rational being; and, though

3   it does not raise it above nature, nor has any tendency to make us pleasing to our Maker, yet is it nothing to substitute what is in itself harmless for what is, to say the least, inexpressibly dangerous? is it a little thing to exchange a circle of ideas which are certainly sinful, for others which are certainly not so? You will say, perhaps, in the words of the Apostle, "Knowledge puffeth up:"* and doubtless this mental cultivation, even when it is successful for the purpose for which I am applying it, may be from the first nothing more than the substitution of pride for sensuality. I grant it, I think I shall have something to say on this point presently; but this is not a necessary result, it is but an incidental evil, a danger which may be realized or may be averted, whereas we may in most cases predicate guilt, and guilt of a heinous kind, where the mind is suffered to run wild and indulge its thoughts without training or law of any kind; and surely to turn away a soul from mortal sin is a good and a gain so far, whatever comes of it. And therefore, if a friend in need is twice a friend, I conceive that intellectual employments, though they do no more than occupy the mind with objects naturally noble or innocent, have a special claim upon our consideration and gratitude.

"Knowledge puffeth up" · 1 Corinthians 8:1

Frederick Douglass

⊸(1 8 1 8 – 1 8 9 5)⊸

Frederick Augustus Washington Bailey (later Douglass) was born in Maryland. His mother was a slave and his father an unknown white slaveholder. After several heartrending attempts for freedom, he was finally victorious on September 3, 1838, when he escaped to New York. While there, Douglass married Anna Murray, a free black woman, and the one who was instrumental in helping him escape. They journeyed to New Bedford, Massachusetts, where Douglass began a career that would dramatically change his life. While attending a convention of the Massachusetts Anti-Slavery Society in Nantucket, Douglass was overheard sharing his experiences as a slave with some of his friends. A leading abolitionist was drawn to his story, and he persuaded the reluctant Douglass to share it at the convention. He was so nervous that he made several blunders during the address. He thought his speech was a disaster, but the assembly thought otherwise. Those present loved his sincere passion and his captivating voice. They were so impressed with his story that they immediately employed him as a traveling lecturer and a social activist for their cause. After the publication of his narrative, he fled to Great Britain to avoid persecution and capture. In 1847, he returned to the United States, buying his own freedom and establishing a newspaper for the black race, the North Star. *During the Civil War, he was invited several times by President Lincoln to discuss matters concerning black soldiers in the Union Army. In 1877, he was appointed United States Marshal for the District of Columbia and in 1881, Recorder of Deeds. In 1884, Douglass married again. His second wife, Helen Pitts, was a white woman, and this marriage brought criticism and controversy. Douglass was an activist to the very end of his life. On February 20, 1895, after delivering a passionate speech at a woman-suffrage convention, he died of a heart attack.*

from THE LIFE OF FREDERICK DOUGLASS

I HAVE HAD TWO MASTERS. My first master's name was Anthony. I do not remember his first name. He was generally called Captain Anthony – a title which, I presume, he acquired by sailing a craft on the Chesapeake Bay. He was not considered a rich slaveholder. He owned two or three farms, and about thirty slaves. His farms and slaves were under the care of an overseer. The overseer's name was Plummer. Mr. Plummer was a miserable drunkard, a profane swearer, and a savage monster. He always went armed with a cowskin* and a heavy cudgel.* I have known him to cut and slash the women's heads so horribly, that even master would be enraged at his cruelty, and would threaten to whip him if he did not mind himself. Master, however, was not a humane slaveholder. It required extraordinary barbarity on the part of an overseer to affect him. He was a cruel man, hardened by a long life of slaveholding. He would at times seem to take great pleasure in whipping a slave. I have often been awakened at the dawn of day by the most heart-rending shrieks of an old aunt of mine, whom he used to tie up to a joist, and whip upon her naked back till she was literally covered with blood. No words, no tears, no prayers, from his gory victim, seemed to move his iron heart from its bloody purpose. The louder she screamed, the harder he whipped; and where the blood ran fastest, there he whipped longest. He would whip her to make her scream, and whip her to make her hush; and not until overcome by fatigue, would he cease to swing the blood-clotted cowskin. I remember the first time I ever witnessed this horrible exhibition. I was quite a child, but I well remember it. I never shall forget it whilst I remember any thing. It was the first of a long series of such outrages, of which I was doomed to be a witness and a participant. It struck me with awful force. It was the blood-stained gate, the entrance to the hell of slavery, through which I was about to pass. It was a most terrible spectacle. I wish I could commit to paper the feelings with which I beheld it.

This occurrence took place very soon after I went to live with my old master, and under the following circumstances. Aunt Hester went out one night, – where or for what I do not know – and happened to be absent when my master desired

cowskin · a leather whip

cudgel · a short, heavy club

2 her presence. He had ordered her not to go out evenings and warned her that she must never let him catch her in company with a young man, who was paying attention to her, belonging to Colonel Lloyd. The young man's name was Ned Roberts, generally called Lloyd's Ned. Why master was so careful of her, may be safely left to conjecture. She was a woman of noble form, and of graceful proportions, having very few equals, and fewer superiors, in personal appearance, among the colored or white women of our neighborhood.

3 Aunt Hester had not only disobeyed his orders in going out, but had been found in company with Lloyd's Ned; which circumstance, I found, from what he said while whipping her, was the chief offence. Had he been a man of pure morals himself, he might have been thought interested in protecting the innocence of my aunt; but those who knew him will not suspect him of any such virtue. Before he commenced whipping Aunt Hester, he took her into the kitchen, and stripped her from neck to waist, leaving her neck, shoulders, and back, entirely naked. He then told her to cross her hands, calling her at the same time a d – d b – h. After crossing her hands, he tied them with a strong rope, and led her to a stool under a large hook in the joist, put in for the purpose. He made her get upon the stool, and tied her hands to the hook. She now stood fair for his infernal purpose. Her arms were stretched up at their full length, so that she stood upon the ends of her toes. He then said to her, "Now, you d – d b – h, I'll learn you how to disobey my orders!" and after rolling up his sleeves, he commenced to lay on the heavy cowskin, and soon the warm, red blood (amid heartrending shrieks from her, and horrid oaths from him) came dripping to the floor. I was so terrified and horror-stricken at the sight, that I hid myself in a closet, and dared not venture out till long after the bloody transaction was over. I expected it would be my turn next. It was all new to me. I had never seen any thing like it before. I had always lived with my grandmother on the outskirts of the plantation, where she was put to raise the children of the younger women. I had therefore been, until now, out of the way of the bloody scenes that often occurred on the plantation.

4 I lived with Mr. Covey one year. During the first six months, of that year, scarce a week passed without his whipping me. I was

seldom free from a sore back. My awkwardness was almost always his excuse for whipping me. We were worked fully up to the point of endurance. Long before day we were up, our horses fed, and by the first approach of day we were off to the field with our hoes and ploughing teams. Mr. Covey gave us enough to eat, but scarce time to eat it. We were often less than five minutes taking our meals. We were often in the field from the first approach of day till its last lingering ray had left us; and at saving-fodder time,· midnight often caught us in the field binding blades.

saving-fodder time ·
the late fall, after initial harvest, when corn stalks are gathered to be mixed with hay to make animal feed for the winter

Covey would be out with us. The way he used to stand it, was this. He would spend the most of his afternoons in bed. He would then come out fresh in the evening, ready to urge us on with his words, example, and frequently with the whip. Mr. Covey was one of the few slaveholders who could and did work with his hands. He was a hard-working man. He knew by himself just what a man or a boy could do. There was no deceiving him. His work went on in his absence almost as well as in his presence; and he had the faculty of making us feel that he was ever present with us. This he did by surprising us. He seldom approached the spot where we were at work openly, if he could do it secretly. He always aimed at taking us by surprise. Such was his cunning, that we used to call him, among ourselves, "the snake." When we were at work in the cornfield, he would sometimes crawl on his hands and knees to avoid detection, and all at once he would rise nearly in our midst, and scream out, "Ha, ha! Come, come! Dash on, dash on!" This being his mode of attack, it was never safe to stop a single minute. His comings were like a thief in the night.· He appeared to us as being ever at hand. He was under every tree, behind every stump, in every bush, and at every window, on the plantation. He would sometimes mount his horse, as if bound to St. Michael's, a distance of seven miles, and in half an hour afterwards you would see him coiled up in the corner of the wood-fence, watching every motion of the slaves. He would, for this purpose, leave his horse tied up in the woods. Again, he would sometimes walk up to us, and give us orders as though he was upon the point of starting on a long journey, turn his back upon us, and make as though he was going to the house to get ready; and, before he would get half way thither, he would turn short and crawl into a fence-corner, or behind some tree, and there watch us till the going down of the sun.

His comings … night ·
see 1 Thessalonians 5:20, 2 Peter 3:10

6   Mr. Covey's *forté* consisted in his power to deceive. His life was devoted to planning and perpetrating the grossest deceptions. Every thing he possessed in the shape of learning or religion, he made conform to his disposition to deceive. He seemed to think himself equal to deceiving the Almighty. He would make a short prayer in the morning, and a long prayer at night; and, strange as it may seem, few men would at times appear more devotional than he. The exercises of his family devotions were always commenced with singing; and, as he was a very poor singer himself, the duty of raising the hymn generally came upon me. He would read his hymn, and nod at me to commence. I would at times do so; at others, I would not. My non-compliance would almost always produce much confusion. To show himself independent of me, he would start and stagger through with his hymn in the most discordant manner. In this state of mind, he prayed with more than ordinary spirit. Poor man! such was his disposition, and success at deceiving, I do verily believe that he sometimes deceived himself into the solemn belief, that he was a sincere worshipper of the most high God; and this, too, at a time when he may be said to have been guilty of compelling his woman slave to commit the sin of adultery. The facts in the case are these: Mr. Covey was a poor man; he was just commencing in life; he was only able to buy one slave; and, shocking as is the fact, he bought her, as he said, for a *breeder*. This woman was named Caroline. Mr. Covey bought her from Mr. Thomas Lowe, about six miles from St. Michael's. She was a large, able-bodied woman, about twenty years old. She had already given birth to one child, which proved her to be just what he wanted. After buying her, he hired a married man of Mr. Samuel Harrison, to live with him one year; and him he used to fasten up with her every night! The result was, that, at the end of the year, the miserable woman gave birth to twins. At this result Mr. Covey seemed to be highly pleased, both with the man and the wretched woman. Such was his joy, and that of his wife, that nothing they could do for Caroline during her confinement* was too good, or too hard, to be done. The children were regarded as being quite an addition to his wealth.

confinement · a euphemism referring to the time of pregnancy

7   If at any one time of my life more than another, I was made to drink the bitterest dregs of slavery, that time was during the

first six months of my stay with Mr. Covey. We were worked in 7
all weathers. It was never too hot or too cold; it could never rain,
blow, hail, or snow too hard for us to work in the field. Work,
work, work, was scarcely more the order of the day than of the
night. The longest days were too short for him, and the shortest
nights too long for him. I was somewhat unmanageable when I
first went there, but a few months of this discipline tamed me. Mr.
Covey succeeded in breaking me. I was broken in body, soul, and
spirit. My natural elasticity was crushed, my intellect languished,
the disposition to read departed, the cheerful spark that lingered
about my eye died; the dark night of slavery closed in upon me;
and behold a man transformed into a brute!

Sunday was my only leisure time. I spent this in a sort of 8
beast-like stupor, between sleep and wake, under some large
tree. At times I would rise up, a flash of energetic freedom would
dart through my soul, accompanied with a faint beam of hope,
that flickered for a moment, and then vanished. I sank down
again, mourning over my wretched condition. I was sometimes
prompted to take my life, and that of Covey, but was prevented by
a combination of hope and fear. My sufferings on this plantation
seem now like a dream rather than a stern reality.

a few rods · a rod is a
unit of measure equal
to 5.5 yards (16.5 feet)

Our house stood within a few rods* of the Chesapeake Bay, 9
whose broad bosom was ever white with sails from every quarter
of the habitable globe. Those beautiful vessels, robed in purest
white, so delightful to the eye of freemen, were to me so many
shrouded ghosts, to terrify and torment me with thoughts of
my wretched condition. I have often, in the deep stillness of a
summer's Sabbath, stood all alone upon the lofty banks of that
noble bay, and traced, with saddened heart and tearful eye, the
countless number of sails moving off to the mighty ocean. The
sight of these always affected me powerfully. My thoughts would
compel utterance; and there, with no audience but the Almighty,
I would pour out my soul's complaint, in my rude* way, with an
apostrophe* to the moving multitude of ships:—

rude · uncouth, with-
out formal training

apostrophe · a digres-
sion, often addressed to
an absent or imagined
other

"You are loosed from your moorings, and are free; I am fast in 10
my chains, and am a slave! You move merrily before the gentle
gale, and I sadly before the bloody whip! You are freedom's swift-
winged angels, that fly round the world; I am confined in bands
of iron! O that I were free! O, that I were on one of your gallant

10 decks, and under your protecting wing! Alas! betwixt me and you, the turbid waters roll. Go on, go on. O that I could also go! Could I but swim! If I could fly! O, why was I born a man, of whom to make a brute! The glad ship is gone; she hides in the dim distance. I am left in the hottest hell of unending slavery. O God, save me! God, deliver me! Let me be free! Is there any God? Why am I a slave? I will run away. I will not stand it. Get caught, or get clear, I'll try it. I had as well die with ague as the fever. I have only one life to lose. I had as well be killed running as die standing. Only think of it; one hundred miles straight north, and I am free! Try it? Yes! God helping me, I will. It cannot be that I shall live and die a slave. I will take to the water. This very bay shall bear me into freedom. The steamboats steered in a north-east course from North Point. I will do the same; and when I get to the head of the bay, I will turn my canoe adrift, and walk straight through Delaware into Pennsylvania. When I get there, I shall not be required to have a pass; I can travel without being disturbed. Let but the first opportunity offer, and, come what will, I am off. Meanwhile, I will try to bear up under the yoke. I am not the only slave in the world. Why should I fret? I can bear as much as any of them. Besides, I am but a boy, and all boys are bound to some one. It may be that my misery in slavery will only increase my happiness when I get free. There is a better day coming."

11 Thus I used to think, and thus I used to speak to myself; goaded almost to madness at one moment, and at the next reconciling myself to my wretched lot.

APPENDIX

12 I FIND, SINCE READING OVER the foregoing Narrative that I have, in several instances, spoken in such a tone and manner, respecting religion, as may possibly lead those unacquainted with my religious views to suppose me an opponent of all religion. To remove the liability of such misapprehension, I deem it proper to append the following brief explanation. What I have said respecting and against religion, I mean strictly to apply to the *slaveholding religion* of this land, and with no possible reference to Christianity proper; for, between the Christianity of this land, and the Christianity of Christ, I recognize the

widest possible difference – so wide, that to receive the one as ¹²
good, pure, and holy, is of necessity to reject the other as bad,
corrupt, and wicked. To be the friend of the one, is of necessity
to be the enemy of the other. I love the pure, peaceable, and
impartial Christianity of Christ: I therefore hate the corrupt,
slaveholding, women-whipping, cradle-plundering, partial and
hypocritical Christianity of this land. Indeed, I can see no reason,
but the most deceitful one, for calling the religion of this land
Christianity. I look upon it as the climax of all misnomers, the
boldest of all frauds, and the grossest of all libels. Never was
there a clearer case of "stealing the livery* of the court of heaven
to serve the devil in." I am filled with unutterable loathing when
I contemplate the religious pomp and show, together with the
horrible inconsistencies, which everywhere surround me. We
have men-stealers for ministers, women worshippers for missionaries, and cradle-plunderers for church members. The man
who wields the blood-clotted cowskin during the week fills the
pulpit on Sunday, and claims to be a minister of the meek and
lowly Jesus. The man who robs me of my earnings at the end
of each week meets me as a class-leader on Sunday morning,
to show me the way of life, and the path of salvation. He who
sells my sister, for purposes of prostitution, stands forth as the
pious advocate of purity. He who proclaims it a religious duty to
read the Bible denies me the right of learning to read the name
of the God who made me. He who is the religious advocate of
marriage robs whole millions of its sacred influence, and leaves
them to the ravages of wholesale pollution. The warm defender
of the sacredness of the family relation is the same that scatters
whole families, – sundering husbands and wives, parents and
children, sisters and brothers, – leaving the hut vacant, and the
hearth desolate. We see the thief preaching against theft, and the
adulterer against adultery. We have men sold to build churches,
women sold to support the gospel, and babes sold to purchase
Bibles for the *poor heathen*! *all for the glory of God and the good
of souls*! The slave auctioneer's bell and the church-going bell
chime in with each other, and the bitter cries of the heart-broken
slave are drowned in the religious shouts of his pious master.
Revivals of religion and revivals in the slave-trade go hand in
hand together. The slave prison and the church stand near each

livery · the uniform or distinctive dress worn by the servants of a lord or master. The quotation is taken from *The Course of Time* by popular Scottish religious poet Robert Pollok (1798–1827)

12 other. The clanking of fetters and the rattling of chains in the prison, and the pious psalm and solemn prayer in the church, may be heard at the same time. The dealers in the bodies and souls of men erect their stand in the presence of the pulpit, and they mutually help each other. The dealer gives his blood-stained gold to support the pulpit, and the pulpit, in return, covers his infernal business with the garb of Christianity. Here we have religion and robbery the allies of each other – devils dressed in angels' robes, and hell presenting the semblance of paradise.

12a   Just God! and these are they,
      Who minister at thine altar, God of right!
      Men who their hands, with prayer and blessing, lay
      On Israel's ark of light.

12b   What! preach, and kidnap men?
      Give thanks, and rob thy own afflicted poor?
      Talk of thy glorious liberty, and then
      Bolt hard the captive's door?

12c   What! servants of thy own
      Merciful son, who came to seek and save
      The homeless and the outcast, fettering down
      The tasked and plundered slave!

12d   Pilate* and Herod* friends!
      Chief priests and rulers, as of old, combine!
      Just God and holy! is that church which lends
      Strength to the spoiler thine?

Pilate · Pontius Pilate (d 36), Roman prefect of Judea under the emperor Tiberius; he presided at the trial of Jesus and gave the order for his crucifixion

Herod · Herod Antipas (21 BC–39), tetrarch of Galilee who ruled throughout Jesus' life. When Pilate sent Jesus to Herod for condemnation, Herod was unwilling to pass judgment

votaries · those bound to live a life of religious service, those who have affiliated themselves formally with a particular religious movement

scribes and Pharisees · members of the religious elite whom Jesus routinely condemned for their hypocrisy and evil ways

13   The Christianity of America is a Christianity, of whose votaries* it may be as truly said, as it was of the ancient scribes and Pharisees,* "They bind heavy burdens, and grievous to be borne, and lay them on men's shoulders, but they themselves will not move them with one of their fingers. All their works they do for to be seen of men. – They love the uppermost rooms at feasts, and the chief seats in the synagogues, …and to be called by men, Rabbi, Rabbi. – But woe unto you, scribes and Pharisees, hypocrites! for ye shut up the kingdom of heaven against men; for ye neither go in yourselves, neither suffer ye them that are entering to go in. Ye devour widows' houses, and for a pretence

"They bind ... in-iquity" · this lengthy passage is taken from Matthew 23:4–29

make long prayers; therefore ye shall receive the greater dam- 13 nation. Ye compass sea and land to make one proselyte, and when he is made, ye make him twofold more the child of hell than yourselves. – Woe unto you, scribes and Pharisees, hypocrites! for ye pay tithe of mint, and anise, and cumin, and have omitted the weightier matters of the law, judgment, mercy, and faith; these ought ye to have done, and not to leave the other undone. Ye blind guides! which strain at a gnat, and swallow a camel. Woe unto you, scribes and Pharisees, hypocrites! for ye make clean the outside of the cup and of the platter; but within, they are full of extortion and excess. Woe unto you, scribes and Pharisees, hypocrites! for ye are like unto whited sepulchres, which indeed appear beautiful outward, but are within full of dead men's bones, and of all uncleanness. Even so ye also outwardly appear righteous unto men, but within ye are full of hypocrisy and iniquity."•

Dark and terrible as is this picture, I hold it to be strictly true of 14 the overwhelming mass of professed Christians in America. They strain at a gnat, and swallow a camel. Could any thing be more true of our churches? They would be shocked at the proposition of fellowshipping a sheep-stealer; and at the same time they hug to their communion a man-stealer, and brand me with being an infidel, if I find fault with them for it. They attend with Pharisaical strictness to the outward forms of religion, and at the same time neglect the weightier matters of the law, judgment, mercy, and faith. They are always ready to sacrifice, but seldom to show mercy. They are they who are represented as professing to love God whom they have not seen, whilst they hate their brother whom they have seen. They love the heathen on the other side of the globe. They can pray for him, pay money to have the Bible put into his hand, and missionaries to instruct him; while they despise and totally neglect the heathen at their own doors.

Such is, very briefly, my view of the religion of this land; and 15 to avoid any misunderstanding, growing out of the use of general terms, I mean, by the religion of this land, that which is revealed in the words, deeds, and actions, of those bodies, north and south, calling themselves Christian churches, and yet in union with slaveholders. It is against religion, as presented by these bodies, that I have felt it my duty to testify.

Langston Hughes

❧(1 9 0 2 – 1 9 6 7)❧

Multiple childhood influences shaped Hughes's writing. The Christian faith of his grandmother, with whom he spent his early years in Lawrence, Kansas, had a profound impact on his artistic sensibilities and linguistic development. His urban experience living with his mother and stepfather, moreover, would provide him with the material he eventually used to present the emergent "New Negro" to readers. His father's expatriation to Mexico to escape racial prejudice – Hughes spent a year with him there – further affected his worldview, helping to free him from American provincialism. After a period of international travel as a merchant seaman, Hughes entered and graduated from Lincoln University, in Pennsylvania. Unlike many African American writers of the 1920s, Hughes focused less on rural Southern blacks, preferring instead to treat the lives of black city dwellers. As an adult, Hughes was drawn to Communism, visiting Russia for a year (1932–1933). He applauded Marxism's ostensible respect for the working class and disdain for racial boundaries. During the "red scare" of the McCarthy era, therefore, Hughes was considered a security risk and was restricted by the government of the United States from traveling abroad. The ban was lifted in the 1960s, and the writer resumed his travels, reading and lecturing to international audiences. Though Hughes is perhaps best remembered for poetry, his literary output was varied and included the collecting and editing of black folklore. Perhaps more than any other artist of the Harlem Renaissance, the cultural movement of which he was part, Langston Hughes presented and embodied a portrait of the African American in ideological transition.

SALVATION

1 I WAS SAVED FROM SIN when I was going on thirteen. But not really saved. It happened like this. There was a big revival at my

47

Auntie Reed's church. Every night for weeks there had been much preaching, singing, praying, and shouting, and some very hardened sinners had been brought to Christ, and the membership of the church had grown by leaps and bounds. Then just before the revival ended, they held a special meeting for children, "to bring the young lambs to the fold." My aunt spoke of it for days ahead. That night I was escorted to the front row and placed on the mourners' bench* with all the other young sinners, who had not yet been brought to Jesus.

mourners' bench · a special seat on the front row of a church reserved for those asking for prayers or responding to a call for repentance

My aunt told me that when you were saved you saw a light, and something happened to you inside! And Jesus came into your life! And God was with you from then on! She said you could see and hear and feel Jesus in your soul. I believed her. I had heard a great many old people say the same thing and it seemed to me they ought to know. So I sat there calmly in the hot, crowded church, waiting for Jesus to come to me.

The preacher preached a wonderful rhythmical sermon, all moans and shouts and lonely cries and dire pictures of hell, and then he sang a song about the ninety and nine safe in the fold, but one little lad was left out in the cold.* Then he said: "Won't you come? Won't you come to Jesus? Young lambs, won't you come?" And he held out his arms to all us young sinners there on the mourners' bench. And the little girls cried. And some of them jumped up and went to Jesus right away. But most of us just sat there.

the ninety and nine ... cold · the hymn "The Ninety and Nine" (words E. C. Clephane, music I. D. Sankey, 1874) is based on Christ's parable of the lost sheep (Luke 15:3–7)

A great many old people came and knelt around us and prayed, old women with jet-black faces and braided hair, old men with work-gnarled hands. And the church sang a song about the lower lights are burning, some poor sinners to be saved.* And the whole building rocked with prayer and song.

lower lights are burning ... be saved · "Let the Lower Lights Be Burning" (words and music P. P. Bliss, 1871) uses the metaphor of a lighthouse to encourage Christian witness and evangelism

Still I kept waiting to *see* Jesus.

Finally all the young people had gone to the altar and were saved, but one boy and me. He was a rounder's son named Westley. Westley and I were surrounded by sisters and deacons praying. It was very hot in the church, and getting late now. Finally Westley said to me in a whisper:

"God damn! I'm tired o' sitting here. Let's get up and be saved." So he got up and was saved.

Then I was left all alone on the mourners' bench. My aunt came and knelt at my knees and cried, while prayers and songs

8   swirled all around me in the little church. The whole congregation prayed for me alone, in a mighty wail of moans and voices. And I kept waiting serenely for Jesus, waiting, waiting – but he didn't come. I wanted to see him, but nothing happened to me. Nothing! I wanted something to happen to me, but nothing happened.

9   I heard the songs and the minister saying: "Why don't you come? My dear child, why don't you come to Jesus? Jesus is waiting for you. He wants you. Why don't you come? Sister Reed, what is this child's name?"

10   "Langston," my aunt sobbed.

11   "Langston, why don't you come? Why don't you come and be saved? Oh, Lamb of God! Why don't you come?"

12   Now it was really getting late. I began to be ashamed of myself, holding everything up so long. I began to wonder what God thought about Westley, who certainly hadn't seen Jesus either, but who was now sitting proudly on the platform, swinging his knickerbockered* legs and grinning down at me, surrounded by deacons and old women on their knees praying. God had not struck Westley dead for taking his name in vain or for lying in the temple. So I decided that maybe to save further trouble, I'd better lie, too, and say that Jesus had come, and get up and be saved.

knickerbockered · knickerbockers are short pants gathered just below the knee, commonly worn at that time by young boys

13   So I got up.

14   Suddenly the whole room broke into a sea of shouting, as they saw me rise. Waves of rejoicing swept the place. Women leaped in the air. My aunt threw her arms around me. The minister took me by the hand and led me to the platform.

15   When things quieted down, in a hushed silence, punctuated by a few ecstatic "Amens," all the new young lambs were blessed in the name of God. Then joyous singing filled the room.

16   That night, for the last time in my life but one – for I was a big boy twelve years old – I cried. I cried, in bed alone, and couldn't stop. I buried my head under the quilts, but my aunt heard me. She woke up and told my uncle I was crying because the Holy Ghost had come into my life, and because I had seen Jesus. But I was really crying because I couldn't bear to tell her that I had lied, that I had deceived everybody in the church, that I hadn't seen Jesus, and that now I didn't believe there was a Jesus any more, since he didn't come to help me.

Thomas Merton

◀(1 9 1 5 – 1 9 6 8)▶

*Born in France, orphaned at sixteen, and educated at Clare College,
Cambridge, Merton emigrated to the United States in 1934. Merton
attended Columbia University, where he became a Catholic. In 1941
he entered the Cistercians of the Strict Observance (Trappist). He
spent the rest of his life writing works of poetry, spirituality, and
theology. His best-selling autobiography,* The Seven Storey Mountain
*(1948), helped make him a public figure. Merton succeeded in intro-
ducing large numbers of readers to the value of the spiritual life
and the disciplines of meditation and prayer without their having
to enter the monastic life (themes reiterated and extended by Henri
Nouwen). Merton emphasized the deep connection between the
spiritual life and service to humanity: "Go into the desert not to
escape other men but in order to find them in God," he writes in*
New Seeds of Contemplation *(1961). "There is no true solitude except
interior solitude. And interior solitude is not possible for anyone
who does not accept his true place in relation to other men." Merton
died in an accident in Bangkok, Thailand, in December 1968.*

PRAY FOR YOUR OWN DISCOVERY

1 THERE EXISTS SOME POINT at which I can meet God in a real
and experimental* contact with His infinite actuality. This is the
"place" of God, His sanctuary – it is the point where my contingent
being depends upon His love. Within myself is a metaphorical apex
of existence at which I am held in being by my Creator.

2 God utters me like a word containing a partial thought of
Himself.

3 A word will never be able to comprehend the voice that utters it.

4 But if I am true to the concept that God utters in me, if I am
true to the thought of Him I was meant to embody, I shall be

experimental ·
experiential

full of His actuality and find Him everywhere in myself, and find 4
myself nowhere. I shall be lost in Him: that is, I shall find myself.
I shall be "saved."

It is a pity that the beautiful Christian metaphor "salvation" 5
has come to be so hackneyed and therefore so despised. It has
been turned into a vapid synonym for "piety"– not even a truly
ethical concept. "Salvation" is something far beyond ethical
propriety. The word connotes a deep respect for the fundamental metaphysical reality of man. It reflects God's own infinite
concern for man, God's love and care for man's inmost being,
God's love for all that is His own in man, His son. It is not only
human nature that is "saved" by the divine mercy, but above all
the human person. The object of salvation is that which is unique,
irreplaceable, incommunicable – that which is myself alone. This
true inner self must be drawn up like a jewel from the bottom
of the sea, rescued from confusion, from indistinction, from
immersion in the common, the nondescript, the trivial, the
sordid, the evanescent.*

evanescent · vanishing or fleeting

We must be saved from immersion in the sea of lies and pas- 6
sions which is called "the world." And we must be saved above
all from that abyss of confusion and absurdity which is our own
worldly self. The person must be rescued from the individual.
The free son of God must be saved from the conformist slave of
fantasy, passion and convention. The creative and mysterious
inner self must be delivered from the wasteful, hedonistic* and
destructive ego that seeks only to cover itself with disguises.

hedonistic · hedonism holds pleasure to be the greatest good

To be "lost" is to be left to the arbitrariness and pretenses of 7
the contingent ego, the smoke-self that must inevitably vanish.
To be "saved" is to return to one's inviolate and eternal reality
and to live in God.

❧ ❧ ❧

WHAT ONE OF YOU CAN ENTER into himself and find the 8
God Who utters him?

"Finding God" means much more than just abandoning all things 9
that are not God, and emptying oneself of images and desires.

If you succeed in emptying your mind of every thought and 10
every desire, you may indeed withdraw into the center of yourself
and concentrate everything within you upon the imaginary point

10 where your life springs out of God: yet you will not really find God. No natural exercise can bring you into vital contact with Him. Unless He utters Himself in you, speaks His own name in the center of your soul, you will no more know Him than a stone knows the ground upon which it rests in its inertia.

⊕   ⊕   ⊕

11 OUR DISCOVERY OF GOD IS, in a way, God's discovery of us. We cannot go to heaven to find Him because we have no way of knowing where heaven is or what it is. He comes down from heaven and finds us.

12 He looks at us from the depths of His own infinite actuality, which is everywhere, and His seeing us gives us a new being and a new mind in which we also discover Him. We only know Him in so far as we are known by Him, and our contemplation of Him is a participation in His contemplation of Himself.

13 We become contemplatives when God discovers* Himself in us.

discovers · reveals

14 At that moment the point of our contact with Him opens out and we pass through the center of our own nothingness and enter into infinite reality, where we awaken as our true self.

15 It is true that God knows Himself in all the things that exist. He sees them, and it is because He sees them that they exist. It is because He loves them that they are good. His love in them is their intrinsic goodness. The value He sees in them is their value. Insofar as He sees and loves them, all things reflect Him.

16 But although God is present in all things by His knowledge and His love and His power and His care of them, He is not necessarily realized and known by them. He is only known and loved by those to whom He has freely given a share in His own knowledge and love of Himself.

17 In order to know and love God as He is, we must have God dwelling in us in a new way, not only in His creative power but in His mercy, not only in His greatness but in His littleness, by which He empties Himself* and comes down to us to be empty in our emptiness, and so fill us in His fullness. God bridges the infinite distances between Himself and the spirits created to love Him, by supernatural missions of His own life. The Father, dwelling in the depths of all things and in my own depths, communicates to me His Word and His Spirit. Receiving them I am

He empties Himself · the New Testament doctrine of *kenosis*, Christ's voluntary surrender of divine prerogatives. See Philippians 2:5–11

drawn into His own life and know God in His own Love, being   17
one with Him in His own Son.

My discovery of my identity begins and is perfected in these   18
missions, because it is in them that God Himself, bearing in
Himself the secret of who I am, begins to live in me not only as
my Creator but as my other and true self. *Vivo, iam non ego, vivit*
vero in me Christus ("I live, now not I, but Christ lives in me").·

"I live … me" ·
Galatians 2:20

✢ ✢ ✢

THESE MISSIONS BEGIN at Baptism. But they do not take on   19
any practical meaning in the life of our spirit until we become
capable of conscious acts of love. From then on God's special presence in us corresponds to our own free decisions. From then on our
life becomes a series of choices between the fiction of our false self,
whom we feed with the illusions of passion and selfish appetite, and
our loving consent to the purely gratuitous mercy of God.

When I consent to the will and the mercy of God as it "comes"   20
to me in events of life, appealing to my inner self and awakening
my faith, I break through the superficial exterior appearances that
form my routine vision of the world and of my own self, and I find
myself in the presence of hidden majesty. It may appear to me
that this majesty and presence is something objective, "outside

primitive · original
or early

cherubim · see Exodus
25:18–22

myself." Indeed, the primitive· saints and prophets saw this divine
presence in vision as a light or an angel or a man or a burning
fire, or a blazing glory upheld by cherubim.· Only thus could
their minds do justice to the supreme reality of what they experienced. Yet this is a majesty we do not see with our eyes and it is
all within ourselves. It is the mission of the Word and the Spirit,
from the Father, in the depths of our own being. It is a majesty
communicated to us, shared with us, so that our whole being is
filled with the gift of glory and responds with adoration.

This is the "mercy of God" revealed to us by the secret mis-   21
sions in which He gives Himself to us, and awakens our identity
as sons and heirs of His Kingdom. This is the Kingdom of God

Kingdom … within
us · "the kingdom of God
is within you" (Luke 17:21)

"Our Father" · The Lord's
Prayer (Matthew 6:9–13)

within us,· and for the coming of this Kingdom we pray each
time we say the "Our Father."· In the revelation of mercy and
majesty we come to an obscure intuition of our own personal
secret, our true identity. Our inner self awakens, with a momentary flash, in the instant of recognition when we say "Yes!" to

21   the indwelling Divine Persons. We are only really ourselves when we completely consent to "receive" the glory of God into ourselves. Our true self is, then, the self that receives freely and gladly the missions that are God's supreme gift to His sons. Any other "self" is only an illusion.

22   As long as I am on earth my mind and will remain more or less impervious to the missions of God's Word and His Spirit. I do not easily receive His light.

23   Every movement of my own natural appetite, even though my nature is good in itself, tends in one way or another to keep alive in me the illusion that is opposed to God's reality living within me.

24   Even though my natural acts are good they have a tendency, when they are only natural, to concentrate my faculties on the man that I am not, the one I cannot be, the false self in me, the character that God does not know. This is because I am born in selfishness. I am born self-centered. And this is original sin.*

25   Even when I try to please God, I tend to please my own ambition, His enemy. There can be imperfection even in the ardent love of great perfection, even in the desire of virtue, of sanctity. Even the desire of contemplation can be impure, when we forget that true contemplation means the complete destruction of all selfishness – the most pure poverty and cleanness of heart.

original sin · doctrine developed by Augustine of Hippo (354–430) that all humans are born sinful, carrying the taint of Adam's primal disobedience

✦   ✦   ✦

26   ALTHOUGH GOD LIVES in the souls of men who are unconscious of Him, how can I say that I have found Him and found myself in Him if I never know Him or think of Him, never take any interest in Him or seek Him or desire His presence in my soul? What good does it do to say a few formal prayers to Him and then turn away and give all my mind and all my will to created things, desiring only ends that fall far short of Him? Even though my soul may be justified, yet if my mind does not belong to Him then I do not belong to Him either. If my love does not reach out toward Him but scatters itself in His creation, it is because I have reduced His life in me to the level of a formality, forbidding it to move me with a truly vital influence.

27   Justify my soul, O God, but also from Your fountains fill my will with fire. Shine in my mind, although perhaps this means

"be darkness to my experience," but occupy my heart with Your 27 tremendous Life. Let my eyes see nothing in the world but Your glory, and let my hands touch nothing that is not for Your service. Let my tongue taste no bread that does not strengthen me to praise Your great mercy. I will hear Your voice and I will hear all harmonies You have created, singing Your hymns. Sheep's wool and cotton from the field shall warm me enough that I may live in Your service; I will give the rest to Your poor. Let me use all things for one sole reason: to find my joy in giving You glory.

Therefore keep me, above all things, from sin. Keep me from 28 the death of deadly sin which puts hell in my soul. Keep me from the murder of lust that blinds and poisons my heart. Keep me from the sins that eat a man's flesh with irresistible fire until he is devoured. Keep me from loving money in which is hatred, from avarice and ambition that suffocate my life. Keep me from the dead works of vanity and the thankless labor in which artists destroy themselves for pride and money and reputation, and saints are smothered under the avalanche of their own importunate* zeal. Stanch in me the rank wound of covetousness and the hungers that exhaust my nature with their bleeding. Stamp out the serpent envy that stings love with poison and kills all joy.

importunate · stubbornly or unreasonably persistent

Untie my hands and deliver my heart from sloth. Set me free 29 from the laziness that goes about disguised as activity when activity is not required of me, and from the cowardice that does what is not demanded, in order to escape sacrifice.

But give me the strength that waits upon You in silence and 30 peace. Give me humility in which alone is rest, and deliver me from pride which is the heaviest of burdens. And possess my whole heart and soul with the simplicity of love. Occupy my whole life with the one thought and the one desire of love, that I may love not for the sake of merit, not for the sake of perfection, not for the sake of virtue, not for the sake of sanctity, but for You alone.

For there is only one thing that can satisfy love and reward 31 it, and that is You alone.

This then is what it means to seek God perfectly: to withdraw 32 from illusion and pleasure, from worldly anxieties and desires, from the works that God does not want, from a glory that is only human display; to keep my mind free from confusion in

32 order that my liberty may be always at the disposal of His will; to entertain silence in my heart and listen for the voice of God; to cultivate an intellectual freedom from the images of created things in order to receive the secret contact of God in obscure love; to love all men as myself; to rest in humility and to find peace in withdrawal from conflict and competition with other men; to turn aside from controversy and put away heavy loads of judgment and censorship and criticism and the whole burden of opinions that I have no obligation to carry; to have a will that is always ready to fold back within itself and draw all the powers of the soul down from its deepest center to rest in silent expectancy for the coming of God, poised in tranquil and effortless concentration upon the point of my dependence on Him; to gather all that I am, and have all that I can possibly suffer or do or be, and abandon them all to God in the resignation of a perfect love and blind faith and pure trust in God, to do His will.

33 And then to wait in peace and emptiness and oblivion of all things.

34 *Bonum est præstolari cum silentio salutare Dei* ("It is good to wait in silence for the salvation of God").·

"It is ... God".
Lamentations 3:26

Madeleine L'Engle

⟨ 1 9 1 8 – ⟩

L'Engle has written over fifty books in many different genres, including children's fiction, adult fiction, non-fiction prose, prayers, and letters. Her work often deals with science as theology. Perhaps L'Engle is most well known for her beloved A Wrinkle in Time (1962), *which was sent to dozens of publishers before it was accepted and which, in due course, was awarded the Newberry Medal. Born in New York City, the only child of older parents, L'Engle grew up in an adult world and turned to writing to amuse herself. She acted briefly on the stage and was married to an actor, but after she became a mother she launched into writing seriously. For many years L'Engle was the writer-in-residence at the Cathedral of St. John the Divine in New York City.*

ICONS OF THE TRUE

1   IT HAS OFTEN STRUCK ME with awe that some of the most deeply religious people I know have been, on the surface, atheists. Atheism is a peculiar state of mind; you cannot deny the existence of that which does not exist. I cannot say, "That chair is not there," if there is no chair there to say it about.

2   Many atheists deny God because they care so passionately about a caring and personal God and the world around them is inconsistent with a God of love, they feel, and so they say, "There is no God." But even when one denies God, to serve music, or painting, or words is a religious activity, whether or not the conscious mind is willing to accept that fact. Basically there can be no categories such as "religious" art and "secular" art, because all true art is incarnational, and therefore "religious."

3   The problem of pain, of war and the horror of war, of poverty and disease is always confronting us. But a God who allows no pain, no grief, also allows no choice. There is little unfairness in a

59

colony of ants, but there is also little freedom. We human beings
have been given the terrible gift of free will, and this ability to make
choices, to help write our own story, is what makes us human, even
when we make the wrong choices, abusing our freedom and the
freedom of others. The weary and war-torn world around us bears
witness to the wrongness of many of our choices. But lest I stumble
into despair I remember, too, seeing the white, pinched-faced little
children coming to the pediatric floor of a city hospital for open-
heart surgery, and seeing them, two days later, with color in their
cheeks, while the nurses tried to slow down their wheel-chair races.
I remember, too, that there is now a preventative for trachoma,·
still the chief cause of blindness in the world. And I remember that
today few mothers die in childbirth, and our graveyards no longer
contain the mute witness of five little stones in a row, five children
of one family, dead in a week of scarlet fever or diphtheria.

George MacDonald· gives me renewed strength during times
of trouble – times when I have seen people tempted to deny
God – when he says, "The Son of God suffered unto death, not that
men might not suffer, but that their sufferings might be like his."

Jesus, too, had to make choices, and in the eyes of the world
some of his choices were not only contrary to acceptable behavior,
but were foolish in the extreme. He bucked authority by healing
on the Sabbath; when he turned his steps towards Jerusalem he
was making a choice which led him to Calvary.

It is the ability to choose which makes us human.

❖   ❖   ❖

THIS ABILITY, THIS NECESSITY to choose, is an important
element in all story. Which direction will the young man take
when he comes to the cross-roads? Will the girl talk with the
handsome stranger? Should the child open the forbidden door?

Œdipus killed the man he met at the crossroads, and even
though he did not know that the man was his father, that did not
allow him to escape the retribution which followed his choice.
He married a woman he did not know to be his mother, but his
lack of knowledge did not make him "innocent." Though we may
cry out, "But I didn't know!" our anguish does little to forestall
the consequences of our actions. To the non-believer, the person
who sees no cosmos in chaos, we are all the victims of the dark-

trachoma · a form of
conjunctivitis

George MacDonald ·
Scottish author (1824–
1905). See MacDonald's
poem "Obedience" on
pages 433–434

8 ness which surrounds our choices; we have lost our way; we do not know what is right and what is wrong; we cannot tell our left hand from our right. There is no meaning.

9 But to serve any discipline of art, be it to chip a David out of an unwieldy piece of marble, to take oils and put a clown on canvas, to write a drama about a young man who kills his father and marries his mother and suffers for these actions, to hear a melody and set the notes down for a string quartet, is to affirm meaning, despite all the ambiguities and tragedies and misunderstanding which surround us.

10 Æschylus* writes, "In our sleep, pain that cannot forget falls drop by drop upon the heart and in our own despair, against our will, comes wisdom through the awful grace of God."

11 We see that wisdom and that awful grace in the silence of the Pietà*; in Gerard Manley Hopkins' poems*; in Poulenc's organ concerto*; but we do not find it in many places where we would naturally expect to find it This confusion comes about because much so-called religious art is in fact bad art, and therefore bad religion. Those angels rendered by grown-ups who obviously didn't believe in angels and which confused the delegates at Ayia Napa* are only one example. Some of those soppy pictures of Jesus, looking like a tubercular,* fair-haired, blue-eyed *goy*,* are far more secular than a Picasso* mother and child. The Lord Jesus who rules my life is not a sentimental, self-pitying weakling. He was a Jew, a carpenter, and strong. He took into his own heart, for our sakes, that pain which brings "wisdom through the awful grace of God."

12 It is impossible for an artist to attempt a graphic reproduction of Jesus in any way that is meant to be literal. I sympathize with the Hassidic* teaching that it is wrong to try in any way to make pictures of God or his prophets. The Muslims have this philosophy, too, hence the intricate, nonrepresentational designs on the mosques.

13 But in a way both miss the point which the Eastern Orthodox artists are taught when they study the painting of icons. The figure on the icon is not meant to represent literally what Peter or John or any of the apostles looked like, nor what Mary looked like, nor the child, Jesus. But, the orthodox painter feels, Jesus of Nazareth did not walk around Galilee faceless. The icon of Jesus may not look like the man Jesus two thousand years ago, but it represents some *quality* of Jesus, or his mother, or his followers, and so

Æschylus · Greek playwright (525–456 BC)

Pietà · a representation of Mary, Christ's mother, grieving over his corpse

Gerard Manley Hopkins' poems · G. M. Hopkins (1844–1889), Jesuit and English poet. See Hopkins' poems on pages 443–445

Poulenc's organ concerto · Francis Poulenc (1899–1963), French composer

Ayia Napa · resort town in eastern Cyprus featuring a 15th-century monastery where regular ecumenical theological conferences are held

tubercular · weak, pale

goy · "gentile" (Yiddish)

Picasso · Pablo Picasso (1881–1973), Spanish cubist painter and sculptor

Hassidic · The Hassidim are followers of a strict sect of orthodox Judaism

becomes an open window through which we can be given a new   13
glimpse of the love of God. Icons are painted with firm discipline,
much prayer, and anonymity. In this way the iconographer is
enabled to get out of the way, to listen, to serve the work.

An icon is a symbol, rather than a sign. A sign may point the way to   14
something, such as: *Athens – 10 kilometers.* But the sign is not Athens,
even when we reach the city limits and read *Athens.* A symbol, however, unlike a sign, contains within it some quality of what it represents.
An icon of the Annunciation, for instance, does more than point to
the angel and the girl; it contains, for us, some of Mary's acceptance
and obedience and so affects our own ability to accept, to obey.

Francis of Assisi · son
of a noble Italian family,
Francis (1181/2–1226)
renounced his wealth,
became a monk, and
founded the Franciscan
order in the 13th century

Francis of Assisi* says that "In pictures of God and the blessed   15
Virgin painted on wood, God and the blessed Virgin are held in
mind, yet the wood and the painting ascribe nothing to themselves, because they are just wood and paint; so the servant of
God is a kind of painting, that is, a creature of God in which God
is honoured for the sake of his benefits. But he ought to ascribe
nothing to himself, just like the wood or the painting, but should
render honour and glory to God alone."

I travel with a small icon, a picture pasted on wood, which   16
was given to me with love, so that the picture, the wood, and the
love have become for me a Trinity, an icon of God. Of themselves
they are nothing; because they are also part of God's munificent
love they are everything.

(A parenthesis here about quotations and credits. I was taught   17
in college how to footnote, how to give credit where credit is due,
and in the accepted, scholarly way. But most of the writers I want
to quote in this book are writers whose words I've copied down in
a big, brown, Mexican notebook, what is called a commonplace
book. I copy down words and thoughts upon which I want to
meditate, and footnoting is not my purpose; this is a devotional,
not a scholarly notebook. I've been keeping it for many years, and
turn to it for help in prayer, in understanding. All I'm looking for in
it is meaning, meaning which will help me to live life lovingly, and
I am only now beginning to see the usefulness of noting book title
and page, rather than simply jotting down, "Francis of Assisi.")

iconographer · one
who creates or studies
images that represent
sacred figures

An iconographer* is a devout and practising Christian, but all   18
true art has an iconic quality. An Eastern Orthodox theologian,
Timothy Kallistos Ware, writes (and where? in a magazine called

18   *Sobornost*, probably about a decade ago edited by the Rev. Canon
A. M. Allchin, of Canterbury Cathedral, England) that

18a   an abstract composition by Kandinsky* or Van Gogh's* landscape of the cornfield with birds … is a real instance of divine
transfiguration, in which we see matter rendered spiritual and
entering into the "glorious liberty of the children of God." This
remains true, even when the artist does not personally believe
in God. Provided he is an artist of integrity, he is a genuine servant of the glory which he does not recognize, and unknown
to himself there is "something divine" about his work. We
may rest confident that at the last judgment the angels will
produce his works of art as testimony on his behalf.

Kandinsky · Wassily
Kandinsky (1866–1944),
Russian abstract painter

Van Gogh's landscape ·
Vincent Van Gogh
(1853–1890), Dutch post-
impressionist painter

(Angels again!)

19   We may not like that, but we call the work of such artists un-
Christian or non-Christian at our own peril. Christ has always
worked in ways which have seemed peculiar to many men, even
his closest followers. Frequently the disciples failed to understand
him. So we need not feel that we have to understand how he
works through artists who do not consciously recognize him.
Neither should our lack of understanding cause us to assume
that he cannot be present in their work.

20   A sad fact which nevertheless needs to be faced is that a
deeply committed Christian who wants to write stories or paint
pictures or compose music to the glory of God simply may not
have been given the talent, the gift, which a non-Christian, or
even an atheist, may have in abundance. God is no respecter of
persons, and this is something we are reluctant to face.

21   We would like God's ways to be like our ways, his judgments
to be like our judgments. It is hard for us to understand that he
lavishly gives enormous talents to people we would consider
unworthy, that he chooses his artists with as calm a disregard of
surface moral qualifications as he chooses his saints.

22   Often we forget that he has a special gift for each one of us,
because we tend to weigh and measure such gifts with the coin of
the world's market place. The widow's mite was worth more than all
the rich men's gold because it represented the focus of her life. Her
poverty was rich because all she had belonged to the living Lord.
Some unheard-of Elizabethan woman who led a life of selfless love

may well be brought before the throne of God ahead of Shakespeare, 22 for such a person may be a greater force for good than someone on whom God's blessings seem to have been dropped more generously. As Emmanuel, Cardinal Suhard says, "To be a witness does not consist in engaging in propaganda, nor even in stirring people up, but in being a living mystery. It means to live in such a way that one's life would not make sense if God did not exist."

widow's mite · see Mark 12:41–44

Bach's *St. Matthew's Passion* · one of the most famous works by J. S. Bach (1685–1750), composed in 1729

The widow's mite* and Bach's *St. Matthew's Passion** are both 23 "living mysteries," both witness to lives which affirm the loving presence of God.

✦   ✦   ✦

Martin Buber · German-Jewish philosopher (1878–1965)

K ANDINSKY AND VAN GOGH say more than they know in 24 their paintings. So does a devout man who is not a Christian, but a Jew and a philosopher, Martin Buber.* Listen: "You should utter words as though heaven were opened within them and as though you did not put the word into your mouth, but as though you had entered the word." Buber was certainly not consciously thinking of the second Person of the Trinity when he wrote that. Nevertheless his words become richer for me when I set them alongside these: "In the beginning was the Word, and the Word was with God, and the Word was God."*

"In the beginning ... was God" · John 1:1

Plato · Greek philosopher (428/7–348/7 BC)

Plato,* too, all that distance away in time and space from 25 Bethlehem, seems often to be struggling towards an understanding of incarnation, of God's revelation of himself through particularity. Of course, because I am a struggling Christian, it's inevitable that I superimpose my awareness of all that happened in the life of Jesus upon what I'm reading, upon Buber, upon Plato, upon the Book of Daniel. But I'm not sure that's a bad thing. To be truly Christian means to see Christ everywhere, to know him as all in all.

I don't mean to water down my Christianity into a vague kind 26 of universalism, with Buddha and Mohammed all being more or less equal to Jesus – not at all! But neither do I want to tell God (or my friends) where he can and cannot be seen! We human beings far too often tend to codify God, to feel that we know where he is and where he is not, and this arrogance leads to such things as the Spanish Inquisition,* the Salem witch burnings,* and has the result of further fragmenting an already broken Christendom.

Spanish Inquisition · authorized by Pope Sixtus IV in 1478, the Spanish Inquisition punished heretics and non-Christians

Salem witch burnings · Puritan trials in the witchcraft scare of 1692

We live by revelation, as Christians, as artists, which means that 27 we must be careful never to get set into rigid molds. The minute

27 we begin to think we know all the answers, we forget the questions, and we become smug like the Pharisee who listed all his considerable virtues, and thanked God that he was not like other men.

28 Unamuno* might be describing the artist as well as the Christian as he writes, "Those who believe they believe in God, but without passion in the heart, without anguish of mind, without uncertainty, without doubt, and even at times without despair, believe only in the idea of God, and not in God himself."

Unamuno · Miguel de Unamuno (1864–1936), Spanish educator and philosopher

⁌ ⁍ ⁌

29 WHEN I WAS IN COLLEGE I knew that I wanted to be a writer. And to be a writer means, as everyone knows, to be published.

30 And I copied in my journal from Tchekov's letters:* "You must once and for all give up being worried about successes and failures. Don't let that concern you, It's your duty to go on working steadily day by day, quite quietly, to be prepared for mistakes, which are inevitable, and for failures."

Tchekov's letters · Anton Chekhov (1860–1904), Russian author and playwright

31 I believed those words then, and I believe them now, though in the intervening years my faith in them has often been tested. After the success of my first novels I was not prepared for rejections, for the long years of failure. Again I turned to Tchekov. "The thought that I must, that I ought to, write, never leaves me for an instant." Alas, it *did* leave me, when I had attacks of false guilt because I was spending so much time at the typewriter and in no way pulling my own weight financially. But it never left me for long.

32 I've written about that decade of failure in *A Circle of Quiet*. I learned a lot of valuable lessons during that time, but there's no doubt that they were bitter. This past winter I wrote in my journal, "If I'd read these words of Rilke's* during the long years of rejection they might have helped, because I could have answered the question in the affirmative:

Rilke's · Rainer Maria Rilke (1875–1926), German-Austrian poet

32a You are looking outward, and that above all you should not do now. Nobody can counsel and help you, nobody. There is only one single way. Go into yourself. Search for the reason that bids you to write; find out whether it is spreading out its roots in the deepest places of your heart, acknowledge to yourself whether you would have to die if it were denied you to write. This above all – ask yourself

in the stillest hour of your night: Must I write? Delve into   32a
yourself for a deep answer. And if this should be affirmative, if you may meet this earnest question with a strong
and simple "I must," then build your life according to this
necessity; your life even into its most indifferent and slightest hour must be a sign of this urge and testimony to it.

That is from *Letters to a Young Poet*, and surely Rilke speaks to   32
all of us who struggle with a vocation of words.

✤ ✤ ✤

THE WRITER DOES WANT to be published; the painter urgently   33
hopes that someone will see the finished canvas (van Gogh
was denied the satisfaction of having his work bought and appre-
ciated during his life time; no wonder the pain was more than
he could bear); the composer needs his music to be heard. Art is
communication, and if there is no communication it is as though
the work had been still-born.

The reader, viewer, listener, usually grossly underestimates   34
his importance. If a reader cannot create a book along with the
writer, the book will never come to life. Creative involvement:
that's the basic difference between reading a book and watching
TV. In watching TV we are passive; sponges; we *do* nothing. In
reading we must become creators. Once the child has learned to
read alone, and can pick up a book without illustrations, he must
become a creator, imagining the setting of the story, visualizing
the characters, seeing facial expressions, hearing the inflection
of voices. The author and the reader "know" each other; they
meet on the bridge of words.

So there is no evading the fact that the artist yearns for "suc-   35
cess," because that means that there has been a communication
of the vision: that all the struggle has not been invalid.

Yet with each book I write I am weighted with a deep longing   36
for anonymity, a feeling that books should not be signed, reviews
should not be read. But I sign the books; I read the reviews.

Two writers I admire express the two sides of this paradox.   37
They seem to disagree with each other completely, and yet I
believe that each is right.

E. M. Forster · English
novelist (1879–1970)

E. M. Forster* writes,   38

38a …all literature tends towards a condition of anonymity, and that, so far as words are creative, a signature merely distracts from their true significance.

38b I do not say that literature "ought" not to be signed … because literature is alive, and consequently "ought" is the wrong word. It wants not to be signed. That is my point. It is always tugging in that direction … saying, in effect, "I, not the author, really exist."

38c The poet wrote the poem, no doubt. But he forgot himself while he wrote it, and we forget him while we read…. We forget, for ten minutes, his name and our own, and I contend that this temporary forgetfulness, this momentary and mutual anonymity, is sure evidence of good stuff.

38d Modern education promotes the unmitigated study of literature, and concentrates our attention on the relation between a writer's life – his surface life – and his work. That is the reason it is such a curse.

38e Literature wants not to be signed.

And yet I know whom I am quoting, for Forster signed his work.

39 W. H. Auden* writes:

W. H. Auden · English-born author (1907–1973). See Auden's poems on pages 455–456

39a Our judgment of an established author is never simply an æsthetic judgment. In addition to any literary merit it may have, a new book by him has a historic interest for us as the act of a person in whom we have long been interested. He is not only a poet or a novelist; he is also a character in our biography.

39 We cannot seem to escape paradox; I do not think I want to.

✦ ✦ ✦

Jane Austen · English novelist (1775–1817)

40 FORSTER REFERS TO "*his* surface life and *his* work;" Auden says, "*He* is not only a poet or a novelist; *he* is also a character in our biography." That *his* and that *he* refers as much to Jane Austen* and George Sand* as to Flaubert* and Hemingway.* It is a generic *his* and *he,* and not exclusively masculine.

George Sand · literary pseudonym of Aurore Dupin (1804–1876), French Romantic writer

Flaubert · Gustave Flaubert (1821–1880), French Realist novelist

41 I am a female, of the species, man. Genesis is very explicit that it takes both male and female to make the image of God and that the generic word, man, includes both.

Hemingway · Ernest Hemingway (1899–1961), American novelist

God created man in his own image, male and female.   41a

That is Scripture, therefore I refuse to be timid about being part   41
of *man*kind. We of the female sex are half of mankind, and it
is pusillanimous* to resort to he/she, him/her, or even worse,
android words. I have a hunch that those who would do so have
forgotten their rightful heritage.

pusillanimous ·
cowardly

I know that I am fortunate in having grown up in a household   42
where no sexist roles were imposed on me. I lived in an atmosphere
which assumed equality with all its differences. When mankind was
referred to it never occurred to me that I was not part of it, or that
I was in some way being excluded. My great-great-grandmother,
growing up on the St. John's river* in times of violence and hardship,
had seven homes burned down; nevertheless she spoke casually in
seven languages. Her daughter-in-law ran a military hospital, having
been brought up at the court of Spain where she was her ambassador
father's hostess; her closest friend was the princess Eugénie,* soon to
be Empress, and the two young women rode and competed with the
princess's brothers in all sports; to prove their bravery, each drove a
sharp knife into the flesh of the forearm without whimper. Others
of my female forbears crossed the country in covered wagons, and
knew how to handle a gun as well as any man.

St. John's river · river in
northeastern Florida

princess Eugénie ·
Eugénie, Comtesse
de Teba (1826–1920),
Spanish wife of Napoleon
III of France and Empress
of France 1853–1870

Perhaps it is this background which has made me assume   43
casually that of course I am not excluded when anyone refers to a
novelist – or anyone else – as he or him. My closest woman friend
is a physician, and so is my daughter-in-law. Not all women have
been as fortunate as I have been. When my books were being
rejected during the fifties it was not because of my sex, it was
because the editors did not like what I was writing. It was my
words which were being rejected, not my femaleness.

Because I am a story-teller I live by words. Perhaps music   44
is a purer art form. It may be that when we communicate with
life on another planet, it will be through music, not through
language or words.

But I am a story-teller and that involves language, for me the   45
English language, that wonderfully rich, complex, and ofttimes confusing tongue. When language is limited, I am thereby diminished, too.

In time of war language always dwindles, vocabulary is lost;   46
and we live in a century of war. When I took my elder daughter's

46 tenth grade vocabulary cards up to the school from which she had graduated, less than a decade after she had left, the present tenth grade students knew almost none of them. It was far easier for my daughter to read Shakespeare in high school than it was for students coming along just a few years after her.

47 This diminution is world-wide. In Japan, after the Second World War, so many written characters were lost, that it is difficult, if not impossible, for the present day college student to read the works of the great classical masters. In Russia, even if Solzhenytzin* were allowed to be read freely, it would not be easy for the average student to read his novels, for again, after revolution and war, vocabulary fell away. In one of Solzhenytzin's books his hero spends hours at night reading the great Russian dictionary which came out in the late nineteenth century, and Solzhenytzin himself draws on this work, and in his writing he is redeeming language, using the words of Tolstoy* and Dostoyevsky,* using the words of the people of the street, bringing language back to life as he writes.

48 So it has always been. Dante,* writing in exile when dukedoms and principalities were embroiled in wars, was forging language as he wrote his great science-fiction fantasies.

49 We think because we have words, not the other way around. The more words we have, the better able we are to think conceptually. Yet another reason why *Wrinkle* was so often rejected is that there are many words in it which would never be found on a controlled vocabulary list for the age-group of the ten-to-fourteen-year-old. *Tesseract,** for instance. It's a real word, and one essential for the story.

50 As a child, when I came across a word I didn't know, I didn't stop reading the story to look it up, I just went on reading. And after I had come across the word in several books, I knew what it meant; it had been added to my vocabulary. This still happens. When I started to read Teilhard de Chardin's* *The Phenomenon of Man,* I was determined to understand it. I read intelligently, with a dictionary beside me, stopping to look up the scientific words which were not familiar to me. And I bogged down. So I put aside the dictionary and read as though I were reading a story, and quickly I got drawn into the book, fascinated by his loving theology, and understood it far better, at a deeper level, than if I had stuck with the dictionary.

Solzhenytzin · Aleksandr Solzhenytzin (1918–), Russian author who was exiled to Siberia under Stalin and who there embraced the Christian faith

Tolstoy · Count Leo Tolstoy (1828–1910), Russian novelist. See Tolstoy's "How Much Land Does a Man Need" on pages 189–203

Dostoyevsky · Fyodor Dostoyevsky (1821–1881), Russian author. See Dostoyevsky's "The Grand Inquisitor" on pages 169–188

Dante · Dante Alighieri (1265–1321), Italian author of *The Divine Comedy*

Tesseract · a 4-dimensional cube

Teilhard de Chardin's · Pierre Teilhard de Chardin (1881–1955), French philosopher and paleontologist

Is this contradiction? I don't think so. We played with my 51
daughter's vocabulary words during dinner. We kept a dictionary
by the table, just for fun. But when we read, we read. We were
capable of absorbing far more vocabulary when we read straight
on than when we stopped to look up every word. Sometimes I
will jot down words to be looked up later. But we learn words
in many ways, and much of my vocabulary has been absorbed
by my subconscious mind, which then kindly blips it up to my
conscious mind when it is needed.

✣ ✣ ✣

We CANNOT NAME or be Named without language. If our 52
vocabulary dwindles to a few shopworn words, we are
setting ourselves up for takeover by a dictator. When language
becomes exhausted, our freedom dwindles – we cannot think;
we do not recognize danger; injustice strikes us as no more than
"the way things are."

Some of the Ayia Napa delegates came from countries ruled 53
by dictators, either from the right or the left. In both cases,
teachers are suspect; writers are suspect, because people who
use words are able to work out complex ideas, to see injustice,
and perhaps even try to do something about it. Simply being
able to read the Bible in their own language made some of the
delegates suspect.

I might even go to the extreme of declaring that the deliberate 54
diminution of vocabulary by a dictator, or an advertising copy
writer, is anti-Christian.

One cannot have been brought up on the *Book of Common* 55
Prayer,˙ as I was, and not have a feeling for language, willy nilly. In
my first boarding school we had mandatory Morning and Evening
Prayer, through which we sat, bored, looking for divertissement,˙
ready to snicker if someone broke wind or belched. But the language of Cranmer˙ and Coverdale˙ could not but seep through
the interstices.˙ Ready and willing or not, we were enriched.

It is not surprising that there has been considerable discus- 56
sion about the *New Episcopal Book of Common Prayer* in Church
circles, Protestant and Roman Catholic, and by Everyman˙ as well.
The language of the *Book of Common Prayer* is part of our literary heritage, as is the language of the King James translation˙ of

Book of Common Prayer · a book of prayers and liturgy used by churches of the Anglican Communion

divertissement · diversion, amusement

Cranmer · Thomas Cranmer (1489–1556), Archbishop of Canterbury under Henry VIII and Edward VI, he originated the *Book of Common Prayer*

Coverdale · Miles Coverdale (1488?–1569), Bishop of Exeter, his loose translation became the first complete printed Bible in English

interstices · narrow spaces or gaps

Everyman · a refer- ence to the average reader (based on the 15th-century morality play bearing that title)

King James transla- tion · presented to James I in 1611, this translation of the Bible became the *de facto* standard among Protestant churches for centuries thereafter

56 the Bible. Writers throughout centuries of literature have drawn from the Prayer Book as well as the Bible – how many titles come from the Psalms! Novels often contain sentences from Scripture without identification, because it is part of our common heritage; there is no need for footnoting.

57 There was much in the 1928 *Book of Common Prayer* which needed changing; indeed, revision was first talked about in the year of publication. So it is not that all the critics of the new translations are against change (though some are), but against shabby language, against settling for the mediocre and the flabbily permissive. Where language is weak, theology is weakened.

58 I do not want to go back to the 1928 Prayer Book. We can't "go home again." On the whole, the new Prayer Book is a vast improvement over the '28. But I do want us to be aware that not only the '28 Prayer Book had flaws. What has been gained in strength of structure has been lost in poverty of language. Some of the translations of Cranmer's Collects* (those magnificent, one-sentence petitions) or Coverdale's psalms remind me of what Bowdler* did to Shakespeare. Well, Bowdler had his way for a while, but we went back to the richness of Shakespeare.

59 There are some elegant sentences in the new translation ("I myself will awaken the dawn"), but some verses aren't much better than a French translation of Hamlet, in which the famous words Hamlet utters when he first sees the ghost of his father, "Angels and ministers of grace defend us," are rendered, "*Tiens, qu'est que c'est que ça?*"* And surely Shakespeare's words prove his familiarity with Scripture, for they are reminiscent of Saul's encounter with the ghost of Samuel.*

60 *Pelican in the wilderness* has now become *vulture. Praise him, dragons and all deeps,* has become *sea monsters,* which lacks alliteration, to put it mildly. I have been using the new Book for – approximately ten years, I think. It is now thoroughly familiar. In the old language I read, "Be ye sure that the Lord he is God; it is he that hath made us, and not we ourselves." That is a lot more potent theology than "For the Lord himself has made us and we are his." True. But we also need to be reminded in this do-it-yourself age that it is indeed God who has made us, and not we ourselves. We are human and humble and of the earth, and we cannot create until we acknowledge our createdness.

Collects · short prayers

Bowdler · Thomas Bowdler (1754–1825), known for his *Family Shakespeare* (1818), which, through paraphrase, simplification, and editing, sought to provide a version of Shakespeare accessible to all

"Tiens … ça" · "Hey, what's that?" (line 1.4.39, page 573) See *Hamlet* on pages 554–664

Saul's encounter … Samuel · see 1 Samuel 28:7–20

In the old language I read, "O God, make clean our hearts   61
within us, and take not thy Holy Spirit from us." In the new version it is, "Create clean hearts within us, O Lord, and comfort us
with your Holy Spirit." All very well, but we need to know that
if we turn from God, if we are rebellious and stiff-necked we
deeply offend the Holy Spirit; we may not take him for granted;
he indwells us on his own conditions, not ours. We cannot simply
ingest him when we feel like it, like an aspirin.

Although Holy Ghost has been rendered as Holy Spirit   62
throughout, there seems to be considerable fear of the word
"Spirit" and all its implications.

To "The Lord be with you", we used to reply, "And with thy spirit."   63
Now it goes, "The Lord be with you." "And also with you."   64
To which the only suitable response is, "Likewise, I'm sure."   65
We're told that the new Prayer Book is meant to be in the "lan-   66
guage of the people." But which people? And in language which
is left after a century of war, all dwindled and shrivelled? Are we
supposed to bring our language down to the lowest common
denominator in order to be "meaningful"? And, if we want to make
the language contemporary, why not just cut out the *thy* and say,
"And with your spirit?" Why are we afraid of the word *spirit*? Does it
remind us of baffling and incomprehensible and fearful things like

the Annunciation · see   the Annunciation* and the Transfiguration* and the Passover,* those
Luke 1:26–38   mighty acts of God which we forget how to understand because
the Transfiguration ·   our childlike creativity has been corrupted and diminished?
see Matthew 17:1–13

the Passover · see   Perhaps the old Prayer Book dwelt too much on penitence, but   67
Exodus 12   there was also excellent psychology in confessing, "We have left
undone those things which we ought to have done," *before* "We have
done those things which we ought not to have done." In the new confession we confess our sins of commission before our sins of omission.
But I have noticed that when someone dies, those who are left are apt
to cry out, "Oh, if I had only taken her on that picnic!" Or, "If only I'd
gone to see him last Wednesday. "It is the things I have left undone
which haunt me far more than the things which I have done.

In restricting the language in the new translations we have   68
lost that depth and breadth which can give us the kind of *knowing* which is our heritage. This loss has permeated our literature,
and our prayers, not necessarily in that order. College students
of the future will miss many allusions in their surveys of English

68   literature, because the language of the great seventeenth century translators is no longer in their blood stream. I like to read the new translations of Bible and Prayer Book for new insights, for shocks of discovery and humour, but I don't want to discard the old, as though it were as transitory as last year's fashions.

69   Nor do I want to be stuck in the vague androidism which has resulted from the attempts to avoid the masculine pronoun. We are in a state of intense sexual confusion, both in life and language, but the social manipulation is not working. Language is a living thing; it does not stay the same; it is hard for me to read the language of *Piers Plowman*,* for instance, so radical have the changes been. But language is its own creature. It evolves on its own. It follows the language of its great artists, such as Chaucer.* It does not do well when suffering from arbitrary control. Our attempts to change the words which have long been part of a society dominated by males have not been successful; instead of making language less sexist they have made it more so.

Piers Plowman · 14th-century English religio-political poem

Chaucer · Geoffrey Chaucer (1342/3–1400), English poet and author of *The Canterbury Tales*

70   Indeed we are in a bind. For thousands of years we have lived in a paternalistic society, where women have allowed men to make God over in their own, masculine image. But that's anthropomorphism. To think of God in terms of sex at all is a dead end.

71   To substitute *person* for *man* has ruined what used to be a good, theological word, calling up the glory of God's image within us. Now, at best, it's a joke. There's something humiliating and embarrassing about being a chairperson. Or a Chair. A group of earnest women have put together a volume of desexed hymns, and one of my old favorites now begins:

72   "Dear Mother-Father of personkind…"*

"Dear … person-kind…" · a version of the hymn "Dear Lord and Father of Mankind" (words J. G. Whittier, 1872, music F. C. Maker, 1887)

73   No. It won't do. This is not equality. Perhaps we should drop the word *woman* altogether, and use man, recognizing that we need both male and female to be whole. And perhaps, if we ever have real equality with all our glorious differences, the language itself will make the appropriate changes. For language, like a story or a painting, is alive. Ultimately it will be the artists who will change the language (as Chaucer did, as Dante did, as Joyce* did), not the committees. For an artist is not a consumer, as our commercials urge us to be. An artist is a nourisher and a creator who knows that during the act of creation there is collaboration. We do not create alone.

Joyce · James Joyce (1882–1941), Irish novelist and literary innovator

❖ ❖ ❖

A FRIEND OF MINE AT A denominational college reported sadly 74 that one of his students came to complain to him about a visiting professor. This professor was having the students read some twentieth-century fiction, and the student was upset both at the language of this fiction, and the amount of what she considered to be immoral sex.

My friend, knowing the visiting professor to be a person of 75 both intelligence and integrity, urged the student to go and talk with him about these concerns.

"Oh, I couldn't do that," the student said. "He isn't a Christian." 76

"He" is a Roman Catholic. 77

If we fall into Satan's trap of assuming that other people are not 78 Christians because they do not belong to our own particular brand of Christianity, no wonder we become incapable of understanding the works of art produced by so-called non-Christians, whether they be atheists, Jews, Buddhists, or anything else outside a frame of reference we have made into a closed rather than an open door.

If I cannot see evidence of incarnation in a painting of a bridge 79 in the rain by Hokusai,* a book by Chaim Potok* or Isaac Bashevis Singer,* in music by Bloch* or Bernstein,* then I will miss its significance in an Annunciation by Franciabigio,* the final chorus of the St. Matthew Passion, the words of a sermon by John Donne.*

One of the most profoundly moving moments at Ayia Napa 80 came for me when Jesse, a student from Zimbabwe, told me, "I am a good Seventh-day Adventist, but you have shown me God." Jesse will continue to be a good Seventh-day Adventist as he returns to Africa to his family; I will struggle with my own way of belief; neither of us felt the need or desire to change the other's Christian frame of reference. For that moment, at least, all our doors and windows were wide open; we were not carefully shutting out God's purifying light, in order to feel safe and secure; we were bathed in the same light that burned and yet did not consume the bush. We walked barefoot on holy ground.*

❖ ❖ ❖

I HAPPEN TO LOVE SPINACH, but my husband, Hugh, does 81 not; he prefers beets, which I don't much care for – except

Hokusai · Katsushika Hokusai (1760–1849), Japanese master artist of *ukiyo-e* ("pictures of the floating world")

Chaim Potok · American Jewish author (1929–2002)

Isaac Bashevis Singer · American Jewish writer (1904–1991). See Singer's "Gimpel the Fool" on pages 233–246

Bloch · Ernest Bloch (1880–1959), Swiss-born Jewish composer

Bernstein · Leonard Bernstein (1918–1990), American Jewish composer and director of the New York Philharmonic

Franciabigio · Italian Renaissance painter (1482/3–1525)

John Donne · English Metaphysical poet and minister (1572–1631). See Donne's "Meditation 17" on pages 11–13

burned … ground · see Exodus 3:2–5

81 the greens. Neither of us thinks less of the other because of this difference in taste. Both spinach and beets are vegetables; both are good for us. We do not have to enjoy precisely the same form of balanced meal.

82 We also approach God in rather different ways, but it is the same God we are seeking, just as Jesse and I, in our totally different disciplines, worship the same Lord.

83 Stories, no matter how simple, can be vehicles of truth; can be, in fact, icons. It's no coincidence that Jesus taught almost entirely by telling stories, simple stories dealing with the stuff of life familiar to the Jews of his day. Stories are able to help us to become more whole, to become Named. And Naming is one of the impulses behind all art; to give a name to the cosmos we see despite all the chaos.

84 God asked Adam to name all the animals,• which was asking Adam to help in the creation of their wholeness. When we name each other, we are sharing in the joy and privilege of incarnation, and all great works of art are icons of Naming.

God ... animals · see Genesis 2:18–20

85 When we look at a painting, or hear a symphony, or read a book, and feel more Named, then, for us, that work is a work of Christian art. But to look at a work of art and then to make a judgment as to whether or not it is art, and whether or not it is Christian, is presumptuous. It is something we cannot know in any conclusive way. We can know only if it speaks within our own hearts, and leads us to living more deeply with Christ in God.

86 One of my professors, Dr. Caroline Gordon, a deeply Christian woman, told our class, "We do not judge great art. It judges us." And that very judgment may enable us to change our lives, and to renew our commitment to the Lord of Creation.

⁜ ⁜ ⁜

87 BUT HOW DIFFICULT IT IS for us not to judge; to make what, in the current jargon, is called "a value judgment!" And here we blunder into paradox again. Jesus said, "Judge not, that you be not judged."• And yet daily we must make decisions which involve judgments:

"Judge not ... judged" · Matthew 7:1

88 We had peanut butter sandwiches yesterday because they are Tod's favorites. Today it's Sarah's turn and we'll have bologna with lots of mustard.

I will not let my child take this book of fairy tales out of the library because fairy tales are untrue. 89

I will share these wonderful fairy tales with my child because they are vehicles of hidden truths. 90

I will not talk with the Roman Catholic professor lest he make me less Christian than I think I am. 91

I will not talk to the Jewish scientist in the next apartment or Hitler and the Storm Troopers might send me to a concentration camp. 92

I will not read this book because it might shake my belief in the answers I am so comfortable with. 93

Zeal ... up · Psalm 69:9   Zeal for thine house hath eaten me up.* 94

Bertrand Russell · English philosopher and pacifist (1872–1970)

But Bertrand Russell* says, "Zeal is a bad mark for a cause. Nobody has any zeal about arithmetic. It is not the vaccinationists but the antivaccinationists who generate zeal. People are zealous for a cause when they are not quite positive that it is true." 95

Dr. Semmelweis · Ignaz Philipp Semmelweis (1818–1865), German-Hungarian physician

It is hard for us to believe now that there were antivaccination- 96 ists, when vaccinations have succeeded in wiping small-pox from the planet. It is hard for us to believe that Dr. Semmelweis* was almost torn to pieces when he suggested that physicians should wash their hands before delivering babies in order to help prevent the septicemia or puerperal fever which killed so many women after childbirth. It is hard for us to believe that Bach was considered heretical when he put the thumb under instead of over the fingers on the keyboard. It is hard for us to believe that Shakespeare was considered a trivial playwright because he was too popular. But great negative zeal was expended in all of these cases.

We all tend to make zealous judgments, and thereby close 97 ourselves off from revelation. If we feel that we already know something in its totality, then we fail to keep our ears and eyes open to that which may expand or even change that which we so zealously think we know.

My non-Christian friends and acquaintances are zealous in 98 what they "know" about Christianity, and which bears little or no relationship to anything I believe.

A friend of mine, Betty Beckwith, in her book, *If I Had the* 99 *Wings of the Morning,* writes about taking her brain-damaged child to a Jewish doctor. He said, "You people think of us as the people who killed your Christ." Spontaneously she replied, "Oh, no. We think of you as the people who gave him to us."

❖ ❖ ❖

100 IN THE LITERARY WORLD TODAY, Christianity has pretty well replaced sex as the present pet taboo, not only because Christianity is so often distorted by Christians as well as non-Christians, but because it is too wild and free for the timid.

101 How many of us really want life, life more abundant,* life which does not promise any fringe benefits or early retirement plans? Life which does not promise the absence of pain, or love which is not vulnerable and open to hurt? The number of people who attempt to withdraw from life through the abuse of alcohol, tranquilizers, barbiturates, is statistically shocking.

life more abundant · see John 10:10

102 How many of us dare to open ourselves to that truth which would make us free? Free to talk to Roman Catholics or charismatics or Jews, as Jesus was free to talk to tax collectors or publicans* or Samaritans. Free to feast at the Lord's table with those whose understanding of the Body and Blood may be a little different from ours. Free to listen to angels. Free to run across the lake when we are called.

publicans · see Mark 2:15–17 and John 4:4–42

103 What is a true icon of God to one person may be blasphemy to another. And it is not possible for us flawed human beings to make absolute, zealous judgments as to what is and what is not religious art. I know what is religious art for me. You know what is religious art for you. And they are not necessarily the same. Not everybody feels pulled up to heavenly heights in listening to the pellucid,* mathematically precise structure of a Bach fugue. The smarmy* picture of Jesus which I find nauseating may be for someone else, a true icon.

pellucid · clear

smarmy · emotionally manipulative

❖ ❖ ❖

104 ANOTHER PROBLEM ABOUT identifying what is and what is not religious art, is that religious art transcends its culture and reflects the eternal, and while we are alive we are caught within our culture. All artists reflect the time in which they live, but whether or not their work also has that universality which lives in any generation or culture is nothing we can know for many years. Also, art which is truly iconographic for one period may have little to say to another. My parents, who were in their thirties at the time of the First World War, loved Romantic music, Chopin,* Wagner*—how they loved Wagner! But Wagner has

Chopin · Frédéric Chopin (1810–1849), Polish-French Romantic composer

Wagner · Richard Wagner (1813–1883), German Romantic composer

little to say to me. The reasonable, peaceful world in which my [104]
parents grew up, the world which was far too civilized for war,
was broken forever by the horror of World War I. My father went
to fight in the war to end war, and for the rest of his life he had
to live with the knowledge that not only had his war not ended
war, it was the beginning of a century of near-total war.

My generation, and my children's, living in this embattled and [105]
insane period, find more nourishment in the structure of Bach
and Mozart* than the lush romanticism of Wagner. Wagner is fine
if the world around one is stable. But when the world is, indeed,
in chaos, then an affirmation of cosmos becomes essential.

Usually, after the death of a well-known artist, there comes [106]
a period of eclipse of his work. If the artist reflects only his own
culture, then his works will die with that culture. But if his works
reflect the eternal and universal, they will revive. It's difficult to
believe that for several centuries after Shakespeare's death he
was virtually unknown. William Green,* his contemporary, was
considered a better playwright than the too popular Will, who
pandered to public taste. But was it pandering? Art should communicate with as many people as possible, not just with a group
of the esoteric elite. And who remembers Green today?

Bach, too, was eclipsed, and remembered as a good church [107]
organist rather than a composer, and for a long time that putting
of the thumb under the fingers was held against him; no wonder
the thumb had been very little used in keyboard music until Bach
came along with this "radical" departure from custom.

Bach might have been forgotten forever had not Mendelssohn* [108]
discovered some monks wrapping parcels in music manuscript – and gave the St. Matthew Passion back to the world.

The St. Matthew Passion is an icon of the highest quality [109]
for me, an open door into the realm of the numinous. Bach, of
course, was a man of deep and profound religious faith, a faith
which shines through his most secular music. As a matter of fact,
the melody of his moving chorale, *O sacred head now wounded*,
was the melody of a popular street song of the day, but Bach's
religious genius was so great that it is now recognized as one of
the most superb pieces of religious music ever written.

There is nothing so secular that it cannot be sacred, and that [110]
is one of the deepest messages of the Incarnation.

Mozart · Wolfgang
Amadeus Mozart
(1756–1791), Austrian
composer

William Green ·
L'Engle is perhaps
referring to English playwright and poet Robert
Greene (1558–1592)

Mendelssohn ·
Felix Mendelssohn
(1809–1847), German
composer of the early
Romantic period

Flannery O'Connor

⊀ 1 9 2 5 - 1 9 6 4 ⊱

O'Connor was under no illusions as to how odd her overt Christian emphases might appear to non-religious readers. Her subject in writing, she once remarked, "is the action of grace in territory held largely by the devil. I have also found that what I write is read by an audience which puts little stock either in grace or the devil." However, the author was neither defensive nor abrasive in her approach to those who did not share her beliefs. In her fiction, essays, and letters, in fact, O'Connor was deeply compassionate about the crisis of faith in a religionless age: "Nihilism is the gas we breathe," she once observed. "I think there is no suffering greater than what is caused by the doubts of those who want to believe. I know what torment this is, but I can only see it, in myself anyway, as the process by which faith is deepened. What people don't realize is how much religion costs. They think it is a big electric blanket, when of course it is the cross." O'Connor frequently lectured on university campuses, often addressing the tension between intellect and religious convictions. The following letter, published posthumously in a collection of letters under the title The Habit of Being *(1979), is O'Connor's response to an Emory University student who had written to her concerning his doubts about the truth of Christianity.*

A LETTER TO ALFRED CORN

30 MAY 1962

1   I THINK THAT THIS EXPERIENCE you are having of losing your faith, or as you think, of having lost it, is an experience that in the long run belongs to faith; or at least it can belong to faith if it is still valuable to you, and it must be or you would not have written me about this.

2   I don't know how the kind of faith required of a Christian living in the 20th century can be at all if it is not grounded on

this experience that you are having right now of unbelief. This 2
may be the case always and not just in the 20th century. Peter
said, "Lord, I believe. Help my unbelief."• It is the most natural
and most human and most agonizing prayer in the gospels, and
I think it is the foundation prayer of faith.

As a freshman in college you are bombarded with new ideas, or 3
rather pieces of ideas, new frames of reference, an activation of the
intellectual life which is only beginning, but which is already running
ahead of your lived experience. After a year of this, you think you
cannot believe. You are just beginning to realize how difficult it is to
have faith and the measure of a commitment to it, but you are too
young to decide you don't have faith just because you feel you can't
believe. About the only way we know whether we believe or not is
by what we do, and I think from your letter that you will not take
the path of least resistance in this matter and simply decide that you
have lost your faith and that there is nothing you can do about it.

One result of the stimulation of your intellectual life that 4
takes place in college is usually a shrinking of the imaginative
life. This sounds like a paradox, but I have often found it to be
true. Students get so bound up with difficulties such as reconciling the clashing of so many different faiths such as Buddhism,
Mohammedanism,• etc., that they cease to look for God in other
ways. Bridges• once wrote Gerard Manley Hopkins and asked
him to tell him how he, Bridges, could believe. He must have
expected from Hopkins a long philosophical answer. Hopkins
wrote back, "Give alms." He was trying to say to Bridges that God
is to be experienced in Charity (in the sense of love for the divine
image in human beings). Don't get so entangled with intellectual
difficulties that you fail to look for God in this way.

The intellectual difficulties have to be met, however, and you will 5
be meeting them for the rest of your life. When you get a reasonable
hold on one, another will come to take its place. At one time, the clash
of the different world religions was a difficulty for me. Where you
have absolute solutions, however, you have no need of faith. Faith
is what you have in the absence of knowledge. The reason this clash
doesn't bother me any longer is because I have got, over the years, a
sense of the immense sweep of creation, of the evolutionary process
in everything, of how incomprehensible God must necessarily be to
be the God of heaven and earth. You can't fit the Almighty into your

"Lord … unbelief"·
O'Connor is perhaps
recalling the plea of an
anguished father whose
son was afflicted, "I
believe; help thou mine
unbelief" (Mark 9:24)

Mohammedanism·
Islam

Bridges·Robert
Bridges (1844–1930),
English poet and life-
long friend of poet G. M.
Hopkins (1844–1889).
See Hopkins' poems on
pages 443–445

5   intellectual categories. I might suggest that you look into some of the works of Pierre Teilhard de Chardin* (*The Phenomenon of Man* et al.). He was a paleontologist – helped to discover Peking man – and also a man of God. I don't suggest you go to him for answers but for different questions, for that stretching of the imagination that you need to make you a skeptic in the face of much that you are learning, much of what is new and shocking but which when boiled down becomes less so and takes its place in the general scheme of things. What kept me a skeptic in college was precisely my Christian faith. It always said: wait, don't bite on this, get a wider picture, continue to read.

6   If you want your faith, you have to work for it. It is a gift, but for very few is it a gift given without any demand for equal time devoted to its cultivation. For every book you read that is anti-Christian, make it your business to read one that presents the other side of the picture; if one isn't satisfactory read others. Don't think that you have to abandon reason to be a Christian. A book that might help you is *The Unity of Philosophical Experience* by Étienne Gilson.* Another is Newman's *The Grammar of Assent.** To find out about faith, you have to go to the people who have it and you have to go to the most intelligent ones if you are going to stand up intellectually to agnostics and the general run of pagans that you are going to find in the majority of people around you. Much of the criticism of belief that you find today comes from people who are judging it from the standpoint of another and narrower discipline. The Biblical criticism of the 19th century, for instance, was the product of historical disciplines. It has been entirely revamped in the 20th century by applying broader criteria to it, and those people who lost their faith in the 19th century because of it, could better have hung on in blind trust.

7   Even in the life of a Christian, faith rises and falls like the tides of an invisible sea. It's there, even when he can't see it or feel it, if he wants it to be there. You realize, I think, that it is more valuable, more mysterious, altogether more immense than anything you can learn or decide upon in college. Learn what you can, but cultivate Christian skepticism. It will keep you free – not to do anything you please, but free to be formed by something larger than your own intellect or the intellects of those around you.

8   I don't know if this is the kind of answer that can help you, but any time you care to write me, I can try to do better.

Pierre Teilhard de Chardin · Jesuit French philosopher and paleontologist (1881–1955)

Étienne Gilson · French professor of medieval philosophy (1884–1978)

Newman's *The Grammar of Assent* · John Henry Newman (1801–1890), English theologian and philosopher. See Newman's *The Idea of a University* on pages 29–33

Frederick Buechner

《 1 9 2 6 - 》

Buechner is a rarity on the literary scene, being both an ordained minister ("the most quoted living writer among Christians of influence," according to one critic) and a respected novelist, author of The Book of Bebb *(1979),* Godric *(1980), and* Brendan *(1987). He was reared in a secular home in New York and the Bahamas, then attended Princeton University and Union Theological Seminary. Buechner believes that the signs of God's presence may be seen and heard everywhere, especially in our ordinary lives: "There is no place or time so lowly and earthbound but that holiness can be there too," Buechner writes. "Listen to your life. See it for the fathomless mystery that it is... because in the last analysis all moments are key moments, and life itself is grace." In this respect, Buechner continues a longstanding Christian tradition of spiritual self-examination. The "inner frontier" of the soul, "where doubt is pitted against faith, hope against despair, grief against joy," is the domain that most fascinates Buechner both as fiction writer and theologian. The excerpt which follows is the opening chapter of Buechner's third autobiographical work,* Telling Secrets *(1991).*

THE DWARVES IN THE STABLE

1 ONE NOVEMBER MORNING IN 1936 when I was ten years old, my father got up early, put on a pair of gray slacks and a maroon sweater, opened the door to look in briefly on my younger brother and me, who were playing a game in our room, and then went down into the garage where he turned on the engine of the family Chevy and sat down on the running board to wait for the exhaust to kill him. Except for a memorial service for his Princeton class the next spring, by which time we had moved away to another part of the world altogether, there was no

funeral because on both my mother's side and my father's there   1
was no church connection of any kind and funerals were simply
not part of the tradition. He was cremated, his ashes buried in
a cemetery in Brooklyn, and I have no idea who if anybody was
present. I know only that my mother, brother, and I were not.

There was no funeral to mark his death and put a period at   2
the end of the sentence that had been his life, and as far as I can
remember, once he had died my mother, brother, and I rarely
talked about him much ever again, either to each other or to
anybody else. It made my mother too sad to talk about him, and
since there was already more than enough sadness to go round,
my brother and I avoided the subject with her as she avoided
it for her own reasons also with us. Once in a while she would
bring it up but only in very oblique ways. I remember her saying
things like "You're going to have to be big boys now," and "Now
things are going to be different for all of us," and to me, "You're
the man of the family now," with that one little three-letter adverb
freighted with more grief and anger and guilt and God knows
what all else than it could possibly bear.

We didn't talk about my father with each other, and we didn't   3
talk about him outside the family either partly at least because
suicide was looked on as something a little shabby and shameful
in those days. Nice people weren't supposed to get mixed up with
it. My father had tried to keep it a secret himself by leaving his
note to my mother in a place where only she would be likely to
find it and by saying a number of times the last few weeks of his
life that there was something wrong with the Chevy's exhaust
system, which he was going to see if he could fix. He did this partly
in hopes that his life insurance wouldn't be invalidated, which of
course it was, and partly too, I guess, in hopes that his friends
wouldn't find out how he had died, which of course they did.
His suicide was a secret we nonetheless tried to keep as best we
could, and after a while my father himself became such a secret.
There were times when he almost seemed a secret we were trying
to keep from each other. I suppose there were occasions when
one of us said, "Remember the time he did this," or, "Remember
the time he said that," but if so, I've long since forgotten them.
And because words are so much a part of what we keep the past
alive by, if only words to ourselves, by not speaking of what we

3 remembered about him we soon simply stopped remembering at all, or at least I did.

4 Within a couple of months of his death we moved away from New Jersey, where he had died, to the island of Bermuda of all places – another house, another country even – and from that point on I can't even remember remembering him. Within a year of his death I seem to have forgotten what he looked like except for certain photographs of him, to have forgotten what his voice sounded like and what it had been like to be with him. Because none of the three of us ever talked about how we had felt about him when he was alive or how we felt about him now that he wasn't, those feelings soon disappeared too and went underground along with the memories. As nearly as I can find out from people who knew him, he was a charming, good-looking, gentle man who was down on his luck and drank too much and had a great number of people who loved him and felt sorry for him. Among those people, however inadequately they may have showed it, I can only suppose were his wife and two sons; but in almost no time at all, it was as if, at least for me, he had never existed.

5 "Don't talk, don't trust, don't feel" is supposed to be the unwritten law of families that for one reason or another have gone out of whack, and certainly it was our law. We never talked about what had happened. We didn't trust the world with our secret, hardly even trusted each other with it. And as far as my ten-year-old self was concerned anyway, the only feeling I can remember from that distant time was the blessed relief of coming out of the dark and unmentionable sadness of my father's life and death into fragrance and greenness and light.

6 Don't talk, trust, feel was the law we lived by, and woe to the one who broke it. Twenty-two years later in a novel called *The Return of Ansel Gibbs* I told a very brief and fictionalized version of my father's death, and the most accurate word I can find to describe my mother's reaction to it is fury. For days she could hardly bring herself to speak to me, and when she did, it was with words of great bitterness. As she saw it, I had betrayed a sacred trust, and though I might have defended myself by saying that the story was after all as much mine as his son to tell as it was hers as his widow to keep hidden, I not only didn't say

any such things but never even considered such things. I felt ⁶
as much of a traitor as she charged me with being, and at the
age of thirty-two was as horrified at what I had done as if I had
been a child of ten. I was full of guilt and remorse and sure that
in who-knows-what grim and lasting way I would be made to
suffer for what I had done.

I was in my fifties and my mother in her eighties before I dared ⁷
write on the forbidden subject again. It was in an autobiographical
book called *The Sacred Journey* that I did so, and this time I told
the story straight except that out of deference to her, or perhaps
out of fear of her, I made no reference to her part in it. Otherwise
I set it down as fully and accurately as I could, and the only reason
I was able to do so was that I suspected that from *Ansel Gibbs* on
my mother had never really read any other book I had written
for fear of what she might find there. I was sure that she wouldn't
read this one either. And I turned out to be right. She never read
the book or the second autobiographical one that followed it even
though, or precisely because, it was the story of her son's life and
in that sense a part of her own story too. She was a strong and
brave woman in many ways, but she was not brave and strong
enough for that. We all have to survive as best we can.

She survived to within eleven days of her ninety-second birth- ⁸
day and died in her own bed in the room that for the last year or
so of her life when her arthritic knees made it virtually impossible
for her to walk became the only world that really interested her.
She kept track more or less of the world outside. She had a rough
idea what her children and grandchildren were up to. She read
the papers and watched the evening news. But such things as that
were dim and far away compared to the news that was breaking
around her every day. Yvonne, who came days, had been trying
to tell her something but God only knew what, her accent was so
thick. Marge, who came nights, was an hour late because of delays
on the subway, or so she said. My mother's cane had fallen behind
the radiator, and the super was going to have to come do something about it. Where was her fan? Where was the gold purse she
kept her extra hearing aids in? Where was the little peach-colored
pillow, which of all the pillows she had was the only one that kept
her tray level when they brought in her meals? In the world where
she lived, these were the things that made headlines.

9   "If I didn't have something to look for, I would be lost," she said once. It was one of her most shimmering utterances. She hunted for her lost pills, lost handkerchief, lost silver comb, the little copy of *Les Malheurs de Sophie** she had lost, because with luck she might even find them. There was a better chance of it anyway than of finding her lost beauty or the friends who had mostly died or the life that had somehow gotten mislaid in the debris of her nonlife, all the aches and pains and indignities of having outlived almost everything including herself. But almost to the end she could laugh till the tears ran down and till our tears ran down. She loved telling how her father in the confusion of catching a train handed the red-cap* his wallet once, or how one of her beaux had stepped through somebody's straw hat in the hall closet and was afraid to come out. Her laughter came from deep down in herself and deep down in the past, which in one way was lost and gone and in other ways was still as much within her reach as the can of root beer with a straw sticking in it which she always had on her bedside table because she said it was the only thing that helped her dry throat. The sad times she kept locked away never to be named, but the funny, happy times, the glamorous, romantic, young times, continued to be no less a part of her life than the furniture.

10   She excoriated the ravages of old age but never accepted them as the inevitable consequence of getting old. "I don't know what's wrong with me today," she must have said a thousand days as she tried once, then again, then a third time, to pull herself out of her chair into her walker. It never seemed to occur to her that what was wrong with her was that she was on her way to pushing a hundred. Maybe that was why some part of her remained unravaged. Some surviving lightness of touch let her stand back from the wreckage and see that among other things it was absurdly funny. When I told her the last time she was mobile enough to visit us in Vermont that the man who had just passed her window was the gardener, she said, "Tell him to come in and take a look at the last rose of summer."

11   She liked to paste gold stars on things or to antique things with gold paint – it was what she did with the past too of course – and lampshades, chairs, picture frames, tables, gleamed like treasure in the crazy little museum of her bedroom. The *chaise longue**

Les Malheurs de Sophie · "Sophie's Misfortunes" (French), written by the Comtesse de Ségur (1799–1874) and published in 1864, featured a naughty 4-year-old girl

red-cap · a railroad porter

chaise longue · "long chair" (French), a lounge for reclining

was heaped with pillows, a fake leopard-skin throw, a velvet quilt, 11
fashion magazines, movie magazines, catalogues stacked on a
table beside it, stories by Dorothy Parker• and Noël Coward,•
Kahlil Gibran's *The Prophet*.• Victorian beadwork pincushions
hung from the peach-colored walls along with pictures of happier times, greener places. The closet was a cotillion• of pretty
clothes she hadn't been able to wear for years, and her bureau
overflowed with more of them – blouses, belts, costume jewelry,
old evening purses, chiffon scarves, gloves. On top of the bureau
stood perfume bottles, pill bottles, jars, tubes, boxes of patent
medicine, a bowl of M & MS, which she said were good for her.
She had a theory that when you have a craving for something,
including M & MS, it means that your system needs it.

The living heart and command center of that room was the 12
dressing table. When she was past getting out of her bed to sit
at it any longer, what she needed from it was brought to her on
a tray as soon as she woke up every morning, before breakfast
even – the magnifying mirror, the lipsticks, eyebrow pencils,
tweezers, face powder, hair brush, combs, cold cream, mascara.
Before she did anything else, she did that and did it with such
artistry that even within weeks of her end she managed a not
implausible version of the face that since girlhood had been her
principal fame and fairest fortune.

Over that dressing table there hung for years a mirror that 13
I can remember from childhood. It was a mirror with an olive
green wooden frame which she had once painted in oils with a
little garland of flowers and medallions bearing the French words:
Il faut souffrir pour être belle. It was the motto of her life: You
have to suffer in order to be beautiful. What she meant, of course,
was all the pains she took in front of the mirror: the plucking and
primping and powdering, the brushing and painting – that kind of
suffering. But it seems clear that there was another kind too. To
be born as blonde and blue-eyed and beautiful as she was can be
as much of a handicap in its way as to be born with a cleft palate
because if you are beautiful enough you don't really have to be
anything much else to make people love you and want to be near
you. You don't have to be particularly kind or unselfish or generous
or compassionate because people will flock around you anyway
simply for the sake of your *beaux yeux*.• My mother could be all

Dorothy Parker · American writer and wit (1893–1967)

Noël Coward · English comic playwright (1899–1973)

Kahlil Gibran's *The Prophet* · Kahlil Gibran (1883–1931) Lebanese-American essayist and poet. *The Prophet* was first published in 1923

cotillion · a formal ballroom dance

beaux yeux · "beautiful eyes" (French)

13 of those good things when she took a notion to, but she never made a habit of it. She never developed the giving, loving side of what she might have been as a human being, and, needless to say, that was where the real suffering came – the two failed marriages after the death of my father, the fact that among all the friends she had over the course of her life, she never as far as I know had one whom she would in any sense have sacrificed herself for and by doing so might perhaps have begun to find her best and truest self. W. B. Yeats* in his poem "A Prayer for My Daughter" writes, "Hearts are not had as a gift but hearts are earned/By those that are not entirely beautiful." My almost entirely beautiful mother was by no means heartless, but I think hers was a heart that, who knows why, was rarely if ever touched in its deepest place. To let it be touched there was a risk that for reasons known only to her she was apparently not prepared to take.

W. B. Yeats · Irish poet and playwright (1865–1939)

14 For the twenty years or so she lived in New York she made no new friends because she chose to make none and lost all contact with the few old ones who were still alive. She believed in God, I think. With her eyes shut she would ask me what I thought about the afterlife from time to time, though when I tried to tell her she of course couldn't hear because it is hard to shout anything very much about the afterlife. But she never went to church. It always made her cry, she said. She wouldn't have been caught dead joining a club or group of any kind. "I know I'm queer," she often said. "I'm a very private person." And it was true. Even with the people closest to her she rarely spoke of what was going on inside her skin or asked that question of them. For the last fifteen years or so it reached the point where she saw virtually nobody except her immediate family and most of them not often. But by a miracle it didn't destroy her.

15 She had a cruel and terrible tongue when she was angry. When she struck, she struck to kill, and such killings must have been part of what she closed her eyes to, together with the other failures and mistakes of her life and the guilt they caused her, the shame she felt. But she never became bitter. She turned away from the world but never turned in upon herself. It was a kind of miracle, really. If she was lonely, I never heard her complain about it. Instead it was her looks she complained about: My hair looks like straw. When I wake up in the morning I have

this awful red spot on my cheek. These God-awful teeth don't   15
fit. I don't know what's wrong with me today. From somewhere
she was nourished, in other words, and richly nourished, God
only knows how, God only knows. That was the other part of
the miracle. Something deep within her stayed young, stayed
beautiful even, was never lost. And till the end of her life she was
as successful at not facing the reality of being a very old woman
as for almost a century she was successful at not facing her dark
times as a young one.

Being beautiful was her business, her art, her delight, and it   16
took her a long way and earned her many dividends, but when,
as she saw it, she lost her beauty – you stand a better chance of
finding your cane behind the radiator than ever finding blue eyes
and golden hair again – she was like a millionaire who runs out
of money. She took her name out of the phone book and got an
unlisted number. She eventually became so deaf that it became
almost impossible to speak to her except about things simple
enough to shout – her health, the weather, when you would be
seeing her next. It was as if deafness was a technique she mastered for not hearing anything that might threaten her peace. She
developed the habit of closing her eyes when she spoke to you
as if you were a dream she was dreaming. It was as if she chose
not to see in your face what you might be thinking behind the
simple words you were shouting, or as if, ostrich-like, closing
her eyes was a way of keeping you from seeing her. With her
looks gone she felt she had nothing left to offer the world, to
propitiate the world. So what she did was simply to check out of

Greta Garbo · a movie
star of the 1920s and
1930s, Garbo (1905–1990)
lived in seclusion in New
York for almost 50 years

Marlene Dietrich ·
a movie star, Dietrich
(1901–1992) was active
from the 1920s through
the 1950s, but became
increasingly reclusive in
later life

the world – that old, last rose of summer – the way Greta Garbo*
and Marlene Dietrich* checked out of it, holing themselves up
somewhere and never venturing forth except in disguise. My
mother holed herself up in her apartment on 79th Street, then
in just one room of that apartment, then in just one chair in that
room, and finally in the bed where one morning a few summers
ago, perhaps in her sleep, she died at last.

It is so easy to sum up other people's lives like this, and nec-   17
essary too, of course, especially our parents' lives. It is a way of
reducing their giant figures to a size we can manage, I suppose, a
way of getting even maybe, of getting on, of saying goodbye. The
day will come when somebody tries to sum you up the same way

17 and also me. Tell me about old Buechner then. What was he really like? What made him tick? How did his story go? Well, you see, this happened and then that happened, and then that, and that is why he became thus and so, and why when all is said and done it is not so hard to understand why things turned out for him as they finally did. Is there any truth at all in the patterns we think we see, the explanations and insights that fall so readily from our tongues? Who knows. The main thing that leads me to believe that what I've said about my mother has at least a kind of partial truth is that I know at first hand that it is true of the mother who lives on in me and will always be part of who I am.

18   In the mid 1970s, as a father of three teenage children and a husband of some twenty years standing by then, I would have said that my hearing was pretty good, that I could hear not only what my wife and children were saying but lots of things they weren't saying too. I would have said that I saw fairly well what was going on inside our house and what was going on inside me. I would also have said if anybody had asked me that our family was a close and happy one – that we had our troubles like every-body else but that we loved each other and respected each other and understood each other better than most. And in a hundred ways, praise God, I believe I was right. I believe that is the way it was. But in certain other ways, I came to learn, I was as deaf as my mother was with her little gold purse full of hearing aids none of which really ever worked very well, and though I did not shut my eyes when I talked to people the way she did, I shut them without knowing it to a whole dimension of the life that my wife and I and our children were living together on a green hillside in Vermont during those years.

19   There are two pieces of stained glass that sit propped up in one of the windows in the room where I write – a room paneled in old barn siding gone silvery gray with maybe as much as two centuries of weathering and full of a great many books, many of them considerably older than that which I've collected over the years and try to keep oiled and repaired because books are my passion, not only writing them and every once in a while even reading them but just having them and moving them around and feeling the comfort of their serene presence. One of those pieces of stained glass, which I think I asked somebody to give me one

Christmas, shows the Cowardly Lion from *The Wizard of Oz* with his feet bound with rope and his face streaming with tears as a few of the Winged Monkeys who have bound him hover around in the background. The other is a diptych* that somebody gave me once and that always causes me a twinge of embarrassment when I notice it because it seems a little too complacently religious. On one of its panels are written the words "May the blessing of God crown this house" and on the other "Fortunate is he whose work is blessed and whose household is prospered by the Lord."

diptych · a painting made on 2 hinged panels

I have never given either the lion or the diptych much thought as they've sat there year after year gathering dust, but I happened to notice them as I was preparing these pages and decided they might well serve as a kind of epigraph for this part of the story I'm telling. The Cowardly Lion is me, of course – crying, tied up, afraid. I am crying because at the time I'm speaking of, some fifteen years ago, a lot of sad and scary things were going on in our house that I felt helpless either to understand or to do anything about. Yet despite its rather self-satisfied religiosity, I believe the diptych is telling a truth about that time too.

I believe the blessing of God was indeed crowning our house in the sense that the sad and scary things themselves were, as it turned out, a fearsome blessing. And all the time those things were happening, the very fact that I was able to save my sanity by continuing to write among other things a novel called *Godric* made my work blessed and a means of grace at least for me. Nothing I've ever written came out of a darker time or brought me more light and comfort. It also – far more than I realized at the time I wrote it – brought me a sharper glimpse than I had ever had before of the crucial role my father has always played in my life and continues to play in my life even though in so many ways I have long since lost all but a handful of conscious memories of him.

I did not realize until after I wrote it how much of this there is in the book. When Godric is about to leave home to make his way in the world and his father Ædlward raises his hand to him in farewell, Godric says, "I believe my way went from that hand as a path goes from a door, and though many a mile that way has led me since, with many a turn and crossroad in between, if ever I should trace it back, it's to my father's hand that it would lead."

22 And later, when he learns of his father's death, he says, "The sadness was I'd lost a father I had never fully found. It's like a tune that ends before you've heard it out. Your whole life through you search to catch the strain, and seek the face you've lost in strangers' faces." In writing passages like that, I was writing more than I had known I knew with the result that the book was not only a word *from* me – my words painstakingly chosen and arranged into sentences by me alone – but also a word out of such a deep and secret part of who I am that it seemed also a word *to* me.

23 If writers write not just with paper and ink or a word processor but with their own life's blood, then I think something like this is perhaps always the case. A book you write out of the depths of who you are, like a dream you dream out of those same depths, is entirely your own creation. All the words your characters speak are words that you alone have put into their mouths, just as every situation they become involved in is one that you alone have concocted for them. But it seems to me nonetheless that a book you write, like a dream you dream, can have more healing and truth and wisdom in it at least for yourself than you feel in any way responsible for.

24 A large part of the truth that *Godric* had for me was the truth that although death ended my father, it has never ended my relationship with my father – a secret that I had never so clearly understood before. So forty-four years after the last time I saw him, it was to my father that I dedicated the book – *In memoriam patris mei.* I wrote the dedication in Latin solely because at the time it seemed appropriate to the medieval nature of the tale, but I have come to suspect since that Latin was also my unconscious way of remaining obedient to the ancient family law that the secret of my father must be at all costs kept secret.

In memoriam patris mei · "in memory of my father" (Latin)

25 The other half of the diptych's message – "whose household is prospered by the Lord" – was full of irony. Whether because of the Lord or good luck or the state of the stock market, we were a prosperous family in more ways than just economic, but for all the good our prosperity did us when the chips were down, we might as well have been paupers.

26 What happened was that one of our daughters began to stop eating. There was nothing scary about it at first. It was just the sort of thing any girl who thought she'd be prettier if she lost a

few pounds might do – nothing for breakfast, maybe a carrot or 26
a Diet Coke for lunch, for supper perhaps a little salad with low
calorie dressing. But then, as months went by, it did become scary.
Anorexia nervosa is the name of the sickness she was suffering
from, needless to say, and the best understanding of it that I have
been able to arrive at goes something like this. Young people crave
to be free and independent. They crave also to be taken care of
and safe. The dark magic of *anorexia* is that it satisfies both of
these cravings at once. By not eating, you take your stand against
the world that is telling you what to do and who to be. And by not
eating you also make your body so much smaller, lighter, weaker
that in effect it becomes a child's body again and the world flocks
to your rescue. This double victory is so great that apparently not
even self-destruction seems too high a price to pay.

Be that as it may, she got more and more thin, of course, till she 27
began to have the skull-like face and fleshless arms and legs of a
victim of Buchenwald,* and at the same time the Cowardly Lion
got more and more afraid and sad, felt more and more helpless.
No rational argument, no dire medical warning, no pleading or
cajolery or bribery would make this young woman he loved eat
normally again but only seemed to strengthen her determination not to, this young woman on whose life his own in so many
ways depended. He could not solve her problem because he was
of course himself part of her problem. She remained very much
the same person she had always been – creative, loving, funny,
bright as a star – but she was more afraid of gaining weight than
she was afraid of death itself because that was what it came to
finally. Three years were about as long as the sickness lasted in its
most intense form with some moments when it looked as though
things were getting better and some moments when it was hard
to imagine they could get any worse. Then finally, when she had
to be hospitalized, a doctor called one morning to say that unless
they started feeding her against her will, she would die. It was
as clear-cut as that. Tears ran down the Cowardly Lion's face as
he stood with the telephone at his ear. His paws were tied. The
bat-winged monkeys hovered.

I will not try to tell my daughter's story for two reasons. One 28
is that it is not mine to tell but hers. The other is that of course I
do not know her story, not the real story, the inside story, of what

Buchenwald · one of
the first and largest of
the Nazi concentration
camps

28 it was like for her. For the same reasons I will not try to tell what it was like for my wife or our other two children, each of whom in her own way was involved in that story. I can tell only my part in it, what happened to me, and even there I can't be sure I have it right because in many ways it is happening still. The fearsome blessing of that hard time continues to work itself out in my life in the same way we're told the universe is still hurtling through outer space under the impact of the great cosmic explosion that brought it into being in the first place. I think grace sometimes explodes into our lives like that – sending our pain, terror, astonishment hurtling through inner space until by grace they become Orion, Cassiopeia, Polaris to give us our bearings, to bring us into something like full being at last.

29 My anorectic daughter was in danger of starving to death, and without knowing it, so was I. I wasn't living my own life any more because I was so caught up in hers. If in refusing to eat she was mad as a hatter, I was if anything madder still because whereas in some sense she knew what she was doing to herself, I knew nothing at all about what I was doing to myself. She had given up food. I had virtually given up doing anything in the way of feeding myself humanly. To be at peace is to have peace inside yourself more or less in spite of what is going on outside yourself. In that sense I had no peace at all. If on one particular day she took it into her head to have a slice of toast, say, with her dietetic supper, I was in seventh heaven. If on some other day she decided to have no supper at all, I was in hell.

30 I choose the term *hell* with some care. Hell is where there is no light but only darkness, and I was so caught up in my fear for her life, which had become in a way my life too, that none of the usual sources of light worked any more, and light was what I was starving for. I had the companionship of my wife and two other children. I read books. I played tennis and walked in the woods. I saw friends and went to the movies. But even in the midst of such times as that I remained so locked inside myself that I was not really present in them at all. Toward the end of C. S. Lewis's *The Last Battle** there is a scene where a group of dwarves sit huddled together in a tight little knot thinking that they are in a pitch black, malodorous stable when the truth of it is that they are out in the midst of an endless grassy countryside as green as Vermont with

C. S. Lewis's *The Last Battle* · part of the "Chronicles of Narnia" series written by Lewis (1898–1963), English writer and popular theologian. For some of Lewis's poetry, see pages 449–451

the sun shining and blue sky overhead. The huge golden lion, 30
Aslan* himself, stands nearby with all the other dwarves "kneeling
in a circle around his forepaws" as Lewis writes, "and burying
their hands and faces in his mane as he stooped his great head
to touch them with his tongue." When Aslan offers the dwarves
food, they think it is offal.* When he offers them wine, they take
it for ditch water. "Perfect love casteth out fear," John writes
(1 John 4:18), and the other side of that is that fear like mine
casteth out love, even God's love. The love I had for my daughter
was lost in the anxiety I had for my daughter.

The only way I knew to be a father was to take care of her, as 31
my father had been unable to take care of me, to move heaven and
earth if necessary to make her well, and of course I couldn't do
that. I didn't have either the wisdom or the power to make her well.
None of us has the power to change other human beings like that,
and it would be a terrible power if we did, the power to violate the
humanity of others even for their own good. The psychiatrists we
consulted told me I couldn't cure her. The best thing I could do
for her was to stop trying to do anything. I think in heart I knew
they were right, but it didn't stop the madness of my desperate
meddling, it didn't stop the madness of my trying. Everything I
could think to do or say only stiffened her resolve to be free from,
among other things, me. Her not eating was a symbolic way of
striking out for that freedom. The only way she would ever be well
again was if and when she freely chose to be. The best I could do
as her father was to stand back and give her that freedom even at
the risk of her using it to choose for death instead of life.

Love your neighbor as yourself* is part of the great command- 32
ment. The other way to say it is, Love yourself as your neighbor.
Love yourself not in some egocentric, self-serving sense but
love yourself the way you would love your friend in the sense of
taking care of yourself, nourishing yourself, trying to understand,
comfort, strengthen yourself. Ministers in particular, people in
the caring professions in general, are famous for neglecting their
selves with the result that they are apt to become in their own
way as helpless and crippled as the people they are trying to care
for and thus no longer selves who can be of much use to anybody.
If your daughter is struggling for life in a raging torrent, you do
not save her by jumping into the torrent with her, which leads

Aslan · In Lewis's "Narnia" series, Aslan is the Christ figure

offal · trimmings of a slaughtered animal; rotting material or rubbish unfit for food

Love … yourself · see Leviticus 19:18, Matthew 22:37–39

32   only to your both drowning together. Instead you keep your feet on the dry bank – you maintain as best you can your own inner peace, the best and strongest of who you are – and from that solid ground reach out a rescuing hand. "Mind your own business" means butt out of other people's lives because in the long run they must live their lives for themselves, but it also means pay mind to your own life, your own health and wholeness, both for your own sake and ultimately for the sake of those you love too. Take care of yourself so you can take care of them. A bleeding heart is of no help to anybody if it bleeds to death.

33   How easy it is to write such words and how impossible it was to live them. What saved the day for my daughter was that when she finally had to be hospitalized in order to keep her alive, it happened about three thousand miles away from me. I was not there to protect her, to make her decisions, to manipulate events on her behalf, and the result was that she had to face those events on her own. There was no one to shield her from those events and their consequences in all their inexorability. In the form of doctors, nurses, social workers, the judge who determined that she was a danger to her own life and thus could be legally hospitalized against her will, society stepped in. Those men and women were not haggard, dithering, lovesick as I was. They were realistic, tough, conscientious, and in those ways, though they would never have put it in such terms themselves, loved her in a sense that I believe is closer to what Jesus meant by love than what I had been doing.

34   God loves in something like their way, I think. The power that created the universe and spun the dragonfly's wing and is beyond all other powers holds back, in love, from overpowering us. I have never felt God's presence more strongly than when my wife and I visited that distant hospital where our daughter was. Walking down the corridor to the room that had her name taped to the door, I felt that presence surrounding me like air – God in his very stillness, holding his breath, loving her, loving us all, the only way he can without destroying us. One night we went to compline* in an Episcopal cathedral, and in the coolness and near emptiness of that great vaulted place, in the remoteness of the choir's voices chanting plainsong, in the grayness of the stone, I felt it again – the passionate restraint and hush of God.

compline · an evening service of the Episcopal church

Little by little the young woman I loved began to get well, 35
emerging out of the shadows finally as strong and sane and wise
as anybody I know, and little by little as I watched her healing
happen, I began to see how much I was in need of healing and
getting well myself. Like Lewis's dwarves, for a long time I had
sat huddled in the dark of a stable of my own making. It was
only now that I started to suspect the presence of the green
countryside, the golden lion in whose image and likeness even
cowardly lions are made.

This is all part of the story about what it has been like for the 36
last ten years or so to be me, and before anybody else has the
chance to ask it, I will ask it myself: Who cares? What in the world
could be less important than who I am and who my father and
mother were, the mistakes I have made together with the occasional discoveries, the bad times and good times, the moments of
grace. If I were a public figure and my story had had some impact
on the world at large, that might be some justification for telling
it, but I am a very private figure indeed, living very much out of
the mainstream of things in the hills of Vermont, and my life has
had very little impact on anybody much except for the people
closest to me and the comparative few who have read books I've
written and been one way or another touched by them.

But I talk about my life anyway because if, on the one hand, 37
hardly anything could be less important, on the other hand,
hardly anything could be more important. My story is important
not because it is mine, God knows, but because if I tell it anything
like right, the chances are you will recognize that in many ways
it is also yours. Maybe nothing is more important than that we
keep track, you and I, of these stories of who we are and where
we have come from and the people we have met along the way
because it is precisely through these stories in all their particularity, as I have long believed and often said, that God makes himself
known to each of us most powerfully and personally. If this is
true, it means that to lose track of our stories is to be profoundly
impoverished not only humanly but also spiritually.

The God of biblical faith is a God who started history going 38
in the first place. He is also a God who moment by moment, day
by day continues to act in history always, which means both the
history that gets written down in the *New York Times* and the *San*

38 *Francisco Chronicle* and at the same time my history and your history, which for the most part don't get written down anywhere except in the few lines that may be allotted to us some day on the obituary page. The Exodus, the Covenant, the entry into the Promised Land•— such mighty acts of God as these appear in Scripture, but no less mighty are the acts of God as they appear in our own lives. I think of my father's death as in its way his exodus, his escape from bondage, and of the covenant that my mother made with my brother and me never to talk about him, and of the promised land of pre-World War II Bermuda that we reached through the wilderness and bewilderness of our first shock and grief at losing him.

Exodus … Promised Land · see Exodus 12:31–14:31, Exodus 20:1–40:33, and Joshua 3–4, respectively

39 As I understand it, to say that God is mightily present even in such private events as these does not mean that he makes events happen to us which move us in certain directions like chessmen. Instead, events happen under their own steam as random as rain, which means that God is present in them not as their cause but as the one who even in the hardest and most hair-raising of them offers us the possibility of that new life and healing which I believe is what salvation is. For instance I cannot believe that a God of love and mercy in any sense willed my father's suicide; it was only father himself who willed it as the only way out available to him from a life that for various reasons he had come to find unbearable. God did not will what happened that early November morning in Essex Falls, New Jersey, but I believe that God was present in what happened. I cannot guess how he was present with my father – I can guess much better how utterly abandoned by God my father must have felt if he thought about God at all – but my faith as well as my prayer is that he was and continues to be present with him in ways beyond my guessing. I can speak with some assurance only of how God was present in that dark time for me in the sense that I was not destroyed by it but came out of it with scars that I bear to this day, to be sure, but also somehow the wiser and the stronger for it. Who knows how I might have turned out if my father had lived, but through the loss of him all those long years ago I think that I learned something about how even tragedy can be a means of grace that I might never have come to any other way. As I see it, in other words, God acts in history and in your and my brief

histories not as the puppeteer who sets the scene and works the strings but rather as the great director who no matter what role fate casts us in conveys to us somehow from the wings,* if we have our eyes, ears, hearts open and sometimes even if we don't, how we can play those roles in a way to enrich and ennoble and hallow the whole vast drama of things including our own small but crucial parts in it.

wings · the areas at either side of a stage, backstage and out of sight

In fact I am inclined to believe that God's chief purpose in giving us memory is to enable us to go back in time so that if we didn't play those roles right the first time round, we can still have another go at it now. We cannot undo our old mistakes or their consequences any more than we can erase old wounds that we have both suffered and inflicted, but through the power that memory gives us of thinking, feeling, imagining our way back through time we can at long last finally finish with the past in the sense of removing its power to hurt us and other people and to stunt our growth as human beings.

The sad things that happened long ago will always remain part of who we are just as the glad and gracious things will too, but instead of being a burden of guilt, recrimination, and regret that make us constantly stumble as we go, even the saddest things can become, once we have made peace with them, a source of wisdom and strength for the journey that still lies ahead. It is through memory that we are able to reclaim much of our lives that we have long since written off by finding that in everything that has happened to us over the years God was offering us possibilities of new life and healing which, though we may have missed them at the time, we can still choose and be brought to life by and healed by all these years later.

Another way of saying it, perhaps, is that memory makes it possible for us both to bless the past, even those parts of it that we have always felt cursed by, and also to be blessed by it. If this kind of remembering sounds like what psychotherapy is all about, it is because of course it is, but I think it is also what the forgiveness of sins is all about – the interplay of God's forgiveness of us and our forgiveness of God and each other. To see how God's mercy was for me buried deep even in my father's death was not just to be able to forgive my father for dying and God for letting him die so young and without hope and all the

42   people like my mother who were involved in his death but also to be able to forgive myself for all the years I had failed to air my crippling secret so that then, however slowly and uncertainly, I could start to find healing. It is in the experience of such healing that I believe we experience also God's loving forgiveness of us, and insofar as memory is the doorway to both experiences, it becomes not just therapeutic but sacred.

43   In a book called *The Wizard's Tide* I wrote the story of my father's death the way I would tell it to a child, in other words the way I need to tell it to the child who lives on inside me as the children we were live on inside all of us. By telling it as a story, I told it not from the outside as an observer, the way I have told it in these pages, but from the inside as a participant. By telling it in language a child could understand, I told it as the child who I both was in 1936 and still am in 1990. I relived it for that child and as that child with the difference that this time I was able to live it right.

44   The father in the story dies in much the way my father did, and the mother and the children in the story hushed it up in much the way my mother and her two children did, but there comes the difference. At the end of the story, on Christmas eve, the boy Teddy, who is me, comes to a momentous conclusion.

44a   He thought about how terrible it was that nobody talked about [his father] any more so that it was almost as if there had never been any such person. He decided that from now on he wanted to talk about him a lot. He wanted to remember everything about him that he could remember so someday he could tell about him to other people who had never seen him.

44   And then, just before turning off the lights, Teddy actually does this. For the first time since his father's death, Teddy brings the subject up to his younger sister, Bean. He doesn't say anything about his father, he just mentions his name, but as I wrote the story, I knew that was enough. It was enough to start a healing process for the children in the story that for me didn't start till I was well into my fifties. Stranger still, it was enough also to start healing the child in me the way he might have been healed in 1936 if his real story had only turned out like the make-believe story in the book. By a kind of miracle, the make-believe story

became the real story or vice versa. The unalterable past was in 44
some extraordinary way altered. Maybe the most sacred function of memory is just that: to render the distinction between
past, present, and future ultimately meaningless; to enable us at
some level of our being to inhabit that same eternity which it is
said that God himself inhabits.

We believe in God – such as it is, we have faith – because cer- 45
tain things happened to us once and go on happening. We work
and goof off, we love and dream, we have wonderful times and
awful times, are cruelly hurt and hurt others cruelly, get mad and
bored and scared stiff and ache with desire, do all such human
things as these, and if our faith is not mainly just window dressing
or a rabbit's foot or fire insurance, it is because it grows out of
precisely this kind of rich human compost. The God of biblical
faith is the God who meets us at those moments in which for
better or worse we are being most human, most ourselves, and if
we lose touch with those moments, if we don't stop from time to
time to notice what is happening to us and around us and inside
us, we run the tragic risk of losing touch with God too.

Sad to say, the people who seem to lose touch with themselves 46
and with God most conspicuously are of all things ministers. As
a minister myself I am peculiarly aware of this. I don't say they do
it more than other people but they do it more publicly. It could
hardly be more ironic. First of all, ministers give preeminence
to of all books the Bible whose absolutely central and unifying
thesis is that God makes himself known in historical experience.
Secondly, they call their congregations to examine their own
experience as human beings in that most intimate and searching
of all ways which is known as prayer. Thirdly, in their sermons,
if they do it right, they proclaim above all else the staggeringly
good news that God so loves the world that he is continually at
work in our lives in the world in order to draw us, in love, closer
and closer to himself and to each other. In other words, a major
part of their ministry is to remind us that there is nothing more
important than to pay attention to what is happening to us, yet
again and again they show little sign of doing so themselves.
There is precious little in most of their preaching to suggest that
they have rejoiced and suffered with the rest of mankind. If they
draw on their own experience at all, it is usually for some little

46 anecdote to illustrate a point or help make the pill go down but rarely if ever for an authentic, first-hand, flesh-and-blood account of what it is like to love Christ, say, or to feel spiritually bankrupt, or to get fed up with the whole religious enterprise.

47 Along with much of the rest of mankind, ministers have had such moments, we can only assume, but more often than not they don't seem to trust them, don't draw on them, don't talk about them. Instead they keep setting them aside for some rea- son – maybe because they seem too private to share or too trivial or too ambiguous or not religious enough; maybe because what God seems to be saying to them through their flesh-and-blood experience has a depth and mystery and power to it which make all their homiletical pronouncements about God sound empty by comparison. The temptation then is to stick to the homiletical* pronouncements. Comparatively empty as they may be, they are at least familiar. They add up. Congregations have come to expect homiletical pronouncements and to take comfort from them, and the preachers who pronounce them can move them around in various thought-provoking and edifying ways which nobody will feel unsettled or intimidated by because they have heard them so often.

homiletical · relating to a sermon

48 Ministers run the awful risk, in other words, of ceasing to be witnesses to the presence in their own lives – let alone in the lives of the people they are trying to minister to – of a living God who transcends everything they think they know and can say about him and is full of extraordinary surprises. Instead they tend to become professionals who have mastered all the techniques of institutional religion and who speak on religious matters with what often seems a maximum of authority and a minimum of vital personal involvement. Their sermons often sound as bland as they sound bloodless. The faith they proclaim appears to be no longer rooted in or nourished by or challenged by their own lives but instead free-floating, secondhand, passionless. They sound, in other words, burnt out.

49 Obviously ministers are not called to be in that sense profes- sionals. God forbid. I believe that they are called instead, together with all other Christians and would-be Christians, to consider the lilies of the field, to consider the least of these my brethren, to consider the dead sparrow by the roadside.* Maybe prerequisite

consider . . . road- side · see Luke 12:6–28, Luke 9:48

to all those, they are called upon to consider themselves – what 49
they love and what they fear, what they are ashamed of, what
makes them sick to their stomachs, what rejoices their hearts. I
believe that ministers and everyone are called also to consider
Jesus of Nazareth in whom God himself showed how crucial
human life is by actually living one and hallowed human death
by actually dying one and who lives and dies still with us and for
us and in spite of us. I believe that we are called to see that the
day-by-day lives of all of us – the things that happened long ago,
the things that happened only this morning – are also hallowed
and crucial and part of a great drama in which souls are lost and
souls are saved including our own.

That is why to keep track of these lives we live is not just a 50
means of enriching our understanding and possibly improving
our sermons but a truly sacred work. In these pages I tell secrets
about my parents, my children, myself because that is one way of
keeping track and because I believe that it is not only more honest
but also vastly more interesting than to pretend that I have no
such secrets to tell. I not only have my secrets, I am my secrets.
And you are your secrets. Our secrets are human secrets, and
our trusting each other enough to share them with each other
has much to do with the secret of what it is to be human.

Henri Nouwen

⟨ 1 9 3 2 – 1 9 9 6 ⟩

Nouwen was a Dutch theologian, priest, and professor of psychology who spent much of his adult life in North America, where he preached and wrote about the virtues of service to the poor and the weak and the practice of the spiritual disciplines. Although he taught at Notre Dame, Yale, and Harvard, he found his greatest fulfillment living and working at Daybreak – a community for the severely handicapped near Toronto. Nouwen was a prolific writer on the spiritual life. In such books as Life of the Beloved, In the Name of Jesus, The Road to Daybreak, Way of the Heart, *and* Return of the Prodigal Son, *he emphasizes the paradoxes of the Christian faith – that the Divine Presence is evident in the "downward way" taught by Jesus. Nouwen tries to counter the forces of secularism with the story of a loving God who waits patiently for the return of his rebellious creatures. The writer died of a heart attack while visiting in the Netherlands in the fall of 1996.*

ADAM'S PEACE

1 IN THE MIDDLE OF THIS DECADE I moved from Harvard to Daybreak – from an institution for very bright people to a community for mentally handicapped ones.

2 Daybreak, situated near Toronto, is part of an international federation of communities called *l'Arche* – the Ark – where mentally handicapped men and women and their assistants try to live together in the spirit of the beatitudes* of Jesus.

beatitudes · see Matthew 5:3–12

3 I live in a house with six handicapped people and four assistants. We live together as a family. None of the assistants is specially trained to work with people with a mental handicap, but we receive all the help we need from nearby professionals.

4 When there are no special crises we live just as a family, gradually forgetting who is handicapped and who is not. All have their

gifts, all have their struggles. We eat together, play together, pray together and go out together. We all have our own preferences in terms of work, food and movies, and we all have our problems getting along with someone in the house, whether handicapped or not. We laugh a lot. We cry a lot too. Sometimes both at the same time. That is *l'Arche*, that is Daybreak, that is the family of ten I live with day in and day out.

When asked to return to Harvard to speak about peace, I suddenly realized that speaking about peace from this tiny family is not like speaking about peace as a professor. I need a new perspective and a new sensibility, a new language. It is not easy. It is even quite painful. I feel so vulnerable and so naked. But I will tell you the story of Adam, one of the ten people in our home, and let him become the silent witness for the peace that is not of this world.

Adam is the weakest person in our family. He is a 25-year-old man who cannot speak, cannot dress or undress himself, cannot walk alone, cannot eat without much help. He does not cry or laugh. Only occasionally does he make eye contact. His back is distorted. His arm and leg movements are twisted. He suffers from severe epilepsy and, despite heavy medication, sees few days without grand-mal seizures. Sometimes, as he grows suddenly rigid, he utters a howling groan. On a few occasions I've seen one big tear roll down his cheek.

It takes me about an hour and a half to wake Adam up, give him his medication, carry him into his bath, wash him, shave him, clean his teeth, dress him, walk him to the kitchen, give him his breakfast, put him in his wheelchair and bring him to the place where he spends most of the day with therapeutic exercises.

I tell you this not to give you a nursing report, but to share with you something quite intimate. After a month of working this way with Adam, something happened to me. This deeply handicapped young man, who is considered by many outsiders a vegetable, a distortion of humanity, a useless animal-like creature who shouldn't have been born, started to become my dearest companion.

As my fears gradually lessened, a love emerged in me so full of tender affection that most of my other tasks seemed boring and superficial compared with the hours spent with Adam. Out

9 of his broken body and broken mind emerged a most beautiful human being offering me a greater gift than I would ever offer him: Somehow Adam revealed to me who he is, and who I am, and how we can love each other.

10 When I carried him into his bath, made big waves to let the water run fast around his chest and neck, rubbed noses with him and told him all sorts of stories about him and me, I knew that two friends were communicating far beyond the realm of thought or emotion. Deep speaks to deep, spirit speaks to spirit, heart speaks to heart. I started to realize that ours was a mutual love based not on shared knowledge or shared feelings, but on shared humanity. The longer I stayed with Adam the more clearly I saw him as my gentle teacher, teaching me what no book, school or professor could ever teach me.

11 The gift of peace hidden in Adam's utter weakness is a gift not of this world, but certainly for this world. For this gift to become known, someone has to lift it up and pass it on. That may be the deepest meaning of being an assistant to handicapped people: helping them to share their gifts.

12 Adam's peace is first of all a peace rooted in being. Being is more important than doing. How simple a truth, but how hard to live.

13 Adam can do nothing. He is completely dependent on others. His gift is purely being with us. Every evening when I run home to take care of Adam – to help him with his supper and put him to bed – I realize that the best thing I can do for him is to be with him. And indeed, that is the great joy: paying total attention to his breathing, his eating, his careful steps; noticing how he tries to lift a spoon to his mouth or offers his left arm a little to make it easier for me to take off his shirt.

14 Most of my life has been built around the idea that my value depends on what I do. I made it through school. I earned my degrees and awards and I made my career. Yes, with many others, I fought my way up to a little success, a little popularity and a little power. But as I sit beside the slow and heavy-breathing Adam, I start to see how violent that journey was. So marked by rivalry and competition, so pervaded with compulsion and obsession, so spotted with moments of suspicion, jealousy, resentment and revenge.

15 Oh sure, most of what I did was called ministry, the ministry of justice and peace, the ministry of forgiveness and reconcilia-

tion, the ministry of healing and wholeness. But when those who 15
want peace are as interested in success, popularity and power
as those who want war, what then is the real difference between
war and peace? When the peace is as much of this world as the
war is, the choice is between a war which we euphemistically call
pacification and a peace in which the peacemakers violate each
other's deepest values.

Adam says to me: Peace is first of all the art of being. I know 16
he is right because, after four months of being a little with Adam,
I am discovering in myself the beginning of an inner at-homeness
that I didn't know before.

When I cover him with his sheets and blankets, turn out the 17
lights and pray with Adam, he is always very quiet. It's as if he
knows my praying voice from my speaking voice. I whisper in his
ear: "May all the angels protect you," and often he looks up to me
from his pillow and seems to know what I am saying.

Ever since I've been praying with Adam I've known better 18
than before that praying is being with Jesus, simply "wasting
time" with him. Adam keeps teaching me that.

Adam's peace is not only a peace rooted in being, but also a 19
peace rooted in the heart. Somehow through the centuries we
have come to believe that what makes us human is our mind.
Many people define a human being as a rational animal. But
Adam keeps telling me over and over again that what makes us
human is not our mind but our heart, not our ability to think but
our ability to love. Whoever speaks about Adam as a vegetable or
an animal-like creature misses the sacred mystery that Adam is
fully capable of receiving and giving love. He is not half human,
not nearly human, but fully, completely human because he is all
heart and it is the heart that is made in the likeness of God.

Let me quickly add that by "heart" I do not mean the seat of 20
human emotions, in contrast to the mind as the seat of human
thought. No, by "heart" I mean the center of our being, where
God has hidden the divine gifts of trust, hope and love. Whereas
the mind tries to understand, grasp problems, discern different
aspects of reality and probe mysteries, the heart allows us to
become sons and daughters of God and brothers and sisters of
each other. Long before the mind is able to exercise its power, the
heart is already able to develop a trusting human relationship.

21   When I say that I believe deeply that Adam can give and receive love and that there is a true mutuality between us, I make no naïve psychological statement overlooking his severe handicaps; I speak of a love between us that transcends all thoughts and feelings, precisely because it is rooted in God's first love, a love that precedes all human loves. The mystery of Adam is that in his deep mental and emotional brokenness he has become so empty of all human pride that he has become the preferable mediator of that first love. Maybe this will help you see why Adam is giving me a whole new understanding of God's love for the poor and the oppressed.

22   The peace that flows from Adam's broken heart is not of this world. It is not the result of political analysis, roundtable debates, discernment of the signs of the times or well advised strategies. All these activities of the mind have their role in peacemaking. But they are all easily perverted to a new way of warmaking if they are not in the service of the divine peace that flows from the broken heart of those who are called the poor in spirit.* Adam's peace, while rooted more in being than in doing, and more in the heart than in the mind, is a peace that calls forth community. At *l'Arche* the people hold us together as a family; in fact, the most handicapped people are the true center of gravity. Adam in his total vulnerability calls us together as a family.

poor in spirit · see Matthew 5:3.

23   The weakest members are not the handicapped residents but the assistants. Our commitments are ambiguous at best. Some stay longer than others, but most move on after one or two years. Closer to the center are Raymond, Bill, John, and Trevor, each of whom is relatively independent, but still in need of much help and attention. They are permanent family members; they are with us for life; they keep us honest. Because of them, conflicts never last very long, tensions are talked out, disagreements are resolved. But in the heart of our community are Rose and Adam, both deeply handicapped, and the weaker of the two is Adam. Adam, the most broken of us all, is without any doubt the strongest bond among us.

24   Because of Adam there is always someone home. Because of Adam there is a quiet rhythm in the house. Because of Adam there are words of affection, gentleness and tenderness. Because of Adam there is always space for mutual forgiveness and healing. Adam, the weakest among us, is our true peacemaker. How mysterious are God's ways!

Most of my adult life I have tried to show the world that I 25
could do it on my own, that I needed others only to get me back
on my lonely road as a strong, independent, creative man. And
most of my fellow intellectuals joined me in that desire. But all
of us highly trained individuals today are facing a world on the
brink of total destruction. Now we wonder how we might join
forces to make peace!

What kind of peace can this possibly be? Who can paint a 26
group portrait of people who all want the center seat? When
all want the honor of being the final peacemaker, there will be
no peace.

Adam needs many people, none of whom can boast of any 27
success. Adam will never be better. Medically, he will only grow
worse. Each person who works with him does only a little bit.
My part in his life is very small. Some cook for him, some do his
laundry, some give him massages, some let him listen to music
or take him for a walk or a swim or a ride. Others look after his
blood pressure, regulate his medicine, look after his teeth. Even
with all this assistance Adam often slips into total exhaustion. Yet
a community of peace has emerged around him, a peace community not just for Adam, but for all who belong to Adam's race.
It's a community that proclaims that God has chosen to reveal
his glory in complete weakness and vulnerability.

I've told you about Adam and about his peace. But you're not 28
part of *l'Arche*, you don't live at Daybreak, you're not a member
of Adam's family. Like me, however, you search for peace in your
heart, in your family and in your world.

I've told you about Adam and his peace to offer you a quiet guide 29
with a gentle heart, a little light for walking through this dark world.
In Adam's name, therefore, I say to you: Do not give up working for
peace. But remember that the peace you seek is not of this world.
Don't be distracted by the great noises of war, the dramatic descrip-
tions of misery, the sensational exploitation of cruelty. Newspapers,
movies and war novels may numb you, but they do not create a
true desire for peace. They mostly create feelings of shame, guilt
and powerlessness – the worst motives for peace work.

refuses ... temporal power · see Matthew 4:1–11, Luke 4:1–12

Keep your eyes on the one who refuses to turn stones into 30
bread, jump from great heights or rule with great temporal
power.* Keep your eyes on the one who says,

30a   Blessed are the poor, the gentle, those who mourn and those who hunger and thirst for righteousness; blessed are the merciful, the pure of heart, the peacemakers and those who are persecuted in the cause of uprightness.•

Blessed … uprightness · Matthew 5:3–10

31   Keep your eyes on the one who touches the lame and the blind, the one who speaks forgiveness and encouragement, the one who dies alone. Keep your eyes on the one who is poor with the poor, weak with the weak and rejected with the rejected. That one is the source of all peace.

32   As long as we think and live as if there is no peace and that it all depends on ourselves to make it come about, we are on the road to self-destruction. But when we trust that the God of love has already given the peace we are searching for, we will see this peace poking through the broken soil of our human condition and we will be able to let it grow fast, even to heal the economic and political maladies of our time.

33   An old Hassidic• tale summarizes much of what I have tried to say.

Hassidic · The Hassidim are followers of a strict sect of orthodox Judaism

34   The Rabbi asks his students, "How can we determine the hour of dawn, when the night ends and the day begins?"

35   One student suggests, "When, from a distance, you can distinguish between a dog and a sheep?"

36   "No," the Rabbi answers.

37   "Is it when you can distinguish between a fig tree and a grapevine?" asks a second student.

38   "No," the Rabbi says.

39   "Please tell us the answer, then," say the students .

40   "It is," says the wise teacher, "when you have enough light to look human beings in the face and recognize them as your brothers and sisters. Until then the darkness is still with us."

41   Let us pray for that light. It is the peace that the world cannot give.

Wendell Berry

⟨ 1 9 3 4 - ⟩

Berry is a farmer, a teacher, an essayist, a novelist, and a poet, in addition to being a respected environmental activist. Born in rural Kentucky, he has denounced the "industrial vandalism" his home state has suffered at the hands of coal companies. For Berry, as he has argued in A Continuous Harmony *(1972), there are two irreconcilable philosophies of land management. One philosophy, that of Christian stewardship, begins with a commitment that the earth is the Lord's. The current stewards, according to this viewpoint, hold natural resources in trust, using them with restraint in the knowledge that as-yet-unborn generations must also depend upon those same resources for survival. The other philosophy, one Berry terms "exploitation," begins with a commitment to immediate profit: whatever is profitable is good. This approach to nature, of course, Berry opposes vehemently. Perhaps because his environmental ethic is based upon his Christian beliefs, Berry has also opposed views like those expounded by entomologist E. O. Wilson in* Consilience *(1998), views which tend to reduce humanity's religious instinct to a mere biological survival trait and a useful product of natural evolution. In his response to Wilson, Berry insists upon the limited validity of scientific explanations. "Science cannot replace art or religion," Berry writes in* Life is a Miracle *(2001), "for the same reason that you cannot loosen a nut with a saw or cut a board in two with a wrench."*

GOD AND COUNTRY

1 THE SUBJECT OF CHRISTIANITY and ecology is endlessly, perhaps infinitely, fascinating. It is fascinating theologically and artistically because of our never-to-be-satisfied curiosity about the relation between a made thing and its maker. It is fascinating practically because we are unrelentingly required to honor in all

113

things the relation between the world and its Maker, and because that requirement implies another, equally unrelenting, that we ourselves, as makers, should always honor that greater making; we are required, that is, to study the ways of working well, and those ways are endlessly fascinating. The subject of Christianity and ecology also is politically fascinating, to those of us who are devoted both to biblical tradition and to the defense of the earth, because we are always hankering for the support of the churches, which seems to us to belong, properly and logically, to our cause.

This latter fascination, though not the most difficult and fearful, is certainly the most frustrating, for the fact simply is that the churches, which claim to honor God as the "maker of heaven and earth,"* have lately shown little inclination to honor the earth or to protect it from those who would dishonor it.

Organized Christianity seems, in general, to have made peace with "the economy" by divorcing itself from economic issues, and this, I think, has proved to be a disaster, both religious and economic. The reason for this, on the side of religion, is suggested by the adjective "organized." It is clearly possible that, in the condition of the world as the world now is, organization can force upon an institution a character that is alien or even antithetical to it. The organized church comes immediately under a compulsion to think of itself, and identify itself to the world, not as an institution synonymous with its truth and its membership, but as a hodgepodge of funds, properties, projects, and offices, all urgently requiring economic support. The organized church makes peace with a destructive economy and divorces itself from economic issues because it is economically compelled to do so. Like any other public institution so organized, the organized church is dependent on "the economy"; it cannot survive apart from those economic practices that its truth forbids and that its vocation is to correct. If it comes to a choice between the extermination of the fowls of the air and the lilies of the field* and the extermination of a building fund, the organized church will elect — indeed, has already elected — to save the building fund. The irony is compounded and made harder to bear by the fact that the building fund can be preserved by crude applications of money, but the fowls of the air and the lilies of the field can

"maker … earth" · a quotation from the Apostles' Creed

fowls … field · see Matthew 5:25–34, Luke 12:24–31

3 be preserved only by true religion, by the practice of a proper love and respect for them as the creatures of God. No wonder so many sermons are devoted exclusively to "spiritual" subjects. If one is living by the tithes* of history's most destructive economy, then the disembodiment of the soul becomes the chief of worldly conveniences.

tithes · a tenth of one's income which is contributed for religious purposes

4 There are many manifestations of this tacit* alliance between the organized churches and "the economy," but I need to speak only of two in order to make my point. The first is the phrase "full-time Christian service," which the churches of my experience have used exclusively to refer to the ministry, thereby at once making of the devoted life a religious specialty or career and removing the possibility of devotion from other callings. Thus the $50,000-a-year preacher is a "full-time Christian servant," whereas a $20,000 or a $10,000-a-year farmer, or a farmer going broke, so far as the religious specialists are concerned, must serve "the economy" in his work or in his failure and serve God in his spare time. The professional class is likewise free to serve itself in its work and to serve God by giving the church its ten per-cent. The churches in this way excerpt sanctity from the human economy and its work just as Cartesian* science has excerpted it from the material creation. And it is easy to see the interde-pendence of these two desecrations: the desecration of nature would have been impossible without the desecration of work, and vice versa.

tacit · unspoken, silent

Cartesian · named for French philosopher, mathematician and scientist René Descartes (1596–1650)

5 The second manifestation I want to speak of is the practice, again common in the churches of my experience, of using the rural ministry as a training ground for young ministers and as a means of subsidizing their education. No church official, appar-ently, sees any logical, much less any spiritual, problem in sending young people to minister to country churches before they have, according to their institutional superiors, become eligible to be ministers. These student ministers invariably leave the rural congregations that have sponsored or endured their educations as soon as possible once they have their diplomas in hand. The denominational hierarchies, then, evidently regard country places in exactly the same way as "the economy" does: as sources of economic power to be exploited for the advantage of "better" places. The country people will be used to educate ministers for

the benefit of city people (in wealthier churches) who, obviously, 5
are thought more deserving of educated ministers. This, I am
well aware, is mainly the fault of the church organizations; it is
not a charge that can be made to stick to any young minister in
particular: not all ministers should be country ministers, just
as not all people should be country people. And yet it is a fact
that in the more than fifty years that I have known my own rural
community, many student ministers have been "called" to serve
in its churches, but not one has ever been "called" to stay. The
message that country people get from their churches, then, is
the same message that they get from "the economy": that, as
country people, they do not matter much and do not deserve
much consideration. And this inescapably imposes an economic
valuation on spiritual things. According to the modern church, as
one of my Christian friends said to me, "The soul of the plowboy
ain't worth as much as the soul of the delivery boy."

If the churches are mostly indifferent to the work and the 6
people by which the link between economy and ecosystem must
be enacted, it is no wonder that they are mostly indifferent to the
fate of the ecosystems themselves. One must ask, then: is this
state of affairs caused by Christian truth or by the failures and
errors of Christian practice? My answer is that it is caused by
the failures and errors of Christian practice. The evident ability
of most church leaders to be "born again in Christ" without in
the least discomforting their faith in the industrial economy's
bill of goods, however convenient and understandable it may
be, is not scriptural.

Anyone making such a statement must deal immediately with 7
the belief of many non-Christian environmentalists as well as at
least some Christians that Genesis 1:28, in which God instructs
Adam and Eve to "be fruitful and multiply and replenish the earth,
and subdue it," gives unconditional permission to humankind
to use the world as it pleases. Such a reading of Genesis 1:28 is
contradicted by virtually all the rest of the Bible, as many people
by now have pointed out. The ecological teaching of the Bible
is simply inescapable: God made the world because He wanted
it made. He thinks the world is good, and He loves it. It is His
world; He has never relinquished title to it. And He has never
revoked the conditions, bearing on His gift to us of the use of it,

7   that oblige us to take excellent care of it. If God loves the world, then how might any person of faith be excused for not loving it or justified in destroying it?

8   But of course, those who see in Genesis 1:28 the source of all our abuse of the natural world (most of them apparently having read no more of the Bible than that verse) are guilty of an extremely unintelligent misreading of Genesis 1:28 itself. How, for example, would one arrange to "replenish the earth" if "subdue" means, as alleged, "conquer" or "defeat" or "destroy"?

9   We have in fact in the biblical tradition, rooted in the Bible but amplified in agrarian, literary, and other cultural traditions stemming from the Bible, the idea of stewardship as conditioned by the idea of *usufruct*. George Perkins Marsh* was invoking biblical tradition when he wrote, in 1864, that "man has too long forgotten that the earth was given to him for *usufruct* alone, not for consumption, still less for profligate waste." The Mormon essayist Hugh Nibley* invoked it explicitly when he wrote that "man's dominion is a call to service, not a license to exterminate."

10 That service, stewardship, is the responsible care of property belonging to another. And by this the Bible does not mean an absentee landlord, but one living on the property, profoundly and intimately involved in its being and its health, as Elihu says to Job: "if he gather unto himself his spirit and his breath; All flesh shall perish together."* All creatures live by God's spirit, portioned out to them, and breathe His breath. To "lay up ... treasures in heaven,"* then, cannot mean to be spiritual at the earth's expense, or to despise or condemn the earth for the sake of heaven. It means exactly the opposite: do not desecrate or depreciate these gifts, which take part with us in the being of God, by turning them into worldly "treasure"; do not reduce life to money or to any other mere quantity.

11 The idea of *usufruct* gives this point to the idea of stewardship, and makes it practical and economic. *Usufruct*, the *Oxford English Dictionary* says, is "the right of temporary possession, use, or enjoyment of the advantages of property belonging to another, so far as may be had without causing damage or prejudice to this." It is hardly a "free-market economy" that the Bible prescribes. Large accumulations of land were, and are, forbidden because the dispossession and privation of some cannot be an acceptable or

George Perkins Marsh · American conservationist and scholar (1801–1882)

Hugh Nibley · American historian and Mormon apologist (1910–)

"if he ... together" · Job 34:14–15

"lay up ... heaven" · Matthew 6:20

Usury · the practice of charging interest for lending money. See Exodus 22:25, Leviticus 25:36–37

normal result of the economic activity of others, for that destroys a people as a people; it destroys the community. Usury* was, and is, forbidden because the dispossession and privation of some should not be regarded by others as an economic opportunity, for that is contrary to neighborliness; it destroys the community. And the greed that destroys the community also destroys the land. What the Bible proposes is a moral economy, the standard of which is the health of properties belonging to God. 11

But we have considered so far only those things of the Creation that can be included within the human economy – the usable properties, so to speak. What about the things that are outside the human economy? What about the things that from the point of view of human need are useless or only partly usable? What about the places that, as is increasingly evident, we should not use at all? Obviously we must go further, and the Bible can take us further. Many passages take us beyond a merely economic stewardship, but the one that has come to seem most valuable to me is Revelation 4:11, because I think it proposes an indispensable standard for the stewardship both of things in use and of useless things and things set aside from use: "Thou art worthy, O Lord, to receive glory and honour and power: for thou hast created all things, and for thy pleasure they are and were created." 12

The implications of this verse are relentlessly practical. The ideas that we are permitted to use things that are pleasing to God, that we have nothing at all to use that is not pleasing to Him, and that necessarily implicated in the power to use is the power to misuse and destroy are troubling, and indeed frightening, ideas. But they are consoling, too, precisely insofar as we have the ability to use well and the goodness or the character required to limit use or to forbear to use. 13

Our responsibility, then, as stewards, the responsibility that inescapably goes with our dominion over the other creatures, according to Revelation 4:11, is to safeguard God's pleasure in His work. And we can do that, I think (I don't know how else we could do it), by safeguarding our pleasure in His work, and our pleasure in our own work. Or, if we no longer can trust ourselves to be more than economic machines, then we must do it by safeguarding the pleasure of children in God's work and in ours. It is impossible, admittedly, to give an accurate economic 14

14 value to the goodness of good work, much less to the goodness of an unspoiled forest or prairie or desert, or to the goodness of pure sunlight or water or air. And yet we are required to make an economy that honors such goods and is conversant with them. An economy that ignores them, as our present one does, "builds a Hell in Heaven's despite."•

15   As a measure of how far we have "progressed" in our industrial economy, let me quote a part of a sentence from the prayer "For Every Man in His Work" from the 1928 *Book of Common Prayer:*• "Deliver us, we beseech thee, in our several callings, from the service of mammon,• that we may do the work which thou givest us to do, in truth, in beauty, and in righteousness, with singleness of heart as thy servants, and to the benefit of our fellow men." What is astonishing about that prayer is that it is a relic. Throughout the history of the industrial revolution, it has become steadily less prayable. The industrial nations are now divided, almost entirely, into a professional or executive class that has not the least intention of working in truth, beauty, and righteousness, as God's servants, or to the benefit of their fellow men, and an underclass that has no choice in the matter. Truth, beauty, and righteousness now have, and can have, nothing to do with the economic life of most people. This alone, I think, is sufficient to account for the orientation of most churches to religious feeling, increasingly feckless, as opposed to religious thought or religious behavior.

16   I acknowledge that I feel deeply estranged from most of the manifestations of organized religion, partly for reasons that I have mentioned. Yet I am far from thinking that one can somehow become righteous by carrying Protestantism to the logical conclusion of a one-person church. We all belong, at least, to the problem. "There is … a price to be paid," Philip Sherrard says, "for fabricating around us a society which is as artificial and as mechanized as our own, and this is that we can exist in it only on condition that we adapt ourselves to it. This is our punishment."•

17   We all, obviously, are to some extent guilty of this damnable adaptation. We all are undergoing this punishment. But as Philip Sherrard well knows, it is a punishment that we can set our hearts against, an adaptation that we can try with all our might to undo. We can ally ourselves with those things that are

"builds … despite" • the quotation comes from "The Clod and the Pebble" by English Romantic poet William Blake (1757–1827)

Book of Common Prayer • a book of prayers and liturgy used by Anglican and Episcopal churches

mammon • material goods, worldly wealth

"There is … punishment" • Philip Sherrard (1922–1995) religious thinker and Christian apologist. The quotation is from Sherrard's *The Rape of Man and Nature* (1987)

worthy: light, air, water, earth; plants and animals; human fami- 17
lies and communities; the traditions of decent life, good work,
and responsible thought; the religious traditions; the essential
stories and songs.

It is presumptuous, personally and historically, to assume that 18
one is a part of a "saving remnant."* One had better doubt that one
deserves such a distinction, and had better understand that there
may, after all, be nothing left to save. Even so, if one wishes to save
anything not protected by the present economy – topsoil, groves
of old trees, the possibility of the goodness or health of anything,
even the economic relevance of the biblical tradition – one is a
part of a remnant, and a dwindling remnant too, though not
without hope, and not without the necessary instructions, the
most pertinent of which, perhaps, is this, also from Revelation:
"Be watchful, and strengthen the things which remain, that are
ready to die."*

"saving remnant"·
see Romans 9:27

"Be watchful ... die"·
Revelation 3:2

Annie Dillard

(1945-)

Dillard was born in Pittsburgh and educated at Hollins College, Virginia. Her collection of meditative essays on nature, Pilgrim at Tinker Creek, *earned her the Pulitzer Prize in 1974. One of America's leading prose stylists, Dillard composes essays noted for their vivid metaphors and singular lyricism. She characteristically explores the inherent mystery of the natural world, her vision imbued with the intuition that what she sees there is a hieroglyph of sorts. Extending and enlarging the naturalist tradition of Emerson and Thoreau, Dillard resensitizes readers to the numinous quality of their embodied existence. If the natural world cloaks horror, as every diligent observer must concede, it also veils an intense glory – overwhelming evidence, in other words, that mystery is at the heart of the cosmos. Dillard has written a book on her craft,* The Writing Life *(1989), and an autobiography of her early years,* An American Childhood *(1987), from which the following selection is taken. She currently serves as writer-in-residence at Wesleyan University (Connecticut).*

from AN AMERICAN CHILDHOOD

1 THAT MORNING IN CHURCH after our first subscription dance,* we reconvened on the balcony of the Shadyside Presbyterian Church. I sat in the first balcony row, and resisted the impulse to stretch my Charleston-stiff legs on the balcony's carved walnut rail. The blond boy I'd met at the dance was on my mind, and I intended to spend the church hour recalling his every word and gesture, but I couldn't concentrate. Beside me sat my friend Linda. Last night at the dance she had been a laughing, dimpled girl with an advanced sense of the absurd. Now in church she was grave, and didn't acknowledge my remarks.

> subscription dance ·
> a dance held to raise
> money, often for a
> charitable organization

Near us in the balcony's first row, and behind us, were the boys – the same boys with whom we had traveled on a bus to and from the Sewickley Country Club dance. Below us spread the main pews, filling with adults. Almost everyone in the church was long familiar to me. But this particular Sunday in church bore home to me with force a new notion: that I did not really know any of these people at all. I thought I did – but, being now a teenager, I thought I knew almost everything. Only the strongest evidence could penetrate this illusion, which distorted everything I saw. I knew I approved almost nothing. That is, I liked, I adored, I longed for, everyone on earth, especially India and Africa, and particularly everyone on the streets of Pittsburgh – all those friendly, democratic, openhearted, sensible people – and at Forbes Field,* and in all the office buildings, parks, streetcars, churches, and stores, excepting only the people I knew, none of whom was up to snuff.

Forbes Field · home stadium of the Pittsburgh Pirates baseball team from 1909 until 1970

The church building, where the old Scotch-Irish families assembled weekly, was a Romanesque* chunk of rough, carved stone and panes of dark slate. Covered in creeper, long since encrusted into its quietly splendid site, it looked like a Scottish rock in the rain.

Romanesque · an artistic and architectural style that flourished in medieval Europe

Everywhere outside and inside the church and parish hall, sharp carved things rose from the many dim tons of stone. There were grainy crossed keys, pelicans, anchors, a phoenix, ivy vines, sheaves of wheat, queer and leering mammal heads like gargoyles, thistles for Scotland, lizards, scrolls, lions, and shells. It looked as if someone had once in Pittsburgh enjoyed a flight or two of fancy. If your bare hand or arm brushed against one of the stone walls carelessly, the stone would draw blood.

My wool coat sat empty behind me; its satin lining felt cool on the backs of my arms. I hated being here. It looked as if the boys did, too. Their mouths were all open, and their eyelids half down. We were all trapped. At home before church, I had been too rushed to fight about it.

I imagined the holy war each boy had fought with his family this morning, and lost, resulting in his sullen and suited presence in church. I thought of Dan there, ruddy* cheeked, and of wild, sweet Jamie beside him, each flinging his silk tie at his hypocrite father after breakfast, and making a desperate stand in some dark dining room lighted upward by snowlight from the lawns

ruddy · red

6   outside – struggling foredoomed to raise the stone and walnut weight of this dead society's dead institutions, battling for liberty, freedom of conscience, and so forth.

7   The boys, at any rate, slumped. Possibly they were hung over.

8   While the nave* filled we examined, or glared at, the one thing before our eyes: the apse's* enormous gold mosaic of Christ. It loomed over the chancel;* every pew in the nave and on the balcony looked up at it. It was hard to imagine what long-ago board of trustees had voted for this Romish* looking mosaic, so glittering, with which we had been familiarizing ourselves in a lonely way since infancy, when our eyes could first focus on distance.

9   Christ stood barefoot, alone and helpless-looking, his palms outcurved at his sides. He was wearing his robes. He wasn't standing on anything, but instead floated loose and upright inside a curved, tiled dome. The balcony's perspective foreshortened the dome's curve, so Christ appeared to drift flattened and clumsy, shriveled but glorious. Barefoot as he was, and with the suggestion of sandstone scarps* behind him, he looked rural. Below me along the carpeted marble aisles crept the church's families; the women wore mink and sable stoles. Hushed, they sat and tilted their hatted heads and looked at the rural man. His skies of shattered gold widened over the sanctuary and almost met the square lantern tower, gold-decorated, over the nave.

10   The mosaic caught the few church lights – lights like tapers* in a castle – and spread them dimly, a dusting of gold like pollen, throughout the vast and solemn space. There was nothing you could see well in this rich, Rembrandt* darkness – nothing save the minister's shining face and Christ's gold vault – and yet there was no corner, no scratchy lily work, you couldn't see at all.

11   It was a velvet cord, maroon, with brass fittings, that reserved our ninth-grade balcony section for us. We sat on velvet cushions. Below us, filling the yellow pews with dark furs, were the rest of the families of the church, who seemed to have been planted here in dignity – by a God who could see how hard they worked and how few pleasures they took for themselves – just after the Flood* went down. There were Linda's parents and grandparents and one of her great-grandparents. Always, the same old Pittsburgh families ran this church. The men, for whose forefathers streets all over town were named, served as deacons,

nave · the chief part of a Christian church, extending from the entrance (the narthex) to the area just before the altar

apse · the area behind the altar

chancel · also known as the choir, the chancel is the area just before the altar

Romish · Roman Catholic

scarps · cliffs

tapers · long, slender candles

Rembrandt · Rembrandt van Rijn (1606–1669), Dutch painter

the Flood · see Genesis 6:13–9:17

trustees, and elders. The women served in many ways, and ran 11
the Christmas bazaar.

I knew these men; they were friends and neighbors. I knew 12
what they lived for, I thought. The men wanted to do the right
thing, at work and in the community. They wore narrow, tight
neckties. Close-mouthed, they met, in volunteer boardrooms
and in club locker rooms, the same few comfortable others they
had known since kindergarten. Their wives and children, in those
days, lived around them on their visits home. Some men found
their families bewildering, probably; a man might wonder, wak-
ened by reports of the outstanding misdeeds of this son or that
son, how everyone had so failed to understand what he expected.
Some of these men held their shoulders and knuckles tight; their
laughter was high and embarrassed; they seemed to be looking
around for the entrance to some other life. Only some of the
doctors, it seemed to me, were conspicuously interested and glad.
During conversations, they looked at people calmly, even at their
friends' little daughters; their laughter was deep, long, and joyful;
they asked questions; and they knew lots of words.

I knew the women better. The women were wise and strong. 13
Even among themselves, they prized gaiety and irony, gaiety and
irony come what may. They coped. They sighed, they permitted
themselves a remark or two, they lived essentially alone. They
reared their children with their own two hands, and did all their
own cooking and driving. They had no taste for waste or idleness.
They volunteered their considerable energies, wisdom, and ideas at
the church or the hospital or the service organization or charity.

Life among these families partook of all the genuine serious-
ness of life in time. A child's birth was his sole entrée, just as it
is to life itself. His birthright was a regiment of families and a
phalanx · a tightly   phalanx· of institutions which would accompany him, solidly but
packed mass   at a distance, through this vale of tears.·

this vale of tears ·   Families whose members have been acquainted with each 14
the world as a place of   other for as long as anyone remembers grow not close, but
sorrow and loss   respectful. They accumulate dignity by being seen at church
every Sunday for the duration of life, despite their troubles and
sorrows. They accumulate dignity at club luncheons, dinners,
and dances, by gracefully and persistently, with tidy hair and
fitted clothes, occupying their slots.

15   In this world, some grown women went carefully wild from time to time. They appeared at parties in outlandish clothes, hair sticking out, faces painted in freckles. They shrieked, sang, danced, and parodied anything – that is, anything at all outside the tribe – so that nothing, almost, was sacred. These clowns were the best-loved women, and rightly so, for their own sufferings had taught them what dignity was worth, and every few years they reminded the others, and made them laugh till they cried.

16   My parents didn't go to church. I practically admired them for it. Father would drive by at noon and scoop up Amy and me, saying, "Hop in quick!" so no one would see his weekend khaki pants and loafers.

17   Now, in unison with the adults in the dimness below, we read responsively, answering the minister. Our voices blended low, so their joined sound rose muffled and roaring, rhythmic, like distant seas, and soaked into the rough stone vaults and plush fittings, and vanished, and rose again:

17a   The heavens declare the glory of God:
        and the firmament showeth his handywork.
    Day unto day uttereth speech,
        and night unto night showeth knowledge.
    There is no speech nor language, where their voice is
      not heard.

> **The heavens ... not heard** · see Psalm 19:1–3

18   The minister was a florid, dramatic man who commanded a batch of British vowels, for which I blamed him absolutely, not knowing he came from a Canadian farm. His famous radio ministry attracted letters and even contributions from Alaskan lumberjacks and fishermen. The poor saps. What if one of them, a lumberjack, showed up in Pittsburgh wearing a lumberjack shirt and actually tried to enter the church building? Maybe the ushers were really bouncers.

19   I had got religion at summer camp, and had prayed nightly there and in my bed at home, to God, asking for a grateful heart, and receiving one insofar as I requested it. Inasmuch as I despised everything and everyone about me, of course, it was taken away, and I was left with the blackened heart I had chosen instead. As the years wore on, the intervals between Julys at camp stretched, and filled with country-club evenings, filled with the slang of us girls, our

gossip, and our intricately shifting friendships, filled with the sight of the boys whose names themselves were a litany,* and with the absorbing study of their nonchalance and gruff ease. All of which I professed, from time to time, when things went poorly, to disdain. 19

litany · a repetitive chant or prayer

Nothing so inevitably blackened my heart as an obligatory Sunday at the Shadyside Presbyterian Church: the sight of orphan-girl Liz's "Jesus" tricked out in gilt; the minister's Britishy accent; the putative hypocrisy of my parents, who forced me to go, though they did not; the putative hypocrisy of the expensive men and women who did go. I knew enough of the Bible to damn these people to hell, citing chapter and verse. My house shall be called the house of prayer; but ye have made it a den of thieves.* Every week I had been getting madder; now I was going to plain quit. One of these days, when I figured out how. 20

My house … thieves · see Matthew 21:13, Mark 11:17, Luke 19:46

After the responsive reading there was a pause, an expectant hush. It was the first Sunday of the month, I remembered, shocked. Today was Communion. I would have to sit through Communion, with its two species,* embarrassment and tedium – and I would be late getting out and Father would have to drive around the block a hundred times. I had successfully avoided Communion for years. 21

two species · the two eucharistic elements, bread and wine, are sometimes termed "species"

From their pews below rose the ushers and elders – everybody's father and grandfather, from Mellon Bank & Trust *et cetera* – in tailcoats. They worked the crowd smoothly, as always. When they collected money, I noted, they were especially serene. Collecting money was, after all, what they did during the week; they were used to it. Down each pew an usher thrust a long-handled velvet butterfly net, into the invisible interior of which we each inserted a bare hand to release a crushed, warm dollar bill we'd stored in a white glove's palm. 22

Now with dignity the ushers and elders hoisted the round sterling silver trays which bore Communion. A loaded juice tray must have weighed ten pounds. From a cunning array of holes in its top layer hung wee, tapered, lead-crystal glasses. Each held one-half ounce of Welch's grape juice. 23

The seated people would pass the grape-juice trays down the pews. After the grape juice came bread: flat silver salvers* bore heaps of soft bread cubes, as if for stuffing a turkey. The elders and ushers spread swiftly and silently over the marble aisles in discreet pairs, some for bread cubes, some for grape juice, communicating by eyebrow only. 24

salvers · large serving trays

24 An unseen organist, behind stone screens, played a muted series of single notes, a restless, breathy strain in a minor key, to kill time.

25 Soon the ushers reached the balcony where we sat. There our prayers had reached their intensest pitch, so fervent were we in our hopes not to drop the grape-juice tray.

26 I passed up the Welch's grape juice, I passed up the cubed bread, and sat back against my coat. Was all this not absurd? I glanced at Linda beside me. Apparently it was not. Her hands lay folded in her lap. Both her father and her uncle were elders.

27 It was not surprising, really, that I alone in this church knew what the barefoot Christ, if there had been such a person, would think about things – grape juice, tailcoats, British vowels, sable stoles. It was not surprising because it was becoming quite usual. After all, I was the intelligentsia around these parts, single-handedly. The intelligentsium. I knew why these people were in church: to display to each other their clothes. These were sophisticated men and women, such as we children were becoming. In church they made business connections; they saw and were seen. The boys, who, like me, were starting to come out for freedom and truth, must be having fits, now that the charade of Communion was in full swing.

28 I stole a glance at the boys, then looked at them outright, for I had been wrong. The boys, if mine eyes did not deceive me, were praying. Why? The intelligentsia, of course, described itself these days as "agnostic" – a most useful word. Around me, in seeming earnest, the boys prayed their unthinkable private prayers. To whom? It was wrong to watch, but I watched.

29 On the balcony's first row, to my right, big Dan had pressed his ruddy cheeks into his palms. Beside him, Jamie bent over his knees. Over one eye he had jammed a fist; his other eye was crinkled shut. Another boy, blond Robert, lay stretched over his arms, which clasped the balcony rail. His shoulders were tight; the back of his jacket rose and fell heavily with his breathing. It had been a long time since I'd been to Communion. When had this praying developed?

30 Dan lowered his hands and leaned back slowly. He opened his eyes, unfocused to the high, empty air before him. Wild Jamie moved his arm; he picked up a fistful of hair from his forehead and held it. His eyes fretted tightly shut; his jaws worked. Robert's head still lay low on his outstretched sleeves; it moved once from side to side and back again. So they struggled on. I finally looked away.

Below the balcony, in the crowded nave, men and women 31
were also concentrating, it seemed. Were they perhaps pretending to pray? All heads were bent; no one moved. I began to doubt
my own omniscience. If I bowed my head, too, and shut my eyes,
would this be apostasy?* No, I'd keep watching the people, in case
I'd missed some clue that they were actually doing something
else – bidding bridge hands.

apostasy · the abandonment of Christian faith

For I knew these people, didn't I? I knew their world, which 32
was, in some sense, my world, too, since I could not, outside of
books, name another. I knew what they loved: their families, their
houses, their country clubs, hard work, the people they knew best,
and summer parties with old friends full of laughter. I knew what
they hated: labor unions, laziness, spending, wildness, loudness.
They didn't buy God. They didn't buy anything if they could help
it. And they didn't work on spec.*

on spec · on specula-tion, without a contract or formal agreement

Nevertheless, a young father below me propped his bowed 33
head on two fists stacked on a raised knee. The ushers and
their trays had vanished. The people had taken Communion.
No one moved. The organist hushed. All the men's heads were
bent – black, white, red, yellow, and brown. The men sat absolutely still. Almost all the women's heads were bent down, too,
and some few tilted back. Some hats wagged faintly from side
to side. All the people seemed scarcely to breathe.

Moment of insight ⭐

I was alert enough now to feel, despite myself, some faint, 34
thin stream of spirit braiding forward from the pews. Its flawed
and fragile rivulets pooled far beyond me at the altar. I felt, or
saw, its frail strands rise to the wide tower ceiling, and mass in
the gold mosaic's dome.

tesseræ · the fragments composing a mosaic

The gold tesseræ* scattered some spirit like light back over the 35
cavernous room, and held some of it, like light, in its deep curve.
Christ drifted among floating sandstone ledges and deep, absor-
bent skies. There was no speech nor language. The people had
been praying, praying to God, just as they seemed to be praying.
That was the fact. I didn't know what to make of it.

Who *is* my neighbor? · see Luke 10:25–37

I left Pittsburgh before I had a grain of sense. Who *is* my 36
neighbor?* I never learned what the strangers around me had
known and felt in their lives – those lithe, sarcastic boys in the
balcony, those expensive men and women in the pews below – but
it was more than I knew, after all.

Robert A. Fink

⟨ 1 9 4 6 - ⟩

A native Texan, Robert Fink is an award-winning poet and veteran of the Vietnam War. His experience as a first lieutenant in the United States Marine Corps often figures in his poetry and essays. Fink's three books of poetry, Azimuth Points *(1981),* The Ghostly Hitchhiker *(1989), and* The Tongues of Men and of Angels *(1995), often describe passionate wrestlings with moral and spiritual questions. His works cover a wide range of topics – family, marriage, baseball, war, religion – and often reveal a happy blend of humor and spiritual insight. Fink is the Bond Professor of English and director of the Creative Writing Workshops at Hardin-Simmons University.*

HOW I FOUND RELIGION AT A BASEBALL GAME

1   I ALWAYS SIT FOUR ROWS UP, directly behind home plate. It's important to be in position to see the whole picture. I discovered this spot several years ago when I recognized the invisible line connecting home plate to the pitching rubber, to second base, to the middle of the twenty-foot green monster wall in dead center. This is the line dividing the playing field into halves resembling angels' wings. The line originates at my fourth-row position.

2   The poet Theodore Rœthke* is supposed to have said he never realized he could think until he turned forty. There's something to this. The view from forty is similar to my fourth-row vantage point. It's more of an introspective look at what's happening around me, and I'm not as important to the picture as I used to think, and this doesn't bother me as much as I expected. My past begins to look like design, not mine. It's more like religion. Not a bad place to be on a sunny, March afternoon in West Texas, the temperature in the high 70s, the flags at ease above the center

Theodore Rœthke·
American poet
(1908–1963)

129

field wall. This is the kind of day you would select if you knew 2 something extraordinary was about to happen.

I recognized the mood because I had felt it seven months earlier. 3 My wife, two teenage sons, and I had spent the summer at Phillips Academy, Andover, Massachusetts, where my sons took course-work, and I taught a couple of classes. It was the evening before we were to start back to Texas early the next morning. We were rushing around packing the car and cleaning up the house we had stayed in for the summer. Just outside our back door was the school's baseball field. This was not your ordinary ballpark. First of all, it really was a field. When we arrived in June, the outfield grass was higher than our ankles and so thick that until you took off after a fly ball in the gap between right and center, you wouldn't notice the ground had never been leveled but rose and fell like the undulations of waves twelve miles out in the ocean. There were no fences, the outfield rising toward the distant tennis courts. Five hundred feet out in center, a solitary grandfather oak had been left for æsthetics or possibly as a reminder that the focal point of this picture had always been nature. Instead of dugouts for each team, two green benches had been placed along the first-base and the third-base foul lines. There were no bleachers for the fans. I watched most of the American Legion games played on the field that summer, and the moms and dads, the girlfriends and younger brothers of the ball-players brought folding lawn chairs or stretched out on the grassy slope running the length of the right field foul line. I preferred to lie back and shut my eyes, taking in the sounds of the game, especially the players' chatter, soothing as surf rolling into shore.

Wednesday afternoons, a couple of my friends and I would 4 meet on the field and throw the ball around. We had grown up playing baseball, and the poet-in-residence had even spent several years in the Phillies' minor-league system. When the word got around, other middle-aged faculty started showing up with gloves no one would believe existed, much less still had some magic in the pocket. We took turns lobbing batting practice fast balls to each other, and every now and then someone would slip in what he announced was a curve. The rest of us would fan out across the outfield, often gathering in clusters of two and three to visit but always with an eye on the batter, always ready to call out "Mine" or "I got it" and amble off after a can of corn,* working hard to

can of corn · an easily-caught fly-ball

4 make the catch look routine, then rainbow the ball back toward the pitcher's mound. When we took our turn at bat, every hit was a rope,* every fly outta here or at least deep enough to have easily scored a runner tagging at third.

a rope · a hard, line-drive hit

5 A light rain was falling our last afternoon at Andover. The car was pretty much packed, and my wife and my sons were checking the house for any items we had overlooked. It was about 7:00 PM, and as I squeezed my glove into a corner of our Honda Civic's trunk, I decided to walk down to the baseball field. Fog had started to settle around the tennis courts, and the oak in center seemed diaphanous as a vision. I sat down on the Visitor's bench, leaned back and pulled the bill of my shapeless Washington Senators cap lower across my eyes; the rain had become a steady drizzle. I couldn't say how long I sat there staring at the field, at all that green. I don't remember thinking or feeling anything. I couldn't move, didn't want to. It was almost like 1973 on a Santa Monica beach when I lay back in the sand and for a moment couldn't recall what day it was or what I had to do tomorrow. The Andover field was a holy place. Had I been able, I would have removed my shoes. When I could rise from the bench, I had to rediscover my limbs, slowly recognize that I was walking back to the house, my family asking where I had been; why I was soaked to the skin.

6 On that occasion I didn't feel particularly wise, just peaceful; but on a March afternoon, fourth-row up behind home plate, the president of our university sitting beside me, I recalled Herman Melville's statement* that we can't know greatness until we've failed. I had just finished grading a set of Freshman poetry explications of Sylvia Plath's "Metaphors."* The essays had been much better than I expected, and several of the interpretations had bordered on brilliant. One twenty-six-year-old mother of a couple of pre-schoolers had even argued that the poem's last line – "Boarded the train there's no getting off" – didn't mean the speaker of the poem, a pregnant woman, was depressed about becoming a mother. On this day I needed to believe her and didn't write in the margin of the essay – "Then how do you explain Plath's love affair with Death, her later suicide?" I needed the wife in the poem to affirm the life within her, growing larger day by day. I left my third-floor office and walked over to the baseball stadium to take in the first game of a double header.

Herman Melville's statement · Herman Melville (1819–1891), American novelist

Sylvia Plath's "Metaphors" · Sylvia Plath (1932–1963), American poet

Bottom of the second inning, our university president came up   7
the steps leading to the bleachers. He started down the walkway
in front of the first row of seats. From the corner of my eye, I
watched him wave to the three or four students on the third-base
side; then he shook hands with one of the ballplayer's parents.
Not many fans show up for Wednesday afternoon games. Our
record was 3 and 17, but we weren't that bad; we started the
season against the University of Texas, Texas A&M, Baylor, and
Oklahoma. After each loss, the coach and the sportswriters
emphasized our lack of pitching.

I could tell the president was looking for someone, and that   8
person had failed to show, so I waved and asked if he would like to
join me. He sat down, inquired about the score and made a comment
about the poor officiating we'd been having. He seemed eager to yell
at "Blue" about his lack of good judgment. I grinned and pointed
out the similarity between umpires and university presidents – how
we needed to loudly shout their sins, a catharsis for fans and faculty
members. He smiled and took off his coat, said he'd have to be going
soon. He loosened his tie and yelled a word of encouragement to
the batter quickly behind in the count, 0 and 2. The president had
announced he would be stepping down from office at the end of the
school year. After fourteen years, he wanted to concentrate on writing, maybe teach a class or two. When he arrived on campus he had a
head of thick, black hair and often ran with students in 5K races. Now
what hair still ringed his crown was gray, and he had back problems.
I was hired the same year he was, both of us just starting out.

I was thinking about this connection when our catcher   9
launched a light-stanchion-clearing shot down the left field line.
The ball almost disappeared into the western sun but stayed fair
by at least ten feet. Everyone but the umpire could see it was
a home run. The pitcher knew it. He slammed his fist into his
glove and stomped off the mound. Our on-deck batter leaped
high and jabbed at the air; the rest of our players burst from the
dugout as if a trumpet had sounded calling the dead from their
graves. The batter was halfway to first base, easing into his victory trot, when the home plate umpire threw both arms to his
left and shouted, "Foul Ball!"

Our coach slammed his cap into the dirt and ran toward the   10
umpire. Each time the ump turned his back, the coach would

10   scoot around to keep his nose and his index finger about an inch in front of the umpire's face. The president jumped up and shouted "Blue!" as if this were the vilest of epithets. Our second baseman, the team captain, stepped in front of the coach and threw his glove against the umpire's shins. He said the call was "Tragic!" Having no comeback for such a word, the umpire aimed his arm at the bench and tossed our second baseman. The coach took up his cause. The president shouted "Blue! Blue!"

11   We ended up losing the game by one run. Now we were 3 and 18, but everyone seemed more exhilarated by this loss than by the three wins. We had been robbed. We could glory in our defeat. We had a cause to champion over coffee in the faculty lounge. Our sports reporter would have a two-column diatribe for the school paper. The president could finally rage with us on an issue; he had found a higher official to sacrifice on the altar of righteous indignation.

12   What really amazed me was that while everyone was shouting and leaping and throwing equipment, I wasn't. I did not feel superior to the participants in this dance; nor did I feel like the only one without a partner. I was thinking of a scene from the movie *Meatballs* where the summer-camp olympics team of klutzes is about to face the champion team from a rival camp. Bill Murray, one of the klutz team's camp counselors, fires up his enervated players by pulling them to their feet and leading a hand-clapping, tent-revival rally. By the end of the scene, all twenty-odd team members are snake dancing around the camp lodge, chanting with Murray, "It just doesn't matter! It just doesn't matter!" Unable to lift myself from my spot in the bleachers, I believed everything mattered. I believed nothing mattered. I was invigorated and exhausted. I somehow knew God had forgiven me for always demanding that things turn out right, that winning bring salvation.

13   In seventh grade, my best friend and I spent hours perfecting our pitches on the narrow strip of lawn, west side of my house. Or we'd take the football and play kick over in the street in front of his house. Sometimes his dad would quarterback pass patterns with us. Sometimes we'd pitch a tent in his backyard and camp out overnight laughing at everything; if we got lucky and uncovered one of his older sister's dirty novels, we'd sneak it from her

room to read the sex scenes, one of us turning the pages while [13] the other held the flashlight. We were not as close in high school, and in college we only dropped each other a line once or twice a year. We sent invitations to our weddings, announcements when our first child was born.

I never believed my friend would die, not from bone cancer, [14] not at twenty-seven, his dad staying at his side the last weeks in the hospital, twice a day lifting his son from the bed and hugging him close, stumbling around the room in a pantomime of exercise. My friend wrote he was running down-and-out pass patterns, juking* the plastic hospital chairs. He swore he was getting better; I didn't need to leave my graduate studies, my wife and my new-born twins, and fly to see him. I was relieved. I mailed him a funny greeting card every day. His wife called to talk after the funeral. She said he had looked forward to the cards.

juking · avoiding defending football players

The year I was in Vietnam, the Marines were packing to leave. [15] Nobody was supposed to die; our operations were designed to show discretion, not valor. Everybody died. The first was one of the guys from my Officer Candidate School platoon. He casually opened the door of a village hut. I remembered his having to stand in front of our OCS platoon of recent college graduates and sing, "I'm a little teapot, short and stout. Here is my handle. Here is my spout." Our platoon sergeant was displeased with him for failing to shine the coffee urn in the officers' lounge. Now he was dead, like the lance corporal who just happened to walk into the Military Police office at the same instant one of his buddies forgot to eject the ammo clip from his .45 automatic, chambering a round instead of clearing the pistol. When the slide shot home, the gun discharged its bullet into the forehead of the lance corporal.

During a two-week period, five helicopters from Marine Air [16] Group 16 disappeared for no good reason – four exploding in mid-air, one vanishing over the China Sea. A sixth had a steel cable snap extracting a Recon* unit out of triple-canopy jungle north of Da Nang. Four of the team were safe in the chopper when the cable broke and the lieutenant, who was almost close enough for the door gunner to touch, fell a hundred feet back into the canopy, the cable trailing from his waist like an umbilical cord.

Recon · short for reconnaissance, a unit sent to gain preliminary information on enemy territory and movements

Viet Cong · the communist guerrilla force that aided the North Vietnamese Army in fighting against South Vietnam

Da Nang · chief port of the central lowlands of Vietnam

The night the Viet Cong* finally got lucky and hit the fuel [17] dump at the Da Nang* Air Base, one of their rockets fell short

17   and exploded in MAG-11.· I had the duty at First Marine Air Wing. I waited at our helicopter Landing Zone for the evacuation chopper called in to rush the seriously wounded to the battalion hospital. When the first ambulance from MAG-11 arrived, the young Marine tucked under the clean sheet didn't look injured at all. I had been expecting blood and gaping wounds; all I saw was a teenager with the whitest face I had seen in my six months in 'Nam. The corpsmen didn't speak. One of them handed me an IV bottle, then each grabbed an end of the stretcher and rushed toward the chopper. I held the bottle high and jogged along beside the stretcher. Keeping my head ducked to try and avoid the helicopter's rotor wash, I looked directly into the boy's eyes. He was scared, so I shouted that he would be all right. I believed it. No blood. He was dead before the chopper reached the hospital. The corpsmen told me the boy was scheduled to rotate back to the states that morning. Things like that didn't happen. Things like that always happened.

> **MAG-11**· Marine Aircraft Group 11

18   Like my poetry-writing student who told me she had asthma, trained for marathons, and taught ærobic dance at the Y· three times a week. She was always bringing cookies to class to share with the writing workshop members. Her face looked like a skull, her arms and legs little more than bones. Everyone but me knew she was anorexic. Everyone but me knew not to push her to stop writing about birds and flowers, knew not to insist she revise the three-page, incoherent poem about the high school cheerleader who found her father's body in his Cadillac idling in the closed garage. Everyone but me understood she wasn't taking the course to improve her writing.

> **the Y**· The YMCA and YWCA (Young Men's and Young Women's Christian Associations, respectively) sponsor athletic and personal-development activities

19   I always believed in winning. A good loser was still a loser. All you'd learn from losing was why you didn't win. I was wrong. Nobody needs to learn from winning. Failure tempers us for tomorrow; this must be why Jesus warned his followers to concern themselves only with the sufficient evil of each day· and offered forgiveness for yesterday's failures.

> **sufficient evil of each day**· see Matthew 6:34

20   No theologian understands this better than baseball people; that's why coaches schedule as many games as possible each week, sometimes even slipping in a double header. Should you go 0 for 3 at the plate and make two run-scoring errors in the field, you can turn your shame around in the next game. Coaches are fond

of saying that if you screw up in the field, make up for it with 20
your bat; if you couldn't hit a beach ball floated to the plate, then
look flashy at third. Baseball is religion because it admonishes
its converts to accept a second chance, taking comfort in the
knowledge that everyone expects you to fail at least seven out of
ten times at bat. You can always rely on drawing the farsighted
umpire, on getting the bad hop, on having to play the sun field.
Gravity is always pulling at your bones.

On that sunny, March afternoon in the bleachers, I under- 21
stood. God expected Adam and Eve to eat the apple.*

Adam … apple · see
Genesis 3:1–6

A. N. Wilson

⟪ 1 9 5 0 - ⟫

Wilson, a prolific biographer and novelist, attended New College, Oxford, where he earned the MA in 1976. His novels, including The Sweets of Pimlico *(1977) and* The Healing Art *(1980), are noted for their excellent characterization, irony, and black humor. Wilson has written full-length portraits of several great figures, including John Milton, Leo Tolstoy, C. S. Lewis, and Jesus, among others. Though unfailingly interesting, his biographies have been criticized for their sometimes idiosyncratic judgments. Wilson is also a social critic with a quick eye for the comic. He describes himself as "congenitally irascible." That very irascibility appears in the following essay, the first chapter from* How Can We Know *(1985), an unusual personal view of Christianity – a religion which he finds difficult to accept but impossible to ignore. In this essay Wilson offers an account of his own youthful quest for truth, as it was ignited by the life of Leo Tolstoy and Jesus' Sermon on the Mount.*

THE CALL

1 RATHER LESS THAN TWENTY years ago, when I was a school boy, I belonged to a sixth-form society* to which we invited visiting speakers. Someone came and told us how the City of London worked. On another week, a politician might come to speak, or a journalist or a writer. One week, a man came and told us about Tolstoy.* He spoke, not about Tolstoy's genius as a novelist (which I think I had begun to discover) but about the great act of renunciation which Tolstoy undertook after he had finished *Anna Karenina.* As he spoke, I felt my "heart burn within me," like the disciples walking to Emmaus after the first Easter.* I felt more excited by the story than by any I had ever heard. Here was the greatest genius who had ever written a novel. He was a Russian aristocrat,

sixth-form society · academic organization in the English school system

Tolstoy · Leo Tolstoy (1828–1910), Russian novelist. See Tolstoy's "How Much Land Does a Man Need" on pages 189–203

"heart …" … Easter · see Luke 24:32

an ex-soldier, a sensualist, one of the richest characters (in all senses of those words) in the history of literature. And yet, at the very summit of his fame, he wanted to renounce everything, to abandon his estates, his money, the practice of literature, the exercise of his carnal appetites, and to live a life of poverty, like the peasants on his estates. And why? Because he had become convinced that the Sermon preached by Jesus on the mountain* towards the beginning of St. Matthew's Gospel was simply and literally true.

At the time, I was very young for my fifteen or sixteen years, very impressionable and very enthusiastic. I had already been by turns, a convert to a simple sort of evangelical Christianity; an atheist; a Marxist with particular devotion to the teachings of Chairman Mao.* I do not remember in what order I adopted and discarded these enthusiasms. I expect I went through about three or four creeds in each school term. But the Tolstoy thing took hold of me for longer. Strange as it seems to me now, for about two years I tried to practice some of the simpler dictates of the Tolstoyan creed such as vegetarianism. I joined the Peace Pledge Union.* I absorbed and re-read as much of his writing as I could. Then, when a few years passed, I found that I had moved on. "It is the concrete being that reasons," Newman* wrote; "pass a number of years and I find my mind in a new place. How? The whole man moves, paper logic is but the record of it." I stumbled on, zig-zagging my way down the road of faith, now believing, now disbelieving, and increasingly concerned with the spiritual journey of Newman himself. Tolstoy was not forgotten. He was put on one side, always haunting my memory.

Lately, for a number of reasons, I have returned to Tolstoy, and once again, I have been overwhelmed by the sheer grandeur and simplicity of his writings on the subject of Christianity. Coming to the story as a grown-up, I am furthermore haunted by his appalling domestic sufferings. Everything about him was great – larger than life – including his faults and his mistakes. How, for instance, could somebody of his extraordinary knowledge of human character have been so foolish as to show all his private diaries to his wife? Much of his quest for the Kingdom of God was obscured by his ludicrously Luddite* and philistine* prejudices. Why, for instance, was it more Christian to travel in a cart than by train? What lunacy can have prompted him to think

---

Sermon . . . mountain · see Matthew 5–7

Chairman Mao · Mao Zedong (1893–1976), leader of the Chinese Communist Party

Peace Pledge Union · founded in 1934 by Richard Sheppard, a chaplain in World War I, the Union campaigned for pacifist causes

Newman · John Henry Newman (1801–1890), English author and theologian. See Newman's *The Idea of a University* on pages 29–33

Luddite · British workers who in 1811–1816 rioted, destroying labor-saving machinery they feared would result in the loss of their jobs

philistine · one lacking in taste or culture

3 his own greatest novels (no modesty, here, he was a stranger to modesty) *War and Peace* and *Anna Karenina* were simply piffle? How could he have been so arrogant as to dismiss Shakespeare? Oh yes, the faults are all obvious enough to the grown-up reader. And we can read with a lofty cynicism of the great Tolstoy's moral failings. What rows* there were at Yasnaya Polyana* after he had resolved to put all anger out of his heart! Nor was it necessarily safe for the young peasant girls to get too close to the Count after he had made his notorious vow of complete celibacy.

rows · fights, arguments

Yasnaya Polyana · the Tolstoy estate

4 But Tolstoy himself had an answer which shames any of his detractors:

4a "Well, but you, Leo Nikolayevich; you preach – but how about practice?" People always put it to me and always triumphantly shut my mouth with it. You preach, but how do you live? And I reply that I do not preach and cannot preach, though I passionately desire to do so. I could only preach by deeds; and my deeds are bad. What I say is not a sermon, but only a refutation of a false understanding of the Christian teaching and an explanation of its real meaning. Its meaning is not that we should in its name rearrange society by violence: its purpose is to find the meaning of our life in this world. The performance of Christ's five commandments* gives that meaning. If you wish to be a Christian, you must fulfill those commands. If you do not wish to fulfill them, don't talk of Christianity.... I do not fulfill a ten-thousandth part it is true, and I am to blame for that; but it is not because I do not wish to fulfill them that I fail, but because I do not know how to. Teach me how to escape from the nets of temptation that have ensnared me, help me, and I will fulfill them; but even without help I desire and hope to do so. Blame me – I do that myself – but blame me, and not the path I tread, and show to those who ask me where in my opinion the road lies! If I know the road home and go along it drunk, staggering from side to side – does that make the road along which I go a wrong one?...

Christ's five commandments · see Matthew 5:21–48

4 Reading those words again after a gap of nearly twenty years, I was arrested once more by their extraordinary power. They

The Sermon on the Mount · see Matthew 5–7

made me read The Sermon on the Mount* again, and to see it 4
with fresh eyes. As a young reader of Tolstoy, I was chiefly struck
by his failure to live as Jesus said we should. Twenty years later,
I am much more astonished by his attempt to do so, than I am
by his failure. Most reasonable, decent, Western readers in the
latter half of the twentieth century would find the Christ of Saint
Matthew's Gospel romantic, but repellent. The brutal paradoxes
of the Beatitudes* seem inimical to contemporary moral values.
Sometimes good agnostics say that they are unable to accept
the supernatural elements of the New Testament but that they
would like to think that their lives approximate to the values of
the Sermon on the Mount. The life of Tolstoy is a vivid illustra-
tion of what it would be like if we truly wished to live as Jesus
taught. The modern, unchristian wisdom, for instance, would
consider it impracticable and simply unhealthy to worry about
the lustful thoughts which happen to pass through our heart. In
the scale of values enunciated by Jesus, "he who casts his eyes on
a woman so as to lust after her has already committed adultery
with her in his heart" (Matthew 5:28). Even if we thought that we
could prevent ourselves having such thoughts, how many of us
believe that we should? Certainly many an analyst would be out
of business if we truly thought it was possible to banish the very
feelings of anger (Matthew 5:22). As for the teachings of Jesus
about money and poverty, could anyone who was not, like Tolstoy,
a rich aristocrat, contemplate giving up everything, and living as
the flowers of the field,* dependent wholly on the Providence of
God? Perhaps a few young men and women nowadays embrace
the comparative security of a religious order and believe that
they have become poor for Christ's sake. But what of us, who live
in the world? Do bills pay themselves? Christ told his disciples
to pay tax to Cæsar,* so presumably he did not expect them to
be penniless. The renunciation of Tolstoy, when watched from
afar, unfolds like a great tragedy, and we can, at this historical
distance, be uplifted by its drama. But of us: what of us, with
our humdrum carnal and economic needs? Surely it would be
madness to emulate him, pure insanity to put into practice the
self-destructive teachings of Christ.

But, I find that the words of Tolstoy won't be dismissed or 5
ignored. "If you wish to be a Christian, you must fulfill these

Beatitudes · see Matthew 5:3–11

flowers of the field · see Matthew 6:28

Christ ... Cæsar · see Matthew 22:15–22

5 commands," he said. And when one turns to the New Testament itself, the paradox of it all becomes even harsher. What would we say of a man who tried to bottle up all his anger, to suppress his sexual nature, who abandoned all earthly security, closed his deposit account and gave the money to the poor? Would we not think that such a person was storing up trouble, behaving in a way which was calculated to produce a total personal collapse? Jesus says this about such a man:

5a Whoever, then, hears these commandments of mine and carries them out, is like a wise man who built his house upon rock; and the rain fell and the floods came and the winds blew and beat upon that house, but it did not fall; it was founded upon rock. But whoever hears these commandments of mine and does not carry them out is like a fool, who built his house upon sand; and the rain fell and the floods came and the winds blew and beat upon that house, and it fell; and great was the fall of it. (Matthew 7:24–28)

6 These words at the end of the Sermon on the Mount are perhaps the most shocking and preposterous of all. For, whatever else Christ appears to offer in his manifesto for the Kingdom, it is not rock-like security. From the very opening words, *Blessed are the poor in spirit,*· the paradox is with us. *Blessed are the poor in spirit* does not mean the same, precisely, as blessed are the poor. And it is conspicuous that those who are professionally engaged in teaching the truth of the Incarnation,· the clergy, should have spent so much of their energy over the years in denying the truth of these words, *Blessed are the poor in spirit*, the very first words uttered, in St. Matthew's Sermon, by the Incarnate God. We have been told that there is such a thing as "evangelical poverty" which is somehow different from real poverty, or that the words mean, "Blessed are the needy": that is, Blessed are those who recognize their need for God's grace. But this Beatitude, *Blessed are the poor in spirit*, is really no more than an introduction to the other sayings of Christ in the same Sermon.

Blessed ... spirit·
Matthew 5:3

6a Do not lay up treasure for yourselves on earth, where there is moth and rust to consume it, where there are thieves to break in and steal it; lay up treasure for yourselves in

heaven.... A man cannot be the slave of two masters at 6a
once; either he will hate the one and love the other, or
he will devote himself to the one and despise the other.
You must serve God or money; you cannot serve both.
(Matthew 6:19–20, 24)

And there is abundant evidence in the Gospels that Jesus believed 6
that "it is easier for a camel to pass through a needle's eye, than for
a man to enter the kingdom of heaven when he is rich" (Matthew
19:24). One can reserve for the moment the casuist's* discussion of
"how poor is poor," or the common-sense notion that we have "got
to live" and provide for the future, the children, and old age. Christ
specifically tells his disciples not to do those things. He says that
we should take no thought for the morrow (Matthew 6:34) and not
worry about how we are to be clothed or fed (Matthew 6:28).

"The poor have the good news preached to them" (Matthew 7
11:5). It came as the climax of his message to John the Baptist in
prison. It seems from its rhetorical placing in that sentence to
be more important, in Christ's scale of values, than the blind
seeing, or the lame walking, or the lepers being made clean;
more important, or more miraculous. So indeed it is. The great
Christian miracle for St. Paul was that God dispossessed himself
and became like a poor slave in order to teach the human race
the way of dispossession (Philippians 2:7).

But in common-sense terms, we know that the poor aren't 8
blessed. What is blessed about the filth of shanty-towns? What
is blessed about a disease-ridden African village full of starving children? What can the poor in such places hope for, live
for? We suffer in the West from the deadening effects of materialism. But we can at least see that wealth, rightly used, has
enabled us to lift ourselves above the purely material level of the
beasts. Shakespeare* was patronized by a rich man, the Earl of
Southampton.* Michelangelo* painted his masterpieces at the
behest of rich popes. The sublime masses and symphonies of
Haydn* were paid for. The great Gothic cathedrals,* the swooping,
well-planted parks of eighteenth century noblemen, the great can-
vases of Tintoretto* or Rembrandt* were all produced by money,
and they would not have existed if everyone in Christian Europe
had followed purely the dictates of the Christian religion.

casuist's · a person
who studies questions
of right and wrong
conduct, often in a false
or deceptive manner

Shakespeare · William
Shakespeare (1564–1616)

Earl of Southampton ·
Henry Wriothesley
(1573–1624), a wealthy
patron of the arts

Michelangelo · Italian
sculptor, painter, architect,
and poet (1475–1564)

Haydn · Franz Joseph
Haydn (1732–1809),
Austrian Classical
composer

Gothic cathedrals ·
flourishing between the
12th and 16th centuries,
gothic architecture is
characterized by ribbed
vaults and flying but-
tresses, which allowed
soaring heights and the
extensive use of windows

Tintoretto · Italian
Mannerist painter
(1518–1594)

Rembrandt · Rembrandt
van Rijn (1606–1669),
Dutch painter

9   There is nothing bland about the Beatitudes. They are all hard: hard in the sense of flinty – as the final metaphor of the Sermon would suggest; hard in the sense of difficult; hard, even, in the sense of merciless. For the fifth beatitude, *Blessed are the merciful,*· sounds easy enough until Christ expounds it. We are not merely to show mercy comparatively in the manner of a magistrate reducing a poacher's sentence from hanging to penal servitude. Mercy in the moral universe of the Sermon seems to demand total open-heartedness.

Blessed ... merciful · Matthew 5:7

9a   You have heard that it was said, An eye for an eye and a tooth for a tooth. But I tell you that you should not offer resistance to injury; if a man strikes thee on thy right cheek, turn the other cheek also towards him; if he is ready to go to law with thee over thy coat, let him have it and thy cloak with it. (Matthew 5:38-41)

10   One feature of the debate about nuclear weapons which goes on at the moment, is how vociferously certain church leaders have returned to the Christian pacifism of the Sermon on the Mount. It would seem (though papal utterances are always hard to disentangle) as though the Pope had now discarded the old notion of a "just war." Many churchmen seem to say that they object to nuclear weapons but they do not object to "conventional warfare," by which they presumably mean things like the Battle of the Somme· and the bombing of Dresden.· Others have casu-istically, and perhaps wisely, argued that Our Lord's Sermon on the Mount was not directed to nations but to *individuals*. But how does that alter the morality of the case? It is an individual and not a nation who pulls the trigger, or presses the button. The pacifism of Christ was obviously absolute. It was not of a "militant" kind. He did not hurl abuse at centurions.· On the contrary, he conversed with them; one of them, he regarded as being a man of greater faith than his own fellow-Israelites (Matthew 8:10). It is also true that he told his disciples that they should not set themselves up as judges of other people (Matthew 7:1). But if it is true that St. Matthew's Gospel does not anticipate the moral complexities of the nuclear debate, there can be no escaping its absolute rejection of reprisal as a moral principle. If a society were ordered along the lines of the Sermon, it would be neces-

Battle of the Somme · a massively costly yet ineffectual Allied offensive on the Western Front during World War I

bombing of Dresden · the German city of Dresden was almost completely destroyed by massive Allied fire-bombing raids in 1945

centurions · professional Roman soldiers, each centurion commanded 100 men

sary not merely to abolish the armed forces, but also the police 10
and the law-courts. In social terms, it is a recipe for anarchy. In
personal terms, it is loudly and inescapably obvious that Our Lord
forbade his followers to defend themselves against attack, just as
he forbade them to provide for the future by saving up money.

Then again, in the sixth beatitude, Jesus says, *Blessed are the* 11
clean of heart. "In Hebrew psychology, the heart is the seat of
thought and will rather than of emotion," says one modern commentary on this verse. If that is so, it means that Jesus makes a
greater, not a lesser demand. We could all get into a *mood* of
piety if we wanted to, in which we felt, or persuaded ourselves
that we felt, as pure as driven snow. It is much less easy to control the movement of the mind. It is harder yet to purify the will.
If by *heart* is really meant the whole inner man, his affections,
his prejudices, his habits of mind, his emotional history, all that
we mean by his *character*, these things are to a large degree
unchangeable. By the time that our "characters are formed," there
is very little we can do about them. We can resolve to do better;
we can undertake a major programme of reform. But all the scars
and shapes of our old existence will still be there.

Common sense rebels against the call to poverty. (It rebels in 12
vain, but it rebels.) In this saying, by contrast, the human heart
itself is reproached by Christ. It shows that his standards are
meant to be impossibly high. In the course of the Sermon, he says
(scholars tell us that the author of St. Matthew's Gospel makes
him say) that he does not want to overthrow the old Judaic law.
Whether or not that verse has been invented by an early Jewish
Christian anxious not to lose contact with the practices of his old
faith, we cannot escape the searching perfectionism of what follows. The old law had said that it was wrong to commit murder.

> But I tell you that any man who is angry with his brother 12a
> must answer for it before the court of justice, and any man
> who says *Raca* to his brother must answer for it before the
> Council; and any man who says to his brother, Thou fool,
> must answer for it in Hell fire. (Matthew 5:22–23)

Raca · "empty-headed"
or "good-for-nothing"
(Aramaic)

For someone like myself who is not merely congenitally 13
irascible, but also professionally committed, as a journalist, to
commenting upon human folly, this is perhaps the most dis-

13 turbing passage in the entire sermon. In his story of Dives and Lazarus, Jesus tells us that the rich man, who ignored his warning to embrace holy poverty, was sent to hell (Luke 16:22). Likewise, in the sermon on the Mount, he implies that hell is the reward of those who commit the sins of the flesh.

13a
> If thy right eye is the occasion of thy falling into sin, pluck it out and cast it away from thee; better to lose one part of thy body than to have the whole cast into hell. (Matthew 5:29)

13 And, more generally,

13b
> It is a broad gate and a wide road that leads on to perdition. (Matthew 7:13)

14 It is the narrow way which leads on to salvation. It is the chaste, meek-hearted pacifist with no money in the world who builds his house on a rock. It is the libidinous, aggressive man, storing up quantities of this world's riches, who is building his house on the sand.

15 When I contemplate the lives of other people, I am just about prepared to concede the romantic appeal of all this. Sitting on a commuter train, perhaps, and watching everyone going to work, I see the lecherous business-men, giving themselves ulcers by overwork, their minds perpetually engaged, even when at home, by the threats of auditors and the hopes of foreign contracts, changes in interest rates and all the arcane movements and mysteries of money. I compare their worried, pampered faces with the quiet serenity that I have seen on the faces of monks who – mad by the standards of the world – have abandoned the hope of riches and the gratifications of the flesh. I think of promiscuous young women I know, their young faces already raddled with late nights, messy love affairs and too much dope and drink, and compare them with the radiant calm of some of the Christian women I know. In such reveries, the Sermon on the Mount, with all its apparent reversal of common sense, seems luminously sane.

16 But, to tell the truth, only momentarily so. For the Sermon very specifically tells us not to judge other people. It is not addressed to the others. It is addressed to me. And this

explains, perhaps, its abiding power over the centuries. I know 16 with perfect certainty that I have not lived my life according to the dictates of this Sermon. The example of the great Tolstoy would seem to suggest that these counsels of perfection could not even be attempted without failure. But as soon as the words of Christ shine like a spotlight on one's own condition, rather than on the lives of others, their effect is different. It may well be the case that I have not tried to practice Christianity, but I am not certain that life has been any the better for that omission. Here I am, stuck in my mid-thirties with the responsibilities of earning a living and providing for a family. It should be very easy to shrug and say that I have no intention of plunging my children into poverty or adopting the Simple Life. But Christ's words do not go away as easily as that. Nor do I think it is simply because I have heard them since childhood and formed a sentimental attachment to them, while doing next to nothing to put them into practice.

Why is it that, the older one grows, the more topsy-turvy 17 the wisdom of Christ appears; and yet the more it appears to be wisdom? He seems to be looking at life upside down; he tells us that the poor have security, the mourners will be happy, the sexually deprived will be the most fulfilled. It seems, by the wisdom of this world, as if he got everything the wrong way round. But live a bit, and one discovers that this is not necessarily the case at all. If the world itself is inverted, then the only way to see it clearly is upside down. If the values of the world are the wrong way round, then the only way to wisdom is to stand those values on their head. When we say that we lose the idealism of our youth, we often add that moral choice becomes more complicated with age. We speak as if complexity were a good thing and as though moral sight, like eyesight, got better with age. But some of us could see more clearly when we were sixteen than when we are sixty. I remember something about accepting the Kingdom as a little child. And I remember my first excitement at Tolstoy's words, "If you wish to be a Christian, you must fulfill these commands. If you do not wish to fulfill them, don't talk of Christianity." The words won't go away. Jesus said, "Heaven and earth shall pass away, but my words shall not pass away."*

"Heaven ... away" ·
Matthew 24:35

John Philip Santos

◀(1 9 5 7 -)▶

A native of San Antonio, Texas, Santos has written widely on Latino culture, publishing articles in, among other venues, the Los Angeles Times *and the* New York Times. *Television documentaries written and produced by Santos have appeared on* CBS *and* PBS. *In addition to his other honors, Santos holds the distinction of being the first Mexican American to be appointed a Rhodes scholar. In* Places Left Unfinished At the Time of Creation (*1999*), *a journalistic memoir, Santos investigates his grandfather's 1939 suicide. Tracing the clues surrounding his ancestor's death, the author is led to an exploration of the Mexican people's dual heritage, of their ties both to Spain and the pre-Columbian culture of the American continents. Mexican mythology, European colonial history, and the Texas present here meld, much as Santos's ancestors melded with the contradictory cultural influences in which they lived.*

from PLACES LEFT UNFINISHED AT THE TIME OF CREATION

1 I WENT BACK TO SAN ANTONIO, having received a letter from the city's fire department helping me locate Mr. A. G. Pompa, one of the two now long-retired firemen who had tried to revive my *abuelo** Juan José on that January morning in 1939. Their names, Rathke and Pompa, had appeared in all of the press accounts of his death, and Mr. Pompa was one of the figures in the photograph in the *San Antonio Light*, crouching alongside my grandfather's body by the bank of the San Antonio River. Along with my father and Uncle Chale, Pompa was the last living witness of the circumstances of that day. The other fireman, a Mr. A. L. Rathke, had died in the early '70s.

abuelo · "grandfather" (Spanish)

When I arrived in San Antonio, the front pages of the news- 2
papers were announcing in banner headlines the report of a
visitation of the Virgin Mary in the city, where she had appeared
to a young witness in the illumination of a porchlight, reflected
off the polished chrome fender of a 1975 Chevrolet Impala. It
happened in an old *barrio** sub-development on the far south side
of the city, off the Pleasanton Road, which had once been a stage-
coach route but was now a long, faceless asphalt trail of strip malls,
feed stores, and massage parlors. The houses there are flat and
weathered from the tea-colored sandstorms that blow through
that part of the San Antonio River plain in the summers.

barrio · "neighborhood" (Spanish), the Spanish-speaking area of a city or town

The "Chevrolet Madonna" was first seen by a Chicano boy on his 3
sixteenth birthday, after taking out the trash around ten that night.
For some weeks, he had been having nightmares that he would be
shot in a drive-by killing on his birthday. In his dream, he would be
taking out the trash, walking across the dry, straw-colored carpet
grass of the front yard, when he would notice a gray Ford Pinto
coming around the corner toward his house. As he saw someone
leaning out of the back window with a pistol in hand, he would try
to run for his front door, but found he was suddenly paralyzed by
a mysterious force. He turned toward the house, but the air was
as dense as deep water. And each night, the dream would end just
after he heard the explosion of the gun firing from behind him.

When he went out to empty the garbage the night of the 4
vision, he said he saw a bright white light descend swiftly onto
a neighbor's lawn across the street, He watched as it moved
down the street, zig-zagging between ash trees and pickup
trucks like a spinning top, veering sharply in the middle of the
street in front of his house and coming directly for him. Before
he could move away, he screamed as he felt what he called "the
icy light" pass directly through him and float farther on the
night air, finally coming to rest against the clapboard wall of
the neighbor's house.

When his mother and sister found him kneeling in the yard 5
just minutes later, his hands were clasped in prayer and his gaze
was fixed on the house next door. As he looked at the large, jagged
splash of light before him, he recognized in it a clearly defined
shape where the light was brighter.

"It's our Holy Lady, kneeling, reading the Bible," he told them. 6

7   They looked at the wall and saw the same shape there, and they were awestruck. There was a pool of light that might be a bowed head, one edge that could be a large book held open, a wavy glimmer toward the ground that could seem to some to be a kneeling torso. But you had to look deep into the light, deliberately unfocusing your eyes, to see any of this. After holding hands and saying prayers together, the family went inside and built an altar to receive the blessings the Divine Mother was bestowing on them.

8   Along with the cataclysms, natural and man-made, this has been a century of miracles and visions. The epic of magic remains incomplete. *Promesas** are still being fulfilled. Before an apocalyptic vortex of killing and recrimination descended on Bosnia-Herzegovina,* there were daily visions of Mary taking place in the mountain village of Medjugorje. Three youths, two girls and a boy, carried on a years-long conversation with their vision, whom they described as the Virgin Mary, Mother of God. After the attending crowd for the punctual afternoon apparitions grew too large, the venue was moved by begrudging church authorities to the local church rectory, where only a few witnesses were allowed. Appearing so routinely, the Virgin was able to address herself to such otherwise quotidian matters as the inefficiency of public waterworks in the village and the penurious local property tax rates. An uncle went on a pilgrimage there and claimed, along with other followers, to have looked straight at the sun at midday without harming his eyes. Instead, he saw a rapid dance of many-colored light, as if filtered through a prism in the sky. The visions at Medjugorje ended without fanfare when one of the visionaries went off to join the Bosnian army. Another developed brain cancer. Then the war arrived, and it became too dangerous to even gather at the rectory for daily prayers.

Promesas · "promises" or "pledges" (Spanish)

Bosnia-Herzegovina · a region of the former Yugoslavia where civil war broke out between people of different faiths and ethnicities and where "ethnic cleansing" was practiced from 1992–1995

9   The San Antonio papers reported that after the Chevrolet apparition, the family began a marathon of Rosaries devoted to the Virgin Mary. The son fainted and began speaking in a high-pitched voice, while his family held a minicorder to his mouth, recording his every utterance. When he declared the tapwater in the house was blessed, they placed roses in a vase filled with the water, and the entire house was filled with an intoxicating scent of the flowers.

10   As word spread through the neighborhood and the news media started to report the story, hundreds of people arrived

every evening to see the light for themselves. It didn't take the   10
skeptics long to discern that the light of this apparition was
nothing more than the reflection of the family's porch light off
the front bumper of a maroon Impala, parked in the driveway.
On the second night of the apparition, a couple of *pachuco*•
homeboys who had been sniffing glue all afternoon, started
rocking the car and howling with laughter as the apparition
bobbed up and down against the beige house siding, startling
the devoted onlookers.

pachuco · a young
tough or thug

Nonetheless, on crutches, in wheelchairs, and in large groups,   11
the hopeful, the devout, the sick, and the curious kept coming. A
man with acute colitis was rumored to have rid himself of crippling
abdominal pain by touching the wall. Many swooned while just
standing along the chain-link fence of the neighbor's backyard.

Then, another neighbor caught a pilgrim urinating on his lawn.   12
Another found a couple, *in flagrante delicto*,• in their own parked
car as they had come to attempt to conceive a child in the apparition's glow, unable to do so before without divine intervention.

in flagrante delicto ·
"in passionate delight"
(Latin), to be caught
in the very act; to be
caught red-handed: a
euphemism for sexual
activity

A local Bishop said the church was "cautiously skeptical" about   13
the matter. "I see the Blessed Mother every day," he told the
newspaper. "But I don't necessarily invite the whole community.
If it isn't from God, it will die a natural death."

✦ ✦ ✦

A FTER UNCOVERING HIS NAME in the microfilm archives of   14
the newspapers, I had tried to find Mr. Pompa. It seemed he
had left the city. For years the fire department had been unable
to locate him, until they received a notification of a change of
address through his insurance company. After several days'
more of inquiries with the San Antonio Fireman's Benevolent
Association, I learned he was living in Kerrville, Texas, about an
hour and a half north of San Antonio, in the Texas hill country.
Mr. Pompa was a patient at the State Hospital in Kerrville, the
end-of-the-line facility in the Texas State mental health system.
Identifying myself on the phone only as a friend of the family, the
nurse I spoke to there would not discuss his condition with me,
but said I was welcome to visit, with an appointment.

"You can come on up," she said. "He has good days and bad   15
days, but he don't talk much with nobody."

16   I dreaded that hospital from one summer during college when I had a job there doing art therapy with the patients, many of whom are elderly, long-term internees of the state mental health system. The hospital grounds are nestled in the hills outside of Kerrville, and the campus is laid out like a little village unto itself, with its own streets, named after heroes of Texas Independence, and imitation shops meant to give the patients the reassuring feeling of being at home in a real place. After only two weeks of work there, I was haunted by the sounds and scenes from the hospital. While watching a movie, I'd hear the jagged laughter of one of the patients I had been with during the day. I recoiled when I saw the downy translucent flesh hanging from the underarms of patients who had taken prescriptions for decades that had that eerie side effect. I had quit shortly thereafter, and the doctor overseeing the arts program scolded me for leaving, telling me, "It's not so easy to escape these things. You can't quit *them*."

17   When I was shown to the patio in the ward where Mr. Pompa was waiting, I remembered walking through that solarium* years before, encountering a group of patients there who were watching the film *The Alamo*, with John Wayne and Richard Widmark, in reverse, after some lazy orderly had improperly spooled the projector. But none of the members of the audience seemed to mind, staring silently at the sheet that had been hung as a screen as John Wayne walked backward along the parapets of the fort under siege.

solarium · a sunroom

18   That afternoon, the cicadas were singing at an eardrum-piercing volume as a nurse led me to Mr. Pompa at one end of a covered patio, dressed only in a cotton robe and sitting in a La-Z-Boy recliner, with his bare feet up on the raised footrest. The nurse pulled his seat back upright, and his old, unshaven face was round and freckled, his soft, dark eyes both blank and querulous. His hands were large and rough-scaled, quivering on his bare knees, protruding from his robe. He looked like Diego Rivera* as an old man, his white hair standing up like plumes on the back of his head. At first, he took no notice as the nurse introduced me, taking pains to pronounce every syllable with a shout.

Diego Rivera · Mexican Social Realist Muralist (1886–1957), husband of artist Frida Kahlo

19   "He understands everything. He just mainly don't want to talk. That's all it is, right, Mr. Pompa?"

20   Mr. Pompa had two Q-Tips hanging from his nostrils, and two sticking out of his ears. The nurse gathered them quickly

with a *tsk* and set off back for the ward. Alone on the patio, I 20
pulled up a chair and introduced myself to Mr. Pompa again,
which he responded to with only a blink in his wide open stare.
I explained to him how I had gotten his whereabouts, and why
I had looked for him in the first place. I told him he was one
of the last living witnesses of that morning in 1939, when, as a
young man of twenty-five, he had tried to revive my grandfather.
I showed him the photograph from the January 1939 *San Antonio
Light,* where he was pictured.

"Juan – José – Santos. You are that A. G. Pompa, aren't you?" 21

The Fireman's Association said that, already twenty years 22
retired, he had had a decorated career as a *bombero.** He had
put out a lot of San Antonio fires. He had run into hundreds
of burning houses to bring out the living. Maybe he had been
able to revive untold others of the would-be drowned. But all
of that was lost to him now, including the morning of January 9,
1939. Whatever faint echo of that day remained deep inside of
him and was beyond his grasp. If he was aware of anything, he
was unable or unwilling to let anyone else know. We sat staring
at each other silently for another few moments. In his eyes, he
seemed present, but abandoned, as if a fire had left only the shell
of the building standing. Then he took a long, deep breath and
began singing with a still-noticeable Spanish accent, *"The eyes
of Texas are upon you… all the livelong day…."*

bombero · "firefighter"
(Spanish)

On my way back, I thought I might drive past San Antonio, 23
past Uvalde, Hondo, and La Pryor, past Piedras Negras and Nava,
and on into the center of Mexico to where all the roads began.

The news from the radio was that it hadn't mattered much 24
to the faithful that the "Chevrolet Madonna" had a perfectly
explicable source. Hundreds of believers were still coming to
the simple neighborhood every night. Was it not a miracle that
the lamplight from the porch had even caught the dented fender
of the Impala in the first place? What was the probability of
those few shafts of light reflecting off that long, curved chrome
surface in precisely the way necessary to project the Madonna's
silhouette? Out of the million chance encounters in the ordinary
running on of the everyday, this beam was a light breaking suddenly through a curtain, creating an aperture between worlds,
showing just how incomplete our own world really was.

25   But the neighbor on whose wall the apparition reflected was growing desperate as hordes of devotees trampled greater swaths of his lawn and carried on singing and chanting all night long. He decided to illuminate the apparition with two gigantic mercury floodlights, thereby bathing the amber-toned reflection in a fluorescent silver glare that erased any hint of the Virgin Mary's outline and drew gasps and angry shouts from the crowd.

26   One reporter heard a woman scream at the neighbor, "If you have any love in your heart you will let us see the Virgin!"

27   "If you believe in Mary, the mother of God, you will turn out the light," yelled another.

28   The mother of the family of the young visionary collapsed.

29   In the days that followed, the family repositioned their Impala in the driveway and used camping flashlights to try, without success, to cast the Virgin's reflection against their own garage door. All they managed were jittery Rorschach blots* of a shapeless milky light. Once the car was moved, the image of the Blessed Virgin Mary reading the Bible was to disappear forever. For several days, the devout and the nosy continued to come after sunset. For months after they stopped coming, the neighbor kept his modest house saturated in as much light as the Lincoln Memorial.

Rorschach blots · Hermann Rorschach (1884–1922), a Swiss psychiatrist, devised the ink blot test

30   She had not been a Virgin who had come with much to say. As always, she had chosen an obscure place under humble circumstances to manifest herself. This time there were no clouds, no cherubim,* no starry mantle. As apparitions go, she was more of a chimera* or a cipher* rather than an interlocutor* between worlds. For those who believed in her light, she brought the message that the interaction between the mortal and the divine in those lands has not ended.

cherubim · see Exodus 25:18–22

chimera · an imaginary creature or illusory idea

cipher · a nonentity, a meaningless sign

interlocutor · one who takes part in a conversation or dialogue

31   From her debut in the Americas on a sacred hill in Mexico City more than four hundred years ago,* here at end of the twentieth century, she came to a parched, rundown Texas suburb. The faithful had congregated to see in the apparition's low-wattage glow that the enchantment of the homelands is not over.

debut … years ago · Mary ("Our Lady of Guadalupe") appeared to a poor native near Mexico City in 1531, leading to the swift conversion of millions of indigenous people

32   On the night the miracle-busting floodlights were turned on, when the mother of the young seer of Pleasanton Road passed out, some of the devotees had gathered around her, holding hands, and improvised a song they sang over her as she lay unconscious, *"Stay with me, Lord, stay with me, the spirit of the Lord is moving through my heart, stay with me, Lord, stay with me."*

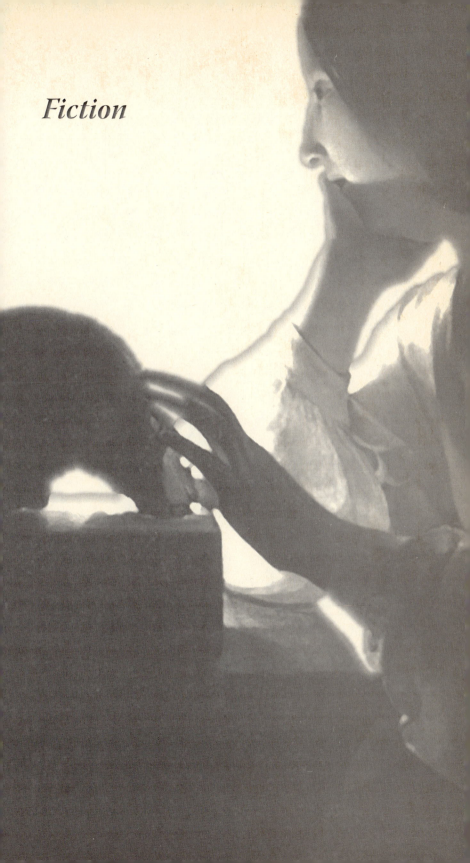

Fiction

Nathaniel Hawthorne

◀ 1 8 0 4 – 1 8 6 4 ▶

Long considered a giant in 19th-century American literature, Hawthorne has more recently been noted for his key role in interpreting the spiritual complexion of colonial America. Hawthorne came by his interest in Puritan New England honestly: not only was he born in Salem, Massachusetts, but one of his ancestors served as judge in the Salem witchcraft trials. As a young man, Hawthorne systematically studied colonial history and explored the implications of Puritan theology. His contemporary Herman Melville observed that a "Calvinistic sense of Innate Depravity and Original Sin" permeates Hawthorne's fiction, a judgment supported by readers of short stories such as "Young Goodman Brown," "The Minister's Black Veil," and "The May-Pole of Merry Mount," as well as longer works such as The Scarlet Letter *(1850). His true subject is the human heart tortured by an innate awareness of sinfulness and an obsessive desire to conceal that guilt. Though some characters transcend the debilitating effects of sin to achieve partial redemption, more common is the experience of young Goodman Brown, whose ultimate inability to recognize his own weakness leads to despair.*

YOUNG GOODMAN BROWN

1 YOUNG GOODMAN* BROWN came forth at sunset into the street at Salem village; but put his head back, after crossing the threshold, to exchange a parting kiss with his young wife. And Faith, as the wife was aptly named, thrust her own pretty head into the street, letting the wind play with the pink ribbons of her cap while she called to Goodman Brown.

2 "Dearest heart," whispered she, softly and rather sadly, when her lips were close to his ear, "prithee* put off your journey until sunrise and sleep in your own bed to-night. A lone woman is

Goodman · a title referring to men of humble birth

prithee · a contraction for "I pray thee"; "I beg you"

157

troubled with such dreams and such thoughts that she's afeared 2
of herself sometimes. Pray tarry with me this night, dear husband,
of all nights in the year."

"My love and my Faith," replied young Goodman Brown, "of 3
all nights in the year, this one night must I tarry away from thee.
My journey, as thou callest it, forth and back again, must needs
be done 'twixt now and sunrise. What, my sweet, pretty wife, dost
thou doubt me already, and we but three months married?"

"Then God bless you!" said Faith, with the pink ribbons; "and 4
may you find all well when you come back."

"Amen!" cried Goodman Brown. "Say thy prayers, dear Faith, 5
and go to bed at dusk, and no harm will come to thee."

So they parted; and the young man pursued his way until, 6
being about to turn the corner by the meeting-house, he looked
back and saw the head of Faith still peeping after him with a
melancholy air, in spite of her pink ribbons.

"Poor little Faith!" thought he, for his heart smote him. "What 7
a wretch am I to leave her on such an errand! She talks of dreams,
too. Methought as she spoke there was trouble in her face, as if a
dream had warned her what work is to be done to-night. But no, no;
't would kill her to think it. Well, she's a blessed angel on earth; and
after this one night I'll cling to her skirts and follow her to heaven."

With this excellent resolve for the future, Goodman Brown felt 8
himself justified in making more haste on his present evil purpose.
He had taken a dreary road, darkened by all the gloomiest trees of
the forest, which barely stood aside to let the narrow path creep
through, and closed immediately behind. It was all as lonely as
could be; and there is this peculiarity in such a solitude, that the
traveller knows not who may be concealed by the innumerable
trunks and the thick boughs overhead; so that, with lonely footsteps, he may yet be passing through an unseen multitude.

"There may be a devilish Indian behind every tree," said 9
Goodman Brown to himself; and he glanced fearfully behind
him as he added, "What if the devil himself should be at my
very elbow!"

His head being turned back, he passed a crook of the road, and, 10
looking forward again, beheld the figure of a man, in grave and
decent attire, seated at the foot of an old tree. He arose at Goodman
Brown's approach and walked onward side by side with him.

11   "You are late, Goodman Brown," said he. "The clock of the Old South* was striking as I came through Boston, and that is full fifteen minutes agone."

12   "Faith kept me back a while," replied the young man, with a tremor in his voice, caused by the sudden appearance of his companion, though not wholly unexpected.

13   It was now deep dusk in the forest, and deepest in that part of it where these two were journeying. As nearly as could be discerned, the second traveller was about fifty years old, apparently in the same rank of life as Goodman Brown, and bearing a considerable resemblance to him, though perhaps more in expression than features. Still they might have been taken for father and son. And yet, though the elder person was as simply clad as the younger, and as simple in manner too, he had an indescribable air of one who knew the world, and who would not have felt abashed at the governor's dinner table or in King William's court,* were it possible that his affairs should call him thither. But the only thing about him that could be fixed upon as remarkable was his staff, which bore the likeness of a great black snake, so curiously wrought that it might almost be seen to twist and wriggle itself like a living serpent. This, of course, must have been an ocular deception, assisted by the uncertain light.

King William's court · William III, king of England from 1689–1702

14   "Come, Goodman Brown," cried his fellow traveller, "this is a dull pace for the beginning of a journey. Take my staff, if you are so soon weary."

15   "Friend," said the other, exchanging his slow pace for a full stop, "having kept covenant by meeting thee here, it is my purpose now to return whence I came. I have scruples touching the matter thou wot'st* of."

wot'st · to become aware of, to know

16   "Sayest thou so?" replied he of the serpent, smiling apart. "Let us walk on, nevertheless, reasoning as we go; and if I convince thee not thou shalt turn back. We are but a little way in the forest yet."

17   "Too far, too far!" exclaimed the goodman, unconsciously resuming his walk. "My father never went into the woods on such an errand, nor his father before him. We have been a race of honest men and good Christians since the days of the martyrs;* and shall I be the first of the name of Brown that ever took this path and kept—"

martyrs · Christian martyrs, probably Protestants executed during the reign of Mary Tudor, Catholic queen of England from 1553–1558

18   "Such company, thou wouldst say," observed the elder person, interpreting his pause. "Well said, Goodman Brown! I have been

as well acquainted with your family as with ever a one among the Puritans; and that's no trifle to say. I helped your grandfather, the constable, when he lashed the Quaker* woman so smartly through the streets of Salem; and it was I that brought your father a pitch-pine knot, kindled at my own hearth, to set fire to an Indian village, in King Philip's war.* They were my good friends, both; and many a pleasant walk have we had along this path, and returned merrily after midnight. I would fain* be friends with you for their sake." 18

"If it be as thou sayest," replied Goodman Brown, "I marvel they never spoke of these matters; or, verily, I marvel not, seeing that the least rumor of the sort would have driven them from New England. We are a people of prayer, and good works to boot, and abide no such wickedness." 19

"Wickedness or not," said the traveller with the twisted staff, "I have a very general acquaintance here in New England. The deacons of many a church have drunk the communion wine with me; the selectmen* of divers towns make me their chair-man; and a majority of the Great and General Court* are firm supporters of my interest. The governor and I, too – But these are state secrets." 20

"Can this be so?" cried Goodman Brown, with a stare of amaze-ment at his undisturbed companion. "Howbeit, I have nothing to do with the governor and council; they have their own ways, and are no rule for a simple husbandman* like me. But, were I to go on with thee, how should I meet the eye of that good old man, our minister, at Salem village? Oh, his voice would make me tremble both Sabbath day and lecture day."* 21

Thus far the elder traveller had listened with due gravity; but now burst into a fit of irrepressible mirth, shaking himself so violently that his snake-like staff actually seemed to wriggle in sympathy. 22

"Ha! ha! ha!" shouted he again and again; then composing himself, "Well, go on, Goodman Brown, go on; but, prithee, don't kill me with laughing." 23

"Well, then, to end the matter at once," said Goodman Brown, considerably nettled, "there is my wife, Faith. It would break her dear little heart; and I'd rather break my own." 24

"Nay, if that be the case," answered the other, "e'en go thy ways, Goodman Brown. I would not for twenty old women like the one hobbling before us that Faith should come to any harm." 25

Quaker · Quakers were considered heretical by Puritans of the American colonies and suffered persecution

King Philip's war · Metacomet (or "King Philip," as settlers named him) was leader of an Indian uprising in New England (1675–1676)

fain · happily, gladly

selectmen · a board of town officers chosen annually to manage local affairs

Great … Court · the legislative assembly

husbandman · farmer

lecture day · a religious lecture was offered at the midweek church assembly, usually on Thursdays

26　　As he spoke he pointed his staff at a female figure on the path, in whom Goodman Brown recognized a very pious and exemplary dame, who had taught him his catechism* in youth, and was still his moral and spiritual adviser, jointly with the minister and Deacon Gookin.

27　　"A marvel, truly, that Goody* Cloyse should be so far in the wilderness at nightfall," said he. "But with your leave, friend, I shall take a cut through the woods until we have left this Christian woman behind. Being a stranger to you, she might ask whom I was consorting with and whither I was going."

28　　"Be it so," said his fellow-traveller. "Betake you to the woods, and let me keep the path."

29　　Accordingly the young man turned aside, but took care to watch his companion, who advanced softly along the road until he had come within a staff's length of the old dame. She, meanwhile, was making the best of her way, with singular speed for so aged a woman, and mumbling some indistinct words – a prayer, doubtless – as she went. The traveller put forth his staff and touched her withered neck with what seemed the serpent's tail.

30　　"The devil!" screamed the pious old lady.

31　　"Then Goody Cloyse knows her old friend?" observed the traveller, confronting her and leaning on his writhing stick.

32　　"Ah, forsooth,* and is it your worship indeed?" cried the good dame. "Yea, truly is it, and in the very image of my old gossip,* Goodman Brown, the grandfather of the silly fellow that now is. But – would your worship believe it? – my broomstick hath strangely disappeared, stolen, as I suspect, by that unhanged witch, Goody Cory, and that, too, when I was all anointed with the juice of smallage, and cinquefoil, and wolf's bane –"*

33　　"Mingled with fine wheat and the fat of a new-born babe," said the shape of old Goodman Brown.

34　　"Ah, your worship knows the recipe," cried the old lady, cackling aloud. "So, as I was saying, being all ready for the meeting, and no horse to ride on, I made up my mind to foot it; for they tell me there is a nice young man to be taken into communion tonight. But now your good worship will lend me your arm, and we shall be there in a twinkling."

35　　"That can hardly be," answered her friend. I may not spare you my arm, Goody Cloyse; but here is my staff, if you will."

catechism · a short book or form of verbal instruction that uses questions and answers to teach the basic principles of faith

Goody · a contraction of "good wife," a title of address for a wife of humble rank. Goody Cloyse was one of the "witches" executed by Salem's Puritan officials in 1692

forsooth · in truth, indeed

gossip · close friend or companion

smallage ... wolf's-bane · plants traditionally associated with sorcery and witchcraft

So saying, he threw it down at her feet, where, perhaps, it   36
assumed life, being one of the rods which its owner had formerly lent to the Egyptian magi.* Of this fact, however, Goodman
Brown could not take cognizance. He had cast up his eyes in
astonishment, and, looking down again, beheld neither Goody
Cloyse nor the serpentine staff, but his fellow-traveller alone, who
waited for him as calmly as if nothing had happened.

"That old woman taught me my catechism,"* said the young man;   37
and there was a world of meaning in this simple comment.

They continued to walk onward, while the elder traveller   38
exhorted his companion to make good speed and persevere
in the path, discoursing so aptly that his arguments seemed
rather to spring up in the bosom of his auditor than to be suggested by himself. As they went, he plucked a branch of maple
to serve for a walking stick, and began to strip it of the twigs and
little boughs, which were wet with evening dew. The moment
his fingers touched them they became strangely withered and
dried up as with a week's sunshine. Thus the pair proceeded, at
a good free pace, until suddenly, in a gloomy hollow of the road,
Goodman Brown sat himself down on the stump of a tree and
refused to go any farther.

"Friend," said he, stubbornly, "my mind is made up. Not   39
another step will I budge on this errand. What if a wretched
old woman do choose to go to the devil when I thought she was
going to heaven: is that any reason why I should quit my dear
Faith and go after her?"

"You will think better of this by and by," said his acquaintance,   40
composedly. "Sit here and rest yourself a while; and when you
feel like moving again, there is my staff to help you along."

Without more words, he threw his companion the maple   41
stick, and was as speedily out of sight as if he had vanished into
the deepening gloom. The young man sat a few moments by the
roadside, applauding himself greatly, and thinking with how clear
a conscience he should meet the minister in his morning walk,
nor shrink from the eye of good old Deacon Gookin. And what
calm sleep would be his that very night, which was to have been
spent so wickedly, but so purely and sweetly now, in the arms
of Faith! Amidst these pleasant and praiseworthy meditations,
Goodman Brown heard the tramp of horses along the road, and

41 deemed it advisable to conceal himself within the verge of the forest, conscious of the guilty purpose that had brought him thither, though now so happily turned from it.

42 On came the hoof tramps and the voices of the riders, two grave old voices, conversing soberly as they drew near. These mingled sounds appeared to pass along the road, within a few yards of the young man's hiding-place; but, owing doubtless to the depth of the gloom at that particular spot, neither the travellers nor their steeds were visible. Though their figures brushed the small boughs on the wayside, it could not be seen that they intercepted, even for a moment, the faint gleam from the strip of bright sky athwart which they must have passed. Goodman Brown alternately crouched and stood on tiptoe, pulling aside the branches and thrusting forth his head as far as he durst without discerning so much as a shadow. It vexed him the more, because he could have sworn, were such a thing possible, that he recognized the voices of the minister and Deacon Gookin, jogging along quietly, as they were wont to do, when bound to some ordination or ecclesiastical council. While yet within hearing, one of the riders stopped to pluck a switch.

43 "Of the two, reverend sir," said the voice like the deacon's, "I had rather miss an ordination dinner than to-night's meeting. They tell me that some of our community are to be here from Falmouth· and beyond, and others from Connecticut and Rhode Island, besides several of the Indian powwows,· who, after their fashion, know almost as much deviltry as the best of us. Moreover, there is a goodly young woman to be taken into communion."

44 "Mighty well, Deacon Gookin!" replied the solemn old tones of the minister. "Spur up, or we shall be late. Nothing can be done, you know, until I get on the ground."

45 The hoofs clattered again; and the voices, talking so strangely in the empty air, passed on through the forest, where no church had ever been gathered or solitary Christian prayed. Whither, then, could these holy men be journeying so deep into the heathen wilderness? Young Goodman Brown caught hold of a tree for support, being ready to sink down on the ground, faint and overburdened with the heavy sickness of his heart. He looked up to the sky, doubting whether there really was a heaven above him. Yet there was the blue arch, and the stars brightening in it.

Falmouth · a town on Cape Cod, about seventy miles from Salem

Indian powwows · Indian shamans, medicine men

"With heaven above and Faith below, I will yet stand firm   46
against the devil!" cried Goodman Brown.

While he still gazed upward into the deep arch of the firma-   47
ment and had lifted his hands to pray, a cloud, though no wind
was stirring, hurried across the zenith and hid the brightening
stars. The blue sky was still visible, except directly overhead,
where this black mass of cloud was sweeping swiftly northward.
Aloft in the air, as if from the depths of the cloud, came a confused and doubtful sound of voices. Once the listener fancied
that he could distinguish the accents of townspeople of his own,
men and women, both pious and ungodly, many of whom he
had met at the communion table, and had seen others rioting at
the tavern. The next moment, so indistinct were the sounds, he
doubted whether he had heard aught but the murmur of the old
forest, whispering without a wind. Then came a stronger swell of
those familiar tones, heard daily in the sunshine at Salem village,
but never until now from a cloud of night. There was one voice,
of a young woman, uttering lamentations, yet with an uncertain
sorrow, and entreating for some favor, which, perhaps, it would
grieve her to obtain; and all the unseen multitude, both saints
and sinners, seemed to encourage her onward.

"Faith!" shouted Goodman Brown, in a voice of agony and   48
desperation; and the echoes of the forest mocked him, crying,
"Faith! Faith!" as if bewildered wretches were seeking her all
through the wilderness.

The cry of grief, rage, and terror was yet piercing the night,   49
when the unhappy husband held his breath for a response. There
was a scream, drowned immediately in a louder murmur of voices,
fading into far-off laughter, as the dark cloud swept away, leaving
the clear and silent sky above Goodman Brown. But something
fluttered lightly down through the air and caught on the branch
of a tree. The young man seized it, and beheld a pink ribbon.

"My Faith is gone!" cried he, after one stupefied moment.   50
"There is no good on earth; and sin is but a name. Come, devil;
for to thee is this world given."

And, maddened with despair, so that he laughed loud and   51
long, did Goodman Brown grasp his staff and set forth again,
at such a rate that he seemed to fly along the forest path rather
than to walk or run. The road grew wilder and drearier and more

51 faintly traced, and vanished at length, leaving him in the heart of the dark wilderness, still rushing onward with the instinct that guides mortal man to evil. The whole forest was peopled with frightful sounds – the creaking of the trees, the howling of wild beasts, and the yell of Indians; while sometimes the wind tolled like a distant church bell, and sometimes gave a broad roar around the traveller, as if all Nature were laughing him to scorn. But he was himself the chief horror of the scene, and shrank not from its other horrors.

52 "Ha! ha! ha!" roared Goodman Brown when the wind laughed at him. "Let us hear which will laugh loudest. Think not to frighten me with your deviltry. Come witch, come wizard, come Indian powwow, come devil himself, and here comes Goodman Brown. You may as well fear him as he fear you."

53 In truth, all through the haunted forest there could be nothing more frightful than the figure of Goodman Brown. On he flew among the black pines, brandishing his staff with frenzied gestures, now giving vent to an inspiration of horrid blasphemy, and now shouting forth such laughter as set all the echoes of the forest laughing like demons around him. The fiend* in his own shape is less hideous than when he rages in the breast of man. Thus sped the demoniac on his course, until, quivering among the trees, he saw a red light before him, as when the felled trunks and branches of a clearing have been set on fire, and throw up their lurid blaze against the sky, at the hour of midnight. He paused, in a lull of the tempest that had driven him onward, and heard the swell of what seemed a hymn, rolling solemnly from a distance with the weight of many voices. He knew the tune; it was a familiar one in the choir of the village meeting-house. The verse died heavily away, and was lengthened by a chorus, not of human voices, but of all the sounds of the benighted wilderness pealing in awful harmony together. Goodman Brown cried out, and his cry was lost to his own ear, by its unison with the cry of the desert.

fiend · the devil

54 In the interval of silence he stole forward until the light glared full upon his eyes. At one extremity of an open space, hemmed in by the dark wall of the forest, arose a rock, bearing some rude, natural resemblance either to an altar or a pulpit, and surrounded by four blazing pines, their tops aflame, their stems untouched, like candles at an evening meeting. The mass of foliage that had

overgrown the summit of the rock was all on fire, blazing high   54
into the night and fitfully illuminating the whole field. Each
pendent · hanging   pendent* twig and leafy festoon was in a blaze. As the red light
arose and fell, a numerous congregation alternately shone forth,
then disappeared in shadow, and again grew, as it were, out of the
darkness, peopling the heart of the solitary woods at once.

"A grave and dark-clad company," quoth Goodman Brown.   55

In truth they were such. Among them, quivering to and fro   56
between gloom and splendor, appeared faces that would be seen
next day at the council board of the province, and others which,
Sabbath after Sabbath, looked devoutly heavenward, and benig-
nantly over the crowded pews, from the holiest pulpits in the
land. Some affirm that the lady of the governor was there. At least
there were high dames well known to her, and wives of honored
husbands, and widows, a great multitude, and ancient maidens,
all of excellent repute, and fair young girls, who trembled lest
their mothers should espy them. Either the sudden gleams of
light flashing over the obscure field bedazzled Goodman Brown,
or he recognized a score of the church members of Salem village famous for their especial sanctity. Good old Deacon Gookin
had arrived, and waited at the skirts of that venerable saint, his
revered pastor. But, irreverently consorting with these grave,
reputable, and pious people, these elders of the church, these
chaste dames and dewy virgins, there were men of dissolute lives
spotted fame ·   and women of spotted fame,* wretches given over to all mean and
immoral, lascivious, of   filthy vice, and suspected even of horrid crimes. It was strange
poor reputation   to see that the good shrank not from the wicked, nor were the
sinners abashed by the saints. Scattered also among their pale-
faced enemies were the Indian priests, or powwows, who had
often scared their native forest with more hideous incantations
than any known to English witchcraft.

"But where is Faith?" thought Goodman Brown; and, as hope   57
came into his heart, he trembled.

Another verse of the hymn arose, a slow and mournful strain,   58
such as the pious love, but joined to words which expressed all
that our nature can conceive of sin, and darkly hinted at far more.
Unfathomable to mere mortals is the lore of fiends. Verse after
verse was sung; and still the chorus of the desert swelled between
like the deepest tone of a mighty organ; and with the final peal of

58 that dreadful anthem there came a sound, as if the roaring wind, the rushing streams, the howling beasts, and every other voice of the unconcerted wilderness were mingling and according with the voice of guilty man in homage to the prince of all. The four blazing pines threw up a loftier flame, and obscurely discovered shapes and visages of horror on the smoke wreaths above the impious assembly. At the same moment the fire on the rock shot redly forth and formed a glowing arch above its base, where now appeared a figure. With reverence be it spoken, the figure bore no slight similitude, both in garb and manner, to some grave divine of the New England churches.

59   "Bring forth the converts!" cried a voice that echoed through the field and rolled into the forest.

60   At the word, Goodman Brown stepped forth from the shadow of the trees and approached the congregation, with whom he felt a loathful brotherhood by the sympathy of all that was wicked in his heart. He could have well-nigh sworn that the shape of his own dead father beckoned him to advance, looking downward from a smoke wreath, while a woman, with dim features of despair, threw out her hand to warn him back. Was it his mother? But he had no power to retreat one step, nor to resist, even in thought, when the minister and good old Deacon Gookin seized his arms and led him to the blazing rock. Thither came also the slender form of a veiled female, led between Goody Cloyse, that pious teacher of the catechism, and Martha Carrier, who had received the devil's promise to be queen of hell. A rampant hag was she. And there stood the proselytes beneath the canopy of fire.

61   "Welcome, my children," said the dark figure, "to the communion of your race. Ye have found thus young your nature and your destiny. My children, look behind you!"

62   They turned; and flashing forth, as it were, in a sheet of flame, the fiend worshippers were seen; the smile of welcome gleamed darkly on every visage.

63   "There," resumed the sable* form, "are all whom ye have reverenced from youth. Ye deemed them holier than yourselves and shrank from your own sin, contrasting it with their lives of righteousness and prayerful aspirations heavenward. Yet here are they all in my worshipping assembly. This night it shall be granted you to know their secret deeds: how hoary-bearded elders of the church

sable · very dark

have whispered wanton words to the young maids of their house- 63
holds; how many a woman, eager for widows' weeds, has given
her husband a drink at bedtime and let him sleep his last sleep in
her bosom; how beardless youths have made haste to inherit their
fathers' wealth; and how fair damsels, – blush not, sweet ones – have
dug little graves in the garden, and bidden me, the sole guest, to
an infant's funeral. By the sympathy of your human hearts for sin
ye shall scent out all the places – whether in church, bedchamber,
street, field, or forest – where crime has been committed, and shall
exult to behold the whole earth one stain of guilt, one mighty blood
spot. Far more than this. It shall be yours to penetrate, in every
bosom, the deep mystery of sin, the fountain of all wicked arts,
and which inexhaustibly supplies more evil impulses than human
power – than my power at its utmost – can make manifest in deeds.
And now, my children, look upon each other."

They did so; and, by the blaze of the hell-kindled torches, 64
the wretched man beheld his Faith, and the wife her husband,
trembling before that unhallowed altar.

"Lo, there ye stand, my children," said the figure, in a deep 65
and solemn tone, almost sad with its despairing awfulness, as if
his once angelic nature* could yet mourn for our miserable race.
"Depending upon one another's hearts, ye had still hoped that
virtue were not all a dream. Now are ye undeceived. Evil is the
nature of mankind. Evil must be your only happiness. Welcome
again, my children, to the communion of your race."

"Welcome," repeated the fiend worshippers, in one cry of 66
despair and triumph.

And there they stood, the only pair, as it seemed, who were yet 67
hesitating on the verge of wickedness in this dark world. A basin
was hollowed, naturally, in the rock. Did it contain water, red-
dened by the lurid light? or was it blood? or, perchance, a liquid
flame? Herein did the shape of evil dip his hand and prepare to
lay the mark of baptism upon their foreheads,* that they might
be partakers of the mystery of sin, more conscious of the secret
guilt of others, both in deed and thought, than they could now
be of their own. The husband cast one look at his pale wife, and
Faith at him. What polluted wretches would the next glance show
them to each other, shuddering alike at what they disclosed and
what they saw!

once angelic nature ·
tradition holds that
Lucifer is a fallen angel

mark … foreheads ·
a perversion of the
ritual marking of the
cross on the foreheads
of those being baptized,
perhaps here a refer-
ence to the mark of the
Beast (Revelation 20:4)

68   "Faith! Faith!" cried the husband, "look up to heaven, and resist the wicked one."*

resist the wicked one · see James 4:7

69   Whether Faith obeyed he knew not. Hardly had he spoken when he found himself amid calm night and solitude, listening to a roar of the wind which died heavily away through the forest. He staggered against the rock, and felt it chill and damp; while a hanging twig, that had been all on fire, besprinkled his cheek with the coldest dew.

70   The next morning young Goodman Brown came slowly into the street of Salem village, staring around him like a bewildered man. The good old minister was taking a walk along the grave-yard to get an appetite for breakfast and meditate his sermon, and bestowed a blessing, as he passed, on Goodman Brown. He shrank from the venerable saint as if to avoid an anathema.* Old Deacon Gookin was at domestic worship, and the holy words of his prayer were heard through the open window. "What God doth the wizard pray to?" quoth Goodman Brown. Goody Cloyse, that excellent old Christian, stood in the early sunshine at her own lattice, catechizing a little girl who had brought her a pint of morning's milk. Goodman Brown snatched away the child as from the grasp of the fiend himself. Turning the corner by the meeting-house, he spied the head of Faith, with the pink ribbons, gazing anxiously forth, and bursting into such joy at sight of him that she skipped along the street and almost kissed her husband before the whole village. But Goodman Brown looked sternly and sadly into her face, and passed on without a greeting.

anathema · a formal ecclesiastical ban or denunciation, excommunication

71   Had Goodman Brown fallen asleep in the forest and only dreamed a wild dream of a witch-meeting?

72   Be it so if you will; but, alas! it was a dream of evil omen for young Goodman Brown. A stern, a sad, a darkly meditative, a distrustful, if not a desperate man did he become from the night of that fearful dream. On the Sabbath day, when the congregation were singing a holy psalm, he could not listen because an anthem of sin rushed loudly upon his ear and drowned all the blessed strain. When the minister spoke from the pulpit with power and fervid eloquence, and, with his hand on the open Bible, of the sacred truths of our religion, and of saint-like lives and triumphant deaths, and of future bliss or misery unutterable, then did Goodman Brown turn pale, dreading lest the roof

should thunder down upon the gray blasphemer and his hearers. 72
Often, awaking suddenly at midnight, he shrank from the bosom
of Faith; and at morning or eventide, when the family knelt down
at prayer, he scowled and muttered to himself, and gazed sternly
at his wife, and turned away. And when he had lived long, and
was borne to his grave a hoary corpse, followed by Faith, an aged
woman, and children and grandchildren, a goodly procession,
besides neighbors not a few, they carved no hopeful verse upon
his tombstone, for his dying hour was gloom.

Fyodor Dostoyevsky

⟨1 8 2 1 – 1 8 8 1⟩

Dostoyevsky, the son of an army surgeon, became a sublieutenant in the army in 1841 after earning a degree in engineering. In 1849 he was accused of a conspiracy and was sentenced to death before a firing squad. Just before he was to be shot, his sentence was commuted by the Czar. Exiled to a Siberian prison, Dostoyevsky immersed himself in the New Testament and became convinced of the greatness of Christ: "There is only one positively beautiful man in the world – Christ," he wrote to his sister. Dostoyevsky wrote some of the world's greatest novels, including Crime and Punishment *(1866) and* The Brothers Karamazov *(1879), the latter the source of the famous passage below. In "The Grand Inquisitor" two brothers are in conversation. Ivan, a rationalist atheist, is explaining the reasons for his atheism to his brother Alyosha, a devoted Christian. Through this parable or fantasy, Ivan explains what might have happened if Jesus had returned to the earth during the Spanish Inquisition in the 16th century. Since this passage is a small excerpt from a long and complicated novel, one should remember that Ivan's argument, though powerful, is not the final word. Some critics find a reply to Ivan in the mysterious kiss given by Christ; others find a reply in the sermon by a monk (Father Zossima) which follows this passage. In any case, it is important to note that Dostoyevsky believed that authentic belief emerges from "the crucible of doubt."*

THE GRAND INQUISITOR

1 "...Do YOU KNOW, Alyosha – don't laugh! I made a poem* about a year ago. If you can waste another ten minutes on me, I'll tell it to you."

2 "You wrote a poem?"

3 "Oh, no, I didn't write it," laughed Ivan, "and I've never written two lines of poetry in my life. But I made up this poem in prose

poem · a parable, a fiction

171

and I remembered it. I was carried away when I made it up. You 3
will be my first reader – that is, listener. Why should an author
forego even one listener?" smiled Ivan. "Shall I tell it to you?"

"I am all attention," said Alyosha. 4

"My poem is called 'The Grand Inquisitor'; it's a ridiculous 5
thing, but I want to tell it to you."

"Even this must have a preface – that is, a literary preface," 6
laughed Ivan, "and I am a poor hand at making one. You see,
my action takes place in the sixteenth century."...

⁑ ⁑ ⁑

"...FIFTEEN CENTURIES have passed since He promised to come 7
in His glory, fifteen centuries since His prophet wrote, 'Behold,
I come quickly'*; 'Of that day and that hour knoweth no man,
neither the Son, but the Father,'* as He Himself predicted on earth.
But humanity awaits him with the same faith and with the same
love. Oh, with greater faith, for it is fifteen centuries since man
has ceased to see signs from heaven.

'Behold ... quickly' ·
Revelation 3:11

'Of that ... Father' ·
Matthew 24:36

> No signs from heaven come to-day 7a
> To add to what the heart doth say.

There was nothing left but faith in what the heart doth say. It 8
is true there were many miracles in those days. There were saints
who performed miraculous cures; some holy people, according to
their biographies, were visited by the Queen of Heaven* herself.
But the devil did not slumber, and doubts were already arising
among men of the truth of these miracles. And just then there
appeared in the north of Germany a terrible new heresy.* 'A huge
star like to a torch' (that is, to a church) 'fell on the sources of
the waters and they became bitter.'* These heretics began blas-
phemously denying miracles. But those who remained faithful
were all the more ardent in their faith. The tears of humanity rose
up to Him as before, awaited His coming, loved Him, hoped for
Him, yearned to suffer and die for Him as before. And so many
ages mankind had prayed with faith and fervor, 'O Lord our
God, hasten Thy coming'; so many ages called upon Him, that
in His infinite mercy He deigned to come down to His servants.
Before that day He had come down, He had visited some holy
men, martyrs, and hermits, as is written in their lives. Among

Queen of Heaven ·
Mary, Christ's mother

Germany ... heresy ·
Lutheranism, originally
considered to be a heretical movement by the
Roman Catholic church

'A huge star ... bitter' ·
see Revelation 8:10–11

8 us, Tyutchev, with absolute faith in the truth of his words, bore witness that

8a
> Bearing the Cross, in slavish dress,
> Weary and worn, the Heavenly King
> Our mother, Russia, came to bless,
> And through our land went wandering.

And that certainly was so, I assure you.

9 "And behold, He deigned to appear for a moment to the people, to the tortured, suffering people, sunk in iniquity, but loving Him like children. My story is laid in Spain, in Seville, in the most terrible time of the Inquisition, when fires were lighted every day to the glory of God, and 'in the splendid *auto-da-fé*· the wicked heretics were burnt.' Oh, of course, this was not the coming in which He will appear, according to His promise, at the end of time in all His heavenly glory, and which will be sudden 'as lightning flashing from east to west.' No, He visited His children only for a moment, and there where the flames were crackling round the heretics. In His infinite mercy He came once more among men in that human shape in which He walked among men for three years fifteen centuries ago. He came down to the 'hot pavement' of the southern town in which on the day before almost a hundred heretics had, *ad majorem gloriam Dei*,· been burnt by the cardinal, the Grand Inquisitor, in a magnificent *auto-da-fé* in the presence of the king, the court, the knights, the cardinals, the most charming ladies of the court, and the whole population of Seville.

auto-da-fé · "act of faith" (Spanish), a ceremonial punishment of heretics

ad … Dei · "to the greater glory of God" (Latin), a phrase associated with the Catholic Jesuit Order

10 "He came softly, unobserved, and yet, strange to say, every one recognized Him. That might be one of the best passages in the poem. I mean, why they recognized Him. The people are irresistibly drawn to Him, they surround Him, they flock about Him, follow Him. He moves silently in their midst with a gentle smile of infinite compassion. The sun of love burns in His heart, light and power shine from His eyes, and their radiance, shed on the people, stirs their hearts with responsive love. He holds out His hands to them, blesses them, and a healing virtue comes from contact with Him, even with His garments. An old man in the crowd, blind from childhood, cries out, 'O Lord, heal me and I shall see Thee!' and, as it were, scales fall from his eyes· and the blind

An old man … eyes · see Mark 10:46–52 and Acts 9:17–19

man sees Him. The crowd weeps and kisses the earth under His 10
feet. Children throw flowers before Him, sing, and cry hosannah.
'It is He – it is He!' all repeat. 'It must be He, it can be no one but
Him!' He stops at the steps of the Seville cathedral at the moment
when the weeping mourners are bringing in a little open white
coffin. In it lies a child of seven, the only daughter of a prominent
citizen. The dead child lies hidden in flowers. 'He will raise your
child,' the crowd shouts to the weeping mother. The priest, coming
to meet the coffin, looks perplexed, and frowns, but the mother
of the dead child throws herself at His feet with a wail. 'If it is
Thou, raise my child!' she cries, holding out her hands to Him.
The procession halts, the coffin is laid on the steps at His feet. He
looks with compassion, and His lips once more softly pronounce,
'Maiden, arise!' and the maiden arises. The little girl sits up in the
coffin and looks round, smiling with wide-open wondering eyes,
holding a bunch of white roses they had put in her hand.*

In it lies . . . her hand ·
a retelling of Jesus'
miraculous restoration of
Jairus' daughter (Mark
5:22–24, 35–42)

"There are cries, sobs, confusion among the people, and at that 11
moment the cardinal himself, the Grand Inquisitor,* passes by the
cathedral. He is an old man, almost ninety, tall and erect, with a
withered face and sunken eyes, in which there is still a gleam of
light. He is not dressed in his gorgeous cardinal's robes, as he was
the day before, when he was burning the enemies of the Roman
Church – at that moment he was wearing his coarse, old, monk's
cassock.* At a distance behind him come his gloomy assistants
and slaves and the 'holy guard.' He stops at the sight of the crowd
and watches it from a distance. He sees everything; he sees them
set the coffin down at His feet, sees the child rise up, and his face
darkens. He knits his thick grey brows and his eyes gleam with
a sinister fire. He holds out his finger and bids the guards take
Him. And such is his power, so completely are the people cowed
into submission and trembling obedience to him, that the crowd
immediately makes way for the guards, and in the midst of death-
like silence they lay hands on Him and lead Him away. The crowd
instantly bows down to the earth, like one man, before the old
inquisitor. He blesses the people in silence and passes on.

Grand Inquisitor ·
the lead clerical
investigator of a panel
formed under papal
authority to discover
and eliminate heresy

cassock · a simple,
ankle-length garment
that serves as the
primary habit of clerics

"The guards lead their prisoner to the close, gloomy vaulted 12
prison in the ancient palace of the Holy Inquisition and shut Him
in it. The day passes and is followed by the dark, burning 'breathless' night of Seville. The air is 'fragrant with laurel and lemon.' In

12 the pitch darkness the iron door of the prison is suddenly opened and the Grand Inquisitor himself comes in with a light in his hand. He is alone; the door is closed at once behind him. He stands in the doorway and for a minute or two gazes in His face. At last he goes up slowly, sets the light on the table and speaks.

※ ※ ※

1 · THE GRAND INQUISITOR SPEAKS TO THE PRISONER

13 "'Is it Thou? Thou?' but receiving no answer, he adds at once, 'Don't answer, be silent. What canst Thou say, indeed? I know too well what Thou wouldst say. And Thou hast no right to add anything to what Thou hadst said of old. Why, then, art Thou come to hinder us? For Thou hast come to hinder us, and Thou knowest that. But dost Thou know what will be tomorrow? I know not who Thou art and care not to know whether it is Thou or only a semblance of Him, but tomorrow I shall condemn Thee and burn Thee at the stake as the worst of heretics. And the very people who have today kissed Thy feet, tomorrow at the faintest sign from me will rush to heap up the embers of Thy fire. Knowest Thou that? Yes, maybe Thou knowest it,' he added with thoughtful penetration, never for a moment taking his eyes off the Prisoner."

14 "I don't quite understand, Ivan. What does it mean?" Alyosha, who had been listening in silence, said with a smile. "Is it simply a wild fantasy, or a mistake on the part of the old man – some impossible *quid pro quo*?"•

> *quid pro quo* · "this for that" (Latin), a mutually dependent arrangement or agreement

15 "Take it as the last," said Ivan, laughing, "if you are so corrupted by modern realism and can't stand anything fantastic. If you like it to be a case of mistaken identity, let it be so. It is true," he went on, laughing, "the old man was ninety, and he might well be crazy over his set idea. He might have been struck by the appearance of the Prisoner. It might, in fact, be simply his ravings, the delusion of an old man of ninety, overexcited by the *auto-da-fé* of a hundred heretics the day before. But does it matter to us after all whether it was a mistake of identity or a wild fantasy? All that matters is that the old man should speak out, should speak openly of what he has thought in silence for ninety years."

16 "And the Prisoner too is silent? Does He look at him and not say a word?"•

> silent … word · see Isaiah 53:7

"That's inevitable in any case," Ivan laughed again. "The old [17] man has told Him He hasn't the right to add anything to what He has said of old. One may say it is the most fundamental feature of Roman Catholicism, in my opinion at least. 'All has been given by Thee to the Pope,' they say 'and all, therefore, is still in the Pope's hands, and there is no need for Thee to come now at all. Thou must not meddle for the time, at least.' That's how they speak and write too — the Jesuits,* at any rate. I have read it myself in the works of their theologians."

Jesuits · members of the Society of Jesus, a Roman Catholic order founded by Ignatius Loyola in 1534 and dedicated to teaching and missionary work

"'Hast Thou the right to reveal to us one of the mysteries of that [18] world from which Thou hast come?' my old man asks Him, and answers the question for Him. 'No, Thou hast not; that Thou mayest not add to what has been said of old, and mayest not take from men the freedom which Thou didst exalt when Thou wast on earth. Whatsoever Thou revealest anew will encroach on men's freedom of faith; for it will be manifest as a miracle, and the freedom of their faith was dearer to Thee than anything in those days fifteen hundred years ago. Didst Thou not often say then, "I will make you free"? But now Thou hast seen these "free" men,' the old man adds suddenly, with a pensive smile. 'Yes, we've paid dearly for it,' he goes on, looking sternly at Him, 'but at last we have completed that work in Thy name. For fifteen centuries we have been wrestling with Thy freedom, but now it is ended and over for good. Dost Thou not believe that it's over for good? Thou lookest meekly at me and deignest not even to be wroth with me. But let me tell Thee that now, today, people are more persuaded than ever that they have perfect freedom, yet they have brought their freedom to us and laid it humbly at our feet. But that has been our doing. Was this what Thou didst? Was this Thy freedom?'"

"I don't understand again," Alyosha broke in. "Is he ironical, is [19] he jesting?"

"Not a bit of it! He claims it as a merit for himself and his [20] Church that at last they have vanquished freedom and have done so to make men happy."

"'For now' (he is speaking of the Inquisition, of course) 'for the [21] first time it has become possible to think of the happiness of

21 men. Man was created a rebel; and how can rebels be happy? Thou wast warned,' he says to Him. 'Thou hast had no lack of admonitions, and warnings, but Thou didst not listen to those warnings; Thou didst reject the only way by which men might be made happy. But, fortunately, departing Thou didst hand on the work to us. Thou hast promised, Thou hast established by Thy word. Thou hast given to us the right to bind and to unbind, and now, of course, Thou canst not think of taking it away. Why, then, hast Thou come to hinder us?' "

22 "And what's the meaning of 'no lack of admonitions and warnings'?" asked Alyosha.

23 "Why, that's the chief part of what the old man must say."

2 · THE THREE TEMPTATIONS FORESHADOWED THE WHOLE SUBSEQUENT HISTORY OF MANKIND

24 "'THE WISE AND DREAD SPIRIT, the spirit of self-destruction and non-existence,' the old man goes on, 'the great spirit talked with Thee in the wilderness, and we are told in the books that he "tempted" Thee. Is that so? And could anything truer be said than what he revealed to Thee in three questions and what Thou didst reject, and what in the books is called "the temptation"? And yet if there has ever been on earth a real stupendous miracle, it took place on that day, on the day of the three temptations. The statement of those three questions was itself the miracle. If it were possible to imagine simply for the sake of argument that those three questions of the dread spirit had perished utterly from the books, and that we had to restore them and to invent them anew, and to do so had gathered together all the wise men of the earth – rulers, chief priests, learned men, philosophers, poets – and had set them the task to invent three questions, such as would not only fit the occasion, but express in three words, three human phrases, the whole future history of the world and of humanity – dost Thou believe that all the wisdom of the earth united could have invented anything in depth and force equal to the three questions which were actually put to Thee then by the wise and mighty spirit in the wilderness? From those questions alone, from the miracle of their statements, we can see that we

wilderness … three temptations · see Matthew 4:1–11

have here to do not with the fleeting human intelligence, but with 24
the absolute and eternal. For in those three questions the whole
subsequent history of mankind is, as it were, brought together into
one whole, and foretold, and in them are united all the unsolved
historical contradictions of human nature. At the time it could not
be so clear, since the future was unknown; but now that fifteen
hundred years have passed, we see that everything in those three
questions was so justly divined and foretold, and has been so truly
fulfilled that nothing can be added to them or taken from them.

3 · THE FIRST TEMPTATION: THE PROBLEM OF BREAD

"JUDGE THYSELF WHO WAS RIGHT – Thou or he who questioned 25
Thee then? Remember the first question; its meaning, in other
words, was this: "Thou wouldst go into the world, and art going
with empty hands, with some promise of freedom which men
in their simplicity and their natural unruliness cannot even
understand, which they fear and dread – for nothing has ever
been more insupportable for a man and a human society than
freedom. But seest Thou these stones in this parched and barren
wilderness? Turn them into bread,· and mankind will run after
Thee like a flock of sheep, grateful and obedient, though for
ever trembling, lest Thou withdraw Thy hand and deny them
Thy bread." But Thou wouldst not deprive man of freedom and
didst reject the offer, thinking, what is that freedom worth, if
obedience is bought with bread? Thou didst reply that man lives
not by bread alone. But dost Thou know that for the sake of that
earthly bread the spirit of the earth will rise up against Thee
and will strive with Thee and overcome Thee, and all will follow
him, crying, "Who can compare with this beast? He has given
us fire from heaven!"· Dost Thou know that the ages will pass,
and humanity will proclaim by the lips of their sages that there
is no crime, and therefore no sin; there is only hunger? "Feed
men, and then ask of them virtue!" that's what they'll write on
the banner, which they will raise against Thee, and with which
they will destroy Thy temple. Where Thy temple stood will rise
a new building; the terrible tower of Babel· will be built again,
and though, like the one of old, it will not be finished, yet Thou
mightest have prevented that new tower and have cut short the
sufferings of men for a thousand years; for they will come back

stones ... bread ·
see Matthew 4:3–4

"Who ... heaven!" ·
see Revelation 13:4

tower of Babel · see
Genesis 11:4–9

25 to us after a thousand years of agony with their tower. They will seek us again, hidden underground in the catacombs, for we shall be again persecuted and tortured. They will find us and cry to us, "Feed us, for those who have promised us fire from heaven haven't given it!" And then we shall finish building their tower, for he finishes the building who feeds them. And we alone shall feed them in Thy name, declaring falsely that it is in Thy name. Oh, never, never can they feed themselves without us! No science will give them bread so long as they remain free. In the end they will lay their freedom at our feet, and say to us, "Make us your slaves, but feed us." They will understand themselves, at last, that freedom and bread enough for all are inconceivable together, for never, never will they be able to share between them! They will be convinced, too, that they can never be free, for they are weak, vicious, worthless and rebellious.

26 "'Thou didst promise them the bread of Heaven,* but, I repeat again, can it compare with earthly bread in the eyes of the weak, ever sinful and ignoble race of man? And if for the sake of the bread of Heaven thousands and tens of thousands shall follow Thee, what is to become of the millions and tens of thousands of millions of creatures who will not have the strength to forego the earthly bread for the sake of the heavenly? Or dost Thou care only for the tens of thousands of the great and strong, while the millions, numerous as the sands of the sea, who are weak but love Thee, must exist only for the sake of the great and strong? No, we care for the weak too. They are sinful and rebellious, but in the end they too will become obedient. They will marvel at us and look on us as gods, because we are ready to endure the freedom which they have found so dreadful to rule over them – so awful it will seem to them to be free. But we shall tell them that we are Thy servants and rule them in Thy name. We shall deceive them again, for we will not let Thee come to us again. That deception will be our suffering, for we shall be forced to lie.

27 "'This is the significance of the first question in the wilderness, and this is what Thou hast rejected for the sake of that freedom which Thou hast exalted above everything. Yet in this question lies hid the great secret of this world.

28 "'Choosing "bread," Thou wouldst have satisfied the universal and everlasting craving and humanity – to find some one to worship.

bread of Heaven · see John 6:48–58

"'So long as man remains free he strives for nothing so inces- 29
santly and so painfully as to find some one to worship. But man
seeks to worship what is established beyond dispute, so that all
men would agree at once to worship it. For these pitiful creatures
are concerned not only to find what one or the other can worship,
but to find something that all would believe in and worship; what
is essential is that all may be *together* in it. This craving for *community* of worship is the chief misery of every man individually
and of all humanity from the beginning of time. For the sake of
common worship they've slain each other with the sword. They
have set up gods and challenged one another, "Put away your
gods and come and worship ours, or we will kill you and your
gods!" And so it will be to the end of the world, even when gods
disappear from the earth; they will fall down before idols just the
same. Thou didst know, Thou couldst not but have known, this
fundamental secret of human nature, but Thou didst reject the
one infallible banner which was offered Thee to make all men bow
down to Thee alone – the banner of earthly bread; and Thou hast
rejected it for the sake of freedom and the bread of Heaven.

4 · THE SECOND TEMPTATION: THE PROBLEM OF CONSCIENCE

"'BEHOLD WHAT THOU didst further. And all again in the name 30
of freedom! I tell Thee that man is tormented by no greater
anxiety than to find some one quickly to whom he can hand over
that gift of freedom with which the ill-fated creature is born. But
only one who can appease their conscience can take over their
freedom. In bread there was offered Thee an invincible banner; give
bread, and man will worship Thee, for nothing is more certain than
bread. But if some one else gains possession of his conscience – oh!
then he will cast away Thy bread and follow after him who has
ensnared his conscience. In that Thou wast right. For the secret
of man's being is not only to live but to have something to live for.
Without a stable conception of the object of life, man would not
consent to go on living, and would rather destroy himself than
remain on earth, though he had bread in abundance. That is true.

"'But what happened? 31

"'Instead of taking men's freedom from them, Thou didst 32
make it greater than ever! Didst Thou forget that man prefers

32 peace, and even death, to freedom of choice in the knowledge of good and evil? Nothing is more seductive for man than his freedom of conscience, but nothing is a greater cause of suffering. And behold, instead of giving a firm foundation for setting the conscience of man at rest for ever, Thou didst choose all that is exceptional, vague and enigmatic; Thou didst choose what was utterly beyond the strength of men, acting as though Thou didst not love them at all – Thou who didst come to give Thy life for them! Instead of taking possession of men's freedom, Thou didst increase it, and burdened the spiritual kingdom of mankind with its sufferings for ever. Thou didst desire man's free love, that he should follow Thee freely, enticed and taken captive by Thee. In place of the rigid ancient law, man must hereafter with free heart decide for himself what is good and what is evil, having only Thy image before him as his guide. But didst Thou not know he would at last reject even Thy image and Thy truth, if he is weighed down with the fearful burden of free choice? They will cry aloud at last that the truth is not in Thee, for they could not have been left in greater confusion and suffering than Thou hast caused, laying upon them so many cares and unanswerable problems.

33 "'So that, in truth, Thou didst Thyself lay the foundation for the destruction of Thy kingdom, and no one is more to blame for it. Yet what was offered Thee? There are three powers, three powers alone, able to conquer and to hold captive for ever the conscience of these impotent rebels for their happiness – those forces are miracle, mystery and authority. Thou hast rejected all three and hast set the example for doing so. When the wise and dread spirit set Thee on the pinnacle of the temple and said to Thee, "If Thou wouldst know whether Thou art the Son of God then cast Thyself down, for it is written: the angels shall hold him up lest he fall and bruise himself,* and Thou shalt know then whether Thou art the Son of God and shalt prove then how great is Thy faith in Thy father." But Thou didst refuse and wouldst not cast Thyself down. Oh! of course, Thou didst proudly and well like God; but the weak, unruly race of men, are they gods? Oh, Thou didst know then that in taking one step, in making one movement to cast Thyself down, Thou wouldst be tempting God and have lost all Thy faith in Him, and wouldst have been dashed to pieces against that earth which Thou didst come to save. And the wise

cast ... himself · see
Matthew 4:5–7

spirit that tempted Thee would have rejoiced. But I ask again, are 33
there many like Thee? And couldst Thou believe for one moment
that men, too, could face such a temptation? Is the nature of men
such, that they can reject miracle, and at the great moments of
their life, the moments of their deepest, most agonizing spiritual
difficulties, cling only to the free verdict of the heart?

"'Oh, Thou didst know that Thy deed would be recorded in 34
books, would be handed down to remote times and the utmost
ends of the earth, and Thou didst hope that man, following Thee,
would cling to God and not ask for a miracle. But Thou didst not
know that when man rejects miracle he rejects God too; for man
seeks not so much God as the miraculous. And as man cannot
bear to be without the miraculous, he will create new miracles
of his own for himself, and will worship deeds of sorcery and
witchcraft, though he might be a hundred times over a rebel,
heretic, and infidel. Thou didst not come down from the Cross

"Come down … He"·
See Mark 15:29–32,
Matthew 27:39–43

when they shouted to Thee, mocking and reviling Thee. "Come
down from the cross and we will believe that Thou art He."· Thou
didst not come down, for again Thou wouldst not enslave man by
a miracle, and didst crave faith given freely, not based on miracle.
Thou didst crave for free love and not the base raptures of the
slave before the might that has overawed him for ever.

"'But Thou didst think too highly of men therein, for they are 35
slaves, of course, though rebellious by nature. Look around and
judge; fifteen centuries have passed, look upon them. Whom
hast Thou raised up to Thyself? I swear, man is weaker and baser
by nature than Thou hast believed him! Can he, can he do what
Thou didst? By showing him so much respect, Thou didst, as it
were, cease to feel for him, for Thou didst ask far too much from
him – Thou who hast loved him more than Thyself! Respecting
him less, Thou wouldst have asked less of him. That would have
been more like love, for his burden would have been lighter. He
is weak and vile. What though he is everywhere now rebelling
against our power, and proud of his rebellion? It is the pride of a
child and a schoolboy. They are little children rioting and barring
out the teacher at school. But their childish delight will end; it
will cost them dear. They will cast down temples and drench the
earth with blood. But they will see at last, the foolish children,
that, though they are rebels, they are impotent rebels, unable to

35 keep up their own rebellion. Bathed in their foolish tears, they will recognize at last that He who created them rebels must have meant to mock at them. They will say this in despair, and their utterance will be a blasphemy which will make them more unhappy still, for man's nature cannot bear blasphemy, and in the end always avenges it on itself. And so unrest, confusion and unhappiness – that is the present lot of man after Thou didst bear so much for their freedom!

36 "'Thy great prophet tells in vision and in image, that he saw all those who took part in the first resurrection and that there were of each tribe twelve thousand.' But if there were so many of them, they must have been not men but gods. They had borne Thy cross, they had endured scores of years in the barren, hungry wilderness, living upon locusts and roots' – and Thou mayest indeed point with pride at those children of freedom, of free love, of free and splendid sacrifice for Thy name. But remember that they were only some thousands; and what of the rest? And how are the other weak ones to blame, because they could not endure what the strong have endured? How is the weak soul to blame that it is unable to receive such terrible gifts? Canst Thou have simply come to the elect' and for the elect? But if so, it is a mystery and we cannot understand it. And if it is a mystery, we too have a right to preach a mystery, and to teach them that it's not the free judgment of their hearts, not love that matters, but a mystery which they must follow blindly, even against their conscience. So we have done. We have corrected Thy work and have founded it upon *miracle*, *mystery* and *authority*. And men rejoiced that they were again led like sheep, and that the terrible gift that had brought them such suffering, was, at last, lifted from their hearts.

37 "'Were we right teaching them this?

38 "'Speak!

39 "'Did we not love mankind, so meekly acknowledging their feebleness, lovingly lightening their burden, and permitting their weak nature even sin with our sanction? Why hast Thou come now to hinder us? And why dost Thou look silently and searchingly at me with Thy mild eyes? Be angry. I don't want Thy love, for I love Thee not. And what use is it for me to hide anything from Thee? Don't I know to Whom I am speaking? All that I can

Thy great ... thousand · see Revelation 7:4–8

wilderness ... roots · see Matthew 3:4

the elect · those chosen by God for salvation

say is known to Thee already. And is it for me to conceal from 39
Thee our mystery? Perhaps it is Thy will to hear it from my lips.

5 · THE THIRD TEMPTATION: THE PROBLEM OF UNITY

"'LISTEN, THEN. WE ARE NOT working with Thee, but with 40
him – that is our mystery. It's long – eight centuries – since
we have been on his side and not on Thine. Just eight centuries
ago, we took from him what Thou didst reject with scorn, that
last gift he offered Thee, showing Thee all the kingdoms of the
earth.* We took from him Rome and the sword of Cæsar, and
proclaimed ourselves sole rulers of the earth, though hitherto
we have not been able to complete our work. But whose fault
is that? Oh, the work is only beginning, but it has begun. It has
long to await completion and the earth has yet much to suffer,
but we shall triumph and shall be Cæsar's, and then we shall plan
the universal happiness of man. But Thou mightest have taken
even the sword of Cæsar.

showing … earth ·
see Matthew 4:8–10

"'Why didst Thou reject that last gift? 41

"'Hadst Thou accepted that last counsel of the mighty 42
spirit, Thou wouldst have accomplished all that man seeks on
earth – that is, some one to worship, some one to keep his conscience, and some means of uniting all in one unanimous and
harmonious antheap, for the craving for universal unity is the
third and last anguish of men. Mankind as a whole has always
striven to organize a universal state. There have been many
great nations with great histories, but the more highly they
were developed the more unhappy they were, for they felt more
acutely than other people the craving for worldwide union. The
great conquerors, Timours and Ghenghis-Khans,* whirled like
hurricanes over the face of the earth striving to subdue its people,
and they too were but the unconscious expression of the same
craving for universal unity. Hadst Thou taken the world and
Cæsar's purple,* Thou wouldst have founded the universal state
and have given universal peace. For who can rule men if not he
who holds their conscience and their bread in his hands.

Timours and
Ghenghis-Khans ·
Timour (1336?–1405),
who was also known as
Tamerlane or Tamburlaine
the Great, and Ghenghis
Kahn (1162?–1227) were
Mongol emperors known
for their cruelty and
expansionism

Cæsar's purple · royal
color signifying high
rank and rule

"'We have taken the sword of Cæsar, and in taking it, of course, 43
have rejected Thee and followed *him*.

"'Oh, ages are yet to come of the confusion of free thought, of 44
their science and cannibalism. For having begun to build their

44 tower of Babel without us, they will end, of course, with cannibalism. But then the beast will crawl to us and lick our feet and
spatter them with tears of blood. And we shall sit upon the beast
and raise the cup, and on it will be written, "Mystery." But then, and
only then, the reign of peace and happiness will come for men.

45 "'Thou art proud of Thine elect, but Thou hast only the elect,
while we give rest to all. And besides, how many of those elect,
those mighty ones who could become elect, have grown weary
waiting for Thee, and have transferred and will transfer the powers
of their spirit and the warmth of their heart to the other camp, and
end by raising their *free* banner against Thee. Thou didst Thyself
lift up that banner. But with us all will be happy and will no more
rebel nor destroy one another as under Thy freedom.

46 "'Oh, we shall persuade them that they will only become free
when they renounce their freedom to us and submit to us. And
shall we be right or shall we be lying? They will be convinced
that we are right, for they will remember the horrors of slavery
and confusion to which Thy freedom brought them. Freedom,
free thought and science, will lead them into such straits and will
bring them face to face with such marvels and insoluble mysteries,
that some of them, the fierce and rebellious, will destroy themselves, others, rebellious but weak, will destroy one another, while
the rest, weak and unhappy, will crawl fawning to our feet and
whine to us: "Yes, you were right, you alone possess His mystery,
and we come back to you, save us from ourselves!"

6 · SUMMARY: THE INQUISITOR'S UTOPIA

47 "'RECEIVING BREAD FROM US, they will see clearly that we take
the bread made by their hands from them, to give it to
them, without any miracle. They will see that we do not change
the stones to bread, but in truth they will be more thankful for
taking it from our hands than for the bread itself! For they will
remember only too well that in old days, without our help, even
the bread they made turned to stones in their hands, while since
they have come back to us, the very stones have turned to bread
in their hands. Too, too well they know the value of complete
submission! And until men know that, they will be unhappy. Who
is most to blame for their not knowing it, speak? Who scattered
the flock and sent it astray on unknown paths? But the flock will

come together again and will submit once more, and then it will   47
be once for all. Then we shall give them the quiet humble happiness of weak creatures such as they are by nature. Oh, we shall
persuade them at last not to be proud, for Thou didst lift them up
and thereby taught them to be proud. We shall show them that
they are weak, that they are only pitiful children, but that childlike
happiness is the sweetest of all. They will become timid and will
look to us and huddle close to us in fear, as chicks to the hen. They
will marvel at us and will be awe-stricken before us, and will be
proud at our being so powerful and clever, that we have been able
to subdue such a turbulent flock of thousands of millions. They
will tremble impotently before our wrath, their minds will grow
fearful, they will be quick to shed tears like women and children,
but they will be just as ready at a sign from us to pass to laughter
and rejoicing, to happy mirth and childish song. Yes, we shall set
them to work, but in their leisure hours we shall make their life
like a child's game, with children's songs and innocent dance. Oh,
we shall allow them even sin, they are weak and helpless, and
they will love us like children because we allow them to sin. We
shall tell them that every sin will be expiated, if it is done with
our permission, that we allow them to sin because we love them,
and the punishment for these sins we take upon ourselves. And
we shall take it upon ourselves, and they will adore us as their
saviours who have taken on themselves their sins before God.
And they will have no secrets from us. We shall allow or forbid
them to live with their wives and mistresses, to have or not to
have children – according to whether they have been obedient or
disobedient – and they will submit to us gladly and cheerfully. The
most painful secrets of their conscience, all, all they will bring to
us, and we shall have an answer for all. And they will be glad to
believe our answer, for it will save them from the great anxiety and
terrible agony they endure at present in making a free decision
for themselves. And all will be happy, all the millions of creatures
except the hundred thousand who rule over them. For only we,
we who guard the mystery, shall be unhappy.

"'There will be thousands of millions of happy babes, and a   48
hundred thousand sufferers who have taken upon themselves the
curse of the knowledge of good and evil. Peacefully they will die,
peacefully they will expire in Thy name, and beyond the grave

48   they will find nothing but death. But we shall keep the secret, and for their happiness we shall allure them with the reward of heaven and eternity. Though if there were anything in the other world, it certainly would not be for such as they.

49   "'It is prophesied that Thou wilt come again in victory, Thou wilt come with Thy chosen, the proud and strong, but we will say that they have only saved themselves, but we have saved all. We are told that the harlot who sits upon the beast, and holds in her hands the *mystery*, shall be put to shame, that the weak will rise up again, and will rend her royal purple and will strip naked her loathsome body. But then I will stand up and point out to Thee the thousand millions of happy children who have known no sin. And we who have taken their sins upon us for their happiness will stand up before Thee and say: "Judge us if Thou canst and darest." Know that I fear Thee not. Know that I too have been in the wilderness, I too have lived on roots and locusts, I too prized the freedom with which Thou hast blessed men, and I too was striving to stand among Thy elect, among the strong and powerful, thirsting "to make up the number." But I awakened and would not serve madness. I turned back and joined the ranks of those *who have corrected Thy work*. I left the proud and went back to the humble, for the happiness of the humble. What I say to Thee will come to pass, and our dominion will be built up. I repeat, tomorrow Thou shalt see that obedient flock who at a sign from me will hasten to heap up the hot cinders about the pile on which I shall burn Thee for coming to hinder us. For if any one has ever deserved our fires, it is Thou. Tomorrow I shall burn Thee. *Dixi*.'"•

Dixi · "I have spoken" (Latin), the final word of a formal finding or pronouncement

50   Ivan stopped. He was carried away as he talked and spoke with excitement; when he had finished, he suddenly smiled.

51   Alyosha had listened in silence; toward the end he was greatly moved and seemed several times on the point of interrupting, but restrained himself. Now his words came with a rush.

Orthodox Church · the Christian body predominant in Eastern Europe and Western Asia that is presided over by the Patriarch of Constantinople, a body often at odds with Roman Catholicism

52   "But … that's absurd!" he cried, flushing. "Your poem is in praise of Jesus, not in blame of Him – as you meant it to be. And who will believe you about freedom? Is that the way to understand it? That's not the idea of it in the Orthodox Church•…. That's Rome, and not even the whole of Rome, it's false – those are the worst of the Catholics,

the Inquisitors, the Jesuits! ...And there could not be such a fantastic 52
creature as your Inquisitor. What are these sins of mankind they take
on themselves? Who are these keepers of the mystery who have
taken some curse upon themselves for the happiness of mankind?
When have they been seen? We know the Jesuits, they are spoken
ill of, but surely they are not what you describe? They are not that
at all, not at all.... They are simply the Romish army for the earthly
sovereignty of the world in the future, with the Pontiff of Rome* for
Emperor ... that's their ideal, but there's no sort of mystery or lofty
melancholy about it.... It's simple lust of power, of filthy earthly gain,
of domination – something like a universal serfdom* with them as
masters – that's all they stand for. They don't even believe in God
perhaps. Your suffering inquisitor is a mere fantasy."

"Stay, stay," laughed Ivan, "how hot you are! A fantasy you say, 53
let it be so! Of course it's a fantasy. But allow me to say: do you
really think that the Roman Catholic movement of the last centuries is actually nothing but the lust of power, of filthy earthly
gain? Is that Father Païssy's teaching?"

"No, no, on the contrary, Father Païssy did once say something 54
the same as you ... but of course it's not the same, not a bit the
same," Alyosha hastily corrected himself.

"A precious admission, in spite of your 'not a bit the same.' 55
I ask you why your Jesuits and Inquisitors have united simply
for vile material gain? Why can there not be among them one
martyr oppressed by great sorrow and loving humanity? You
see, only suppose that there was one such man among all those
who desire nothing but filthy material gain – if there's only one
like my old inquisitor, who had himself eaten roots in the desert
and made frenzied efforts to subdue his flesh to make himself
free and perfect. But yet all his life he loved humanity, and suddenly his eyes were opened, and he saw that it is no great moral
blessedness to attain perfection and freedom, if at the same time
one gains the conviction that billions of God's creatures have
been created as a mockery, that they will never be capable of
using their freedom, that these poor rebels can never turn into
giants to complete the tower, that it was not for such geese that
the great idealist dreamt his dream of harmony. Seeing all that
he turned back and joined – the clever people. Surely that could
have happened?"

Pontiff of Rome ·
the Pope

serfdom · a form of
slavery in which people
are bound to the land
and owned by a lord,
common in feudal
Europe and Russia

56   "Joined whom, what clever people?" cried Alyosha, completely carried away. "They have no such great cleverness and no mysteries and secrets.... Perhaps nothing but Atheism, that's all their secret. Your inquisitor does not believe in God, that's his secret!"

57   "What if it is so! At last you have guessed it. It's perfectly true that that's the whole secret, but isn't that suffering, at least for a man like that, who has wasted his whole life in the desert and yet could not shake off his incurable love of humanity? In his old age he reached the clear conviction that nothing but the advice of the great dread spirit could build up any tolerable sort of life for the feeble, unruly 'incomplete, empirical creatures created in jest.' And so, convinced of this, he sees that he must follow the council of the wise spirit, the dread spirit of death and destruction, and therefore accept lying and deception, and lead men consciously to death and destruction, and yet deceive them all the way so that they may not notice where they are being led, that the poor blind creatures may at least on the way think themselves happy. And note, the deception is in the name of Him in Whose ideal the old man had so fervently believed all his life long. Is not that tragic? And if only one such stood at the head of the whole army 'filled with the lust of power only for the sake of filthy gain' – would not one such be enough to make a tragedy? More than that, one such standing at the head is enough to create the actual leading idea of the Roman Church with all its armies and Jesuits, its highest idea. I tell you frankly that I firmly believe that there has always been such a man among those who stood at the head of the movement. Who knows, there may have been some such even among the Roman Popes. Who knows, perhaps the spirit of that accursed old man who loves mankind so obstinately in his own way, is to be found even now in a whole multitude of such old men, existing not by chance but by agreement, as a secret league formed long ago for the guarding of the mystery, to guard it from the weak and the unhappy, so as to make them happy. No doubt it is so, and so it must be indeed. I fancy that even among the Masons˙ there's something of the same mystery at the bottom, and that that's why the Catholics so detest the Masons as their rivals breaking up the unity of the idea, while it is so essential that there should be one flock and one shepherd.... But from

Masons · Freemasonry, a secret international charitable fraternity

the way I defend my idea I might be an author impatient of your   57
criticism. Enough of it."

"You are perhaps a Mason yourself!" broke suddenly from   58
Alyosha. "You don't believe in God," he added, speaking this
time very sorrowfully. He fancied besides that his brother was
looking at him ironically. "How does your poem end?" he asked,
suddenly looking down. "Or was it the end?"

"I meant it to end like this: 59

"When the Inquisitor ceased speaking he waited some time for   60
his Prisoner to answer him. His silence weighed down upon him.
He saw the Prisoner had listened intently all the time, looking
gently in his face and evidently not wishing to reply. The old man
longed for Him to say something, however bitter and terrible. But
He suddenly approached the old man in silence and softly kissed
him on his bloodless aged lips. That was all His answer. The old
man shuddered. His lips moved. He went to the door, opened
it, and said to Him: 'Go, and come no more.... Come not at all,
never, never!' And he let Him out into the dark alleys of the town.
The Prisoner went away."

"And the old man?"   61

"The kiss glows in his heart, but the old man adheres to   62
his idea...."

Leo Tolstoy

⟨ 1 8 2 8 – 1 9 1 0 ⟩

Born into an aristocratic family, Count Tolstoy served in the army and later taught school before experiencing a major religious crisis in the 1870s, which led him to question the meaning of his life. The crisis was resolved when Tolstoy discovered a new way of life based upon Jesus' Sermon on the Mount. While rejecting the teachings and authority of the Russian Orthodox Church, Tolstoy preached a gospel of simplicity, forgiveness, love, and pacifism, which he believed could restructure society. Tolstoy's ideas were widely admired, eventually influencing the thought of Mahatma Gandhi and Martin Luther King, Jr. Tolstoy's post-conversion fiction (including the selection which follows) is noted for its profound moral vision expressed through a deceptively simple narrative form. Tolstoy's late short stories are virtual parables emphasizing the need to live one's life with the awareness that death is near and always certain. Tolstoy, author of War and Peace *(1863–1869),* Anna Karenina *(1875–1877), and* Resurrection *(1899), is one of the monumental Russian novelists.*

HOW MUCH LAND DOES A MAN NEED?

1

1   AN ELDER SISTER CAME to visit her younger sister in the country. The elder was married to a tradesman in town, the younger to a peasant in the village. As the sisters sat over their tea talking, the elder began to boast of the advantages of town life: saying how comfortably they lived there, how well they dressed, what fine clothes her children wore, what good things they ate and drank, and how she went to the theater, promenades, and entertainments.

2   The younger sister was piqued,* and in turn disparaged the life of a tradesman, and stood up for that of a peasant.

piqued · annoyed

"I would not change my way of life for yours," said she. "We may live roughly, but at least we are free from anxiety. You live in better style than we do, but though you often earn more than you need, you are very likely to lose all you have. You know the proverb, "Loss and gain are brothers twain." It often happens that people who are wealthy one day are begging their bread the next. Our way is safer. Though a peasant's life is not a fat one, it is a long one. We shall never grow rich, but we shall always have enough to eat." 3

The elder sister said sneeringly: 4

"Enough? Yes, if you like to share with the pigs and the calves! 5 What do you know of elegance or manners! However much your goodman* may slave, you will die as you are living – on a dung heap – and your children the same."

goodman · a peasant, a man of humble birth

"Well, what of that?" replied the younger. "Of course our work 6 is rough and coarse. But, on the other hand, it is sure, and we need not bow to any one. But you, in your towns, are surrounded by temptations; today all may be right, but tomorrow the Evil One may tempt your husband with cards, wine, or women, and all will go to ruin. Don't such things happen often enough?"

Pakhom, the master of the house, was lying on the top of the 7 stove and he listened to the women's chatter.

"It is perfectly true," thought he. "Busy as we are from childhood 8 tilling mother earth, we peasants have no time to let any nonsense settle in our heads. Our only trouble is that we haven't land enough. If I had plenty of land, I shouldn't fear the Devil himself!"

The women finished their tea, chatted a while about dress, and 9 then cleared away the tea-things and lay down to sleep.

But the Devil had been sitting behind the stove, and had heard 10 all that was said. He was pleased that the peasant's wife had led her husband into boasting, and that he had said that if he had plenty of land he would not fear the Devil himself. "All right," thought the Devil. "We will have a tussle. I'll give you land enough; and by means of that land I will get you into my power."

2

CLOSE TO THE VILLAGE there lived a lady, a small landowner 11 who had an estate of about three hundred acres. She had always lived on good terms with the peasants until she engaged as her steward an old soldier, who took to burdening the people

11 with fines. However careful Pakhom tried to be, it happened again and again that now a horse of his got among the lady's oats, now a cow strayed into her garden, now his calves found their way into her meadows – and he always had to pay a fine.

12   Pakhom paid up, but grumbled, and going home in a temper, was rough with his family. All through that summer, Pakhom had much trouble because of this steward, and he was even glad when winter came and the cattle had to be stabled. Though he grudged the fodder* when they could no longer graze on the pasture-land, at least he was free from anxiety about them.

fodder · livestock feed

13   In the winter the news got about that the lady was going to sell her land and that the keeper of the inn on the high road was bargaining for it. When the peasants heard this they were very much alarmed.

14   "Well," thought they, "if the innkeeper gets the land, he will worry us with fines worse than the lady's steward. We all depend on that estate."

15   So the peasants went on behalf of their commune, and asked the lady not to sell the land to the innkeeper, offering her a better price for it themselves. The lady agreed to let them have it. Then the peasants tried to arrange for the commune to buy the whole estate, so that it might be held by them all in common. They met twice to discuss it, but could not settle the matter; the Evil One sowed discord among them and they could not agree. So they decided to buy the land individually, each according to his means; and the lady agreed to this plan as she had to the other.

16   Presently Pakhom heard that a neighbor of his was buying fifty acres, and that the lady had consented to accept one half in cash and to wait a year for the other half. Pakhom felt envious.

17   "Look at that," thought he, "the land is all being sold, and I shall get none of it." So he spoke to his wife.

18   "Other people are buying," said he, "and we must also buy twenty acres or so. Life is becoming impossible. That steward is simply crushing us with his fines."

19   So they put their heads together and considered how they could manage to buy it. They had one hundred rubles laid by. They sold a colt and one half of their bees, hired out one of their sons as a labourer and took his wages in advance; borrowed the rest from a brother-in-law, and so scraped together half the purchase money.

Having done this, Pakhom chose out a farm of forty acres, 20
some of it wooded, and went to the lady to bargain for it. They
came to an agreement, and he shook hands with her upon it and
paid her a deposit in advance. Then they went to town and signed
the deeds; he paying half the price down, and undertaking to pay
the remainder within two years.

So now Pakhom had land of his own. He borrowed seed, and 21
sowed it on the land he had bought. The harvest was a good one, and
within a year he had managed to pay off his debts both to the lady
and to his brother-in-law. So he became a landowner, ploughing and
sowing his own land, making hay on his own land, cutting his own
trees, and feeding his cattle on his own pasture. When he went out
to plough his fields, or to look at his growing corn, or at his grass
meadows, his heart would fill with joy. The grass that grew and the
flowers that bloomed there seemed to him unlike any that grew elsewhere. Formerly, when he had passed by that land, it had appeared
the same as any other land, but now it seemed quite different.

3

So Pakhom was well-contented, and everything would 22
have been right if the neighboring peasants would only not
have trespassed on his corn-fields and meadows. He appealed
to them most civilly, but they still went on: now the communal
herdsmen would let the village cows stray into his meadows, then
horses from the night pasture would get among his corn. Pakhom
turned them out again and again, and forgave their owners, and
for a long time he forbore to prosecute any one. But at last he
lost patience and complained to the district court. He knew it
was the peasants' want of land, and no evil intent on their part,
that caused the trouble, but he thought:

"I cannot go on overlooking it or they will destroy all I have. 23
They must be taught a lesson."

had them up · to be
brought before a local
council or court for
judgment

So he had them up,· gave them one lesson, and then another, 24
and two or three of the peasants were fined. After a time
Pakhom's neighbors began to bear him a grudge for this, and
would now and then let their cattle onto his land on purpose.
One peasant even got into Pakhom's wood at night and cut down
five young lime trees for their bark. Pakhom passing through the
wood one day noticed something white. He came nearer and saw

24 the stripped trunks lying on the ground, and close by stood the stumps where the trees had been. Pakhom was furious.

25 "If he had only cut one here and there it would have been bad enough," thought Pakhom, "but the rascal has actually cut down a whole clump. If I could only find out who did this, I would pay him out."

pay him out · to get revenge, to call to account

26 He racked his brains as to who it could be. Finally he decided: "It must be Simon – no one else could have done it." So he went to Simon's homestead to have a look round, but he found nothing, and only had an angry scene. However, he now felt more certain than ever that Simon had done it, and he lodged a complaint. Simon was summoned. The case was tried, and retried, and at the end of it all Simon was acquitted, there being no evidence against him. Pakhom felt still more aggrieved, and let his anger loose upon the elder and the judges.

27 "You let thieves grease your palms," said he. "If you were honest folk yourselves you would not let a thief go free."

28 So Pakhom quarrelled with the judges and with his neighbors. Threats to burn his building began to be uttered. So though Pakhom had more land, his place in the commune was much worse than before.

29 About this time a rumor got about that many people were moving to new parts.

30 "There's no need for me to leave my land," thought Pakhom. "But some of the others might leave our village and then there would be more room for us. I would take over their land myself and make my estate a bit bigger. I could then live more at ease. As it is, I am still too cramped to be comfortable."

31 One day Pakhom was sitting at home when a peasant, passing through the village, happened to call in. He was allowed to stay the night, and supper was given him. Pakhom had a talk with this peasant and asked him where he came from. The stranger answered that he came from beyond the Volga, where he had been working. One word led to another, and the man went on to say that many people were settling in those parts. He told how some people from his village had settled there. They had joined the commune, and had had twenty-five acres per man granted them. The land was so good, he said, that the rye sown on it grew as high as a horse, and so thick that five cuts of a sickle made a sheaf. One

the Volga · a river in western Russia that originates northwest of Moscow and flows into the Caspian Sea

peasant, he said, had brought nothing with him but his bare hands, 31
and now he had six horses and two cows of his own.

Pakhom's heart kindled with desire. He thought: 32

"Why should I suffer in this narrow hole, if one can live so well 33
elsewhere? I will sell my land and my homestead here, and with
the money I will start afresh over there and get everything new.
In this crowded place one is always having trouble. But I must
first go and find out all about it myself."

Towards summer he got ready and started. He went down 34
the Volga on a steamer to Samara,* then walked another three
hundred miles on foot, and at last reached the place. It was just
as the stranger had said. The peasants had plenty of land: every
man had twenty-five acres of communal land given him for his
use, and anyone who had money could buy, besides, at two shil-
lings an acre as much good freehold land* as he wanted.

Having found out all he wished to know, Pakhom returned 35
home as autumn came on, and began selling off his belongings.
He sold his land at a profit, sold his homestead and all his cattle,
and withdrew from membership of the commune. He only
waited till the spring, and then started with his family for the
new settlement.

4

As soon as Pakhom and his family reached their new abode, 36
he applied for admission into the commune of a large village. He stood treat to* the elders and obtained the necessary
documents. Five shares of communal land were given him for his
own and his sons' use: that is to say – 125 acres (not all together,
but in different fields) besides the use of the communal pasture.
Pakhom put up the buildings he needed, and bought cattle. Of
the communal land alone he had three times as much as at his
former home, and the land was good cornland. He was ten times
better off than he had been. He had plenty of arable* land and
pasturage, and could keep as many head of cattle as he liked.

At first, in the bustle of building and settling down, Pakhom 37
was pleased with it all, but when he got used to it he began to
think that even here he had not enough land. The first year, he
sowed wheat on his share of the communal land and had a good
crop. He wanted to go on sowing wheat, but had not enough com-

Samara · a city in southwestern Russia on the banks of the Samara river

freehold land · land not associated with a manor that is held by a tenant for life

stood treat to · to negotiate or bargain

arable · fit for cultivation and farming

37 munal land for the purpose, and what he had already used was not available; for in those parts wheat is only sown on virgin soil or on fallow* land. It is sown for one or two years, and then the land lies fallow till it is again overgrown with prairie grass. There were many who wanted such land and there was not enough for all; so that people quarrelled about it. Those who were better off wanted it for growing wheat, and those who were poor wanted it to let* to dealers, so that they might raise money to pay their taxes. Pakhom wanted to sow more wheat, so he rented land from a dealer for a year. He sowed much wheat and had a fine crop, but the land was too far from the village – the wheat had to be carted more than ten miles. After a time Pakhom noticed that some peasant-dealers were living on separate farms and were growing wealthy; and he thought:

fallow · land plowed but left unplanted to allow the soil to rest

to let · to rent out

38 "If I were to buy some freehold land and have a homestead on it, it would be a different thing altogether. Then it would all be nice and compact."

39 The question of buying freehold land recurred to him again and again.

40 He went on in the same way for three years, renting land and sowing wheat. The seasons turned out well and the crops were good, so that he began to lay money by. He might have gone on living contentedly, but he grew tired of having to rent other people's land every year, and having to scramble for it. Wherever there was good land to be had, the peasants would rush for it and it was taken up at once, so that unless you were sharp about it you got none. It happened in the third year that he and a dealer together rented a piece of pasture land from some peasants; and they had already ploughed it up, when there was some dispute and the peasants went to law about it, and things fell out so that the labour was all lost.

41 "If it were my own land," thought Pakhom, "I should be independent, and there would not be all this unpleasantness."

42 So Pakhom began looking out for land which he could buy; and he came across a peasant who had bought thirteen hundred acres, but having got into difficulties was willing to sell again cheap. Pakhom bargained and haggled with him, and at last they settled the price at 1,500 rubles, part in cash and part to be paid later. They had all but clinched the matter when a passing dealer happened to stop at Pakhom's one day to get a feed for his horses. He drank

tea with Pakhom and they had a talk. The dealer said that he was 42
just returning from the land of the Bashkirs,· far away, where he
had bought thirteen thousand acres of land, all for 1,000 rubles.
Pakhom questioned him further, and the tradesman said:

Bashkirs · a nomadic tribe of western Russia who inhabit the region of the southern Ural mountains

"All one need do is to make friends with the chiefs. I gave 43
away about one hundred rubles worth of silk robes and carpets,
besides a case of tea, and I gave wine to those who would drink it;
and I got the land for less than a penny an acre." And he showed
Pakhom the title-deeds, saying:

"The land lies near a river, and the whole prairie is virgin soil." 44
Pakhom plied him with questions, and the tradesman said:

"There is more land there than you could cover if you walked 45
a year, and it all belongs to the Bashkirs. They are as simple as
sheep, and land can be got almost for nothing."

"There now," thought Pakhom, "with my one thousand rubles, 46
why should I get only thirteen hundred acres, and saddle myself
with a debt besides? If I take it out there, I can get more than ten
times as much for the money."

5

PAKHOM INQUIRED HOW TO GET to the place, and as soon as 47
the tradesman had left him, he prepared to go there himself. He
left his wife to look after the homestead, and started on his journey
taking his man with him. They stopped at a town on their way and
bought a case of tea, some wine, and other presents, as the tradesman had advised. On and on they went until they had gone more
than three hundred miles, and on the seventh day they came to a
place where the Bashkirs had pitched their tents. It was all just as
the tradesman had said. The people lived on the steppes,· by a river,
in felt-covered tents. They neither tilled the ground, nor ate bread.
Their cattle and horses grazed in herds on the steppe. The colts
were tethered behind the tents, and the mares were driven to them
twice a day. The mares were milked, and from the milk *kumiss*· was
made. It was the women who prepared *kumiss*, and they also made
cheese. As far as the men were concerned, drinking *kumiss* and
tea, eating mutton, and playing on their pipes, was all they cared
about. They were all stout and merry, and all the summer long they
never thought of doing any work. They were quite ignorant, and
knew no Russian, but were good-natured enough.

steppes · a region of semiarid, grass-covered plains

kumiss · (also *kumys*), a fermented drink made from mare's milk

48   As soon as they saw Pakhom, they came out of their tents and gathered round their visitor. An interpreter was found, and Pakhom told them he had come about some land. The Bashkirs seemed very glad; they took Pakhom and led him into one of the best tents, where they made him sit on some down cushions placed on a carpet, while they sat round him. They gave him some tea and *kumiss*, and had a sheep killed, and gave him mutton to eat. Pakhom took presents out of his cart and distributed them among the Bashkirs, and divided the tea amongst them. The Bashkirs were delighted. They talked a great deal among themselves, and then told the interpreter to translate.

      "They wish to tell you," said the interpreter, "that they like you,
49   and that it is our custom to do all we can to please a guest and to repay him for his gifts. You have given us presents, now tell us which of the things we possess please you best, that we may present them to you."

50   "What pleases me best here", answered Pakhom, "is your land. Our land is crowded and the soil is exhausted; but you have plenty of land and it is good land. I never saw the like of it."

51   The interpreter translated. The Bashkirs talked among themselves for a while. Pakhom could not understand what they were saying, but saw that they were much amused and that they shouted and laughed. Then they were silent and looked at Pakhom while the interpreter said:

52   "They wish me to tell you that in return for your presents they will gladly give you as much land as you want. You have only to point it out with your hand and it is yours."

53   The Bashkirs talked again for a while and began to dispute. Pakhom asked what they were disputing about, and the interpreter told him that some of them thought they ought to ask their chief about the land and not act in his absence, while others thought there was no need to wait for his return.

6

54   WHILE THE BASHKIRS were disputing, a man in a large fox-fur cap appeared on the scene. They all became silent and rose to their feet. The interpreter said, "This is our chief himself."

55   Pakhom immediately fetched the best dressing-gown and five pounds of tea, and offered these to the chief. The chief accepted them, and seated himself in the place of honour. The Bashkirs

at once began telling him something. The chief listened for a 55
while, then made a sign with his head for them to be silent, and
addressing himself to Pakhom, said in Russian:

"Well, let it be so. Choose whatever piece of land you like; we 56
have plenty of it."

"How can I take as much as I like?" thought Pakhom. "I must 57
get a deed to make it secure, or else they may say, 'It is yours,'
and afterwards may take it away again."

"Thank you for your kind words," he said aloud. "You have 58
much land, and I only want a little. But I should like to be sure
which bit is mine. Could it not be measured and made over to
me? Life and death are in God's hands. You good people give it
to me, but your children might wish to take it away again."

"You are quite right," said the chief. "We will make it over to you." 59

"I heard that a dealer had been here," continued Pakhom, "and 60
that you gave him a little land, too, and signed title-deeds to that
effect. I should like to have it done in the same way."

The chief understood. 61

"Yes," replied he, "that can be done quite easily. We have 62
a scribe, and we will go to town with you and have the deed
properly sealed."

"And what will be the price?" asked Pakhom. 63

"Our price is always the same: one thousand rubles a day." 64
Pakhom did not understand.

"A day? What measure is that? How many acres would that be?" 65

"We do not know how to reckon it out," said the chief. "We 66
sell it by the day. As much as you can go round on your feet in a
day is yours, and the price is one thousand rubles a day."

Pakhom was surprised. 67

"But in a day you can get round a large tract of land," he said. 68

The chief laughed. 69

"It will all be yours!" said he. "But there is one condition: If 70
you don't return on the same day to the spot whence you started,
your money is lost."

"But how am I to mark the way that I have gone?" 71

"Why, we shall go to any spot you like, and stay there. You must 72
start from that spot and make your round, taking a spade with you.
Wherever you think necessary, make a mark. At every turning,
dig a hole and pile up the turf; then afterwards we will go round

72 with a plough from hole to hole. You may make as large a circuit as you please, but before the sun sets you must return to the place you started from. All the land you cover will be yours." Pakhom was delighted. It was decided to start early next morning. They talked a while, and after drinking some more *kumiss* and eating some more mutton, they had tea again, and then the night came on. They gave Pakhom a feather-bed to sleep on, and the Bashkirs dispersed for the night, promising to assemble the next morning at day-break and ride out before sunrise to the appointed spot.

7

73 PAKHOM LAY ON THE feather-bed, but could not sleep. He kept thinking about the land.

74 "What a large tract I will mark off!" thought he. "I can easily do thirty-five miles in a day. The days are long now, and within a circuit of thirty-five miles what a lot of land there will be! I will sell the poorer land, or let it to peasants, but I'll pick out the best and farm it. I will buy two ox-teams, and hire two more labourers. About a hundred and fifty acres shall be plough-land, and I will pasture cattle on the rest."

75 Pakhom lay awake all night, and dozed off only just before dawn. Hardly were his eyes closed when he had a dream. He thought he was lying in that same tent and heard somebody chuckling outside. He wondered who it could be, and rose and went out, and he saw the Bashkir chief sitting in front of the tent holding his sides and rolling about with laughter. Going nearer to the chief, Pakhom asked: "What are you laughing at?" But he saw that it was no longer the chief, but the dealer who had recently stopped at his house and had told him about the land. Just as Pakhom was going to ask, "Have you been here long?" he saw that it was not the dealer, but the peasant who had come up from the Volga, long ago, to Pakhom's old home. Then he saw that it was not the peasant either, but the Devil himself with hoofs and horns, sitting there and chuckling, and before him lay a man barefoot, prostrate on the ground, with only trousers and a shirt on. And Pakhom dreamt that he looked more attentively to see what sort of a man it was that was lying there, and he saw that the man was dead, and that it was himself! He awoke horror-struck.

76 "What things one does dream," thought he.

Looking round he saw through the open door that the dawn   77
was breaking.

"It's time to wake them up," thought he. "We ought to be starting."   78

He got up, roused his man (who was sleeping in his cart), bade   79
him harness; and went to call the Bashkirs.

"It's time to go to the steppe to measure the land," he said.   80

The Bashkirs rose and assembled, and the chief came too. Then   81
they began drinking *kumiss* again, and offered Pakhom some tea,
but he would not wait.

"If we are to go, let us go. It is high time," said he.   82

8

T HE BASHKIRS GOT READY and they all started: some   83
mounted on horses, and some in carts. Pakhom drove in
his own small cart with his servant and took a spade with him.
When they reached the steppe, the morning red was beginning to
kindle. They ascended a hillock (called by the Bashkirs a *shikhan*)
and dismounting from their carts and their horses, gathered in
one spot. The chief came up to Pakhom and stretching out his
arm towards the plain;

"See," said he, "all this, as far as your eye can reach, is ours.   84
You may have any part of it you like."

Pakhom's eyes glistened: it was all virgin soil, as flat as the   85
palm of your hand, as black as the seed of a poppy, and in the
hollows different kinds of grasses grew breast high.

The chief took off his fox-fur cap, placed it on the ground   86
and said:

"This will be the mark. Start from here, and return here again.   87
All the land you go round shall be yours."

Pakhom took out his money and put it on the cap. Then he   88
took off his outer coat, remaining in his sleeveless under-coat. He
unfastened his girdle and tied it tight below his stomach, put a little
bag of bread into the breast of his coat, and tying a flask of water to
his girdle, he drew up the tops of his boots, took the spade from his
man, and stood ready to start. He considered for some moments
which way he had better go – it was tempting everywhere.

"No matter," he concluded, "I will go towards the rising sun."   89

He turned his face to the east, stretched himself, and waited   90
for the sun to appear above the rim.

91   "I must lose no time," he thought, "and it is easier walking while it is still cool."

92   The sun's rays had hardly flashed above the horizon, before Pakhom, carrying the spade over his shoulder, went down into the steppe.

93   Pakhom started walking neither slowly nor quickly. After having gone a thousand yards he stopped, dug a hole, and placed pieces of turf one on another to make it more visible. Then he went on; and now that he had walked off his stiffness he quickened his pace. After a while he dug another hole.

94   Pakhom looked back. The hillock could be distinctly seen in the sunlight, with the people on it, and the glittering tires of the cartwheels. At a rough guess Pakhom concluded that he had walked three miles. It was growing warmer; he took off his under-coat, flung it across his shoulder, and went on again. It had grown quite warm now; he looked at the sun, it was time to think of breakfast.

95   "The first shift is done, but there are four in a day, and it is too soon yet to turn. But I will just take off my boots," said he to himself.

96   He sat down, took off his boots, stuck them into his girdle, and went on. It was easy walking now.

97   "I will go on for another three miles," thought he, "and then turn to the left. This spot is so fine, that it would be a pity to lose it. The further one goes, the better the land seems."

98   He went straight on for a while, and when he looked round, the hillock was scarcely visible and the people on it looked like black ants, and he could just see something glistening there in the sun.

99   "Ah," thought Pakhom, "I have gone far enough in this direction, it is time to turn. Besides I am in a regular sweat, and very thirsty."

100   He stopped, dug a large hole, and heaped up pieces of turf. Next he untied his flask, had a drink, and then turned sharply to the left. He went on and on; the grass was high, and it was very hot.

101   Pakhom began to grow tired: he looked at the sun and saw that it was noon.

102   "Well," he thought, "I must have a rest."

103   He sat down and ate some bread and drank some water; but he did not lie down, thinking that if he did he might fall asleep. After sitting a little while, he went on again. At first he walked easily: the food had strengthened him; but it had become terribly hot and he felt sleepy, still he went on, thinking: "An hour to suffer, a life-time to live."

He went a long way in this direction also, and was about to turn   104
to the left again, when he perceived a damp hollow: "It would be a
pity to leave that out," he thought. "Flax would do well there." So
he went on past the hollow, and dug a hole on the other side of it
before he turned the corner. Pakhom looked towards the hillock.
The heat made the air hazy: it seemed to be quivering, and through
the haze the people on the hillock could scarcely be seen.

"Ah!" thought Pakhom, "I have made the sides too long; I must   105
make this one shorter." And he went along the third side, stepping faster. He looked at the sun: it was nearly half-way to the
horizon, and he had not yet done two miles of the third side of
the square. He was still ten miles from the goal.

"No," he thought, "though it will make my land lop-sided, I   106
must hurry back in a straight line now. I might go too far, and
as it is I have a great deal of land."

So Pakhom hurriedly dug a hole, and turned straight towards   107
the hillock.

9

PAKHOM WENT STRAIGHT towards the hillock, but he now   108
walked with difficulty. He was done up with the heat, his bare
feet were cut and bruised, and his legs began to fail. He longed to
rest, but it was impossible if he meant to get back before sunset.
The sun waits for no man, and it was sinking lower and lower.

"Oh dear," he thought, "if only I have not blundered trying for   109
too much! What if I am too late?"

He looked towards the hillock and at the sun. He was still far   110
from his goal, and the sun was already near the rim.

Pakhom walked on and on; it was very hard walking but he   111
went quicker and quicker. He pressed on, but was still far from
the place. He began running, threw away his coat, his boots,
his flask, and his cap, and kept only the spade which he used
as a support.

"What shall I do?" he thought again, "I have grasped too much   112
and ruined the whole affair. I can't get there before the sun sets."

And this fear made him still more breathless. Pakhom went   113
on running, his soaking shirt and trousers stuck to him and his
mouth was parched. His breast was working like a blacksmith's
bellows, his heart was beating like a hammer, and his legs were

113   giving way as if they did not belong to him. Pakhom was seized with terror lest he should die of the strain.

114   Though afraid of death, he could not stop. "After having run all that way they will call me a fool if I stop now," thought he. And he ran on and on, and drew near and heard the Bashkirs yelling and shouting to him, and their cries inflamed his heart still more. He gathered his last strength and ran on.

115   The sun was close to the rim, and cloaked in mist looked large, and red as blood. Now, yes now, it was about to set! The sun was quite low, but he was also quite near his aim. Pakhom could already see the people on the hillock waving their arms to hurry him up. He could see the fox-fur cap on the ground and the money on it, and the chief sitting on the ground holding his sides. And Pakhom remembered his dream.

116   "There is plenty of land," thought he, "but will God let me live on it? I have lost my life, I have lost my life! I shall never reach that spot!"

117   Pakhom looked at the sun, which had reached the earth: one side of it had already disappeared. With all his remaining strength he rushed on, bending his body forward so that his legs could hardly follow fast enough to keep him from falling. Just as he reached the hillock it suddenly grew dark. He looked up – the sun had already set! He gave a cry: "All my labour has been in vain," thought he, and was about to stop, but he heard the Bashkirs still shouting, and remembered that though to him, from below, the sun seemed to have set, they on the hillock could still see it. He took a long breath and ran up the hillock. It was still light there. He reached the top and saw the cap. Before it sat the chief laughing and holding his sides. Again Pakhom remembered his dream, and he uttered a cry: his legs gave way beneath him, he fell forward and reached the cap with his hands.

118   "Ah, that's a fine fellow!" exclaimed the chief. "He has gained much land!"

119   Pakhom's servant came running up and tried to raise him, but he saw that blood was flowing from his mouth. Pakhom was dead!

120   The Bashkirs clicked their tongues to show their pity.

121   His servant picked up the spade and dug a grave long enough for Pakhom to lie in, and buried him in it. Six feet from his head to his heels was all he needed.

I. L. Peretz

⟨ 1 8 5 2 – 1 9 1 5 ⟩

Isaac Leib Peretz – "father of the Yiddish Renaissance," poet, essayist, political activist, and playwright – was born in Zamość, a city of eastern Poland, then part of the Russian Empire. Peretz was devoted to the Jewish Enlightenment, a movement to bring Eastern European Jewish culture into direct conversation with science and Western humanist values. The writer came to believe that he could best aid the cause by writing in Yiddish, the household language of Polish Jews. He rejected the popular mysticism of Hassidic Judaism, arguing for a modern, enlightened approach to life and faith. A socialist who advocated radical political reform, he suffered persecution by the Russian government, losing his license to practice law and enduring a brief imprisonment. Though sympathetic with the socialist rebellions on the horizon, he feared the rise of new, dehumanizing ideologies worse than Russian imperialism. He predicted a new world in which bodies would be fed, but in which spirits would starve. He feared the human spirit would "stand with clipped wings at the same trough beside the cow and ox." The Yiddish literary culture of which Peretz was the chief architect was largely destroyed by three forces: the Holocaust, the assimilation of Jewish culture in America, and the triumph of modern Hebrew in contemporary Israel. Though Yiddish is a dying language, I. L. Peretz left elegant stories whose beauty and ethical idealism endure through translation.

IF NOT HIGHER

1 EARLY EVERY FRIDAY morning, at the time of the Penitential Prayers, the rabbi of Nemirov would vanish.

2 He was nowhere to be seen – neither in the synagogue nor in the two study houses nor at a *minyan.** And he was certainly not at home. His door stood open: whoever wished could go

minyan · a meeting involving a minimum of ten Jewish males above thirteen years of age, the number required for a public religious service

207

in and out; no one would steal from the rabbi. But not a living creature was within. [2]

Where could the rabbi be? Where should he be? In heaven, no doubt. A rabbi has plenty of business to take care of just before the Days of Awe.* Jews, God bless them, need livelihood, peace, health, and good matches. They want to be pious and good, but our sins are so great, and Satan of the thousand eyes watches the whole earth from one end to the other. What he sees, he reports; he denounces, informs. Who can help us if not the rabbi! [3]

That's what the people thought. [4]

But once, a *Litvak** came, and he laughed. You know the *Litvaks.* They think little of the holy books but stuff themselves with *Talmud** and law. So this *Litvak* points to a passage in the *Gemara** – it sticks in your eyes – where it is written that even Moses our Teacher did not ascend to heaven during his lifetime but remained suspended two and a half feet below. Go argue with a *Litvak*! [5]

So where can the rabbi be? [6]

"That's not my business," said the *Litvak*, shrugging. Yet all the while – what a *Litvak* can do! – he is scheming to find out. [7]

That same night, right after the evening prayers, the *Litvak* steals into the rabbi's room, slides under the rabbi's bed, and waits. He'll watch all night and discover where the rabbi vanishes and what he does during the Penitential Prayers. [8]

Someone else might have gotten drowsy and fallen asleep, but the *Litvak* is never at a loss; he recites a whole tractate of the *Talmud* by heart. [9]

At dawn he hears the call to prayers. [10]

The rabbi has already been awake for a long time. The *Litvak* heard him groaning for a whole hour. [11]

Whoever has heard the rabbi of Nemirov groan knows how much sorrow for all Israel, how much suffering, lies in each groan. A man's heart might break, hearing it. But a *Litvak* is made of iron; he listens and remains where he is. The rabbi – long life to him! – lies on the bed, and the *Litvak* under the bed. [12]

Then the *Litvak* hears the beds in the house begin to creak; he hears people jumping out of their beds, mumbling a few Jewish words, pouring water on their fingernails,* banging doors. Everyone has left. It is again quiet and dark, a bit of light from the moon shines through the shutters. [13]

Days of Awe · the "Ten Days of Repentance" begin on *Rosh Hashanah* (Jewish New Year) and end on *Yom Kippur* (the Day of Atonement). Special penitential prayers are said before morning devotionals on these days

Litvak · a Lithuanian Jew

Talmud · a collection of ancient rabbinic writings, the basis of religious authority for traditional Judaism

Gemara · a commentary and elaboration upon the *Mishnah*, a Jewish code of laws. Together, the *Mishnah* and the *Gemara* constitute the *Talmud*

pouring ... fingernails · part of the ritual cleansing performed by Orthodox Jews

14 (Afterward, the *Litvak* admitted that when he found himself alone with the rabbi a great fear took hold of him. Goose pimples spread across his skin, and the roots of his sidelocks* pricked him like needles. A trifle: to be alone with the rabbi at the time of the Penitential Prayers! But a *Litvak* is stubborn. So he quivered like a fish in water and remained where he was.)

15 Finally the rabbi – long life to him! – arises. First, he does what befits a Jew. Then he goes to the clothes closet and takes out a bundle of peasant clothes: linen trousers, high boots, a coat, a big felt hat, and a long, wide leather belt studded with brass nails. The rabbi gets dressed. From his coat pocket dangles the end of a heavy peasant rope.

16 The rabbi goes out, and the *Litvak* follows him.

17 On the way the rabbi stops in the kitchen, bends down, takes an ax from under the bed, puts it into his belt, and leaves the house. The *Litvak* trembles but continues to follow.

18 The hushed dread of the Days of Awe hangs over the dark streets. Every once in a while a cry rises from some *minyan* reciting the Penitential Prayers, or from a sickbed. The rabbi hugs the sides of the streets, keeping to the shade of the houses. He glides from house to house, and the *Litvak* after him. The *Litvak* hears the sound of his heartbeats mingling with the sound of the rabbi's heavy steps. But he keeps on going and follows the rabbi to the outskirts of the town.

19 A small wood stands just outside the town.

20 The rabbi – long life to him! – enters the wood. He takes thirty or forty steps and stops by a small tree. The *Litvak*, overcome with amazement, watches the rabbi take the ax out of his belt and strike the tree. He hears the tree creak and fall. The rabbi chops the tree into logs and the logs into sticks. Then he makes a bundle of the wood and ties it with the rope in his pocket. He puts the bundle of wood on his back, shoves the ax back into his belt, and returns to the town.*

He takes ... to the town · the rabbi's labor in traveling such a distance, cutting down the tree, chopping and bundling the wood and carrying it back to town was expressly prohibited by Talmudic law, as is all work during holy days

21 He stops at a back street beside a small, broken-down shack and knocks at the window.

22 "Who is there?" asks a frightened voice. The *Litvak* recognizes it as the voice of a sick Jewish woman.

23 "I" answers the rabbi in the accent of a peasant.

24 "Who is I?"

Again the rabbi answers in Russian. "Vassil." 25

"Who is Vassil, and what do you want?" 26

"I have wood to sell, very cheap." And not waiting for the 27
woman's reply, he goes into the house.

The *Litvak* steals in after him. In the gray light of early morning 28
he sees a poor room with broken, miserable furnishings. A sick
woman, wrapped in rags, lies on the bed. She complains bitterly,
"Buy? How can I buy? Where will a poor widow get money?"

"I'll lend it to you," answers the supposed Vassil. "It's only 29
six cents."

"And how will I ever pay you back?" asks the poor woman, 30
groaning.

"Foolish one," says the rabbi reproachfully. "See, you are a poor, 31
sick Jew, and I am ready to trust you with a little wood. I am sure
you'll pay. While you, you have such a great and mighty God and
you don't trust him for six cents."

"And who will kindle the fire?" asks the widow. "Have I the 32
strength to get up? My son is at work."

"I'll kindle the fire," answers the rabbi. 33

As the rabbi put the wood into the tile oven he recited, in a 34
groan, the first portion of the Penitential Prayers.

As he kindled the fire and the wood burned brightly, he recited, 35
a bit more joyously, the second portion of the Penitential Prayers.
When the fire was set, he recited the third portion, and then he
shut the stove.

The *Litvak* who saw all this became a disciple of the rabbi. 36

And ever after, when another disciple tells how the rabbi of 37
Nemirov ascends to heaven at the time of the Penitential Prayers,
the *Litvak* does not laugh. He only adds quietly, "If not higher."

Willa Cather

⟨1873-1947⟩

Her family's immigration from Virginia to the Nebraska prairie when Cather was nine was a formative event. Following her graduation from the state university in Lincoln, Cather returned to the east, establishing herself there as a successful journalist and magazine editor. But the prairie's mystique still haunted her. The stark, empty landscape, peopled by poor but often highly cultured European immigrants who, like Cather's family, had come in search of farmland, exerted a continuing influence on her art. In Cather's fiction, sensitive souls are traumatized by more hardy personality types and by the harshness of pioneer life. Throughout her twelve novels and fifty-eight stories, a number of them focusing on the heroism of western settlers, Cather displays what friend and literary mentor Sarah Orne Jewett called the "gift of sympathy."

THE JOY OF NELLY DEANE

1 NELL AND I WERE almost ready to go on for the last act of *Queen Esther,* and we had for the moment got rid of our three patient dressers, Mrs. Dow, Mrs. Freeze, and Mrs. Spinny. Nell was peering over my shoulder into the little cracked looking glass that Mrs. Dow had taken from its nail on her kitchen wall and brought down to the church under her shawl that morning. When she realized that we were alone, Nell whispered to me in the quick, fierce way she had:

2 "Say, Peggy, won't you go up and stay with me tonight? Scott Spinny's asked to take me home, and I don't want to walk up with him alone."

3 "I guess so, if you'll ask my mother."

4 "Oh, I'll fix her!" Nell laughed, with a toss of her head which meant that she usually got what she wanted, even from people much less tractable than my mother.

Queen Esther · an oratorio by Georg Friedrich Händel (1685–1759) composed in 1732

tiring-women · assistants who help actors change clothes backstage

In a moment our tiring-women* were back again. The three old ₅ ladies – at least they seemed old to us – fluttered about us, more agitated than we were ourselves. It seemed as though they would never leave off patting Nell and touching her up. They kept trying things this way and that, never able in the end to decide which way was best. They wouldn't hear to her using rouge, and as they powdered her neck and arms, Mrs. Freeze murmured that she hoped we wouldn't get into the habit of using such things. Mrs. Spinny divided her time between pulling up and tucking down the "illusion"* that filled in the square neck of Nelly's dress. She didn't like things much low, she said; but after she had pulled it up, she stood back and looked at Nell thoughtfully through her glasses. While the excited girl was reaching for this and that, buttoning a slipper, pinning down a curl, Mrs. Spinny's smile softened more and more until, just before Esther made her entrance, the old lady tiptoed up to her and softly tucked the illusion down as far as it would go.

"illusion" · a piece of skin-colored cloth used under a low-cut gown to give the appearance of cleavage

"She's so pink; it seems a pity not," she whispered apologetically to Mrs. Dow. ₆

Every one admitted that Nelly was the prettiest girl in ₇ Riverbend, and the gayest – oh, the gayest! When she was not singing, she was laughing. When she was not laid up with a broken arm, the outcome of a foolhardy coasting feat, or suspended from school because she ran away at recess to go buggy-riding with Guy Franklin, she was sure to be up to mischief of some sort. Twice she broke through the ice and got soused in the river because she never looked where she skated or cared what happened so long as she went fast enough. After the second of these duckings our three dressers declared that she was trying to be a Baptist despite herself.

Mrs. Spinny and Mrs. Freeze and Mrs. Dow, who were always ₈ hovering about Nelly, often whispered to me their hope that she would eventually come into our church and not "go with the Methodists"; her family were Wesleyans.* But to me these artless plans of theirs never wholly explained their watchful affection. They had good daughters themselves – except Mrs. Spinny, who had only the sullen Scott – and they loved their plain girls and thanked God for them. But they loved Nelly differently. They were proud of her pretty figure and yellow-brown eyes, which dilated so easily and sparkled with a kind of golden efferves-

Methodists ... Wesleyans · followers of the English minister John Wesley (1703–1791)

8   cence. They were always making pretty things for her, always coaxing her to come to the sewing circle, where she knotted her thread, and put in the wrong sleeve, and laughed and chattered and said a great many things that she should not have said, and somehow always warmed their hearts. I think they loved her for her unquenchable joy.

9   All the Baptist ladies liked Nell, even those who criticized her most severely, but the three who were first in fighting the battles of our little church, who held it together by their prayers and the labor of their hands, watched over her as they did over Mrs. Dow's century plant before it blossomed. They looked for her on Sunday morning and smiled at her as she hurried, always a little late, up to the choir. When she rose and stood behind the organ and sang "There Is a Green Hill,"* one could see Mrs. Dow and Mrs. Freeze settle back in their accustomed seats and look up at her as if she had just come from that hill and had brought them glad tidings.

"There Is a Green Hill" · a hymn (words C. F. Alexander, music G. C. Stebbins, 1878) that describes the crucifixion of Christ

10   It was because I sang contralto, or, as we said, alto, in the Baptist choir that Nell and I became friends. She was so gay and grown up, so busy with parties and dances and picnics, that I would scarcely have seen much of her had we not sung together. She liked me better than she did any of the older girls, who tried clumsily to be like her, and I felt almost as solicitous and admiring as did Mrs. Dow and Mrs. Spinny. I think even then I must have loved to see her bloom and glow, and I loved to hear her sing, in "The Ninety and Nine,"*

"The Ninety and Nine" · a hymn (words E. C. Clephane, music I. D. Sankey, 1874) based on Christ's parable of the lost sheep (Luke 15:3–7)

10a   *But one was out on the hills away*

in her sweet, strong voice. Nell had never had a singing lesson but she had sung from the time she could talk, and Mrs. Dow used fondly to say that it was singing so much that made her figure so pretty.

11   After I went into the choir it was found to be easier to get Nelly to choir practice. If I stopped outside her gate on my way to church and coaxed her, she usually laughed, ran in for her hat and jacket, and went along with me. The three old ladies fostered our friendship, and because I was "quiet," they esteemed me a good influence for Nelly. This view was propounded in a sewing-circle discussion and, leaking down to us through our mothers, greatly amused us. Dear old ladies! It was so manifestly for what

Nell was that they loved her, and yet they were always looking 11
for "influences" to change her.

The *Queen Esther* performance had cost us three months of 12
hard practice, and it was not easy to keep Nell up to attending
the tedious rehearsals. Some of the boys we knew were in the
chorus of Assyrian youths, but the solo cast was made up of older
people, and Nell found them very poky. We gave the cantata in
the Baptist church on Christmas Eve, "to a crowded house," as
the *Riverbend Messenger* truly chronicled. The country folk for
miles about had come in through a deep snow, and their teams
and wagons stood in a long row at the hitch-bars on each side
of the church door. It was certainly Nelly's night, for however
much the tenor – he was her schoolmaster, and naturally thought
poorly of her – might try to eclipse her in his dolorous solos about
the rivers of Babylon* there could be no doubt as to whom the
people had come to hear – and to see.

rivers of Babylon · a
reference to the captivity
of Israel. See Psalm 137:1

After the performance was over, our fathers and mothers came 13
back to the dressing rooms – the little rooms behind the baptistry
where the candidates for baptism were robed – to congratulate
us, and Nell persuaded my mother to let me go home with her.
This arrangement may not have been wholly agreeable to Scott
Spinny, who stood glumly waiting at the baptistry door; though I
used to think he dogged Nell's steps not so much for any pleasure
he got from being with her as for the pleasure of keeping other
people away. Dear little Mrs. Spinny was perpetually in a state
of humiliation on account of his bad manners, and she tried by
a very special tenderness to make up to Nelly for the remissness
of her ungracious son.

Scott was a spare, muscular fellow, good-looking, but with 14
a face so set and dark that I used to think it very like the cast-
ings he sold. He was taciturn and domineering, and Nell rather
liked to provoke him. Her father was so easy with her that she
seemed to enjoy being ordered about now and then. That night,
when every one was praising her and telling her how well she
sang and how pretty she looked, Scott only said, as we came out
of the dressing room:

"Have you got your high shoes on?" 15

"No; but I've got rubbers on over my low ones. Mother 16
doesn't care."

17 "Well, you just go back and put 'em on as fast as you can."

18 Nell made a face at him and ran back, laughing. Her mother, fat, comfortable Mrs. Deane, was immensely amused at this.

19 "That's right, Scott," she chuckled. "You can do enough more with her than I can. She walks right over me an' Jud."

20 Scott grinned. If he was proud of Nelly, the last thing he wished to do was to show it. When she came back he began to nag again. "What are you going to do with all those flowers? They'll freeze stiff as pokers."*

pokers · fireplace pokers

21 "Well, there won't none of *your* flowers freeze, Scott Spinny, so there!" Nell snapped. She had the best of him that time, and the Assyrian youths rejoiced. They were most of them high-school boys, and the poorest of them had "chipped in" and sent all the way to Denver for Queen Esther's flowers. There were bouquets from half a dozen townspeople, too, but none from Scott. Scott was a prosperous hardware merchant and notoriously penurious, though he saved his face, as the boys said, by giving liberally to the church.

22 "There's no use freezing the fool things, anyhow. You get me some newspapers, and I'll wrap 'em up." Scott took from his pocket a folded copy of the *Riverbend Messenger* and began laboriously to wrap up one of the bouquets. When we left the church door he bore three large newspaper bundles, carrying them as carefully as if they had been so many newly frosted wedding cakes, and left Nell and me to shift for ourselves as we floundered along the snow-burdened sidewalk.

23 Although it was after midnight, lights were shining from many of the little wooden houses, and the roofs and shrubbery were so deep in snow that Riverbend looked as if it had been tucked down into a warm bed. The companies of people, all coming from church, tramping this way and that toward their homes and calling "Good night" and "Merry Christmas" as they parted company, all seemed to us very unusual and exciting.

24 When we got home, Mrs. Deane had a cold supper ready, and Jud Deane had already taken off his shoes and fallen to on his fried chicken and pie. He was so proud of his pretty daughter that he must give her her Christmas presents then and there, and he went into the sleeping chamber behind the dining room and from the depths of his wife's closet brought out a short sealskin jacket and a round cap and made Nelly put them on.

Mrs. Deane, who sat busy between a plate of spice cake and   25
a tray piled with her famous whipped cream tarts, laughed inor-
dinately at his behavior. "Ain't he worse than any kid you ever
see? He's been running to that closet like a cat shut away from
her kittens. I wonder Nell ain't caught on before this. I did think
he'd make out now to keep 'em till Christmas morning; but he's
never made out to keep anything yet."

That was true enough, and fortunately Jud's inability to keep   26
anything seemed always to present a highly humorous aspect
to his wife. Mrs. Deane put her heart into her cooking, and said
that so long as a man was a good provider she had no cause
to complain. Other people were not so charitable toward Jud's
failing. I remember how many strictures were passed upon that
little sealskin and how he was censured for his extravagance. But
what a public-spirited thing, after all, it was for him to do! How,
the winter through, we all enjoyed seeing Nell skating on the
river or running about the town with the brown collar turned
up about her bright cheeks and her hair blowing out from under
the round cap! "No seal," Mrs. Dow said, "would have begrudged
it to her. Why should we?" This was at the sewing circle, when
the new coat was under grave discussion.

At last Nelly and I got upstairs and undressed, and the pad of   27
Jud's slippered feet about the kitchen premises – where he was
carrying up from the cellar things that might freeze – ceased. He
called "Good night, daughter," from the foot of the stairs, and the

house grew quiet. But one is not a *prima donna* the first time
for nothing, and it seemed as if we could not go to bed. Our light
must have burned long after every other in Riverbend was out.
The muslin curtains of Nell's bed were drawn back; Mrs. Deane

had turned down the white counterpane and taken off the shams
and smoothed the pillows for us. But their fair plumpness offered
no temptation to two such hot young heads. We could not let
go of life even for a little while. We sat and talked in Nell's cozy
room, where there was a tiny, white fur rug – the only one in
Riverbend – before the bed; and there were white sash curtains,
and the prettiest little desk and dressing table I had ever seen. It
was a warm, gay little room, flooded all day long with sunlight
from east and south windows that had climbing roses all about
them in summer. About the dresser were photographs of ador-

27 ing high school boys; and one of Guy Franklin, much groomed
and barbered, in a dress coat and a boutonnière. I never liked
to see that photograph there. The home boys looked properly
modest and bashful on the dresser, but he seemed to be staring
impudently all the time.

28   I knew nothing definite against Guy, but in Riverbend all
"traveling men" were considered worldly and wicked. He traveled for a Chicago dry-goods firm, and our fathers didn't like
him because he put extravagant ideas into our mothers' heads.
He had very smooth and flattering ways, and he introduced into
our simple community a great variety of perfumes and scented
soaps, and he always reminded me of the merchants in Cæsar,
who brought into Gaul "those things which effeminate the mind,"
as we translated that delightfully easy passage.

> merchants … mind ·
> the quote is from Julius
> Cæsar's *The Gallic Wars* 1.1

29   Nell was sitting before the dressing table in her nightgown,
holding the new fur coat and rubbing her cheek against it, when
I saw a sudden gleam of tears in her eyes. "You know, Peggy," she
said in her quick, impetuous way, "this makes me feel bad. I've
got a secret from my daddy."

30   I can see her now, so pink and eager, her brown hair in two
springy braids down her back, and her eyes shining with tears
and with something even softer and more tremulous.

31   "I'm engaged, Peggy," she whispered, "really and truly."

32   She leaned forward, unbuttoning her nightgown, and there
on her breast, hung by a little gold chain about her neck, was a
diamond ring – Guy Franklin's solitaire; every one in Riverbend
knew it well.

33   "I'm going to live in Chicago, and take singing lessons, and
go to operas, and do all those nice things – oh, everything! I
know you don't like him, Peggy, but you know you are a kid.
You'll see how it is yourself when you grow up. He's so different
from our boys, and he's just terribly in love with me. And then,
Peggy,"– flushing all down over her soft shoulders, – "I'm awfully
fond of him, too. Awfully."

34   "Are you, Nell, truly?" I whispered. She seemed so changed
to me by the warm light in her eyes and that delicate suffusion
of color. I felt as I did when I got up early on picnic mornings in
summer, and saw the dawn come up in the breathless sky above
the river meadows and make all the corn fields golden.

"Sure I do, Peggy; don't look so solemn. It's nothing to look   35
that way about, kid. It's nice." She threw her arms about me suddenly and hugged me.

"I hate to think about your going so far away from us all, Nell."   36

"Oh, you'll love to come and visit me. Just you wait."   37

She began breathlessly to go over things Guy Franklin had   38
told her about Chicago, until I seemed to see it all looming up
out there under the stars that kept watch over our little sleeping
town. We had neither of us ever been to a city, but we knew what
it would be like. We heard it throbbing like great engines, and
calling to us, that faraway world. Even after we had opened the
windows and scurried into bed, we seemed to feel a pulsation
across all the miles of snow. The winter silence trembled with
it, and the air was full of something new that seemed to break
over us in soft waves. In that snug, warm little bed I had a sense
of imminent change and danger. I was somehow afraid for Nelly
when I heard her breathing so quickly beside me, and I put my
arm about her protectingly as we drifted toward sleep.

In the following spring we were both graduated from the   39
Riverbend high school, and I went away to college. My family
moved to Denver, and during the next four years I heard very
little of Nelly Deane. My life was crowded with new people and
new experiences, and I am afraid I held her little in mind. I heard
indirectly that Jud Deane had lost what little property he owned
in a luckless venture in Cripple Creek, and that he had been able
to keep his house in Riverbend only through the clemency of his
creditors. Guy Franklin had his route changed and did not go to
Riverbend anymore. He married the daughter of a rich cattle-
man out near Long Pine, and ran a dry-goods store of his own.
Mrs. Dow wrote me a long letter about once a year, and in one
of these she told me that Nelly was teaching in the sixth grade
in the Riverbend school.

> Dear Nelly does not like teaching very well. The children   39a
> try her, and she is so pretty it seems a pity for her to be
> tied down to uncongenial employment. Scott is still very
> attentive, and I have noticed him look up at the window
> of Nelly's room in a very determined way as he goes
> home to dinner. Scott continues prosperous; he has made

39a money during these hard times and now owns both our hardware stores. He is close, but a very honorable fellow. Nelly seems to hold off, but I think Mrs. Spinny has hopes. Nothing would please her more. If Scott were more careful about his appearance, it would help. He of course gets black about his business, and Nelly, you know, is very dainty. People do say his mother does his courting for him, she is so eager. If only Scott does not turn out hard and penurious like his father! We must all have our schooling in this life, but I don't want Nelly's to be too severe. She is a dear girl, and keeps her color.

40 Mrs. Dow's own schooling had been none too easy. Her husband had long been crippled with rheumatism, and was bitter and faultfinding. Her daughters had married poorly, and one of her sons had fallen into evil ways. But her letters were always cheerful, and in one of them she gently remonstrated with me because I "seemed inclined to take a sad view of life."

41 In the winter vacation of my senior year I stopped on my way home to visit Mrs. Dow. The first thing she told me when I got into her old buckboard* at the station was that "Scott had at last prevailed," and that Nelly was to marry him in the spring. As a preliminary step, Nelly was about to join the Baptist church. "Just think, you will be here for her baptizing! How that will please Nelly! She is to be immersed tomorrow night."

buckboard · an open, flat-bottomed, four-wheeled carriage

42 I met Scott Spinny in the post office that morning and he gave me a hard grip with one black hand. There was something grim and saturnine about his powerful body and bearded face and his strong, cold hands. I wondered what perverse fate had driven him for eight years to dog the footsteps of a girl whose charm was due to qualities naturally distasteful to him. It still seems strange to me that in easygoing Riverbend, where there were so many boys who could have lived contentedly enough with my little grasshopper, it was the pushing ant* who must have her and all her careless ways.

43 By a kind of unformulated etiquette one did not call upon candidates for baptism on the day of the ceremony, so I had my first glimpse of Nelly that evening. The baptistry was a cemented pit directly under the pulpit rostrum, over which we had our stage when we sang *Queen Esther*. I sat through the sermon somewhat

grasshopper ... ant · a reference to the fable by Æsop in which a grasshopper fiddles the summer away while an ant wisely stores food

nervously. After the minister, in his long, black gown, had gone down into the water and the choir had finished singing, the door from the dressing room opened, and, led by one of the deacons, Nelly came down the steps into the pool. Oh, she looked so little and meek and chastened! Her white cashmere robe clung about her, and her brown hair was brushed straight back and hung in two soft braids from a little head bent humbly. As she stepped down into the water I shivered with the cold of it, and I remembered sharply how much I had loved her. She went down until the water was well above her waist, and stood white and small, with her hands crossed on her breast, while the minister said the words about being buried with Christ in baptism. Then, lying in his arm, she disappeared under the dark water. "It will be like that when she dies," I thought, and a quick pain caught my heart. The choir began to sing "Washed in the Blood of the Lamb"* as she rose again, the door behind the baptistry opened, revealing those three dear guardians, Mrs. Dow, Mrs. Freeze, and Mrs. Spinny, and she went up into their arms.

I went to see Nell next day, up in the little room of many memories. Such a sad, sad visit! She seemed changed – a little embarrassed and quietly despairing. We talked of many of the old Riverbend girls and boys, but she did not mention Guy Franklin or Scott Spinny, except to say that her father had got work in Scott's hardware store. She begged me, putting her hands on my shoulders with something of her old impulsiveness, to come and stay a few days with her. But I was afraid – afraid of what she might tell me and of what I might say. When I sat in that room with all her trinkets, the foolish harvest of her girlhood, lying about, and the white curtains and the little white rug, I thought of Scott Spinny with positive terror and could feel his hard grip on my hand again. I made the best excuse I could about having to hurry on to Denver; but she gave me one quick look, and her eyes ceased to plead. I saw that she understood me perfectly. We had known each other so well. Just once, when I got up to go and had trouble with my veil, she laughed her old merry laugh and told me there were some things I would never learn, for all my schooling.

The next day, when Mrs. Dow drove me down to the station to catch the morning train for Denver, I saw Nelly hurrying to school with several books under her arm. She had been working

43

44

45

"Washed … Lamb" · this hymn, also known as "Have You Been to Jesus?" (words and music A. E. Hoffman, 1878), was often associated with baptism

45 up her lessons at home, I thought. She was never quick at her books, dear Nell.

46   It was ten years before I again visited Riverbend. I had been in Rome for a long time, and had fallen into bitter homesickness. One morning, sitting among the dahlias and asters that bloom so bravely upon those gigantic heaps of earth-red ruins that were once the palaces of the Cæsars, I broke the seal of one of Mrs. Dow's long yearly letters. It brought so much sad news that I resolved then and there to go home to Riverbend, the only place that had ever really been home to me. Mrs. Dow wrote me that her husband, after years of illness, had died in the cold spell last March. "So good and patient toward the last," she wrote, "and so afraid of giving extra trouble." There was another thing she saved until the last. She wrote on and on, dear woman, about new babies and village improvements, as if she could not bear to tell me; and then it came:

46a   You will be sad to hear that two months ago our dear Nelly left us. It was a terrible blow to us all. I cannot write about it yet, I fear. I wake up every morning feeling that I ought to go to her. She went three days after her little boy was born. The baby is a fine child and will live, I think, in spite of everything. He and her little girl, now eight years old, whom she named Margaret, after you, have gone to Mrs. Spinny's. She loves them more than if they were her own. It seems as if already they had made her quite young again. I wish you could see Nelly's children.

47   Ah, that was what I wanted, to see Nelly's children! The wish came aching from my heart along with the bitter homesick tears, along with a quick, torturing recollection that flashed upon me, as I looked about and tried to collect myself, of how we two had sat in our sunny seat in the corner of the old bare schoolroom one September afternoon and learned the names of the seven hills* together. In that place, at that moment, after so many years, how it all came back to me – the warm sun on my back, the chattering girl beside me, the curly hair, the laughing yellow eyes, the stubby little finger on the page! I felt as if even then, when we sat in the sun with our heads together, it was all arranged, written out like a story that at this moment I should be sitting among

seven hills · the group of hills on which the ancient city of Rome was built

the crumbling bricks and drying grass, and she should be lying 47
in the place I knew so well, on that green hill far away.

Mrs. Dow sat with her Christmas sewing in the familiar sitting 48
room where the carpet and the wallpaper and the tablecover had
all faded into soft, dull colors, and even the chromo* of Hagar
and Ishmael* had been toned to the sobriety of age. In the bay
window the tall wire flowerstand still bore its little terraces of
potted plants, and the big fuchsia and the Martha Washington
geranium had blossomed for Christmastide. Mrs. Dow herself
did not look greatly changed to me. Her hair, thin ever since I
could remember it, was now quite white, but her spare, wiry little
person had all its old activity, and her eyes gleamed with the old
friendliness behind her silver-bowed glasses. Her gray house
dress seemed just like those she used to wear when I ran in after
school to take her angelfood cake down to the church supper.

The house sat on a hill, and from behind the geraniums I could 49
see pretty much all of Riverbend, tucked down in the soft snow,
and the air above was full of big, loose flakes, falling from a gray sky
which betokened settled weather. Indoors the hard-coal burner
made a tropical temperature, and glowed a warm orange from
its isinglass* sides. We sat and visited, the two of us, with a great
sense of comfort and completeness. I had reached Riverbend only
that morning, and Mrs. Dow, who had been haunted by thoughts
of shipwreck and suffering upon wintry seas, kept urging me to
draw nearer to the fire and suggesting incidental refreshment. We
had chattered all through the winter morning and most of the
afternoon, taking up one after another of the Riverbend girls and
boys, and agreeing that we had reason to be well satisfied with
most of them. Finally, after a long pause in which I had listened
to the contented ticking of the clock and the crackle of the coal,
I put the question I had until then held back:

"And now, Mrs. Dow, tell me about the one we loved best of 50
all. Since I got your letter I've thought of her every day. Tell me
all about Scott and Nelly."

The tears flashed behind her glasses, and she smoothed the 51
little pink bag on her knee.

"Well, dear, I'm afraid Scott proved to be a hard man, like his 52
father. But we must remember that Nelly always had Mrs. Spinny.
I never saw anything like the love there was between those two.

chromo · chromolitho-
graph; a color lithograph
Hagar and Ishmael ·
see Genesis 16:1–16

isinglass · thin, transparent sheets of mica, a
mineral resistant to heat

52 After Nelly lost her own father and mother, she looked to Mrs. Spinny for everything. When Scott was too unreasonable, his mother could 'most always prevail upon him. She never lifted a hand to fight her own battles with Scott's father, but she was never afraid to speak up for Nelly. And then Nelly took great comfort of her little girl. Such a lovely child!"

53 "Had she been very ill before the little baby came?"

54 "No, Margaret; I'm afraid 't was all because they had the wrong doctor. I feel confident that either Doctor Tom or Doctor Jones could have brought her through. But, you see, Scott had offended them both, and they'd stopped trading at his store, so he would have young Doctor Fox, a boy just out of college and a stranger. He got scared and didn't know what to do. Mrs. Spinny felt he wasn't doing right, so she sent for Mrs. Freeze and me. It seemed like Nelly had got discouraged. Scott would move into their big new house before the plastering was dry, and though 't was summer, she had taken a terrible cold that seemed to have drained her, and she took no interest in fixing the place up. Mrs. Spinny had been down with her back again and wasn't able to help, and things was just anyway. We won't talk about that, Margaret; I think 't would hurt Mrs. Spinny to have you know. She nearly died of mortification when she sent for us, and blamed her poor back. We did get Nelly fixed up nicely before she died. I prevailed upon Doctor Tom to come in at the last, and it 'most broke his heart. 'Why, Mis' Dow,' he said, 'if you'd only have come and told me how 't was, I'd have come and carried her right off in my arms.'"

55 "Oh, Mrs. Dow," I cried, "then it needn't have been? "

56 Mrs. Dow dropped her needle and clasped her hands quickly. "We mustn't look at it that way, dear," she said tremulously and a little sternly; "we mustn't let ourselves. We must just feel that our Lord wanted her then, and took her to Himself. When it was all over, she did look so like a child of God, young and trusting, like she did on her baptizing night, you remember?"

57 I felt that Mrs. Dow did not want to talk any more about Nelly then, and, indeed, I had little heart to listen; so I told her I would go for a walk, and suggested that I might stop at Mrs. Spinny's to see the children.

58 Mrs. Dow looked up thoughtfully at the clock. "I doubt if you'll find little Margaret there now. It's half-past four, and she'll

have been out of school an hour and more. She'll be most likely   58
coasting on Lupton's Hill. She usually makes for it with her sled
the minute she is out of the schoolhouse door. You know, it's the
old hill where you all used to slide. If you stop in at the church
about six o'clock, you'll likely find Mrs. Spinny there with the
baby. I promised to go down and help Mrs. Freeze finish up the
tree, and Mrs. Spinny said she'd run in with the baby, if 't wasn't
too bitter. She won't leave him alone with the Swede girl. She's
like a young woman with her first."

Lupton's Hill was at the other end of town, and when I got   59
there the dusk was thickening, drawing blue shadows over the
snowy fields. There were perhaps twenty children creeping up
the hill or whizzing down the packed sled track. When I had
been watching them for some minutes, I heard a lusty shout, and
a little red sled shot past me into the deep snow drift beyond.
The child was quite buried for a moment, then she struggled out
and stood dusting the snow from her short coat and red woolen
comforter. She wore a brown fur cap, which was too big for her
and of an old-fashioned shape, such as girls wore long ago, but
I would have known her without the cap. Mrs. Dow had said a
beautiful child, and there would not be two like this in Riverbend.
She was off before I had time to speak to her, going up the hill at
a trot, her sturdy little legs plowing through the trampled snow.
When she reached the top she never paused to take breath, but
threw herself upon her sled and came down with a whoop that
was quenched only by the deep drift at the end.

"Are you Margaret Spinny?" I asked as she struggled out in a   60
cloud of snow.

"Yes, 'm." She approached me with frank curiosity, pulling her   61
little sled behind her. "Are you the strange lady staying at Mrs.
Dow's?" I nodded, and she began to look my clothes over with
respectful interest.

"Your grandmother is to be at the church at six o'clock,   62
isn't she?"

"Yes, 'm."   63

"Well, suppose we walk up there now. It's nearly six, and all   64
the other children are going home." She hesitated, and looked
up at the faintly gleaming track on the hill slope. "Do you want
another slide? Is that it?" I asked.

65   "Do you mind?" she asked shyly.

66   "No. I'll wait for you. Take your time; don't run."

67   Two little boys were still hanging about the slide, and they cheered her as she came down, her comforter streaming in the wind.

68   "Now," she announced, getting up out of the drift, "I'll show you where the church is."

69   "Shall I tie your comforter again?"

70   "No, 'm, thanks. I'm plenty warm." She put her mittened hand confidingly in mine and trudged along beside me.

71   Mrs. Dow must have heard us tramping up the snowy steps of the church, for she met us at the door. Every one had gone except the old ladies. A kerosene lamp flickered over the Sunday school chart, with the lesson-picture of the Wise Men, and the little barrel stove threw out a deep glow over the three white heads that bent above the baby. There the three friends sat, patting him, and smoothing his dress, and playing with his hands, which made theirs look so brown.

72   "You ain't seen nothing finer in all your travels," said Mrs. Spinny, and they all laughed.

73   They showed me his full chest and how strong his back was; had me feel the golden fuzz on his head, and made him look at me with his round, bright eyes. He laughed and reared himself in my arms as I took him up and held him close to me. He was so warm and tingling with life, and he had the flush of new beginnings, of the new morning and the new rose. He seemed to have come so lately from his mother's heart! It was as if I held her youth and all her young joy. As I put my cheek down against his, he spied a pink flower in my hat, and making a gleeful sound, he lunged at it with both fists.

74   "Don't let him spoil it," murmured Mrs. Spinny. "He loves color so – like Nelly."

Katherine Anne Porter

◀(1890–1980)▶

Porter was born in a log cabin in Indian Creek, Texas. Her early life was marked by poverty and little formal education. Marriage brought Porter into contact with Roman Catholicism, and she was baptized into the church in 1910. Many of her stories are set in the South, the Southwest, or in Mexico – "my familiar country," as she called it. Despite her assertions that Catholicism was not a significant intellectual influence, a wistful Catholic consciousness is sometimes detectable in her work. In her twenties, Porter wrote and burned "trunksful" of manuscripts, making no attempt to publish until she was thirty. This rigorous apprenticeship and ruthless selectivity account for the stylistic excellence of her work, an estimate on which virtually all critics agree. Of her literary art Porter has said, "My whole attempt has been to discover and understand human motives, human feeling, to make a distillation of what human relations and experiences my mind has been able to absorb." The Collected Stories *(1965) won a Pulitzer Prize, and her only novel,* Ship of Fools *(1962), was converted into an award-winning movie.*

ROPE

1   O N THE THIRD DAY after they moved to the country he came walking back from the village carrying a basket of groceries and a twenty-four-yard coil of rope. She came out to meet him, wiping her hands on her green smock. Her hair was tumbled, her nose was scarlet with sunburn; he told her that already she looked like a born country woman. His gray flannel shirt stuck to him, his heavy shoes were dusty. She assured him he looked like a rural character in a play.

2   Had he brought the coffee? She had been waiting all day long for coffee. They had forgot it when they ordered at the store the first day.

Gosh, no, he hadn't. Lord, now he'd have to go back. Yes, he 3
would if it killed him. He thought, though, he had everything else.
She reminded him it was only because he didn't drink coffee himself.
If he did he would remember it quick enough. Suppose they ran
out of cigarettes? Then she saw the rope. What was that for? Well,
he thought it might do to hang clothes on, or something. Naturally
she asked him if he thought they were going to run a laundry? They
already had a fifty-foot line hanging right before his eyes? Why,
hadn't he noticed it, really? It was a blot on the landscape to her.

He thought there were a lot of things a rope might come in 4
handy for. She wanted to know what, for instance. He thought
a few seconds, but nothing occurred. They could wait and see,
couldn't they? You need all sorts of strange odds and ends around
a place in the country. She said, yes, that was so; but she thought
just at that time when every penny counted, it seemed funny to
buy more rope. That was all. She hadn't meant anything else. She
hadn't just seen, not at first, why he felt it was necessary.

Well, thunder, he had bought it because he wanted to, and that 5
was all there was to it. She thought that was reason enough, and
couldn't understand why he hadn't said so, at first. Undoubtedly it
would be useful, twenty-four yards of rope, there were hundreds of
things, she couldn't think of any at the moment, but it would come
in. Of course. As he had said, things always did in the country.

But she was a little disappointed about the coffee, and oh, look, 6
look, look at the eggs! Oh, my, they're all running! What had he
put on top of them? Hadn't he known eggs mustn't be squeezed?
Squeezed, who had squeezed them, he wanted to know. What a
silly thing to say. He had simply brought them along in the basket
with the other things. If they got broke it was the grocer's fault.
He should know better than to put heavy things on top of eggs.

She believed it was the rope. That was the heaviest thing in 7
the pack, she saw him plainly when he came in from the road,
the rope was a big package on top of everything. He desired the
whole wide world to witness that this was not a fact. He had
carried the rope in one hand and the basket in the other, and
what was the use of her having eyes if that was the best they
could do for her?

Well, anyhow, she could see one thing plain: no eggs for break- 8
fast. They'd have to scramble them now, for supper. It was too

8   damned bad. She had planned to have steak for supper. No ice, meat wouldn't keep. He wanted to know why she couldn't finish breaking the eggs in a bowl and set them in a cool place.

9   Cool place! If he could find one for her, she'd be glad to set them there. Well, then, it seemed to him they might very well cook the meat at the same time they cooked the eggs and then warm up the meat for tomorrow. The idea simply choked her. Warmed-over meat, when they might as well have had it fresh. Second best and scraps and makeshifts, even to the meat! He rubbed her shoulder a little. It doesn't really matter so much, does it, darling? Sometimes when they were playful, he would rub her shoulder and she would arch and purr. This time she hissed and almost clawed. He was getting ready to say that they could surely manage somehow when she turned on him and said, if he told her they could manage somehow she would certainly slap his face.

10   He swallowed the words red hot, his face burned. He picked up the rope and started to put it on the top shelf. She would not have it on the top shelf, the jars and tins belonged there; positively she would not have the top shelf cluttered up with a lot of rope. She had borne all the clutter she meant to bear in the flat in town, there was space here at least and she meant to keep things in order.

11   Well, in that case, he wanted to know what the hammer and nails were doing up there? And why had she put them there when she knew very well he needed that hammer and those nails upstairs to fix the window sashes?* She simply slowed down everything and made double work on the place with her insane habit of changing things around and hiding them.

window sashes · the wooden casements that hold the glass panes

12   She was sure she begged his pardon, and if she had had any reason to believe he was going to fix the sashes this summer she would have left the hammer and nails right where he put them; in the middle of the bedroom floor where they could step on them in the dark. And now if he didn't clear the whole mess out of there she would throw them down the well.

13   Oh, all right, all right – could he put them in the closet? Naturally not, there were brooms and mops and dustpans in the closet, and why couldn't he find a place for his rope outside her kitchen? Had he stopped to consider there were seven God-forsaken rooms in the house, and only one kitchen?

He wanted to know what of it? And did she realize she was 14
making a complete fool of herself? And what did she take him
for, a three-year-old idiot? The whole trouble with her was she
needed something weaker than she was to heckle and tyrannize
over. He wished to God now they had a couple of children she
could take it out on. Maybe he'd get some rest.

Her face changed at this, she reminded him he had forgot 15
the coffee and had bought a worthless piece of rope. And when
she thought of all the things they actually needed to make the
place even decently fit to live in, well, she could cry, that was all.
She looked so forlorn, so lost and despairing he couldn't believe
it was only a piece of rope that was causing all the racket. What
was the matter, for God's sake?

Oh, would he please hush and go away, and *stay* away, if he 16
could, for five minutes? By all means, yes, he would. He'd stay
away indefinitely if she wished. Lord, yes, there was nothing he'd
like better than to clear out and never come back. She couldn't
for the life of her see what was holding him, then. It was a swell
time. Here she was, stuck, miles from a railroad, with a half-
empty house on her hands, and not a penny in her pocket, and
everything on earth to do; it seemed the God-sent moment for
him to get out from under. She was surprised he hadn't stayed
in town as it was until she had come out and done the work and
got things straightened out. It was his usual trick.

It appeared to him that this was going a little far. Just a touch 17
out of bounds, if she didn't mind his saying so. Why the hell had
he stayed in town the summer before? To do a half-dozen extra
jobs to get the money he had sent her. That was it. She knew perfectly well they couldn't have done it otherwise. She had agreed
with him at the time. And that was the only time so help him he
had ever left her to do anything by herself.

Oh, he could tell that to his great-grandmother. She had her 18
notion of what had kept him in town. Considerably more than a
notion, if he wanted to know. So, she was going to bring all that
up again, was she? Well, she could just think what she pleased.
He was tired of explaining. It may have looked funny but he had
simply got hooked in, and what could he do? It was impossible to
believe that she was going to take it seriously. Yes, yes, she knew
how it was with a man: if he was left by himself a minute, some

18 woman was certain to kidnap him. And naturally he couldn't hurt her feelings by refusing!

19   Well, what was she raving about? Did she forget she had told him those two weeks alone in the country were the happiest she had known for four years? And how long had they been married when she said that? All right, shut up! If she thought that hadn't stuck in his craw.

20   She hadn't meant she was happy because she was away from him. She meant she was happy getting the devilish house nice and ready for him. That was what she had meant, and now look! Bringing up something she had said a year ago simply to justify himself for forgetting her coffee and breaking the eggs and buying a wretched piece of rope they couldn't afford. She really thought it was time to drop the subject, and now she wanted only two things in the world. She wanted him to get that rope from underfoot, and go back to the village and get her coffee, and if he could remember it, he might bring a metal mitt for the skillets, and two more curtain rods, and if there were any rubber gloves in the village, her hands were simply raw, and a bottle of milk of magnesia* from the drugstore.

milk of magnesia · a common medication used as a laxative

21   He looked out at the dark blue afternoon sweltering on the slopes, and mopped his forehead and sighed heavily and said, if only she could wait a minute for *anything*, he was going back. He had said so, hadn't he, the very instant they found he had overlooked it?

22   Oh, yes, well … run along. She was going to wash windows. The country was so beautiful! She doubted they'd have a moment to enjoy it. He meant to go, but he could not until he had said that if she wasn't such a hopeless melancholiac* she might see that this was only for a few days. Couldn't she remember anything pleasant about the other summers? Hadn't they ever had any fun? She hadn't time to talk about it, and now would he please not leave that rope lying around for her to trip on? He picked it up, somehow it had toppled off the table, and walked out with it under his arm.

melancholiac · depressive personality

23   Was he going this minute? He certainly was. She thought so. Sometimes it seemed to her he had second sight about the precisely perfect moment to leave her ditched. She had meant to put the mattresses out to sun, if they put them out this minute

they would get at least three hours, he must have heard her say 23
that morning she meant to put them out. So of course he would
walk off and leave her to it. She supposed he thought the exercise
would do her good.

Well, he was merely going to get her coffee. A four-mile walk 24
for two pounds of coffee was ridiculous, but he was perfectly
willing to do it. The habit was making a wreck of her, but if she
wanted to wreck herself there was nothing he could do about it.
If he thought it was coffee that was making a wreck of her, she
congratulated him: he must have a damned easy conscience.

Conscience or no conscience, he didn't see why the mattresses 25
couldn't very well wait until tomorrow. And anyhow, for God's
sake, were they living in the house, or were they going to let the
house ride them to death? She paled at this, her face grew livid
about the mouth, she looked quite dangerous, and reminded
him that housekeeping was no more her work than it was his:
she had other work to do as well, and when did he think she was
going to find time to do it at this rate?

Was she going to start on that again? She knew as well as he 26
did that his work brought in the regular money, hers was only
occasional, if they depended on what *she* made – and she might
as well get straight on this question once for all!

That was positively not the point. The question was, when 27
both of them were working on their own time, was there going
to be a division of the housework, or wasn't there? She merely
wanted to know, she had to make her plans. Why, he thought that
was all arranged. It was understood that he was to help. Hadn't
he always, in summers?

Hadn't he, though? Oh, just hadn't he? And when, and where, 28
and doing what? Lord, what an uproarious joke!

It was such a very uproarious joke that her face turned slightly 29
purple, and she screamed with laughter. She laughed so hard
she had to sit down, and finally a rush of tears spurted from her
eyes and poured down into the lifted corners of her mouth. He
dashed towards her and dragged her up to her feet and tried
to pour water on her head. The dipper hung by a string on a
nail and he broke it loose. Then he tried to pump water with
one hand while she struggled in the other. So he gave it up and
shook her instead.

30   She wrenched away, crying out for him to take his rope and go
to hell, she had simply given him up: and ran. He heard her high-
heeled bedroom slippers clattering and stumbling on the stairs.

31   He went out around the house and into the lane; he suddenly
realized he had a blister on his heel and his shirt felt as if it were
on fire. Things broke so suddenly you didn't know where you
were. She could work herself into a fury about simply nothing.
She was terrible, damn it: not an ounce of reason. You might as
well talk to a sieve as that woman when she got going. Damned if
he'd spend his life humoring her! Well, what to do now? He would
take back the rope and exchange it for something else. Things
accumulated, things were mountainous, you couldn't move them
or sort them out or get rid of them. They just lay and rotted
around. He'd take it back. Hell, why should he? He wanted it.
What was it anyhow? A piece of rope. Imagine anybody caring
more about a piece of rope than about a man's feelings. What
earthly right had she to say a word about it? He remembered
all the useless, meaningless things she bought for herself: Why?
because I wanted it, that's why! He stopped and selected a large
stone by the road. He would put the rope behind it. He would
put it in the tool-box when he got back. He'd heard enough about
it to last him a life-time.

32   When he came back she was leaning against the post box
beside the road waiting. It was pretty late, the smell of broiled
steak floated nose high in the cooling air. Her face was young
and smooth and fresh-looking. Her unmanageable funny black
hair was all on end. She waved to him from a distance, and he
speeded up. She called out that supper was ready and waiting,
was he starved?

33   You bet he was starved. Here was the coffee. He waved it at
her. She looked at his other hand. What was that he had there?

34   Well, it was the rope again. He stopped short. He had meant
to exchange it but forgot. She wanted to know why he should
exchange it, if it was something he really wanted. Wasn't the air
sweet now, and wasn't it fine to be here?

35   She walked beside him with one hand hooked into his leather
belt. She pulled and jostled him a little as he walked, and leaned
against him. He put his arm clear around her and patted her
stomach. They exchanged wary smiles. Coffee, coffee for the

Ootsum Wootsums! He felt as if he were bringing her a beauti- 35
ful present.

He was a love, she firmly believed, and if she had had her coffee 36
in the morning, she wouldn't have behaved so funny…. There was
a whippoorwill still coming back, imagine, clear out of season,
sitting in the crab-apple tree calling all by himself. Maybe his girl
stood him up. Maybe she did. She hoped to hear him once more,
she loved whippoorwills…. He knew how she was, didn't he?

Sure, he knew how she was. 37

Isaac Bashevis Singer

◄(1904–1991)►

Singer was educated in a rabbinical seminary in Warsaw, Poland, and immigrated to New York City in 1935, thereby escaping the Holocaust. His writing career began with sketches of village life, composed in Yiddish and collaboratively translated, in The Jewish Daily Forward. *In his artistic maturity, these sketches broadened into the 19th century Jewish society of Eastern Europe, a society characterized by fervent otherworldly faith but simultaneously by the doubt and materialism brought about by Western Enlightenment. Singer's world is one in which characters are often forced to acknowledge that unbelief, intellectually tempting though it may be, is inimical to human happiness. His most memorable creations are Jewish doubters who eventually flee to their religious heritage as a bastion of human worth and meaning in the face of Western society's atheistic drift. Though not morality tales, his works are constructed, Singer has said, around a moral point of view: "I even would go so far as to say that any writer who does not think in terms of good and evil cannot go very far in his writing." Singer was awarded the Nobel Prize for Literature in 1978.*

GIMPEL THE FOOL

1

1 I AM GIMPEL THE FOOL. I don't think myself a fool. On the contrary. But that's what folks call me. They gave me the name while I was still in school. I had seven names in all: imbecile, donkey, flax-head, dope, glump, ninny, and fool. The last name stuck. What did my foolishness consist of? I was easy to take in. They said, "Gimpel, you know the rabbi's wife has been brought to childbed?" So I skipped school. Well, it turned out to be a lie. How was I supposed to know? She hadn't had a big belly. But I

never looked at her belly. Was that really so foolish? The gang laughed and hee-hawed, stomped and danced and chanted a good-night prayer. And instead of the raisins they give when a woman's lying in, they stuffed my hand full of goat turds. I was no weakling. If I slapped someone he'd see all the way to Cracow.• But I'm really not a slugger by nature. I think to myself: Let it pass. So they take advantage of me.

I was coming home from school and heard a dog barking. I'm not afraid of dogs, but of course I never want to start up with them. One of them may be mad, and if he bites there's not a Tartar• in the world who can help you. So I made tracks. Then I looked around and saw the whole market place wild with laughter. It was no dog at all but Wolf-Leib the Thief. How was I supposed to know it was he? It sounded like a howling bitch.

When the pranksters and leg-pullers found that I was easy to fool, every one of them tried his luck with me. "Gimpel, the Czar• is coming to Frampol; Gimpel, the moon fell down in Turbeen; Gimpel, little Hodel Furpiece found a treasure behind the bath-house." And I like a *golem*• believed everyone. In the first place, everything is possible, as it is written in The Wisdom of the Fathers,• I've forgotten just how. Second, I had to believe when the whole town came down on me! If I ever dared to say, "Ah, you're kidding!" there was trouble. People got angry. "What do you mean! You want to call everyone a liar?" What was I to do? I believed them, and I hope at least that did them some good.

I was an orphan. My grandfather who brought me up was already bent toward the grave. So they turned me over to a baker, and what a time they gave me there! Every woman or girl who came to bake a batch of noodles had to fool me at least once. "Gimpel, there's a fair in heaven; Gimpel, the rabbi gave birth to a calf in the seventh month; Gimpel, a cow flew over the roof and laid brass eggs." A student from the *yeshiva*• came once to buy a roll, and he said, "You, Gimpel, while you stand here scraping with your baker's shovel the Messiah has come. The dead have arisen." "What do you mean?" I said. "I heard no one blowing the ram's horn!" He said, "Are you deaf?" And all began to cry, "We heard it, we heard!" Then in came Rietze the Candle-dipper and called out in her hoarse voice, "Gimpel, your father and mother have stood up from the grave. They're looking for you."

Cracow • the city of Kraków, on the Vistula river in southern Poland

Tarter • named for a warlike tribe that settled in west-central Russia, a notably strong, resource-ful or violent person

Czar • the ruler of Russia under the monarchial system

golem • an artificial person; a human simulacrum (Hebrew)

Wisdom of the Fathers • the *Mishna*, a collection of rabbinic sayings and wisdom

yeshiva • an academy of Talmudic learning, where students study biblical and legal exegesis and the appli-cation of Scripture

5   To tell the truth, I knew very well that nothing of the sort had happened, but all the same, as folks were talking, I threw on my wool vest and went out. Maybe something had happened. What did I stand to lose by looking? Well, what a cat music went up! And then I took a vow to believe nothing more. But that was no go either. They confused me so that I didn't know the big end from the small.

6   I went to the rabbi to get some advice. He said, "It is written, better to be a fool all your days than for one hour to be evil. You are not a fool. They are the fools. For he who causes his neighbor to feel shame loses Paradise himself." Nevertheless the rabbi's daughter took me in. As I left the rabbinical court she said, "Have you kissed the wall yet?" I said, "No; what for?" She answered, "It's the law; you've got to do it after every visit." Well, there didn't seem to be any harm in it. And she burst out laughing. It was a fine trick. She put one over on me, all right.

7   I wanted to go off to another town, but then everyone got busy matchmaking, and they were after me so they nearly tore my coat tails off. They talked at me and talked until I got water on the ear. She was no chaste maiden, but they told me she was virgin pure. She had a limp, and they said it was deliberate, from coyness. She had a bastard, and they told me the child was her little brother. I cried, "You're wasting your time. I'll never marry that whore." But they said indignantly, "What a way to talk! Aren't you ashamed of yourself? We can take you to the rabbi and have you fined for giving her a bad name." I saw then that I wouldn't escape them so easily and I thought: They're set on making me their butt. But when you're married the husband's the master, and if that's all right with her it's agreeable to me too. Besides, you can't pass through life unscathed, nor expect to.

8   I went to her clay house, which was built on the sand, and the whole gang, hollering and chorusing, came after me. They acted like bear-baiters.* When we came to the well they stopped all the same. They were afraid to start anything with Elka. Her mouth would open as if it were on a hinge, and she had a fierce tongue. I entered the house. Lines were strung from wall to wall and clothes were drying. Barefoot she stood by the tub, doing the wash. She was dressed in a worn hand-me-down gown of plush. She had her hair put up in braids and pinned across her head. It took my breath away, almost, the reek of it all.

bear-baiters · bear-baiting is a sport (now outlawed) in which dogs are allowed to harass a chained bear

Evidently she knew who I was. She took a look at me and said, 9
"Look who's here! He's come, the drip. Grab a seat."

I told her all; I denied nothing. "Tell me the truth," I said, "are 10
you really a virgin, and is that mischievous Yechiel actually your
little brother? Don't be deceitful with me, for I'm an orphan."

"I'm an orphan myself," she answered, "and whoever tries to
twist you up, may the end of his nose take a twist. But don't let
them think they can take advantage of me. I want a dowry of fifty
guilders, and let them take up a collection besides. Otherwise
they can kiss my you-know-what." She was very plainspoken. I
said, "It's the bride and not the groom who gives a dowry." Then
she said, "Don't bargain with me. Either a flat 'yes' or a flat
'no'– Go back where you came from."

I thought: No bread will ever be baked from *this* dough. But 11
ours is not a poor town. They consented to everything and
proceeded with the wedding. It so happened that there was a
dysentery epidemic at the time. The ceremony was held at the
cemetery gates, near the little corpse-washing hut. The fellows
got drunk. While the marriage contract was being drawn up I
heard the most pious high rabbi ask, "Is the bride a widow or a
divorced woman?" And the sexton's wife answered for her, "Both
a widow and divorced." It was a black moment for me. But what
was I to do, run away from under the marriage canopy?

There was singing and dancing. An old granny danced oppo- 12
site me, hugging a braided white *chalah.* The master of revels
made a "God 'a mercy" in memory of the bride's parents. The
schoolboys threw burrs, as on *Tishe b'Av* fast day. There were a
lot of gifts after the sermon: a noodle board, a kneading trough,
a bucket, brooms, ladles, household articles galore. Then I took a
look and saw two strapping young men carrying a crib. "What do
we need this for?" I asked. So they said, "Don't rack your brains
about it. It's all right, it'll come in handy." I realized I was going
to be rooked. Take it another way though, what did I stand to
lose? I reflected: I'll see what comes of it. A whole town can't go
altogether crazy.

chalah · a type of
braided bread eaten on
ceremonial occasions
(Hebrew)

Tishe b'Av fast day · a
Jewish fast that takes
place in late July or early
August commemorat-
ing the destruction of
the Temple

2

AT NIGHT I CAME WHERE MY wife lay, but she wouldn't let me 13
in. "Say, look here, is this what they married us for?" I said.

13 And she said, "My monthly has come." "But yesterday they took you to the ritual bath, and that's afterward, isn't it supposed to be?" "Today isn't yesterday," said she, "and yesterday's not today. You can beat it if you don't like it." In short, I waited.

14 Not four months later she was in childbed. The townsfolk hid their laughter with their knuckles. But what could I do? She suffered intolerable pains and clawed at the walls. "Gimpel," she cried, "I'm going. Forgive me!" The house filled with women. They were boiling pans of water. The screams rose to the welkin.·

welkin · the sky, viewed as a curved roof above the earth

The thing to do was to go to the House of Prayer to repeat Psalms, and that was what I did.

15 The townsfolk liked that, all right. I stood in a corner saying Psalms and prayers, and they shook their heads at me. "Pray, pray!" they told me. "Prayer never made any woman pregnant." One of the congregation put a straw to my mouth and said, "Hay for the cows." There was something to that too, by God!

16 She gave birth to a boy. Friday at the synagogue the sexton·stood up before the Ark,· pounded on the reading table, and announced, "The wealthy Reb Gimpel invites the congregation to a feast in honor of the birth of a son." The whole House of Prayer rang with laughter. My face was flaming. But there was nothing I could do. After all, I *was* the one responsible for the circumcision honors and rituals.

sexton · the caretaker of the synagogue who announces worship

the Ark · in Jewish synagogues, an ornate cabinet that enshrines the sacred Torah scrolls used for public worship

17 Half the town came running. You couldn't wedge another soul in. Women brought peppered chick-peas, and there was a keg of beer from the tavern. I ate and drank as much as anyone, and they all congratulated me. Then there was a circumcision, and I named the boy after my father, may he rest in peace. When all were gone and I was left with my wife alone, she thrust her head through the bed-curtain and called me to her.

18 "Gimpel," said she, "why are you silent? Has your ship gone and sunk?"

19 "What shall I say?" I answered. "A fine thing you've done to me! If my mother had known of it she'd have died a second time."

20 She said, "Are you crazy, or what?"

21 "How can you make such a fool," I said, "of one who should be the lord and master?"

22 "What's the matter with you?" she said. "What have you taken it into your head to imagine?"

I saw that I must speak bluntly and openly. "Do you think this   23
is the way to use an orphan?" I said. "You have borne a bastard."
She answered, "Drive this foolishness out of your head. The
child is yours."

"How can he be mine?" I argued. "He was born seventeen   24
weeks after the wedding."

She told me then that he was premature. I said, "Isn't he a   25
little too premature?" She said, she had had a grandmother who
carried just as short a time and she resembled this grandmother
of hers as one drop of water does another. She swore to it with
such oaths that you would have believed a peasant at the fair if
he had used them. To tell the plain truth, I didn't believe her; but
when I talked it over next day with the schoolmaster he told me
that the very same thing had happened to Adam and Eve. Two
they went up to bed, and four they descended.

"There isn't a woman in the world who is not the granddaugh-   26
ter of Eve," he said.

That was how it was; they argued me dumb. But then, who   27
really knows how such things are?

I began to forget my sorrow. I loved the child madly, and he   28
loved me too. As soon as he saw me he'd wave his little hands
and want me to pick him up, and when he was colicky I was
the only one who could pacify him. I bought him a little bone
teething ring and a little gilded cap. He was forever catching the
evil eye from someone, and then I had to run to get one of those
abracadabras for him that would get him out of it. I worked like
an ox. You know how expenses go up when there's an infant in
the house. I don't want to lie about it; I didn't dislike Elka either,
for that matter. She swore at me and cursed, and I couldn't get
enough of her. What strength she had! One of her looks could rob
you of the power of speech. And her orations! Pitch and sulphur,
that's what they were full of, and yet somehow also full of charm.
I adored her every word. She gave me bloody wounds though.

In the evening I brought her a white loaf as well as a dark   29
one, and also poppyseed rolls I baked myself. I thieved because
of her and swiped everything I could lay hands on: macaroons,
raisins, almonds, cakes. I hope I may be forgiven for stealing from
the Saturday pots the women left to warm in the baker's oven.
I would take out scraps of meat, a chunk of pudding, a chicken

29 leg or head, a piece of tripe, whatever I could nip quickly. She ate and became fat and handsome.

30 I had to sleep away from home all during the week, at the bakery. On Friday nights when I got home she always made an excuse of some sort. Either she had heartburn, or a stitch in the side, or hiccups, or headaches. You know what women's excuses are. I had a bitter time of it. It was rough. To add to it, this little brother of hers, the bastard, was growing bigger. He'd put lumps on me, and when I wanted to hit back she'd open her mouth and curse so powerfully I saw a green haze floating before my eyes. Ten times a day she threatened to divorce me. Another man in my place would have taken French leave* and disappeared. But I'm the type that bears it and says nothing. What's one to do? Shoulders are from God, and burdens too.

French leave · to leave the army without permission, to desert

31 One night there was a calamity in the bakery; the oven burst, and we almost had a fire. There was nothing to do but go home, so I went home. Let me, I thought, also taste the joy of sleeping in bed in mid-week. I didn't want to wake the sleeping mite and tiptoed into the house. Coming in, it seemed to me that I heard not the snoring of one but, as it were, a double snore, one a thin enough snore and the other like the snoring of a slaughtered ox. Oh, I didn't like that! I didn't like it at all. I went up to the bed, and things suddenly turned black. Next to Elka lay a man's form. Another in my place would have made an uproar, and enough noise to rouse the whole town, but the thought occurred to me that I might wake the child. A little thing like that – why frighten a little swallow, I thought. All right then, I went back to the bakery and stretched out on a sack of flour and till morning I never shut an eye. I shivered as if I had had malaria. "Enough of being a donkey," I said to myself. "Gimpel isn't going to be a sucker all his life. There's a limit even to the foolishness of a fool like Gimpel."

32 In the morning I went to the rabbi to get advice, and it made a great commotion in the town. They sent the beadle* for Elka right away. She came, carrying the child. And what do you think she did? She denied it, denied everything, bone and stone! "He's out of his head," she said. "I know nothing of dreams or divinations." They yelled at her, warned her, hammered on the table, but she stuck to her guns: it was a false accusation, she said.

beadle · a minor synagogue official whose duties include ushering and keeping order

33 The butchers and the horse-traders took her part. One of the lads from the slaughterhouse came by and said to me, "We've

got our eye on you, you're a marked man." Meanwhile the child 33
started to bear down and soiled itself. In the rabbinical court
there was an Ark of the Covenant, and they couldn't allow that,
so they sent Elka away. I said to the rabbi, "What shall I do?"

"You must divorce her at once," said he. 34

"And what if she refuses?" I asked. 35

He said, "You must serve the divorce. That's all you'll have to do." 36

I said, "Well, all right, Rabbi. Let me think about it." 37

"There's nothing to think about," said he. "You mustn't remain 38
under the same roof with her."

"And if I want to see the child?" I asked. 39

"Let her go, the harlot," said he, "and her brood of bastards 40
with her."

The verdict he gave was that I mustn't even cross her thresh- 41
old – never again, as long as I should live.

During the day it didn't bother me so much. I thought: It was 42
bound to happen, the abscess had to burst. But at night when I
stretched out upon the sacks I felt it all very bitterly. A longing
took me, for her and for the child. I wanted to be angry, but that's
my misfortune exactly, I don't have it in me to be really angry. In
the first place – this was how my thoughts went – there's bound to
be a slip sometimes. You can't live without errors. Probably that
lad who was with her led her on and gave her presents and what
not, and women are often long on hair and short on sense, and so
he got around her. And then since she denies it so, maybe I was
only seeing things? Hallucinations do happen. You see a figure or a
mannikin or something, but when you come up closer it's nothing,
there's not a thing there. And if that's so, I'm doing her an injustice.
And when I got so far in my thoughts I started to weep. I sobbed so
that I wet the flour where I lay. In the morning I went to the rabbi
and told him that I had made a mistake. The rabbi wrote on with
his quill, and he said that if that were so he would have to reconsider
the whole case. Until he had finished I wasn't to go near my wife,
but I might send her bread and money by messenger.

3

NINE MONTHS PASSED before all the rabbis could come to 43
an agreement. Letters went back and forth. I hadn't realized
that there could be so much erudition about a matter like this.

44   Meanwhile Elka gave birth to still another child, a girl this time. On the Sabbath I went to the synagogue and invoked a blessing on her. They called me up to the *Torah,** and I named the child for my mother-in-law — may she rest in peace. The louts and loudmouths of the town who came into the bakery gave me a going over. All Frampol refreshed its spirits because of my trouble and grief. However, I resolved that I would always believe what I was told. What's the good of *not* believing? Today it's your wife you don't believe; tomorrow it's God Himself you won't take stock in.

Torah · the written scroll of Scriptures housed in the Ark

45   By an apprentice who was her neighbor I sent her daily a corn or a wheat loaf, or a piece of pastry, rolls or bagels, or, when I got the chance, a slab of pudding, a slice of honeycake, or wedding strudel — whatever came my way. The apprentice was a good-hearted lad, and more than once he added something on his own. He had formerly annoyed me a lot, plucking my nose and digging me in the ribs, but when he started to be a visitor to my house he became kind and friendly. "Hey, you, Gimpel," he said to me, "you have a very decent little wife and two fine kids. You don't deserve them."

46   "But the things people say about her," I said.

47   "Well, they have long tongues," he said, "and nothing to do with them but babble. Ignore it as you ignore the cold of last winter." One day the rabbi sent for me and said, "Are you certain, Gimpel, that you were wrong about your wife?"

48   I said, "I'm certain."

49   "Why, but look here! You yourself saw it."

50   "It must have been a shadow," I said.

51   "The shadow of what?"

52   "Just of one of the beams, I think."

53   "You can go home then. You owe thanks to the Yanover rabbi. He found an obscure reference in Maimonides** that favored you."

Maimonides · Moses Maimonides (1135–1204), Jewish scholastic philosopher

54   I seized the rabbi's hand and kissed it.

55   I wanted to run home immediately. It's no small thing to be separated for so long a time from wife and child. Then I reflected: I'd better go back to work now, and go home in the evening. I said nothing to any one, although as far as my heart was concerned it was like one of the Holy Days. The women teased and twitted me as they did every day, but my thought was: Go on, with your loose

talk. The truth is out, like the oil upon the water. Maimonides   55
says it's right, and therefore it is right!

At night, when I had covered the dough to let it rise, I took   56
my share of bread and a little sack of flour and started homeward.
The moon was full and the stars were glistening, something to
terrify the soul. I hurried onward, and before me darted a long
shadow. It was winter, and a fresh snow had fallen. I had a mind
to sing, but it was growing late and I didn't want to wake the
householders. Then I felt like whistling, but I remembered that
you don't whistle at night because it brings the demons out. So
I was silent and walked as fast as I could.

Dogs in the Christian yards barked at me when I passed, but   57
I thought: Bark your teeth out! What are you but mere dogs?
Whereas I am a man, the husband of a fine wife, the father of
promising children.

As I approached the house my heart started to pound as   58
though it were the heart of a criminal. I felt no fear, but my heart
went thump! thump! Well, no drawing back. I quietly lifted the
latch and went in. Elka was asleep. I looked at the infant's cradle.
The shutter was closed, but the moon forced its way through the
cracks. I saw the newborn child's face and loved it as soon as I
saw it – immediately – each tiny bone.

Then I came nearer to the bed. And what did I see but the   59
apprentice lying there beside Elka. The moon went out all at once. It
was utterly black, and I trembled. My teeth chattered. The bread fell
from my hands, and my wife waked and said, "Who is that, ah?"

I muttered, "It's me."   60

"Gimpel?" she asked. "How come you're here? I thought it   61
was forbidden."

"The rabbi said," I answered and shook as with a fever.   62

"Listen to me, Gimpel," she said, "go out to the shed and see   63
if the goat's all right. It seems she's been sick." I have forgotten
to say that we had a goat. When I heard she was unwell I went
into the yard. The nannygoat was a good little creature. I had a
nearly human feeling for her.

With hesitant steps I went up to the shed and opened the door.   64
The goat stood there on her four feet. I felt her everywhere, drew
her by the horns, examined her udders, and found nothing wrong.
She had probably eaten too much bark. "Good night, little goat,"

64 I said. "Keep well." And the little beast answered with a "maa" as though to thank me for the good will.

65 I went back. The apprentice had vanished.

66 "Where," I asked, "is the lad?"

67 "What lad?" my wife answered.

68 "What do you mean?" I said. "The apprentice. You were sleeping with him."

69 "The things I have dreamed this night and the night before," she said, "may they come true and lay you low, body and soul! An evil spirit has taken root in you and dazzles your sight." She screamed out, "You hateful creature! You moon calf!* You spook! You uncouth man! Get out, or I'll scream all Frampol out of bed!"

moon calf · an unnatural or dangerous magical creature

70 Before I could move, her brother sprang out from behind the oven and struck me a blow on the back of the head. I thought he had broken my neck. I felt that something about me was deeply wrong, and I said, "Don't make a scandal. All that's needed now is that people should accuse me of raising spooks and *dybbuks.*"* For that was what she had meant. "No one will touch bread of my baking."

dybbuks · wandering spirits of the dead (Yiddish)

71 In short, I somehow calmed her.

72 "Well," she said, "that's enough. Lie down, and be shattered by wheels."

73 Next morning I called the apprentice aside. "Listen here, brother!" I said. And so on and so forth. "What do you say?" He stared at me as though I had dropped from the roof or something. "I swear," he said, "you'd better go to an herb doctor or some healer. I'm afraid you have a screw loose, but I'll hush it up for you." And that's how the thing stood.

74 To make a long story short, I lived twenty years with my wife. She bore me six children, four daughters and two sons. All kinds of things happened, but I neither saw nor heard. I believed, and that's all. The rabbi recently said to me, "Belief in itself is beneficial. It is written that a good man lives by his faith."

75 Suddenly my wife took sick. It began with a trifle, a little growth upon the breast. But she evidently was not destined to live long; she had no years. I spent a fortune on her. I have forgotten to say that by this time I had a bakery of my own and in Frampol was considered to be something of a rich man. Daily the healer came, and every witch doctor in the neighborhood was brought.

cupping · a medical practice in which heated glass cups are applied to the skin to draw toxins from the blood

Lublin · a city in eastern Poland on the Bystrzyca River

They decided to use leeches, and after that to try cupping.˙ They 75 even called a doctor from Lublin,˙ but it was too late. Before she died she called me to her bed and said, "Forgive me, Gimpel."

I said, "What is there to forgive? You have been a good and 76 faithful wife."

"Woe, Gimpel!" she said. "It was ugly how I deceived you all 77 these years. I want to go clean to my Maker, and so I have to tell you that the children are not yours."

If I had been clouted on the head with a piece of wood it 78 couldn't have bewildered me more.

"Whose are they?" I asked. 79

"I don't know," she said. "There were a lot … but they're not 80 yours." And as she spoke she tossed her head to the side, her eyes turned glassy, and it was all up with Elka. On her whitened lips there remained a smile.

I imagined that, dead as she was, she was saying, "I deceived 81 Gimpel. That was the meaning of my brief life."

4

ONE NIGHT, WHEN THE PERIOD of mourning was done, as 82 I lay dreaming on the flour sacks, there came the Spirit of Evil himself and said to me, "Gimpel, why do you sleep?"

I said, "What should I be doing? Eating *kreplach*?"˙ 83

kreplach · a dumpling stuffed with meat or cheese, often served in soup

"The whole world deceives you," he said, "and you ought to 84 deceive the world in your turn."

"How can I deceive all the world?" I asked him. 85

He answered, "You might accumulate a bucket of urine every 86 day and at night pour it into the dough. Let the sages of Frampol eat filth."

"What about the judgment in the world to come?" I said. 87 "There is no world to come," he said. "They've sold you a bill of goods and talked you into believing you carried a cat in your belly. What nonsense!"

"Well then," I said, "and is there a God?" 88

He answered, "There is no God either." 89

"What," I said, "*is* there, then?" 90

"A thick mire." 91

He stood before my eyes with a goatish beard and horn, long- 92 toothed, and with a tail. Hearing such words, I wanted to snatch

92   him by the tail, but I tumbled from the flour sacks and nearly broke a rib. Then it happened that I had to answer the call of nature, and, passing, I saw the risen dough, which seemed to say to me, "Do it!" In brief, I let myself be persuaded.

93   At dawn the apprentice came. We kneaded the bread, scattered caraway seeds on it, and set it to bake. Then the apprentice went away, and I was left sitting in the little trench by the oven, on a pile of rags. Well, Gimpel, I thought, you've revenged yourself on them for all the shame they've put on you. Outside the frost glittered, but it was warm beside the oven. The flames heated my face. I bent my head and fell into a doze.

94   I saw in a dream, at once, Elka in her shroud. She called to me, "What have you done, Gimpel?"

95   I said to her, "It's all your fault," and started to cry.

96   "You fool!" she said. "You fool! Because I was false is everything false too? I never deceived anyone but myself. I'm paying for it all, Gimpel. They spare you nothing here."

97   I looked at her face. It was black; I was startled and waked, and remained sitting dumb. I sensed that everything hung in the balance. A false step now and I'd lose Eternal Life. But God gave me His help. I seized the long shovel and took out the loaves, carried them into the yard, and started to dig a hole in the frozen earth.

98   My apprentice came back as I was doing it. "What are you doing boss?" he said, and grew pale as a corpse. "I know what I'm doing," I said, and I buried it all before his very eyes.

99   Then I went home, took my hoard from its hiding place, and divided it among the children. "I saw your mother tonight," I said. "She's turning black, poor thing."

100   They were so astounded they couldn't speak a word.

101   "Be well," I said, "and forget that such a one as Gimpel ever existed." I put on my short coat, a pair of boots, took the bag that held my prayer shawl in one hand, my stock in the other, and kissed the *mezzuzah*.* When people saw me in the street they were greatly surprised.

102   "Where are you going?" they said.

103   I answered, "Into the world." And so I departed from Frampol.

mezzuzah · a case containing Hebrew scriptures, attached to doorframes of Jewish homes (Hebrew)

I wandered over the land, and good people did not neglect   104
me. After many years I became old and white; I heard a great
deal, many lies and falsehoods, but the longer I lived the more
I understood that there were really no lies. Whatever doesn't
really happen is dreamed at night. It happens to one if it doesn't
happen to another, tomorrow if not today, or a century hence if
not next year. What difference can it make? Often I heard tales
of which I said, "Now this is a thing that cannot happen." But
before a year had elapsed I heard that it actually had come to
pass somewhere.

Going from place to place, eating at strange tables, it often   105
happens that I spin yarns – improbable things that could never
have happened – about devils, magicians, windmills, and the like.
The children run after me, calling, "Grandfather, tell us a story."
Sometimes they ask for particular stories, and I try to please them.
A fat young boy once said to me, "Grandfather, it's the same story
you told us before." The little rogue, he was right.

So it is with dreams too. It is many years since I left Frampol,   106
but as soon as I shut my eyes I am there again. And whom do
you think I see? Elka. She is standing by the washtub, as at our
first encounter, but her face is shining and her eyes are as radiant as the eyes of a saint, and she speaks outlandish words to
me, strange things. When I wake I have forgotten it all. But while
the dream lasts I am comforted. She answers all my queries, and
what comes out is that all is right. I weep and implore, "Let me
be with you." And she consoles me and tells me to be patient. The
time is nearer than it is far. Sometimes she strokes and kisses
me and weeps upon my face. When I awaken I feel her lips and
taste the salt of her tears.

No doubt the world is entirely an imaginary world, but it   107
is only once removed from the true world. At the door of the
hovel where I lie, there stands the plank on which the dead are
taken away. The gravedigger Jew has his spade ready. The grave
waits and the worms are hungry; the shrouds are prepared – I
carry them in my beggar's sack. Another *shnorrer** is waiting to
inherit my bed of straw. When the time comes I will go joyfully.
Whatever may be there, it will be real, without complication,
without ridicule, without deception. God be praised: there even
Gimpel cannot be deceived.

schnorrer · a beggar,
freeloader, or parasite
(Yiddish)

Eudora Welty

⊰ 1 9 0 9 – 2 0 0 1 ⊱

*Regionalism is a powerful shaping influence in Welty's fiction.
Born in Jackson, Mississippi, where she resided for much of her life,
Welty rendered, most memorably perhaps in her short stories, the
courage and nobility of poverty-besieged Southerners whose rich
interior lives belie external want. Drawing on regional gossip and
storytelling, and later recording the Depression experiences of fellow
Mississippians as a* WPA *photographer, Welty developed an understanding of the quiet heroism and altruism of ordinary lives. Her
artistic vision, as one critic has noted, "affirms the sustaining power
of community and family life and at the same time explores the
need for solitude." Her awards include a number of O. Henry Prizes
for individual stories, a Pulitzer Prize for* The Optimist's Daughter
(1972), *and the Howells Medal for her* Collected Stories (1980).

DEATH OF A TRAVELING SALESMAN

1 R.J. BOWMAN, WHO FOR FOURTEEN years had traveled for
a shoe company through Mississippi, drove his Ford along a
rutted dirt path. It was a long day! The time did not seem to clear
the noon hurdle and settle into soft afternoon. The sun, keeping its
strength here even in winter, stayed at the top of the sky, and every
time Bowman stuck his head out of the dusty car to stare up the
road, it seemed to reach a long arm down and push against the top
of his head, right through his hat – like the practical joke of an old
drummer, long on the road. It made him feel all the more angry and
helpless. He was feverish, and he was not quite sure of the way.

2 This was his first day back on the road after a long siege of
influenza. He had had very high fever, and dreams, and had
become weakened and pale, enough to tell the difference in
the mirror, and he could not think clearly.... All afternoon, in

the midst of his anger, and for no reason, he had thought of his 2
dead grandmother. She had been a comfortable soul. Once more
Bowman wished he could fall into the big feather bed that had
been in her room.... Then he forgot her again.

This desolate hill country! And he seemed to be going the 3
wrong way – it was as if he were going back, far back. There was
not a house in sight.... There was no use wishing he were back
in bed, though. By paying the hotel doctor his bill he had proved
his recovery. He had not even been sorry when the pretty trained
nurse said good-bye. He did not like illness, he distrusted it, as
he distrusted the road without signposts. It angered him. He had
given the nurse a really expensive bracelet, just because she was
packing up her bag and leaving.

But now – what if in fourteen years on the road he had never 4
been ill before and never had an accident? His record was broken,
and he had even begun almost to question it.... He had gradually
put up at better hotels, in the bigger towns, but weren't they all,
eternally, stuffy in summer and drafty in winter? Women? He
could only remember little rooms within little rooms, like a nest
of Chinese paper boxes, and if he thought of one woman he saw
the worn loneliness that the furniture of that room seemed built
of. And he himself – he was a man who always wore rather wide-
brimmed black hats, and in the wavy hotel mirrors had looked
something like a bullfighter, as he paused for that inevitable instant
on the landing, walking downstairs to supper.... He leaned out of
the car again, and once more the sun pushed at his head.

Bowman had wanted to reach Beulah by dark, to go to bed 5
and sleep off his fatigue. As he remembered, Beulah was fifty
miles away from the last town, on a graveled road. This was only
a cow trail. How had he ever come to such a place? One hand
wiped the sweat from his face, and he drove on.

He had made the Beulah trip before. But he had never seen 6
this hill or this petering-out path before – or that cloud, he
thought shyly, looking up and then down quickly – any more
than he had seen this day before. Why did he not admit he was
simply lost and had been for miles? ... He was not in the habit of
asking the way of strangers, and these people never knew where
the very roads they lived on went to; but then he had not even
been close enough to anyone to call out. People standing in the

6 fields now and then, or on top of the haystacks, had been too far away, looking like leaning sticks or weeds, turning a little at the solitary rattle of his car across their countryside, watching the pale sobered winter dust where it chunked out behind like big squashes down the road. The stares of these distant people had followed him solidly like a wall, impenetrable, behind which they turned back after he had passed.

7 The cloud floated there to one side like the bolster* on his grandmother's bed. It went over a cabin on the edge of a hill, where two bare chinaberry trees clutched at the sky. He drove through a heap of dead oak leaves, his wheels stirring their weightless sides to make a silvery melancholy whistle as the car passed through their bed. No car had been along this way ahead of him. Then he saw that he was on the edge of a ravine that fell away, a red erosion, and that this was indeed the road's end.

bolster · a long pillow or cushion extending the full width of a bed

8 He pulled the brake. But it did not hold, though he put all his strength into it. The car, tipped toward the edge, rolled a little. Without doubt, it was going over the bank.

9 He got out quietly, as though some mischief had been done him and he had his dignity to remember. He lifted his bag and sample case out, set them down, and stood back and watched the car roll over the edge. He heard something – not the crash he was listening for, but a slow, unuproarious crackle. Rather distastefully he went to look over, and he saw that his car had fallen into a tangle of immense grapevines as thick as his arm, which caught it and held it, rocked it like a grotesque child in a dark cradle, and then, as he watched, concerned somehow that he was not still inside it, released it gently to the ground.

10 He sighed.

11 Where am I? he wondered with a shock. Why didn't I do something? All his anger seemed to have drifted away from him. There was the house, back on the hill. He took a bag in each hand and with almost childlike willingness went toward it. But his breathing came with difficulty, and he had to stop to rest.

12 It was a shotgun house,* two rooms and an open passage between, perched on the hill. The whole cabin slanted a little under the heavy heaped-up vine that covered the roof, light and green, as though forgotten from summer. A woman stood in the passage.

shotgun house · a narrow, one-story dwelling

He stopped still. Then all of a sudden his heart began to behave 13
strangely. Like a rocket set off, it began to leap and expand into
uneven patterns of beats which showered into his brain, and he
could not think. But in scattering and falling it made no noise.
It shot up with great power, almost elation, and fell gently, like
acrobats into nets. It began to pound profoundly, then waited
irresponsibly, hitting in some sort of inward mockery first at
his ribs, then against his eyes, then under his shoulder blades,
and against the roof of his mouth when he tried to say, "Good
afternoon, madam." But he could not hear his heart – it was as
quiet as ashes falling. This was rather comforting; still, it was
shocking to Bowman to feel his heart beating at all.

Stock-still in his confusion, he dropped his bags, which seemed 14
to drift in slow bulks gracefully through the air and to cushion
themselves on the gray prostrate grass near the doorstep.

As for the woman standing there, he saw at once that she was 15
old. Since she could not possibly hear his heart, he ignored the
pounding and now looked at her carefully, and yet in his distraction dreamily, with his mouth open.

She had been cleaning the lamp, and held it, half blackened, 16
half clear, in front of her. He saw her with the dark passage
behind her. She was a big woman with a weather-beaten but
unwrinkled face; her lips were held tightly together, and her eyes
looked with a curious dulled brightness into his. He looked at
her shoes, which were like bundles. If it were summer she would
be barefoot.... Bowman, who automatically judged a woman's
age on sight, set her age at fifty. She wore a formless garment of
some gray coarse material, rough-dried from a washing, from
which her arms appeared pink and unexpectedly round. When
she never said a word, and sustained her quiet pose of holding
the lamp, he was convinced of the strength in her body.

"Good afternoon, madam," he said. 17

She stared on, whether at him or at the air around him he 18
could not tell, but after a moment she lowered her eyes to show
that she would listen to whatever he had to say.

"I wonder if you would be interested –" He tried once more. 19
"An accident – my car...."

Her voice emerged low and remote, like a sound across a lake. 20
"Sonny he ain't here."

21   "Sonny?"

22   "Sonny ain't here now."

23   Her son — a fellow able to bring my car up, he decided in blurred relief. He pointed down the hill. "My car's in the bottom of the ditch. I'll need help."

24   "Sonny ain't here, but he'll be here."

25   She was becoming clearer to him and her voice stronger, and Bowman saw that she was stupid.

26   He was hardly surprised at the deepening postponement and tedium of his journey. He took a breath, and heard his voice speaking over the silent blows of his heart. "I was sick. I am not strong yet.... May I come in?"

27   He stooped and laid his big black hat over the handle on his bag. It was a humble motion, almost a bow, that instantly struck him as absurd and betraying of all his weakness. He looked up at the woman, the wind blowing his hair. He might have continued for a long time in this unfamiliar attitude; he had never been a patient man, but when he was sick he had learned to sink submissively into the pillows, to wait for his medicine. He waited on the woman.

28   Then she, looking at him with blue eyes, turned and held open the door, and after a moment Bowman, as if convinced in his action, stood erect and followed her in.

29   Inside, the darkness of the house touched him like a professional hand, the doctor's. The woman set the half-cleaned lamp on a table in the center of the room and pointed, also like a professional person, a guide, to a chair with a yellow cowhide seat. She herself crouched on the hearth, drawing her knees up under the shapeless dress.

30   At first he felt hopefully secure. His heart was quieter. The room was enclosed in the gloom of yellow pine boards. He could see the other room, with the foot of an iron bed showing, across the passage. The bed had been made up with a red-and-yellow pieced quilt that looked like a map or a picture, a little like his grandmother's girlhood painting of Rome burning. He had ached for coolness, but in this room it was cold. He stared at the hearth with dead coals lying on it and iron pots in the corners. The hearth and smoked chimney were of the stone he had seen ribbing the hills, mostly slate. Why is there no fire? he wondered.

And it was so still. The silence of the fields seemed to enter 31 and move familiarly through the house. The wind used the open hall. He felt that he was in a mysterious, quiet, cool danger. It was necessary to do what? ... To talk.

"I have a nice line of women's low-priced shoes..." he said. 32

But the woman answered, "Sonny'll be here. He's strong. 33 Sonny'll move your car."

"Where is he now?" 34

"Farms for Mr. Redmond." 35

Mr. Redmond. Mr. Redmond. That was someone he would never 36 have to encounter, and he was glad. Somehow the name did not appeal to him.... In a flare of touchiness and anxiety, Bowman wished to avoid even mention of unknown men and their unknown farms.

"Do you two live here alone?" He was surprised to hear his 37 old voice, chatty, confidential, inflected for selling shoes, asking a question like that – a thing he did not even want to know.

"Yes. We are alone." 38

He was surprised at the way she answered. She had taken a 39 long time to say that. She had nodded her head in a deep way too. Had she wished to affect him with some sort of premonition? he wondered unhappily. Or was it only that she would not help him, after all, by talking with him? For he was not strong enough to receive the impact of unfamiliar things without a little talk to break their fall. He had lived a month in which nothing had happened except in his head and his body – an almost inaudible life of heartbeats and dreams that came back, a life of fever and privacy, a delicate life which had left him weak to the point of – what? Of begging. The pulse in his palm leapt like a trout in a brook.

He wondered over and over why the woman did not go ahead 40 with cleaning the lamp. What prompted her to stay there across the room, silently bestowing her presence upon him? He saw that with her it was not a time for doing little tasks. Her face was grave; she was feeling how right she was. Perhaps it was only politeness. In docility he held his eyes stiffly wide; they fixed themselves on the woman's clasped hands as though she held the cord they were strung on.

Then, "Sonny's coming," she said. 41

He himself had not heard anything, but there came a man 42 passing the window and then plunging in at the door, with two

42 hounds beside him. Sonny was a big enough man, with his belt slung low about his hips. He looked at least thirty. He had a hot, red face that was yet full of silence. He wore muddy blue pants and an old military coat stained and patched. World War? Bowman wondered. Great God, it was a Confederate coat. On the back of his light hair he had a wide filthy black hat which seemed to insult Bowman's own. He pushed down the dogs from his chest. He was strong, with dignity and heaviness in his way of moving.... There was the resemblance to his mother.

43 They stood side by side.... He must account again for his presence here.

44 "Sonny, this man, he had his car to run off over the prec'pice an' wants to know if you will git it out for him," the woman said after a few minutes.

45 Bowman could not even state his case.

46 Sonny's eyes lay upon him.

47 He knew he should offer explanations and show money – at least appear either penitent or authoritative. But all he could do was to shrug slightly.

48 Sonny brushed by him going to the window, followed by the eager dogs, and looked out. There was effort even in the way he was looking, as if he could throw his sight out like a rope. Without turning Bowman felt that his own eyes could have seen nothing: it was too far.

49 "Got me a mule out there an' got me a block an' tackle," said Sonny meaningfully. "I *could* catch me my mule an' git me my ropes, an' before long I'd git your car out the ravine."

50 He looked completely around the room, as if in meditation, his eyes roving in their own distance. Then he pressed his lips firmly and yet shyly together, and with the dogs ahead of him this time, he lowered his head and strode out. The hard earth sounded, cupping to his powerful way of walking – almost a stagger.

51 Mischievously, at the suggestion of those sounds, Bowman's heart leapt again. It seemed to walk about inside him.

52 "Sonny's goin' to do it," the woman said. She said it again, singing it almost, like a song. She was sitting in her place by the hearth.

53 Without looking out, he heard some shouts and the dogs barking and the pounding of hoofs in short runs on the hill. In a few minutes Sonny passed under the window with a rope, and there was a brown

mule with quivering, shining, purple-looking ears. The mule actu- 53
ally looked in the window. Under its eyelashes it turned target-like
eyes into his. Bowman averted his head and saw the woman looking
serenely back at the mule, with only satisfaction in her face.

She sang a little more, under her breath. It occurred to him, 54
and it seemed quite marvelous, that she was not really talking to
him, but rather following the thing that came about with words
that were unconscious and part of her looking.

So he said nothing, and this time when he did not reply he felt 55
a curious and strong emotion, not fear, rise up in him.

This time, when his heart leapt, something – his soul – seemed 56
to leap too, like a little colt invited out of a pen. He stared at the
woman while the frantic nimbleness of his feeling made his head
sway. He could not move; there was nothing he could do, unless
perhaps he might embrace this woman who sat there growing
old and shapeless before him.

But he wanted to leap up, to say to her, I have been sick and 57
I found out then, only then, how lonely I am. Is it too late? My
heart puts up a struggle inside me, and you may have heard it,
protesting against emptiness.... It should be full, he would rush
on to tell her, thinking of his heart now as a deep lake, it should
be holding love like other hearts. It should be flooded with love.
There would be a warm spring day.... Come and stand in my
heart, whoever you are, and a whole river would cover your feet
and rise higher and take your knees in whirlpools, and draw you
down to itself, your whole body, your heart too.

But he moved a trembling hand across his eyes, and looked 58
at the placid crouching woman across the room. She was still
as a statue. He felt ashamed and exhausted by the thought that
he might, in one more moment, have tried by simple words and
embraces to communicate some strange thing – something which
seemed always to have just escaped him.... Sunlight touched the
furthest pot on the hearth. It was late afternoon. This time tomorrow he would be somewhere on a good graveled road, driving
his car past things that happened to people, quicker than their
happening. Seeing ahead to the next day, he was glad, and knew
that this was no time to embrace an old woman. He could feel in
his pounding temples the readying of his blood for motion and
for hurrying away.

59   "Sonny's hitched up your car by now," said the woman. "He'll git it out the ravine right shortly."

60   "Fine!" he cried with his customary enthusiasm.

61   Yet it seemed a long time that they waited. It began to get dark. Bowman was cramped in his chair. Any man should know enough to get up and walk around while he waited. There was something like guilt in such stillness and silence.

62   But instead of getting up, he listened.... His breathing restrained, his eyes powerless in the growing dark, he listened uneasily for a warning sound, forgetting in wariness what it would be. Before long he heard something – soft, continuous, insinuating.

63   "What's that noise?" he asked, his voice jumping into the dark. Then wildly he was afraid it would be his heart beating so plainly in the quiet room, and she would tell him so.

64   "You might hear the stream," she said grudgingly.

65   Her voice was closer. She was standing by the table. He wondered why she did not light the lamp. She stood there in the dark and did not light it.

66   Bowman would never speak to her now, for the time was past. I'll sleep in the dark, he thought, in his bewilderment pitying himself.

67   Heavily she moved on to the window. Her arm, vaguely white, rose straight from her full side and she pointed out into the darkness.

68   "That white speck's Sonny," she said, talking to herself.

69   He turned unwillingly and peered over her shoulder; he hesitated to rise and stand beside her. His eyes searched the dusky air. The white speck floated smoothly toward her finger, like a leaf on a river, growing whiter in the dark. It was as if she had shown him something secret, part of her life, but had offered no explanation. He looked away. He was moved almost to tears, feeling for no reason that she had made a silent declaration equivalent to his own. His hand waited upon his chest.

70   Then a step shook the house, and Sonny was in the room. Bowman felt how the woman left him there and went to the other man's side.

71   "I done got your car out, mister," said Sonny's voice in the dark. "She's settin' a-waitin' in the road, turned to go back where she come from."

"Fine!" said Bowman, projecting his own voice to loudness. 72
"I'm surely much obliged – I could never have done it myself – I
was sick...."

"I could do it easy," said Sonny. 73

Bowman could feel them both waiting in the dark, and he 74
could hear the dogs panting out in the yard, waiting to bark
when he should go. He felt strangely helpless and resentful.
Now that he could go, he longed to stay. Of what was he being
deprived? His chest was rudely shaken by the violence of his
heart. These people cherished something here that he could not
see, they withheld some ancient promise of food and warmth
and light. Between them they had a conspiracy. He thought of
the way she had moved away from him and gone to Sonny, she
had flowed toward him. He was shaking with cold, he was tired,
and it was not fair. Humbly and yet angrily he stuck his hand
into his pocket.

"Of course I'm going to pay you for everything –" 75

"We don't take money for such," said Sonny's voice belligerently. 76

"I want to pay. But do something more.... Let me stay – tonight...." 77
He took another step toward them. If only they could see him, they
would know his sincerity, his real need! His voice went on, "I'm not
very strong yet, I'm not able to walk far, even back to my car, maybe,
I don't know – I don't know exactly where I am –"

He stopped. He felt as if he might burst into tears. What would 78
they think of him!

Sonny came over and put his hands on him. Bowman felt them 79
pass (they were professional too) across his chest, over his hips.
He could feel Sonny's eyes upon him in the dark.

"You ain't no revenuer* come sneakin' here, mister, ain't got 80
no gun?"

To this end of nowhere! And yet he had come. He made a 81
grave answer. "No."

"You can stay." 82

"Sonny," said the woman, "you'll have to borry some fire." 83

"I'll go git it from Redmond's," said Sonny. 84

"What?" Bowman strained to hear their words to each other. 85

"Our fire, it's out, and Sonny's got to borry some, because its 86
dark an' cold," she said.

"But matches – I have matches –" 87

revenuer · a tax officer who seeks to collect revenues on illegally produced liquor

88   "We don't have no need for 'em," she said proudly. "Sonny's goin' after his own fire."

89   "I'm goin' to Redmond's," said Sonny with an air of importance, and he went out.

90   After they had waited a while, Bowman looked out the window and saw a light moving over the hill. It spread itself out like a little fan. It zigzagged along the field, darting and swift, not like Sonny at all.... Soon enough, Sonny staggered in, holding a burning stick behind him in tongs, fire flowing in his wake, blazing light into the corners of the room.

91   "We'll make a fire now," the woman said, taking the brand.

92   When that was done she lit the lamp. It showed its dark and light. The whole room turned golden-yellow like some sort of flower, and the walls smelled of it and seemed to tremble with the quiet rushing of the fire and the waving of the burning lampwick in its funnel of light.

93   The woman moved among the iron pots. With the tongs she dropped hot coals on top of the iron lids. They made a set of soft vibrations, like the sound of a bell far away.

94   She looked up and over at Bowman, but he could not answer. He was trembling....

95   "Have a drink, mister?" Sonny asked. He had brought in a chair from the other room and sat astride it with his folded arms across the back. Now we are all visible to one another, Bowman thought, and cried, "Yes sir, you bet, thanks!"

96   "Come after me and do just what I do," said Sonny.

97   It was another excursion into the dark. They went through the hall, out to the back of the house, past a shed and a hooded well. They came to a wilderness of thicket.

98   "Down on your knees," said Sonny.

99   "What?" Sweat broke out on his forehead.

100   He understood when Sonny began to crawl through a sort of tunnel that the bushes made over the ground. He followed, startled in spite of himself when a twig or a thorn touched him gently without making a sound, clinging to him and finally letting him go.

101   Sonny stopped crawling and, crouched on his knees, began to dig with both his hands into the dirt. Bowman shyly struck matches and made a light. In a few minutes Sonny pulled up a jug. He poured out some of the whisky into a bottle from his

coat pocket, and buried the jug again. "You never know who's 101
liable to knock at your door," he said, and laughed. "Start back,"
he said, almost formally. "Ain't no need for us to drink outdoors,
like hogs."

At the table by the fire, sitting opposite each other in their 102
chairs, Sonny and Bowman took drinks out of the bottle, passing
it across. The dogs slept; one of them was having a dream.

"This is good," said Bowman. "This is what I needed." It was 103
just as though he were drinking the fire off the hearth.

"He makes it," said the woman with quiet pride. 104

She was pushing the coals off the pots, and the smells of corn 105
bread and coffee circled the room. She set everything on the
table before the men, with a bone-handled knife stuck into one
of the potatoes, splitting out its golden fiber. Then she stood for
a minute looking at them, tall and full above them where they
sat. She leaned a little toward them.

"You all can eat now," she said, and suddenly smiled. 106

Bowman had just happened to be looking at her. He set his 107
cup back on the table in unbelieving protest. A pain pressed at
his eyes. He saw that she was not an old woman. She was young,
still young. He could think of no number of years for her. She
was the same age as Sonny, and she belonged to him. She stood
with the deep dark corner of the room behind her, the shifting
yellow light scattering over her head and her gray formless dress,
trembling over her tall body when it bent over them in its sudden
communication. She was young. Her teeth were shining and her
eyes glowed. She turned and walked slowly and heavily out of the
room, and he heard her sit down on the cot and then lie down.
The pattern on the quilt moved.

"She's goin' to have a baby," said Sonny, popping a bite into 108
his mouth.

Bowman could not speak. He was shocked with knowing 109
what was really in this house. A marriage, a fruitful marriage.
That simple thing. Anyone could have had that.

Somehow he felt unable to be indignant or protest, although 110
some sort of joke had certainly been played upon him. There
was nothing remote or mysterious here – only something private.
The only secret was the ancient communication between two
people. But the memory of the woman's waiting silently by the

110 cold hearth, of the man's stubborn journey a mile away to get fire, and how they finally brought out their food and drink and filled the room proudly with all they had to show, was suddenly too clear and too enormous within him for response....

111 "You ain't as hungry as you look," said Sonny.

112 The woman came out of the bedroom as soon as the men had finished, and ate her supper while her husband stared peacefully into the fire.

113 Then they put the dogs out, with the food that was left.

114 "I think I'd better sleep here by the fire, on the floor," said Bowman.

115 He felt that he had been cheated, and that he could afford now to be generous. Ill though he was, he was not going to ask them for their bed. He was through with asking favors in this house, now that he understood what was there.

116 "Sure, mister."

117 But he had not known yet how slowly he understood. They had not meant to give him their bed. After a little interval they both rose and looking at him gravely went into the other room.

118 He lay stretched by the fire until it grew low and dying. He watched every tongue of blaze lick out and vanish. "There will be special reduced prices on all footwear during the month of January," he found himself repeating quietly, and then he lay with his lips tight shut.

119 How many noises the night had! He heard the stream running, the fire dying, and he was sure now that he heard his heart beating, too, the sound it made under his ribs. He heard breathing, round and deep, of the man and his wife in the room across the passage. And that was all. But emotion swelled patiently within him, and he wished that the child were his.

120 He must get back to where he had been before. He stood weakly before the red coals and put on his overcoat. It felt too heavy on his shoulders. As he started out he looked and saw that the woman had never got through with cleaning the lamp. On some impulse he put all the money from his billfold under its fluted glass base, almost ostentatiously.

121 Ashamed, shrugging a little, and then shivering, he took his bags and went out. The cold of the air seemed to lift him bodily. The moon was in the sky.

On the slope he began to run, he could not help it. Just as he   122
reached the road, where his car seemed to sit in the moonlight
like a boat, his heart began to give off tremendous explosions
like a rifle, bang bang bang.

He sank in fright onto the road, his bags falling about him. He   123
felt as if all this had happened before. He covered his heart with
both hands to keep anyone from hearing the noise it made.

But nobody heard it.   124

Bernard Malamud

《1914 – 1986》

*Malamud is one of the writers in what literary critics have called
the Jewish Renaissance. He was born in Brooklyn to Russian immi-
grant parents, and grew up a street kid during the Depression. These
were unhappy times, but they provided him with experience for
most of his best writing, including* The Assistant *(1957), considered
to be his best work, though it was not as popular as* The Fixer
*(1966), a gripping story about a victim of anti-Semitism in Czarist
Russia. It received the National Book Award and the Pulitzer Prize.
While most of his works have Jewish protagonists, he considered
his themes to be universal. In this regard two statements he made
about his writing stand out: "All men are Jews," and "I'm in defense
of the human." His best works concern meaningful suffering, particularly as that suffering is a consequence of love betrayed, rejected,
misplaced, or misinterpreted. Though his work is rich in religious
images, figures, and themes, he was an atheistic existentialist.*

THE JEWBIRD

1 THE WINDOW WAS OPEN so the skinny bird flew in. Flappity-
flap with its frazzled black wings. That's how it goes. It's open,
you're in. Closed, you're out and that's your fate. The bird wearily
flapped through the open kitchen window of Harry Cohen's top-
floor apartment on First Avenue near the lower East River.* On a
rod on the wall hung an escaped canary cage, its door wide open,
but this black-type long-beaked bird – its ruffled head and small dull
eyes, crossed a little, making it look like a dissipated crow – landed if
not smack on Cohen's thick lamb chop, at least on the table, close by.
The frozen foods salesman was sitting at supper with his wife and
young son on a hot August evening a year ago. Cohen, a heavy man
with hairy chest and beefy shorts; Edie, in skinny yellow shorts and

lower East River ·
this river runs between
the lower East side
of Manhattan and
Brooklyn in New
York City, an area of
traditionally Jewish
neighborhoods

red halter; and their ten-year-old Morris (after his father) – Maurie, they called him, a nice kid though not overly bright – were all in the city after two weeks out, because Cohen's mother was dying. They had been enjoying Kingston, New York, but drove back when Mama got sick in her flat* in the Bronx.

"Right on the table," said Cohen, putting down his beer glass and swatting at the bird. "Son of a bitch."

"Harry, take care with your language," Edie said, looking at Maurie, who watched every move.

The bird cawed hoarsely and with a flap of its bedraggled wings – feathers tufted this way and that – rose heavily to the top of the open kitchen door, where it perched staring down.

"*Gevalt,** a *pogrom*!"*

"It's a talking bird," said Edie in astonishment.

"In Jewish," said Maurie.

"Wise guy," muttered Cohen. He gnawed on his chop, then put down the bone. "So if you can talk, say what's your business. What do you want here?"

"If you can't spare a lamb chop," said the bird, "I'll settle for a piece of herring with a crust of bread. You can't live on your nerve forever."

"This ain't a restaurant," Cohen replied. "All I'm asking is what brings you to this address?"

"The window was open," the bird sighed; adding after a moment, "I'm running. I'm flying but I'm also running."

"From whom?" asked Edie with interest.

"Anti-Semeets."

"Anti-Semites?" they all said.

"That's from who."

"What kind of anti-Semites bother a bird?" Edie asked.

"Any kind," said the bird, "also including eagles, vultures, and hawks. And once in a while some crows will take your eyes out."

"But aren't you a crow?"

"Me? I'm a Jewbird."

Cohen laughed heartily. "What do you mean by that?"

The bird began dovening.* He prayed without Book or *tallith*,* but with passion. Edie bowed her head though not Cohen. And Maurie rocked back and forth with the prayer, looking up with one wide-open eye.

---

flat · apartment

Gevalt · an expression of astonishment (Yiddish)

pogrom · "like thunder" (Russian), an organized and often officially sanctioned persecution or massacre of a minority group, especially persecutions conducted against Jews

dovening · praying

tallith · a fringed prayer shawl with bands of black or blue (Hebrew)

22 When the prayer was done Cohen remarked, "No hat, no phylacteries?"•

23 "I'm an old radical."

24 "You're sure you're not some kind of a ghost or *dybbuk*?"•

25 "Not a *dybbuk*," answered the bird, "though one of my relatives had such an experience once. It's all over now, thanks God. They freed her from a former lover, a crazy jealous man. She's now the mother of two wonderful children."

26 "Birds?" Cohen asked slyly.

27 "Why not?"

28 "What kind of birds?"

29 "Like me. Jewbirds."

30 Cohen tipped back in his chair and guffawed. "That's a big laugh. I've heard of a Jewfish• but not a Jewbird."

31 "We're once removed." The bird rested on one skinny leg, then on the other. "Please, could you spare maybe a piece of herring with a small crust of bread?"

32 Edie got up from the table.

33 "What are you doing?" Cohen asked her.

34 "I'll clear the dishes."

35 Cohen turned to the bird. "So what's your name, if you don't mind saying?"

36 "Call me Schwartz."

37 "He might be an old Jew changed into a bird by somebody," said Edie, removing a plate.

38 "Are you?" asked Harry, lighting a cigar.

39 "Who knows?" answered Schwartz. "Does God tell us everything?"

40 Maurie got up on his chair. "What kind of herring?" he asked the bird in excitement.

41 "Get down, Maurie, or you'll fall," ordered Cohen.

42 "If you haven't got *matjes*, I'll take *schmaltz*,"• said Schwartz.

43 "All we have is marinated, with slices of onion – in a jar," said Edie.

44 "If you'll open for me the jar I'll eat marinated. Do you have also, if you don't mind, a piece of rye bread – the *spitz*?"•

45 Edie thought she had.

46 "Feed him out on the balcony," Cohen said. He spoke to the bird. "After that take off."

47 Schwartz closed both bird eyes. "I'm tired and it's a long way."

48 "Which direction are you headed, north or south?"

phylacteries · two small leather boxes containing quotations from the Hebrew scriptures, worn by Jewish men while praying

dybbuk · a wandering spirit of the dead (Yiddish)

Jewfish · any of several large fishes of the sea bass family

matjes ... schmaltz · *matjes* (Dutch) and *schmaltz* (Yiddish) are two types of herring, the former superior in quality to the latter

spitz · the heel (Yiddish)

Schwartz, barely lifting his wings, shrugged. 49

"You don't know where you're going?" 50

"Where there's charity I'll go." 51

"Let him stay, papa," said Maurie. "He's only a bird." 52

"So stay the night," Cohen said, "but no longer." 53

In the morning Cohen ordered the bird out of the house but 54
Maurie cried, so Schwartz stayed for a while. Maurie was still on
vacation from school and his friends were away. He was lonely
and Edie enjoyed the fun he had, playing with the bird.

"He's no trouble at all," she told Cohen, "and besides his appe- 55
tite is very small."

"What'll you do when he makes dirty?" 56

"He flies across the street in a tree when he makes dirty, and 57
if nobody passes below, who notices?"

"So all right," said Cohen, "but I'm dead set against it. I warn 58
you he ain't gonna stay here long."

"What have you got against the poor bird?" 59

"Poor bird, my ass. He's a foxy bastard. He thinks he's a Jew." 60
"What difference does it make what he thinks?"

"A Jewbird, what a *chutzpah.*• One false move and he's out on 61
his drumsticks."

At Cohen's insistence Schwartz lived out on the balcony in a 62
new wooden birdhouse Edie had bought him.

"With many thanks," said Schwartz, "though I would rather 63
have a human roof over my head. You know how it is at my age. I
like the warm, the windows, the smell of cooking. I would also be
glad to see once in a while the *Jewish Morning Journal* and have
now and then a schnapps because it helps my breathing, thanks
God. But whatever you give me, you won't hear complaints."

However, when Cohen brought home a bird feeder full of 64
dried corn, Schwartz said, "Impossible."

Cohen was annoyed. "What's the matter, crosseyes, is your life 65
getting too good for you? Are you forgetting what it means to be
migratory? I'll bet a helluva lot of crows you happen to be acquainted
with, Jews or otherwise, would give their eyeteeth to eat this corn."

Schwartz did not answer. What can you say to a *grubber yung*?• 66

"Not for my digestion," he later explained to Edie. "Cramps. 67
Herring is better even if it makes you thirsty. At least rainwater
don't cost anything." He laughed sadly in breathy caws.

chutzpah • brazenness, gall, an affront (Yiddish)

grubber yung • a crude type of boot (Yiddish), used here as a term of derision

68   And herring, thanks to Edie, who knew where to shop, was what Schwartz got, with an occasional piece of potato pancake, and even a bit of soupmeat when Cohen wasn't looking.

69   When school began in September, before Cohen would once again suggest giving the bird the boot, Edie prevailed on him to wait a little while until Maurie adjusted.

70   "To deprive him right now might hurt his school work, and you know what trouble we had last year."

71   "So okay, but sooner or later the bird goes. That I promise you."

72   Schwartz, though nobody had asked him, took on full responsibility for Maurie's performance in school. In return for favors granted, when he was let in for an hour or two at night, he spent most of his time overseeing the boy's lessons. He sat on top of the dresser near Maurie's desk as he laboriously wrote out his homework. Maurie was a restless type and Schwartz gently kept him to his studies. He also listened to him practice his screechy violin, taking a few minutes off now and then to rest his ears in the bathroom. And they afterwards played dominoes. The boy was an indifferent checker player and it was impossible to teach him chess. When he was sick, Schwartz read him comic books though he personally disliked them. But Maurie's work improved in school and even his violin teacher admitted his playing was better. Edie gave Schwartz credit for these improvements though the bird pooh-poohed them.

73   Yet he was proud there was nothing lower than C-minuses on Maurie's report card, and on Edie's insistence celebrated with a little schnapps.

74   "If he keeps up like this," Cohen said, "I'll get him in any Ivy League college for sure."

75   "Oh I hope so," sighed Edie.

76   But Schwartz shook his head. "He's a good boy — you don't have to worry. He won't be a *shicker** or a wifebeater, God forbid, but a scholar he'll never be, if you know what I mean, although maybe a good mechanic. It's no disgrace in these times."

shicker · "drunkard" (Yiddish)

77   "If I were you," Cohen said, angered, "I'd keep my big snoot out of other people's private business."

78   "Harry, please," said Edie.

79   "My goddamn patience is wearing out. That crosseyes butts into everything."

Though he wasn't exactly a welcome guest in the house, Schwartz 80
gained a few ounces although he did not improve in appearance. He
looked bedraggled as ever, his feathers unkempt, as though he had
just flown out of a snowstorm. He spent, he admitted, little time
taking care of himself. Too much to think about. "Also outside plumb-
ing," he told Edie. Still there was more glow to his eyes so that though
Cohen went on calling him crosseyes he said it less emphatically.

Liking his situation, Schwartz tried tactfully to stay out of 81
Cohen's way, but one night when Edie was at the movies and
Maurie was taking a hot shower, the frozen foods salesman began
a quarrel with the bird.

"For Christ sake, why don't you wash yourself sometimes? 82
Why must you always stink like a dead fish?"

"Mr. Cohen, if you'll pardon me, if somebody eats garlic he 83
will smell from garlic. I eat herring three times a day. Feed me
flowers and I will smell like flowers."

"Who's obligated to feed you anything at all? You're lucky to 84
get herring."

"Excuse me, I'm not complaining," said the bird. "You're 85
complaining."

"What's more," said Cohen, "Even from out on the balcony I can 86
hear you snoring away like a pig. It keeps me awake at night."

"Snoring," said Schwartz, "isn't a crime, thanks God." 87

"All in all you are a goddamn pest and freeloader. Next thing 88
you'll want to sleep in bed next to my wife."

"Mr. Cohen," said Schwartz, "on this rest assured. A bird is a bird." 89

"So you say, but how do I know you're a bird and not some 90
kind of a goddamn devil?"

"If I was a devil you would know already. And I don't mean 91
because your son's good marks."

"Shut up, you bastard bird," shouted Cohen. 92

"*Grubber yung*," cawed Schwartz, rising to the tips of his talons, 93
his long wings outstretched.

Cohen was about to lunge for the bird's scrawny neck but Maurie 94
came out of the bathroom, and for the rest of the evening until
Schwartz's bedtime on the balcony, there was pretended peace.

But the quarrel had deeply disturbed Schwartz and he slept 95
badly. His snoring woke him, and awake, he was fearful of what
would become of him. Wanting to stay out of Cohen's way, he kept

95   to the birdhouse as much as possible. Cramped by it, he paced back and forth on the balcony ledge, or sat on the birdhouse roof, staring into space. In evenings, while overseeing Maurie's lessons, he often fell asleep. Awakening, he nervously hopped around exploring the four corners of the room. He spent much time in Maurie's closet, and carefully examined his bureau drawers when they were left open. And once when he found a large paper bag on the floor, Schwartz poked his way into it to investigate what possibilities were. The boy was amused to see the bird in the paper bag.

96   "He wants to build a nest," he said to his mother.

97   Edie, sensing Schwartz's unhappiness, spoke to him quietly.

98   "Maybe if you did some of the things my husband wants you, you would get along better with him."

99   "Give me a for instance," Schwartz said.

100   "Like take a bath, for instance."

101   "I'm too old for baths," said the bird. "My feathers fall out without baths."

102   "He says you have a bad smell."

103   "Everybody smells. Some people smell because of their thoughts or because who they are. My bad smell comes from the food I eat. What does his come from?"

104   "I better not ask him or it might make him mad," said Edie.

105   In late November Schwartz froze on the balcony in the fog and cold, and especially on rainy days he woke with stiff joints and could barely move his wings. Already he felt twinges of rheumatism. He would have liked to spend more time in the warm house, particularly when Maurie was in school and Cohen at work. But though Edie was good-hearted and might have sneaked him in in the morning, just to thaw out, he was afraid to ask her. In the meantime Cohen, who had been reading articles about the migration of birds, came out on the balcony one night after work when Edie was in the kitchen preparing pot roast, and peeking into the birdhouse, warned Schwartz to be on his way soon if he knew what was good for him. "Time to hit the flyways."

106   "Mr. Cohen, why do you hate me so much?" asked the bird. "What did I do to you?"

107   "Because you're an A-number-one trouble maker, that's why. What's more, whoever heard of a Jewbird! Now scat or it's open war."

But Schwartz stubbornly refused to depart so Cohen 108
embarked on a campaign of harassing him, meanwhile hiding it
from Edie and Maurie. Maurie hated violence and Cohen didn't
want to leave a bad impression. He thought maybe if he played
dirty tricks on the bird he would fly off without being physically
kicked out. The vacation was over, let him make his easy living
off the fat of somebody else's land. Cohen worried about the
effect of the bird's departure on Maurie's schooling but decided
to take the chance, first, because the boy now seemed to have
the knack of studying – give the black bird-bastard credit – and
second, because Schwartz was driving him bats by being there
always, even in his dreams.

The frozen foods salesman began his campaign against 109
the bird by mixing watery cat food with the herring slices in
Schwartz's dish. He also blew up and popped numerous paper
bags outside the birdhouse as the bird slept, and when he got
Schwartz good and nervous, though not enough to leave, he
brought a full-grown cat into the house, supposedly a gift for
little Maurie, who had always wanted a pussy. The cat never
stopped springing up at Schwartz whenever he saw him, one
day managing to claw out several of his tailfeathers. And
even at lesson time, when the cat was usually excluded from
Maurie's room, though somehow or other he quickly found
his way in at the end of the lesson, Schwartz was desperately
fearful of his life and flew from pinnacle to pinnacle – light
fixture to clothes-tree to door-top – in order to elude the
beast's wet jaws.

Once when the bird complained to Edie how hazardous 110
his existence was, she said, "Be patient, Mr. Schwartz. When
the cat gets to know you better he won't try to catch you
any more."

"When he stops trying we will both be in Paradise," Schwartz 111
answered. "Do me a favor and get rid of him. He makes my whole
life worry. I'm losing feathers like a tree loses leaves."

"I'm awfully sorry but Maurie likes the pussy and sleeps with it." 112

What could Schwartz do? He worried but came to no deci- 113
sion, being afraid to leave. So he ate the herring garnished with
cat food, tried hard not to hear the paper bags bursting like fire
crackers outside the birdhouse at night, and lived terror-stricken

113 closer to the ceiling than the floor, as the cat, his tail flicking, endlessly watched him.

114 Weeks went by. Then on the day after Cohen's mother had died in her flat in the Bronx, when Maurie came home with a zero on an arithmetic test, Cohen, enraged, waited until Edie had taken the boy to his violin lesson, then openly attacked the bird. He chased him with a broom on the balcony and Schwartz frantically flew back and forth, finally escaping into his birdhouse. Cohen triumphantly reached in, and grabbing both skinny legs, dragged the bird out, cawing loudly, his wings wildly beating. He whirled the bird around and around his head. But Schwartz, as he moved in circles, managed to swoop down and catch Cohen's nose in his beak, and hung on for dear life. Cohen cried out in great pain, punched the bird with his fist, and tugging at its legs with all his might, pulled his nose free. Again he swung the yawking Schwartz around until the bird grew dizzy, then with a furious heave, flung him into the night. Schwartz sank like stone into the street. Cohen then tossed the birdhouse and feeder after him, listening at the ledge until they crashed on the sidewalk below. For a full hour, broom in hand, his heart palpitating and nose throbbing with pain, Cohen waited for Schwartz to return but the broken-hearted bird didn't.

115 That's the end of that dirty bastard, the salesman thought and went in. Edie and Maurie had come home.

116 "Look," said Cohen, pointing to his bloody nose swollen three times its normal size, "what that sonofabitch bird did. It's a permanent scar."

117 "Where is he now?" Edie asked, frightened.

118 "I threw him out and he flew away. Good riddance."

119 Nobody said no, though Edie touched a handkerchief to her eyes and Maurie rapidly tried the nine times table and found he knew approximately half.

120 In the spring when the winter's snow had melted, the boy, moved by a memory, wandered in the neighborhood, looking for Schwartz. He found a dead black bird in a small lot near the river, his two wings broken, neck twisted, and both bird-eyes plucked clean.

121 "Who did it to you, Mr. Schwartz?" Maurie wept.

122 "Anti-Semeets," Edie said later.

Shusako Endo

❮ 1 9 2 3 – 1 9 9 6 ❯

Christianity came to Japan in 1549 and flourished briefly, but thereafter adherents were often a persecuted minority. Endo was baptized young but had little faith. He thought his difficulty developing strong faith in a foreign deity was typically Japanese because he and his compatriots preferred a warm, maternal god. Eventually, he realized that Jesus, who helped the sick and the outcast, was just such a deity, and he determined to write about this realization. "Unzen" (1965) – named for an active volcano – is an early sketch for Endo's greatest novel, Silence *(1966). The story depicts the aftermath of the Shimabara Rebellion of 1637–1638, an uprising of peasants and Christians over taxes. The local warlord saw only Christians at the root of the insurrection and began torturing and killing them unless they denied their faith. This denial haunts Endo, probably because he came so close to it. The typical Endo character, partly autobiographical and often named Suguro, is caught between weak faith and denial of it. Suguro becomes aware of the historical Kichijirō, who watches fellow Christians suffer boiling-water torture and horrible death in Mt. Unzen's Valley of Hell but cannot overcome fear of joining them. Endo believes Kichijirō suffers terribly in ways the dying faithful cannot understand. Though apostate, Kichijirō must learn that Jesus has not given up on him. This lesson gives Suguro a new identity because, despite the three-hundred-year gap, he – and Endo – are Kichijirō's spiritual doubles.*

UNZEN

1   As HE SAT ON THE BUS FOR UNZEN, he drank a bottle of milk and gazed blankly at the rain-swept sea. The frosty waves washed languidly against the shore just beneath the coastal highway.

The bus had not yet left the station. The scheduled hour of departure had long since passed, but a connecting bus from Nagasaki* still had not arrived, and their driver was chatting idly with the woman conductor and displaying no inclination to switch on the engine. Even so the tolerant passengers uttered no word of complaint, but merely pressed their faces against the window glass. A group of bathers from the hot springs walked by, dressed in large, thickly-padded *kimonos*. They shielded themselves from the rain with umbrellas borrowed from their inn. The counters of the gift shops were lined with all sorts of decorative shells and souvenir bean-jellies from the local hot springs, but there were no customers around to buy their wares.

"This place reminds me of Atagawa in Izu,"* Suguro grumbled to himself as he snapped the cardboard top back onto the milk bottle. "What a disgusting landscape."

He had to chuckle a bit at himself for coming all the way to this humdrum spot at the western edge of Kyūshū.* In Tokyo he had not had the slightest notion that this village of Obama, home of many of the Christian martyrs and some of the participants in the Shimabara Rebellion, would be so commonplace a town.

From his studies of the Christian era in Japan, Suguro knew that around 1630 many of the faithful had made the climb from Obama towards Unzen, which a Jesuit* of the day had called "one of the tallest mountains in Japan." The Valley of Hell high up on Unzen was an ideal place for torturing Christians. According to the records, after 1629, when the Nagasaki Magistrate Takenaka Shigetsugu hit upon the idea of abusing the Christians in this hot spring inferno, sixty or seventy prisoners a day were roped together and herded from Obama to the top of this mountain.

Now tourists strolled the streets of the village, and popular songs blared out from loudspeakers. Nothing remained to remind one of that sanguinary* history. But precisely three centuries before the present month of January, on a day of misty rain, the man whose footsteps Suguro now hoped to retrace had undoubtedly climbed up this mountain from Obama.

Finally the engine started up, and the bus made its way through the village. They passed through a district of two-and three-storey Japanese inns where men leaned with both hands on the railings of the balconies and peered down into the bus. Even

---

Nagasaki · largest city of western Kyūshū, Portuguese traders introduced Roman Catholicism to Nagasaki in the mid-16th century. Authorities soon began persecuting Christians, crucifying 26 believers there in 1597

Atagawa in Izu · located on the east coast of the Izu peninsula of Honshu, Atagawa features volcanic hot springs and has been a popular destination since its discovery in the 15th century

Kyūshū · southernmost and third largest of the four main islands of Japan

a Jesuit · member of the Society of Jesus, a Roman Catholic order founded by Ignatius Loyola in 1534 and dedicated to teaching and missionary work

sanguinary · bloody, murderous

7　those windows which were deserted were draped with pink and white washcloths and towels. When the bus finally passed beyond the hotel district, both sides of the mountain road were lined with old stone walls and squat farmhouses with thatched roofs.

8　　Suguro had no way of knowing whether these walls and farmhouses had existed in the Christian century. Nor could he be sure that this road was the one travelled by the Christians, the officers, and the man he was pursuing. The only certain thing was that, during their fitful stops along the path, they had looked up at this same Mount Unzen wrapped in grey mist.

9　　He had brought a number of books with him from Tokyo, but he now regretted not including a collection of letters from Jesuits of the day who had reported on the Unzen martyrdoms to their superiors in Rome. He had thoughtlessly tossed into his bag one book that would be of no use to him on this journey – Collado's *Christian Confessions.*•

10　The air cooled as the bus climbed into the hills, and the passengers, peeling skins from the *mikans*• they had bought at Obama, listened half-heartedly to the sing-song travelogue provided by the conductor.

11　"Please look over this way," she said with a waxy smile. "There are two large pine trees on top of the hill we are about to circle. It's said that at about this spot, the Christians of olden days would turn around and look longingly back at the village of Obama. These trees later became known as the Looking-Back Pines."

12　Collado's *Christian Confessions* was published in Rome in 1632, just five years before the outbreak of the Shimabara Rebellion. By that time the Shōgunate's persecution• of the Christians had grown fierce, but a few Portuguese and Italian missionaries had still managed to steal into Japan from Macao• or Manila.• The *Christian Confessions* were printed as a practical guide to Japanese grammar for the benefit of these missionaries. But what Suguro found hard to understand was why Collado had made public the confessions of these Japanese Christians, when a Catholic priest was under no circumstances permitted to reveal the innermost secrets of the soul shared with him by members of his flock.

13　Yet the night he read the *Confessions*, Suguro felt as though a more responsive chord had been struck within him than with any

---

Collado's *Christian Confessions* · a Spanish missionary, Diego Collado (d 1641) was a Dominican friar who first went to Japan in 1619 and returned to Europe in 1622 following the martyrdom of Luis Flóres. *Christian Confessions* was first published in Madrid in 1632

mikans · mandarin oranges

Shōgunate's persecution · the government office of a Shōgun, a military commander of Japan whose power, prior to the revolution of the mid-1800s, exceeded even that of the emperor. The Shōgun attempted to eliminate Christianity in the 17th century

Macao · a region of the southern coast of China

Manila · capital and chief city of the Philippines

other history of the Christian era he had encountered. Every study 13
he had read was little more than a string of pæans* to the noble
acts of priests and martyrs and common believers inspired by faith.
They were without exception chronicles of those who had sustained
their beliefs and their testimonies no matter what sufferings or
tortures they had to endure. And each time he read them, Suguro
had to sigh, "There's no way I can emulate people like this."

He had been baptized as a child, along with the rest of his family. 14
Since then he had passed through many vicissitudes and somehow
managed to arrive in his forties without rejecting his religion. But
that was not due to firm resolve or unshakable faith. He was more
than adequately aware of his own spiritual slovenliness and pusillanimity.* He was certain that an unspannable gulf separated him from
the ancient martyrs of Nagasaki, Edo and Unzen who had effected
glorious martyrdoms. Why had they all been so indomitable?

Suguro diligently searched the Christian histories for someone
like himself. But there was no one to be found. Finally he had 15
stumbled across the *Christian Confessions* one day in a second-
hand bookshop, and as he flipped indifferently through the pages
of the book, he had been moved by the account of a man whose
name Collado had concealed. The man had the same feeble will and
tattered integrity as Suguro. Gradually he had formed in his mind
an image of this man – genuflecting like a camel before the priest
nearly three hundred years earlier, relishing the almost desperate
experience of exposing his own filthiness to the eyes of another.

> I stayed for a long time with some heathens. I didn't want 15a
> the innkeeper to realize I was a Christian, so I went with
> him often to the heathen temples and chanted along
> with them. Many times when they praised the gods and
> buddhas, I sinned greatly by nodding and agreeing with
> them. I don't remember how many times I did that. Maybe
> twenty or thirty times – more than twenty, anyway.
>
> And when the heathens and the apostates* got together 15b
> to slander us Christians and blaspheme against God, I
> was there with them. I didn't try to stop them talking or
> to refute them.
>
> Just recently, at the Shōgun's orders the Magistrate came 15c
> to our fief* from the capital, determined to make all the

pæans · joyous songs of praise, tribute, thanks-giving, or triumph

pusillanimity · cowardliness

apostates · those who have renounced their faith

fief · a feudal estate

15c Christians here apostatize. Everyone was interrogated and pressed to reject the Christian codes, or at least apostatize in form* only. Finally, in order to save the lives of my wife and children, I told them I would abandon my beliefs.

16 Suguro did not know where this man had been born, or what he had looked like. He had the impression he was a *samurai,** but there was no way to determine who his master might have been. The man would have had no inkling that his private confession would one day be published in a foreign land, and eventually fall into the hands of one of his own countrymen again, to be read by a person like Suguro. Though he did not have a clear picture of how the man looked, Suguro had some idea of the assortment of facial expressions he would have had to employ in order to evade detection. If he had been born in that age, Suguro would have had no qualms about going along with the Buddhist laymen to worship at their temples, if that meant he would not be exposed as a Christian. When someone mocked the Christian faith, he would have lowered his eyes and tried to look unconcerned. If so ordered, he might even have written out an oath of apostasy, if that would mean saving the lives of his family as well as his own.

※ ※ ※

17 A FAINT RAY OF LIGHT tentatively penetrated the clouds that had gathered over the summit of Unzen. Maybe it will clear up, he thought. In summer this paved road would no doubt be choked by a stream of cars out for a drive, but now there was only the bus struggling up the mountain with intermittent groans. Groves of withered trees shivered all around. A cluster of rain-soaked bungalows huddled silently among the trees, their doors tightly shut.

18 "Listen, martyrdom is no more than a matter of pride."

19 He had had this conversation in the corner of a bar in Shinjuku.* A pot of Akita salted-fish broth* simmered in the center of the *sake*-stained* table. Seated around the pot, Suguro's elders in the literary establishment had been discussing the hero of a novel he had recently published. The work dealt with some Christian martyrs in the 1870s. The writers at the gathering claimed that they could not swallow the motivations behind those martyrdoms the way Suguro had.

20 "At the very core of this desire to be a martyr you'll find pride, pure and simple."

apostatize in form · to say words or take actions that indicate apostasy without actually changing one's beliefs

samurai · a member of the Japanese warrior caste

Shinjuku · the main retail and entertainment district in Tokyo

Akita salted-fish broth · fish and salt combined into "shotturu," a kind of fish sauce

sake-stained · *sake* is an alcoholic fermented rice beverage which is usually served hot

"I'm sure pride plays a part in it. Along with the desire to 21 become a hero, and even a touch of insanity, perhaps. But – "

Suguro fell silent and clutched his glass. It was a simple task to 22 pinpoint elements of heroism and pride among the motives for martyrdom. But when those elements were obliterated, residual motives still remained. Those residual motives were of vital importance.

"Well, if you're going to look at it that way, you can find pride 23 and selfishness underlying virtually every human endeavour, every single act of good faith."

In the ten years he had been writing fiction, Suguro had grown 24 increasingly impatient with those modern novelists who tried to single out the egotism and pride in every act of man. To Suguro's mind, such a view of humanity entailed the loss of something of consummate value, like water poured through a sieve.

The road wound its way to the summit through dead grass and 25 barren woods. In days past, lines of human beings had struggled up this path. Both pride and madness had certainly been part of their make-up, but there must have been something more to it.

"The right wing during the war, for instance, had a certain 26 martyr mentality. I can't help thinking there's something impure going on when people are intoxicated by something like that. But perhaps I feel that way because I experienced the war myself," one of his elders snorted as he drank down his cup of tepid *sake*. Sensing an irreconcilable misunderstanding between himself and this man, Suguro could only grin acquiescently.

Before long he caught sight of a column of white smoke rising 27 like steam from the belly of the mountain. Though the windows of the bus were closed, he smelled a faintly sulphuric odor. Milky white crags and sand came into clear focus.

"Is that the Valley of Hell?" 28

"No." The conductor shook her head. "It's a little further up." 29

A tiny crack in the clouds afforded a glimpse of blue sky. The 30 bus, which up until now had panted along, grinding its gears, suddenly seemed to catch its breath and picked up speed. The road had levelled off, then begun to drop. A series of arrows tacked to the leafless trees, apparently to guide hikers, read "Valley of Hell." Just ahead was the red roof of the rest-house.

Suguro did not know whether the man mentioned in the 31 *Confessions* had come here to the Valley of Hell. But, as if before

31 Suguro's eyes, the image of another individual had overlapped with that of the first man and now stumbled along with his head bowed. There was a little more detailed information about this second man. His name was Kichijirō, and he first appeared in the historical records on the fifth day of December, 1631, when seven priests and Christians were tortured at the Valley of Hell. Kichijirō came here to witness the fate of the fathers who had cared for him. He had apostatized much earlier, so he had been able to blend in with the crowd of spectators. Standing on tiptoe, he had witnessed the cruel punishments which the officers inflicted on his spiritual mentors.

32 Father Christovão Ferreira, who later broke under torture and left a filthy smudge on the pages of Japanese Christian history, sent to his homeland a letter vividly describing the events of that day. The seven Christians arrived at Obama on the evening of December the second, and were driven up the mountain all the following day. There were several look-out huts on the slope, and that evening the seven captives were forced into one of them, their feet and hands still shackled. There they awaited the coming of dawn.

32a The tortures commenced on the fifth of December in the following manner. One by one each of the seven was taken to the brink of the seething pond. There they were shown the frothy spray from the boiling water, and ordered to renounce their faith. The air was chilly and the hot water of the pond churned so furiously that, had God not sustained them, a single look would have cause them to faint away. They all shouted, "Torture us! We will not recant!" At this response, the guards stripped the garments from the prisoners' bodies and bound their hands and feet. Four of them held down a single captive as a ladle holding about a quarter of a liter was filled with the boiling water. Three ladlesful were slowly poured over each body. One of the seven, a young girl called Maria, fainted from the excruciating pain and fell to the ground. In the space of thirty-three days, each of them was subjected to this torture a total of six times.

33 Suguro was the last one off when the bus came to a stop. The cold, taut mountain air blew a putrid odor into his nostrils. White steam poured onto the highway from the tree-ringed valley.

"How about a photograph? Photographs, anyone?" a young 34
man standing beside a large camera on a tripod called out to
Suguro. "I'll pay the postage wherever you want to send it."

At various spots along the road stood women proffering eggs 35
in baskets and waving clumsily-lettered signs that read "Boiled
Eggs." They too touted loudly for business.

Weaving their way among these hawkers, Suguro and the rest 36
of the group from the bus walked towards the valley. The earth,
overgrown with shrubbery, was virtually white, almost the color
of flesh stripped clean of its layer of skin. The rotten-smelling
steam gushed ceaselessly from amid the trees. The narrow path
stitched its way back and forth between springs of hot, bubbling
water. Some parts of the white-speckled pools lay as calm and
flat as a wall of plaster; others eerily spewed up slender sprays
of gurgling water. Here and there on the hillocks formed from
sulphur flows stood pine trees scorched red by the heat.

The bus passengers extracted boiled eggs from their paper 37
sacks and stuffed them into their mouths. They moved forward
like a column of ants.

"Come and look over here. There's a dead bird." 38

"So there is. I suppose the gas fumes must have asphyxiated it." 39

All he knew for certain was that Kichijirō had been a witness to 40
those tortures. Why had he come? There was no way of knowing
whether he had joined the crowd of Buddhist spectators in the hope
of rescuing the priests and the faithful who were being tormented.
The only tangible piece of information he had about Kichijirō was
that he had forsworn his religion to the officers, "so that his wife and
children might live." Nevertheless, he had followed in the footsteps of
those seven Christians, walking all the way from Nagasaki to Obama,
then trudging to the top of the bitterly cold peak of Unzen.

Suguro could almost see the look on Kichijirō's face as he 41
stood at the back of the crowd, furtively watching his former
companions with the tremulous gaze of a dog, then lowering his
eyes in humiliation. That look was very like Suguro's own. In any
case, there was no way Suguro could stand in chains before these
loathsomely bubbling pools and make any show of courage.

A momentary flash of white lit up the entire landscape; then 42
a fierce eruption burst forth with the smell of noxious gas. A
mother standing near the surge quickly picked up her crouching

42 child and retreated. A placard reading "Dangerous Beyond This Point" was thrust firmly into the clay. Around it the carcasses of three dead swallows were stretched out like mummies.

43 This must be the spot where the Christians were tortured, he thought. Through a crack in the misty, shifting steam, Suguro saw the black outlines of a cross. Covering his nose and mouth with a handkerchief and balancing precariously near the warning sign, he peered below him. The mottled water churned and sloshed before his eyes. The Christians must have stood just where he was standing now when they were tortured. And Kichijirō would have stayed behind, standing about where the mother and her child now stood at a cautious distance, watching the spectacle with the rest of the crowd. Inwardly, did he ask them to forgive him? Had Suguro been in his shoes, he would have had no recourse but to repeat over and over again, "Forgive me! I'm not strong enough to be a martyr like you. My heart melts just to think about this dreadful torture."

44 Of course, Kichijirō could justify his attitude. If he had lived in a time of religious freedom, he would never have become an apostate. He might not have qualified for sainthood, but he could have been a man who tamely maintained his faith. But to his regret, he had been born in an age of persecution, and out of fear he had tossed away his beliefs. Not everyone can become a saint or a martyr. Yet must those who do not qualify as saints be branded forever with the mark of the traitor? Perhaps he had made such a plea to the Christians who vilified him. Yet, despite the logic of his argument, he surely suffered pangs of remorse and cursed his own faint resolve.

45 "The apostate endures a pain none of you can comprehend."

46 Over the span of three centuries this cry, like the shriek of a wounded bird, reached Suguro's ears. That single line recorded in the *Christian Confessions* cut at Suguro's chest like a sharp sword. Surely those were the words Kichijirō must have shouted to himself here at Unzen as he looked upon his tormented friends.

❖ ❖ ❖

47 THEY REBOARDED THE BUS. The ride from Unzen to Shimabara took less than an hour. A fistful of blue finally appeared in the sky, but the air remained cold. The same conductor forced her usual smile and commented on the surroundings in a sing-song voice.

The seven Christians, refusing to bend to the tortures at 48
Unzen, had been taken down the mountain to Shimabara, along
the same route Suguro was now following. He could almost see
them dragging their scalded legs, leaning on walking-sticks and
enduring lashes from the officers.

Leaving some distance between them, Kichijirō had timo- 49
rously followed behind. When the weary Christians stopped to
catch their breath, Kichijirō also halted, a safe distance behind.
He hurriedly crouched down like a rabbit in the overgrowth, lest
the officers suspect him, and did not rise again until the group
had resumed their trek. He was like a jilted woman plodding
along in pursuit of her lover.

Half-way down the mountain he had a glimpse of the dark sea. 50
Milky clouds veiled the horizon; several wan beams of sunlight
filtered through the cracks. Suguro thought how blue the ocean
would appear on a clear day.

"Look – you can see a blur out there that looks like an island. 51
Unfortunately, you can't see it very well today. This is Dangō
Island, where Amakusa Shirō, the commander of the Christian
forces, planned the Shimabara Rebellion with his men."

At this the passengers took a brief, apathetic glance towards 52
the island. Before long the view of the distant sea was blocked
by a forest of trees.

What must those seven Christians have felt as they looked at 53
this ocean? They knew they would soon be executed at Shimabara.
The corpses of martyrs were swiftly reduced to ashes and cast
upon the seas. If that were not done, the remaining Christians
would surreptitiously worship the clothing and even locks of
hair from the martyrs as though they were holy objects. And so
the seven, getting their first distant view of the ocean from this
spot, must have realized that it would be their grave. Kichijirō
too would have looked at the sea, but with a different kind of
sorrow – with the knowledge that the strong ones in the world
of faith were crowned with glory, while the cowards had to carry
their burdens with them throughout their lives.

When the group reached Shimabara, four of them were placed 54
in a cell barely three feet tall and only wide enough to accommodate one *tatami*.* The other three were jammed into another
room equally cramped. As they awaited their punishment, they

tatami · a straw mat
used as a floor covering
in Japanese homes

54 persistently encouraged one another and went on praying. There is no record of where Kichijirō stayed during this time.

55 The village of Shimabara was dark and silent. The bus came to a stop by a tiny wharf where the rickety ferry-boat to Amakusa* was moored forlornly. Wood chips and flotsam bobbed on the small waves that lapped at the breakwater. Among the debris floated an object that resembled a rolled-up newspaper; it was the corpse of a cat.

56 The town extended in a thin band along the seafront. The fences of local factories stretched far into the distance, while the odor of chemicals wafted all the way to the highway.

57 Suguro set out towards the reconstructed Shimabara Castle. The only signs of life he encountered along the way were a couple of high-school girls riding bicycles.

58 "Where is the execution ground where the Christians were killed?" he asked them.

59 "I didn't know there was such a place," said one of them, blushing. She turned to her friend. "Have you heard of anything like that? You don't know, do you?" Her friend shook her head.

60 He came to a neighborhood identified as a former *samurai* residence. It had stood behind the castle, where several narrow paths intersected. A crumbling mud wall wound its way between the paths. The drainage ditch was as it had been in those days. Summer *mikans* poked their heads above the mud wall, which had already blocked out the evening sun. All the buildings were old, dark and musty. They had probably been the residence of a low-ranking *samurai*, built at the end of the Tokugawa period.* Many Christians had been executed at the Shimabara grounds, but Suguro had not come across any historical documents identifying the location of the prison.

61 He retraced his steps, and after a short walk came out on a street of shops where popular songs were playing. The narrow street was packed with a variety of stores, including gift shops. The water in the drainage ditch was as limpid as water from a spring.

62 "The execution ground? I know where that is." The owner of a tobacco shop directed Suguro to a pond just down the road. "If you go straight on past the pond, you'll come to a nursery school. The execution ground was just to the side of the school."

63 Though they say nothing of how he was able to do it, the records indicate that Kichijirō was allowed to visit the seven

Amakusa · the Amakusa Islands are part of Unzen-Amakusa National Park. The archipelago was long the gateway for Western culture and was an early center of Christianity. Following the massacre of Japanese Christians in the Shimabara Rebellion, the islands became a refuge for remaining Christians

Tokugawa period · also called the Edo period (1603–1867), it was the final period of traditional Japan, a time of internal peace, political stability, and economic growth under the shōgunate founded by Tokugawa Ieyasu

prisoners on the day before their execution. Possibly he put some 63
money into the hands of the officers.

Kichijirō offered a meager plate of food to the prisoners, who 64
were prostrate from their ordeal.

"Kichijirō, did you retract your oath?" one of the captives asked 65
compassionately. He was eager to know if the apostate had finally
informed the officials that he could not deny his faith. "Have you
come here to see us because you have retracted?"

Kichijirō looked up at them timidly and shook his head. 66

"In any case, Kichijirō, we can't accept this food." 67

"Why not?" 68

"Why not?" The prisoners were mournfully silent for a moment. 69
"Because we have already accepted the fact that we will die."

Kichijirō could only lower his eyes and say nothing. He knew 70
that he himself could never endure the sort of agony he had
witnessed at the Valley of Hell on Unzen.

Through his tears he whimpered, "If I can't suffer the same 71
pain as you, will I be unable to enter Paradise? Will God forsake
someone like me?"

He walked along the street of shops as he had been instructed 72
and came to the pond. A floodgate blocked the overflow from the
pond and the water poured underground and into the drainage
ditch in the village. Suguro read a sign declaring that the purity
of the water in Shimabara village was due to the presence of
this pond.

He heard the sounds of children at play. Four or five young 73
children were tossing a ball back and forth in the nursery school
playground. The setting sun shone feebly on the swings and sand-
box in the yard. He walked around behind a drooping hedge of
rose bushes and located the remains of the execution ground,
now the only barren patch within a grove of trees.

It was a deserted plot some three hundred square yards in 74
size, grown rank with brown weeds; pines towered over a heap of
refuse. Suguro had come all the way from Tokyo to have a look at
this place. Or had he made the journey out of a desire to understand better Kichijirō's emotions as he stood in this spot?

The following morning the seven prisoners were hoisted 75
onto the unsaddled horses and dragged through the streets of
Shimabara to this execution ground.

76   One of the witnesses to the scene has recorded the events of the day: "After they were paraded about, they arrived at the execution ground, which was surrounded by a palisade. They were taken off their horses and made to stand in front of stakes set three metres apart. Firewood was already piled at the base of the stakes, and straw roofs soaked in sea water had been placed on top of them to prevent the flames from raging too quickly and allowing the martyrs to die with little agony. The ropes that bound them to the stakes were tied as loosely as possible, to permit them, up to the very moment of death, to twist their bodies and cry out that they would abandon their faith.

77   "When the officers began setting fire to the wood, a solitary man broke through the line of guards and dashed towards the stakes. He was shouting something, but I could not hear what he said over the roar of the fires. The fierce flames and smoke prevented the man from approaching the prisoners. The guards swiftly apprehended him and asked if he was a Christian. At that, the man froze in fear, and jabbering, "I am no Christian. I have nothing to do with these people! I just lost my head in all the excitement," he skulked away. But some in the crowd had seen him at the rear of the assemblage, his hands pressed together as he repeated over and over, "Forgive me! Forgive me!"

78   "The seven victims sang a hymn until the flames enveloped their stakes. Their voices were exuberant, totally out of keeping with the cruel punishment they were even then enduring. When those voices suddenly ceased, the only sound was the dull crackling of wood. The man who had darted forward could be seen walking lifelessly away from the execution ground. Rumors spread through the crowd that he too had been a Christian."

79   Suguro noticed a dark patch at the very center of the execution ground. On closer inspection he discovered several charred stones half buried beneath the black earth. Although he had no way of knowing whether these stones had been used here three hundred years before, when seven Christians had been burned at the stake, he hurriedly snatched up one of the stones and put it in his pocket. Then, his spine bent like Kichijirō's, he walked back towards the road.

Flannery O'Connor

⟨ 1 9 2 5 – 1 9 6 4 ⟩

Born in Savannah and reared in a minority Roman Catholic community in Milledgeville, Georgia, O'Connor bore the impress of both her regional and religious environment. Her short stories are often set in the dark grotesquerie of the South, and her most memorable characters grapple with intense spiritual crises. After attending the Women's College of Georgia, O'Connor studied writing at the State University of Iowa, earning an MFA *in 1947. She went on to produce a succession of carefully crafted stories and two novels,* Wise Blood *(1952) and* The Violent Bear It Away *(1960), before succumbing to lupus at thirty-eight. O'Connor was posthumously awarded the National Book Award in 1972 for* The Complete Stories. *In* Mystery and Manners *(1969), a collection of essays on the writer's craft, O'Connor has said that life and thus true-to-life fiction is essentially mysterious: "a story does not begin except at a depth where adequate motivation and adequate psychology and the various determinations have been exhausted." It is in this mysterious region, a space in which supernatural powers of good and evil vie for the soul, that the author's characters confront life-changing spiritual choices. And for O'Connor, volitional choice is a reality. Her work is marked by "the redemptive act," by the demand "that what falls at least be offered the chance to be restored."*

REVELATION

1   THE DOCTOR'S WAITING ROOM, which was very small, was almost full when the Turpins entered and Mrs. Turpin, who was very large, made it look even smaller by her presence. She stood looming at the head of the magazine table set in the center of it, a living demonstration that the room was inadequate and ridiculous. Her little bright black eyes took in all the patients as

she sized up the seating situation. There was one vacant chair 1
and a place on the sofa occupied by a blond child in a dirty blue
romper who should have been told to move over and make room
for the lady. He was five or six, but Mrs. Turpin saw at once that
no one was going to tell him to move over. He was slumped down
in the seat, his arms idle at his sides and his eyes idle in his head;
his nose ran unchecked.

Mrs. Turpin put a firm hand on Claud's shoulder and said in 2
a voice that included anyone who wanted to listen, "Claud, you
sit in that chair there," and gave him a push down into the vacant
one. Claud was florid and bald and sturdy, somewhat shorter
than Mrs. Turpin, but he sat down as if he were accustomed to
doing what she told him to.

Mrs. Turpin remained standing. The only man in the room 3
besides Claud was a lean stringy old fellow with a rusty hand
spread out on each knee, whose eyes were closed as if he were
asleep or dead or pretending to be so as not to get up and offer
her his seat. Her gaze settled agreeably on a well-dressed gray-
haired lady whose eyes met hers and whose expression said: if that
child belonged to me, he would have some manners and move
over – there's plenty of room there for you and him too.

Claud looked up with a sigh and made as if to rise. 4

"Sit down," Mrs. Turpin said. "You know you're not supposed 5
to stand on that leg. He has an ulcer on his leg," she explained.

Claud lifted his foot onto the magazine table and rolled his 6
trouser leg up to reveal a purple swelling on a plump marble-
white calf.

"My!" the pleasant lady said. "How did you do that?" 7

"A cow kicked him," Mrs. Turpin said. 8

"Goodness!" said the lady. 9

Claud rolled his trouser leg down. 10

"Maybe the little boy would move over," the lady suggested, 11
but the child did not stir.

"Somebody will be leaving in a minute," Mrs. Turpin said. 12
She could not understand why a doctor – with as much money
as they made charging five dollars a day to just stick their head
in the hospital door and look at you – couldn't afford a decent-
sized waiting room. This one was hardly bigger than a garage.
The table was cluttered with limp-looking magazines and at one

12   end of it there was a big green glass ashtray full of cigarette butts and cotton wads with little blood spots on them. If she had had anything to do with the running of the place, that would have been emptied every so often. There were no chairs against the wall at the head of the room. It had a rectangular-shaped panel in it that permitted a view of the office where the nurse came and went and the secretary listened to the radio. A plastic fern in a gold pot sat in the opening and trailed its fronds down almost to the floor. The radio was softly playing gospel music.

13   Just then the inner door opened and a nurse with the highest stack of yellow hair Mrs. Turpin had ever seen put her face in the crack and called for the next patient. The woman sitting beside Claud grasped the two arms of her chair and hoisted herself up; she pulled her dress free from her legs and lumbered through the door where the nurse had disappeared.

14   Mrs. Turpin eased into the vacant chair, which held her tight as a corset. "I wish I could reduce," she said, and rolled her eyes and gave a comic sigh.

15   "Oh, you aren't fat," the stylish lady said.

16   "Ooooo I am too," Mrs. Turpin said. "Claud he eats all he wants to and never weighs over one hundred and seventy-five pounds, but me I just look at something good to eat and I gain some weight," and her stomach and shoulders shook with laughter. "You can eat all you want to, can't you, Claud?" she asked, turning to him.

17   Claud only grinned.

18   "Well, as long as you have such a good disposition," the stylish lady said, "I don't think it makes a bit of difference what size you are. You just can't beat a good disposition."

19   Next to her was a fat girl of eighteen or nineteen, scowling into a thick blue book which Mrs. Turpin saw was entitled *Human Development*. The girl raised her head and directed her scowl at Mrs. Turpin as if she did not like her looks. She appeared annoyed that anyone should speak while she tried to read. The poor girl's face was blue with acne and Mrs. Turpin thought how pitiful it was to have a face like that at that age. She gave the girl a friendly smile but the girl only scowled the harder. Mrs. Turpin herself was fat but she had always had good skin, and, though she was forty-seven years old, there was not a wrinkle in her face except around her eyes from laughing too much.

Next to the ugly girl was the child, still in exactly the same posi- 20
tion, and next to him was a thin leathery old woman in a cotton
print dress. She and Claud had three sacks of chicken feed in their
pump house that was in the same print.* She had seen from the
first that the child belonged with the old woman. She could tell by
the way they sat – kind of vacant and white-trashy, as if they would
sit there until Doomsday if nobody called and told them to get up.
And at right angles but next to the well-dressed pleasant lady was
a lank-faced woman who was certainly the child's mother. She
had on a yellow sweat shirt and wine-colored slacks, both gritty
looking, and the rims of her lips were stained with snuff.* Her
dirty yellow hair was tied behind with a little piece of red paper
ribbon. Worse than niggers any day, Mrs. Turpin thought.

The gospel hymn playing was, "When I looked up and He 21
looked down,"* and Mrs. Turpin, who knew it, supplied the last
line mentally, "And wona these days I know I'll we-eara crown."

Without appearing to, Mrs. Turpin always noticed people's 22
feet. The well-dressed lady had on red and gray suede shoes
to match her dress. Mrs. Turpin had on her good black patent
leather pumps. The ugly girl had on Girl Scout shoes and heavy
socks. The old woman had on tennis shoes and the white-trashy
mother had on what appeared to be bedroom slippers, black
straw with gold braid threaded through them – exactly what you
would have expected her to have on.

Sometimes at night when she couldn't go to sleep, Mrs. Turpin 23
would occupy herself with the question of who she would have
chosen to be if she couldn't have been herself. If Jesus had said
to her before he made her, "There's only two places available for
you. You can either be a nigger or white-trash," what would she
have said? "Please, Jesus, please," she would have said, "just let me
wait until there's another place available," and he would have said,
"No, you have to go right now and I have only those two places so
make up your mind." She would have wiggled and squirmed and
begged and pleaded but it would have been no use and finally
she would have said, "All right, make me a nigger then – but that
don't mean a trashy one." And he would have made her a neat
clean respectable Negro woman, herself but black.

Next to the child's mother was a red-headed youngish 24
woman, reading one of the magazines and working a piece of

---

in the same print ·
flour and animal feed
were often shipped in
cotton bags which poor
or rural people used
to make clothing and
other furnishings

snuff · a smokeless
tobacco product

**"When I … looked
down" ·** the hymn
(words and music
A. E. Brumley, 1955)
describes an epiphany
when one who "had
reached a sorry station
in this wilderness below"
looks up to heaven and
realizes salvation

24 chewing gum, hell for leather, as Claud would say. Mrs. Turpin
could not see the woman's feet. She was not white-trash, just
common. Sometimes Mrs. Turpin occupied herself at night
naming the classes of people. On the bottom of the heap were
most colored people, not the kind she would have been if she
had been one, but most of them; then next to them – not above,
just away from – were the white-trash; then above them were
the home-owners, and above them the home-and-land owners,
to which she and Claud belonged. Above she and Claud were
people with a lot of money and much bigger houses and much
more land. But here the complexity of it would begin to bear in
on her, for some of the people with a lot money were common
and ought to be below she and Claud and some of the people
who had good blood had lost their money and had to rent and
then there were colored people who owned their homes and
land as well. There was a colored dentist in town who had two
red Lincolns and a swimming pool and a farm with registered
white-face cattle on it. Usually by the time she had fallen asleep
all the classes of people were moiling and roiling around in her
head, and she would dream they were all crammed in together
in a box car, being ridden off to be put in a gas oven.

25 "That's a beautiful clock," she said and nodded to her right. It
was a big wall clock, the face encased in a brass sunburst.

26 "Yes, it's very pretty," the stylish lady said agreeably. "And right
on the dot too," she added, glancing at her watch.

27 The ugly girl beside her cast an eye upward at the clock,
smirked, then looked directly at Mrs. Turpin and smirked again.
Then she returned her eyes to her book. She was obviously the
lady's daughter because, although they didn't look anything
alike as to disposition, they both had the same shape of face
and the same blue eyes. On the lady they sparkled pleasantly
but in the girl's seared face they appeared alternately to smolder
and to blaze.

28 What if Jesus had said, "All right, you can be white-trash or
a nigger or ugly!"

29 Mrs. Turpin felt an awful pity for the girl, though she thought
it was one thing to be ugly and another to act ugly.

30 The woman with the snuff-stained lips turned around in her
chair and looked up at the clock. Then she turned back and

appeared to look a little to the side of Mrs. Turpin. There was a 30
cast in one of her eyes. "You want to know wher you can get you
one of themther clocks?" she asked in a loud voice.

"No, I already have a nice clock," Mrs. Turpin said. Once 31
somebody like her got a leg in the conversation, she would be
all over it.

"You can get you one with green stamps,"* the woman said. 32
"That's most likely wher he got hisn. Save you up enough, you
can get you most anythang. I got me some joo'ry."

Ought to have got you a wash rag and some soap, Mrs. Turpin 33
thought.

"I get contour sheets with mine," the pleasant lady said. 34

The daughter slammed her book shut. She looked straight 35
in front of her, directly through Mrs. Turpin and on through
the yellow curtain and the plate glass window which made the
wall behind her. The girl's eyes seemed lit all of a sudden with a
peculiar light, an unnatural light like night road signs give. Mrs.
Turpin turned her head to see if there was anything going on outside that she should see, but she could not see anything. Figures
passing cast only a pale shadow through the curtain. There was
no reason the girl should single her out for her ugly looks.

"Miss Finley," the nurse said, cracking the door. The gum- 36
chewing woman got up and passed in front of her and Claud
and went into the office. She had on red high-heeled shoes.

Directly across the table, the ugly girl's eyes were fixed on Mrs. 37
Turpin as if she had some very special reason for disliking her.

"This is wonderful weather, isn't it?" the girl's mother said. 38

"It's good weather for cotton if you can get the niggers to pick 39
it," Mrs. Turpin said, "but niggers don't want to pick cotton any
more. You can't get the white folks to pick it and now you can't
get the niggers – because they got to be right up there with the
white folks."

"They gonna *try* anyways," the white-trash woman said, lean- 40
ing forward.

"Do you have one of the cotton-picking machines?" the pleas- 41
ant lady asked.

"No," Mrs. Turpin said, "they leave half the cotton in the 42
field. We don't have much cotton anyway. If you want to make
it farming now, you have to have a little of everything. We got a

42 couple of acres of cotton and a few hogs and chickens and just enough white-face that Claud can look after them himself, for merchandise of various types."

43 "One thang I don't want," the white-trash woman said, wiping her mouth with the back of her hand. "Hogs. Nasty stinking things, a-gruntin and a-rootin all over the place."

44 Mrs. Turpin gave her the merest edge of her attention. "Our hogs are not dirty and they don't stink," she said. "They're cleaner than some children I've seen. Their feet never touch the ground. We have a pig-parlor – that's where you raise them on concrete," she explained to the pleasant lady, "and Claud scoots them down with the hose every afternoon and washes off the floor." Cleaner by far than that child right there, she thought. Poor nasty little thing. He had not moved except to put the thumb of his dirty hand into his mouth.

45 The woman turned her face away from Mrs. Turpin. "I know I wouldn't scoot down no hog with no hose," she said to the wall.

46 You wouldn't have no hog to scoot down, Mrs. Turpin said to herself.

47 "A-gruntin and a-rootin and a-groanin," the woman muttered.

48 "We got a little of everything," Mrs. Turpin said to the pleasant lady. "It's no use in having more than you can handle yourself with help like it is. We found enough niggers to pick our cotton this year but Claud he has to go after them and take them home again in the evening. They can't walk that half a mile. No they can't. I tell you," she said and laughed merrily, "I sure am tired of buttering up niggers, but you got to love em if you want em to work for you. When they come in the morning, I run out and I say, 'Hi yawl this morning?' and when Claud drives them off to the field I just wave to beat the band and they just wave back." And she waved her hand rapidly to illustrate.

49 "Like you read out of the same book," the lady said, showing she understood perfectly.

50 "Child, yes," Mrs. Turpin said. "And when they come in from the field, I run out with a bucket of icewater. That's the way it's going to be from now on," she said. "You may as well face it."

51 "One thang I know," the white-trash woman said. "Two thangs I ain't going to do: love no niggers or scoot down no hog with no hose." And she let out a bark of contempt.

The look that Mrs. Turpin and the pleasant lady exchanged 52 indicated they both understood that you had to *have* certain things before you could *know* certain things. But every time Mrs. Turpin exchanged a look with the lady, she was aware that the ugly girl's peculiar eyes were still on her, and she had trouble bringing her attention back to the conversation.

"When you got something," she said, "you got to look after 53 it." And when you ain't got a thing but breath and britches, she added to herself, you can afford to come to town every morning and just sit on the Court House coping and spit.

A grotesque revolving shadow passed across the curtain 54 behind her and was thrown palely on the opposite wall. Then a bicycle clattered down against the outside of the building. The door opened and a colored boy glided in with a tray from the drugstore. It had two large red and white paper cups on it with tops on them. He was a tall, very black boy in discolored white pants and a green nylon shirt. He was chewing gum slowly, as if to music. He set the tray down in the office opening next to the fern and stuck his head through to look for the secretary. She was not in there. He rested his arms on the ledge and waited, his narrow bottom stuck out, swaying to the left and right. He raised a hand over his head and scratched the base of his skull.

"You see that button there, boy?" Mrs. Turpin said. "You can punch 55 that and she'll come. She's probably in the back somewhere."

"Is thas right?" the boy said agreeably, as if he had never seen 56 the button before. He leaned to the right and put his finger on it. "She sometime out," he said and twisted around to face his audience, his elbows behind him on the counter. The nurse appeared and he twisted back again. She handed him a dollar and he rooted in his pocket and made the change and counted it out to her. She gave him fifteen cents for a tip and he went out with the empty tray. The heavy door swung to slowly and closed at length with the sound of suction. For a moment no one spoke.

"They ought to send all them niggers back to Africa," the white 57 trash woman said. "That's wher they come from in the first place."

"Oh, I couldn't do without my good colored friends," the 58 pleasant lady said.

"There's a heap of things worse than a nigger," Mrs. Turpin 59 agreed. "It's all kinds of them just like it's all kinds of us."

60   "Yes, and it takes all kinds to make the world go round," the lady said in her musical voice.

61   As she said it, the raw-complexioned girl snapped her teeth together. Her lower lip turned downwards and inside out, revealing the pale pink inside of her mouth. After a second it rolled back up. It was the ugliest face Mrs. Turpin had ever seen anyone make and for a moment she was certain that the girl had made it at her. She was looking at her as if she had known and disliked her all her life – all of Mrs. Turpin's life, it seemed too, not just all the girl's life. Why, girl, I don't even know you, Mrs. Turpin said silently.

62   She forced her attention back to the discussion. "It wouldn't be practical to send them back to Africa," she said. "They wouldn't want to go. They got it too good here."

63   "Wouldn't be what they wanted – if I had anythang to do with it," the woman said.

64   "It wouldn't be a way in the world you could get all the niggers back over there," Mrs. Turpin said. "They'd be hiding out and lying down and turning sick on you and wailing and hollering and raring and pitching. It wouldn't be a way in the world to get them over there."

65   "They got over here," the trashy woman said. "Get back like they got over."

66   "It wasn't so many of them then," Mrs. Turpin explained.

67   The woman looked at Mrs. Turpin as if here was an idiot indeed but Mrs. Turpin was not bothered by the look, considering where it came from.

68   "Nooo," she said, "they're going to stay here where they can go to New York and marry white folks and improve their color. That's what they all want to do, every one of them, improve their color."

69   "You know what comes of that, don't you?" Claud asked.

70   "No, Claud, what?" Mrs. Turpin said.

71   Claud's eyes twinkled. "White-faced niggers," he said with never a smile.

72   Everybody in the office laughed except the white-trash and the ugly girl. The girl gripped the book in her lap with white fingers. The trashy woman looked around her from face to face as if she thought they were all idiots. The old woman in the feed sack dress continued to gaze expressionless across the floor at

the high-top shoes of the man opposite her, the one who had 72
been pretending to be asleep when the Turpins came in. He was
laughing heartily, his hands still spread out on his knees. The
child had fallen to the side and was lying now almost face down
in the old woman's lap.

While they recovered from their laughter, the nasal chorus 73
on the radio kept the room from silence.

"You go to blank blank 73a
And I'll go to mine
But we'll all blank along
To-geth-ther,
And all along the blank
We'll hep eachother out
Smile-ling in any kind of
Weath-ther!"*

"You go ... Weather!" · a version of the bluegrass song "You Go To Your Church (And I'll Go To Mine)" (lyrics by Phillips H. Lord) which calls for "separate but equal" tolerance among Christians despite doctrinal differences

Mrs. Turpin didn't catch every word but she caught enough 74
to agree with the spirit of the song and it turned her thoughts
sober. To help anybody out that needed it was her philosophy of
life. She never spared herself when she found somebody in need,
whether they were white or black, trash or decent. And of all she
had to be thankful for, she was most thankful that this was so. If
Jesus had said, "You can be high society and have all the money
you want and be thin and svelte-like,* but you can't be a good
woman with it," she would have had to say, "Well don't make
me that then. Make me a good woman and it don't matter what
else, how fat or how ugly or how poor!" Her heart rose. He had
not made her a nigger or white-trash or ugly! He had made her
herself and given her a little of everything. Jesus, thank you! she
said. Thank you thank you thank you! Whenever she counted her
blessings she felt as buoyant as if she weighed one hundred and
twenty-five pounds instead of one hundred and eighty.

svelte-like · graceful and suave, refined in form

"What's wrong with your little boy?" the pleasant lady asked 75
the white-trashy woman.

"He has a ulcer," the woman said proudly. "He ain't give me a 76
minute's peace since he was born. Him and her are just alike," she
said, nodding at the old woman, who was running her leathery
fingers through the child's pale hair. "Look like I can't get nothing
down them two but Co' Cola and candy."

77   That's all you try to get down em, Mrs. Turpin said to herself. Too lazy to light the fire. There was nothing you could tell her about people like them that she didn't know already. And it was not just that they didn't have anything. Because if you gave them every-thing, in two weeks it would all be broken or filthy or they would have chopped it up for lightwood. She knew all this from her own experience. Help them you must, but help them you couldn't.

78   All at once the ugly girl turned her lips inside out again. Her eyes fixed like two drills on Mrs. Turpin. This time there was no mistaking that there was something urgent behind them.

79   Girl, Mrs. Turpin exclaimed silently, I haven't done a thing to you! The girl might be confusing her with somebody else. There was no need to sit by and let herself be intimidated. "You must be in college," she said boldly, looking directly at the girl. "I see you reading a book there."

80   The girl continued to stare and pointedly did not answer.

81   Her mother blushed at this rudeness. "The lady asked you a question, Mary Grace," she said under her breath.

82   "I have ears," Mary Grace said.

83   The poor mother blushed again. "Mary Grace goes to Wellesley College,"* she explained. She twisted one of the but-tons on her dress. "In Massachusetts," she added with a grimace. "And in the summer she just keeps right on studying. Just reads all the time, a real book worm. She's done real well at Wellesley; she's taking English and Math and History and Psychology and Social Studies," she rattled on, "and I think it's too much. I think she ought to get out and have fun."

Wellesley College · a private women's college in Wellesley, Massachusetts, known for its rigorous liberal arts curriculum

84   The girl looked as if she would like to hurl them all through the plate glass window.

85   "Way up north," Mrs. Turpin murmured and thought, well, it hasn't done much for her manners.

86   "I'd almost rather to have him sick," the white-trash woman said, wrenching the attention back to herself. "He's so mean when he ain't. Look like some children just take natural to meanness. It's some gets bad when they get sick but he was the opposite. Took sick and turned good. He don't give me no trouble now. It's me waitin to see the doctor," she said.

87   If I was going to send anybody back to Africa, Mrs. Turpin thought, it would be your kind, woman. "Yes, indeed," she said

aloud, but looking up at the ceiling, "it's a heap of things worse 87
than a nigger." And dirtier than a hog, she added to herself.

"I think people with bad dispositions are more to be pitied 88
than anyone on earth," the pleasant lady said in a voice that was
decidedly thin.

"I thank the Lord he has blessed me with a good one," Mrs. 89
Turpin said. "The day has never dawned that I couldn't find
something to laugh at."

"Not since she married me anyways," Claud said with a comical 90
straight face.

Everybody laughed except the girl and the white-trash. 91

Mrs. Turpin's stomach shook. "He's such a caution," she said, 92
"that I can't help but laugh at him."

The girl made a loud ugly noise through her teeth. 93

Her mother's mouth grew thin and tight. "I think the worst 94
thing in the world," she said, "is an ungrateful person. To have
everything and not appreciate it. I know a girl," she said, "who has
parents who would give her anything, a little brother who loves
her dearly, who is getting a good education, who wears the best
clothes, but who can never say a kind word to anyone, who never
smiles, who just criticizes and complains all day long."

"Is she too old to paddle?" Claud asked. 95

The girl's face was almost purple. 96

"Yes," the lady said, "I'm afraid there's nothing to do but leave 97
her to her folly. Some day she'll wake up and it'll be too late."

"It never hurt anyone to smile," Mrs. Turpin said. "It just makes 98
you feel better all over."

"Of course," the lady said sadly, "but there are just some people 99
you can't tell anything to. They can't take criticism."

"If it's one thing I am," Mrs. Turpin said with feeling, "it's grate- 100
ful. When I think who all I could have been besides myself and
what all I got, a little of everything, and a good disposition besides,
I just feel like shouting, 'Thank you, Jesus, for making everything
the way it is!' It could have been different!" For one thing, somebody else could have got Claud. At the thought of this, she was
flooded with gratitude and a terrible pang of joy ran through her.
"Oh thank you, Jesus, Jesus, thank you!" she cried aloud.

The book struck her directly over her left eye. It struck almost 101
at the same instant that she realized the girl was about to hurl

101   it. Before she could utter a sound, the raw face came crashing across the table toward her, howling. The girl's fingers sank like clamps into the soft flesh of her neck. She heard the mother cry out and Claud shout, "Whoa!" There was an instant when she was certain that she was about to be in an earthquake.

102   All at once her vision narrowed and she saw everything as if it were happening in a small room far away, or as if she were looking at it through the wrong end of a telescope. Claud's face crumpled and fell out of sight. The nurse ran in, then out, then in again. Then the gangling figure of the doctor rushed out of the inner door. Magazines flew this way and that as the table turned over. The girl fell with a thud and Mrs. Turpin's vision suddenly reversed itself and she saw everything large instead of small. The eyes of the white-trashy woman were staring hugely at the floor. There the girl, held down on one side by the nurse and on the other by her mother, was wrenching and turning in their grasp. The doctor was kneeling astride her, trying to hold her arm down. He managed after a second to sink a long needle into it.

103   Mrs. Turpin felt entirely hollow except for her heart which swung from side to side as if it were agitated in a great empty drum of flesh.

104   "Somebody that's not busy call for the ambulance," the doctor said in the off-hand voice young doctors adopt for terrible occasions.

105   Mrs. Turpin could not have moved a finger. The old man who had been sitting next to her skipped nimbly into the office and made the call, for the secretary still seemed to be gone.

106   "Claud!" Mrs. Turpin called.

107   He was not in his chair. She knew she must jump up and find him but she felt like some one trying to catch a train in a dream, when everything moves in slow motion and the faster you try to run the slower you go.

108   "Here I am," a suffocated voice, very unlike Claud's, said.

109   He was doubled up in the corner on the floor, pale as paper, holding his leg. She wanted to get up and go to him but she could not move. Instead, her gaze was drawn slowly downward to the churning face on the floor, which she could see over the doctor's shoulder.

110   The girl's eyes stopped rolling and focused on her. They seemed a much lighter blue than before, as if a door that had

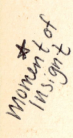

been tightly closed behind them was now open to admit light 110
and air.

Mrs. Turpin's head cleared and her power of motion returned. 111
She leaned forward until she was looking directly into the fierce
brilliant eyes. There was no doubt in her mind that the girl did
know her, knew her in some intense and personal way, beyond
time and place and condition. "What you got to say to me?" she
asked hoarsely and held her breath, waiting, as for a revelation.

The girl raised her head. Her gaze locked with Mrs. Turpin's. 112
"Go back to hell where you came from, you old wart hog," she whispered. Her voice was low but clear. Her eyes burned for a moment
as if she saw with pleasure that her message had struck its target.

Mrs. Turpin sank back in her chair. 113

After a moment the girl's eyes closed and she turned her head 114
wearily to the side.

The doctor rose and handed the nurse the empty syringe. He 115
leaned over and put both hands for a moment on the mother's
shoulders, which were shaking. She was sitting on the floor, her
lips pressed together, holding Mary Grace's hand in her lap. The
girl's fingers were gripped like a baby's around her thumb. "Go on
to the hospital," he said. "I'll call and make the arrangements."

"Now let's see that neck," he said in a jovial voice to Mrs. Turpin. 116
He began to inspect her neck with his first two fingers. Two little
moon-shaped lines like pink fish bones were indented over her
windpipe. There was the beginning of an angry red swelling above
her eye. His fingers passed over this also.

"Lea' me be," she said thickly and shook him off. "See about 117
Claud. She kicked him."

"I'll see about him in a minute," he said and felt her pulse. He 118
was a thin gray-haired man, given to pleasantries. "Go home and
have yourself a vacation the rest of the day," he said and patted
her on the shoulder.

Quit your pattin' me, Mrs. Turpin growled to herself. 119

"And put an ice pack over that eye," he said. Then he went and 120
squatted down beside Claud and looked at his leg. After a moment
he pulled him up and Claud limped after him into the office.

Until the ambulance came, the only sounds in the room were 121
the tremulous moans of the girl's mother, who continued to sit
on the floor. The white-trash woman did not take her eyes off the

121 girl. Mrs. Turpin looked straight ahead at nothing. Presently the ambulance drew up, a long dark shadow, behind the curtain. The attendants came in and set the stretcher down beside the girl and lifted her expertly onto it and carried her out. The nurse helped the mother gather up her things. The shadow of the ambulance moved silently away and the nurse came back in the office.

122 "That ther girl is going to be a lunatic, ain't she?" the white-trash woman asked the nurse, but the nurse kept on to the back and never answered her.

123 "Yes, she's going to be a lunatic," the white-trash woman said to the rest of them.

124 "Po' critter," the old woman murmured. The child's face was still in her lap. His eyes looked idly out over her knees. He had not moved during the disturbance except to draw one leg up under him.

125 "I thank Gawd," the white-trash woman said fervently, "I ain't a lunatic."

126 Claud came limping out and the Turpins went home.

127 As their pick-up truck turned into their own dirt road and made the crest of the hill, Mrs. Turpin gripped the window ledge and looked out suspiciously. The land sloped gracefully down through a field dotted with lavender weeds and at the start of the rise their small yellow frame house, with its little flower beds spread out around it like a fancy apron, sat primly in its accustomed place between two giant hickory trees. She would not have been startled to see a burnt wound between two blackened chimneys.

128 Neither of them felt like eating so they put on their house clothes and lowered the shade in the bedroom and lay down, Claud with his leg on a pillow and herself with a damp washcloth over her eye. The instant she was flat on her back, the image of a razorbacked hog with warts on its face and horns coming out behind its ears snorted into her head. She moaned, a low quiet moan.

129 "I am not," she said tearfully, "a wart hog. From hell." But the denial had no force. The girl's eyes and her words, even the tone of her voice, low but clear, directed only to her, brooked no repudiation. She had been singled out for the message, though there was trash in the room to whom it might justly have been applied. The full force of this fact struck her only now. There was

a woman there who was neglecting her own child but she had   129
been overlooked. The message had been given to Ruby Turpin,
a respectable, hard-working, church-going woman. The tears
dried. Her eyes began to burn instead with wrath.

She rose on her elbow and the washcloth fell into her hand.   130
Claud was lying on his back, snoring. She wanted to tell him what
the girl had said. At the same time, she did not wish to put the
image of herself as a wart hog from hell into his mind.

"Hey, Claud," she muttered and pushed his shoulder.   131

Claud opened one pale baby blue eye.   132

She looked into it warily. He did not think about anything.   133
He just went his way.

"Wha, whasit?" he said and closed the eye again.   134

"Nothing," she said. "Does your leg pain you?"   135

"Hurts like hell," Claud said.   136

"It'll quit terreckly," she said and lay back down. In a moment   137
Claud was snoring again. For the rest of the afternoon they lay
there. Claud slept. She scowled at the ceiling. Occasionally she
raised her fist and made a small stabbing motion over her chest as
if she was defending her innocence to invisible guests who were
like the comforters of Job,· reasonable-seeming but wrong.

About five-thirty Claud stirred. "Got to go after those niggers,"   138
he sighed, not moving.

She was looking straight up as if there were unintelligible   139
handwriting on the ceiling. The protuberance over her eye had
turned a greenish-blue. "Listen here," she said.

"What?"   140

"Kiss me."   141

Claud leaned over and kissed her loudly on the mouth. He   142
pinched her side and their hands interlocked. Her expression of
ferocious concentration did not change. Claud got up, groaning
and growling, and limped off. She continued to study the ceiling.

She did not get up until she heard the pick-up truck coming   143
back with the Negroes. Then she rose and thrust her feet in her
brown oxfords, which she did not bother to lace, and stumped
out onto the back porch and got her red plastic bucket. She
emptied a tray of ice cubes into it and filled it half full of water
and went out into the back yard. Every afternoon after Claud
brought the hands in, one of the boys helped him put out hay

---

comforters of Job ·
for most of the book
of Job, his three friends
attempt to convince
him that he is being
punished for evil things
he has done or good
things he has left
undone. They argue
with Job extensively,
but are finally rebuked
by God (see Job 37:1)

143 and the rest waited in the back of the truck until he was ready to take them home. The truck was parked in the shade under one of the hickory trees.

144 "Hi yawl this evening?" Mrs. Turpin asked grimly, appearing with the bucket and the dipper. There were three women and a boy in the truck.

145 "Us doin nicely," the oldest woman said. "Hi you doin?" and her gaze stuck immediately on the dark lump on Mrs. Turpin's forehead. "You done fell down, ain't you?" she asked in a solicitous voice. The old woman was dark and almost toothless. She had on an old felt hat of Claud's set back on her head. The other two women were younger and lighter and they both had new bright green sunhats. One of them had hers on her head; the other had taken hers off and the boy was grinning beneath it.

146   Mrs. Turpin set the bucket down on the floor of the truck. "Yawl hep yourselves," she said. She looked around to make sure Claud had gone. "No, I didn't fall down," she said, folding her arms. "It was something worse than that."

147 "Ain't nothing bad happen to you!" the old woman said. She said it as if they all knew that Mrs. Turpin was protected in some special way by Divine Providence. "You just had you a little fall."

148 "We were in town at the doctor's office for where the cow kicked Mr. Turpin," Mrs. Turpin said in a flat tone that indicated they could leave off their foolishness. "And there was this girl there. A big fat girl with her face all broke out. I could look at that girl and tell she was peculiar but I couldn't tell how. And me and her mama was just talking and going along and all of a sudden WHAM! She throws this big book she was reading at me and...."

149 "Naw!" the old woman cried out.

150 "And then she jumps over the table and commences to choke me."

151 "Naw!" they all exclaimed, "naw!"

152 "Hi come she do that?" the old woman asked. "What ail her?"

153   Mrs. Turpin only glared in front of her.

154 "Somethin ail her," the old woman said.

155 "They carried her off in an ambulance," Mrs. Turpin continued, "but before she went she was rolling on the floor and they were trying to hold her down to give her a shot and she said something to me." She paused. "You know what she said to me?"

"What she say?" they asked. 156

"She said," Mrs. Turpin began, and stopped, her face very dark 157
and heavy. The sun was getting whiter and whiter, blanching the
sky overhead so that the leaves of the hickory tree were black in
the face of it. She could not bring forth the words. "Something
real ugly," she muttered.

"She sho shouldn't said nothin ugly to you," the old woman 158
said. "You so sweet. You the sweetest lady I know."

"She pretty too," the one with the hat on said. 159

"And stout," the other one said. "I never knowed no sweeter 160
white lady."

"That's the truth befo' Jesus," the old woman said. "Amen! You 161
des as sweet and pretty as you can be."

Mrs. Turpin knew exactly how much Negro flattery was 162
worth and it added to her rage. "She said," she began again and
finished this time with a fierce rush of breath, "that I was an old
wart hog from hell."

There was an astounded silence. 163

"Where she at?" the youngest woman cried in a piercing voice. 164

"Lemme see her. I'll kill her!" 165

"I'll kill her with you!" the other one cried. 166

"She b'long in the 'sylum," the old woman said emphatically. 167
"You the sweetest white lady I know."

"She pretty too," the other two said. "Stout as she can be and 168
sweet. Jesus satisfied with her!"

"'Deed he is," the old woman declared. 169

Idiots! Mrs. Turpin growled to herself. You could never say 170
anything intelligent to a nigger. You could talk at them but not
with them. "Yawl ain't drunk your water," she said shortly. "Leave
the bucket in the truck when you're finished with it. I got more
to do than just stand around and pass the time of day," and she
moved off and into the house.

She stood for a moment in the middle of the kitchen. The dark 171
protuberance over her eye looked like a miniature tornado cloud
which might any moment sweep across the horizon of her brow.
Her lower lip protruded dangerously. She squared her massive
shoulders. Then she marched into the front of the house and out the
side door and started down the road to the pig parlor. She had the
look of a woman going single-handed, weaponless, into battle.

172   The sun was a deep yellow now like a harvest moon and was riding westward very fast over the far tree line as if it meant to reach the hogs before she did. The road was rutted and she kicked several good-sized stones out of her path as she strode along. The pig parlor was on a little knoll at the end of a lane that ran off from the side of the barn. It was a square of concrete as large as a small room, with a board fence about four feet high around it. The concrete floor sloped slightly so that the hog wash could drain off into a trench where it was carried to the field for fertilizer. Claud was standing on the outside, on the edge of the concrete, hanging onto the top board, hosing down the floor inside. The hose was connected to the faucet of a water trough nearby.

173   Mrs. Turpin climbed up beside him and glowered down at the hogs inside. There were seven long-snouted bristly shoats* in it – tan with liver-colored spots – and an old sow a few weeks off from farrowing.* She was lying on her side grunting. The shoats were running about shaking themselves like idiot children, their little slit pig eyes searching the floor for anything left. She had read that pigs were the most intelligent animal. She doubted it. They were supposed to be smarter than dogs. There had even been a pig astronaut. He had performed his assignment perfectly but died of a heart attack afterwards because they left him in his electric suit, sitting upright throughout his examination when naturally a hog should be on all fours.

shoats · young hogs

farrowing · giving birth to pigs

174   A-gruntin and a-rootin and a-groanin.

175   "Gimme that hose," she said, yanking it away from Claud. "Go on and carry them niggers home and then get off that leg."

176   "You look like you might have swallowed a mad dog," Claud observed, but he got down and limped off. He paid no attention to her humors.

177   Until he was out of earshot, Mrs. Turpin stood on the side of the pen, holding the hose and pointing the stream of water at the hind quarters of any shoat that looked as if it might try to lie down. When he had had time to get over the hill, she turned her head slightly and her wrathful eyes scanned the path. He was nowhere in sight. She turned back again and seemed to gather herself up. Her shoulders rose and she drew in her breath.

178   "What do you send me a message like that for?" she said in a low fierce voice, barely above a whisper but with the force of a shout in its

concentrated fury. "How am I a hog and me both? How am I saved 178
and from hell too?" Her free fist was knotted and with the other she
gripped the hose, blindly pointing the stream of water in and out of
the eye of the old sow whose outraged squeal she did not hear.

The pig parlor commanded a view of the back pasture where 179
their twenty beef cows were gathered around the hay-bales Claud
and the boy had put out. The freshly cut pasture sloped down to
the highway. Across it was their cotton field and beyond that a
dark green dusty wood which they owned as well. The sun was
behind the wood, very red, looking over the paling* of trees like
a farmer inspecting his own hogs.

paling · a fence of
regularly spaced pickets

"Why me?" she rumbled. "It's no trash around here, black or 180
white, that I haven't given to. And break my back to the bone
every day working. And do for the church."

She appeared to be the right size woman to command the 181
arena before her. "How am I a hog?" she demanded. "Exactly how
am I like them?" and she jabbed the stream of water at the shoats.
"There was plenty of trash there. It didn't have to be me."

"If you like trash better, go get yourself some trash then," she 182
railed. "You could have made me trash. Or a nigger. If trash is what
you wanted why didn't you make me trash?" She shook her fist with
the hose in it and a watery snake appeared momentarily in the air.
"I could quit working and take it easy and be filthy," she growled.
"Lounge about the sidewalks all day drinking root beer. Dip snuff and
spit in every puddle and have it all over my face. I could be nasty.

"Or you could have made me a nigger. It's too late for me to 183
be a nigger," she said with deep sarcasm, "but I could act like
one. Lay down in the middle of the road and stop traffic. Roll
on the ground."

In the deepening light everything was taking on a mysterious 184
hue. The pasture was growing a peculiar glassy green and the
streak of highway had turned lavender. She braced herself for a
final assault and this time her voice rolled out over the pasture.
"Go on," she yelled, "call me a hog! Call me a hog again. From
hell. Call me a wart hog from hell. Put that bottom rail on top.
There'll still be a top and bottom!"

A garbled echo returned to her. 185

A final surge of fury shook her and she roared, "Who do you 186
think you are?"

187   The color of everything, field and crimson sky, burned for a moment with a transparent intensity. The question carried over the pasture and across the highway and the cotton field and returned to her clearly like an answer from beyond the wood.

188   She opened her mouth but no sound came out of it.

189   A tiny truck, Claud's, appeared on the highway, heading rapidly out of sight. Its gears scraped thinly. It looked like a child's toy. At any moment a bigger truck might smash into it and scatter Claud's and the niggers' brains all over the road.

190   Mrs. Turpin stood there, her gaze fixed on the highway, all her muscles rigid, until in five or six minutes the truck reappeared, returning. She waited until it had had time to turn into their own road. Then like a monumental statue coming to life, she bent her head slowly and gazed, as if through the very heart of mystery, down into the pig parlor at the hogs. They had settled all in one corner around the old sow who was grunting softly. A red glow suffused them. They appeared to pant with a secret life.

191   Until the sun slipped finally behind the tree line, Mrs. Turpin remained there with her gaze bent to them as if she were absorbing some abysmal life-giving knowledge. At last she lifted her head. There was only a purple streak in the sky, cutting through a field of crimson and leading, like an extension of the highway, into the descending dusk. She raised her hands from the side of the pen in a gesture hieratic* and profound. A visionary light settled in her eyes. She saw the streak as a vast swinging bridge extending upward from the earth through a field of living fire. Upon it a vast horde of souls were rumbling toward heaven. There were whole companies of white-trash, clean for the first time in their lives, and bands of black niggers in white robes, and battalions of freaks and lunatics shouting and clapping and leaping like frogs. And bringing up the end of the procession was a tribe of people whom she recognized at once as those who, like herself and Claud, had always had a little of everything and the God-given wit to use it right. She leaned forward to observe them closer. They were marching behind the others with great dignity, accountable as they had always been for good order and common sense and respectable behavior. They alone were on key. Yet she could see by their shocked and altered faces that even their virtues were being burned away. She lowered her hands and gripped the rail

hieratic · a symbolic gesture whose meaning is hidden

of the hog pen, her eyes small but fixed unblinkingly on what lay 191 ahead. In a moment the vision faded but she remained where she was, immobile.

At length she got down and turned off the faucet and made 192 her slow way on the darkening path to the house. In the woods around her the invisible cricket choruses had struck up, but what she heard were the voices of the souls climbing upward into the starry field and shouting hallelujah.

Alice Munro

⟨ 1 9 3 1 – ⟩

Munro chronicles the intense and private worlds of small town characters in Midwestern Canada. Set in familiar places like skating rinks and school book rooms, her stories are poignant with experiences most of us recognize, such as the smell of disinfectant and the taste of root beer. These details are not only present; they are significant because they live in the imagination and memory of the characters. Within the borders of Munro's fiction, a tea strainer means something, for example, because the character who uses it understands it in a certain way. Perhaps no one since Chekhov has catalogued so powerfully and with such strangeness the mundane lives of ordinary people. Her fiction, which is regularly published in such magazines as The Atlantic Monthly *and* The New Yorker, *has been gathered in award-winning collections, including* The Moons of Jupiter *(1983),* The Progress of Love *(1986), and* Open Secrets *(1994).*

MRS. CROSS AND MRS. KIDD

1   Mrs. Cross and Mrs. Kidd have known each other eighty years, ever since Kindergarten, which was not called that then, but Primary. Mrs. Cross's first picture of Mrs. Kidd is of her standing at the front of the class reciting some poem, her hands behind her back and her small black-eyed face lifted to let out her self-confident voice. Over the next ten years, if you went to any concert, any meeting that featured entertainment, you would find Mrs. Kidd (who was not called Mrs. Kidd then but Marian Botherton), with her dark, thick bangs cut straight across her forehead, and her pinafore sticking up in starched wings, reciting a poem with the greatest competence and no hitch of memory. Even today with hardly any excuse, sitting in her wheelchair, Mrs. Kidd will launch forth.

Today ... Ratisbon ·
the opening line of
"Incident of the French
Camp" by English
poet Robert Browning
(1812–1889)

Where ... tide? · the
opening lines of "The
Ships of Saint John" by
Canadian poet Bliss
Carman (1861–1929)

Today we French stormed Ratisbon,*   1a

she will say, or: 1

Where are the ships I used to know   1b
That came to port on the Fundy tide?*

She stops not because she doesn't remember how to go on but in   1
order to let somebody say, "What's that one?" or, "Wasn't that in
the Third Reader?" which she takes as a request to steam ahead.

Half a century ago   1c
In beauty and stately pride.

Mrs. Kidd's first memory of Mrs. Cross (Dolly Grainger) is of   2
a broad red face and a dress with a droopy hem, and thick fair
braids, and a bellowing voice, in the playground on a rainy day
when they were all crowded under the overhang. The girls played
a game that was really a dance, that Mrs. Kidd did not know how
to do. It was a Virginia reel and the words they sang were:

Jolting up and down in the old Brass Wagon   2a
Jolting up and down in the old Brass Wagon
Jolting up and down in the old Brass Wagon
You're the One my Darling!"

Nobody whirled and stomped and sang more enthusiastically   3
than Mrs. Cross, who was the youngest and smallest allowed to play.
She knew it from her older sisters. Mrs. Kidd was an only child.

Younger people, learning that these two women have known   4
each other for more than three-quarters of a century, seem to
imagine this gives them everything in common. They themselves
are the only ones who can recall what separated them, and to a
certain extent does yet: the apartment over the Post Office and
Customs house, where Mrs. Kidd lived with her mother and
her father who was the Postmaster; the row-house on Newgate
Street where Mrs. Cross lived with her mother and father and
two sisters and four brothers; the fact that Mrs. Kidd went to the
Anglican Church and Mrs. Cross to the Free Methodist; that Mrs.
Kidd married, at the age of twenty-three, a high-school teacher
of science, and Mrs. Cross married, at the age of seventeen, a
man who worked on the lake boats and never got to be a captain.

4 Mrs. Cross had six children, Mrs. Kidd had three. Mrs. Cross's husband died suddenly at forty-two with no life insurance; Mrs. Kidd's husband retired to Goderich with a pension after years of being principal of the high school in a nearby town. Only recently has the gap closed. The children equalled things out; Mrs. Cross's children, on the average, make as much money as Mrs. Kidd's children, though they do not have as much education. Mrs. Cross's grandchildren make more money.

5 Mrs. Cross has been in Hilltop Home three years and two months, Mrs. Kidd three years less a month. They both have bad hearts and ride around in wheelchairs to save their energy. During their first conversation, Mrs. Kidd said, "I don't notice any hilltop."

6 "You can see the highway," said Mrs. Cross. "I guess that's what they mean. Where did they put you?" she asked.

7 "I hardly know if I can find my way back. It's a nice room, though. It's a single."

8 "Mine is too, I have a single. Is it the other side of the dining-room or this?"

9 "Oh. The other side."

10 "That's good. That's the best part. Everybody's in fairly good shape down there. It costs more, though. The better you are, the more it costs. The other side of the dining-room is out of their head."

11 "Senile?"

12 "Senile. This side is the younger ones that have something like that the matter with them. For instance." She nodded at a mongoloid* man of about fifty, who was trying to play the mouth organ. "Down in our part there's also younger ones, but nothing the matter up here," she tapped her head. "Just some disease. When it gets to the point they can't look after themselves upstairs. That's where you get the far-gone ones. Then the crazies is another story. Locked up in the back wing. That's the real crazies. Also, I think there is some place they have the ones that walk around but soil all the time. "

13 "Well, we are the top drawer," said Mrs. Kidd with a tight smile. "I knew there would be plenty of senile ones, but I wasn't prepared for the others. Such as." She nodded discreetly at the mongoloid who was doing a step-dance in front of the window.

mongoloid · someone with Down's syndrome

Unlike most mongoloids, he was thin and agile, though very pale   13
and brittle-looking.

"Happier than most," said Mrs. Cross, observing him. "This is   14
the only place in the county, everything gets dumped here. After
a while it doesn't bother you."

"It doesn't *bother* me."   15

Mrs. Kidd's room is full of rocks and shells, in boxes and in   16
bottles. She has a case of brittle butterflies and a case of stuffed
songbirds. Her bookshelves contain *Ferns and Mosses of North
America, Peterson's Guide to the Birds of Eastern North America,
How to Know the Rocks and Minerals,* and a book of *Star Maps.* The
case of butterflies and the songbirds once hung in the classroom
of her husband, the science teacher. He bought the songbirds, but
he and Mrs. Kidd collected the butterflies themselves. Mrs. Kidd
was a good student of botany and zoology. If she had not had what
was perceived at the time as delicate health, she would have gone
on and studied botany at a university, though few girls did such
a thing then. Her children, who all live at a distance, send her
beautiful books on subjects they are sure will interest her, but for
the most part these books are large and heavy and she can't find
a way to look at them comfortably, so she soon relegates them to
her bottom shelf. She would not admit it to her children, but her
interest has waned, it has waned considerably. They say in their
letters that they remember how she taught them about mushrooms; do you remember when we saw the destroying angel[*] in
Petrie's Bush when we were living in Logan? Their letters are full
of remembering. They want her fixed where she was forty or fifty
years ago, these children who are aging themselves. They have a
notion of her that is as fond and necessary as any notion a parent
ever had of a child. They celebrate what would in a child be called
precocity: her brightness, her fund of knowledge, her atheism
(a secret all those years her husband was in charge of the minds
of young), all the ways in which she differs from the average, or
expected, old lady. She feels it a duty to hide from them the many
indications that she is not so different as they think.

Mrs. Cross also gets presents from her children, but not   17
books. Their thoughts run to ornaments, pictures, cushions. Mrs.
Cross has a bouquet of artificial roses in which are set tubes of
light, always shooting and bubbling up like a fountain. She has

destroying angel ·
among the deadliest of
all mushrooms

17 a Southern Belle whose satin skirts are supposed to form an enormous pincushion. She has a picture of the Lord's Supper, in which a light comes on to form a halo around Jesus's head. (Mrs. Kidd, after her first visit, wrote a letter to one of her children in which she described this picture and said she had tried to figure out what the Lord and his Disciples were eating and it appeared to be hamburgers. This is the sort of thing her children love to hear from her.) There is also, near the door, a life-size plaster statue of a collie dog which resembles a dog the Cross family had when the children were small: old Bonnie. Mrs. Cross finds out from her children what these things cost and tells people. She says she is shocked.

18 Shortly after Mrs. Kidd's arrival, Mrs. Cross took her along on a visit to the Second Floor. Mrs. Cross has been going up there every couple of weeks to visit a cousin of hers, old Lily Barbour.

19 "Lily is not running on all cylinders," she warned Mrs. Kidd, as they wheeled themselves into the elevator. "Another thing, it doesn't smell like Sweet Violets, in spite of them always spraying. They do the best they can."

20 The first thing Mrs. Kidd saw as they got off the elevator was a little wrinkled-up woman with wild white hair, and a dress rucked up high on her bare legs (Mrs. Kidd snatched her eyes away from that) and a tongue she couldn't seem to stuff back inside her mouth. The smell was of heated urine – you would think they had had it on the stove – as well as of floral sprays. But here was a smooth-faced sensible-looking person with a topknot, wearing an apron over a clean pink dress.

21 "Well, did you get the papers?" this woman said in a familiar way to Mrs. Cross and Mrs. Kidd.

22 "Oh, they don't come in till about five o'clock," said Mrs. Kidd politely, thinking she meant the newspaper.

23 "Never mind her," said Mrs. Cross.

24 "I have to sign them today," the woman said. "Otherwise it'll be a catastrophe. They can put me out. You see I never knew it was illegal." She spoke so well, so plausibly and confidentially, that Mrs. Kidd was convinced she had to make sense, but Mrs. Cross was wheeling vigorously away. Mrs. Kidd went after her.

25 "Don't get tied up in that rigamarole," said Mrs. Cross when Mrs. Kidd caught up to her. A woman with a terrible goitre,* such

goitre · an enlargement of the thyroid gland

as Mrs. Kidd had not seen for years, was smiling winningly at 25
them. Up here nobody had teeth.

"I thought there was no such thing as a goitre any more," Mrs. 26
Kidd said. "With the iodine."

They were going in the direction of a hollering voice. 27

"George!" the voice said. "George! Jessie! I'm here! Come and 28
pull me up! George!"

Another voice was weaving cheerfully in and out of these yells. 29
"Bad-bad-bad, "it said. "Bad-Bad-bad. Bad-bad-bad. Bad-*bad*. "

The owners of both these voices were sitting around a long 30
table by a row of windows halfway down the hall. Nine or ten
women were sitting there. Some were mumbling or singing softly
to themselves. One was tearing apart a little embroidered cushion
somebody had made. Another was eating a chocolate-covered ice-
cream bar. Bits of chocolate had caught on her whiskers, dribbles
of ice cream ran down her chin. None of them looked out the
windows, or at each other. None of them paid any attention to
George-and-Jessie, or to Bad-bad-bad, who were carrying on
without a break.

Mrs. Kidd halted. 31

"Where is this Lily?" 32

"She's down at the end. They don't get her out of bed." 33

"Well, you go on and see her," said Mrs. Kidd. "I'm going 34
back."

"There's nothing to get upset about," said Mrs. Cross. "They're 35
all off in their own little world. They're happy as clams. "

"They may be, but I'm not," said Mrs. Kidd. "I'll see you in the 36
Recreation Room." She wheeled herself around and down the hall
to the elevator where the pink lady was still inquiring urgently
for her papers. She never came back.

Mrs. Cross and Mrs. Kidd used to play cards in the Recreation 37
Room every afternoon. They put on earrings, stockings, afternoon dresses. They took turns treating for tea. On the whole,
these afternoons were pleasant. They were well matched at cards.
Sometimes they played Scrabble, but Mrs. Cross did not take
Scrabble seriously, as she did cards. She became frivolous and
quarrelsome, defending words that were her own invention. So
they went back to cards; they played rummy, most of the time.
It was like school here. People paired off, they had best friends.

37 The same people always sat together in the dining-room. Some people had nobody.

38   The first time Mrs. Cross took notice of Jack, he was in the Recreation Room, when she and Mrs. Kidd were playing cards. He had just come in a week or so before. Mrs. Kidd knew about him.

39   "Do you see that red-haired fellow by the window?" said Mrs. Kidd. "He's in from a stroke. He's only fifty-nine years old. I heard it in the dining-room before you got down.

40   "Poor chap. That young."

41   "He's lucky to be alive at all. His parents are still alive, both of them, they're still on a farm. He was back visiting them and he took the stroke and was lying face down in the barnyard when they found him. He wasn't living around here, he's from out west."

42   "Poor chap," said Mrs. Cross. "What did he work at?"

43   "He worked on a newspaper.

44   "Was he married?"

45   "That I didn't hear. He's supposed to have been an alcoholic, then he joined AA and got over it. You can't trust all you hear in this place. "

46   (That was true. There was usually a swirl of stories around any newcomer; stories about the money people had, or the places they had been, or the number of operations they have had and the plastic repairs or contrivances they carry around in or on their bodies. A few days later Mrs. Cross was saying that Jack had been the editor of a newspaper. First she heard it was in Sudbury,* then she heard Winnipeg.* She was saying he had had a nervous breakdown due to overwork; that was the truth, he had never been an alcoholic. She was saying he came from a good family. His name was Jack MacNeil.)

Sudbury · located in southeastern Ontario

Winnipeg · capital of Manitoba

47   At present Mrs. Cross noticed how clean and tended he looked in his gray pants and light shirt. It was unnatural, at least for him; he looked like something that had gone soft from being too long in the water. He was a big man, but he could not hold himself straight, even in the wheelchair. The whole left side of his body was loose, emptied, powerless. His hair and moustache were not even gray yet, but fawn-colored. He was white as if just out of bandages.

48   A distraction occurred. The Gospel preacher who came every week to conduct a prayer service, with hymns (the more estab-

lished preachers came, in turn, on Sundays), was walking through   48
the Recreation Room with his wife close behind, the pair of them
showering smiles and greetings wherever they could catch an
eye. Mrs. Kidd looked up when they had passed and said softly
but distinctly, "Joy to the World."

At this, Jack, who was wheeling himself across the room in a   49
clumsy way – he tended to go in circles – smiled. The smile was
intelligent, ironic, and did not go with his helpless look. Mrs.
Cross waved him over and wheeled part of the way to meet him.
She introduced herself, and introduced Mrs. Kidd. He opened
his mouth and said, "Anh-anh-anh,"

"Yes," said Mrs. Cross encouragingly. "Yes?"   50

"Anh-anh-*anh*," said Jack. He flapped his right hand. Tears   51
came into his eyes.

"Are we playing cards?" said Mrs. Kidd.   52

"I have to get on with this game," said Mrs. Cross. "You're   53
welcome to sit and watch. Were you a card player?"

His right hand came out and grabbed her chair, and he bent   54
his head weeping. He tried to get the left hand up to wipe his face.
He could lift it a few inches, then it fell back in his lap.

"Oh, well," said Mrs. Cross softly. Then she remembered what   55
you do when children cry; how to josh them out of it. "How can I
tell what you're saying if you're going to cry? You just be patient.
I have known people that have had strokes and got their speech
back. Yes I have. You mustn't cry, that won't accomplish anything.
You just take it slow. "Boo-hoo-hoo," she said, bending towards
him. "Boo-hoo-hoo. You'll have Mrs. Kidd and me crying next."

That was the beginning of Mrs. Cross's takeover of Jack. She   56
got him to sit and watch the card game and to dry up, more or
less, and make a noise which was a substitute for conversation
(an-anh) rather than a desperate attempt at it (anh-anh-*anh*). Mrs.
Cross felt something stretching in her. It was her old managing,
watching power, her capacity for strategy, which if properly exer-
cised could never be detected by those it was used on.

Mrs. Kidd could detect it, however.   57

"This isn't what I call a card game," she said.   58

Mrs. Cross soon found out that Jack could not stay interested in   59
cards and there was no use trying to get him to play; it was conversation he was after. But trying to talk brought on the weeping.

60   "Crying doesn't bother me," she said to him. "I've seen tears
and tears. But it doesn't do you any good with a lot of people, to
get a reputation for being a cry-baby.

61   So she started to ask him questions to which he could give
yes-and-no answers. That brightened him up and let her test out
her information.

62   Yes, he had worked on a newspaper. No, he was not married. No,
the newspaper was not in Sudbury. Mrs. Cross began to reel off
the name of every city she could think of but was unable to hit on
the right one. He became agitated, tried to speak, and this time the
syllables got close to a word, but she couldn't catch it. She blamed
herself, for not knowing enough places. Then, inspired, she ordered
him to stay right where he was, not to move, she would be back, and
she wheeled herself down the hall to the Library. There she looked
for a book with maps in it. To her disgust there was not such a thing,
there was nothing but love stories and religion. But she did not give
up. She took off down the hall to Mrs. Kidd's room. Since their card
games had lapsed (they still played some days, but not every day),
Mrs. Kidd spent many afternoons in her room. She was there now,
lying on top of her bed, wearing an elegant purple dressing-gown
with a high embroidered neck. She had a headache.

63   "Have you got one of those, like a geography book?" Mrs. Cross
said. "A book with maps in it." She explained that she wanted it
for Jack.

64   "An atlas, you mean, "said Mrs. Kidd. "I think there may be.
I can't remember. You can look on the bottom shelf. I can't
remember what's there."

65   Mrs. Cross parked by the bookcase and began to lift the heavy
books onto her lap one by one, reading the titles at close range.
She was out of breath from the speed of her trip.

66   "You're wearing yourself out," said Mrs. Kidd. "You'll get yourself upset and you'll get him upset, and what is the point of it?"

67   "I'm not upset. It just seems a crime to me."

68   "What does?"

69   "Such an intelligent man, what's he doing in here? They should
have put him in one of those places they teach you things, teach
you how to talk again. What's the name of them? You know. Why
did they just stick him in here? I want to help him and I don't
know what to do. Well, I just have to try. If it was one of my boys

like that and in a place where nobody knew him, I just hope some 69
woman would take the same interest in him."

"Rehabilitation," said Mrs. Kidd. "The reason they put him in 70
here is more than likely that the stroke was too bad for them to
do anything for him."

"Everything under the sun but a map-book," said Mrs. Cross, 71
not choosing to answer this. "He'll think I'm not coming back."
She wheeled out of Mrs. Kidd's room without a thank-you or
good-bye. She was afraid Jack would think she hadn't meant to
come back, all she intended to do was to get rid of him. Sure
enough, when she got to the Recreation Room he was gone.
She did not know what to do. She was near tears herself. She
didn't know where his room was. She thought she would go to
the office and ask; then she saw that it was five past four and the
office would be closed. Lazy, those girls were. Four o'clock, get
their coats on and go home, nothing matters to them. She went
wheeling slowly along the corridor, wondering what to do. Then
in one of the dead-end side corridors she saw Jack.

"There you are, what a relief! I didn't know where to look for 72
you. Did you think I wasn't ever coming back? I'll tell you what
I went for. I was going to surprise you. I went to look for one of
those books with maps in, what do you call them, so you could
show me where you used to live. Atlases!"

He was sitting looking at the pink wall as if it was a window. 73
Against the wall was a whatnot* with a vase of plastic daffodils on it,
and some figurines, dwarfs and dogs; on the wall were three paint-
by-number pictures that had been done in the Craft Room.

whatnot · a display
case for knickknacks

"My friend Mrs. Kidd has more books than the Library. She has 74
a book on nothing but bugs. Another nothing but the moon, when
they went there, close up. But not such a simple thing as a map."

Jack was pointing at one of the pictures. 75

"Which one are you pointing at?" said Mrs. Cross. "The one 76
with the church with the cross? No? The one above that? The
pine trees? Yes? What about it? The pine trees and the red deer?"
He was smiling, waving his hand. She hoped he wouldn't get
too excited and disappointed this time. "What about it? This
is like one of those things on television. Trees? Green? Pine
trees? Is it the deer? Three deer? No? Yes. Three red deer?" He
flapped his arm up and down and she said, "I don't know, really.

76　Three – red – deer. Wait a minute. That's a place. I've heard it on the news. Red Deer.* Red Deer! That's the place! That's the place you lived in! That's the place where you worked on the newspaper! *Red Deer.*"

Red Deer · a city in central Alberta

77　They were both jubilant. He waved his arm around in celebration, as if he was conducting an orchestra, and she leaned forward, laughing, clapping her hands on her knees.

78　"Oh, if everything was in pictures like that, we could have a lot of fun! You and me could have a lot of fun, couldn't we?"

79　Mrs. Cross made an appointment to see the doctor.

80　"I've heard of people that had a very bad stroke and their speech came back, isn't that so?"

81　"It can happen. It depends. Are you worrying a lot about this man?"

82　"It must be a terrible feeling. No wonder he cries."

83　"How many children did you have?"

84　"Six."

85　"I'd say you'd done your share of worrying."

86　She could see he didn't mean to tell her anything. Either he didn't remember much about Jack's case or he was pretending he didn't.

87　"I'm here to take care of people," the doctor said. "That's what I'm here for, that's what the nurses are here for. So you can leave all the worrying to us. That's what we get paid for. Right?"

88　And how much worrying do you do? she wanted to ask.

89　She would have liked to talk to Mrs. Kidd about this visit because she knew Mrs. Kidd thought the doctor was a fool, but once Mrs. Kidd knew Jack was the reason for the visit she would make some impatient remark. Mrs. Cross never talked to her any more about Jack. She talked to other people, but she could see them getting bored. Nobody cares about anybody else's misfortunes in here, she thought. Even when somebody dies they don't care, it's just *me, I'm still alive, what's for dinner?* The selfishness. They're all just as bad as the ones on the Second Floor, only they don't show it yet.

90　She hadn't been up to the Second Floor, hadn't visited Lily Barbour, since she took up with Jack.

91　They liked sitting in the corner with the Red Deer picture, the scene of their first success. That was established as their place, where they could be by themselves. Mrs. Cross brought a pencil

and paper, fixed the tray across his chair, tried to see how Jack 91
made out with writing. It was about the same as talking. He would
scrawl a bit, push the pencil till he broke it, start to cry. They didn't
make progress, either in writing or talking, it was useless. But
she was learning to talk to him by the yes-and-no method, and it
seemed sometimes she could pick up what was in his mind.

"If I was smarter I would be more of a help to you," she said. "Isn't 92
it the limit? I can get it all out that's in my head, but there never
was so much in it, and you've got your head crammed full but you
can't get it out. Never mind. We'll have a cup of coffee, won't we?
Cup of coffee, that's what you like. My friend Mrs. Kidd and I used
to drink tea all the time, but now I drink coffee. I prefer it too."

"So you never got married? Never?" 93

Never. 94

"Did you have a sweetheart?" 95

Yes. 96

"Did you? Did you? Was it long ago? Long ago or recently?" 97

Yes. 98

"Long ago or recently? Both. Long ago and recently. Different 99
sweethearts. The same? The same. The same woman. You were
in love with the same woman years and years but you didn't get
married to her. Oh, Jack. Why didn't you? Couldn't she marry
you? She couldn't. Why not? Was she married already? Was she?
Yes. Yes. Oh, my."

She searched his face to see if this was too painful a subject 100
or if he wanted to go on. She thought he did want to. She was
eager to ask where this woman was now, but something warned
her not to. Instead she took a light tone.

"I wonder if I can guess her name? Remember Red Deer? 101
Wasn't that funny? I wonder. I could start with A and work
through the alphabet. Anne? Audrey? Annabelle? No. I think
I'll just follow my intuition. Jane? Mary? Louise?"

The name was Pat, Patricia, which she hit on maybe her 102
thirtieth try.

"Now, in my mind a Pat is always fair. Not dark. You know how 103
you have a picture in your mind for a name? Was she fair? Yes?
And tall, in my mind a Pat is always tall. Was she? Well! I got it
right. Tall and fair. A good-looking woman. A lovely woman."

Yes. 104

105   She felt ashamed of herself, because she had wished for a moment that she had somebody to tell this to.

106   "That is a secret then. It's between you and me. Now. If you ever want to write Pat a letter you come to me. Come to me and I'll make out what you want to say to her and I'll write it.

107   No. No letter. Never.

108   "Well. I have a secret too. I had a boy I liked, he was killed in the First World War. He walked me home from a skating-party, it was our school skating-party. I was in the Senior Fourth. I was fourteen. That was before the war. I did like him, and I used to think about him, you know, and when I heard he was killed, that was after I was married, I was married at seventeen, well, when I heard he was killed I thought, now I've got something to look forward to, I could look forward to meeting him in Heaven. That's true that's how childish I was.

109   "Marian was at that skating-party too. You know who I mean by Marian. Mrs. Kidd. She was there and she had the most beautiful outfit. It was sky-blue trimmed with white fur and a hood on it. Also she had a muff. She had a white fur muff. I never saw anything I would've like to have for myself as much as that muff."

110   Lying in the dark at night, before she went to sleep, Mrs. Cross would go over everything that had happened with Jack that day: how he had looked; how his color was; whether he had cried and how long and how often; whether he had been in a bad temper in the dining-room, annoyed with so many people around him or perhaps not liking the food; whether he had said good-night to her sullenly or gratefully.

111   Meanwhile Mrs. Kidd had taken on a new friend of her own. This was Charlotte, who used to live down near the dining-room but had recently moved in across the hall. Charlotte was a tall, thin, deferential woman in her mid-forties. She had multiple sclerosis. Sometimes her disease was in remission, as it was now; she could have gone home, if she had wanted to, and there had been a place for her. But she was happy where she was. Years of institutional life had made her childlike, affectionate, good-humored. She helped in the hairdressing shop, she loved doing that, she loved brushing and pinning up Mrs. Kidd's hair, marvelling at how much black there still was in it. She put an ash-blond rinse on her own hair and wore it in a bouffant, stiff

with spray. Mrs. Kidd could smell the hairspray from her room 111
and she would call out, "Charlotte! Did they move you down
here for the purpose of asphyxiating us?"

Charlotte giggled. She brought Mrs. Kidd a present. It was 112
a red felt purse, with an appliquéd design of green leaves and
blue and yellow flowers; she had made it in the Craft Room. Mrs.
Kidd thought how much it resembled those recipe-holders her
children used to bring home from school; a whole cardboard pie-
plate and a half pie-plate, stitched together with bright yarn. They
didn't hold enough to be really useful. They were painstakingly
created frivolities, like the crocheted potholders through which
you could burn yourself; the cut-out wooden horse's head with
a hook not quite big enough to hold a hat.

Charlotte made purses for her daughters, who were married, and 113
for her small granddaughter, and for the woman who lived with her
husband and used his name. The husband and this woman came
regularly to see Charlotte; they were all good friends. It had been a
good arrangement for the husband, for the children, and perhaps for
Charlotte herself. Nothing was being put over on Charlotte. Most
likely she had given in without a whimper. Glad of the chance.

"What do you expect?" said Mrs. Cross. "Charlotte's easygoing." 114

Mrs. Cross and Mrs. Kidd had not had any falling-out or any 115
real coolness. They still had some talks and card games. But it
was difficult. They no longer sat at the same table in the dining-
room because Mrs. Cross had to watch to see if Jack needed help
cutting up his meat. He wouldn't let anyone else cut it; he would
just pretend he didn't want any and miss out on his protein. Then
Charlotte moved into the place Mrs. Cross had vacated. Charlotte
had no problems cutting her meat. In fact she cut her meat, toast,
egg, vegetables, cake, whatever she was eating that would cut,
into tiny regular pieces before she started on it. Mrs. Kidd told
her that was not good manners. Charlotte was crestfallen but
stubborn and continued to do it.

"Neither you nor I would have given up so quickly," said 116
Mrs. Kidd, still speaking about Charlotte to Mrs. Cross. "We
wouldn't've had the choice."

"That's true. There weren't places like this. Not pleasant places. 117
They couldn't have kept us alive the way they do her. The drugs
and so on. Also it may be the drugs makes her silly."

118 Mrs. Kidd remained silent, frowning at hearing Charlotte called silly, though that was just the blunt way of putting what she had been trying to say herself. After a moment she spoke lamely.

119 "I think she has more brains than she shows."

120 Mrs. Cross said evenly, "I wouldn't know."

121 Mrs. Kidd sat with her head bent forward, thoughtfully. She could sit that way for half an hour, easily, letting Charlotte brush and tend her hair. Was she turning into one of those old ladies that love to be waited on? Those old ladies also needed somebody to boss. They were the sort who went around the world on cruise ships, she had read about them in novels. They went around the world, and stayed at hotels, or they lived in grand decaying houses, with their companions. It was so easy to boss Charlotte, to make her play Scrabble and tell her when her manners were bad. Charlotte was itching to be somebody's slave. So why did Mrs. Kidd hope to restrain herself? She did not wish to be such a recognizable sort of old lady. Also, slaves cost more than they were worth. In the end, people's devotion hung like rocks around your neck. Expectations. She wanted to float herself clear. Sometimes she could do it by lying on her bed and saying in her head all the poems she knew, or the facts, which got harder and harder to hold in place. Other times she imagined a house on the edge of some dark woods or bog, bright fields in front of it running down to the sea. She imagined she lived there alone, like an old woman in a story.

122 Mrs. Cross wanted to take Jack on visits. She thought it was time for him to learn to associate with people. He didn't cry so often now, when they were alone. But sometimes at meals she was ashamed of him and had to tell him so. He would take offense at something, often she didn't know what, and sometimes his sulk would proceed to the point where he would knock over the sugar bowl, or sweep all his cutlery on to the floor. She thought that if only he could get used to a few more people as he was to her, he would calm down and behave decently.

123 The first time she took him to Mrs. Kidd's room Mrs. Kidd said she and Charlotte were just going out, they were going to the Crafts Room. She didn't ask them to come along. The next time they came, Mrs. Kidd and Charlotte were sitting there playing Scrabble, so they were caught.

"You don't mind if we watch you for a little while," Mrs. Cross said. 124

"Oh no. But don't blame me if you get bored. Charlotte takes 125
a week from Wednesday to make up her mind."

"We're not in any hurry. We're not expected anywhere. Are 126
we, Jack?"

She was wondering if she could get Jack playing Scrabble. She 127
didn't know the extent of his problem when he tried to write. Was
it that he couldn't form the letters, was that all? Or couldn't he see
how they made the words? This might be the very thing for him.

At any rate he was taking an interest. He edged his chair up 128
beside Charlotte, who picked up some letters, put them back,
picked them up, looked at them in her hand, and finally made
wind, working down from the *w* in Mrs. Kidd's word *elbow*.
Jack seemed to understand. He was so pleased that he patted
Charlotte's knee in congratulation. Mrs. Cross hoped Charlotte
would realize that was just friendliness and not take offense.

She needn't have worried. Charlotte did not know how to 129
take offense.

"Well good for you," said Mrs. Kidd, frowning, and right 130
away she made *demon* across from the *d*. "Triple word!" she
said, and was writing down the score. "Pick up your letters,
Charlotte."

Charlotte showed her new letters to Jack, one by one, and 131
he made a noise of appreciation. Mrs. Cross kept an eye on him,
hoping nothing would happen to turn him bad-tempered and
spoil this show of friendliness. Nothing did. But he was not having
a good effect on Charlotte's concentration.

"You want to help?" Charlotte said, and moved the little stand 132
with the letters on it so that it was in front of both of them. He
bent over so that he almost had his head on her shoulder.

"Anh-anh-anh," said Jack, but he sounded cheerful. 133

"Anh-anh-anh?" said Charlotte, teasing him. "What kind of a 134
word is that, *anh-anh-anh*?"

Mrs. Cross waited for the skies to fall, but the only thing Jack 135
did was giggle, and Charlotte giggled, so that there was a sort of
giggling-match set up between the two of them.

"Aren't you the great friends," said Mrs. Kidd. 136

Mrs. Cross thought it would be just as well not to exasperate 137
Mrs. Kidd if they wanted to make a habit of visiting.

138   "Now Jack, don't distract Charlotte," she said affably. "You let her play."

139   Even as she finished saying this, she saw Jack's hand descend clumsily on the Scrabble board. The letters went flying. He turned and showed her his ugly look, worse than she had ever seen it. She was amazed and even frightened, but she did not mean to let him see.

140   "Now what have you done?" she said. "Fine behavior!" He made a sound of disgust and pushed the Scrabble board and all the letters to the floor, all the time looking at Mrs. Cross so that there could be no doubt that this disgust and fury had been aroused by her. She knew that it was important at this moment to speak coldly and firmly. That was what you must do with a child or an animal; you must show them that your control has not budged and that you are not hurt or alarmed by such displays. But she was not able to say a word, such a feeling of grief, and shock, and helplessness rose in her heart. Her eyes filled with tears, and at the sight of her tears his expression grew even more hateful and menacing as if the feelings he had against her were boiling higher every moment.

141   Charlotte was smiling, either because she could not switch out of her giggling mood of a moment before or because she did not know how to do anything but smile, no matter what happened. She was pink-faced, apologetic, excited.

142   Jack managed to turn his chair around, with a violent, awkward motion. Charlotte stood up. Mrs. Cross made herself speak.

143   "Yes, you better push him home now. He better go home and cool off and repent of his bad manners. He better."

144   Jack made a taunting sound, which seemed to point out that Mrs. Cross was just telling Charlotte to do what Charlotte was going to do anyway; Mrs. Cross was just pretending to have control of things. Charlotte had hold of the wheelchair and was pushing it towards the door, her smiling lips pressed together in concentration as she avoided the bookshelves and the butterfly case leaning against the wall. Perhaps it was hard for her to steer, perhaps the ordinary reflexes and balances of her body were not there for her to rely on. But she looked pleased; she raised her hand to them and released her smile, and set off down the corridor. She was just like one of those old-fashioned dolls, not the kind Mrs. Cross and Mrs. Kidd used to have but the kind their

mothers had, with the long, limp bodies and pink-and-white faces 144
and crimped china hair and ladylike smiles. Jack kept his face
turned away; the bit of it Mrs. Cross could see was flushed red.

"It would be easy for any man to get the better of Charlotte," 145
said Mrs. Kidd when they were gone.

"I don't think he's so much of a danger," said Mrs. Cross. She 146
spoke in a dry tone but her voice was shaking.

Mrs. Kidd looked at the Scrabble board and the letters scat- 147
tered all over the floor.

"We can't do much about picking them up," she said. "If either 148
one of us bends over we black out." That was true.

"Useless old crocks, aren't we?" said Mrs. Cross. Her voice was 149
under better control now.

"We won't try. When the girl comes in with the juice I'll ask her 150
to do it. We don't need to say how it happened. That's what we'll
do. We won't bend over and end up smashing our noses."

Mrs. Cross felt her heart give a big flop. Her heart was like 151
an old crippled crow, flopping around in her chest. She crossed
her hands there, to hold it.

"Well, I never told you, I don't think I did," said Mrs. Kidd, 152
with her eyes on Mrs. Cross's face. "I never told you what happened that time I got out of bed too fast in my apartment, and I
fell over on my face. I blacked out. Fortunately the woman was
home, in the apartment underneath me, and she heard the crash
and got the whatyamacallit, the man with the keys, the superin-
tendent. They came and found me out cold and took me in the
ambulance. I don't remember a thing about it. I can't remember
anything that happened throughout the next three weeks. I wasn't
unconscious. I wish I had been. I was conscious and saying a lot
of foolish things. Do you know the first thing I remember? The
psychiatrist coming to see me! They had got a psychiatrist in to
determine whether I was loony. But nobody told me he was a
psychiatrist. That's part of it, they don't tell you. He had a thing
like an army jacket on. He was quite young. So I thought he was
just some fellow who had walked in off the street.

"'What is the name of the Prime Minister?' he said to me. 153

"Well! I thought *he* was loony. So I said, 'Who cares?' And I 154
turned my back on him as if I was going to sleep, and from that
time on I remember everything."

155 *"Who cares!"*

156 As a matter of fact, Mrs. Cross had heard Mrs. Kidd tell this story before, but it was a long time ago and she laughed now not just to be obliging; she laughed with relief. Mrs. Kidd's firm voice had spread a numbing ointment over her misery.

157 Out of their combined laughter, Mrs. Kidd shot a quick serious question.

158 "Are you all right?"

159 Mrs. Cross lifted her hands from her chest, waited.

160 "I think so. Yes. But I think I'll go and lie down."

161 In this exchange it was understood that Mrs. Kidd also said, "Your heart is weak, you shouldn't put it at the mercy of these emotions," and Mrs. Cross replied, "I will do as I do, though there may be something in what you say."

162 "You haven't got your chair," Mrs. Kidd said. Mrs. Cross was sitting on an ordinary chair. She had come here walking slowly behind Jack's chair, to help him steer.

163 "I can walk," she said. "I can walk if I take my time."

164 "No. You ride. You get in my chair and I'll push you."

165 "You can't do that."

166 "Yes I can. If I don't use my energy I'll get mad about my Scrabble game."

167 Mrs. Cross heaved herself up and into Mrs. Kidd's wheelchair. As she did so she felt such weakness in her legs that she knew Mrs. Kidd was right. She couldn't have walked ten feet.

168 "Now then," said Mrs. Kidd, and she negotiated their way out of the room into the corridor.

169 "Don't strain yourself. Don't try to go too fast."

170 "No."

171 They proceeded down the corridor, turned left, made their way successfully up a very gentle ramp. Mrs. Cross could hear Mrs. Kidd's breathing.

172 "Maybe I can manage the rest by myself.

173 "No you can't."

174 They made another left turn at the top of the ramp. Now Mrs. Cross's room was in sight. It was three doors ahead of them.

175 "What I am going to do now," said Mrs. Kidd, with emphasis and pauses to hide her breathlessness, "is give you a push. I can give you a push that will take you exactly to your own door."

"Can you?" said Mrs. Cross doubtfully.   176

"Certainly. Then you can turn yourself in and get on the bed   177
and take your time to get yourself settled, then ring for the girl
and get her to deliver the chair back to me.

"You won't bash me into anything?"   178

"You watch."   179

With that Mrs. Kidd gave the wheelchair a calculated, deli-   180
cately balanced push. It rolled forward smoothly and came to a
stop just where she had said it would, in exactly the right place
in front of Mrs. Cross's door. Mrs. Cross had hastily raised her
feet and hands for this last bit of the ride. Now she dropped them.
She gave a single, satisfied, conceding nod and turned and glided
safely into her own room.

Mrs. Kidd, as soon as Mrs. Cross was out of sight, sank down   181
and sat with her back against the wall, her legs stuck straight out
in front of her on the cool linoleum. She prayed no nosy person
would come along until she could recover her strength and get
started on the trip back.

John Updike

◄(1 9 3 2 -)►

*Updike's prolific output of fiction, essays, poetry, and literary/
social criticism repeatedly engages religious concerns, often with a
Protestant sensibility. Influenced in early life by Søren Kierkegaard's
Christian existentialism and by Karl Barth's neo-orthodoxy, Updike
has created a succession of fictional characters who struggle to
achieve or maintain Christian faith in the face of profound personal
sin, doubt-inducing mentors, and the rampant hedonism of the
20th century. To lose faith, for Updike, is to lose a basis for action.
"I've felt in myself and in those around me a failure of nerve – a
sense of doubt as to the worth of any action," the author has said
in a Life interview. "At such times one has nothing but the ancient
assertions of Christianity to give one the will to act, even if the
act is only the bringing in of the milk bottles off the front porch." A
New England native, Updike seems especially concerned with the
fate of the Puritan mentality in post-Christian America. He was
awarded the Pulitzer Prize for* Rabbit Is Rich *in 1982, and again
for* Rabbit at Rest *in 1991. A recent novel,* In the Beauty of the Lilies
*(1996), demonstrates once again the writer's concern with crises of
faith. "Pigeon Feathers" appeared in Updike's second collection of
short stories, published in 1962.*

PIGEON FEATHERS

1   WHEN THEY MOVED TO FIRETOWN, things were upset, dis-
placed, rearranged. A red cane-back sofa that had been the
chief piece in the living room at Olinger was here banished, too big
for the narrow country parlor, to the barn, and shrouded under a
tarpaulin. Never again would David lie on its length all afternoon
eating raisins and reading mystery novels and science fiction and
P. G. Wodehouse.* The blue wing chair that had stood for years in

P. G. Wodehouse ·
English-born writer
(1881–1975), best
known as the creator
of Jeeves, the supreme
"gentleman's gentleman"

329

the ghostly, immaculate guest bedroom, gazing through the windows curtained with dotted swiss toward the telephone wires and horse-chestnut trees and opposite houses, was here established importantly in front of the smutty little fireplace that supplied, in those first cold April days, their only heat. As a child, David had been afraid of the guest bedroom – it was there that he, lying sick with the measles, had seen a black rod the size of a yardstick jog along at a slight slant beside the edge of the bed and vanish when he screamed – and it was disquieting to have one of the elements of its haunted atmosphere basking by the fire, in the center of the family, growing sooty with use. The books that at home had gathered dust in the case beside the piano were here hastily stacked, all out of order, in the shelves that the carpenters had built along one wall below the deep-silled windows. David, at fourteen, had been more moved than a mover; like the furniture, he had to find a new place, and on the Saturday of the second week he tried to work off some of his disorientation by arranging the books.

It was a collection obscurely depressing to him, mostly books his mother had acquired when she was young: college anthologies of Greek plays and Romantic poetry, Will Durant's *Story of Philosophy*,* a soft-leather set of Shakespeare with string bookmarks sewed to the bindings, *Green Mansions** boxed and illustrated with woodcuts, *I, the Tiger*, by Manuel Komroff,* novels by names like Galsworthy* and Ellen Glasgow* and Irvin S. Cobb* and Sinclair Lewis* and "Elizabeth."* The odor of faded taste made him feel the ominous gap between himself and his parents, the insulting gulf of time that existed before he was born. Suddenly he was tempted to dip into this time. From the heaps of books piled around him on the worn old floorboards, he picked up Volume II of a four-volume set of *The Outline of History*, by H. G. Wells.* Once David had read *The Time Machine** in an anthology; this gave him a small grip on the author. The book's red binding had faded to orange-pink on the spine. When he lifted the cover, there was a sweetish, attic-like smell, and his mother's maiden name written in unfamiliar handwriting on the flyleaf – an upright, bold, yet careful signature, bearing a faint relation to the quick scrunched backslant that flowed with marvellous consistency across her shopping lists and budget accounts and Christmas cards to college friends from this same, vaguely menacing long ago.

Will Durant's *Story of Philosophy* · popular reference book by the American writer (1885–1981)

Green Mansions · romantic novel by English author and naturalist W. H. Hudson (1841–1922)

***I, The Tiger*, by Manuel Komroff** · novel from a tiger's perspective first published in 1933 by the American author (1890–1974)

Galsworthy · John Galsworthy (1867–1933), English novelist and playwright

Ellen Glasgow · American novelist (1873–1945)

Irvin S. Cobb · American writer and humorist (1876–1944)

Sinclair Lewis · American novelist and social critic (1885–1951)

"Elizabeth" · pen-name of English author Mary Annette, Countess Russell (1866–1941)

***The Outline of History*, by H. G. Wells** · first published in 1920, a text promoting the theory of social evolution touted by the English author and atheist (1866–1946)

The Time Machine · Wells' post-apocalyptic first novel published in 1895

3   He leafed through, pausing at drawings, done in an old-fashioned stippled style, of bas-reliefs,* masks, Romans without pupils
in their eyes, articles of ancient costume, fragments of pottery
found in unearthed homes. He knew it would be interesting
in a magazine, sandwiched between ads and jokes, but in this
undiluted form history was somehow sour. The print was deter-
minedly legible, and smug, like a lesson book. As he bent over the
pages, yellow at the edges, they seemed rectangles of dusty glass
through which he looked down into unreal and irrelevant worlds.
He could see things sluggishly move, and an unpleasant fullness
came into his throat. His mother and grandmother fussed in the
kitchen; the puppy, which they had just acquired, for "protection
in the country," was cowering, with a sporadic panicked scrabble
of claws, under the dining table that in their old home had been
reserved for special days but that here was used for every meal.

> **bas-reliefs** · a form of sculpture, often on plaques or walls, in which the design is raised slightly from the background

4   Then, before he could halt his eyes, David slipped into Wells's
account of Jesus. He had been an obscure political agitator, a kind
of hobo, in a minor colony of the Roman Empire. By an accident
impossible to construct, he (the small *h* horrified David) survived
his own crucifixion and presumably died a few weeks later. A
religion was founded on the freakish incident. The credulous
imagination of the times retrospectively assigned miracles and
supernatural pretensions to Jesus; a myth grew, and then a church,
whose theology at most points was in direct contradiction of the
simple, rather communistic teachings of the Galilean.

5   It was as if a stone that for weeks and even years had been
gathering weight in the web of David's nerves snapped them and
plunged through the page and a hundred layers of paper underneath. These fantastic falsehoods – plainly untrue; churches stood
everywhere, the entire nation was founded "under God"– did not
at first frighten him; it was the fact that they had been permitted
to exist in an actual human brain. This was the initial impact – that
at a definite spot in time and space a brain black with the denial
of Christ's divinity had been suffered to exist; that the universe
had not spit out this ball of tar but allowed it to continue in its
blasphemy, to grow old, win honors, wear a hat, write books that,
if true, collapsed everything into a jumble of horror. The world
outside the deep-silled windows – a rutted lawn, a whitewashed
barn, a walnut tree frothy with fresh green – seemed a haven from

which he was forever sealed off. Hot washrags seemed pressed 5
against his cheeks.

He read the account again. He tried to supply out of his igno- 6
rance objections that would defeat the complacent march of these
black words, and found none. Survivals and misunderstandings
more far-fetched were reported daily in the papers. But none
of them caused churches to be built in every town. He tried to
work backwards through the churches, from their brave high
fronts through their shabby, ill attended interiors back into the
events at Jerusalem, and felt himself surrounded by shifting gray
shadows, centuries of history, where he knew nothing. The thread
dissolved in his hands. Had Christ ever come to him, David Kern,
and said, "Here. Feel the wound in My side"?* No; but prayers had
been answered. What prayers? He had prayed that Rudy Mohn,
whom he had purposely tripped so he cracked his head on their
radiator, not die, and he had not died. But for all the blood, it
was just a cut; Rudy came back the same day, wearing a bandage
and repeating the same teasing words. He could never have died.
Again, David had prayed for two separate war-effort posters he
had sent away for to arrive tomorrow, and though they did not,
they did arrive, some days later, together, popping through the
clacking letter slot like a rebuke from God's mouth: *I answer your
prayers in My way, in My time.* After that, he had made his prayers
less definite, less susceptible of being twisted into a scolding. But
what a tiny, ridiculous coincidence this was, after all, to throw
into battle against H. G. Wells's engines of knowledge! Indeed, it
proved the enemy's point: Hope bases vast premises on foolish
accidents, and reads a word where in fact only a scribble exists.

His father came home. Though Saturday was a free day for him, 7
he had been working. He taught school in Olinger and spent all
his days performing, with a curious air of panic, needless errands.
Also, a city boy by birth, he was frightened of the farm and seized
any excuse to get away. The farm had been David's mother's
birthplace; it had been her idea to buy it back. With an ingenuity
and persistence unparalleled in her life, she had gained that end,
and moved them all here – her son, her husband, her mother.
Granmom, in her prime, had worked these fields alongside her
husband, but now she dabbled around the kitchen futilely, her
hands waggling with Parkinson's disease. She was always in the

"Here ... My side" ·
see John 20:25–29

7   way. Strange, out in the country, amid eighty acres, they were crowded together. His father expressed his feelings of discomfort by conducting with Mother an endless argument about organic farming. All through dusk, all through supper, it rattled on.

8   "Elsie, I know, I know from my education, the earth is nothing but chemicals. It's the only damn thing I got out of four years of college, so don't tell me it's not true."

9   "George, if you'd just walk out on the farm you'd know it's not true. The land has a *soul*."

10 "Soil, has, no, soul," he said, enunciating stiffly, as if to a very stupid class. To David he said, "You can't argue with a *femme*.• Your mother's a real *femme*. That's why I married her, and now I'm suffering for it."

femme · "woman" (French), here used as a superlative

11 "*This* soil has no soul," she said, "because it's been killed with superphosphate.• It's been burned bare by Boyer's tenant farmers." Boyer was the rich man they had bought the farm from. "It used to have a soul, didn't it, Mother? When you and Pop farmed it?"

superphosphate · a kind of liquid fertilizer

12 "Ach, yes; I guess." Granmom was trying to bring a forkful of food to her mouth with her less severely afflicted hand. In her anxiety she brought the other hand up from her lap. The crippled fingers, dull red in the orange light of the kerosene lamp in the center of the table, were welded by paralysis into one knobbed hook.

13 "Only human indi-vidu-als have souls," his father went on, in the same mincing, lifeless voice. "Because the Bible tells us so." Done eating, he crossed his legs and dug into his ear with a match miserably; to get at the thing inside his head he tucked in his chin, and his voice came out low-pitched at David. "When God made your mother, He made a real *femme*."

14 "George, don't you read the papers? Don't you know that between the chemical fertilizers and the bug sprays we'll all be dead in ten years? Heart attacks are killing every man in the country over forty-five."

15 He sighed wearily; the yellow skin of his eyelids wrinkled as he hurt himself with the match. "There's no connection," he stated, spacing his words with pained patience, "between the heart – and chemical fertilizers. It's alcohol that's doing it. Alcohol and milk. There is too much – cholesterol – in the tissues of the American heart. Don't tell me about chemistry, Elsie; I majored in the damn stuff for four years."

"Yes and I majored in Greek and I'm not a penny wiser. Mother, ¹⁶
put your waggler a*way*!" The old woman started, and the food
dropped from her fork. For some reason, the sight of her bad hand
at the table cruelly irritated her daughter. Granmom's eyes, worn
bits of crazed crystal embedded in watery milk, widened behind
her cockeyed spectacles. Circles of silver as fine as thread, they
clung to the red notches they had carved over the years into her
little white beak. In the orange flicker of the kerosene lamp her
dazed misery seemed infernal. David's mother began, without
noise, to cry. His father did not seem to have eyes at all; just
jaundiced sockets of wrinkled skin. The steam of food clouded the
scene. It was horrible but the horror was particular and familiar,
and distracted David from the formless dread that worked, sticky
and sore, within him, like a too large wound trying to heal.

He had to go to the bathroom, and took a flashlight down ¹⁷
through the wet grass to the outhouse. For once, his fear of spiders there felt trivial. He set the flashlight, burning, beside him,
and an insect alighted on its lens, a tiny insect, a mosquito or flea,
made so fine that the weak light projected its x-ray onto the wall
boards: the faint rim of its wings, the blurred strokes, magnified,
of its long hinged legs, the dark cone at the heart of its anatomy.
The tremor must be its heart beating. Without warning, David
was visited by an exact vision of death: a long hole in the ground,
no wider than your body, down which you are drawn while the
white faces above recede. You try to reach them but your arms
are pinned. Shovels pour dirt into your face. There you will be
forever, in an upright position, blind and silent, and in time no
one will remember you, and you will never be called. As strata
of rock shift, your fingers elongate, and your teeth are distended
sideways in a great underground grimace indistinguishable from
a strip of chalk. And the earth tumbles on, and the sun expires,
and unaltering darkness reigns where once there were stars.

Sweat broke out on his back. His mind seemed to rebound off ¹⁸
a solidness. Such extinction was not another threat, a graver sort
of danger, a kind of pain; it was qualitatively different. It was not
even a conception that could be voluntarily pictured; it entered
him from outside. His protesting nerves swarmed on its surface
like lichen on a meteor. The skin of his chest was soaked with
the effort of rejection. At the same time that the fear was dense

18 and internal, it was dense and all around him; a tide of clay had swept up to the stars; space was crushed into a mass. When he stood up, automatically hunching his shoulders to keep his head away from the spider webs, it was with a numb sense of being cramped between two huge volumes of rigidity. That he had even this small freedom to move surprised him. In the narrow shelter of that rank shack, adjusting his pants, he felt – his first spark of comfort – too small to be crushed.

19 But in the open, as the beam of the flashlight skidded with frightened quickness across the remote surfaces of the barn and the grape arbor and the giant pine that stood by the path to the woods, the terror descended. He raced up through the clinging grass pursued, not by one of the wild animals the woods might hold, or one of the goblins his superstitious grandmother had communicated to his childhood, but by spectres out of science fiction, where gigantic cinder moons fill half the turquoise sky. As David ran, a gray planet rolled inches behind his neck. If he looked back, he would be buried. And in the momentum of his terror, hideous possibilities – the dilation of the sun, the triumph of the insects, the crabs on the shore in *The Time Machine* – wheeled out of the vacuum of make-believe and added their weight to his impending oblivion.

20 He wrenched the door open; the lamps within the house flared. The wicks burning here and there seemed to mirror one another. His mother was washing the dishes in a little pan of heated pump-water; Granmom fluttered near her elbow apprehensively. In the living room – the downstairs of the little square house was two long rooms – his father sat in front of the black fireplace restlessly folding and unfolding a newspaper as he sustained his half of the argument. "Nitrogen, phosphorus, potash: these are the three replaceable constituents of the soil. One crop of corn carries away hundreds of pounds of"– he dropped the paper into his lap and ticked them off on three fingers –"nitrogen, phosphorus, potash."

21 "Boyer didn't grow corn."

22 "*Any* crop, Elsie. The human animal –"

23 "You're killing the *earth*worms, George!"

24 "The human animal, after thousands and *thou*sands of years, learned methods whereby the chemical balance of the soil may be maintained. Don't carry me back to the Dark Ages."

"When we moved to Olinger the ground in the garden was 25
like slate. Just one summer of my cousin's chicken dung and the
earthworms came back."

"I'm sure the Dark Ages were a fine place to the poor devils 26
born in them, but I don't want to go there. They give me the
creeps." Daddy stared into the cold pit of the fireplace and clung
to the rolled newspaper in his lap as if it alone were keeping him
from slipping backwards and down, down.

Mother came into the doorway brandishing a fistful of wet 27
forks. "And thanks to your DDT· there soon won't be a bee left
in the country. When I was a girl here you could eat a peach
without washing it."

DDT· an insecticide
banned for most uses
in the United States
since 1972 because of its
harmful effects on the
ecosystem

"It's primitive, Elsie. It's Dark Age stuff." 28

"Oh what do *you* know about the Dark Ages?" 29

"I know I don't want to go back to them." 30

David took from the shelf, where he had placed it this 31
afternoon, the great unabridged Webster's Dictionary that his
grandfather had owned. He turned the big thin pages, floppy as
cloth, to the entry he wanted, and read

> soul…I. An entity conceived as the essence, substance, 31a
> animating principle, or actuating cause of life, or of the
> individual life, esp. of life manifested in psychical activities;
> the vehicle of individual existence, separate in nature from
> the body and usually held to be separable in existence.

The definition went on, into Greek and Egyptian conceptions, 32
but David stopped short on the treacherous edge of antiquity. He
needed to read no further. The careful overlapping words shin-
gled a temporary shelter for him. "Usually held to be separable
in existence"– what could be fairer, more judicious, surer?

His father was saying, "The modern farmer can't go around 33
sweeping up after his cows. The poor devil has thousands and
*thou*sands of acres on his hands. Your modern farmer uses a
scientifically-arrived-at mixture, like five-ten-five, or six-twelve-
six, or *three*-twelve-six,· and spreads it on with this wonderful
modern machinery which of course we can't afford. Your modern
farmer can't *afford* medieval methods."

five-ten-five…*three-*
twelve-six· formulations
for fertilizers

Mother was quiet in the kitchen; her silence radiated waves 34
of anger.

35   "No now Elsie; don't play the *femme* with me. Let's discuss this calmly like two rational twentieth-century people. Your organic farming nuts aren't attacking five-ten-five; they're attacking the chemical fertilizer crooks. The monster firms."

36   A cup clinked in the kitchen. Mother's anger touched David's face; his cheeks burned guiltily. Just by being in the living room he was associated with his father. She appeared in the doorway with red hands and tears in her eyes, and said to the two of them, "I knew you didn't want to come here but I didn't know you'd torment me like this. You talked Pop into his grave and now you'll kill me. Go ahead, George, more power to you; at least I'll be buried in good ground." She tried to turn and met an obstacle and screamed, "Mother, stop hanging on my *back*! Why don't you go to *bed?*"

37   "Let's all go to bed," David's father said, rising from the blue wing chair and slapping his thigh with a newspaper. "This reminds me of death." It was a phrase of his that David had heard so often he never considered its sense.

38   Upstairs, he seemed to be lifted above his fears. The sheets on his bed were clean. Granmom had ironed them with a pair of flatirons saved from the Olinger attic; she plucked them hot off the stove alternately, with a wooden handle called a goose. It was a wonder, to see how she managed. In the next room, his parents grunted peaceably; they seemed to take their quarrels less seriously than he did. They made comfortable scratching noises as they carried a little lamp back and forth. Their door was open a crack, so he saw the light shift and swing. Surely there would be, in the last five minutes, in the last second, a crack of light, showing the door from the dark room to another, full of light. Thinking of it this vividly frightened him. His own dying, in a specific bed in a specific room, specific walls mottled with wallpaper, the dry whistle of his breathing, the murmuring doctors, the nervous relatives going in and out, but for him no way out but down into the funnel. *Never touch a doorknob again.* A whisper, and his parents' light was blown out. David prayed to be reassured. Though the experiment frightened him, he lifted his hands high into the darkness above his face and begged Christ to touch them. Not hard or long: the faintest, quickest grip would be final for a lifetime. His hands waited in the air, itself a

substance, which seemed to move through his fingers; or was it 38
the pressure of his pulse? He returned his hands to beneath the
covers uncertain if they had been touched or not. For would not
Christ's touch *be* infinitely gentle?

Through all the eddies of its aftermath, David clung to this 39
thought about his revelation of extinction: that there, in the outhouse, he had struck a solidness qualitatively different, a rock of
horror firm enough to support any height of construction. All he
needed was a little help; a word, a gesture, a nod of certainty, and
he would be sealed in, safe. The assurance from the dictionary
had melted in the night. Today was Sunday, a hot fair day. Across
a mile of clear air the church bells called, *Celebrate, celebrate.*
Only Daddy went. He put on a coat over his rolled-up shirtsleeves
and got into the little old black Plymouth parked by the barn
and went off, with the same pained hurried grimness of all his
actions. His churning wheels, as he shifted too hastily into second,
raised plumes of red dust on the dirt road. Mother walked to the
far field, to see what bushes needed cutting. David, though he
usually preferred to stay in the house, went with her. The puppy
followed at a distance, whining as it picked its way through the
stubble but floundering off timidly if one of them went back to
pick it up and carry it. When they reached the crest of the far
field, his mother asked, "David, what's troubling you?"

"Nothing. Why?" 40

She looked at him sharply. The greening woods cross-hatched 41
the space beyond her half-gray hair. Then she showed him her
profile, and gestured toward the house, which they had left a
half-mile behind them. "See how it sits in the land? They don't
know how to build with the land any more. Pop always said the
foundations were set with the compass. We must try to get a
compass and see. It's supposed to face due south; but south feels
a little more *that* way to me." From the side, as she said these
things, she seemed handsome and young. The smooth sweep of
her hair over her ear seemed white with a purity and calm that
made her feel foreign to him. He had never regarded his parents
as consolers of his troubles; from the beginning they had seemed
to have more troubles than he. Their confusion had flattered
him into an illusion of strength; so now on this high clear ridge
he jealously guarded the menace all around them, blowing like

41 a breeze on his fingertips, the possibility of all this wide scenery sinking into darkness. The strange fact that though she came to look at the brush she carried no clippers, for she had a fixed prejudice against working on Sundays, was the only consolation he allowed her to offer.

42 As they walked back, the puppy whimpering after them, the rising dust behind a distant line of trees announced that Daddy was speeding home from church. When they reached the house he was there. He had brought back the Sunday paper and the vehement remark, "Dobson's too intelligent for these farmers. They just sit there with their mouths open and don't hear a thing the poor devil's saying."

43 "What makes you think farmers are unintelligent? This country was made by farmers. George Washington was a farmer."

44 "They are, Elsie. They are unintelligent. George Washington's dead. In this day and age only the misfits stay on the farm. The lame, the halt, the blind. The morons with one arm. Human garbage. They remind me of death, sitting there with their mouths open."

45 "My *father* was a farmer."

46 "He was a frustrated man, Elsie. He never knew what hit him. The poor devil meant so well, and he never knew which end was up. Your mother'll bear me out. Isn't that right, Mom? Pop never knew what hit him?"

47 "Ach, I guess not," the old woman quavered, and the ambiguity for the moment silenced both sides.

48 David hid in the funny papers and sports section until one-thirty. At two, the catechetical class met at the Firetown church. He had transferred from the catechetical class of the Lutheran church in Olinger, a humiliating comedown. In Olinger they met on Wednesday nights, spiffy and spruce,* in the atmosphere of a dance. Afterwards, blessed by the brick-faced minister from whose lips the word "Christ" fell like a burning stone, the more daring of them went with their Bibles to a luncheonette and smoked. Here in Firetown, the girls were dull white cows and the boys narrow-faced brown goats in old men's suits, herded on Sunday afternoons into a threadbare church basement that smelled of stale hay. Because his father had taken the car on one of his endless errands to Olinger, David walked, grateful for the open air and the silence. The catechetical class embarrassed

spruce · neat in appearance

him, but today he placed hope in it, as the source of the nod, the 48
gesture, that was all he needed.

Reverend Dobson was a delicate young man with great dark 49
eyes and small white shapely hands that flickered like protesting doves when he preached; he seemed a bit misplaced in the
Lutheran ministry. This was his first call. It was a split parish; he
served another rural church twelve miles away. His iridescent
green Ford, new six months ago, was spattered to the windows
with red mud and rattled from bouncing on the rude back roads,
where he frequently got lost, to the malicious satisfaction of many.
But David's mother liked him, and, more pertinent to his success,
the Haiers, the sleek family of feed merchants and innkeepers
and tractor salesmen who dominated the Firetown church, liked
him. David liked him, and felt liked in turn; sometimes in class,
after some special stupidity, Dobson directed toward him out of
those wide black eyes a mild look of disbelief, a look that, though
flattering, was also delicately disquieting.

Catechetical instruction consisted of reading aloud from a work 50
booklet answers to problems prepared during the week, problems like, "'I am the _____, the _____, and the _____,' saith
the Lord.'" Then there was a question period in which no one
ever asked any questions. Today's theme was the last third of the
Apostles' Creed. When the time came for questions, David blushed
and asked, "About the Resurrection of the Body – are we conscious
between the time when we die and the Day of Judgment?"

Dobson blinked, and his fine little mouth pursed, suggest- 51
ing that David was making difficult things more difficult. The
faces of the other students went blank, as if an indiscretion had
been committed.

"No, I suppose not," Reverend Dobson said. 52

"Well, where is our soul, then, in this gap?" 53

The sense grew, in the class, of a naughtiness occurring. 54
Dobson's shy eyes watered, as if he were straining to keep up
the formality of attention, and one of the girls, the fattest, sim-
pered' toward her twin, who was a little less fat. Their chairs
were arranged in a rough circle. The current running around
the circle panicked David. Did everybody know something he
didn't know?

"I suppose you could say our souls are asleep," Dobson said. 55

56 "And then they wake up, and there is the earth like it always is, and all the people who have ever lived? Where will Heaven be?"

57 Anita Haier giggled. Dobson gazed at David intently, but with an awkward, puzzled flicker of forgiveness, as if there existed a secret between them that David was violating. But David knew of no secret. All he wanted was to hear Dobson repeat the words he said every Sunday morning. This he would not do. As if these words were unworthy of the conversational voice.

58 "David, you might think of Heaven this way: as the way the goodness Abraham Lincoln did lives after him."

59 "But is Lincoln conscious of it living on?" He blushed no longer with embarrassment but in anger; he had walked here in good faith and was being made a fool.

60 "Is he conscious now? I would have to say no; but I don't think it matters." His voice had a coward's firmness; he was hostile now.

61 "You don't."

62 "Not in the eyes of God, no." The unction,* the stunning impudence, of this reply sprang tears of outrage in David's eyes. He bowed them to his book, where short words like Duty, Love, Obey, Honor, were stacked in the form of a cross.

> **unction** · exaggerated or superficial earnestness, condescension

63 "Were there any other questions, David?" Dobson asked with renewed gentleness. The others were rustling, collecting their books.

64 "No." He made his voice firm, though he could not bring up his eyes.

65 "Did I answer your question fully enough?"

66 "Yes."

67 In the minister's silence the shame that should have been his crept over David: the burden and fever of being a fraud were placed upon *him*, who was innocent, and it seemed, he knew, a confession of this guilt that on the way out he was unable to face Dobson's stirred gaze, though he felt it probing the side of his head.

68 Anita Haier's father gave him a ride down the highway as far as the dirt road. David said he wanted to walk the rest, and figured that his offer was accepted because Mr. Haier did not want to dirty his bright blue Buick with dust. This was all right; everything was all right, as long as it was clear. His indignation at being betrayed, at seeing Christianity betrayed, had hardened him. The straight dirt road reflected his hardness. Pink stones thrust up through its packed surface. The April sun beat down from the center of

the afternoon half of the sky; already it had some of summer's 68
heat. Already the fringes of weeds at the edges of the road were
bedraggled with dust. From the reviving grass and scruff of the
fields he walked between, insects were sending up a monotonous,
automatic chant. In the distance a tiny figure in his father's coat was
walking along the edge of the woods. His mother. He wondered
what joy she found in such walks; to him the brown stretches of
slowly rising and falling land expressed only a huge exhaustion.

Flushed with fresh air and happiness, she returned from her walk 69
earlier than he had expected, and surprised him at his grandfather's
Bible. It was a stumpy black book, the boards worn thin where the
old man's fingers had held them; the spine hung by one weak hinge
of fabric. David had been looking for the passage where Jesus says to
the one thief on the cross, "Today shalt thou be with me in paradise."*
He had never tried reading the Bible for himself before. What was
so embarrassing about being caught at it, was that he detested the
apparatus of piety. Fusty* churches, creaking hymns, ugly Sunday-
school teachers and their stupid leaflets – he hated everything about
them but the promise they held out, a promise that in the most
perverse way, as if the homeliest crone in the kingdom were given
the Prince's hand, made every good and real thing, ball games and
jokes and pert-breasted girls, possible. He couldn't explain this to
his mother. There was no time. Her solicitude was upon him.

"David, what are you doing?" 70

"Nothing." 71

"What are you doing at Grandpop's Bible?" 72

"Trying to read it. This is supposed to be a Christian country, 73
isn't it?"

She sat down on the green sofa, which used to be in the sun 74
parlor at Olinger, under the fancy mirror. A little smile still lingered on her face from the walk.

"David, I wish you'd talk to me." 75

"What about?" 76

"About whatever it is that's troubling you. Your father and I 77
have both noticed it."

"I asked Reverend Dobson about Heaven and he said it was 78
like Abraham Lincoln's goodness living after him."

He waited for the shock to strike her. "Yes?" she said, expect- 79
ing more.

80 "That's all."

81 "And why didn't you like it?"

82 "Well, don't you see? It amounts to saying there isn't any Heaven at all."

83 "I don't see that it amounts to that. What do you want Heaven to be?"

84 "Well, I don't know. I want it to be *some*thing. I thought he'd tell me what it was. I thought that was his job." He was becoming angry, sensing her surprise at him. She had assumed that Heaven had faded from his head years ago. She had imagined that he had already entered, in the secrecy of silence, the conspiracy that he now knew to be all around him.

85 "David," she asked gently, "don't you ever want to rest?"

86 "No. Not forever."

87 "David, you're so young. When you get older, you'll feel differently."

88 "Grandpa didn't. Look how tattered this book is."

89 "I never understood your grandfather."

90 "Well I don't understand ministers who say it's like Lincoln's goodness going on and on. Suppose you're not Lincoln?"

91 "I think Reverend Dobson made a mistake. You must try to forgive him."

92 "It's not a *question* of his making a mistake! It's a question of dying and never moving or seeing or hearing anything ever again."

93 "But"—in exasperation—"darling, it's so *greedy* of you to want more. When God has given us this wonderful April day, and given us this farm, and you have your whole life ahead of you —"

94 "You think, then, that there is God?"

95 "Of course I do"—with deep relief, that smoothed her features into a reposeful oval. He had risen and was standing too near her for his comfort. He was afraid she would reach out and touch him.

96 "He made everything? You feel that?"

97 "Yes."

98 "Then who made Him?"

99 "Why, Man. Man." The happiness of this answer lit up her face radiantly, until she saw his gesture of disgust. She was so simple, so illogical; such a *femme*.

100 "Well that amounts to saying there is none."

Her hand reached for his wrist but he backed away. "David, it's a mystery. A miracle. It's a miracle more beautiful than any Reverend Dobson could have told you about. You don't say houses don't exist because Man made them." 101

"No. God has to be different." 102

"But, David, you have the *evidence*. Look out the window at the sun; at the fields." 103

"Mother, good grief. Don't you see"—he rasped away the roughness in his throat—"if when we die there's nothing, all your sun and fields and what not are all, ah, *horror*? It's just an ocean of horror." 104

"But David, it's not. It's so clearly not that." And she made an urgent opening gesture with her hands that expressed, with its suggestion of a willingness to receive his helplessness, all her grace, her gentleness, her love of beauty, gathered into a passive intensity that made him intensely hate her. He would not be wooed away from the truth. *I am the Way, the Truth....* · 105

I am ... Truth.... ·
John 14:6

"No," he told her. "Just let me alone." 106

He found his tennis ball behind the piano and went outside to throw it against the side of the house. There was a patch high up where the brown stucco that had been laid over the sandstone masonry was crumbling away; he kept trying with the tennis ball to chip more pieces off. Superimposed upon his deep ache was a smaller but more immediate worry; that he had hurt his mother. He heard his father's car rattling on the straightaway, and went into the house, to make peace before he arrived. To his relief, she was not giving off the stifling damp heat of her anger, but instead was cool, decisive, maternal. She handed him an old green book, her college text of Plato. · 107

Plato · Greek philosopher
(428/7–348/7 BC)

Parable of the Cave ·
Plato's allegory argues
that the spiritual realm
constitutes ultimate
reality while the mate-
rial realm is an inferior
reflection of it

"I want to read the Parable of the Cave," · she said. 108

"All right," he said, though he knew it would do no good. Some story by a dead Greek just vague enough to please her. "Don't worry about it, Mother." 109

"I *am* worried. Honestly, David, I'm sure there will be something for us. As you get older, these things seem to matter a great deal less." 110

"That may be. It's a dismal thought, though." 111

His father bumped at the door. The locks and jambs stuck here. But before Granmom could totter to the latch and let him 112

112 in, he had knocked it open. He had been in Olinger dithering with track meet tickets. Although Mother usually kept her talks with David a confidence, a treasure between them, she called instantly, "George, David is worried about death!"

113   He came to the doorway of the living room, his shirt pocket bristling with pencils, holding in one hand a pint box of melting ice cream and in the other the knife with which he was about to divide it into four sections, their Sunday treat. "Is the kid worried about death? Don't give it a thought, David. I'll be lucky if I live till tomorrow, and I'm not worried. If they'd taken a buckshot gun and shot me in the cradle I'd be better off. The *world*'d be better off. Hell, I think death is a wonderful thing. I look forward to it. Get the garbage out of the way. If I had the man here who invented death, I'd pin a medal on him."

114   "Hush, George. You'll frighten the child worse than he is."

115   This was not true; he never frightened David. There was no harm in his father, no harm at all. Indeed, in the man's steep self-disgust the boy felt a kind of ally. A distant ally. He saw his position with a certain strategic coldness. Nowhere in the world of other people would he find the hint, the nod, he needed to begin to build his fortress against death. They none of them believed. He was alone. In that deep hole.

116   In the months that followed, his position changed little. School was some comfort. All those sexy, perfumed people, wisecracking, chewing gum, all of them doomed to die, and none of them noticing. In their company David felt that they would carry him along into the bright, cheap paradise reserved for them. In any crowd, the fear ebbed a little; he had reasoned that somewhere in the world there must exist a few people who believed what was necessary, and the larger the crowd, the greater the chance that he was near such a soul, within calling distance, if only he was not too ignorant, too ill-equipped, to spot him. The sight of clergymen cheered him; whatever they themselves thought, their collars were still a sign that somewhere, at some time, someone had recognized that we cannot, *cannot*, submit to death. The sermon topics posted outside churches, the flip, hurried pieties of disc jockeys, the cartoons in magazines showing angels or devils – on such scraps he kept alive the possibility of hope.

For the rest, he tried to drown his hopelessness in clatter and 117
jostle. The pinball machine at the luncheonette was a merciful
distraction; as he bent over its buzzing, flashing board of flippers
and cushions, the weight and constriction in his chest lightened
and loosened. He was grateful for all the time his father wasted
in Olinger. Every delay postponed the moment when they must
ride together down the dirt road into the heart of the dark farmland, where the only light was the kerosene lamp waiting on the
dining-room table, a light that drowned their food in shadow
and made it sinister.

He lost his appetite for reading. He was afraid of being 118
ambushed again. In mystery novels people died like dolls being
discarded; in science fiction enormities of space and time con-
spired to crush the humans; and even in P. G. Wodehouse he felt a
hollowness, a turning away from reality that was implicitly bitter,
and became explicit in the comic figures of futile clergymen. All
gaiety seemed minced out on the skin of a void. All quiet hours
seemed invitations to dread.

Even on weekends, he and his father contrived to escape the 119
farm; and when, some Saturdays, they did stay home, it was to do
something destructive – tear down an old henhouse or set huge
brush fires that threatened, while Mother shouted and flapped
her arms, to spread to the woods. Whenever his father worked,
it was with rapt violence; when he chopped kindling, fragments
of the old henhouse boards flew like shrapnel and the ax-head
was always within a quarter of an inch of flying off the handle.
He was exhilarating to watch, sweating and swearing and sucking
bits of saliva back into his lips.

School stopped. His father took the car in the opposite direc- 120
tion, to a highway construction job where he had been hired
for the summer as a timekeeper, and David was stranded in the
middle of acres of heat and greenery and blowing pollen and the
strange, mechanical humming that lay invisibly in the weeds and
alfalfa and dry orchard grass.

For his fifteenth birthday his parents gave him, with jokes 121
about him being a hillbilly now, a Remington .22. It was somewhat
like a pinball machine to take it out to the old kiln in the woods
where they dumped their trash, and set up tin cans on the kiln's
sandstone shoulder and shoot them off one by one. He'd take

121 the puppy, who had grown long legs and a rich coat of reddish fur – he was part chow. Copper hated the gun but loved the boy enough to accompany him. When the flat acrid crack rang out, he would race in terrified circles that would tighten and tighten until they brought him, shivering, against David's legs. Depending upon his mood, David would shoot again or drop to his knees and comfort the dog. Giving this comfort to a degree returned comfort to him. The dog's ears, laid flat against his skull in fear, were folded so intricately, so – he groped for the concept – *surely*. Where the dull-studded collar made the fur stand up, each hair showed a root of soft white under the length, black-tipped, of the metal-color that had lent the dog its name. In his agitation Copper panted through nostrils that were elegant slits, like two healed cuts, or like the key-holes of a dainty lock of black, grained wood. His whole whorling, knotted, jointed body was a wealth of such embellishments. And in the smell of the dog's hair David seemed to descend through many finely differentiated layers of earth: mulch, soil, sand, clay, and the glittering mineral base.

122 But when he returned to the house, and saw the books arranged on the low shelves, fear returned. The four adamant volumes of Wells like four thin bricks, the green Plato that had puzzled him with its queer softness and tangled purity, the dead Galsworthy and "Elizabeth," Grandpa's mammoth dictionary, Grandpa's Bible, the Bible that he himself had received on becoming a member of the Firetown Lutheran Church – at the sight of these, the memory of his fear reawakened and came around him. He had grown stiff and stupid in its embrace. His parents tried to think of ways to entertain him.

123 "David, I have a job for you to do," his mother said one evening at the table.

124 "What?"

125 "If you're going to take that tone perhaps we'd better not talk."

126 "What tone? I don't take any tone."

127 "Your grandmother thinks there are too many pigeons in the barn."

128 "Why?" David turned to look at his grandmother, but she sat there staring at the burning lamp with her usual expression of bewilderment.

129 Mother shouted, "Mom, he wants to know why!"

Granmom made a jerky, irritable motion with her bad hand, 130 as if generating the force for utterance, and said, "They foul the furniture."

"That's right," Mother said. "She's afraid for that old Olinger fur- 131 niture that we'll never use. David, she's been after me for a month about those poor pigeons. She wants you to shoot them."

"I don't want to kill anything especially," David said. 132

Daddy said, "The kid's like you are, Elsie. He's too good for 133 this world. Kill or be killed, that's my motto."

His mother said loudly, "Mother, he doesn't want to do it." 134

"Not?" The old lady's eyes distended as if in horror and her 135 claw descended slowly to her lap.

"Oh, I'll do it, I'll do it tomorrow," David snapped, and a pleas- 136 ant crisp taste entered his mouth with the decision.

"And I had thought, when Boyer's men made the hay, it would 137 be better if the barn doesn't look like a rookery," his mother added needlessly.

A barn, in day, is a small night. The splinters of light between the 138 dry shingles pierce the high roof like stars, and the rafters and cross-beams and built-in ladders seem, until your eyes adjust, as mysterious as the branches of a haunted forest. David entered silently, the gun in one hand. Copper whined desperately at the door, too frightened to come in with the gun yet unwilling to leave the boy. David stealthily turned, said "Go away," shut the door on the dog, and slipped the bolt across. It was a door within a door; the double door for wagons and tractors was as high and wide as the face of a house.

The smell of old straw scratched his sinuses. The red sofa, half- 139 hidden under its white-splotched tarpaulin, seemed assimilated into this smell, sunk in it, buried. The mouths of empty bins gaped like caves. Rusty oddments of farming – coils of baling wire, some spare tines for a harrow, a handleless shovel – hung on nails driven here and there in the thick wood. He stood stock-still a minute; it took a while to separate the cooing of the pigeons from the rustling in his ears. When he had focused on the cooing, it flooded the vast interior with its throaty, bubbling outpour: there seemed no other sound. They were up behind the beams. What light there was leaked through the shingles and the dirty glass windows at the far end and the small round holes, about as big as basketballs, high on the opposite stone side walls, under the ridge of the roof.

140   A pigeon appeared in one of these holes, on the side toward the house. It flew in, with a battering of wings, from the outside, and waited there, silhouetted against its pinched bit of sky, preening and cooing in a throbbing, thrilled, tentative way. David tiptoed four steps to the side, rested his gun against the lowest rung of a ladder pegged between two upright beams, and lowered the gunsight into the bird's tiny, jauntily cocked head. The slap of the report seemed to come off the stone wall behind him, and the pigeon did not fall. Neither did it fly. Instead it stuck in the round hole, pirouetting rapidly and nodding its head as if in frantic agreement. David shot the bolt back and forth and had aimed again before the spent cartridge had stopped jingling on the boards by his feet. He eased the tip of the sight a little lower, into the bird's breast, and took care to squeeze the trigger with perfect evenness. The slow contraction of his hand abruptly sprang the bullet; for a half-second there was doubt, and then the pigeon fell like a handful of rags, skimming down the barn wall into the layer of straw that coated the floor of the mow* on this side.

mow · the part of a barn where hay or straw is stored

141   Now others shook loose from the rafters, and whirled in the dim air with a great blurred hurtle of feathers and noise. They would go for the hole; he fixed his sight on the little moon of blue, and when a pigeon came to it, shot him as he was walking the ten inches of stone that would have carried him into the open air. This pigeon lay down in that tunnel of stone, unable to fall either one way or the other, although he was alive enough to lift one wing and cloud the light. It would sink back, and he would suddenly lift it again, the feathers flaring. His body blocked that exit. David raced to the other side of the barn's main aisle, where a similar ladder was symmetrically placed, and rested his gun on the same rung. Three birds came together to this hole; he got one, and two got through. The rest resettled in the rafters.

142   There was a shallow triangular space behind the cross beams supporting the roof. It was here they roosted and hid. But either the space was too small, or they were curious, for now that his eyes were at home in the dusty gloom, David could see little dabs of gray popping in and out. The cooing was shriller now; its apprehensive tremolo made the whole volume of air seem liquid. He noticed one little smudge of a head that was especially persistent in peeking out; he marked the place, and fixed his gun

on it, and when the head appeared again, had his finger tightened 142
in advance on the trigger. A parcel of fluff slipped off the beam
and fell the barn's height onto a canvas covering some Olinger
furniture, and where its head had peeked out there was a fresh
prick of light in the shingles.

Standing in the center of the floor, fully master now, disdain- 143
ing to steady the barrel with anything but his arm, he killed two
more that way. He felt like a beautiful avenger. Out of the shadowy ragged infinity of the vast barn roof these impudent things
dared to thrust their heads, presumed to dirty its starred silence
with their filthy timorous life, and he cut them off, tucked them
back neatly into the silence. He had the sensation of a creator;
these little smudges and flickers that he was clever to see and
even cleverer to hit in the dim recesses of the rafters – out of
each of them he was making a full bird. A tiny peek, probe, dab
of life, when he hit it, blossomed into a dead enemy, falling with
good, final weight.

The imperfection of the second pigeon he had shot, who was 144
still lifting his wing now and then up in the round hole, nagged
him. He put a new clip into the stock. Hugging the gun against
his body, he climbed the ladder. The barrel sight scratched his
ear; he had a sharp, garish vision, like a color slide, of shooting
himself and being found tumbled on the barn floor among his
prey. He locked his arm around the top rung – a fragile, gnawed
rod braced between uprights – and shot into the bird's body from
a flat angle. The wing folded, but the impact did not, as he had
hoped, push the bird out of the hole. He fired again, and again,
and still the little body, lighter than air when alive, was too heavy
to budge from its high grave. From up here he could see green
trees and a brown corner of the house through the hole. Clammy
with the cobwebs that gathered between the rungs, he pumped
a full clip of eight bullets into the stubborn shadow, with no
success. He climbed down, and was struck by the silence in the
barn. The remaining pigeons must have escaped out the other
hole. That was all right; he was tired of it.

He stepped with his rifle into the light. His mother was coming 145
to meet him, and it tickled him to see her shy away from the
carelessly held gun. "You took a chip out of the house," she said.
"What were those last shots about?"

146   "One of them died up in that little round hole and I was trying to shoot it down."

147   "Copper's hiding behind the piano and won't come out. I had to leave him."

148   "Well don't blame me. *I* didn't want to shoot the poor devils."

149   "Don't smirk. You look like your father. How many did you get?"

150   "Six."

151   She went into the barn, and he followed. She listened to the silence. Her hair was scraggly, perhaps from tussling with the dog. "I don't suppose the others will be back," she said wearily. "Indeed, I don't know why I let Mother talk me into it. Their cooing was such a comforting noise." She began to gather up the dead pigeons. Though he didn't want to touch them, David went into the mow and picked up by its tepid, horny, coral-colored feet the first bird he had killed. Its wings unfolded disconcertingly, as if the creature had been held together by threads that now were slit. It did not weigh much. He retrieved the one on the other side of the barn; his mother got the three in the middle and led the way across the road to the little southern slope of land that went down toward the foundations of the vanished tobacco shed. The ground was too steep to plant and mow; wild strawberries grew in the tangled grass. She put her burden down and said, "We'll have to bury them. The dog will go wild."

152   He put his two down on her three; the slick feathers let the bodies slide liquidly on one another. He asked, "Shall I get you the shovel?"

153   "Get it for yourself; *you* bury them. They're your kill. And be sure to make the hole deep enough so he won't dig them up." While he went to the tool shed for the shovel, she went into the house. Unlike her, she did not look up, either at the orchard to the right of her or at the meadow on her left, but instead held her head rigidly, tilted a little, as if listening to the ground.

154   He dug the hole, in a spot where there were no strawberry plants, before he studied the pigeons. He had never seen a bird this close before. The feathers were more wonderful than dog's hair, for each filament was shaped within the shape of the feather, and the feathers in turn were trimmed to fit a pattern that flowed without error across the bird's body. He lost himself in the geometrical tides as the feathers now broadened and stiffened to

make an edge for flight, now softened and constricted to cup 154
warmth around the mute flesh. And across the surface of the
infinitely adjusted yet somehow effortless mechanics of the feathers played idle designs of color, no two alike, designs executed, it
seemed, in a controlled rapture, with a joy that hung level in the
air above and behind him. Yet these birds bred in the millions
and were exterminated as pests. Into the fragrant open earth he
dropped one broadly banded in slate shades of blue, and on top of
it another, mottled all over in rhythms of lilac and gray. The next
was almost wholly white, but for a salmon glaze at its throat. As
he fitted the last two, still pliant, on the top, and stood up, crusty
coverings were lifted from him, and with a feminine, slipping
sensation along his nerves that seemed to give the air hands, he
was robed in this certainty[that the God who had lavished such
craft upon these worthless birds would not destroy His whole
Creation by refusing to let David live forever.]

V. Divinly crafted creations
· to us they are meaningless
  ⇒ if God is this crafty w/ a
Piegon (lowly animal) then surly
    ~~God~~ ~~will~~ there is a heaven for his ppl

N. Scott Momaday

《1 9 3 4 -》

Momaday is the product of at least three cultures: the Kiowa culture of his birth, the Southwest Indian cultures of his early years, and, from his adult training, 20th-century Anglo-American literary culture. Momaday was born Navarro Scott Mammedaty in 1934, in Kiowa country, Oklahoma, the son of full-blooded Kiowa artist, Alfred Morris Mammedaty (Alfred later changed the spelling of the family name). When Momaday was two, his family moved to the Southwest, where his parents taught in several places, ending up in the tiny school of Jemez Pueblo, New Mexico. Leaving Jemez, Momaday took his initial degree from the University of New Mexico, then went on to earn the doctorate in American literature from Stanford University (1963). Momaday's first novel, House Made of Dawn *(1968), was awarded the Pulitzer Prize and profoundly influenced the emerging movement of contemporary Native American writing. This novel illustrates Momaday's fusion of the various cultures of his background and training to produce a literature at once complex, challenging, and truly multi-cultural. The influence of such Anglo-American modernists as William Faulkner is evidenced in Momaday's use of the stream-of-consciousness technique, with its confusion of time and space. Its Jemez (or Walatowa) protagonist and setting give Momaday the opportunity to explore Pueblo tradition and ceremony, as well as the problems created for contemporary Pueblo people by the intersecting cultures of their world. But Tosamah, the title character of "Priest of the Sun" (part 2 of the novel, from which our selection is taken), is an urban Kiowa. In his ceremonies and sermons, Tosamah combines the Plains tribes' reverence for place and the spoken word with Christianity. This fusion of worldviews is evidenced, for example, in his highly unusual reading of the first chapter of the Gospel of John.*

THE PRIEST OF THE SUN

THE PRIEST OF THE SUN lived with his disciple Cruz on the first floor of a two-story red-brick building in Los Angeles. The upstairs was maintained as a storage facility by the A. A. Kaul Office Supply Company. The basement was a kind of church. There was a signboard on the wall above the basement steps, encased in glass. In neat, movable white block letters on a black field it read:

1

LOS ANGELES
HOLINESS PAN-INDIAN RESCUE MISSION
Rev. J. B. B. Tosamah, Pastor & Priest of the Sun
Saturday 8:30 PM
"The Gospel According to John"
Sunday 8:30 PM
"The Way to Rainy Mountain"
Be kind to a white man today

1a

The basement was cold and dreary, dimly illuminated by two 40-watt bulbs which were screwed into the side walls above the dais. This platform was made out of rough planks of various woods and dimensions, thrown together without so much as a hammer and nails; it stood seven or eight inches above the floor, and it supported the tin firebox and the crescent altar. Off to one side was a kind of lectern, decorated with red and yellow symbols of the sun and moon. In back of the dais there was a screen of purple drapery, threadbare and badly faded. On either side of the aisle which led to the altar there were chairs and crates, fashioned into pews. The walls were bare and gray and streaked with water. The only windows were small, rectangular openings near the ceiling, at ground level; the panes were covered over with a thick film of coal oil and dust, and spider webs clung to the frames or floated out like smoke across the room. The air was heavy and stale; odors of old smoke and incense lingered all around. The people had filed into the pews and were waiting silently.

2

Cruz, a squat, oily man with blue-black hair that stood out like spines from his head, stepped forward on the platform and raised his hands as if to ask for the quiet that already was. Everyone watched him for a moment; in the dull light his skin shone yellow with sweat. Turning slightly and extending his arm behind him, he said, "The Right Reverend John Big Bluff Tosamah."

3

4   There was a ripple in the dark screen; the drapes parted and the Priest of the Sun appeared, moving shadow-like to the lectern. He was shaggy and awful-looking in the thin, naked light: big, lithe as a cat, narrow-eyed, suggesting in the whole of his look and manner both arrogance and agony. He wore black like a cleric; he had the voice of a great dog:

5   "*In principio erat Verbum.*" Think of Genesis. Think of how it was before the world was made. There was nothing, the Bible says. 'And the earth was without form, and void; and darkness was upon the face of the deep.' It was dark, and there was nothing. There were no mountains, no trees, no rocks, no rivers. There was nothing. But there was darkness all around, and in the darkness something happened. Something happened! There was a single sound. Far away in the darkness there was a single sound. Nothing made it, but it was there; and there was no one to hear it, but it was there. It was there, and there was nothing else. It rose up in the darkness, little and still, almost nothing in itself – like a single soft breath, like the wind arising; yes, like the whisper of the wind rising slowly and going out into the early morning. But there was no wind. There was only the sound, little and soft. It was almost nothing in itself, the smallest seed of sound – but it took hold of the darkness and there was light; it took hold of the stillness and there was motion forever; it took hold of the silence and there was sound. It was almost nothing in itself, a single sound, a word – a word broken off at the darkest center of the night and let go in the awful void, forever and forever. And it was almost nothing in itself. It scarcely was; but it was, and everything began."

6   Just then a remarkable thing happened. The Priest of the Sun seemed stricken; he let go of his audience and withdrew into himself, into some strange potential of himself. His voice, which had been low and resonant, suddenly became harsh and flat; his shoulders sagged and his stomach protruded, as if he had held his breath to the limit of endurance; for a moment there was a look of amazement, then utter carelessness in his face. Conviction, caricature, callousness: the remainder of his sermon was a going back and forth among these.

7   "Thank you so much, Brother Cruz. Good evening, blood brothers and sisters, and welcome, welcome. Gracious me, I see

'In principio … Verbum' · "In the beginning was the Word" (Latin), John 1:1

'And the … deep' · Genesis 1:2

lots of new faces out there tonight. Gracious me! May the Great
Spirit – can we knock off that talking in the back there? – be with
you always.

"'In the beginning was the Word.' I have taken as my text this
evening the almighty Word itself. Now get this: 'There was a
man sent from God, whose name was John. The same came
for a witness, to bear witness of the Light, that all men through
him might believe!'" Amen, brothers and sisters, Amen. And the
riddle of the Word, 'In the beginning was the Word....' Now what
do you suppose old John *meant* by that? That cat was a preacher,
and, well, you know how it is with preachers; he had something
big on his mind. Oh my, it was big; it was the *Truth*, and it was
heavy, and old John hurried to set it down. And in his hurry he
said too much. 'In the beginning was the Word, and the Word
was with God, and the Word was God!' It was the Truth, all right,
but it was more than the Truth. The Truth was overgrown with
fat, and the fat was God. The fat was *John's* God, and God stood
between John and the Truth. Old John, see, he got up one morning and caught sight of the Truth. It must have been like a bolt of
lightning, and the sight of it made him blind. And for a moment
the vision burned on in back of his eyes, and he *knew* what it
was. In that instant he saw something he had never seen before
and would never see again. That was the instant of revelation,
inspiration, Truth. And old John, he must have fallen down on
his knees. Man, he must have been shaking and laughing and
crying and yelling and praying – all at the same time – and he
must have been drunk and delirious with the Truth. You see, he
had lived all his life waiting for that one moment, and it came,
and it took him by surprise, and it was gone. And he said, 'In
the beginning was the Word....' And, man, right then and there
he should have stopped. There was nothing more to say, but he
went on. He had said all there was to say, everything, but he went
on. 'In the beginning was the Word....' Brothers and sisters, *that*
was the Truth, the whole of it, the essential and eternal Truth,
the bone and blood and muscle of the Truth. But he went on, old
John, because be was a preacher. The perfect vision faded from
his mind, and he went on. The instant passed, and then he had
nothing but a memory. He was desperate and confused, and in
his confusion be stumbled and went on. 'In the beginning was the

7

8

**'There was ... be-
lieve'** · John 1:6–7

8   Word, and the Word was with God, and the Word was God.' He
went on to talk about Jews and Jerusalem, Levites and Pharisees,
Moses and Philip and Andrew and Peter. Don't you see? Old John
had to go on. That cat had a whole lot at stake. He couldn't let
the Truth alone. He couldn't see that he had come to the end of
the Truth, and he went on. He tried to make it bigger and better
than it was, but instead he only demeaned and encumbered it. He
made it soft and big with fat. He was a preacher, and he made a
complex sentence of the Truth, two sentences, three, a paragraph.
He made a sermon and theology of the Truth. He imposed his
idea of God upon the everlasting Truth. 'In the beginning was
the Word....' And that is all there was, and it was enough.

9   "Now, brothers and sisters, old John was a white man, and the
white man has his ways. Oh gracious me, he has his ways. He
talks about the Word. He talks through it and around it. He builds
upon it with syllables, with prefixes and suffixes and hyphens and
accents. He adds and divides and multiplies the Word. And in
all of this he subtracts the Truth. And, brothers and sisters, you
have come here to live in the white man's world. Now the white
man deals in words, and he deals easily, with grace and sleight
of hand. And in his presence, here on his own ground, you are
as children, mere babes in the woods. You must not mind, for in
this you have a certain advantage. A child can listen and learn.
The Word is sacred to a child.

10   "My grandmother was a storyteller; she knew her way around
words. She never learned to read and write, but somehow she
knew the good of reading and writing; she had learned how to
listen and delight. She had learned that in words and in language,
and there only, she could have whole and consummate being. She
told me stories, and she taught me how to listen. I was a child
and I listened. She could neither read nor write, you see, but
she taught me how to live among her words, how to listen and
delight. 'Storytelling; to utter and to hear....' And the simple act
of listening is crucial to the concept of language, more crucial
even than reading and writing, and language in turn is crucial to
human society. There is proof of that, I think, in all the histories
and prehistories of human experience. When that old Kiowa
woman told me stories, I listened with only one ear. I was a
child, and I took the words for granted. I did not know what all

of them meant, but somehow I held on to them; I remembered 10 them, and I remember them now. The stories were old and dear; they meant a great deal to my grandmother. It was not until she died that I knew how much they meant to her. I began to think about it, and then I knew. When she told me those old stories, something strange and good and powerful was going on. I was a child, and that old woman was asking me to come directly into the presence of her mind and spirit; she was taking hold of my imagination, giving me to share in the great fortune of her wonder and delight. She was asking me to go with her to the confrontation of something that was sacred and eternal. It was a timeless, timeless thing; nothing of her old age or of my childhood came between us.

"Children have a greater sense of the power and beauty of 11 words than have the rest of us in general. And if that is so, it is because there occurs – or reoccurs – in the mind of every child something like a reflection of all human experience. I have heard that the human fetus corresponds in its development, stage by stage, to the scale of evolution. Surely it is no less reasonable to suppose that the waking mind of a child corresponds in the same way to the whole evolution of human thought and perception.

"In the white man's world, language, too – and the way in which 12 the white man thinks of it – has undergone a process of change. The white man takes such things as words and literatures for granted, as indeed he must, for nothing in his world is so commonplace. On every side of him there are words by the millions, an unending succession of pamphlets and papers, letters and books, bills and bulletins, commentaries and conversations. He has diluted and multiplied the Word, and words have begun to close in upon him. He is sated and insensitive; his regard for language – for the Word itself – as an instrument of creation has diminished nearly to the point of no return. It may be that he will perish by the Word.

"But it was not always so with him, and it is not so with you. 13 Consider for a moment that old Kiowa woman, my grandmother, whose use of language was confined to speech. And be assured that her regard for words was always keen in proportion as she depended upon them. You see, for her words were medicine; they were magic and invisible. They came from nothing into sound

13   and meaning. They were beyond price; they could neither be
bought nor sold. And she never threw words away.

14   "My grandmother used to tell me the story of *Tai-me*, of how
Tai-me came to the Kiowas. The Kiowas were a sun dance culture,
and *Tai-me* was their sun dance doll, their most sacred fetish;
no medicine was ever more powerful. There is a story about the
coming of *Tai-me*. This is what my grandmother told me:

14a   Long ago there were bad times. The Kiowas were hungry
and there was no food. There was a man who heard his
children cry from hunger, and he began to search for
food. He walked four days and became very weak. On
the fourth day he came to a great canyon. Suddenly there
was thunder and lightning. A Voice spoke to him and said,
"Why are you following me? What do you want?" The man
was afraid. The thing standing before him had the feet of
a deer, and its body was covered with feathers. The man
answered that the Kiowas were hungry. "Take me with
you," the Voice said, "and I will give you whatever you want."
From that day *Tai-me* has belonged to the Kiowas.

15   "Do you see? There, far off in the darkness, something happened. Do you see? Far, far away in the nothingness something
happened. There was a voice, a sound, a word – and everything
began. The story of the coming of *Tai-me* has existed for hundreds
of years by word of mouth. It represents the oldest and best idea
that man has of himself. It represents a very rich literature, which,
because it was never written down, was always but one generation from extinction. But for the same reason it was cherished
and revered. I could see that reverence in my grandmother's eyes,
and I could hear it in her voice. It was that, I think, that old Saint
John had in mind when he said, 'In the beginning was the Word....'
But he went on. He went on to lay a scheme about the Word. He
could find no satisfaction in the simple fact that the Word was; he
had to account for it, not in terms of that sudden and profound
insight, which must have devastated him at once, but in terms of
the moment afterward, which was irrelevant and remote; not in
terms of his imagination, but only in terms of his prejudice.

16   "Say this: 'In the beginning was the Word....' There was nothing. There was *nothing*! Darkness. There was darkness, and there

was no end to it. You look up sometimes in the night and there   16
are stars; you can see all the way to the stars. And you begin to
know the universe, how awful and great it is. The stars lie out
against the sky and do not fill it. A single star, flickering out in
the universe, is enough to fill the mind, but it is nothing in the
night sky. The darkness looms around it. The darkness flows
among the stars, and beyond them forever. In the beginning
that is how it was, but there were no stars. There was only the
dark infinity in which nothing was. And something happened.
At the distance of a star something happened, and everything
began. The Word did not come into being, but *it was*. It did not
break upon the silence, but *it was older than the silence and the
silence was made of it*.

"Old John caught sight of something terrible. The thing stand-   17
ing before him said, 'Why are you following me? What do you
want?' And from that day the Word has belonged to us, who have
heard it for what it is, who have lived in fear and awe of it. In the
Word was the beginning; *'In the beginning was the Word....'*"

The Priest of the Sun appeared to have spent himself. He   18
stepped back from the lectern and hung his head, smiling. In
his mind the earth was spinning and the stars rattled around in
the heavens. The sun shone, and the moon. Smiling in a kind of
transport, the Priest of the Sun stood silent for a time while the
congregation waited to be dismissed.

"Good night," he said, at last, "and get yours."   19

Larry Woiwode

◀(1 9 4 1 -)▶

*The fiction of Larry Woiwode has been described as possessing a
"mannered, traditional, realistic style," a technique better compared
to that of D. H. Lawrence or Hemingway than to more contemporary American writers. Yet the simplicity of his prose carries power,
especially when Woiwode engages one of his recurring concerns: the
out-of-reach past and the at times painful attempts of memory to
probe the mysteries of that past. There is, moreover, a sacramental sensibility in Woiwode's fiction, an awareness, in other words,
that material objects and physical scenery – perhaps a weathered
house in the bleak landscape of his North Dakota birthplace – can
be vehicles of spiritual power and meaning. Woiwode's first novel,*
What I'm Going to Do, I Think *(1969), received the William Faulkner
Foundation Award. In 1980 he received an Award in Literature
from the American Academy of Arts and Letters.*

THE OLD HALVORSON PLACE

1   A FAMILY OF FOURTEEN HAD LIVED in the house before the
Neumillers. Their name was Russell. Mr. Russell, who was
the sexton* of St. Mary Margaret's Catholic Church and the janitor
of the parochial school,* had seven sons and five daughters ranging
in age from eleven to thirty-six. Two of the sons were ordained
into the priesthood and three of the daughters became nuns. One
daughter was said to be an accomplished musician and another
had literary leanings, and together they composed the music and
lyrics of the school song that is still sung in Hyatt, North Dakota.

2   Martin Neumiller, the principal of the high school, had been
annoyed for years by the stilted words of the old song (sung to
the tune of "On, Wisconsin!") and he persuaded the Russell girls
to write the new one. It begins

sexton · the caretaker
of the church who
announces worship

parochial school ·
education offered
by a religious group
and often featuring a
religious component

> *We'll raise a lofty, mighty cheer for you,*   2a
> *Straight from the hearts of students fond and true*

and its concluding lines are   2

> *Deep as the ocean, our love and devotion*   2b
> *For the Hy – ! Hy – ! Hyatt High School!*

The parish owned the Russell house and everybody in the   3
parish had expected the Russells to live out their lives in it, a
monument to the faith. But one day old Mr. Russell went to Father
Schimmelpfennig and said that he was giving up both jobs and
moving out of town.

What?   4

He was grateful for all the parish had done for him, but he felt   5
there were better opportunities in South Dakota for him and the
children who remained at home.

Father Schimmelpfennig offered him the house rent-free.   6

Mr. Russell said he couldn't accept charity. Hyatt wasn't growing   7
and would never grow, he felt, and he wanted to take advantage of
the boom down at Rapid City, maybe even go into business for himself, and hoped the younger kids could attend bigger schools.

Two months later the Russells were gone. They were a   8
cloistered · shut
off from the world,
protected

cloistered,· close-knit family, and other than the song, they
left little trace of themselves behind when they moved. Father
Schimmelpfennig let their house stand vacant for a year, as if
he found it impossible to admit their absence, and then the
Neumillers needed a place.

Martin Neumiller, who was devoted to home life and ambi-   9
tious for his family, but without guile, nearly biblical in his purity
of motive and character, was Father Schimmelpfennig's friend and
confidant, and Martin had three bright, promising young sons.

The Neumillers had lived in several other houses in Hyatt,   10
none of them satisfactory. One they rented from a widow, who
continued to live on in a separate wing and promised to make
herself "so scarce you won't know I'm here," but didn't. In another,
the furnace never worked properly, and a smell that originated
in one of the kitchen walls was amazing in its rankness. Rather
than break into the wall of a house that didn't belong to them,
they kept wondering, What could it be?

11   In their present house, the basement flooded to the floor joists in the spring (bringing up buried salamanders that went floating out into the yard), and the foundation eroded so badly several walls began to part from the ceiling. And all of these places had contained noisy populations of mice and rats, driven indoors by the bitter, drawn-out winters, and none of the houses had been large enough. At this time, the Neumillers' three sons – Jerome, Charles, and Timothy – were sharing the same room to sleep and play in, and although Jerome, the oldest, was only five, Alpha Neumiller was pregnant again.

12   There were ten rooms in the old Russell house – three bedrooms upstairs, plus a large attic, and three more bedrooms downstairs; a living room, with a big bay window, and a dining room; a kitchen; a pantry as large as the kitchen; a basement with vegetable bins and rows of shelves for canned food; an indoor bathroom (a rarity in Hyatt – there was no running water in the village and only the drains were plumbed in) with all of the fixtures; a front porch, with turned posts and gingerbread trim; an enclosed porch on the south side; and, attached to the rear of the house, a lean-to porch which had once been used to stable a pony and was now a coal shed. The rent was twenty-five dollars a month.

13   Alpha Neumiller was ecstatic. She pirouetted through the rooms of the empty house, saying, "The space, the space, the space!" And several months later, on Charles's fifth birthday, she leaned against a wall with her arms folded, smiling as she watched a dozen birthday guests play Red Rover – *Red Rover!* – in her living room. The room was so large that her upright piano, which had always been in the way, seemed to have shrunk three sizes. Her piano! She sat down and began playing "*Clair de Lune*,"* and all the children stopped their game and stared at her as she played.

"Clair de Lune" · one of the most famous works by French impressionist composer Claude Debussy (1862–1918)

14   Martin could appreciate the depth of her satisfaction; there were articles close to her heart, family heirlooms and wedding presents, that they hadn't unpacked since their marriage, and some of their furniture – a dining-room set with inlays of bird's-eye maple, a handmade gateleg table – had never been used. But around town and at the Friday-night pinochle* games at Father Schimmelpfennig's, Martin was heard to say, "Sometimes I can't understand that woman. She loves the place, sure, how could she

pinochle · a popular card game

help it? But it's always been like this. The happiest times of her   14
life are when we move."

✦ ✦ ✦

Martin's father, who had settled in Illinois several   15
years ago, was in North Dakota visiting relatives and
friends, and he drove up to Hyatt to help them move. Somehow
he got stuck with the job of bringing in the basement things, and
toward the end of the day he turned to Alpha with a solemn face
and said, "I've carried nine hundred and ninety-nine empty fruit
jars down these stairs." He was a building contractor. He made
minor repairs around the house, and persuaded Martin to pour a
concrete slab that began at the outside wall of the lean-to, went in
a curve around the corner of the house, past the enclosed porch,
and abutted against the bay window. It was a full day's work for
five men, excluding Martin and his father, and when the slab was
finally poured, and Martin's father had finished troweling it by
the light of a floor lamp Martin held above him, he said, "There.
Now the boys have a place to ride their tricycles."

While they were still getting settled into the house, Martin   16
took Jerome and Charles upstairs and led them into a room
overlooking the street corner. Against one wall was an enormous
rolltop desk of oak. "Look!" Martin said, and turned to them
as though offering a gift. The boys looked at one another with
questioning frowns, and Jerome shrugged. "Well, don't you see
what's happened here?" Martin asked.

They didn't see.   17

"First of all, you can tell by looking that it couldn't have come   18
up by the stairs. They're too narrow. The door to this room is even
narrower than the stairway, and the windows are narrower yet."

He squatted at the desk and rapped on it with a knuckle.   19
"That's solid oak, you hear? The corners have been dovetailed
and then trimmed over. You can feel the dovetailing here in the
back. Right here. Now, nobody could take this apart, once it was
built, without damaging the wood somewhere – especially where
it's dovetailed – and they certainly would have left a mark on the
finish. But the finish is practically perfect. Isn't it beautiful?"

They nodded, impatient to get their own hands on that feath-   20
ery dovetail stuff.

21   "There's only one possibility," Martin said, and smiled at them
in conclusion. "When this place was built, an elderly cabinet-
maker came to the house, carried his hand tools and materials
up to this room, and built this desk on the spot where we're
standing. But why? Why would anybody want to build a desk
way up here?"

22   Mysteries, for Martin, were a source of delight; there was
nothing unnatural about them, as he saw it. They were a major
ingredient of life, meant to be explored and marveled at, but
never feared, and seldom explained. Where others overlooked
mystery, he could find it, and this kept him in a state of childlike
wonder, exuberance, and joy.

✦ ✦ ✦

23   ALPHA WAS SURPRISED THAT the interior of the house wasn't
more beat up. From the outside it appeared that it would be;
paint was flaking from the second story, the roof of the lean-to
was beginning to sag, and the hedge that bordered the yard on
three sides had been allowed to grow to a height of seven feet.
But Martin's father said that the house was structurally sound,
surprisingly so, and the interior was in excellent condition, even
though fourteen people had lived in the place for a decade.

24   The hardwood floors didn't need refinishing. The baseboards
at toe level were battered, but otherwise the original oak wood-
work, the sliding oak doors to the master bedroom, the turned
posts beneath the oak banister leading upstairs, the bookshelves
around the bottom of the bay window, also of oak, had hardly
a scratch on them. And there were no ink stains or adolescent
carvings on the rolltop desk.

25   The Russells had even left a new-looking chair at the desk. The
Neumillers couldn't understand why, unless it had been standing
there when the Russells moved in, because the Russells left nothing else behind to provide a clue to their life in the house – no old
receipts, letters, or notes, not one stray sock in the bottom of a
closet, not even a drawing or a set of initials on the walls, or, as
Alpha put it, "not a speck of themselves or their dirt."

26   The attic, however, was packed with valuables, so layered with
dust it looked as though the Russells had never touched them.
Was it because they belonged to the family that had built the

house and lived there originally, the Halvorsons? Their name   26
was everywhere in the attic, on the backs of daguerreotypes* and
photographs, in the flyleaves of books, underneath chair seats;
even written, along with a set of measurements, across the bosom
of an old dress form.*

In a large and decaying leather-bound volume, *A Century-*   27
End History and Biography of North Dakota, Martin found an
engraving of a daguerreotype of Mr. Halvorson, a twin to another
picture of him in the attic, along with this information:

> ALVARD J. HALVORSON. This gentleman, of whom a   27a
> portrait will be found on the opposite page, occupies a
> prominent position as a real-estate dealer in Hyatt, Leeds
> County. To his influence is due much of the solid prosper-
> ity of Leeds and Ecklund Counties.
>
> Our subject was born in Hamlin Township, Michigan,   27b
> Aug. 1, 1839, and was the only son of Selmer and Dora
> (Waldorf) Halvorson, the former of Scandinavian and the
> latter of German descent. Mr. Halvorson was raised on his
> father's farm and attended country schools and at the age
> of nineteen went to Indianapolis, Indiana, in company with
> his father and later was engaged in business and also in
> farming with his father in Indiana for about twenty years.
>
> Our subject moved to Valley City, North Dakota, in the   27c
> fall of 1879 and became interested in Leeds County lands
> in 1881, since which time A. J. HALVORSON CO. has added
> as much as perhaps any other firm in the development of
> the possibilities of the agricultural and stock raising inter-
> ests of North Dakota, and he now conducts an extensive
> real-estate business in Hyatt, where the family located in
> 1895, two years after the founding of Hyatt.
>
> Our subject was married at Indianapolis, Indiana,   27d
> in 1865, to Miss Catherine Maxwell, who is of Scottish
> descent. Mr. and Mrs. Halvorson are the parents of
> three children, who bear the following names: Olivia C.,
> Alice N., and Lydia. The two older children were born in
> Indiana and the last named in North Dakota. Politically,
> Mr. Halvorson is a Republican and has taken a highly
> active part in affairs pertaining to local government.

daguerreotypes · the first successful form of photography

dress form · a mannequin

28   Nobody living in Hyatt at present could remember the Halvorsons, much less say why they'd moved and left so much behind. This fascinated Martin. He went to the library in the county seat, McCallister, and conducted his own research in the record books there. He didn't find many allusions to Mr. Halvorson, but he discovered how it was possible for the Halvorson family to be forgotten; the village had changed that much.

29   It was plotted by Richard Hyatt, an English lord, and began as a settlement of wealthy and cultivated Englishmen and Scots (one of whom constructed an artificial lake and a nine-hole golf course at the edge of town), and then it turned into a trading center for the German and Scandinavian and Irish immigrants who homesteaded in the area, and for a while was the county seat. And finally, after the county building was hauled off by the tradesmen of a neighboring town in the dead of the night, and after suffering the effects of the Crash* and the Great Depression,* besides being missed by the main line of the railroad, it became what it was now – a poor village, largely German and Roman Catholic, with only the lake remaining as a reminder of its past. Its present population was two hundred and thirty-two. This figure Martin knew before he began his research; he'd taken the 1940 census.

the Crash · the stock-market crash of October 24–29, 1929 during which stock prices collapsed completely

the Great Depression · a major economic crisis in North America, Europe, and other industrialized areas of the world that began in 1929 and lasted until about 1939

30   Although several other families must have lived in the Neumillers' house since the time of the Halvorsons, it appeared that no one had touched the Halvorsons' belongings in the attic, as though to tamper with them or to remove them were to tamper with the heart of the house. Or perhaps their possessions had been so numerous (wasn't the desk theirs?) that people had merely taken what they wanted without much diminishing the original store. Martin, for instance, as he walked around the attic, said that when they left, if they ever did, he was going to take those candlesticks, that teapot, the horse collar there, and a wheelbarrowful of these books.

31   Alpha said that just to stand in the place made her temperature drop ten degrees, and she'd rather he left everything the way it was.

32   "But what about these?" he said, and held up a set of copper bowls with silver medallions on their handles. "These are collector's items."

"I have more bowls than I know what to do with already." "What 33
about a book? Wouldn't you like to read some of these books?"

"I would if I'd bought them." She picked up Timmy, who was put- 34
ting fluffs of dust into a china commode,* and started out the door.

commode · a move-
able washstand with a
basin and a cupboard
underneath

"Let's have an auction," Jerome said. "Let's sell all this stuff and 35
make a bunch of money." He and Charles were sorting through
a stack of dusty phonograph records.

"Leave those alone," Alpha Neumiller said. "They're not yours. 36
I don't want you two playing in this attic – ever, you understand?
I'm going to keep the hook at the top of this door latched. I bet
that's what Mrs. Russell did. You don't belong in here."

The boys turned to their father, who was rummaging through 37
a round-topped trunk bound with leather straps, and Jerome
asked if they could move this – he rapped on an ancient Victrola*
with his knuckles – and the records into their playroom. The door
was plenty big, Jerome said. Martin looked up, his eyes bright
and abstracted, unaware that Alpha had spoken, and said, "Sure.
Why not? Let's get it in there and see if it works."

Victrola · an early
brand of record player,
often housed in a
decorative cabinet

♦   ♦   ♦

THE VICTROLA SAT IN A CORNER of the second-floor room 38
designated as the boys' playroom, near the door that led to
the attic. It was such a tall machine they had to stand on a stool
to place records on the turntable. On the underside of its cover,
beveled like a coffin lid, *Lydia* had been scratched into the wood
with something sharp, and the name, foreign to them, seemed
strangely appropriate there. No needles had survived with the
machine, so their father fashioned one from the end of a safety
pin. Among the old records from the attic, they found only one
they really liked; the rest, thick Edison records* with hymns on
them, they sailed out a second-story window.

Edison records ·
Thomas Edison invented
wax-cylinder recording
in 1877 and continued to
dominate early record
production

They played that same record over and over, in spite of the 39
scratches on its surface – years of them, layers of them – that
made the metallic tenor sound as though it came out of the
center of a gale, and they never tired of hearing the man sing
about Sal, his maiden fair, singing Polly Wolly Doodle all the day,
with her curly eyes and her laughing hair....*

Sal ... hair · lyrics
from a popular
American folk-song

They stood on the stool and worked the crank, staring at the 40
name scratched on the lid. "Fare thee well! Fare thee well!" the

40 tenor sang. "Fare thee well, my fairy fey!" And no matter how many times it rose up, tinny and frail from the ancient grooves, the image of a grasshopper sitting on a railroad track (singing Polly Wolly Doodle all the day) always made them get down, laughing, and roll around and slap the floor in hysterics.

41 They had their own library in the playroom; they had clay, blocks, marbles, and mallets, dominoes, Lincoln Logs, an electric train, and a handmade alphabet with wooden characters five inches high which they kept in dull-green ammunition boxes an uncle had brought back from the war. But none of these possessions were of the same caliber of interest as the Victrola, and when they weren't playing it, they spent their afternoons at the rolltop desk.

42 Their father had appropriated the desk. Here, he said, was where he intended to sit when he wrote his book – a project he talked about often, especially after any unusual or moving experience, or whenever he sat down and told them a story from his past. He referred to the book simply as "the book of my life," and if he'd been up in the room for the evening, Jerome and Charles would go to the desk the next day, slide its slatted cover up, and search through its drawers and cubbyholes for evidence of the book, in which they hoped to be included.

43 There was always a neat pile of white paper in the center of a green blotter, with a pen and a bottle of ink, plus a bottle of ink eradicator, standing ready. Next to the blotter was the large, leather-bound volume their father had found in the attic. Searching through the pigeonholes of the desk, they found old letters, scripts of dramatic and patriotic readings their father had performed in high school and college, a rubber stamp that reproduced his high, tilted signature, a watch fob* braided from his mother's hair, a broken pocket watch, some rocks from the Badlands,* and a plastic tube they could look into and see a monument of stone and the inscription *Geographical Center of North America, Rugby, North Dakota.*

watch fob · a short ribbon or chain attached to a pocket watch

the Badlands · a region in southwestern South Dakota

44 In one of the drawers was a half-filled box of flaky cigars with IT'S A BOY! printed on the cellophane wrappers, and in another a metal file that contained insurance policies, birth certificates (their own and their parents', too, which was unsettling), government savings bonds in their names (money!), and their father's

baby book. In the center drawer were pens and pencils and a ream 44
of that same white paper, which never seemed to diminish.

Once, they discovered this on the top sheet:

CHAPTER I 45a
– My father's influence on my life (Mom's too)
CHAPTER II
– The Depression Years
CHAPTER III
– I meet Alpha, my wife-to-be
CHAPTER IV
?

Other than some notes to himself and a Christmas card list, 46
they never found anything else their father had written.

◈ ◈ ◈

THEY COULD NOT RESIST the temptation of the attic, although 47
they knew this upset their mother. She disliked the attic, disliked even more the idea of anybody's being in it (she never entered
it herself), and was so adamant and humorless in her dislike that
their father teased her by calling North Dakota "the cold-storage
box way up at the top, the *attic* of the United States!"

They would put their record on the Victrola, move a stool 48
over to the attic door, unlatch the hook, ease the door open, and
step inside, and sunlight, coming through a pair of windows in
the far wall, fell over them with a warmth sunlight had nowhere
else. Old cobwebs powdered with dust, and shining filaments
that spiders had recently strung in place, sparkled in its light,
imparting a summer radiance to the air. The personal effects of
the Halvorsons – the dress form, a brass bedstead, the boxes and
trunks of memorabilia, a wooden wardrobe with a dress sword
and sash hanging from its top, chairs, books, an oval mirror that
held their reflections – stood around in solid eloquence.

settee · a kind of sofa
designed for two or
more people

Charles tiptoed over to a settee,˙ upholstered in red velvet 49
badly damaged by moths and nesting mice, and sat down. He
bounced his weight on its springs. Who had sat here? What had
they talked about? Had anybody cried on it, as he had on their
couch? Or done a flip on it? He looked up at Jerome, who hadn't
moved since they'd stepped into the attic.

50   The surrounding objects were as real and as awesome as a
roomful of strangers, and more compelling; they belonged to
a world removed not only by time – by half a century, as their
father said – but by convention and law: the world of adults.
Here they could handle and examine that world in every detail
(and only through touch would it give up its mystery), without
interference or protest, as they could not examine the world of
their parents.

51   Since any wholehearted examination of the property of others
was forbidden, they held back, hesitant, but all of the objects
seemed to strain toward them, as if to give up their secrets.
Jerome and Charles were not the only ones who sensed this. Only
moments after they'd unhooked the door, they would hear, coming
from the foot of the stairs, "Are you two into that attic again?"

52   "No!" they cried at the same time, a dead giveaway.

53   "You stay out of there when your father's not around! You hear?"

54   "We're not in here," Charles said.

55   "Don't lie to your mother!"

56   They looked at one another, and then Jerome went over and
began to examine the object that had held his attention, and
Charles picked up a wooden doll with most of its limbs missing,
while the dented and tattered dress form – composed of var-
nished strips of paper that were lifting up in orangy translucent
curls – stood above them, as unmoving and silent as a second,
more permissive mother.

57   Jerome studied a wooden box with wires and disklike elec-
trodes dangling from it. Its lid swung open like a little door, and
from what he could understand of the instructions, which were
pasted on the inside of the lid, it was a device for giving shocks
to the head and feet.

58   "Look at this," Charles said. He took a lace dress out of a trunk and
held it in front of him. "This is what they wore then. What would
you think if you saw somebody wearing it? What would you think
if I was a girl?" He wrinkled up his nose and giggled like one.

59   "Quit it," Jerome said. "Put it back." He was more cautious than
Charles, more like his mother, and a dress seemed too personal
to disturb.

60   He picked up a candlestick and pictured the dining room in
a different setting, at night, deep in shadow, with candle flames

lighting the faces around a table, a sound of silver scraping on plates, the rustle of skirts, and then a man's voice, gentle as the candlelight, rising from the shadows: "I have decided –" 60

"Hey, look at this," Charles said. He'd slipped on the rusty jacket of an old suit of tails* that was many sizes too large for him. 61

suit of tails · a tuxedo

"Take it off," Jerome said. "Put it back." 62

"All right. But I'm going to take this." It was a book, *Children of the Garden*, that personified the common species of flowers, giving them human features and appendages and names such as Betsy Bluebell. "We'll keep it in the playroom." 63

"Oh, all right. But don't leave it where Mom'll see it." 64

Jerome went to a box that contained daguerreotypes and old, fading, tea-colored photographs. There were pictures of rural families lined up in front of farmhouses: the farmer, bearded or with long side-whiskers, often sitting in a kitchen chair; his wife, her hair pulled back, standing beside him in a long-sleeved black dress, apparently old enough to be the children's grandmother; and all of the children, even the babies, looked big-headed and mature. 65

There were pictures of houses they recognized, of Main Street as it had once been, with a horse and carriage parked in front of Reiland's Tavern, and several views of their own home. Jerome motioned Charles over, and with an air of solemnity pointed to a rear view of their house, placing his fingertip on the attic window. 66

There were pictures of the Halvorsons, with the subject's name, the year the portrait was taken, and the person's age at the time written in an artistic hand across the back of each. 67

"Look at this," Jerome said, and wiped his forearm across a picture. A plump man in muttonchop whiskers stared up at them with the sparkling eyes of an unrepentant *roué*.* Jerome frowned. "It's Mr. Halvorson. Do you like the way he looks?" 68

roué · one who leads a dissolute life; a rake

"I don't know." 69

"I don't." Jerome shuffled through all the pictures of Mr. Halvorson and his wife, who was broad and square-jawed and looked enough like her husband to be his brother. Two of the daughters looked exactly like her. In a portrait of the third girl, however, Jerome saw what he had hoped to see in the rest of the family. She was reclining at one end of the settee, an open book in her lap, a finger placed along her cheek, her lower lip, with a shine on it, shoved out. Light- 70

70   colored hair fell to her waist, and her dark eyes were staring off at a scene, apparently a heartbreaking one, in the distance.

71   "See," Jerome said, pointing to the lace dress she was wearing. "That was probably hers."

72   "What about it?"

73   "You shouldn't be messing around with it like that."

74   "Why?"

75   "If it was hers—You shouldn't, that's all. Look how pretty she is."

76   "Not anymore."

77   "What do you mean?"

78   "She's probably old and ugly by now."

79   Jerome turned the picture over: "Lydia, at the age of thirteen, in the year of our Lord 1901."

80   "See," Charles said. "That's even before Dad was born, and look how old he is. If she—"

81   But the girl had Jerome in her possession. He saw her running through the downstairs hall on a day as sunlit as this one, running up the steps, her hair streaming behind, and rushing into the playroom to the Victrola. He turned. His mother stood in the doorway, flushed and out of breath from climbing the stairs in her condition.

82   "What did I tell you two? Get out of here! Get out, get out, get out!"

* * *

83   IN AUGUST, ALPHA NEUMILLER gave birth to a daughter, whom she named Marie, after Martin's mother. Jerome and Charles were envious of the attention the girl received, and embarrassed by her. They spent more and more of their time outdoors. But Tim, who was constantly left out of their projects and play, would stand at Marie's bassinet with his hands clasped behind him, sometimes for an hour, as if she were his only hope. Martin was proud of her as only the father of a daughter can be proud, and Alpha, who had always wanted a girl, associated this stroke of good luck with the move into the house. Before the baby arrived, she had decorated a downstairs bedroom in pink and frills.

84   It was becoming Alpha's house. Over the first winter, she had closed off the upstairs to reduce the heating bills and her own

work, but now it was open and a major piece of framework in   84
the home she was building within the house, not merely a place
where the boys went to get off by themselves or make trouble. She

organdy · a very fine,
transparent muslin

put a sleeping cot, white organdy˙ curtains, and glassed-in bookshelves that she'd bought at an auction, and thought she'd never
use, in the room occupied by the rolltop desk, which she referred
to as Martin's office. In a battered box of junk, she unearthed
the shell of a painted turtle that Martin had once found, empty,
along the railroad tracks and had filled with cement – a mislaid,
long-forgotten talisman, which he used to use as a paperweight.
She placed it on the pile of paper on his desk.

    And she had her own room upstairs, a sewing room with an   85
easy chair and a lamp for reading, when she wanted to relax and
read, large closets that accommodated all their winter clothes,

curtain stretchers ·
a device for stretching
curtains to remove
wrinkles

and so much space she was able to keep her curtain stretchers˙
permanently set up.

    She painted, with white enamel, the cupboards in the pantry   86
and the kitchen, and Martin put down new linoleum in every
room. He trimmed the hedge around the house, all of it, down
to four feet, and got blisters and sores and then hands as hard
as horn from the project, which took weeks. He bought and
installed an oil heater in the living room, so they could keep
the chill out of the downstairs on fall days without starting the
furnace in the basement, and when school dismissed for the
summer, he hired a neighbor, William Runyon, as a helper, and
they scraped and wire-brushed and painted the outside of the
house. It was the color Alpha had always wanted her house to
be – warm yellow, with white trim.

    She was unpacked and had found a place for everything, from   87
the rocker she'd inherited from her grandmother to her everyday
soup spoons, and all of her furniture was being used. Then Martin
bought a bedroom set of solid maple she'd dreamed of owning
for five years ("$210," she noted in her diary, "but so what?"), with
a tall dresser for him and a vanity with a mirror big enough to
satisfy her. And still the house looked underfurnished. Which to
her was perfectly all right; nothing or nobody was underfoot.

    She had helped Martin lay out a garden, and as vegetables   88
came into season she canned and preserved them, along with
fruits from the market, jellies and jams, berries picked from

88 the countryside during picnics and outings, and some capons[*] capons · castrated
Martin bought from a neighbor. The shelves in the basement male chickens
were beginning to fill up. The potato bin was full. There were
parsnips, kohlrabi, turnips, and rutabagas, all dipped in paraffin
to preserve them, in the other bins. She brought out the winter
clothes and began to mend them.

✦ ✦ ✦

89 ONE AFTERNOON IN LATE OCTOBER, she was sitting in her
rocker in the alcove formed by the bay window, absorbing
the last of the season's sunlight before winter, and knitting a heavy
pink cardigan for Marie, when she thought she heard a knock at
the front door. She paused in her work and looked up; nobody
ever used that door. The knock came again. She put her work in
the seat of the chair and went to the boys' bedroom and found
all three of them there, up to no mischief. She went through the
living room, down the long hall to the front door, and opened it.
A tall, youthful-looking priest stood on the porch.

90 "Hello. I'm James Russell. Just call me Father Jim."

91 "Oh. Hello."

92 "You must be Mrs. Neumiller."

93 "Yes."

94 "I used to live here."

95 "Well, come in."

96 He stepped inside, and his bright-green eyes traveled over
every area of the entry and stairway, as if following a familiar
course, and stopped; her sons, who had trailed after her through
the living room, were standing at the end of the hall. "Ah," he said,
"I see you have three fine young boys."

97 He strode past her, his cassock[*] smelling of cologne and cassock · a simple,
cigarette smoke, and went up to them and ruffled their hair. ankle-length garment
"Your father's a fine gentleman," he said. "He taught two of my that serves as the
brothers and two of my sisters, and they have nothing but praise primary habit of clerics
for him. You can be proud. Have either of you – not you, little
fellow – made your First Communion[*] yet?"

98 "Me," Jerome said. First Communion ·
a special rite following
99 "'What is God's loving care for us called?'" catechism and confirmation during which the
100 "'God's loving care for us is called Divine Providence.'" participant first partakes
of the Eucharist
101 "'What do we mean when we say that God is almighty?'"

"'When we say that God is almighty we mean that He can do all things.'" 102

"'Is God all-wise, all-holy, all-merciful, and all-just?'" 103

"'Yes. God is all-wise, all-holy, all-merciful, and all-just.'" 104

"You've learned your catechism well. Good, good." He turned to Alpha. "Do you have others?" 105

"A daughter, two and a half months." 106

"Is she asleep?" 107

"Yes." 108

"Ah, that's too bad. I'd like to bless the little tyke. Is your husband here?" 109

"No." 110

"Will he be back soon?" 111

"Later today. He's gone to McCallister." 112

"I'm afraid I won't even have a chance to see him, then, I'm so awfully rushed. That's a disappointment. He's meant a lot to us, you know, the younger ones especially. I haven't been in the area since I was transferred to Minneapolis, nearly three years now. I'm with the Jesuits* there. I believe it was thought best that I not visit the family. We were all quite close." He rubbed and wrung his hands as if washing them as he looked around. "But the family, God bless them, is gone from the area now, and a conference came up in Bismarck* that the Monsignor* couldn't attend – one that might be quite important to the laity, by the way; it deals with sacramentals*– so the Monsignor delegated me to go, and loaned me his car (I left the engine running; I'm already late), and since I was so close, only twenty-five miles off, I couldn't resist. I had to see the old place. Isn't it a lovely house?" 113

He began to pace around the living room, displacing the air in a way that Martin never did, his eyes moving with such speed and restlessness he kept changing direction, turning to look behind, staring up or to the side, turning again. "You've done very well by the old place. It's decorated with taste and is as neat as I can remember. The outside looks fine also – the new paint job, I mean – and the hedge; I think Father let that go the last years. I can't understand why he felt compelled to leave. The hardware store certainly hasn't worked out as he expected, not in that location, and he just suffered a second stroke. Edward and Jackie have left, of course, but Dennis is still at home to help. Dennis is 114

Jesuits · members of the Society of Jesus, a Roman Catholic order founded by Ignatius Loyola in 1534 and dedicated to teaching and missionary work

Bismarck · capital of North Dakota, located in the south-central part of the state

Monsignor · a Roman Catholic prelate or bishop

sacramentals · rites or objects (such as a rosary) that serve as an indirect means of grace by producing religious devotion

114 a good lad. Enid has decided to take her vows*— a surprise to us all, she seemed so involved in the arts – and Margaret graduated valedictorian this year. That makes five in the family so far."He stopped at the bay window.

115 "Isn't this a beautiful view? I've always liked to stand here and admire it. So did Mother. She would look out and pray the Rosary* here at night, when most of us were in bed, and the whole house fell quiet. The lilac bushes there, the garden beyond, that nice oak down the road next to the Runyons'– somehow the arrangement is so pleasing and serene. I hope nobody ever builds on these lots to the corner. It would ruin the view. You can see past the state highway to that far-off Indian mound, or whatever it is. I think it's never been decided for sure, though it certainly couldn't be a hill – not in this territory. Hawk's Nest, it's called. Did you know that it stands nearly in the next county? I used to love to study it and wonder what it could be. Here's where I decided to become a priest."

116 He removed a white handkerchief from the sleeve of his cassock, blew his nose hard, then folded the handkerchief square, still staring out the window, and replaced it in his sleeve. Then he started to pace again, glancing into the dining room, the kitchen, the boys' bedroom, and through a gap in the sliding doors into the master bedroom.

117 "I'm sorry I'm in such an unneighborly rush. I'd like to sit down and visit, have dinner with you all – I can tell by your healthy boys you're a wonderful cook – and I wanted so much to see Martin." He stopped. "I'd love to run up and look at my old bedroom. But I'm afraid that would be imposing."

118 Alpha started to speak, but he held up his hand. "Also, I don't know if I could face it. Too emotional. Patrick and I used to share the room, and we lost him in the war." He crossed himself in a hurried way that appeared involuntary. "Well, boys, remember always to honor your father and mother, don't forget your morning and evening prayers, and keep yourself pure, for there's nothing more honorable in the eyes of God than purity. Now, come here, kneel down, and I'll give you my blessing."

119 Jerome and Charles knelt in front of him with their hands clasped and eyes closed, and Tim, copying them, did the same. Father Jim sketched crosses in the air above their heads and

take her vows · Roman Catholics generally take three vows – poverty, chastity, and obedience – during ordination into a religious order (the process of becoming a priest, monk, or nun)

pray the Rosary · a religious exercise in which ritual prayers are recited and counted on a string of beads or a knotted cord

spoke the Latin in a clear voice, three times, without hurrying the 119
familiar words. He thanked Alpha for her patience and hospitality,
once again apologized for his rush, reminded her to give Martin
his greetings, and then strode to the front door.

Jerome and Charles and Tim stood at the end of the hall and 120
watched while he said goodbye to their mother and, as she bowed
her head, quickly gave her his blessing. Then he walked across
the porch, across the lawn, and out of sight, and they heard the
sound of his car engine echo off a building and grow faint.

Their mother closed the door. She stood with her forehead 121
against it and her hand on the knob, as though examining her
thoughts with an intensity that held her there, and then turned
to them. She looked thinner and older than a moment ago, and
her expression, distant yet resigned, was an expression they'd
never seen. But they knew what she was feeling; now the Russells,
as well as the Halvorsons, would always occupy a part of their
house. And although their mother might resist it, they knew it
would only be a matter of time before they moved.

Alice Walker

◀(1 9 4 4 -)▶

Walker describes herself as an African-American "womanist" writer. She is one of America's most highly regarded novelists and essayists, receiving the Pulitzer Prize and the American Book Award for The Color Purple *(1982). Other novels include* The Third Life of George Copeland *(1970),* Meridian *(1976), and* Possessing the Secret of Joy *(1992). Redemption, the resilience of the human spirit, the sacredness of beauty, and the reconciling power of love are recurring themes in Walker's works, which draw heavily upon her experience of growing up in Eatonton, Georgia. Walker views the transmission of her stories as both an artistic and a moral calling. Committed to preserving an African-American literary tradition, she sees herself as a messenger of reconciliation and a voice for women and minorities who have had little opportunity to speak. The following story is taken from her collection of stories* In Love and Trouble: Stories of Black Women *(1973).*

THE WELCOME TABLE

for sister Clara Ward

> I'm going to sit at the Welcome table
> Shout my troubles over
> Walk and talk with Jesus
> Tell God how you treat me
> One of these days!*

1   THE OLD WOMAN STOOD with eyes uplifted in her Sunday-go-to-meeting clothes: high shoes polished about the tops and toes, a long rusty dress adorned with an old corsage, long withered, and the remnants of an elegant silk scarf as headrag stained with grease from the many oily pigtails underneath. Perhaps she had known suffering. There was a dazed and sleepy

I'm going … these days · the lyrics are from a traditional African-American spiritual

379

look in her aged blue-brown eyes. But for those who searched 1
hastily for "reasons" in that old tight face, shut now like an ancient
door, there was nothing to be read. And so they gazed nakedly
upon their own fear transferred; a fear of the black and the old,
a terror of the unknown as well as of the deeply known. Some of
those who saw her there on the church steps spoke words about
her that were hardly fit to be heard, others held their pious peace;
and some felt vague stirrings of pity, small and persistent and
hazy, as if she were an old collie turned out to die.

She was angular and lean and the color of poor gray Georgia 2
earth, beaten by king cotton and the extreme weather. Her elbows
were wrinkled and thick, the skin ashen but durable, like the bark
of old pines. On her face centuries were folded into the circles
around one eye, while around the other, etched and mapped as
if for print, ages more threatened again to live. Some of them
there at the church saw the age, the dotage,* the missing buttons
down the front of her mildewed black dress. Others saw cooks,
chauffeurs, maids, mistresses, children denied or smothered in
the deferential way she held her cheek to the side, toward the
ground. Many of them saw jungle orgies in an evil place, while
others were reminded of riotous anarchists looting and raping in
the streets. Those who knew the hesitant creeping up on them of
the law, saw the beginning of the end of the sanctuary of Christian
worship, saw the desecration of Holy Church, and saw an invasion
of privacy, which they struggled to believe they still kept.

Still she had come down the road toward the big white church 3
alone. Just herself, an old forgetful woman, nearly blind with
age. Just her and her eyes raised dully to the glittering cross that
crowned the sheer silver steeple. She had walked along the road
in a stagger from her house a half mile away. Perspiration, cold
and clammy, stood on her brow and along the creases by her thin
wasted nose. She stopped to calm herself on the wide front steps,
not looking about her as they might have expected her to do, but
simply standing quite still, except for a slight quivering of her
throat and tremors that shook her cotton-stockinged legs.

The reverend of the church stopped her pleasantly as she 4
stepped into the vestibule. Did he say, as they thought he did,
kindly, "Auntie, you know this is not your church?" As if one could
choose the wrong one. But no one remembers, for they never

dotage · senility

4 spoke of it afterward, and she brushed past him anyway, as if she had been brushing past him all her life, except this time she was in a hurry. Inside the church she sat on the very first bench from the back, gazing with concentration at the stained-glass window over her head. It was cold, even inside the church, and she was shivering. Everybody could see. They stared at her as they came in and sat down near the front. It was cold, very cold to them, too; outside the church it was below freezing and not much above inside. But the sight of her, sitting there somehow passionately ignoring them, brought them up short, burning.

5 The young usher, never having turned anyone out of his church before, but not even considering this job as *that* (after all, she had no right to be there, certainly), went up to her and whispered that she should leave. Did he call her "Grandma," as later he seemed to recall he had? But for those who actually hear such traditional pleasantries and to whom they actually mean something, "Grandma" was not one, for she did not pay him any attention, just muttered, "Go 'way," in a weak sharp *bothered* voice, waving his frozen blond hair and eyes from near her face.

6 It was the ladies who finally did what to them had to be done. Daring their burly indecisive husbands to throw the old colored woman out they made their point. God, mother, country, earth, church. It involved all that, and well they knew it. Leather bagged and shoed, with good calfskin gloves to keep out the cold, they looked with contempt at the bloodless gray arthritic hands of the old woman, clenched loosely, restlessly in her lap. Could their husbands expect them to sit up in church with *that*? No, no, the husbands were quick to answer and even quicker to do their duty.

7 Under the old woman's arms they placed their hard fists (which afterward smelled of decay and musk – the fermenting scent of onionskins and rotting greens). Under the old woman's arms they raised their fists, flexed their muscular shoulders, and out she flew through the door, back under the cold blue sky. This done, the wives folded their healthy arms across their trim middles and felt at once justified and scornful. But none of them said so, for none of them ever spoke of the incident again. Inside the church it was warmer. They sang, they prayed. The protection and promise of God's impartial love grew more not less desirable as the sermon gathered fury and lashed itself out above their penitent heads.

The old woman stood at the top of the steps looking about in 8
bewilderment. She had been singing in her head. They had interrupted her. Promptly she began to sing again, though this time
a sad song. Suddenly, however, she looked down the long gray
highway and saw something interesting and delightful coming.
She started to grin, toothlessly, with short giggles of joy, jumping
about and slapping her hands on her knees. And soon it became
apparent why she was so happy. For coming down the highway
at a firm though leisurely pace was Jesus. He was wearing an
immaculate white, long dress trimmed in gold around the neck
and hem, and a red, a bright red, cape. Over his left arm he carried a brilliant blue blanket. He was wearing sandals and a beard
and he had long brown hair parted on the right side. His eyes,
brown, had wrinkles around them as if he smiled or looked at
the sun a lot. She would have known him, recognized him, anywhere. There was a sad but joyful look to his face, like a candle
was glowing behind it, and he walked with sure even steps in her
direction, as if he were walking on the sea. Except that he was
not carrying in his arms a baby sheep, he looked exactly like the
picture of him that she had hanging over her bed at home. She
had taken it out of a white lady's Bible while she was working
for her. She had looked at that picture for more years than she
could remember, but never once had she really expected to see
him. She squinted her eyes to be sure he wasn't carrying a little
sheep in one arm, but he was not. Ecstatically she began to wave
her arms for fear he would miss seeing her, for he walked looking
straight ahead on the shoulder of the highway, and from time to
time looking upward at the sky.

All he said when he got up close to her was "Follow me," and 9
she bounded down to his side with all the bob and speed of one
so old. For every one of his long determined steps she made two
quick ones. They walked along in deep silence for a long time.
Finally she started telling him about how many years she had
cooked for them, cleaned for them, nursed them. He looked at
her kindly but in silence. She told him indignantly about how
they had grabbed her when she was singing in her head and not
looking, and how they had tossed her out of his church. A old
heifer like me, she said, straightening up next to Jesus, breathing
hard. But he smiled down at her and she felt better instantly and

9   time just seemed to fly by. When they passed her house, forlorn and sagging, weatherbeaten and patched, by the side of the road, she did not even notice it, she was so happy to be out walking along the highway with Jesus.

10   She broke the silence once more to tell Jesus how glad she was that he had come, how she had often looked at his picture hanging on her wall (she hoped he didn't know she had stolen it) over her bed, and how she had never expected to see him down here in person. Jesus gave her one of his beautiful smiles and they walked on. She did not know where they were going; someplace wonderful, she suspected. The ground was like clouds under their feet, and she felt she could walk forever without becoming the least bit tired. She even began to sing out loud some of the old spirituals she loved, but she didn't want to annoy Jesus, who looked so thoughtful, so she quieted down. They walked on, looking straight over the treetops into the sky, and the smiles that played over her dry wind-cracked face were like first clean ripples across a stagnant pond. On they walked without stopping.

11   The people in church never knew what happened to the old woman; they never mentioned her to one another or to anybody else. Most of them heard sometime later that an old colored woman fell dead along the highway. Silly as it seemed, it appeared she had walked herself to death. Many of the black families along the road said they had seen the old lady high-stepping down the highway; sometimes jabbering in a low insistent voice, sometimes singing, sometimes merely gesturing excitedly with her hands. Other times silent and smiling, looking at the sky. She had been alone, they said. Some of them wondered aloud where the old woman had been going so stoutly that it had worn her heart out. They guessed maybe she had relatives across the river, some miles away, but none of them really knew.

Albert Haley

◀ 1 9 5 3 – ▶

Haley was born in Oklahoma but lived much of his life in Alaska. The latter geographical influence may account for the concern his stories show for how human constructions (particularly cities) have separated people from the nourishing qualities of the natural world. He earned his BA *in economics at Yale and an* MFA *at the University of Houston. An advocate of using real-life experience as a source for one's art, he has worked in the oil field, in the banking industry, and for a computer software firm. Haley is a careful crafter of short fiction, beginning with his short story collection* Home Ground: Stories of Two Families and the Land *(1977), which Larry McMurtry called "the best fiction we have about contemporary Alaska." His stories have appeared in* Atlantic Monthly, The New Yorker, Rolling Stone, *and* Image: A Journal of the Arts and Religion. *In 1982 Haley received the John Irving Novel Prize for* Exotic. *"Line of Duty" illustrates Haley's strong sense of identification with injured souls like the traumatized Officer Henning. As the story unfolds, Haley unflinchingly tracks the emotional and spiritual disintegration of Henning. At the same time, in a move characteristic of his more recent work, the writer introduces hope in the form of a Good Samaritan figure, Henning's patrol partner. Haley is currently Associate Professor of English and Writer in Residence at Abilene Christian University.*

LINE OF DUTY

1 · PARTNERS

1   OFFICER HENNING WAS ONE of those big men. He was not a jiggling embarrassment when he started out on the force but came to them as a broad-shouldered athletic type who checked in at a solid six-foot-five and a preferred weight of two twenty-five. With a body like that, Henning dominated the

precinct's beach volleyball team. Whenever the rubbery globe   1
came spinning over the net, he rose into the air and his nylon
shorts flapped and his fists pounded like coordinated jackham-
mers. He was the main point driver for the cops against weekend
teams of blue shirts, firemen, and EMT personnel. Through it all,
including a dismal 6–14 season, Henning remained heroic and
a happy buyer of postgame beer. He had embedded in him the
personality of an easygoing rock until the heart flutter anomaly
began. The problem cropped up about the time Henning was
going through his divorce.

The cardiologist placed the stress test results under the young   2
officer's nose. He told Henning he'd best avoid sand and sweat
gatherings for the remainder of the year. This left Henning with
just the regular forms of non-exercise: sitting squishily on his
behind during long patrol rides, jaw muscle movements when
he yacked over the radio, quick strides up and down concrete
driveways. Unfortunately, his appetite didn't keep tabs on this
sudden reduction in activity.

Every morning they stopped off at *Sweet Heaven!* on Ocean   3
Boulevard. Henning ducked from the cruiser to run inside
and pick up a half-dozen bear claws. Then lunchtime would
roll around and he'd be with the rest of the bunch at *Benito's
Drive-Thru*, helping himself to trio of chimichangas drenched in
green hot goo. By the time Roberta Raye Jones came on board as
Henning's new partner, he had packed on thirty pounds as easily
as a man slipping his arms through an overcoat.

"It's not how much you eat, it's *what* you eat." This was Roberta   4
Raye setting the rehabilitative tone from Day One. She was a
lively acting, Watts-born• Af-Am• who always got into the car
with a flourish. On her lap she set up clean baggies, individually
filled with celery, carrot sticks, bright radish slices. Roberta Raye
fished in and out of the bags as they drove the freeway. "You've
got to put good stuff in you to get good stuff out."

"Are you kidding? Rabbit food?" Henning had taken the off-ramp   5
and they were easing through *barrio*• country with its strange *haciendas*•-on-wheels. Chrome bumpers divided the sun. Across the
street, man-sized graffiti roared and burned on concrete walls.

"Yes, Max, this is *rabbit* food. But don't get ideas. I'm sure not   6
a bunny." It was weird she'd said that, Henning thought. Roberta

Watts-born · Watts is a
largely African American
district of Los Angeles
known for massive riots,
burning, and looting
that occurred in 1965

Af-Am · African
American

barrio · "neighborhood"
(Spanish)

haciendas · estates,
mansions (Spanish)

6 Raye really did have a bod – steely, ærobicized and capped off with a deeply cleaved bust. But her face. It was a departure from the old centerfold ideal guys like Henning had grown up with. Roberta Raye's eyes were set wide apart and her forehead was kinda high. Then there was her nose which had been broken when she was young and not living under circumstances where anyone felt like getting it repaired. The nose had grown nearly flat on one side, resulting in partial nasal blockage. That was why Roberta Raye sounded breathless whenever she talked.

7 Of course, the other white boys kidded Henning fiercely about having a funny looking, double-minority partner, a seaweed smacker on top of all that, and they'd heard that she mumbled prayers before she ate at *Benito's* so she was either a Holy Roller or scared to death of bean burritos, but Henning came back sharply at them. He declared that Roberta Raye was the perfect ride. She was reliable, always smelled good, and because of the racial thing (according to his own conservative lights) he didn't have to worry about falling into the trap of dating her. Add to the final mix Roberta Raye's pleasant chatter and her calm under pressure, and if you were going to have a female in the car, Roberta Raye was tops.

8 "And stop making fun of what she eats," Henning finished up. "She's right, The way you guys chow down will kill you." Of course, it wasn't exactly true that Roberta Raye had converted Henning to the kingdom of whole food. It was more that she had exerted a moderate influence. She was urging him to take into account his poor, neglected heart. His heart really had become a bad thing, and often these days he felt it trying to speak to him. During those night episodes the sweat broke out across Henning's forehead as he lay on his back staring at dark texture swipes on the ceiling. *Flutter*, *flutter* went the strange bird. Henning did not return to the doc or tell anyone. It was frightening, embarrassing, too. After twenty-eight years in Henning's big body, his heart had a single-minded demand. It wanted out. What could he do? He tensed. He gripped both sides of the pillow. The guys noted he looked fatigued. One of the sergeants said something about taking a few days off, adding words about Tamara and having time to recoup. Henning laughed outloud. Who did they think he was? If a big man knew anything, it was how to keep on keeping on.

2 · BANG

Fᴀᴄᴛ ᴡᴀs ʜᴇ ʜᴀᴅ ᴅɪsᴄʜᴀʀɢᴇᴅ the weapon in the line of duty before. A single shot fired into the air outside a North Hollywood convenience store in '99. The following year there had been three frantic rounds squeezed off from the sidewalk at a fleeing suspect's tires, as large and dizzying and unreal as a target at a carnival booth. Most recently the weapon had come into play during a major shootout on Christmas Day in front of a bungalow where they were crouching behind vehicles and firing steadily, pumping lead for half an hour past bougainvillea and beyond shattered window panes, chopping up an artificial Christmas tree among other things. Then sᴡᴀᴛ had broken in and found the place empty, spider webs, the whole bit. 9

This time was different. 10

Roberta Raye was driving and she picked up the guy on the spur road. It was just before midnight and there was lots of hot tire potential, but as soon as they switched on the red and whites it became clear there would be no chase. In less than a quarter mile, Robert Raye had the violator pulled down. From the shotgun seat Henning could see the man sitting calmly behind the wheel. "I'll take him," he said. He flipped the veggie bag over to Roberta. "Save some for me." 11

Except for their headlights and the flashing, silent blare of the roof rack, the road and nearby vacant lots were an unlit pit of blackness. It was out close to the oil patch, an area officially called Holister Hills but known to all as Holiness Hills because that was maybe easier to say and the ugly array of leaning telephone poles and brutal wires suggested an industrial version of Golgotha.· Good for nothing place, known only to contractors and dealers trading bundles and briefcases, Henning thought. The air smelled of ocean and petro, that ol' Long Beach fragrance. He advanced until he was three feet from the car, murking just aft of the driver's window. Behind him Roberta Raye was bent over in the front seat, punching buttons, running the computer check. In the spillover of official light, the violator (male, Caucasian) looked like a mild sort, a bank teller or an accountant. He wore glasses and probably would smell like discount-store aftershave. The car was likewise mundane, a dimly kept K-car· with an empty child seat in back. This was the kind of guy with whom it was easy to 12

Golgotha · the site of Jesus' crucifixion

K-car · an inexpensive, boxy, and utilitarian automobile introduced by Chrysler in the early 1980s

12   break ice: "License and insurance, sir" and "Have any idea how fast you were traveling?"

13   Henning had to rap his knuckles loudly against the glass.

14   The man buzzed down all four windows, an odd or nervous thing to do. Henning ignored it and took the plastic card. He scoped his flashlight over the laminate. He began the rhetorical spiel. The man nodded like the concept of being pulled over for speed drift wasn't new to him. Then he pressed a finger to his nose, as if preventing a sneeze, but within a second he had reached across the dark passenger seat that was as vacant as moonscape.

15   He popped up with something. It was black and not a tissue or handkerchief. Smoothly the man dipped a shoulder so he could fire out the window (or so Henning's reflexes assumed). Henning went for his belt. This had been practiced. Many times. Roll, turn, make yourself gum-wrapper thin. Fast now. Exploit the angle advantage.

16   There didn't seem to be a noise. Just the man pitching suddenly forward over the wheel. Blood foamed at his mouth. Spasms shook the upper body. The bullet had punched cleanly through the neck and trachea. The episode took about fifteen seconds, which to Henning seemed longer. The man's wind sucked and wheezed significantly, much louder than he'd ever heard Roberta Raye breathing through her maimed nostril. When the noises stopped, Henning palmed the fender and hopped to the other side. He placed his warm weapon on the hood and played the flashlight on the pavement. In the flash of muzzle fire he'd seen something go flying. Reaching down he retrieved the man's glasses which somehow (action, reaction?) had gone straight out the open passenger window. When he picked them up, he made sure he didn't let his eyes go back to the interior of the car.

17   Roberta Raye banged out of the patrol car. She hovered by the Chrysler's side, opened the door, jumped back as something poured toward her feet. She came around to Henning. "Are you all right? What – ?"

18   Henning dangled the bifocal glasses in his hands where Roberta Raye could see them.

19   "Not a scratch on these. Don't you think that's amazing? How's Forensics going to explain it?"

Roberta Raye stared at him, ignoring the prescription glasses. 20 "I only heard one shot. He didn't get off a round or anything?" And now she seemed to move like one in a panic as she abruptly unbuttoned Henning's tunic and patted his undershirt. He thought he did feel cold, as if something was gone out of him, but the glasses in his hands made a sort of touchstone. As long as he held onto them he felt steady on his feet. He almost wanted to put them on because things had become blurry. He heard crickets, the most staccato crickets he'd heard in his life, but it couldn't be; this was the Holiness Hills and too close to the ocean for those little stiff-legged creatures. Then he became aware of another sound. Not his heart, which was as steady as a rock chunking down a slope. This sound was something else – wheels whirring, engines thundering, the hum that concrete takes on when weight is flung against it. It was the freeway, a full five miles distant.

"Wow. Listen to that." He'd never had his reflexes reach such a 21 peak. Maybe it was worth sharing. At least with a guy's partner?

"You're pale. I think you need to go over there." Roberta Raye 22 flicked her flashlight toward the weedy shoulder.

At first he didn't understand. He was thinking she meant for 23 him to take a leak. Then it clicked. She thought he might want to be sick.

"Nah," Henning said. For a moment he felt shame. He was so 24 alive. No flutters, nothing. What he'd done or not done didn't affect him at all. Sick? He actually was hungry. As he folded up the pair of glasses and stuck them in his shirt pocket he was thinking basically one thing: "Bear claw."

3 · AFTERMATH

A YEAR EARLIER THERE HAD BEEN a seminar in a downtown 25 hotel, topic: "Use of Deadly Force." A little man with wingtips and a button-down stage presence had hissed into a microphone and peppered the officers with technical talk. What it translated into was, "Don't wax someone unless you or your buddy's life is on the line. Even then be ready for nasty consequences. Internal Affairs, lawyers, civil rights advocates, the press."

With Maxwell Henning it was different. The DA sent the file 26 over and it was revealed that Mr. K-car had indeed been a banker, a mid-level, consumer loan officer. There had been an embezzle-

26 ment going on at the branch for at least eight months and the guy was about to be snagged by the Feds. Better yet, the night of the event the man had left a note behind then headed out to the oceanside to finish the affair. By chance Henning and Roberta Raye had caught him in the midst of his suicide run. So, in a way, Henning hadn't done a thing to alter history. By reaching for the .38 on the seat beside him, the man had hastened the process and spared himself the ammo.

27 With this information the board recognized the shooting as justifiable and cleared Henning. As an afterthought, the department provided him a psychologist to talk to one day a week, even though Henning swore he didn't need couch-deluxe treatment. The twig-like woman with a painted turtle shell on her desk was willing to let him digress, talk about tales of Tamara, so that was fine. This Dr. Berkowitz was adept at exercising the "Big C" (compassion) and she pointed out that Henning's unresolved issues had conflated with the shooting. She said that taking the life of the man was like adding another brick to the destroyed pile of Henning's marriage. "Yes," Henning finally admitted, "I've been a little down lately."

28 He was lying. It was worse. He couldn't get a handle on what was coming over him.

29 What he was starting to feel was so dark that glancing over at Roberta Raye during a long ride failed to offer the normal degree of comfort. He'd look at her and think "Tamara," like he used to, and instead of being a tiny bit warm and tingly, he'd hear a gun going off. He knew he ought to take the killing gracefully, as a sure sign that he was a lucky s.o.b., the guy assigned to the best partner in the world. Roberta Raye had actually sent him flowers. Who else would recognize without a pause that he needed cheering? She was a great one, Roberta Raye was, but unfortunately the daisies and carnations pushed Henning the wrong way. He put the vase on the vanity in the bathroom, close to the porcelain tub. There the flowers sorta blended in with the wrinkled shower curtain. It was cheerful to have that kind of floral life in his nearly barren house, even tucked away in the can, but his mind these days was bent toward the perverse. The pink and white petals allowed him to think the same things over and over. It kept coming back to him: funerals, blossoming wounds, Tamara breaking free of his embrace to announce, "You're noth-

ing like what I thought you were. So much Mr. Wonderful on the 29
outside. Give a gal roses and a box of candy for every occasion.
Thanksgiving even. Roses? Jesus, that's just it, Henning. You're
so automatic. It's click, click, click. Got it done. You shine me up.
Strap me on. That's right. I help you get a job done. You're not
really there for *me*. You can't even begin to imagine what I feel."

Daisies and carnations. Blood red roses. What was the dif- 30
ference, he wondered. He decided to get rid of the flowers and
everything else.

A minute later, his hands. In the mirror. Shaking. He put the vase 31
down on the counter. Quietly, all of him slipped out of the picture.

4 · TWO MONTHS

Today he was sitting in the den in his bathrobe. There 32
had been a bit of incautiousness at a crime scene when he'd
walked heedlessly over the top of the lab woman's strips of
gauze laid out on the sidewalk like tiny surrender flags. There
had been shifts when he was ten minutes late. There had been a
Wednesday, just one Wednesday out of all the Wednesdays he'd
ever lived, when he'd pulled the pepper spray from his belt and
handed the cylinder to a street person who was trying to stop
traffic. "Want them to put on the brakes? This will make them
back up all the way to Nebraska." The department had placed
Henning on leave-of-absence, which was tantamount to ordering
the VCR to become the most important appliance in a man's life.
One filled in gaps with magnetic tape. This time he fed his eyes
a tape he'd made of a mindless game show. Another winner. No,
the doorbell. Roberta Raye standing on the porch. Roberta Raye
out of uniform. Roberta Raye in a green dress and white hose
and high heels. A different perfume. Smiling at him.

"Are you okay, Henning?" 33

"Sure." Hardly any words and she'd already broken down the 34
glassy glaze he'd developed to encase himself. Her voice continued
to chip away, telling him something about dressing smartly pronto-
style and loading himself into the van. She had her kids with her
and she wanted Henning to make the drive to the valley.

"Come on, Max. My folks have a ranch. It's fun and you don't look 35
booked to me. We'll go to church first, then you can have lunch and
babysit while I do some heavy-duty gabbing with my parents."

36   "Church?"

37   "Veggies for the soul," Roberta Raye said. It was a joke he
supposed.

38   The drive took an hour, and for the first time he thought
about Roberta Raye Jones' ethnicity. The reason it came to him
now was because of the two girls and the boy. The dressed-up
children were just as dark-skinned as their mother. So together
they made a black family. Except for Henning, a great bleached
hulk in polo shirt and slacks, the odd man out. "Hi, kids," he said
once. They stared warily at him.

39   At church it wasn't the get-down-in-the-aisle style religion
he'd imagined. The plain buff, steepled building housed something more formal. "Liturgy," Roberta Raye whispered early on in
the service, and sitting next to her on the pew he felt an electric
jolt. The breath from her lips had brushed his ear. He stared at her
long nails, done up especially for the day. He looked down at the
Order of Worship lying in his lap. His eyes couldn't get past the
first title there: "We proclaim the presence of the Lord." What's
that, Henning wondered. God has to be spoken into existence?
Why not simply point at the thing itself? Hey, dude, over there!
Why not catch him bare-handed, as real as a bullet streaking
toward flesh? A fully-intentional God, not one hiding beneath
beds or lodged inside songbooks, waiting for you to say the right
words so he could come out and play.

40   Henning surveyed again the modern stained glass, the light
woods covering the wall, the cushioned pews. By the end of the
service Roberta Raye was smiling like something had passed
through her. He felt nothing. As he walked out he wondered
what he would remember? That it smelled nice in there. Like
furniture polish? Drycleaning? Carpet shampoo? Yes, a clean
place for a dirty person.

41   "What did you think, Max?"

42   "Great. Just great."

43   She smiled like she knew what he was trying to do. "Well,
don't dwell on it. Time to switch gears."

44   "Really?"

45   "That's right. To the ranch!"

46   She didn't really need him to babysit. Instead, she turned the
children over to her parents and rustled up a pair of overalls and

leather boots for both of them. Henning and she got into an old, 46
rusted-up pickup that had a winch in back. It looked almost like
a tow truck, and Henning wondered why they'd need that on a
ranch. There was also a fully stocked gun rack in the cab. "We've
got to go into that field over there and get a cow for my daddy,"
Roberta Raye said.

They bounced over ruts and stopped in front of some 47
Herefords. The cattle looked dumb and suspicious, but didn't do
anything as Roberta Raye stepped out with the rifle. To Henning
it felt like hottest day of the summer; he couldn't be sure having
spent the last week indoors, entirely under air conditioning.
Sweat oozed down Roberta Raye's cheeks. "Here," she said and
handed him the rifle. He heard the whistling noise coming from
her nostril as she spoke faster than normal. "Daddy said to take
that one right there." Roberta Raye wiped her face and pointed.
"The one with the funny patch on her leg."

The rifle was a small-bore job. She advised him to nail the 48
cow between the eyes so it would go down with one pop. Then
she stationed herself behind him.

Henning stumbled upon a hole in the ground and frightened 49
the nearest animals. They stuttered a few yards away. Black Patch
stayed where she was, her head up, chewing, looking at him.
Between the eyes.

"You can do it, Max," Roberta Raye said from the rear. "Taking 50
life is part of preserving life. Kill a beautiful animal and eat it beautifully. That's all it is. We're feeding my kids. You pull the trigger
and you guarantee a good life for someone else. You don't have
to be the judge. The judge has already put you in the situation.
All he is asking you to do is to respond. You hear me, Henning?
Snap out of it! You're not the damn judge! Squeeze!"

A minute later they backed up the truck to the cow. After 51
they'd run the hook through the hocks they turned on the winch.
As the cow dangled and spun at the end of the chain Roberta
Raye used a regular kitchen chef's knife to cut its throat. "There.
Let it drain, then we'll drive it back to the house. Daddy will take
care of the rest."

This was what she'd brought him here for, an event more impor- 52
tant than church or coaxing him into pulling the trigger. She wanted
him to face the blood. It came fast from the body, starting out like a

52 faucet's gush then steadily graduating until, minutes later, it fell in coin-sized drips. A wide red puddle formed on top of the hardened field. Drought conditions. It would be a while before it soaked in. Flies appeared, flirting with the sticky surface. Mostly, Henning was impressed by the odor. The cow's blood smelled hot and dark and even slightly metallic, like a pocketful of change or damp copper pipes in the basement. For a second he thought Roberta Raye might be on the right track, that these qualities could explain everything. Blood inside the animal was what kept it alive. By taking the blood out and putting it into the ground, they weren't so much killing the animal as moving its essence to a new realm. All the pulsing blood effort was going to be transferred into another kind of production. Right here on this spot plants would spring up.

53 He looked at the head-down cow, the carcass that ended in thick, rubbery open lips. He tried to see it as an evacuated bag, a container whose containing job was finished. Yes, he almost had it.

54 "It's bled enough," Roberta Raye said.

55 As he followed her to the truck, she put an arm around him. He hardly felt it. He was thinking about the banker's wife. He'd visited her a few weeks ago. It had been a desperate act. He'd been looking for some kind of story that might suit him. Instead, she gained the wrong impression, that he had come by the house to claim some kind of carnal victory. She caught him curbside as he reached for his car door, trying to get away. "You were looking down at my toe nails in there," she accused. "You want to, don't you?" He said nothing, but they were present just as she asserted: ten fields of ruby red. "See," she said, wiggling each one, "You come back inside, officer, and I'll paint them any color you like. You can help."

56 Any color. He didn't know what. He started to tell Roberta Raye about it. He knew he might start to blubber. He didn't speak. There was no way to make it appropriate. They got in the truck. They carried the beef home to her family. Steaks, roasts, ribs, hamburger. He and Roberta Raye Jones had it all and everyone at the house was gratified that their mission was accomplished so quickly. She took him back to the city and her last words were, "You're going to be okay tonight, huh? I gotta drop the kids off and go on shift."

57 "No rest for the wicked," he said. He meant nothing by the phrase at the time. He was only acting light hearted, giving her

what he thought she wanted which was to see him smile so she   57
might think him cured or at least better behaved for the time being.
He yawned as he waved goodbye. "Going to sleep well tonight." He
thought he sounded convincing. He really hoped he was.

5 · MIDNIGHT

WHO WOULD HAVE GUESSED? He'd never been a boozer,   58
not even during the years when he was deep-sixing his
marriage, so how was a guy to know? That with alcohol-inspired
numbness could come new friends. Energy! Inspiration! It was
true. Why didn't someone put that in a manual for big men? If
you hurt, boy, and don't know what to do, open a quart in the
vacuum of your home. Tip the bottle and cauterize• the wounds
with fire. Before you know it you'll be on your feet and –

cauterize • the process of burning a wound to stop bleeding and destroy damaged or infected tissue

Not exactly dancing but in the bathroom he was tossing the   59
rotting flowers into the waste basket. He packed all his wedding
photos into a large cardboard box and set the box out in the alley
for the garbagemen. He broke open his revolver and emptied it
of bullets. Back to the bathroom where he lifted off the lid on
the back of the toilet so he could turn his hand upside down and
release the ammunition. The bullets sank to the bottom of the
tank. They lay fat and snub-nosed, and everything was so unbear-
ably quiet that he could hear his heavy breaths coming. He felt
his heart, too, and that required a final drink to settle down. He
crashed the bottle into the tub.

With the empty pistol and a single framed photo, he got into his   60
car. He backed out of the driveway and headed toward the beach.
It was growing palpably late. The sun-sunken world that streaked
past him telegraphed shadowy movements: leather armies deploy-
ing on asphalt and concrete. Prime time, crime time.

As soon as he was out of the residential area, Henning applied   61
force to the pedal. He was going 45, 50, 60, then 90. Fast enough
to make streetlights blur into candle flames. The photo beside him
was a strictly composed one, circa• his and Tamara's dating era. It
showed them smiling at the junior prom, three years before they
married, ten years before they divorced. Henning glanced over
at the picture from time to time, but he couldn't see the blond,
smiling girl because it was black inside the car and the revolver
lay atop her. A big gun, it crushed Tamara from head to toe. He

circa • "around" (Latin)

61   drove faster, or so he imagined, until finally, gratefully, he heard a siren and the lights appeared in the mirror, drawing closer and more dramatic, making him swim in a blaze of red and white.

62   What to do? Hit the brakes, but do it smoothly. Decrease speed to a slow roll, then key off the ignition. Sag backwards against the damp seat.

63   A minute later he heard the knuckles lightly tapping on the window. He buzzed down the glass. He didn't look at the officer's face, but he allowed a sliver of hope. It might be her. If it was, she would see him before he handed over his license. The police officer mask would come off and she would speak to him, not as a woman but as a fellow creature. When he failed to answer, Roberta Raye would become even more extreme. She'd reach through the opening and put a hand on his shoulder. "Is that really you? Henning? What are you doing out here?"

64   He continued to stare straight ahead. There were no words yet, just a flashlight playing over his face. His right hand rested on Tamara, on the pistol. The heart palpitations had gone berserk.

65   It was plain now: he could die as easily as he could live. Just like the banker, there would be one ill-advised move and then it would be finished. He found it terrifying that such magnificence should remain within his clumsy grasp. Still he waited for the voice. That was what would settle it. There was a special kind of tone he was waiting for. Some kind of forgiveness not easily obtained. To hear someone say, "Henning, you're okay. Don't do it." That would be good.

66   He waited a few more uneven heartbeats. As long as there was time, most any words would work. He was past being particular. The mere sound of his name might suffice: "Henning, Henning, I see you, Henning, that's you, no one else, Henning, you're alive, come on, get out of the car, Max."

67   It was stupid to let your life get to such a point – dependent on one person out of the whole world. To hope that this one person would care for you where you had failed yourself miserably. To ask, if it came down to it, for that person to save you by pulling you back across the line. It was unacceptable. Unfair to them. Pathetic on your part. Turning yourself into a beggar, a little man with steamy bifocals that were about to fly out the open window. But it was real. He knew now

what it was like. The paralysis, the inability to unbend. Your 67
hand touching death while your ears still sought out life. The
distant freeway. Five miles away and every sound stroke of
the whooshing, speeding traffic registered on his brain. He
could hear them, the midnight people who didn't cut back
on their speed; they just went faster, trying to find that cheap
motel room or get to their six AM bacon and eggs on an oval
plate. Their spinning wheels were as loud as if Henning was
lying on his back on the centerline.

"Please," he thought, "slow down." 68

He turned his bulky body and stared into the officer's blind- 69
ing flashlight. He smelled sweet perfume. His heart seemed to
make a leap.

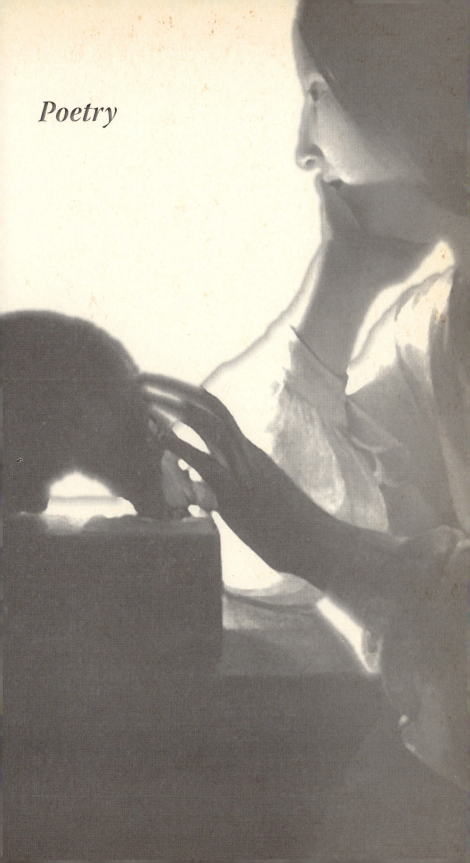

Poetry

Middle English Lyrics

⫷ 1 4 T H   C E N T U R Y ⫸

Designed primarily to be sung and heard rather than read, Middle English lyrics are often brief – yet the themes and images they use can be surprisingly complex. Much of this complexity is achieved through puns and double-meanings, a playfulness with language that allows them to operate on a number of levels simultaneously. These popular lyrics, whose composition flourished from the 13th to the 15th centuries, often focus on religious themes such as Christ's passion or the suffering of Mary, yet they commonly cloak those themes in metaphors and scenes drawn from everyday life. In doing so, they seek to perform two important functions: first, they create in their listeners a personal connection with the central moments of Christianity, seeking to make their audiences feel that "they were there" (an emphasis commonly known as "affective piety"). Second, in linking common experience with religiously significant events, they seek to bridge the gap between the ordinary and the divine. The first two lyrics which follow have been presented in the original Middle English, although spelling has been slightly regularized.

FOWLES IN THE FRITH

1   FOWLES˙ in the frith,˙
     The fisshes in the flod,˙
     And I mon waxe wood:˙
     Much sorwe˙ I walke with
5   For beste˙ of boon˙ and blood.

NOW GOETH SUNNE UNDER WODE

1   NOW GOETH SUNNE under wode˙
     Me reweth,˙ Marye, thy faire rode.˙

Fowles · birds

frith · forest

flod · sea

And I . . . wood · either "and I must go mad" or "and I, man, go mad"

sorwe · sorrow

beste · either "best" or "beast." The ambiguity suggests the tension between Christ and the flesh

boon · bone

wode · wood, forest

Me reweth · I pity

thy faire rode · "rode" may be construed as either "face" or "cross." The line may thus be read as both "I pity, Mary, your fair face" and "I lament, Mary, your fair cross"

Now goeth sunne under tree:
Me reweth, Marye, thy sone and thee.   3

I WOULD BE CLAD

GOLD AND ALL THIS world's wine·
   Is naught but Christ's rood;·   1
I would be clad in Christ's skin
That ran so long with his blood,
And go to his heart, and give to him mine –   5
For he alone is a filling food.
Then I'd care little for kith or kin,·
For in him alone is all that is good. Amen.

Gold ... wine · that is, worldly goods pleasures

rood · cross

Then I'd ... kin · see Luke 14:26

THE SPRING UNDER THE THORN

AT A SPRING, HIDDEN under the thorn,
   Was grief's remedy, so scarce before.   1
There beside it stood a maid,·
Full of love that abounds;
Whosoever will seek true love,   5
In her it shall be found.

a maid · that is, Mary, mother of Christ

William Shakespeare

◖ 1 5 6 4 – 1 6 1 6 ◗

By the 1590s Shakespeare was known in London as an actor, a poet, and a playwright. He wrote thirty-seven plays (or more) and a number of superb nondramatic poems before retiring to Stratford-on-Avon, his birthplace, in about 1610. England's greatest dramatist is seldom thought of as a religious poet, yet he was steeped in the Bible, a book which provides metaphor and framework for many of his themes. His great tragedies, especially Hamlet *(see pages 553–664),* King Lear, *and* Macbeth, *concern profound metaphysical issues such as the nature of justice, good and evil, mystery, temptation, and the presence or absence of God. The sonnets, as well, published in 1609, address such metaphysical themes as love, mutability, and death. The sonnets are intensely personal poems that, in the words of C. S. Lewis, anyone "can walk into and make his own."*

SONNET 146

1 POOR SOUL, THE CENTER of my sinful earth,•
   Thrall to• these rebel powers that thee array,
Why dost thou pine within and suffer dearth,•
Painting thy outward walls so costly gay?
5 Why so large cost, having so short a lease,
Dost thou upon thy fading mansion spend?
Shall worms, inheritors of this excess,•
Eat up thy charge? Is this thy body's end?
Then, soul, live thou upon thy servant's loss,
10 And let that pine to aggravate thy store;•
Buy terms divine in selling hours of dross;•
Within be fed, without be rich no more:
    So shalt thou feed on Death, that feeds on men,
    And Death once dead, there's no more dying then.•

my ... earth · the body

Thrall to · "slave to." This is a conjectural reading due to a fault in the manuscript. Other readings include "Hemmed with," "Fooled by," and "Feeding"

dearth · scarcity, lack

excess · excessive expense

And let ... store · let the body waste away (in self-denial) in order to increase the riches of the soul

dross · baseness, impurity, waste

And death ... then · see 2 Corinthians 15:54

403

Æmilia Lanyer

⟨ 1 5 6 9 – 1 6 4 5 ⟩

Æmilia Lanyer published one book in her lifetime, an original poem on the Passion of Christ, a volume which has earned her the title of the first major feminist in English literary history. Lanyer was a middle class woman who enjoyed the company of the aristocrats of the courts of Queen Elizabeth I and King James I. Her father, Baptiste Bassano, an Italian musician of the Elizabethan court, died when Æmilia was seven. Her mother, Margaret Johnson, died when Æmilia was eighteen. Subsequently, Lanyer became the mistress of Henry Carey, first Lord Hundson and Lord Chamberlain to Queen Elizabeth. In 1592 she married Alphonso Lanyer and at some unknown date underwent a spiritual conversion through the particular influence of the Countess Dowager of Cumberland, to whom (among others) she dedicated her book. In 1611 – the same year in which the Authorized or King James version of the Bible was published – Lanyer published Salve Deus Rex Judæorum ("Hail God, King of the Jews"), a work of over 1,800 lines, which reflects both her conversion and her conviction that previous interpreters of the Bible and the Christian faith have treated women unfairly. The poem attempts to correct the record by showing the extraordinary and positive role of women in the life of Christ. She says in her address to the reader that:

> *it pleased our Lord and Savior Jesus Christ, without the assistance of man, being free from original and all other sins, from the time of his conception, till the hour of his death, to be begotten of a woman, borne of a woman, nourished of a woman, obedient to a woman; and that he healed women, pardoned women, comforted women; yea, even when he was in his greatest agony and bloody sweat, going to be crucified, and also in the last hour of his death, took care to dispose of a woman: after his resurrection, appeared first to a woman,*

405

sent a woman to declare his most glorious resurrection to
the rest of his Disciples.

In a section of the poem entitled "Eve's Apology in Defense of
Women," the poet presents the story of the Passion through the
unique perspective of Pilate's wife, and, by extension through the
point of view of Eve, who represents all women. Lanyer, through this
exceptional narrative poem, establishes herself not only as one of the
first Christian feminists in England but also as one of the first women
to publish a major volume of verse in the English language.

from SALVE DEUS REX JUDÆORUM

EVE'S APOLOGY IN DEFENSE OF WOMEN

cause · court case

Now Pontius Pilate is to judge the cause·   1
   Of faultless Jesus, who before him stands,
Who neither hath offended prince nor laws,
Although he now be brought in woeful bands:
O noble Governor, make thou yet a pause,   5

imbrue · stain, defile

Do not in innocent blood imbrue· thy hands
   But hear the words of thy most worthy wife,·

wife · Pilate's wife, by tradition known as Percula (see "Pilate and Percula," *The Passion*, pages 518–520)

   Who sends to thee to beg her Savior's life:

Let barb'rous cruelty far depart from thee,
And in true justice take afflictions part.   10
Open thine eyes, that thou the truth may'st see,
Do not the thing that goes against thy heart,
Condemn not him that must thy Savior be;
But view his holy life, his good desert.
   Let not us women glory in men's fall,   15
   Who had power given to over-rule us all.

Till now your indiscretion sets us free,
And makes our former fault much less appear.

tree · see Genesis 2:16–17

Our Mother Eve, who tasted of the tree,·
Giving to Adam what she held most dear,   20
Was simply good and had no power to see

after-coming · succeeding

The after-coming· harm did not appear.
   The subtle serpent that our sex betrayed,
   Before our fall so sure a plot had laid.

25 That undiscerning ignorance perceived
No guile or craft that was by him intended,
For had she known of what we were bereaved,˙
To his request she had not condescended.
But she (poor soul) by cunning was deceived,˙
30 No hurt therein her harmless heart intended;
    For she alleged˙ God's word, which he denies
    That they should die but, even as gods, be wise.

But surely Adam cannot be excused.
Her fault though great, yet he was most to blame.
35 What weakness offered, strength might have refused.
Being lord of all, the greater was his shame.
Although Serpent's craft had her abused,
God's holy word ought all his actions frame,
    For he was Lord and King of all the earth,
40   Before poor Eve had either life or breath,

Who, being fram'd by God's eternal hand,
The perfect'st man that ever breath'd on earth,
And from God's mouth receiv'd that strait˙ command,
The breach whereof he knew was present˙ death;
45 Yea, having power to rule both sea and land,
Yet with one apple won˙ to lose that breath
    Which God had breathed in his beauteous face,
    Bringing us all in˙ danger and disgrace.

And then to lay the fault on Patience' back,
50 That we (poor women) must endure it all.
We know right well he did discretion lack,
Being not persuaded thereunto at all.
If Eve did err, it was for knowledge sake,
The fruit being fair persuaded him to fall.
55   No subtle Serpent's falsehood did betray him,
    If he would eat it, who had power to stay˙ him?

Not Eve, whose fault was only too much love,
Which made her give this present to her dear,
That what she tasted, he likewise might prove,˙

bereaved · robbed, deprived

deceived · see 1 Timothy 2:14

alleged · quoted

strait · rigorous, strict

present · immediate

with … won · conquered by one apple (see Genesis 3:6)

in · into

stay · stop

prove · experience (through tasting)

Whereby his knowledge might become more clear. 60
He never sought her weakness to reprove,
With those sharp words, which he of God did hear.
    Yet men will boast of knowledge, which he took
    From Eve's fair hand, as from a learned book.

If any evil did in her remain, 65
Being made of him, he was the ground of all.
If one* of many worlds could lay a stain
Upon our sex, and work so great a fall
To wretched man, by Satan's subtle train,*
What will so foul a fault amongst you all? 70
    Her weakness did the Serpent's words obey,
    But you in malice God's dear Son betray,*

Whom, if unjustly you condemn to die,
Her sin was small, to* what you do commit.
All mortal sins that do for vengeance cry, 75
Are not to be compared unto it.
If many worlds would altogether try,
By all their sins the wrath of God to get,*
    This sin of yours surmounts them all as far
    As doth the sun another little star. 80

Then let us have our liberty again,
And challenge* to yourselves no sovereignty.*
You came not in the world without our pain.
Make that a bar* against your cruelty.
Your fault being greater, why should you disdain 85
Our being your equals, free from tyranny?
    If one weak woman simply did offend,
    This sin* of yours hath no excuse, nor end,

To which (poor souls) we never gave consent.
Witness thy wife (O Pilate) speaks for all 90
Who did but dream,* and yet a message sent,
That thou should'st have nothing to do at all
With that just man, which, if thy heart relent,
Why wilt thou be a reprobate* with Saul*

one · Eve (seen here as a miniature world or cosmos)

train · argument

you ... betray · Pilate and the religious authorities who condemn Jesus

to · compared to

get · receive

challenge · lay claim

sovereignty · superior authority

bar · barrier

This sin · the execution of Christ

dream · see Matthew 27:19

reprobate · lost soul

Saul · King of Israel who sought to kill David, God's anointed

95   To seek the death of him that is so good,
       For thy soul's health to shed his dear blood?

       Yea, so thou may'st these sinful people please,
       Thou art content against all truth and right,
       To seal this act, that may procure thine ease,
100   With blood and wrong, with tyranny and might.
       The multitude thou seekest to appease,
       By base dejection of this heavenly Light,˙
         Demanding which of these that should'st loose,
         Whether the Thief or Christ King of the Jews.

105   Base Barabbas, the Thief, they all desire,˙
       And thou more base than he, perform'st their˙ will;
       Yet when thy thoughts back to themselves retire,
       Thou art unwilling to commit this ill.
       Oh, that thou could'st unto such grace aspire,
110   That thy polluted lips might never kill
         That honor, which right judgment ever graceth,
         To purchase shame, which all true worth defaceth.

⊹   ⊹   ⊹

       Canst thou be innocent, that 'gainst all right
       Wilt yield to what thy conscience doth withstand?
115   Being a man of knowledge, power, and might,
       To let the wicked carry such a hand,
       Before thy face to blindfold Heaven's bright light,
       And thou to yield to what they did demand?
         Washing thy hand, thy conscience cannot clear,
120   But to all worlds this stain must needs appear.

Light · Jesus (see John 1:4–5)

Whether … desire · see Matthew 27:20

their · the rabble calling for Christ's crucifixion

John Donne

⟨ 1 5 7 2 – 1 6 3 1 ⟩

After studying law in London and serving in naval campaigns against Spain, Donne aspired to a career as a dashing courtier in King James' Court. However, his secret elopement with the young niece of his employer, Sir Thomas Egerton, demolished his hopes of worldly success. In 1615, after fourteen years of poverty and despair, Donne made formal the abandonment of his Roman Catholic heritage and was ordained a priest in the Church of England (at the encouragement of King James himself). In 1621 he became the Dean of St. Paul's Cathedral in London and, subsequently, the most famous preacher of his day. In his youth, Donne wrote brilliant, witty, and often patently erotic love poems. After his conversion and ordination, Donne continued to write love poems, though they became love lyrics addressed to God. His "Holy Sonnets" illustrate his intense capacity for religious emotion, illustrated in the twin themes of the mystery of divine union (as figured in marriage) and the universal fact of human mortality.

HOLY SONNET 7

1   At the round earth's imagined corners, blow
      Your trumpets, angels; and arise, arise
From death, you numberless infinities
Of souls, and to your scattered bodies go;
5 All whom the flood did, and fire shall, o'erthrow,
All whom war, dearth,* age, agues,* tyrannies,
Despair, law, chance hath slain, and you whose eyes
Shall behold God, and never taste death's woe.*
But let them sleep, Lord, and me mourn a space,
10 For, if above all these, my sins abound,

dearth · famine

agues · fevers

never taste … woe
some people will
escape death,
according to St. Paul
(1 Thessalonians 4:15–17)

411

'Tis late to ask abundance of thy grace 11
When we are there. Here on this lowly ground,
    Teach me how to repent; for that's as good
    As if thou hadst sealed my pardon with thy blood.

HOLY SONNET 10

DEATH, BE NOT PROUD, though some have called thee 1
    Mighty and dreadful, for, thou art not so,
For, those, whom thou think'st thou dost overthrow,
Die not, poor death, nor yet canst thou kill me;
From rest and sleep, which but thy pictures be, 5
Much pleasure, then from thee, much more must flow,
And soonest our best men with thee do go,
Rest of their bones, and soul's delivery.
Thou art slave to fate, chance, kings, and desperate men,
And dost with poison, war, and sickness dwell, 10
And poppy* or charms can make us sleep as well,
And better than thy stroke; why swell'st thou then?
    One short sleep past, we wake eternally,
    And death shall be no more, Death thou shalt die.

poppy · opium or other drugs that induce sleep

HOLY SONNET 14

BATTER MY HEART, three-personed God; for you 1
    As yet but knock, breathe, shine, and seek to mend;
That I may rise and stand, o'erthrow me, and bend
Your force, to break, blow, burn, and make me new.
I, like an usurped town, to another due, 5
Labor to admit you, but oh, to no end,
Reason, your viceroy in me, me should defend,
But is captived, and proves weak or untrue,
Yet dearly I love you, and would be loved fain,*
But am betrothed* unto your enemy.* 10
Divorce me,* untie, or break that knot again,
Take me to you, imprison me, for I,
    Except you enthrall* me, never shall be free,
    Nor ever chaste, except you ravish* me.

fain · gladly, willingly

betrothed · engaged

your enemy · Satan

Divorce me · the narrator asks God to take the role of King and intervene to break ("divorce") the soul's covenant with Satan

enthrall · to captivate or enslave

ravish · to take by violence, to rape, to overwhelm

George Herbert

⊰ 1 5 9 3 – 1 6 3 3 ⊱

Herbert is one of England's greatest religious poets and a leading member of the "Metaphysical School" of poets, who share themes and stylistic traits with John Donne. After earning the MA at Trinity College, Cambridge, in 1616, the aristocratic Herbert was appointed Reader in Rhetoric at Cambridge (1618), elected Public Orator at Cambridge (1620–1628), and was chosen to serve in Parliament (1625). Ordinarily a man of Herbert's rank, intellect, and experience would have found a career at court, an early ambition that he did in fact pursue. But by a series of events – deaths of friends and his own poor health – Herbert found that God had "cross-biased" him for other ends, and so love of the church superseded his academic and political ambitions. In 1630 he was installed as rector (minister) of Bemerton, a tiny rural congregation near Salisbury. After three years of exemplary service, "Holy Mr. Herbert" died of consumption, leaving behind England's greatest single collection of devotional lyrics, called The Temple *(1633). Herbert's poems are often painfully honest about the sufferings of the Christian pilgrim ("A wonder tortured in the space/Betwixt this world and that of grace"), but they are equally confident of God's presence in struggle "Since here is no place so alone,/The which he doth not fill."*

THE WINDOWS

1   L ORD, HOW CAN MAN preach thy eternal word?
     He is a brittle, crazy* glass;
   Yet in thy temple thou dost him afford
     This glorious and transcendent place,
5   To be a window through thy grace.

   But when thou dost anneal* in glass thy story,*
     Making thy life to shine within

crazy · cracked, flawed

anneal · to heat glass so that an image or a painting may be burned into its surface

thy story · stained glass windows commonly present scenes (the "story") from the Bible or saints' lives

413

The holy preachers, then the light and glory
　　More rev'rend grows, and more doth win;
　　Which else shows wat'rish, bleak, and thin.　　　　10

Doctrine and life, colors and light, in one
　　When they combine and mingle, bring
A strong regard and awe; but speech alone
　　Doth vanish like a flaring thing,
　　And in the ear, not conscience, ring.　　　　15

THE COLLAR˙

Collar · "Collar" suggests both a clerical collar and a slave's shackles

board · table

suit · asking favors

cordial · restorative to the heart

corn · grain

bays · laurel leaves, a symbol of honor

I STRUCK THE BOARD,˙ and cried: "No more.　　　　1
　　　　　I will abroad.
　　What? shall I ever sigh and pine?
My lines and life are free; free as the road,
　　Loose as the wind, as large as store.　　　　5
　　　　　Shall I be still in suit?˙
　　Have I no harvest but a thorn
　　To let me blood, and not restore
What I have lost with cordial˙ fruit?
　　　　　Sure there was wine　　　　10
　　Before my sighs did dry it; there was corn˙
　　Before my tears did drown it.
　　Is the year only lost to me?
　　　　　Have I no bays˙ to crown it?
No flowers, no garlands gay? all blasted?　　　　15
　　　　　All wasted?
　　Not so, my heart; but there is fruit
　　　　　And thou hast hands.
　　Recover all thy sigh-blown age
On double pleasures; leave thy cold dispute　　　　20
Of what is fit, and not. Forsake thy cage,
　　　　　Thy rope of sands,
Which petty thoughts have made, and made to thee
　　Good cable, to enforce and draw,
　　　　　And be thy law,　　　　25
　　While thou didst wink and wouldst not see.
　　　　　Away! Take heed;

I will abroad.
Call in thy death's head there; tie up thy fears.
30   He that forbears•
     To suit and serve his need,
         Deserves his load."
But as I rav'd and grew more fierce and wild
         At every word,
35   Methought• I heard one calling, "Child!"
     And I replied, "My Lord."

forbears · does without

methought · it seemed to me

THE PULLEY

1 WHEN GOD AT first made man,
     Having a glass of blessings standing by,
"Let us," (said he) "pour on him all we can;
Let the world's riches, which dispersed lie,
5   Contract into a span."

     So strength first made a way;
Then beauty flow'd, then wisdom, honour, pleasure.
When almost all was out, God made a stay,
Perceiving that alone of all his treasure
10   Rest in the bottom lay.

     "For if I should," (said he)
"Bestow this jewel also on my creature,
He would adore my gifts instead of me,
And rest in Nature, not the God of Nature:
15   So both should losers be.

     "Yet let him keep the rest,
But keep them with repining• restlessness;
Let him be rich and weary, that at least,
If goodness lead him not, yet weariness
20   May toss him to my breast."

repining · expressing discontentment, complaining

John Milton

◀(1 6 0 8 – 1 6 7 4)▶

Milton, who has been called "the Last Renaissance Man," was born into a well-to-do middle class Protestant home. After earning the MA *at Christ's College, Cambridge, Milton entered the intense religious and political conflicts of the English Civil War. Siding with Cromwell and the Independents, who defeated the Royalists, Milton was rewarded with an office in Cromwell's Council of State. A series of misfortunes soon followed: abandonment by his first wife soon after their wedding in 1642; blindness in 1652; and the dissolution of the Commonwealth and the restoration of the monarchy in 1660, which led to the burning of Milton's books and the writer's temporary imprisonment. Despite these fluctuations of fortune, throughout his life Milton wrote prolifically – a variety of lyric poems in his youth; extensive treatises on religion and politics in the middle years; and his great epics* Paradise Lost *and* Paradise Regained *in his later years. Like dozens of poets before him, Milton tried his hand at the sonnet form. He proved to be a master of the genre, both in Italian and in English, preferring the more difficult Petrarchan rhyme scheme. In addition to the familiar themes of love and friendship, Milton used the sonnet for a variety of subjects including marriage, duty to God, and contemporary political and religious issues. Milton is one of England's greatest writers – second only to Shakespeare in influence – and perhaps England's greatest Christian poet.*

SONNET 7

1 HOW SOON HATH TIME, the subtle thief of youth,
   Stol'n on his wing my three and twentieth year!
  My hasting days fly on with full career,˙
  But my late spring no bud or blossom show'th.
5 Perhaps my semblance might deceive˙ the truth,
   That I to manhood am arriv'd so near,

career · to go at top speed in a reckless way

deceive · misrepresent

And inward ripeness doth much less appear,
That some more timely-happy spirits endu'th.˙

endu'th · endows

Yet be it less or more, or soon or slow,
It shall be still˙ in strictest measure ev'n˙   10
To that same lot, however mean or high,

still · always

ev'n · equal or adequate

Toward which Time leads me, and the will of Heav'n;
All is, if I have grace to use it so,
As ever in my great Task-Master's eye.

SONNET 9

Lady that in the prime of earliest youth,   1
  Wisely hast shunn'd the broad way and the green,
  And with those few art eminently seen
  That labor up the Hill of Heav'nly Truth,
The better part with Mary and with Ruth   5
  Chosen thou hast; and they that overween,˙
  And at thy growing virtues fret their spleen,˙
  No anger find in thee, but pity and ruth.˙

overween · overesti-
mate themselves

spleen · anger, malice

ruth · compassion, pity

Thy care is fixt and zealously attends
  To fill thy odorous lamp with deeds of light,   10
  And Hope that reaps not shame. Therefore, be sure
Thou, when the Bridegroom with his feastful friends
  Passes to bliss at the mid-hour of night,
  Hast gain'd thy entrance, Virgin wise and pure.˙

SONNET 18

Avenge, O Lord, thy slaughtered Saints,˙ whose bones   1
  Lie scattered on the Alpine mountains cold;
  Even them who kept thy truth so pure of old
  When all our fathers worshiped stocks and stones,˙
Forget not: in thy book record their groans   5
  Who were thy sheep, and in their ancient fold
  Slain by the bloody Piedmontese˙ that rolled
  Mother with infant down the rocks. Their moans
The vales redoubled to the hills, and they
  To heaven. Their martyred blood and ashes sow   10

**thy slaughtered
Saints** · the Waldensians,
a sect founded in the
12th century, were
excommunicated by
the Roman Catholic
church in 1215. Considered
early Protestants by
reformers such as Milton,
their Italian communities
were attacked by militant
Catholics seeking to wipe
out the heresy in 1655

stocks and stones ·
idols

Piedmontese ·
Piedmont is the region
in northwest Italy where
the massacre took place

11   O'er all th' Italian fields, where still doth sway
The triple tyrant:* that from these may grow
    A hundredfold* who, having learned thy way
    Early may fly the Babylonian woe.*

SONNET 19

1 WHEN I CONSIDER HOW my light is spent,
    Ere half my days, in this dark world and wide,
And that one talent* which is death to hide
Lodged with me useless, though my soul more bent
5 To serve therewith my Maker, and present
    My true account, lest he returning chide;
    "Doth God exact day-labor, light denied?"
I fondly* ask; but Patience to prevent
That murmur, soon replies, "God doth not need
10   Either man's work or his own gifts, who best
    Bear his mild yoke, they serve him best. His state
Is kingly. Thousands* at his bidding speed
    And post* o'er land and ocean without rest:
    They also serve who only stand and wait."

SONNET 23

1 METHOUGHT* I SAW my late espousèd saint*
    Brought to me like Alcestis* from the grave,
Whom Jove's great son to her glad husband gave,
Rescued from death by force though pale and faint.
5 Mine, as whom washed from spot of childbed taint,
    Purification in the old law did save,*
    And such, as yet once more I trust to have
Full sight of her in heaven without restraint,
Came vested all in white, pure as her mind.
10   Her face was veiled, yet to my fancied sight*
    Love, sweetness, goodness, in her person shined
So clear, as in no face with more delight.
    But O, as to embrace me she inclined,
    I waked, she fled, and day brought back my night.

triple tyrant · like most Protestants of his day, Milton viewed the Pope, whose tiara features 3 crowns, as a religious and political threat

grow ... hundredfold · a reference to a maxim by Tertullian (155?–220?): "the blood of the martyrs is the seed of the church"

Babylonian woe · Babylon signifies sensuality and spiritual corruption (see Revelation 17:4–6). Reformation Protestants often used Babylon as the symbol of a corrupt papacy

talent · both "ability" and a large denomination of money. Milton here refers to the parable of the talents (Matthew 25:14–30)

fondly · foolishly, naïvely

Thousands · the host of angels

post · to travel swiftly

Methought · it seemed to me

late espousèd saint · Milton may be referring to his first wife, Mary Powell, who died in 1652, or his second, Katherine Woodcock, who died in 1657, both shortly after giving birth

Alcestis · wife of Admetus who is rescued from Hades by Hercules ("Jove's great son") and returned to him veiled

as ... did save · after giving birth, women could not enter the temple until they submitted to a rite of purification (Leviticus 12)

fancied sight · Milton was blind by this time

Anne Bradstreet

⟨ca 1616–1672⟩

*Bradstreet, celebrated as the first woman poet in America, was born
in Northampton, England. Her father, Thomas Dudley, a steward
to the Earl of Lincoln, gave Anne access to the Earl's library. The
studious young woman married Simon Bradstreet in 1628 and traveled with her husband and parents to America in 1630. After initial
hardships, her living conditions in America improved considerably.
Eventually, Bradstreet's father and husband became prominent
leaders in Massachusetts. In view of her considerable domestic
duties which included rearing eight children, it is surprising that
Bradstreet had time to write at all. Her early poems, published in*
The Tenth Muse Lately Sprung up in America (1650), *are somewhat
stiff and imitative. She is best known for her later lyrical and meditative poems, expressing her love of children, husband, nature, and
Creator, published posthumously in* Several Poems Compiled with
Great Variety of Wit and Learning, Full of Delight (1678). *While main-
taining her steadfast Puritan point of view, Bradstreet occasionally
expresses a tension between her personal longing for the pleasures
of this world and her desire to submit to God's sovereignty. Anne
was happily married to Simon until her death in 1672.*

A LETTER TO HER HUSBAND, ABSENT UPON PUBLIC EMPLOYMENT

1 MY HEAD, MY HEART, mine eyes, my life, nay, more,
    My joy, my magazine* of earthly store,
If two be one, as surely thou and I,
How stayest thou there, whilst I at Ipswich* lie?
5 So many steps, head from the heart to sever,
If but a neck,* soon should we be together.
I, like the Earth this season,* mourn in black,

magazine · storehouse

Ipswich · town in northeastern Massachusetts
where Bradstreet lived

a neck · that is, if only
the distance were like
a neck that connected
head and heart

this season · winter

in's · in his

zodiac · in astronomy
and astrology, a belt of
12 regions (each with
a corresponding sign)
around the heavens
that mark the sun's
apparent annual path

Capricorn · the tenth
sign of the zodiac
where the sun lingers in
winter from December
22–January 20

Cancer · the fourth
sign of the zodiac that
demarcates high summer
from June 22–July 22

My Sun is gone so far in's• zodiac,•
Whom whilst I 'joyed, nor storms, nor frost I felt,
His warmth such frigid colds did cause to melt.   10
My chilled limbs now numbed lie forlorn;
Return, return, sweet Sol, from Capricorn,•
In this dead time, alas, what can I more
Than view those fruits which through thy heat I bore?
Which sweet contentment yield me for a space,   15
True living pictures of their father's face.
O strange effect! now thou art southward gone,
I weary grow the tedious day so long;
But when thou northward to me shalt return,
I wish my Sun may never set, but burn   20
Within the Cancer• of my glowing breast,
The welcome house of him my dearest guest.
Where ever, ever stay, and go not thence,
Till nature's sad decree shall call thee hence;
Flesh of thy flesh, bone of thy bone,   25
I here, thou there, yet both but one.

Henry Vaughan

ᚕ 1 6 2 1 – 1 6 9 5 ᚕ

Vaughan was born in Wales, and Welsh may have been his first language. He attended Oxford (1638–1640) before moving to London to study law, yet his plans to become a lawyer were interrupted by the English Civil War. Disappointed by the outcome of the war, Vaughan returned to his home in Breconshire where he became a successful, but otherwise obscure, country doctor for the last forty years of his life. Two major events shaped Vaughan's poetic career—first, the discovery of George Herbert's verse, which inspired Vaughan's poetic style and subject matter; second, the tragic death of his younger brother William in 1648, a loss which may have led to Vaughan's conversion. At his best, Vaughan is a poet of stunning visual images built on dramatic contrasts of light and darkness: "There is in God (some say)/A deep and dazzling darkness." "I saw eternity the other night/Like a great ring of pure and endless light,/All calm, as it was bright...." Like his contemporary, Blaise Pascal, Vaughan anticipated the rise of a rationalistic worldview that would reduce the cosmos to a machine, lacking mystery, miracle, and the divine presence.

THE WORLD

1

1 I SAW ETERNITY the other night,
  Like a great ring of pure and endless light,
   All calm, as it was bright;
  And round beneath it, Time in hours, days, years,
5   Driven by the spheres,
  Like a vast shadow moved, in which the world
   And all her train were hurled.

The doting lover* in his quaintest strain
　　Did there complain;
Near him, his lute, his fancy, and his flights,　　　　10
　　Wit's sour delights,
With gloves and knots,* the silly snares of pleasure,
　　Yet his dear treasure
All scattered lay, while he his eyes did pour
　　Upon a flower.　　　　15

The doting lover · in
this and the following
lines, the narrator consid-
ers four common forms of
"madness": erotic passion
("the doting lover"), thirst
for power ("the dark-
some statesman"), greed
("the fearful miser"),
and sensualism ("the
downright epicure")

knots · love tokens

2

THE DARKSOME STATESMAN hung with weights and woe
　　Like a thick midnight-fog moved there so slow
　　He did nor stay, nor go;
　　Condemning thoughts (like sad eclipses) scowl
　　　　Upon his soul,　　　　20
　　And clouds of crying witnesses without
　　　　Pursued him with one shout.
　　Yet digged the mole, and, lest his ways be found
　　　　Worked underground,
　　Where he did clutch his prey. But One did see　　25
　　　　That policy:*
　　Churches and altars fed him; perjuries
　　　　Were gnats and flies;
　　It rained about him blood and tears, but he
　　　　Drank them as free.　　　　30

policy · approach or
strategy

3

THE FEARFUL MISER on a heap of rust*
　　Sat pining all his life there, did scarce trust
　　　　His own hands with the dust;
　　Yet would not place one piece above,* but lives
　　　　In fear of thieves.　　　　35
　　Thousands there were as frantic as himself,
　　　　And hugged each one his pelf:*
　　The downright epicure placed heaven in sense,
　　　　And scorned pretense;
　　While others slipped into a wide excess,　　　　40
　　　　Said little less;
　　The weaker sort slight, trivial wares enslave

heap of rust · wealth
that decays. See
Matthew 6:19–20

place one piece
above · invest to
receive interest

pelf · belongings or
wealth

Who think them brave,•
And poor, despisèd Truth sat counting by•
45   Their victory.

brave · fashionable, showy

counting by · watching

4

Y ET SOME, WHO ALL this while did weep and sing,
And sing and weep, soared up into the Ring;
    But most would use no wing.
"O fools!" (said I) "thus to prefer dark night
50   Before true light!
To live in grots• and caves, and hate the day
    Because it shows the way,
The way which from this dead and dark abode
    Leads up to God,
55 A way where you might tread the sun and be
    More bright than he!"
But as I did their madness so discuss
    One whispered thus:
This ring the bridegroom did for none provide,
60   *But for his bride.•*

grots · grottoes

JOHN 2:16–17

A LL THAT IS IN THE WORLD, *the lust of the flesh, the lust of
the eyes, and the pride of life, is not of the father but is of the
world. And the world passeth away, and the lusts thereof, but he
that doeth the will of God abideth forever.*

RELIGION

1 M Y GOD, WHEN I walk in those groves,
And leaves thy spirit doth still fan,
I see in each shade that there grows
An angel talking with a man.

5 Under a juniper, some house,
Or the cool myrtle's canopy,
Others beneath an oak's green boughs,
Or at some fountain's bubbling eye;•

Under a juniper . . . bubbling eye · in this stanza, the poet summarizes the natural settings where angels meet humans in the Hebrew Bible: under the juniper (1 Kings 19:5), under the myrtle (Zechariah 1:8–11), under the oak (Judges 6:11), and beside a fountain (Genesis 16:7)

Here Jacob dreams and wrestles; there
Elias by a raven is fed,   10
Another time by the angel, where
He brings him water with his bread;

In Abr'ham's tent the winged guests
(O how familiar• then was heaven!)
Eat, drink, discourse, sit down, and rest   15
Until the cool, and shady even;•

Nay thou thyself, my God, in fire,
Whirlwinds and clouds, and the soft voice•
Speak'st there so much, that I admire
We have no conf'rence in these days;   20

Is the truce broke? or 'cause we have
A mediator now with thee,
Dost thou therefore old treaties wave
And by appeals from him decree?•

Or is 't so, as some green heads• say   25
That now all miracles must cease?
Though thou hast promis'd they should stay
The tokens of the Church, and peace;

No, no; Religion is a spring
That from some secret, golden mine   30
Derives her birth, and thence doth bring
Cordials• in every drop and wine;

But in her long, and hidden course
Passing through the earth's dark veins,
Grows still from better unto worse,   35
And both her taste, and color stains,

Then drilling• on, learns to increase
False echoes, and confused sounds,
And unawares doth often seize
On veins of sulfur• under ground;   40

Jacob dreams … shady even · the poet here presents examples of heavenly messengers interacting with people: Jacob wrestles with an angel (Genesis 32:24–30); Elijah (Elias) is fed by the ravens and by an angel (1 Kings 17:6 and 19:6); Abraham entertains three angelic visitors (Genesis 18:1–8)

familiar · close, intimate

Whirlwinds … soft voice · Vaughan seeks to distinguish the angelic visitations from those direct visits by God who appears in fire (Exodus 3:2), in a whirlwind (Job 38:1), in a cloud (Exodus 13:21), and "in a still and soft voice" (1 Kings 19:12)

Is the truce … decree? · the poet here asks whether the coming of Christ the mediator signals the end of God's direct interaction with human beings

green heads · inexperienced people, that is, religious innovators

Cordials · drinks that restore the heart

drilling · dripping

veins of sulfur · the underground stream becomes contaminated

41 So poison'd, breaks forth in some clime,
And at first sight doth many please,
But drunk, is puddle, or mere slime
And 'stead of physic, a disease;

45 Just such a tainted sink* we have
Like that Samaritan's dead well,*
Nor must we for the kernel crave
Because most voices like the shell.*

Heal then these waters, Lord; or bring thy flock,
50 Since these are troubled, to the springing rock,*
Look down great Master of the feast; O shine,
And turn once more our water into wine!*

sink · sewer, cesspool

**Samaritan's dead
well** · The well visited by
the Samaritan woman is
"dead" compared to the
living water offered by
Jesus (John 4:5–15)

shell · outward
appearance

the springing rock ·
Christ (see 1 Corinthians
10:4)

water into wine · a
reference to Christ's first
miracle (John 2)

SONG OF SOLOMON 4:12

M Y SISTER, MY SPOUSE, *is as a garden enclosed, as a spring
shut up, and a fountain sealed up.*

AND DO THEY SO?

*Et enim res Creatæ exerto Capite observantes expectant
revelationem Filiorum Dei.* (Romans 8:19)

Et ... Dei · "For the
creatures, watching with
lifted head, wait for the
revealing of the sons of
God" (Beza's Latin translation of Romans 8:19)

1

1 A ND DO THEY* SO? have they a sense
Of ought but influence?*
Can they their heads lift, and expect,
And groan too?* Why th' Elect*
5 Can do no more: my volumes said
They were all dull, and dead,
They judg'd them senseless, and their state
Wholly inanimate.
Go, go; seal up thy looks,*
10 And burn thy books.

they · earthly creatures

influence · the influence of the stars

Can ... groan too? ·
the poet wonders
whether the creatures
of nature can feel pain
and entertain hope
for Christ's return as
human beings do

Elect · God's chosen

looks · eyes

2

I WOULD I WERE A stone, or tree,
Or flower by pedigree,
Or some poor highway herb, or spring

To flow, or bird to sing!
Then should I (tied to one sure state,)   15

date · day of death　　　All day expect my date;˙
But I am sadly loose, and stray

giddy · showy, wild　　　A giddy˙ blast each way;
O let me not thus range!
Thou canst not change.   20

3

SOMETIMES I SIT with thee, and tarry
　An hour, or so, then vary.

Thy other … mean ·　Thy other creatures in this scene
the lower creatures　　　Thee only aim, and mean;˙
worship and honor
their Creator without　Some rise to seek thee, and with heads   25
fail, unlike human　　　Erect peep from their beds;
beings who are fickle
Others, whose birth is in the tomb,
　And cannot quit the womb,
　Sigh there, and groan for thee,
　Their liberty.   30

4

O LET NOT ME DO less! Shall they
　Watch, while I sleep, or play?
Shall I thy mercies still abuse
　With fancies, friends, or news?

brook · endure　O brook˙ it not! Thy blood is mine,   35
　And my soul should be thine;

stop · withhold　O brook it not! Why wilt thou stop˙
　After whole showers one drop?
　Sure, thou wilt joy to see
　Thy sheep with thee.   40

Edward Taylor

◁(ca 1642–1729)▷

*Born in Sketchley, England, Taylor emigrated to America in 1668
because of the restrictions placed on Puritans. After graduating
from Harvard in 1671, he moved to Westfield, Massachusetts, where
he worked until his death as a minister to the small farming community. In 1674 he married Elizabeth Fitch, who bore him eight
children, five of whom died in infancy. In 1692, he married Ruth
Wyllys, who bore six children. Taylor's work in Westfield included
not only the spiritual tasks of ministering to the community, but also
growing crops to feed his large family. About 1682, he began a series
of poems written to prepare himself for the Lord's Supper. These
poems, composed over a period of 43 years (collected under the title*
Preparatory Meditations), *express Puritan spirituality through rustic
imagery and typology based on Scripture.* Preparatory Meditations
*was unpublished and virtually unknown until 1937 when it was
discovered in the Yale University library. Today Taylor is recognized
as one of the most significant poets in colonial America.*

MEDITATION 8 (*first series*)

John 6:51. I am the living bread.

1 I KENNING* THROUGH astronomy divine
  The world's bright battlement, wherein I spy
A golden path my pencil cannot line,
  From that bright throne unto my threshold lie.
5 And while my puzzled thoughts about it pour,
  I find the bread of life in't at my door.

When that this bird of paradise* put in,
  This wicker cage (my corpse)* to tweedle* praise
Had pecked the fruit forbade: and so did fling

kenning · discovering, discerning

bird of paradise ·
tradition held that this
species of bird never
lands on the ground.
Taylor uses the image
to signify the soul

corpse · body

tweedle · sing

429

Away its food; and lost its golden days;   10
   It fell into celestial famine sore:
And never could attain a morsel more.

Alas! alas! Poor bird, what wilt thou do?
   The creatures' field no food for souls e'er gave.
And if thou knock at angels' doors they show   15
   An empty barrel: they no soul bread have.
   Alas! Poor bird, the world's white loaf is done,
   And cannot yield thee here the smallest crumb.

In this sad state, God's tender bowels• run
   Out streams of grace: and he to end all strife   20
The purest wheat in Heaven, his dear-dear Son
   Grinds, and kneads up into this bread of life.
   Which bread of life from Heaven down came and stands
   Dished on thy table up by angels' hands.

Did God mold up this bread in Heaven, and bake,   25
   Which from his table came, and to thine goeth?
Doth he bespeak thee thus: "This soul bread take.
   Come, eat thy fill of this thy God's white loaf"?
   "It's food too fine for angels, yet come, take
   And eat thy fill. It's Heaven's sugar cake."   30

What grace is this knead in this loaf? This thing
   Souls are but petty things it to admire.
Ye angels, help: This fill would to the brim
   Heav'n's whelm'd-down• crystal meal bowl, yea and higher
   This bread of life dropped in thy mouth, doth cry: 35
   "Eat, eat me, soul, and thou shalt never die."

tender bowels · just as the heart is thought to be the seat of love, the bowels were thought to be the seat of pity and sympathetic emotions

whelm'd-down · turned over

Alfred, Lord Tennyson

⟨ 1 8 0 9 – 1 8 9 2 ⟩

Tennyson, born in Lincolnshire, England, and educated at Cambridge, was made poet laureate of Great Britain in 1850. Although much of his anthologized and most-remembered poetry comes from his collection of Arthurian verse, Idylls of the King, *his collection of poems entitled* In Memoriam *(1850) contains his most passionate and most vulnerable poetry. Like many of his contemporaries, Tennyson encountered scientific revelations which seemed to cast suspicion where once only faith and hope existed. The death of his close friend Arthur Henry Hallam in 1833 inspired an angry, grieving Tennyson to write* In Memoriam, *a collection of 132 separate poems which chronicle his struggle with faith in God, grief at the loss of his friend, and the broader questions of free will, doubt, and the very existence of a benevolent Creator. Ultimately, the work — one of the greatest elegies in the English language — records the growth of faith in the face of fear and uncertainty.*

from IN MEMORIAM A. H. H.

*Obiit** MDCCCXXXIII

1 STRONG SON OF GOD, immortal Love,
    Whom we, that have not seen thy face,
      By faith, and faith alone, embrace,
Believing where we cannot prove;*

5 Thine are these orbs of light and shade;
    Thou madest Life in man and brute;
      Thou madest Death; and lo, thy foot
Is on the skull which thou hast made.

Thou wilt not leave us in the dust:
10   Thou madest man, he knows not why,

Obiit · "died" (Latin). The epigraph cites Hallam's death in 1833

have not seen … cannot prove · see John 20:29

431

He thinks he was not made to die;   11
And thou hast made him: thou art just.

Thou seemest human and divine,
    The highest, holiest manhood, thou.
    Our wills are ours, we know not how;   15
Our wills are ours, to make them thine.

systems · theological or
philosophical paradigms

Our little systems˙ have their day;
    They have their day and cease to be;
    They are but broken lights of thee,
And thou, O Lord, art more than they.   20

We have but faith: we cannot know,
    For knowledge is of things we see;
    And yet we trust it comes from thee,
A beam in darkness: let it grow.

Let knowledge grow from more to more,   25
    But more of reverence in us dwell;
    That mind and soul, according well,
May make one music as before,

But vaster. We are fools and slight;
    We mock thee when we do not fear: 30
    But help thy foolish ones to bear;
Help thy vain worlds to bear thy light.

Forgive what seemed my sin in me,
    What seemed my worth since I began;
    For merit lives from man to man,   35
And not from man, O Lord, to thee.

Forgive my grief for one removed,
    Thy creature, whom I found so fair.
    I trust he lives in thee, and there
I find him worthier to be loved.   40

41 Forgive these wild and wandering cries,
    Confusions of a wasted youth;
    Forgive them where they fail in truth,
And in thy wisdom make me wise.

✦ ✦ ✦

96

1 Y OU SAY, BUT WITH no touch of scorn,
    Sweet-hearted, you,˙ whose light blue eyes
    Are tender over drowning flies,
You tell me, doubt is Devil-born.

5 I know not: one˙ indeed I knew
    In many a subtle question versed,
    Who touched a jarring lyre at first,
But ever strove to make it true;

Perplexed in faith, but pure in deeds,
10   At last he beat his music out.
    There lives more faith in honest doubt,
Believe me, than in half the creeds.

He fought his doubts and gathered strength,
    He would not make his judgment blind,
15   He faced the specters of the mind
And laid them; thus he came at length

To find a stronger faith his own,
    And Power was with him in the night,
    Which makes the darkness and the light,
20 And dwells not in the light alone,

But in the darkness and the cloud,
    As over Sinai's peaks of old,˙
    While Israel made their gods of gold,
Although the trumpet blew so loud.

Sweet-hearted, you · the narrator addresses someone whose faith is serene and uncomplicated

one · Hallam

Sinai's peaks of old · Exodus 32:1–6. See also Deuteronomy 4:11 and 5:23

George MacDonald

♙⟨1842–1905⟩⟩

Poet, mystic, preacher, and novelist, MacDonald was born in Aberdeen, Scotland, to devout Congregationalist parents. After preaching for three years (1850–1853), he resigned in order to devote himself to writing. His most enduring works are symbolic fantasies, including the children's classics At the Back of the North Wind *(1871) and* The Princess and the Goblin *(1872). Through his visionary stories, novels, and poems, MacDonald demonstrated the profound links between faith and imagination. In this respect, he inspired C. S. Lewis, J. R. R. Tolkien, Madeleine L'Engle, and other 20th-century writers of spiritually-endowed fantasy and fiction. "Obedience" plays with a familiar theme in religious verse – "psychomachia" or soul struggle. In this case the struggle is between two goods – the romantic lure of nature and the urgent need to care for oppressed workers in England's nightmarish industrial cities. In this setting, obedience is not oppressive, but liberating. "Obedience is the opener of eyes," writes MacDonald. "Every obedience is the opening of another door into the boundless universe of life."*

OBEDIENCE

1 I SAID, "LET ME walk in the fields."
   He said, "No, walk in the town."
I said, "There are no flowers there."
   He said, "No flowers, but a crown."

5 I said, "But the skies are black;
   There is nothing but noise and din."
And He wept as He sent me back;
   "There is more," He said; "there is sin."

I said, "But the air is thick,
    And fogs are veiling the sun."
He answered, "Yet souls are sick,
    And souls in the dark undone."   10

I said, "I shall miss the light,
    And friends will miss me, they say."
He answered, "Choose to-night
    If I am to miss you, or they."   15

I pleaded for time to be given.
    He said, "Is it hard to decide?
It will not seem hard in heaven
    To have followed the steps of your Guide."   20

I cast one look at the fields,
    Then set my face to the town;
He said, "My child, do you yield?
    Will you leave the flowers for the crown?"

Then into His hand went mine,   25
    And into my heart came He;
And I walk in a light divine
    That path I had feared to see.

Christina Rossetti

Growing up in a home divided between the passions of an Italian father and the moral rigidity of an Anglo-Italian mother, Rossetti's life is marked by two conflicting themes: her unconventional passion for intellect and her search for God and His divine direction. These tensions led her to write some of the most arresting and original religious poems of the Victorian Age. Two men close to Rossetti, William Morris and her brother Dante Gabriel Rossetti, initiated the Pre-Raphaelite Movement, which seems to have affected Rossetti's style—her tendency towards naturalistic detail, pictorialism, symbolism, and sensuousness. In 1871 Christina contracted Graves' Disease, a form of hyperthyroidism, which froze her face like a mask. Though racked by pain for the next twenty years, she continued to publish works of devotional poetry and prose, including a commentary on the book of Revelation, The Face of the Deep, *published two years before her death to cancer.*

GOOD FRIDAY

1   Am I a stone, and not a sheep,
    That I can stand, O Christ, beneath Thy cross,
    To number drop by drop Thy Blood's slow loss,
And yet not weep?

5 Not so those women loved
    Who with exceeding grief lamented Thee;
    Not so fallen Peter weeping bitterly;
Not so the thief was moved;

10 Not so the Sun and Moon
    Which hid their faces in a starless sky.

437

A horror of great darkness at broad noon –
I, only I.

Yet give not o'er
    But seek Thy sheep, true Shepherd of the flock;   15
    Greater than Moses, turn and look once more
And smite a rock.

UP-HILL

Does the road wind up-hill all the way?   1
    Yes, to the very end.
Will the day's journey take the whole long day?
    From morn to night, my friend.

But is there for the night a resting-place?   5
    A roof for when the slow dark hours begin.
May not the darkness hide it from my face?
    You cannot miss that inn.

Shall I meet other wayfarers at night?
    Those who have gone before.   10
Then must I knock, or call when just in sight?
    They will not keep you standing at that door.

Shall I find comfort, travel-sore and weak?
    Of labour you shall find the sum.
Will there be beds for me and all who seek?   15
    Yea, beds for all who come.

Emily Dickinson

(1 8 3 1 – 1 8 8 6)

Dickinson, born and reared in Amherst, Massachusetts, published only a handful of poems in her lifetime. After her death in 1886, it was discovered that she had composed almost 1800 poems, many written on the backs of letters or receipts. Her close friend Thomas Wentworth Higgins found himself baffled when faced with categorizing her poetry since Dickinson delves deeply into nature, glances with irony at society and its functions, and puzzles over questions of faith and will. Her poetry raises far more questions than it answers, for Dickinson found every subject – be it snake, butterfly, bee, or even a closed door – an inspiration, an impetus for thought or emotion. Dickinson is never keen on religious institutions (rarely mentioning organized religion at all), but her poetry is suffused with religious questions. She is notoriously honest about her doubts: "doubt like the mosquito buzzes round my faith," she writes. But she can be serenely confident as well: "I know that He exists. Somewhere – in Silence –." She compares herself to the Old Testament patriarch who wrestles with an angel (Genesis 32:25): "Pugilist and Poet, Jacob was correct." Dickinson seems at her best challenging the deity whose existence she never doubts.

A WOUNDED DEER LEAPS HIGHEST

1 A Wounded Deer – leaps highest –
　　I've heard the Hunter tell
'Tis but the Ecstasy of death –
And then the Brake* is still!

Brake · thicket

5 The Smitten Rock that gushes!
The trampled Steel that springs!
A Cheek is always redder
Just where the Hectic* stings!

Héctic · wasp

Mirth is the Mail* of Anguish –
In which it Cautious Arm,   10
Lest anybody spy the blood
And "you're hurt" exclaim!

Mail · chain mail, a type of armor

❧ THIS WORLD IS NOT CONCLUSION

This World is not Conclusion.   1
A Species* stands beyond –
Invisible, as Music –
But positive, as Sound –
It beckons, and it baffles –   5
Philosophy – don't know –
And through a Riddle, at the last –
Sagacity, must go –
To guess it, puzzles scholars –
To gain it, Men have borne   10
Contempt of Generations
And Crucifixion, shown –
Faith slips – and laughs, and rallies –
Blushes, if any see –
Plucks at a twig of Evidence –   15
And asks a Vane,* the way –
Much Gesture, from the Pulpit –
Strong Hallelujahs roll –
Narcotics cannot still the Tooth
That nibbles at the soul –   20

Species · form

Vane · a weathervane

ɪ MEASURE EVERY GRIEF I MEET

I measure every Grief I meet   1
With narrow, probing, Eyes –
I wonder if It weighs like Mine –
Or has an Easier size.

I wonder if They bore it long –   5
Or did it just begin –
I could not tell the Date of Mine –
It feels so old a pain –

I wonder if it hurts to live –
10 And if They have to try –
And whether – could They choose between –
It would not be – to die –

I note that Some – gone patient long –
At length, renew their smile –
15 An imitation of a Light
That has so little Oil –

I wonder if when Years have piled –
Some Thousands – on the Harm –
That hurt them early – such a lapse
20 Could give them any Balm –

Or would they go on aching still
Through Centuries of Nerve –
Enlightened to a larger Pain –
In Contrast with the Love –

25 The Grieved – are many – I am told –
There is the various Cause –
Death – is but one – and comes but once –
And only nails the eyes –

There's Grief of Want – and Grief of Cold –
30 A sort they call "Despair" –
There's Banishment from native Eyes –
In sight of Native Air –

And though I may not guess the kind –
Correctly – yet to me
35 A piercing Comfort it affords
In passing Calvary –

To note the fashions – of the Cross –
And how they're mostly worn –
Still fascinated to presume
40 That Some – are like My Own –

FAITH — IS THE PIERLESS BRIDGE

Faith — is the Pierless* Bridge   1
Supporting what We see
Unto the Scene that We do not —
Too slender for the eye

It bears the Soul as bold   5
As it were rocked in Steel
With Arms of Steel at either side —
It joins — behind the Veil

To what, could We presume
The Bridge would cease to be   10
To Our far, vacillating Feet
A first Necessity.

Pierless · a pun; both "peerless" (unmatched), and "without piers" (lacking piles or pillars; without support or a concrete foundation)

☙ THERE CAME A DAY

There came a Day at Summer's full,   1
Entirely for me —
I thought that such were for the Saints,
Where Resurrections — be —

The Sun, as common, went abroad,   5
The flowers, accustomed, blew,*
As if no soul the solstice passed
That maketh all things new —

The time was scarce profaned, by speech —
The symbol of a word   10
Was needless, as at Sacrament,
The Wardrobe — of our Lord —

Each was to each The Sealed Church,
Permitted to commune this — time —
Lest we too awkward show   15
At Supper of the Lamb.

blew · bloomed

The Hours slid fast – as Hours will,
Clutched tight, by greedy hands –
So faces on two decks, look back,
20 Bound to opposing lands –

And so when all the time had leaked,
Without external sound
Each bound the Other's Crucifix –
We gave no other Bond –

25 Sufficient troth, that we shall rise –
Deposed – at length, the Grave –
To that new Marriage,
Justified – through Calvaries of Love –

Gerard Manley Hopkins

◈(1844–1889)◈

Hopkins wrote stunningly original poetry, though it was virtually unknown until its posthumous publication in 1918. Born in Stratford, Essex, and educated at Balliol College, Oxford, Hopkins fell under the sway of the Oxford Movement, a religious reform movement that led to Hopkins's decision to enter the Roman Catholic Church in 1866. Soon after, Hopkins joined the Jesuit Order and in 1877 was ordained a priest. He served various parishes, including one in a Liverpool slum. In 1884 he became Classics Professor at University College, Dublin. Hopkins's poems are challenging in their use of word coinages, archaic dialect terms, unusual meter (which he called "sprung rhythm"), extraordinary compactness (including the dropping of unnecessary words), alliteration, and puns. Something of a late Romantic, Hopkins believed that the distinctive designs of nature ultimately lead one to Jesus Christ. Nature, in fact, is the bridge between the finite and the infinite. To experience beauty is to discover the uniqueness of every created form, and therefore to be lifted to God in heart and mind. Not all of Hopkins's poems are celebrations of God in creation; others are wrenching, Job-like inquiries into the reasons for, and God's place in, human suffering.

GOD'S GRANDEUR

1 THE WORLD IS CHARGED with the grandeur of God.·
   It will flame out, like shining from shook foil;·
     It gathers to a greatness, like the ooze of oil
  Crushed.· Why do men then now not reck his rod?·
5 Generations have trod, have trod, have trod;
     And all is seared with trade; bleared, smeared with toil;
     And wears man's smudge and shares man's smell: the soil
  Is bare now, nor can foot feel, being shod.

charged . . . God · Hopkins writes: "All things therefore are charged with love, are charged with God and if we know how to touch them give off sparks and take fire, yield drops and flow, ring and tell of him" (*Sermons and Devotional Writings*)

shook foil · Hopkins explained this image in a letter: "I mean foil in its sense of leaf or tinsel. . . . Shaken goldfoil gives off broad glares like sheet lightning and . . . a sort of fork lightning too"

ooze . . . Crushed · oil flowing from crushed olives

Why . . . his rod? · if nature is so full of God's grandeur, why do men not take heed of ("reck") God's authority ("his rod")?

445

for · despite

And, for* all this, nature is never spent;
    There lives the dearest freshness deep down things;   10
And though the last lights off the black West went
    Oh, morning, at the brown brink eastward, springs –
Because the Holy Ghost over the bent
    World broods with warm breast and with ah! bright wings.

PIED* BEAUTY

pied · multicolored

couple-color · paired
or linked (perhaps
complementary) colors;
consider the polarities
in line 9, "swift, slow;
sweet, sour; adazzle, dim"

brinded · streaked

stipple · speckles
or spots

Fresh-firecoal chest-
nut-falls · a shower of
freshly fallen chestnuts
looks like coals of fire

áll trádes · Hopkins'
spelling includes stresses.
He wrote in what he
called "sprung rhythm,"
by which he meant that
one accented syllable of
the poem often follows
directly upon another

counter · contrary

tucked · plucked

indoors · within

Selves · Hopkins coins
a verb: "to selve" means
"to express one's own
unique being, one's
essential individuality
and particularity"

justices · another of
Hopkins' invented verbs:
"to act in a just, holy,
and gracious manner"

GLORY BE TO GOD for dappled things –   1
    For skies of couple-color* as a brinded* cow;
        For rose-moles all in stipple* upon trout that swim;
Fresh-firecoal chestnut-falls,* finches' wings;
    Landscape plotted and pieced – fold, fallow, and plough;   5
        And áll trádes,* their gear and tackle and trim.

All things counter,* original, spare, strange;
    Whatever is fickle, freckled (who knows how?)
        With swift, slow; sweet, sour; adazzle, dim;
He fathers-forth whose beauty is past change: 10
        Praise him.

AS KINGFISHERS CATCH FIRE

AS KINGFISHERS CATCH FIRE, dragonflies draw flame;   1
    As tumbled over rim in roundy wells
        Stones ring; like each tucked* string tells, each hung bell's
Bow swung finds tongue to fling out broad its name;
Each mortal thing does one thing and the same: 5
    Deals out that being indoors* each one dwells;
    Selves* – goes itself; *myself* it speaks and spells,
Crying *What I do is me: for that I came.*

I say more: the just man justices;*
    Keeps gráce: thát keeps all his goings graces;   10
Acts in God's eye what in God's eye he is –
    Chríst. For Christ plays in ten thousand places,
Lovely in limbs, and lovely in eyes not his
    To the Father through the features of men's faces.

[CARRION COMFORT]*

1 Not, I'll not, carrion comfort, Despair, not feast on thee;
  Not untwist – slack they may be – these last strands of man
  In me ór, most weary, cry *I can no more.* I can;
  Can something, hope, wish day come, not choose not to be.

5 But ah, but O thou terrible, why wouldst thou rude* on me
  Thy wring-world right foot rock?* lay a lionlimb against me? scan.
  With darksome devouring eyes my bruisèd bones? and fan,*
  O in turns of tempest, me heaped there; me frantic to avoid
      thee and flee?

  Why? That my chaff might fly; my grain lie, sheer and clear.
10 Nay in all that toil, that coil,* since (seems) I kissed the rod,*
  Hand rather, my heart lo! lapped strength, stole joy, would laugh,
      chéer.
  Cheer whom though? The hero whose heaven-handling flung
      me, fóot tród
  Me? or mé that fóught him? O which one? is it each one? That
      níght, that year
  Of now done darkness I wretch lay wrestling with (my God!)
      my God.

[Carrion Comfort] · Hopkins did not supply this title; it was given by his friend Robert Bridges (1844–1930)

rude · roughly, violently

why wouldst thou … rock? · why would you, God, who wrings the world with your power, violently rock your foot on me?

fan · to separate the kernel of grain from its husk (chaff) by means of a fan

coil · tumult

kissed the rod · the rod is the symbol of God's chastening; hence Hopkins is describing acceptance of God's authority – including the necessity of one's own suffering

T. S. Eliot

◄(1 8 8 8 – 1 9 6 5)►

Born in St. Louis, Missouri, Eliot studied philosophy at Harvard
and later pursued literary studies in Europe. Settling in England
soon after the outbreak of World War I, Eliot married, accepting a
position with Lloyd's Bank and pursuing his poetry after business
hours. A nervous breakdown was precipitated by his wife's mental
illness – she was eventually confined to an institution, where she
died in 1947 – and in the midst of his personal crisis Eliot turned to
the Christian faith. Confirmed in the Anglican Church in 1927, he
remained a practicing churchman to his death in 1965. In its latter
phase, Eliot's poetry is explicitly Christian, arising from an aware-
ness of how spiritual reality transcends merely human conceptions
of time, place, and temporal purpose. As poet-critic Stephen
Spender has remarked of these works, "Reality is that moment
in time which, for the person experiencing it, stands outside time."
Eliot was awarded the Nobel Prize for Literature in 1948.

JOURNEY OF THE MAGI

1   A COLD COMING we had of it,
      Just the worst time of the year
  For a journey, and such a long journey:
  The ways deep and the weather sharp,˙
5   The very dead of winter.
  And the camels galled, sore-footed, refractory,˙
  Lying down in the melting snow.
  There were times we regretted
  The summer palaces on slopes, the terraces,
10 And the silken girls bringing sherbet.
  Then the camel men cursing and grumbling
  And running away, and wanting their liquor and women,

A cold … sharp ˙
Eliot here quotes from
a sermon by renowned
English preacher
Lancelot Andrewes
(1555–1626)

refractory ˙ stubborn,
resisting control

449

And the night-fires going out, and the lack of shelters,
And the cities hostile and the towns unfriendly
And the villages dirty and charging high prices: 15
A hard time we had of it.
At the end we preferred to travel all night,
Sleeping in snatches,
With the voices singing in our ears, saying
That this was all folly.   20

Then at dawn we came down to a temperate valley,
Wet, below the snow line, smelling of vegetation;
With a running stream and a water-mill beating the darkness,
And three trees on the low sky,
And an old white horse galloped away in the meadow.   25
Then we came to a tavern with vine-leaves over the lintel,
Six hands at an open door dicing for pieces of silver,
And feet kicking the empty wine-skins.•
But there was no information, and so we continued
And arrived at evening, not a moment too soon   30
Finding the place; it was (you may say) satisfactory.

All this was a long time ago, I remember,
And I would do it again, but set down
This set down
This: were we led all that way for   35
Birth or Death? There was a Birth, certainly,
We had evidence and no doubt. I had seen birth and death,
But had thought they were different; this Birth was
Hard and bitter agony for us, like Death, our death.
We returned to our places, these Kingdoms,   40
But no longer at ease here, in the old dispensation,•
With an alien people clutching their gods.
I should be glad of another death.

Then at dawn...wine-skins · a concentration of biblical echoes and allusions occurs in this section (see Hosea 10:1; John 15:1–2; Revelation 6:2; Luke 23:34; Matthew 26:14–15; Luke 5:36–39)

old dispensation · a reference to the social and religious system that existed prior to Christ's coming

C. S. Lewis

⟨ 1 8 9 8 – 1 9 6 3 ⟩

Lewis, perhaps the 20th century's most famous convert to Christianity, has been called "the chief Christian tutor to the English-speaking world." He was born in Belfast, Ireland (now Northern Ireland), but lived most of his adult life in Oxford where he taught at Magdalen College (1925–1954). From 1954 until his death, he was professor of medieval and renaissance literature at Cambridge. A skeptic for many years, Lewis underwent a formal conversion in 1929 (as reported in his auto-biography Surprised by Joy). *Lewis is best known for his science fiction; for his series of children's fantasy,* The Chronicles of Narnia *(1950–1956); and for his witty, intelligent defenses of Christian doctrine such as* The Problem of Pain *(1940),* The Screwtape Letters *(1942),* Miracles *(1947), and* Mere Christianity *(1952). Late in life, Lewis met and married Joy Davidman Gresham, an American poet. Their brief, remarkable mar-riage has been popularized through William Nicholson's stageplay and screenplay* Shadowlands. *Less well-known for his poetry, Lewis is, nonetheless, an accomplished lyricist of Christian conviction.*

NO BEAUTY WE COULD DESIRE

1 YES, YOU ARE ALWAYS everywhere. But I,
   Hunting in such immeasurable forests,
   Could never bring the noble Hart* to bay.*

Hart · an adult male deer

bring … to bay · to corner an animal using dogs

   The scent was too perplexing for my hounds;
5 Nowhere sometimes, then again everywhere.
   Other scents, too, seemed to them almost the same.

   Therefore I turn my back on the unapproachable
   Stars and horizons and all musical sounds,
   Poetry itself, and the winding stair of thought.

Leaving the forests where you are pursued in vain   10
– Often a mere white gleam – I turn instead
To the appointed place where you pursue.

Not in Nature, not even in Man, but in one
Particular Man, with a date, so tall, weighing
So much, talking Aramaic, having learned a trade;   15

Not in all food, not in all bread and wine
(Not, I mean, as my littleness requires)
But this wine, this bread ... no beauty we could desire.˙

no ... desire · of the
Messiah, the prophet
says, "there is no beauty
that we should desire
him" (Isaiah 53:2)

STEPHEN TO LAZARUS

BUT WAS I THE first martyr, who   1
      Gave up no more than life, while you,
Already free among the dead,
Your rags stripped off, your fetters shed,
Surrendered what all other men   5
Irrevocably keep, and when
Your battered ship at anchor lay
Seemingly safe in the dark bay
No ripple stirs, obediently
Put out a second time to sea   10
Well knowing that your death (in vain
Died once) must all be died again?

from FIVE SONNETS

I

YOU THINK THAT WE who do not shout and shake   1
      Our fists at God when youth or bravery die
Have colder blood or hearts less apt to ache
Than yours who rail.˙ I know you do. Yet why?
You have what sorrow always longs to find,   5
Someone to blame, some enemy in chief;
Anger's the anæsthetic of the mind,
It does men good, it fumes away their grief.
We feel the stroke like you; so far our fate

rail · to cry out, criticize

10   Is equal. After that, for us begin
     Half-hopeless labours, learning not to hate,
     And then to want, and then (perhaps) to win
     A high, unearthly comfort, angel's food,
     That seems at first mockery to flesh and blood.

Dietrich Bonhœffer

◀(1906–1945)▶

After a two-year imprisonment, Bonhœffer was hanged in the Flossenburg concentration camp on April 9, 1945, for complicity in an assassination plot against Adolf Hitler. A Lutheran pastor and theologian, Bonhœffer had objected to Germany's anti-Jewish legislation in 1933, consequently being forced from his pulpit and into exile. In London, he temporarily ministered to German congregations. Just before the Second World War, he was invited to the United States for a lecture tour and refused the political asylum that was offered. He returned to Germany as the war began, joining the Resistance forces in his homeland. Bonhœffer's best known works are The Cost of Discipleship *(1948),* Letters and Papers from Prison *(1953), and* Ethics *(1955). His writings attest to an emerging theological system that, though incomplete, is rich in suggestive detail. A pervasive and unifying theme is that there is no separation of the religious realm from the secular. Significantly, when he spoke of the earth, Bonhœffer frequently added "in which the Cross of Jesus Christ is planted." The Christian, in other words, must identify with and suffer for the world as did Christ. In the summer of 1944, while imprisoned in Tegel, Berlin's military prison, Bonhœffer wrote "Who Am I?"*

WHO AM I?

1 Wʜᴏ ᴀᴍ I? They often tell me
　 I stepped from my cell's confinement
calmly, cheerfully, firmly,
like a Squire from his country house.

5 Who am I? They often tell me
I used to speak to my warders˙

warders · guards

455

freely and friendly and clearly,
as though it were mine to command.

Who am I? They also tell me
I bore the days of misfortune   10
equably,* smilingly, proudly,
like one accustomed to win.

equably · evenly,
without harsh extremes

Am I then really that which other men tell of?
Or am I only what I myself know of myself?
Restless and longing and sick, like a bird in a cage,   15
struggling for breath, as though hands were compressing my throat,
yearning for colors, for flowers, for the voices of birds,
thirsting for words of kindness, for neighborliness,
tossing in expectation of great events,
powerlessly trembling for friends at an infinite distance,   20
weary and empty at praying, at thinking, at making,
faint, and ready to say farewell to it all.

Who am I? This or the Other?
Am I one person today and tomorrow another?
Am I both at once? A hypocrite before others,   25
and before myself a contemptible woebegone weakling?
Or is something within me still like a beaten army
fleeing in disorder from victory already achieved?

Who am I? They mock me, these lonely questions of mine.
Whoever I am, Thou knowest, O God, I am thine!   30

W. H. Auden

◀(1907–1973)▶

As the most influential English poet of the 1930s, Auden brought back the public role of poet. A brilliant student at Oxford, he had absorbed the techniques of Modernism, but became tired of its tendency toward obscurity. In his poem, "Twelve Songs," first published as "Funeral Blues" in 1940, he anticipated the "God is Dead" movement among liberal theologians of the 1960s. Experimenting with various philosophies – including Freudianism and Marxism – as solutions to social and personal problems, he eventually worked his way back to Christianity. Auden emigrated to America in 1939, became an American citizen in 1946, and received the Pulitzer Prize in 1948 for The Age of Anxiety. *He taught at numerous universities and served from 1956–1961 as Professor of Poetry at Oxford. Later in life he divided his time between his homes in Austria and New York, completing his great legacy as poet, critic, and dramatist.*

from TWELVE SONGS

9

1   Stop all the clocks, cut off the telephone,
     Prevent the dog from barking with a juicy bone,
   Silence the pianos and with muffled drum
   Bring out the coffin, let the mourners come.

5   Let æroplanes circle moaning overhead
   Scribbling on the sky the message He Is Dead,
   Put crêpe* bows round the white necks of the public doves,
   Let the traffic policemen wear black cotton gloves.*

   He was my North, my South, my East and West,
10 My working week and my Sunday rest,

crêpe · a fine wool or silk fabric often used to make armbands or other signs of mourning

black ... gloves · to be visible, traffic policemen often wore white gloves

My noon, my midnight, my talk, my song;   11
I thought that love would last for ever: I was wrong.

The stars are not wanted now: put out every one;
Pack up the moon and dismantle the sun;
Pour away the ocean and sweep up the wood;   15
For nothing now can ever come to any good.

MUSÉE DES BEAUX ARTS˙

Musée des Beaux Arts · The Museum of Fine Arts, located in Brussels, Belgium, that houses Breughel's (ca 1525–1569) *Icarus*. The painting depicts the legend of Icarus, the son of Dædalus, as the two attempted to escape the palace of Minos on artificial wings made of wax and feathers. When Icarus flew too close to the sun, his wings failed and he plunged to his death

ABOUT SUFFERING THEY were never wrong,   1
   The Old Masters: how well they understood
Its human position; how it takes place
While someone else is eating or opening a window or just walking
      dully along;
How, when the aged are reverently, passionately waiting   5
For the miraculous birth, there always must be
Children who did not specially want it to happen, skating
On a pond at the edge of the wood:
They never forgot
That even the dreadful martyrdom must run its course   10
Anyhow in a corner, some untidy spot
Where the dogs go on with their doggy life and the torturer's horse
Scratches its innocent behind on a tree.

In Breughel's *Icarus*, for instance: how everything turns away
Quite leisurely from the disaster; the ploughman may   15
Have heard the splash, the forsaken cry,
But for him it was not an important failure; the sun shone,
As it had to on the white legs disappearing into the green
Water; and the expensive delicate ship that must have seen
Something amazing, a boy falling out of the sky,   20
Had somewhere to get to and sailed calmly on.

Czesław Miłosz

《 1 9 1 1 – 2 0 0 4 》

A major poet and essayist, Miłosz was a naturalized citizen of the United States who won the Nobel Prize for Literature in 1980. Born in Lithuania and educated in Poland, Miłosz was permanently altered by his observation of totalitarian brutality – first Nazi, then Stalinist – in Warsaw, which he called "the most agonizing spot in the whole of terrorized Europe." Miłosz emigrated to France in 1951 and moved to America a decade later. His poetry often reflects his belief that European civilization inevitably declined when it abandoned its spiritual roots. The poet argues that Europeans were historically nourished by their "Christian imagination," but as scientific theory replaced this sacred understanding, they lost their capacity to see themselves as God-created. The failure of Christian imagination, consequently, rendered Europeans (and all Westerners) helpless in a hostile, alien environment. According to one critic, Miłosz believed that the death of the sacred way of seeing oneself became "the foundation of 20th-century nihilism and subsequently a cradle for totalitarian doctrines." His poems, which Miłosz called "acts of faith," are an effort to repair the damage by rebuilding a divine vision of the world, while fully acknowledging the dark forces that work against this theistic view. With passion, the poet desired to speak for, and to, all victims of persecution: "Now I am homeless – a just punishment. But perhaps I was born so that the 'Eternal Slaves' might speak through my lips." The Russian writer Joseph Brodsky called Miłosz "one of the greatest poets of our time, perhaps the greatest."

albescent · "growing white." Mary Magdalene was traditionally thought to have been a prostitute rescued by Jesus. The painting *The Repentant Magdalene* by Georges de La Tour (1593–1652) is featured on this book's cover

A SKULL

1 Before Mary Magdalen, albescent* in the dusk,
A skull. The candle flickers. Which of her lovers
Is this dried-up bone, she does not try to guess.

She remains like that, for an age or two
In meditation, while sand in the hourglass   5
Has fallen asleep – because once she saw,
And felt on her shoulder the touch of His hand,
Then, at daybreak, when she exclaimed: "Rabboni!"·
I gather dreams of the skull for I am it,
Impetuous, enamored, suffering in the gardens   10
Under a dark window, uncertain whether it's mine
And for no one else, the secret of her pleasure.
Raptures, solemn oaths. She does not quite remember.
And only that moment persists, unrevoked,
When she was almost on the other side.   15

Rabboni · "my teacher" (Aramaic)

A POOR CHRISTIAN LOOKS AT THE GHETTO

Bees build around red liver,   1
Ants build around black bone.
It has begun: the tearing, the trampling on silks,
It has begun: the breaking of glass, wood, copper, nickel, silver, foam
Of gypsum, iron sheets, violin strings, trumpets, leaves, balls,   5
    crystals.
Poof! Phosphorescent fire from yellow walls
Engulfs animal and human hair.

Bees build around the honeycomb of lungs,
Ants build around white bone.
Torn is paper, rubber, linen, leather, flax,   10
Fiber, fabrics, cellulose, snakeskin, wire.
The roof and the wall collapse in flame and heat seizes the
    foundations.
Now there is only the earth, sandy, trodden down,
With one leafless tree.

Slowly, boring a tunnel, a guardian mole makes his way,   15
With a small red lamp fastened to his forehead.
He touches buried bodies, counts them, pushes on,
He distinguishes human ashes by their luminous vapor,
The ashes of each man by a different part of the spectrum.

20 Bees build around a red trace.
Ants build around the place left by my body.

I am afraid, so afraid of the guardian mole.
He has swollen eyelids, like a Patriarch
Who has sat much in the light of candles
25 Reading the great book of the species.

What will I tell him, I, a Jew of the New Testament,
Waiting two thousand years for the second coming of Jesus?
My broken body will deliver me to his sight
And he will count me among the helpers of death:
30 The uncircumcised.

BEFORE MAJESTY   *Redemption*

1 IT IS BITTER TO PRAISE God in misfortune,
thinking that He did not act, though He could have.

The angel of Jehovah did not touch the eyelids
of a man whose hand I hold,
5 I, a passive witness of this suffering for no cause.

Unanswered is our prayer, both his and mine.
Unanswered is my request: strike me
and in exchange give him an ordinary life.

A weak human mercy walks in the corridors of hospitals
10 and is like a half-thawed winter.

While I, who am I, a believer, dancing before the All-Holy?

Dylan Thomas

⟪ 1 9 1 4 – 1 9 5 3 ⟫

Thomas, born in Swansea, Wales, achieved international recogni-
tion as a poet, fiction writer, playwright, critic, and celebrated
public performer of his own compositions. Something like modern
rock stars, Thomas enjoyed a cult following in England, Europe,
and the United States at mid-century. His fame increased through
his bohemian ways that contributed to his early death. Thomas's
poems are often difficult because he believed that modern poetic
language should be "dislocated." Style and themes should be "surre-
alistic." Thomas's best poems succeed through vivid images inspired
by nature, the Bible, and major Romantic and Metaphysical poets.
Thomas viewed himself as a bard in the Welsh Celtic tradition
who celebrates the spiritual forces in nature. Though Thomas
abandoned organized Christianity, his poetic imagination never
quite escaped the Paraclete Congregational Church of his youth.
Thomas was very much like the protagonist of James Joyce's novel A
Portrait of the Artist as a Young Man: *his mind was supersaturated*
with the religion in which he said he disbelieved.

A REFUSAL TO MOURN THE DEATH, BY FIRE, OF
A CHILD IN LONDON

1   NEVER UNTIL THE mankind making
         Bird beast and flower
Fathering and all humbling darkness
Tells with silence the last light breaking
5   And the still hour
Is come of the sea tumbling in harness

And I must enter again the round
Zion* of the water bead

Zion · literally, the east-
ernmost of the two hills
of ancient Jerusalem;
symbolically, the dwell-
ing place of God

463

And the synagogue of the ear of corn
Shall I let pray the shadow of a sound   10
Or sow my salt seed·
In the least valley of sackcloth to mourn

The majesty and burning of the child's death.
I shall not murder
The mankind of her going with a grave truth   15
Nor blaspheme down the stations of the breath
With any further
Elegy of innocence and youth.

Deep with the first dead lies London's daughter,
Robed in the long friends,   20
The grains beyond age, the dark veins of her mother,
Secret by the unmourning water
Of the riding Thames.
After the first death, there is no other.

sow my salt seed ·
literally tears, Thomas
here also alludes to
the ancient practice of
sowing fields with salt to
make them permanently
unfertile, as the Romans
had done in Carthage

Richard Wilbur

《 1 9 2 1 – 2 0 0 1 》

*Born in New York City, Wilbur graduated from Amherst (1942)
and served as an infantryman in World War II. After the war, he
completed an MA at Harvard (1947), where he began a successful teaching career that continued at a number of prestigious
institutions. His first book of poems,* The Beautiful Changes *(1947),
was published when Wilbur was 26. It received affirming critical
responses. Subsequent publications enjoyed equally positive reviews.
His verse is polished in diction, sophisticated in structure, and often
playfully witty in its angle of vision. The admirably smooth surface
Wilbur creates, however, may well distract the reader from noting
unexpected turns in his thought. "The poem," Wilbur has said, "is
an effort to express a knowledge imperfectly felt, to articulate rela-
tionships not quite seen, to make or discover some pattern in the
world." In addition to his two Pulitzer Prizes, Wilbur was honored
with an appointment as Poet Laureate in 1987.*

LOVE CALLS US TO THE THINGS OF THIS WORLD

1 THE EYES OPEN to a cry of pulleys,
   And spirited from sleep, the astounded soul
Hangs for a moment bodiless and simple
As false dawn.
5 Outside the open window
The morning air is all awash with angels.

Some are in bed-sheets, some are in blouses,
Some are in smocks: but truly, there they are.
Now they are rising together in calm swells
10 Of halcyon* feeling, filling whatever they wear
With the deep joy of their impersonal breathing:

halcyon · peaceful
and calm

Now they are flying in place, conveying
The terrible speed of their omnipresence, moving
And staying like white water; and now of a sudden
They swoon down into so rapt a quiet   15
That nobody seems to be there.
The soul shrinks

From all that it is about to remember,
From the punctual rape of every blessed day,
And cries,   20
"Oh, let there be nothing on earth but laundry,
Nothing but rosy hands in the rising steam
And clear dances done in the sight of heaven."

Yet, as the sun acknowledges
With a warm look the world's hunks and colors,   25
The soul descends once more in bitter love
To accept the waking body, saying now
In a changed voice as the man yawns and rises,

"Bring them down from their ruddy gallows;
Let there be clean linen for the backs of thieves: 30
Let lovers go fresh and sweet to be undone,
And the heaviest nuns walk in a pure floating

habits · the characteristic dress worn by nuns

Of dark habits,˙
keeping their difficult balance."

Denise Levertov

⟨ 1 9 2 3 - 1 9 9 7 ⟩

The daughter of a Hassidic Jew who converted to Christianity, Levertov treasured the mysticism of her paternal ancestors. She was born and reared in England, and schooled informally. She began to write at an early age. Moving to New York City in the late 1940s, Levertov became an important voice among the Black Mountain Poets, whose work was open, experimental, and avant-garde. Her poems on social and political themes during the 1960s – particularly those exploring femi-nism and those opposing the Vietnamese War – established her as an important voice in American poetry. During her life she wrote more than twenty books of poetry and a number of volumes of prose. In 1984, Levertov declared herself a Christian, "but not a very orthodox one." In her later years the power of the Incarnation and her search for spiritual depth became a major focus of her work. Denise Levertov's poetry at every stage of her life is clear, concrete, and passionate.

ST. THOMAS DIDYMUS

Redemption

1 In the hot street at noon I saw him
                                        a small man
gray but vivid, standing forth
                            beyond the crowd's buzzing
5 holding in desperate grip his shaking
                                    teethgnashing son,

and thought him my brother.

I heard him cry out, weeping, and speak
                                those words,
10 Lord, I believe, help thou
                    mine unbelief,·

Lord … unbelief·
the prayer of a father
whose son is afflicted
(Mark 9:24)

467

and knew him
              my twin:

a man whose entire being
                    had knotted itself   15
into the one tightdrawn question,
                        Why,
why has this child lost his childhood in suffering,
                  why is this child who will soon be a man
tormented, torn, twisted?   20
                  Why is he cruelly punished
who has done nothing except be born?

The twin of my birth
                was not so close
as that man I heard   25
              say what my heart
sighed with each beat, my breath silently
                      cried in and out,
in and out.

After the healing,   30
              he, with his wondering
newly peaceful boy, receded;
                no one
dwells on the gratitude, the astonished joy,
                    the swift   35
acceptance and forgetting.
                I did not follow
to see their changed lives.
                What I retained
was the flash of kinship.   40
                Despite
all that I witnessed,
              his question remained
my question, throbbed like a stealthy cancer,
                  known   45
only to doctor and patient. To others
              I seemed well enough.

So it was
        that after Golgotha˙
50   my spirit in secret
lurched in the same convulsed writhings
                    that tore that child
before he was healed.
           And after the empty tomb
55 when they told me he lived, had spoken to Magdalen,˙
                    told me
that though He had passed through the door like a ghost
             He had breathed on them
the breath of a living man –
60   even then
when hope tried with a flutter of wings
             to lift me –
still, alone with myself,
        my heavy cry was the same: Lord,
65 *I believe,*
      help thou mine unbelief.

I needed
        blood to tell me the truth,
the touch
70   of blood. Even
my sight of the dark crust of it
           round the nailholes
didn't thrust its meaning all the way through
             to that manifold knot in me
75 that willed to possess all knowledge,
           refusing to loosen
unless that insistence won
        the battle I fought with life.

But when my hand
80   led by His hand's firm clasp
entered the unhealed wound,
        my fingers encountering
rib-bone and pulsing heat,
       what I felt was not

Golgotha · "the place of the skull" (Aramaic), site of Christ's crucifixion

Magdalen · Mary Magdalene was one of Jesus' most celebrated disciples, famous, according to Mark 16:9–10 and John 20:14–17, for being the first person to see the resurrected Christ

scalding pain, shame for my   85
                              obstinate need,
but light, light streaming
                                   into me, over me, filling the room
as if I had lived till then
                              in a cold cave, and now   90
coming forth for the first time,
                                   the knot that bound me unravelling,
I witnessed
                  all things quicken to color, to form,
my question   95
                  not answered but given
                                             its part
in a vast unfolding design lit
                  by a risen sun.

WINDOW-BLIND

MUCH HAPPENS WHEN we're not there.   1
        Many trees, not only that famous one, over and over,
fall in the forest. We don't see, but something sees,
or someone, a different kind of someone,
a different molecular model, or entities   5
not made of molecules anyway; or nothing, no one:
but something has taken place, taken space, been present,
    absent,
returned. Much moves in and out of open windows
when our attention is somewhere else,
just as our souls move in and out of our bodies sometimes.   10
Everyone used to know this,
but for a hundred years or more

molting · to shed
feathers, skin, or horns
for replacement by new
growth

we've been losing our memories, molting,˙ shedding,
like animals or plants that are not well.
Things happen anyway,   15
whether we are aware or whether
the garage door comes down by remote control over our
recognitions, shuts off, cuts off –,
We are animals and plants that are not well.
We are not well but while we look away,   20

21 on the other side of that guillotine or through
the crack of day disdainfully left open below the blind
a very strong luminous arm reaches in,
or from an unsuspected place, in the room with us,
25 where it was calmly waiting, reaches outward.
And though it may have nothing at all to do with us,
and though we can't fathom its designs,
nevertheless our condition thereby changes:
cells shift, a rustling barely audible as of tarlatan*
30 flickers through closed books, one or two leaves
fall, and when we read them we can perceive,
if we are truthful, that we were not dreaming,
not dreaming but once more witnessing.

tarlatan · a thin, stiff, transparent cloth

Galway Kinnell

⟨ 1 9 2 7 – ⟩

Kinnell, poet and novelist, was born in Providence, Rhode Island, earned his BA at Princeton, and served in the United States Navy 1944–1946. He is noted for his experimentation with form and his interest in the spirituality of creation. Because of his subject matter (earthy, natural elements), transcendental philosophy, and personal intensity, Kinnell is sometimes compared to Walt Whitman. Kinnell has been described as "a deeply serious and self-critical poet" who combines the lyrical and the mystical. Since 1949, Kinnell has been poet-in-residence at a variety of universities in the United States and abroad. Kinnell received the Pulitzer Prize for poetry in 1983 and the National Book Award for Selected Poems *in 1984. Today, he lives in New York City.*

SAINT FRANCIS AND THE SOW

1 THE BUD
    stands for all things,
even for those things that don't flower,
for everything flowers, from within, of self-blessing;
5 though sometimes it is necessary
to reteach a thing its loveliness,
to put a hand on its brow
of the flower
and retell it in words and in touch
10 it is lovely
until it flowers again from within, of self-blessing;
as Saint Francis*
put his hand on the creased forehead
of the sow, and told her in words and in touch
15 blessings of earth on the sow, and the sow
began remembering all down her thick length,

Saint Francis · son of a noble Italian family, Francis of Assisi (1181/2–1226), founder of the Franciscan Order, taught the "brotherhood" and "sisterhood" of all creatures

473

from the earthen snout all the way

slops · intestines

through the fodder and slops* to the spiritual curl of the tail,
from the hard spininess spiked out from the spine
down through the great broken heart   20
to the sheer blue milken dreaminess spurting and shuddering
from the fourteen teats into the fourteen mouths sucking and
 blowing beneath them:
the long, perfect loveliness of sow.

WAIT

Wait, for now.
 Distrust everything, if you have to.   1
But trust the hours. Haven't they
carried you everywhere, up to now?
Personal events will become interesting again.   5
Hair will become interesting.
Pain will become interesting.
Buds that open out of season will become interesting.
Second-hand gloves will become lovely again,
their memories are what give them   10
the need for other hands. And the desolation
of lovers is the same: that enormous emptiness
carved out of such tiny beings as we are
asks to be filled; the need
for the new love *is* faithfulness to the old.   15

Wait.
Don't go too early.
You're tired. But everyone's tired.
But no one is tired enough.
Only wait a while and listen.   20
Music of hair,
Music of pain,
music of looms weaving all our loves again.
Be there to hear it, it will be the only time,
most of all to hear,   25
the flute of your whole existence,
rehearsed by the sorrows, play itself into total exhaustion.

Creation

Geoffrey Hill

⟨ 1 9 3 2 - ⟩

Hill was educated at Keble College, Oxford. He served as a professor at Leeds University, as a lecturer at Cambridge, and, most recently, as a professor at Boston University. His verse has been compared to Metaphysical poetry for its intense fusion of intellect and sensuousness, and like many of the Metaphysicals, Hill is a religious poet, a thinker concerned with questions of ultimate meaning. But he is also acquainted with doubt. In some works, in fact, he is virtually an agnostic, honestly confronting human brutality, whether its embodiment be an ancient cross or a modern concentration camp. Hill's honesty, however, will not allow him to ignore the goodness inherent in our world, particularly in the natural world with its rich bounty of blessings.

CHRISTMAS TREES

1   BONHŒFFER* IN HIS skylit cell
      bleached by the flares' candescent fall,
   pacing out his own citadel,

   restores the broken themes of praise,
5   encourages our borrowed days,
   by logic of his sacrifice.

   Against wild reasons of the state
   his words are quiet but not too quiet.
   We hear too late or not too late.

Bonhœffer · Dietrich Bonhœffer (1906–1945), German theologian and martyr. See Bonhœffer's poem "Who Am I?" on pages 453–454

Wendell Berry

⟨ 1 9 3 4 - ⟩

Except for brief study at Stanford University, a year on a Guggenheim fellowship in Europe, and a few years teaching in Europe, Berry has remained close to the place of his origin. Born in Kentucky, he served as a professor at his alma mater, *the State University, until his early forties, and he has continued to live and farm the region inhabited for almost two centuries by his ancestors. Not surprisingly, his poems tend to arise from the land and those who care for it, as do a number of his novels, such as* Nathan Coulter (1960) *and* A Place on Earth (1967). *While his writing tends to be pastoral, Berry also shows social and environmental concerns. In his non-fiction work* The Hidden Wound (1970), *for example, Berry recollects his childhood and the effect of racism upon him. In* The Unsettling of America: Culture and Agriculture (1977), *the problem of responsible land use is addressed. As one biographer has noted, Berry is "a preserver of nature and people," and his writings "attest to his concern for our vanishing world."*

THE SLIP

Fall/Retangsion-

1   THE RIVER TAKES the land, and leaves nothing.
     Where the great slip* gave way in the bank
     and an acre disappeared, all human plans
     dissolve. An aweful clarification occurs
5   where a place was. Its memory breaks
     from what is known now, and begins to drift.
     Where cattle grazed and trees stood, emptiness
     widens the air for birdflight, wind, and rain.
     As before the beginning, nothing is there.
10   Human wrong is in the cause, human
     ruin in the effect – but no matter;

slip · when water undercuts the land's surface, a massive collapse can occur, resulting in a kind of sinkhole

all will be lost, no matter the reason.
Nothing, having arrived, will stay.
The earth, even, is like a flower, so soon
passeth it away. And yet this nothing   15
is the seed of all – heaven's clear
eye, where all the worlds appear.
Where the imperfect has departed, the perfect
begins its struggle to return. The good gift
begins again its descent. The maker moves   20
in the unmade, stirring the water until
it clouds, dark beneath the surface,
stirring and darkening the soul until pain
perceives new possibility.* There is nothing
to do but learn and wait, return to work   25
on what remains. Seed will sprout in the scar.
Though death is in the healing, it will heal.

stirring the water ... possibility · an allusion to the pool of Bethesda, where people could receive healing when the Spirit troubled the waters. See John 5:2–4

Walter McDonald

◀(1 9 3 4 -)▶

Two main territories of McDonald's poetry are west Texas and war-
torn Vietnam. Both are unlikely settings for poetry, the one haunted
by drought and its own vastness, the other by memories of suffering
and disaster. Yet he has drawn sixteen books and over 2,000 poems
mostly from these two places. McDonald grew up in West Texas, flew
jets in the Vietnam War, and later taught at the Air Force Academy.
He earned his doctorate in creative writing at the University of Iowa
and then for many years served as Paul Whitfield Horn Professor of
English and Poet in Residence at Texas Tech. In 2001 he served as Poet
Laureate of Texas. During McDonald's career, he has been honored
with many awards, including six awards from the Texas Institute
of Letters, one of which was the Lon Tinkle Memorial Award for
Excellence Sustained Throughout a Career. McDonald's books include
Climbing the Divide (2003), Great Lonely Places of the Texas Plains
(2003), All Occasions (2000), *and* Blessings the Body Gave (1998).

FAITH IS A RADICAL MASTER

1 GOD BATS ON THE SIDE of the scrubs.*
  With a clean-up hitter like that, who needs
to worry about stealing home, a double squeeze,
cleat-pounding triples? If nothing else works,

5 take a walk, lean into the wicked pitch
careening inside at ninety miles an hour.
At bat, just get on base and pray the next nerd
doesn't pop up. When someone's already on, the coach

 never calls me *Mr. October,** seldom signals *Hit away*.
10 If Johnson with the wicked curve owns the strike zone

scrubs · second-string
players

Mr. October · nickname
of renowned hitter and
Hall-of-Fame player
Reggie Jackson (1946–)

479

or the ump, I'll bunt. No crack of the bat, 11
no wildly cheered Bambino° everyone loves.

Bambino · nickname of George Herman "Babe" Ruth (1895–1948), one of baseball's most famous hitters

Lay it down the line like the weakest kid in school,
disciple of the sacrifice. Some hour my time will come,
late in the game, and I'm on third, wheezing from the run 15
from first after a wild pitch, and Crazy Elmore

waving like a windmill by the third-base line.
Hands on my knees, I'll watch the pitcher
lick two fingers, wipe them on his fancy pin stripes
and try to stare me dead. I'll be almost dead, 20

gasping, wondering how I'll wobble home if someone bunts
or dribbles a slow roller and the coach yells
Go! But there, there in the box is God,
who doesn't pound home plate like an earthquake

points … center field · Ruth sometimes pointed to the part of the field where he intended to hit a home run

but slowly points the bat like the Babe toward center field,° 25
and all my family in the clouds go wild, all friends
I've loved and lost, even the four-eyed scrubs
in the dugout slugging each other and laughing,

tossing their gloves like wild hosannas, and why not —
it's bottom of the ninth, two outs, a run behind 30
and a hall-of-fame fast baller on the mound,
but I'm on third and leaning home, and look who's up.

THE WALTZ WE WERE BORN FOR

WIND CHIMES PING and tangle on the patio. 1
In gusty winds this wild, sparrow hawks° hover

sparrow hawks · a small bird of prey

and bob, always the crash of indigo
hosannas dangling on strings. My wife ties copper
to turquoise from deserts, and bits of steel 5
from engines I tear down. She strings them all
like laces of babies' shoes when the squeal
of their play made joyful noise in the hall.

Her voice is more modest than moonlight,
10 like pearl drops she wears in her lobes.
My hands find the face of my bride.
I stretch her skin smooth and see bone.
Our children bring children to bless her, her face
more weathered than mine. What matters
15 is timeless, dazzling devotion – not rain,
not Eden gardenias, but cactus in drought,
not just moons of deep sleep, not sunlight or stars,
not the blue, but the darkness beyond.

THE DARK, HOLLOW HALO OF SPACE

1 ROCK OF ALL, my marble, stone
of my tomb and my stairs. More firm
than granite in mountains, you are older
than immortal diamond and gold.

5 My body is putty, a tiny blue planet
in the dark, hollow halo of space.
Billions of bonfires are specks
in your eye, maker of fabulous galaxies

far from earth, and all burning. My heart
10 burns slowly, unnoticed, as gold burns,
even novas I've never seen.
I'm numbed by the buckshot of stars,

trillions of tons in each one. When the air
I'm made from is ash, only dust I'll become.
15 And go when You call, where You are,
stone of my tomb and my stairs.

Ann Applegarth

◀ 1 9 3 5 – ▶

Born in McPherson, Kansas, in 1935, Ann Hanchey Applegarth lived in Texas, New Mexico, and Kentucky before following the Oregon Trail to Eugene, Oregon, where she lives, writes, and teaches poetry classes and Sunday School. In 1980 she was awarded the Academy of American Poets prize at the University of New Mexico; in 1990 she earned the BA degree, with honors and distinction in English, at the University of Oregon. Applegarth's poems are noted for their religious symbolism, everyday details, and colloquial dialect. Through simple, spare language, her poems often examine transcendent realities lurking beneath the surface of ordinary experiences.

ALTERNATIVE LIFESTYLE FOR THE QUIETLY DESPERATE

1 O, LET US prance
    through each day
as if it mattered,
heads flung
5 back, toes pointed,
shaking
love sparks
from our fingertips
in time to celestial
10 tambourines,
whirling finally
into that last
glorious pirouette
that spins
15 straight
into
eternity.

483

A HEARTRENDING TALE OF HOW A SIMPLE WOMAN OF FAITH RELINQUISHES TO GOD THE APPLE OF HER EYE WHO IS ON THE VERGE OF ENCOUNTERING WORMS IN THE FLESHPOTS OF MULESHOE, TEXAS*

Muleshoe, Texas · located in the Texas panhandle, a small, agricultural town of about 4,500 people

LORD, YOU KNOW my boy, Harvey, and how I've 1
spoke to you many times about his future, how
I just know you've cut him out to be a missionary or a song
leader (oh, Lord, don't he sing just like a angel?). Lord, that
cute little button's growed up to be a wonderful son, smart, 5
strong, helpin' me carry in groceries and all like that, even
when it rains, but now he's gettin' to the mannish age, Lord,
and that's more than a weary old mama can handle.
I been prayin' hard and long for Harvey, Lord, you know that,
but now it seems to cry for somethin' more, a lightnin' bolt, 10
maybe, or some big thing.

hinsome · handsome

Oh, Lord, Lord, Lord, jerk my Harvey up by the scruff of his
hinsome* young neck and git his attention once and for all
because it's real serious. Lean down now, Lord, and let me
whisper in your ear – I can't hardly stand to say this outright 15
to you, Lord, but you've just got to know:

myrrh and aloes · see Proverbs 7:8–10

my boy come home late last evenin' fairly reekin' of myrrh and aloes,
with creases on his cheek from some Egyptian bedspread.

Nancy Willard

◄(1 9 3 6 -)►

Nancy Willard's poetry looks at the world with the kind of wonder that makes grass and trees and water seem fresh and redemptive. Paging through her nine volumes of poetry, a reader will find a poem about a bride who takes time on her wedding day to feed her pet tortoise, a poem about buying a night light for a child, and a poem about her own bare feet. While Willard has been widely recognized for her poetry, her children's books, essays, and fiction also present common happenings with uncommon grace. Among her many awards is a Newberry Medal for her children's book A Visit to William Blake's Inn *(1982). Nancy Willard was raised in Michigan and educated at The University of Michigan and Stanford University. A Professor at Vassar College, she lives in Poughkeepsie, New York.*

A PSALM FOR RUNNING WATER

1 RUNNING WATER, YOU are remembered and called.
Physician of clover and souls; hock, glove
and slipper* of stones.

Stitch thyme and buttercup to my boots.
5 Make me tread the psalm and sign of water
falling, when I am going the other way,
climbing the mountain for a clear view of home.

After winter's weeding and the fire's gap in the woods,
first ferns, trillium, watercress,*
10 this vivid text, Water, shows your hand.

The trees stand so spare a child may write them.
You, Water, sing them like an old score,

hock … slipper · hock (hollyhock), glove (foxglove), and slipper are all types of flowers, as are clover, thyme, and buttercup

ferns, trillium, watercress · these plants are among the first to appear after the spring thaw

settled, pitched soft and fresh,
and wash our wounds when we fall.

A hundred Baptists, hand in hand,   15
rise and fall in your body and rise again,
praising the Lord, whose hand, I think, wears you.

For all this and more, my grandmother
thumped out of bed on Easter and tramped
over gorse and thorn and wild thistle·   20
to the water smiling through her husband's field.

gorse … thistle ·
all plants that feature
sharp thorns or spines

cruet · a small bottle

She capped some in a cruet;·
the wink of God,
the quick motion of ourselves in time,
flashing! flashing!   25

ANGELS IN WINTER

M ERCY IS WHITER than laundry,   1
great baskets of it, piled like snowmen.
In the cellar I fold and sort and watch
through a squint in the dirty window
the plain bright snow.   5

Unlike the earth, snow is neuter.
Unlike the moon, it stays.
It falls, not from grace, but a silence
which nourishes crystals.
My son catches them on his tongue.   10

Whatever I try to hold perishes.
My son and I lie down in white pastures
of snow and flap like the last survivors
of a species that couldn't adapt to the air.
Jumping free, we look back at   15

ladder of angels ·
see Genesis 28:12

angels, blurred fossils of majesty and justice
from the time when a ladder of angels·

joined the house of the snow
to the houses of those whom it covered
20 with a dangerous blanket or a healing sleep.

As I lift my body from the angel's,
I remember the mad preacher* of Indiana
who chose for the site of his kingdom
the footprint of an angel and named the place
25 New Harmony.* Nothing of it survives.

The angels do not look back
to see how their passing changes the earth,
the way I do, watching the snow,
and the waffles our boots print on its unleavened face,
30 and the nervous alphabet of the pheasant's feet,

and the five-petaled footprint of the cat,
and the shape of snowshoes, white and expensive as tennis,
and the deep ribbons tied and untied by sleds,
I remember the millions who left the earth;
35 it holds no trace of them,

as it holds of us, tracking through snow,
so tame and defenseless
even the air could kill us.

mad preacher · George Rapp (1757–1847), German American pietist preacher who advocated celibacy and attempted to form a religious utopia in southern Indiana

New Harmony · founded as an idealized community in 1814/15 by Rappists, the various utopian schemes failed and it was sold. The town is now a National Historic Landmark

Jeanne Murray Walker

◄(1 9 4 4 –)►

Born in Parkers Prairie, Minnesota, Jeanne Murray Walker grew up in the Midwest before moving to the East Coast. As a college student, she won the Atlantic Monthly Fellowship for both fiction and poetry. After completing her doctorate at the University of Pennsylvania, she began seriously writing poetry – first lyric, then narrative. Walker has also published essays and written scripts, which have been produced in theaters across the United States and abroad. Her work probes issues of time and identity, posing questions about the incongruous self, eternity, and the intersections between generations. She examines the wonder of birth, the struggle between parents and children, the omnipresence of both death and grace. Walker has been honored with numerous prizes and awards, including a National Endowment for the Arts Fellowship, many new play prizes, and the Pew Fellowship in the Arts. Her poetry is collected in six volumes, including Fugitive Angels *(1985)*, Coming Into History *(1990)*, Gaining Time *(1997)*, and* A Deed To the Light *(2004)*.

LITTLE BLESSING FOR MY FLOATER

After George Herbert•

1 THIS TINY RUIN in my eye, small
     flaw in the fabric, little speck
  of blood in the egg, deep chip
  in the windshield, north star,
5 pole star, floater that doesn't
  float, spot where my hand is not,
  even when I'm looking at my hand,
  little piton• that nails every rock
  I see, no matter if the picture
10 turns to sand, or sand to sea,

George Herbert • English poet (1593–1633) best known for his religious lyrics. See Herbert's poems on pages 411–413

piton • a spike or wedge that can be driven into rocks as a support for mountain climbing

489

I embrace you, piece of absence   11
that reminds me what I will be,
all dark some day unless God
rescues me, oh speck
that might yet teach me how to see.   15

A BESTIARY FOR THE BIRTH OF CHRIST

for E. Daniel Larkin

1 · THE FROG

FERNS STEAM AND BOIL beneath the sun.   1
The cypress tree lets down its hair.
The summer lull waits to begin
till gold has fallen everywhere.

I sit beneath a leaf's dark toe   5
and listen to the apples swell.
They ripen to what God must know.
They gaze down on the lowly shell.

I do not know what apples mean
nor what perfume the orchid smells,   10

nor why the bear's eyes flame with sun,
how young lambs foam upon the hills.
But still the garden fills my ear.
The apple nestles in the air
humming its color, bright, gay, dear,   15
till silence loses poise and then

The light lies on us all like doom.
The gold cracks. Look. And through that gap
time pours its minutes. In a dream
I close my bottom eyelid up.   20

The swindle snake slips from his hole.
"Malice, Malice," it is done.

23   With that word, ferns turn into coal
and God becomes a man.

2 · THE COW

1   THE WIND STROLLS and licks my bones
with its rough tongue as I lie dimming
in the moonlight on this desert.

All for me is desert now and I all bone:
5   a thigh whining like a piccolo
on eternal, sound-swallowing sand.

I am the sand's foundering ship.
It barks its glass shins on my skull.
I go down to drowning with my knowledge.

10   Five years ago, in the season when locusts
split their skins, I stood lowing in the stall.
I tell you, he was the son of God.

Now time buzzes through my bridge.
There is no heaven for cattle.
15   My collarbone arches, hollow, hollow.

3 · THE RAVEN

1   I AM THE MOST HIGHLY developed of birds, order *Passeras*,
family *Corvidæ*,·
a bird with a wingspan exceeding a yard
and a well-tailored sense of irony.

5   I flew over the waters for Noah·
and helped Flokki locate Iceland,·
but since Poe, I have argued "Nevermore."·
From my modern height I have surveyed the frog and the cow.
The frog, natural enemy of the snake, has in his own way
10   related the myth that says malice snapped the branch
of eternity which crashed end over end,
scattering us off our perch into lurid time.

Passeras ... Corvidæ · Latin scientific names for the crow

flew ... Noah · the first bird Noah releases after the flood is a Raven; see Genesis 8:7

Flokki ... Iceland · Vikings would release ravens and track where they flew in order to find land. In this manner, the Viking Flokki is said to have discovered Iceland around 870

"Nevermore" · American poet Edgar Allan Poe (1809–1849) wrote "The Raven" in 1845 in which the bird haunts the grieving narrator with the reminder that he would see his beloved "Nevermore"

The cow longs for salvation, believing that such exists.
Not having been present in the stable myself,
how can I authorize the reliability of a witness who was? 15

I, who can fly, know eternity
when my wings slice it.
Time is the meat in the stubble
between hedgerow and wire fence.
If the most capable of all birds 20
cannot pick God out of the air,
we must learn to be satisfied with meat.

Only occasionally the wise, frail eyes of the
fieldmouse disturb me and
sometimes I grow 25
dizzy.

Marjorie Stelmach

(1948 –)

Having taught at the high school and university levels, Stelmach holds an MFA *from the Washington University Writer's Program. Her first book of poems,* Night Drawings, *won the 1994 Marianne Moore Poetry Prize. One of the judges for the contest described it as "a prayerful book," noting the poet's ability to transform everyday speech into "a medium of reverence towards experience." A writer of pronounced spiritual sensitivity, Stelmach seeks meaning in the daily and at times mundane events of life. The poet's recent work has appeared in* Chelsea, Kenyon Review, New Letters, *and* Tampa Review, *as well as in* Florida Review, *in which "Manna" originally appeared. Stelmach lives and teaches in St. Louis, Missouri.*

MANNA

1 SWALLOWS SLICE LOW across the field, feeding
                                 on the unseen.
  Deep in their 200-million-year-old birdness,
  they know precisely what they're doing.
5 But briefly,
              it strikes me as sad
  that they don't know how lovely they are
  to watch, how rare in the world, such accuracy.

  My husband, the agnostic, interrupts
10 to read from *The Bible As History*: manna –
  a secretion of tamarisk bushes pierced by a plant louse,
        and shows me a photo of crystallized honey,
        white when it falls, then turning yellow.
  If it's not collected each morning,· he adds,
15   the ants take it.

each morning · an allusion to Moses's warning that manna should not be kept for more than a day (Exodus 16:19–20)

I guess I prefer those who believe   16
                        in small things,
keeping their large disbeliefs to themselves,
though I like them mostly for their quiet entry into a room
with an odd bit of knowledge,   20
          the way they'll wait for the right moment
          to offer
               the weight of a songbird's blood,
               the stomach contents of the dead pharaohs,
               the titles of books thought to have burned   25
                        in the Alexandria library.
Even if what they bring you is only the ball score,
or the fact that they've seen the egret again
                    out on the Interstate,
mostly they're willing to wait a bit   30
               if you're watching the swallows.

Mark Jarman

《 1 9 5 2 – 》

Born in Kentucky, Mark Jarman spent part of his childhood in Scotland, where his father served as minister to a Church of Christ congregation, and later he spent some years in California. Out of his experience as the son of a minister and the grandson of an evangelist was born his struggle with religious faith. Using his own adolescence as a laboratory, Jarman has written narrative poems that document that struggle. His more recent poems record the intense and immediate questions of a believer. Though Jarman is one of the founders of the New Narrative movement in contemporary poetry, his work is not strictly narrative but combines narrative with lyric, meditative, and dramatic elements. A graduate of the Iowa Writers' Workshop, Jarman taught at Indiana State University, Evansville, the University of California, Irvine, and Murray State University before settling at Vanderbilt University. He has received three National Endowment for the Arts grants in poetry, a Guggenheim Fellowship, and the Lenore Marshall Poetry Prize. His books include Unholy Sonnets (2000), Questions for Ecclesiastes (1997), *and* Body and Soul: Essays on Poetry (2002).

STARS

1   I SIGNED UP FOR astronomy in college
    Just to be close to a girl
  I lost before the course was over. She'd seen me
  Walking below some cherry trees on campus.
5 "The world was blooming," she wrote.
  "And you trudged through, looking at the ground."

  The outrage this inspired in me was like
  The solar wind˙ I imagined—

solar wind · a flow of particles released by the sun's corona that regularly strikes the earth

495

Not the airy plasma of deep space,
But a righteous blast of heat. I telephoned   10
And roared it in her ear.
She answered, "You're not really mad at me."

To this day I get taken by surprise.
I look up and the world
Is clotted with snow or flowers, stars have pricked   15
The breathless, late, blue evening sky, my children
Have tiptoed beside me.
And my response is "Please! Leave me alone!"

Then I have to say, "Don't listen to me."
I repeat it to myself,   20
"Don't listen." And I still confuse the rain,
Seething across a parking lot at dusk,
And the other inner downpour
That I shake off with a curse and an excuse.

I want to be like you, poised, placid stars,   25
Too far away to threaten
With your own throbbing storms and fields of force,
Like you, like lights pinned to a sphere of glass
Turned by love itself –
To give up to your peace, turned by love.   30

UNHOLY SONNET 14

A FTER THE PRAYING, after the hymn-singing,   1
   After the sermon's trenchant* commentary
On the world's ills, which make ours secondary,
After communion, after the hand-wringing,
And after peace descends upon us, bringing   5
Our eyes up to regard the sanctuary
And how the light swords through it, and how, scary
In their sheer numbers, motes of dust ride, clinging –
There is, as doctors say about some pain,
Discomfort knowing that despite your prayers,   10
Your listening and rejoicing, your small part

trenchant · sharp,
penetrating

12 In this communal stab at coming clean,
    There is one stubborn remnant of your cares
    Intact. There is still murder in your heart.

Scott Cairns

⟪ 1 9 5 4 - ⟫

Scott Cairns was born in Tacoma, Washington, and educated at Western Washington University, Hollins College, Bowling Green University, and the University of Utah. He has taught American literature, poetry writing, and poetics courses at Westminster College, the University of North Texas, Old Dominion University, and at the University of Missouri. Cairns' imagination has been deeply influenced by the Greek Orthodox faith he practices, and his poems are replete with images drawn from Greek Orthodox iconography. His early poems, often set in the everyday world, examine questions of faith and practice. Characterized by quick turns of thought, his work has become increasingly centered on Biblical and iconographic subjects. He is interested in the mystical theology of Eastern Christianity and writes about sacramental poetics. Among Cairns' books are The Theology of Doubt *(1985),* The Translation of Babel *(1990),* Figures for the Ghost *(1994),* Recovered Body *(1998), and* Philokalia: New & Selected Poems *(2002).*

THE THEOLOGY OF DELIGHT

1 IMAGINE A WORLD, this ridiculous,
    tentative bud blooming
    in your hand. There in your hand, a world
    opening up, stretching, after the image
5 of your hand. Imagine
    a field of sheep grazing, or a single sheep
    grazing and wandering in the delight
    of grass, of wildflowers
    lifting themselves, after their fashion,
10 to be flowers. Or a woman, lifting her hand
    to touch her brow, and the intricacy
    of the motion that frees her

to set the flat part of her hand carelessly
to her brow. Once, while walking, I happened
across a woman whose walking had brought her   15
to a shaded spot near a field. Enjoying
that cool place together, we sat watching sheep
and the wind moving the wildflowers in the field.
As we rose to set out again, our movement
startled the flock into running; they ran   20
only a little way before settling again
to their blank consideration of the grass.
But one of them continued, its prancing
taking it far into the field where,
free of the others, it leapt for no clear reason,   25
and set out walking through a gathering
of flowers, parting that grip of flowers with its face.

THE THEOLOGY OF DOUBT

I HAVE COME TO BELIEVE this fickleness   1
of belief is unavoidable. As, for these
backlot trees, the annual loss
of leaves and fruit is unavoidable.
I remember hearing that soft-soap   5
about faith being given
only to the faithful – mean trick,
if you believe it. This afternoon,
during my walk, which
I have come to believe is good   10
for me, I noticed one of those
ridiculous leaves hanging
midway up an otherwise naked oak.
The wind did what it could
to bring it down, but the slow   15
learner continued dancing. Then again,
once, hoping for the last good apple,
I reached among bare branches,
pulling into my hand
an apple too soft for anything   20
and warm to the touch, fly-blown.

THE SPITEFUL JESUS

1 Not the one whose courtesy
and kiss unsought are nonetheless
bestowed. Instead, the largely
more familiar blasphemy
5 borne to us in the little boat
that first cracked rock at Plymouth
– petty, plainly man-inflected
demi-god established as a club
with which our paling*
10 generations might be beaten
to a bland consistency.

He is angry. He is just. And while
he may have died for us,
it was not gladly. The way
15 *his* prophets talk, you'd think
the whole affair had left him
queerly out of sorts, unspeakably
indignant, more than a little
needy, and quick to dish out
20 just desserts. I saw him when,
a boy in church, I first
met souls in hell. I made him*
for a corrupt, corrupting fiction when
my own father (mortal that he was)
25 forgave me everything, unasked.

paling · regularly
spaced or dense, like
pickets in a fence

made him · took him
for, understood him
to be

THE MORE EARNEST PRAYER OF CHRIST

"And being in an agony he prayed more earnestly..." Luke 22:44

1 His last prayer in the garden began, as most
of his prayers began – *in earnest*, certainly,
but not without distraction, and habitual ... what?

Distance? Well, yes, a sort of distance, or a mute
5 remove from the genuine distress he witnessed
in the endlessly grasping hands of multitudes

and, often enough, in his own embarrassing
circle of intimates. Even now, he could see
these where they slept, sprawled upon their robes or wrapped

among the arching olive trees. Still, something new,   10
unlikely, uncanny was commencing as he spoke.
As the divine in him contracted to an ache,

a throbbing in the throat, his vision blurred, his voice
grew thick and unfamiliar; his prayer – just before
it fell to silence – became uniquely earnest.   15

And in that moment – perhaps because it was so
new – he *saw* something, had his first taste of what
he would become, first pure taste of the body, and the blood.

Li-Young Lee

⟨ 1 9 5 7 - ⟩

Though born in Jakarta, Indonesia, Lee has spent most of his life in the United States. Lee's father fled Indonesia with his family in 1959 after suffering as a political prisoner under President Sukarno. Traveling through Hong Kong, Macao, and Japan, the family eventually settled in America. In 1979 Lee earned his BA from the University of Pittsburgh. His poems often consider various forms of love – of father, wife, and children, in particular – expressed through original metaphors and images adapted from the Bible. Lee's father, a professor of medicine in China who converted to Christianity while imprisoned in Indonesia, is often a dramatic presence in the poetry. The writer frequently expresses ambivalence towards his loving, patient, demanding father, a man the poet both resists and reveres: "His love for me feels like fire, / feels like doves." Lee's poems, which have been called "testaments of memory and love," also consider the transience and beauty of life, the necessity of cultural and personal memory, the wonder and strangeness of America, and the relation of sacred and earthly loves. "All writing is a form of love," Lee once remarked. "There are just two subjects, love and death … actually, only one, love – the poem is a record of the way we negotiate with death." His first book, Rose *(1986), received the Delmore Schwartz Memorial Poetry Award, and his second volume,* The City in Which I Love You *(1990), received the Lamont Poetry Award.*

FROM BLOSSOMS

1 FROM BLOSSOMS comes
    this brown paper bag of peaches
    we bought from the boy
    at the bend in the road where we turned toward
5 signs painted *Peaches.*

From laden boughs, from hands,   6
from sweet fellowship in the bins,
comes nectar at the roadside, succulent
peaches we devour, dusty skin and all,
comes the familiar dust of summer, dust we eat.   10

O, to take what we love inside,
to carry within us an orchard, to eat
not only the skin, but the shade,
not only the sugar, but the days, to hold
the fruit in our hands, adore it, then bite into   15
the round jubilance of peach.

There are days we live
as if death were nowhere
in the background; from joy
to joy to joy, from wing to wing,   20
from blossom to blossom to
impossible blossom, to sweet impossible blossom.

THE GIFT

To pull the metal splinter from my palm   1
my father recited a story in a low voice.
I watched his lovely face and not the blade.
Before the story ended, he'd removed
the iron sliver I thought I'd die from.   5

I can't remember the tale,
but hear his voice still, a well
of dark water, a prayer.
And I recall his hands,
two measures of tenderness   10
he laid against my face,
the flames of discipline
he raised above my head.
Had you entered that afternoon
you would have thought you saw a man   15
planting something in a boy's palm,

a silver tear, a tiny flame.
Had you followed that boy
you would have arrived here,
20 where I bend over my wife's right hand.

Look how I shave her thumbnail down
so carefully she feels no pain.
Watch as I lift the splinter out.
I was seven when my father
25 took my hand like this.

and I did not hold that shard
between my fingers and think,
Metal that will bury me,
christen it Little Assassin,
30 One Going Deep for My Heart.
And I did not lift up my wound and cry,
Death visited here!
I did what a child does
when he's given something to keep.
35 I kissed my father.

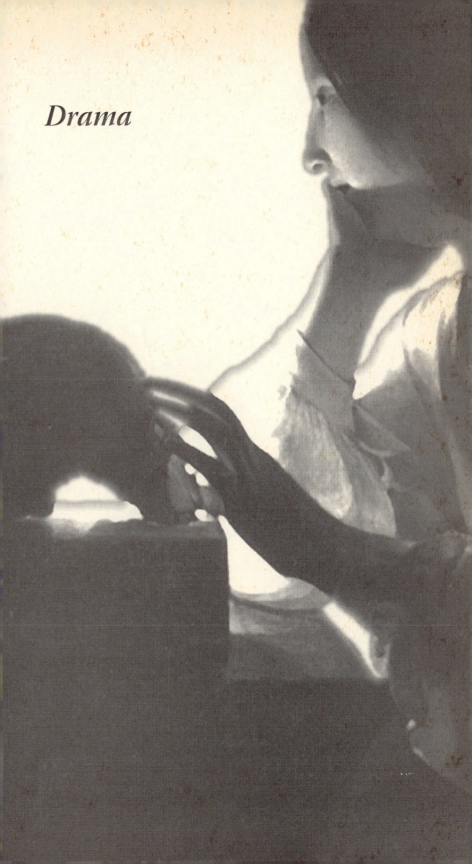

Drama

The York Master

◀(14TH CENTURY)▶

adapted by Tony Harrison

◀(1937-)▶

In the last half of the 1300s, most of the businesses in York, England, were organized into craft guilds (the equivalent of modern trade unions), which collaborated on a brilliant group of plays called The York Cycle. *Starting with* The Creation, *moving to* The Passion, *and ending with* Doomsday, *the York Cycle tells the story of human-kind from beginning to end. The central play,* The Passion, *narrates Christ's death. By calling attention to the daily work of the guilds (for example, the carpenters crucify Christ in* The Passion*), these plays link ordinary town life with the grand design of redemption. In three other English towns, craft guilds wrote and produced cycles of plays, which also remain among our most important medieval literature. Long before theaters were built, these mystery plays were performed once a year in the city streets on large wagons as the central events in city festivals. Tony Harrison's remarkable adaptation of these plays from Middle English emerged from a partnership with actors from England's National Theatre, and that troupe has several times produced these plays with great success. The eloquence of Harrison's powerful rhythms and word sounds become most clear when the plays are read aloud.*

Born in 1937 in Leeds, England to a working class family, Tony Harrison won a scholarship to The University of Leeds and fin-ished his studies there, declining to attend the more prestigious Oxford or Cambridge Universities. He has lived in Africa, Cuba, and Brazil, among other countries, and has long been interested in the struggle of the working class. His poetry has been honored with many prizes, including the Geoffrey Faber Memorial Prize for The Loiners *(1970) and The Whitbread Prize for* Gaze of the Gorgon *(1992). Recognized as England's most accomplished theater and film poet, Harrison has written for The New York Metropolitan Opera, the* BBC, *Channel 4, and for film. His adaptations of historical*

*texts, including the English Mystery Plays and Greek drama, are
so colloquial and electrifying that they have renewed the interest
of contemporary theaters in these important works.*

THE PASSION

adapted from the York Cycle

COMPANY OF CHARACTERS

BAND *musicians*
JOHN BAPTIST *a prophet*
JESUS *the savior*
ANGEL
BLIND MAN ⎱
POOR MAN ⎰ *witnesses of Jesus*
PHILIP
PETER
ANDREW ⎱ *disciples*
JOHN
MARCELLUS ⎰
JUDAS *the betrayer*
BURGHER *a city leader*
PILATE *governor of Judea*
PERCULA *wife of Herod*
CAYPHAS ⎱ *high priests*
ANNAS ⎰
FOUR KNIGHTS *vassals to the high priests*
MALCUS *servant of the high priests*
WOMAN *relative of Malcus*
BARABBAS *a ruffian*
MARY MOTHER *Jesus' mother*
MARY MAGDALENE ⎱ *followers of Jesus*
MARY SALOME ⎰
SIMON OF CYRENE *a traveler*
MINER
DEATH, BOY, THREE WOMEN, THREE MEN

[*The* **COMPANY** *in the various uniforms and overalls of carpenter,
painter, butcher, fireman, bus conductor, ticket collector, fishmonger,*

miner, mechanic, meat-porter, cleaner, gas fitter, construction worker,
etc., help the audience as they arrive to their places and talk to them.
The **Band** *on the stage begins to play a polka tune and some of the*
Company *dance to it, while others clap in rhythm. After the polka,*
the **Band** *sings "All in the Morning" (melody traditional; additional*
lyrics by John Tams).]

1 **Band** "It was on Christmas Day and all in the morning
     Our Savior was born and our Heavenly King.
     And was not this a joyful thing?
     And sweet Jesus we'll call him by name.

5   "It was on the same day and all in the morning
     The shepherds were led to our Heavenly King.
     And was not this a joyful thing?
     And sweet Jesus they called him by name.

     "It was on a Holy Day and all in the morning
10   They baptized our Savior our Heavenly King.
     And was this not a joyful thing?
     And sweet Jesus they called him by name."

[*During the song* **Three Women** *from the* **Company** *and* **Jesus** *move*
into the pit among the audience, and the **Women** *help* **Jesus** *to don a*
simple, rough, oat-colored robe over his overalls. **John Baptist***, also*
in a simple robe over working clothes, gets into position on the steps
above the audience in the pit. The **Company** *moves into position for*
the Baptism of Jesus.]

1 · THE BAPTISM OF JESUS

[*The* **Company** *unfolds a blue silk cloth to represent the water of the*
River Jordan.]

1.1 **John Baptist** Almighty God, and Lord, I say
     Full wonderful is man's failing
     For if I preach them day by day,
     And tell them, Lord, of thy coming
1.5   That all has wrought,
     Men are so dull that my preaching
        Serves for nought.
[*Addressing* **Jesus** *at the other side of the "river."*]
     When I have, Lord, in the name of thee

Baptized the folk in water clear,
Then have I said that after me   1.10
Shall he come that has more power
 Than I can boast
He shall give bapti'm more entire
 In fire and Ghost.

[*The* COMPANY *kneels, holding the edges of the blue cloth and shakes it*
gently to create the flowing of the River Jordan.]

Thus am I come in message right   1.15
And am forerunner in certain,
In witness-bearing of that light,
The which shall lighten every man
 That comes at hand
Into this world; now whoso can   1.20
 May understand.

[*An* ANGEL *appears at an upper level.*]

tak tent · pay attention   ANGEL Now, John, tak tent* what I shall say.
I bring thee tidings wonder good.
My Jesu shall come this day
From Galilee unto this flood   1.25
 Ye Jordan call.
Bapti'm to take mildly with mood,
 This day he shall.

[*The* ANGEL *disappears.*]

wot · know   JOHN BAPTIST But well I wot,* bapti'm is ta'en
To wash and cleanse a man of sin;   1.30
And well I wot that sin is none
In him, without him or within.
 What needs he then
To be baptized for any sin,
 Like sinful men?   1.35

kind · nature   JESUS John, kind* of man is frail,
To which I have me knit,
But I shall show thee reasons two,
That thou shalt know by kindly wit
The cause why I have ordained so;   1.40
 And one is this –
Mankind may not unbaptised go
 To endless bliss.

And since myself have taken mankind,
1.45 Men shall me for their mirror make.
I have their doing in my mind,
And so I do this bapti'm take.
 I will thereby
Myself be baptized for this sake
1.50 Full openly.
JOHN BAPTIST Lord, methinks it were more need
 Thou baptized me.
JESUS Thou sayest full well, John certainly.
But suffer now, that righteousness
1.55 Be fulfilled not in word only
 But als' in deed,
 Through bapti'm clear.
Come, baptize me in my manhood
 Now and here.
[**JOHN BAPTIST** *rises.* **JESUS** *moves towards him.*]
1.60 **JOHN BAPTIST** Ah, Lord; I tremble where I stand,
I am afeard to do that deed.
But save me, Lord that all ordained,
For thee to touch have I great dread,
 For doings dark.
1.65 Now help me, Lord, through thy godhead,
 To do this work.
Jesu, my Lord of mights the most,
I baptize thee here in the name
Of the Father and of the Son and Holy Ghost.
[*The blue cloth is waved over the head of* **JESUS**, *who is thus immersed in the River Jordan.* **JESUS** *rises.* **THREE MEN** *raise* **JOHN BAPTIST** *high into the air.*]
Now, sirs, that bairn⁕ that Mary bore   **bairn** · child
1.70 Be with you all.
[*Music. Exit the* **COMPANY**.]

2 · THE ENTRY INTO JERUSALEM

[*Music. The* **BAND** *leads a procession of the* **COMPANY** *who leave by one exit into the foyer, where they put on the robes of disciples. Only the actors who are to play the* **BLIND MAN** *and the* **POOR MAN** *remain.*]
2.1 **BLIND MAN** Ah lord, that all this world has made,
Both sun and moon and night and day,

What noise is this that makes me glad?
From whence it comes, I cannot say,
    Or what it mean. 2.5
If any man walk in this way,
    Say what is seen.

POOR MAN Why, man, what ails thee so to cry?
Where would thou be? Now tell me here.

BLIND MAN Ah, Sir, a poor blind man am I, 2.10
aye · always   And aye* have been from tender year,
    Since I was born.
I heard a voice of noble cheer,
    Here me before.

POOR MAN Man, wilt thou ought that I can do? 2.15

wit · know   **BLIND MAN** Yea, Sir; for gladly would I, wit,*
If thou would ought declare me true
This mirth I heard, what mean may it?
    Dost understand?

POOR MAN Jesu the prophet full of grace 2.20
    Comes here at hand,
And all the citizens from town
Go him to meet with melody,
With the fairest procession
That was ever seen in this Jewry. 2.25
    He is right near.

BLIND MAN Sir, help me to the street hastily,
    That I may hear
That noise, and that I might through grace –
My sight of him to crave I would. 2.30

[**THREE WOMEN** *enter and unroll a long rubber darts mat to serve as
the path of strewn palms.* **WOMAN 3** *sweeps the mat once it is unrolled.
The* **POOR MAN** *goes to the* **BLIND MAN** *to lead him into the pit to meet*
JESUS*. The* **COMPANY** *enters with four men carrying* **JESUS** *seated on a
wooden donkey. The* **BAND** *leads the procession.*]

POOR MAN Lo, he is here at this same place.
    Cry fast on him; look thou be bold,
high · loud   With voice right high.*

BLIND MAN Jesu, Thou Son of David called,
    Have thou mercy. 2.35
Alas! I cry, he hears me not;

He has no ruth* for my misfare.*

He turns his ear. Where is his thought?

POOR MAN Cry somewhat louder; do not spare.

2.40   So may you speed.

BLIND MAN Jesu, thou salver of all sore,*

To me give good heed.

PHILIP Cease, man, and cry not so.

The prince of the people goes thee by.

2.45   Thou should sit still and attend thereto.

Here passes the prophet of mercy;

Thou dost amiss.

BLIND MAN Ah, David's son, to thee I cry,

The king of bliss.

2.50   **PETER** Lord, have mercy and let him go;

He cannot cease of his crying;

He follows us both to and fro;

Grant him his boon and his asking

And let him wend.*

2.55   We get no rest until this thing

Be brought to end.

JESUS What wouldst thou, man, I to thee did?

In this presence, tell openly.

[*The* **BLIND MAN** *kneels*]

BLIND MAN Lord, mine eyesight from me is hid;

2.60   Grant it to me, I cry mercy.

This would I have.

JESUS Look up now with cheer blithely.

Thy faith can save.

[*The* **BLIND MAN** *looks up slowly and takes in the newly opened world
of sight; then, he rises slowly.*]

BLIND MAN Worship and honor aye to thee,

2.65   With all service that can be done!

The king of bliss, loved might he be,

That thus my sight has sent me soon,

And all through thee.

I was as blind as any stone;

2.70   But now I see.

[*Procession. A* **BURGHER** *steps out of the crowd.*]

BURGHER Hail, blissful babe in Bethleme born!

---

ruth · pity

misfare · misfortune

salver of all sore ·
healer of all sorrow

wend · go

COMPANY Hail!

BURGHER Ransomer of sinners all!

COMPANY Hail!

BURGHER He that shaped both even and morn!   2.75

COMPANY Hail!

BURGHER Welcome of us shall on thee fall!

COMPANY Hail!

BURGHER Royal Jew!

COMPANY Hail!   2.80

BURGHER Comely˙ corse,˙ that we thee call
    With mirth still new

COMPANY Hail!

BURGHER Sun aye shining with bright beams!

COMPANY Hail!   2.85

BURGHER Lamp of life that ne'er goes out!

COMPANY Hail!

BURGHER Lucid lantern's lovely gleams

COMPANY Hail!

BURGHER Salver of our sores so stout!   2.90
    We welcome thee!

COMPANY Hail!

BURGHER And welcome of all about
    To our city!

COMPANY Hail!   2.95

[*Music. The procession continues. The* BAND *returns to its place on the
stage. As the music ends,* JUDAS *jumps down from the bridge onto the
stage.* JUDAS *prowls up and down addressing the audience.*]

JUDAS Unjustly injured, I Judas, by Jesus, that Jew!
    Bursar was I, balancing t' brethren's budgeting book.
    To temptations I tumbled, to tell the tale true.
    And a tenth of each total the treasurer took.

    At Bethany˙ betimes my bale˙ did begin,   2.100
    When Mary brought balm in a beauteous box˙
    In t' best of all alabaster˙ was t' balm brought in
    And she lollopeth˙ the lot on yon lotterell's˙ locks!

    "What waste," wailed I then, "that woman hath wrought!"
    Seeing spikenard˙ so slopped, sir, seres˙ my soul sore.   2.105

Comely · beautiful

corse · body

Bethany · a small village on the eastern slope of the Mount of Olives, just outside of Jerusalem; this was the home of Mary, Martha, and Lazarus

bale · evil

Mary ... box · see John 12:1–4

alabaster · a translucent, ornamental stone

lollopeth · clumsily spills

lotterell's · rascal's

spikenard · a sweet-smelling perfume; one pound sold for nearly a year's wage

seres · sears, blights

2.106　What blessing to t' burdened that balm might have bought.
　　　　Its 300 pence price provide plenty for t' poor.
　　　　Think of folk famished and feeble that fortune would feed.

　　　　Judge ye, gentills all, what that Jesus did jaw —

2.110　"Judas, the needy shall never not need,
　　　　But among ye may I move not a moon* more."
　　　　The poor's plight pricked me not, to play no pretence.
　　　　What pricked me and pined* me was t' loss of my pence.

moon · month

pined · pained

　　　　The cause which that cursed Christ to cumbrance* shall
　　　　　come
2.115　And foiled of my fiddle full fast will I flit,
　　　　Sell that sauntering sawterell* for that selfsame sum
　　　　And thirty pence pocket from Pontius Pilate.

cumbrance · trouble

sawterell · phony saint

　　　　[*Exit* JUDAS *to booing. Music. During the music the* THREE WOMEN *set
　　　　the table for the Last Supper.*]
BAND　On Holy Wednesday and, all in the morning.
　　　　Judas betrayed our Heavenly King.
2.120　And was not this a woeful thing.
　　　　And sweet Jesus they call him by name.

　　　　For thirty silver pieces they sold our savior.
　　　　And Peter thrice denied our Heavenly King.
　　　　And was not this a woeful thing.
2.125　And sweet Jesus they call him by name.

3 · THE LAST SUPPER

　　　　[JESUS *enters the pit and the* DISCIPLES *form a circle.*]
3.1　JESUS　Peace be both by day and night
　　　　Unto this house, and to all that's here.
　　　　Here will I hold, as I have hight,*
　　　　The feast of Pasch* with friends full dear.
3.5　Therefore array you all in row;
　　　　Myself shall part it you between.

hight · said

Pasch · Passover, which
commemorates the
liberation of the Israelites
from Egyptian bondage

　　　　Wherefore I will that ye
　　　　Eat thereof every one;

The remnant parted shall be
To the poor that purveys none.   3.10
Marcell, my own disciple dear,
Do bring us water here in haste.

[MARCELLUS *brings a bowl of water and a towel.*]

MARCELLUS Master, it's already here,
And here a towel clean to taste.

JESUS Come forth with me together here;   3.15
My words shall not be wrought in waste.
Set your feet forth; let's see.
They shall be washen soon.

PETER Ah, Lord by the leave of thee,

That deed ... beseech thee · see John 13:5–9

That deed shall not be done.   3.20
Never I shall make my members meet
Nor see service, Lord, from thee.

JESUS Peter, unless thou let me wash thy feet
Thou gets no part in bliss with me.

PETER Ah mercy, Lord and master sweet!   3.25
Out of that bliss that I not be,
Wash on, my Lord, till all be wet,
Both head and hand, I beseech thee.˙

[*Music.* JESUS *takes the towel from* MARCELLUS *and goes counter-clock-
wise round the circle of* DISCIPLES, *and washes the feet of each one.*
JESUS *forgets* MARCELLUS *who reminds him with a little cough.* JESUS
washes the feet of MARCELLUS *and the other* DISCIPLES *laugh.* JESUS
*then crosses to the table laid for the Last Supper and takes up his posi-
tion behind his place at the center of the table. The* DISCIPLES *follow
to their positions with* JUDAS *at the end of the stage. The* DISCIPLES *sit.*
MARCELLUS *sets bread and wine on the table in front of* JESUS. JESUS
picks up the bread and breaks it in half.]

JESUS This bread, that I do bless and break
It is my corse, no common crust.   3.30
This beaker's t' blood shed for thy sake

ilk · each

And sup of it ilk˙ man you must.

[JESUS *goes behind the disciples with bread and wine. He tears off a
piece of bread for each disciple, and the disciples pass on the goblet of
wine from one to another.*]

One who hath broke bread with me
Shall me into cumbrance cast.

3.35   See where I serve this sop –'tis he!

[JESUS *hands bread to* JUDAS *and addresses him.*]

    What thou must do, do thou full fast.

[*The* DISCIPLES *murmur anxiously among themselves and cast suspicious glances towards* JUDAS *who rises and moves into the pit.*]

JUDAS Now is it time for me to gang,˙   **gang ·** have gone

    For here begins annoy˙ all new.   **annoy ·** trouble

    My fellows mummels,˙ them among,   **mummels ·** murmurs

3.40   That I should all this bargain brew.

    And certes˙ they shall not weep it wrong;   **certes ·** certainly

    To the prince of priests I shall pursue,

    And they shall learn him other ere long,

    That all his saws˙ sore shall him rue.˙   **saws ·** sayings

3.45   I know where he removes˙   **rue ·** regret

    With his fellows ilk one;   **removes ·** withdraws

    I shall tell to the Jews,

    And tite˙ he shall be ta'en.   **tite ·** immediately

[*Exit* JUDAS.]

JESUS I warn you now, my friends so free;

3.50   See to these sayings that I say.

    The fiend is wroth˙ with you and me,   **wroth ·** angry

    And will you mar,˙ if that he may.   **mar ·** ruin

    But Peter, I have prayed for thee,

    So that thou shalt not fear his affray;˙   **affray ·** assault

3.55   And comfort thou this company

    And guide them, when I am gone away.

PETER Ah, Lord, where thou wilt stay

    I shall stay in that stead,

    And with thee make my way

3.60   Evermore, alive or dead.

ANDREW No worldly dread shall me withdraw,

    But I shall with thee live and die.

JOHN Certes, so shall we all on row,˙   **on row ·** all together, united

    Else mickle˙ woe were we worthy.

[*The* DISCIPLES *beat with their hands on the table to show their agreement.* JESUS *addresses* PETER.]   **mickle ·** much

3.65 JESUS Peter, I say to you this saw,

    Which you shall find no fantasy.

    This very night ere the cock crow,

Shalt thou three times my name deny,
And say ye knew me never,
Nor company of mine. 3.70

liever · rather

PETER Alas, lord, I would liever*

pine · pain

Be put to endless pine.*

[*Music (drums).* DISCIPLES *all rise.* PILATE *enters on the bridge above the stage. When he reaches center, the drums stop.* PERCULA *enters on the bridge, meets* PILATE *center. Exeunt** DISCIPLES *from the table.*]

Exeunt · "they go out" (Latin), the plural of exit

4 · PILATE AND PERCULA

PILATE Lo, Pilate am I, proved prince of great pride, 4.1
I was put into Pontius, the people to press;
And then Cæsar himself, with senators by side,
Remitted me to these realms, all ranks to redress.

PERCULA I am Dame Precious Percula, of princesses the prize, 4.5
Wife to Sir Pilate here, prince without peer.
All well of all womanhood am I, witty and wise
Conceive now my countenance so comely and clear.

PILATE Now say may ye safely; I will certify the same.

gramercy · many thanks

PERCULA Gracious lord, gramercy;* your good word is gain. 4.10

PILATE Yet to comfort my corse, I must kiss you, madame.

forward · proposal

PERCULA To fulfil your forward,* my fair lord, I am fain.*

fain · inclined, glad

PILATE How, how, fellows! Now in faith I am fain
Of these lips that so lovely are lapped.

[PILATE *kisses* PERCULA.]

In bed 'tis full blithe to remain. 4.15

PERCULA Yea, sir; it needs must be plain.

PILATE All ladies, we covet them both to be kissed and be clapped.

[*Enter* CAYPHAS *followed by* ANNAS *on to the stage below* PILATE *and* PERCULA.]

CAYPHAS My liberal lord, O leader of laws
I beseech you, my sovereign, assent to my saws —

PERCULA How now! Hearken, jawing and jangling of Jews! 4.20

whoreson · detestable

Why, begone, whoreson* boy, when I bid thee;

carl · churl, lowbrow

Away, cursed carl;* haste thee and hide thee!

PILATE Do mend you, madame, and your mood be amending

meseems · it seems to me

For meseems* it were fitting to hear what he says.

sooth · truth

ANNAS Sir, for to certify the sooth* in your sight 4.25

4.26 To you as our sovereign seemly˙ we seek.   seemly · appropriately

PILATE Why, is there some mischief that musters his might?

ANNAS Yea, Sir; there a rank swain˙   rank swain · corrupt boy

Whose rule is not right

4.30 For he teaches folk him for to call

Great God's son; thus grieves he us all.

CAYPHAS To us, Sir, his law is full loth.   loth · loathsome

PILATE Beware that ye wax not too wroth.

CAYPHAS Sir, without this abating, there hangs as I hope

4.35 A man hilt full of ire,˙ for hasty he is.   ire · anger

PILATE What comes he for?

CAYPHAS I ken˙ him not, but he is clad in a cape.   ken · know

He comes with a keen face, uncomely to kiss.

PILATE Go get him, that his grief we may straitly grope

4.40 So no open language be going amiss.

[ANNAS *to* JUDAS *offstage.*]

ANNAS Come on lively now to my lords, if ye list˙ for to leap,   list · care

But utter so thy language that thou bar not their bliss.

[*Enter* JUDAS.]

JUDAS Sir Pilate most potent a plea I pursue

That Jesus, that Jew, I would sell unto you.

4.45 PILATE What hightest˙ thou?   hightest · to be named

JUDAS Judas Scariot.

PILATE Howgates˙ bought shall he be? Bring forth thy bargain.   Howgates · by what manner

JUDAS But for a little amends to bear hence again.

PILATE Nay, what shall we pay?

4.50 JUDAS Sir, thirty pence, flat; no more then.

[*Music.* PILATE *takes out a bag of coins and drops them one by one to the stage below.* JUDAS *scrabbles about collecting them as they fall. On the final note of the music,* PILATE *throws down a handful of coins which* JUDAS *catches in his outstretched robe.*]

I shall teach you a token him quick for to take.

Where he is ringed in the throng; my word I will keep.

[JUDAS *leaves the stage and begins to enter the pit.* PILATE *calls after him.*]

PILATE We know him not.

[JUDAS *stops and calls up to* PILATE *on the bridge.*]

JUDAS Take care then that caitiff˙ to catch   caitiff · scoundrel

4.55 Whom there I shall kiss.

[*Exit* JUDAS. PILATE *addresses* CAYPHAS *and* ANNAS.]

PILATE Now farewell, and walk on your way.   4.56

[*To* **PERCULA**, *putting his arm round her shoulder*]

I command thee, come near;

I will to my couch.

Have me in your hands handily,

and heave me from here.   4.60

[**PILATE** *and* **PERCULA** *begin their exit,* **PILATE** *leaning heavily on his wife.*]

PERCULA Ah, Sir, ye weigh well.

PILATE Yea, I have wet me with wine.

minion · follower

Look that no man or minion· of mine

With no noise may come nigh me or near.

[*Exeunt* **PILATE** *and* **PERCULA**. *Music. During the music,* **JESUS** *enters and kneels among the standing audience in the pit. Music stops.*]

5 · THE AGONY & THE BETRAYAL

[**JESUS** *kneels.*]

JESUS Thou, Father, that all formed has with food for to fill,   5.1

I feel by my feardness my flesh would full fain

Be turned from this torment and taken thee until,

mazed · confused

in mood and in main ·
in mind and body

For mazed· is my manhood in mood and in main.·

But if thee see soothly· that thy son stiff   5.5

soothly · truly

Withouten surfeit· of sin thus sakless· be slain,

surfeit · excess

Be it worthy wrought even at thy own will,

sakless · without blame

For, Father, at thy bidding am I buxom· and bayne·…

buxom · obedient

Salver of all sore, some succor· me send.

bayne · waiting

The Passion they purpose to put me upon   5.10

succor · comfort

My flesh is full feared and fain would defend.

At Thy will be it wrought and right worthily won.

Have mind of my manhood, my mood for to mend.

Some comfort I crave in this case.

And Father, I shall death taste   5.15

maker unmade · an
echo of the Nicene Creed,
which describes Christ
as "the only Son of God,
eternally begotten of
the Father … begotten,
not made, one in Being
with the Father"

I will it not defend;

Yet if thy will be

Spare me a space.

[*An* **ANGEL** *appears at the upper level.*]

ANGEL Unto thee maker unmade· that most is of might

ay · and

Be loving ay· lasting in light that is lent.   5.20

5.21   Thy Father that in heaven is most, He upon height,
Thy sorrows for to sober, to thee has me sent.
For deeds that man has thy death shall be dight,   **dight** · commanded
And thou with torments be toiled, but take now intent.

5.25   Thy bale' shall be for the best.   **bale** · suffering
Through that shall man's sin be amend;
Then shall thou withouten any end
Reign in thy royalty full of rest.

    [*The* ANGEL *disappears.*]

JESUS Now in my flesh feared be, Father, I am fain
5.30   That mine anguish and my noyes' are near at an end.   **noyes** · injuries

    [JESUS *rises.*]

    Unto my disciples go will I again
Kindly to comfort them that mazed is in their mind.

    [JESUS *moves to* PETER.]

    Now will this hour be nighing full near
That'll certify all the sooth that I've said.

    [*Enter* JUDAS.]

5.35 JUDAS All hail, Master, in faith, and fellows all here.
With great, gracious greeting on t' ground be arrayed.
I would ask you a kiss, Master, if your will were,
For all my love and my liking wholly on you is laid.

JESUS Full heartily, Judas, have it even here.

    [JUDAS *embraces* JESUS.]

5.40   For with this kiss is Man's Son betrayed.

    [FOUR KNIGHTS *surround* JESUS *from all sides.* PETER *moves to defend*
    JESUS.]

KNIGHT 1 Ha! stand, traitor. I tell thee for ta'en.'   **I tell thee for ta'en** ·
    [*A brilliant light shines from the body of* JESUS.]   "that is what I take
                                                  you to be"

KNIGHT 3 Alas! we are lost for gleam of this light.

JESUS Say ye here, whom seek ye? Do tell me; let's see.

KNIGHT 4 One Jesus of Nazareth; I think that name right.

5.45 JESUS Behold ye all hitherward. Lo, here; I am he.

KNIGHT 1 Stand, dastard.' So dreadful thy death shall be dight.   **dastard** · base coward
I'll be no more abashed thy shining to see.

KNIGHT 3 Ah, out! I am amazed almost in main and in might.

KNIGHT 2 And I fear, by my faith, and fain would I flee;
5.50   For such a sight have I not seen.

KNIGHT 3 This gleam, it gleamed so light,   5.51
    I saw ne'er such a sight.
    Me marvel much what it may mean.
JESUS Come, whom seek ye assembled, yet I say?
KNIGHT 1 One Jesus of Naz'reth; him would we nigh now.   5.55
JESUS And I am he soothly, And that shall I say.
    [**MALCUS** *moves towards* **JESUS**.]
MALCUS For that shalt thou die, dastard, Since it is thou.

flay · to strip off the skin   **PETER** And I shall try by my faith thee for to flay.·
lurdan · a stupid person   Here with a lash, lurdan,· I shall thee allow.
    [**PETER** *raises a putty knife and cuts off* **MALCUS**'s *ear.* **MALCUS** *claps*
    his hand to his ear and falls to his knees.]
MALCUS Ah, behold what the dastard hath done!   5.60

trow · believe   **PETER** Nay, traitor, but truly I shall trap thee, I trow.·
JESUS Peace, Peter, I bid thee;

fash thee · trouble   Fash thee· no further, nor frame thee to fight
yourself   If my will were, as thou well wit,
    I might have power in great plenty   5.65
    Of angels full many to muster my might.
    So put thy sword in its sheath, and haste not to hit.
    He that smites with sword, with sword shall be smit.
    [*To* **MALCUS**]

dight · abused   Thou man thus in dread and dolefully dight,·
    Come here to me safely and be salved of thy pain.   5.70
    In the name of my Father that in heaven is most in height,
    Of thy hurts be thou whole in hide and in bone,
    As this virtue in thy veins shall avail.
    [**JESUS** *restores* **MALCUS**'s *ear.* **MALCUS** *touches it in wonder.*]
MALCUS What? All hail! I believe that I be whole!

beshrew · curse   Now beshrew· him this time that gives tale   5.75
    To touch thee for thy travail.
    [**MALCUS** *kisses the robe of* **JESUS**. **KNIGHT 1** *moves towards* **JESUS** *with*
    a noose. **KNIGHT 3** *moves in from the other side.*]
KNIGHT 1 Do, fellows, by your faith, let us hang on all here.

hind · a rustic lad, a   For I have on this hind· firm hold as I can.
fellow (a term of   [**KNIGHT 2**, *moving in to the right of* **JESUS**.]
contempt)   **KNIGHT 2** And I have a lock on him now. How, fellows, draw near.
    [*They seize* **JESUS**.]

ban · curse   **KNIGHT 3** Yea, by the bones that him bare this jest shall he ban.· 5.80

[KNIGHT 4 *clears a way through the audience in the pit, and the* FOUR
KNIGHTS *begin to drag* JESUS *away.*]

5.81 JESUS Even like a thief heinously hurl ye me here.

I taught in your Temple; why took ye me not then?

Now has darkness on earth all his power.

[*The bright light issuing from the body of* JESUS *disappears. Music. The*
FOUR KNIGHTS *drag* JESUS *round the pit and off.*]

6 · THE PALACE OF THE HIGH PRIEST, CAYPHAS

[*Enter* CAYPHAS *on the stage.*]

6.1 CAYPHAS With witchcraft he fares withal

Sirs, that same shall ye see full soon.

Our knights, all forth they went

To take him and betray;

6.5 By this I hold him spent;

He cannot wend away.

[*Enter* ANNAS *bearing a large goblet of wine.*]

ANNAS Would ye, sir, take your rest –

The day is come at hand –

And with wine slake your thirst?

6.10 Then durst I well warrant

Ye should have tidings soon

Of the knights that are gone,

And how they yet have done,

To trap and take him anon.˙   anon · now

6.15 Now put all thought away,

And let your matters rest.

[CAYPHAS, *taking the goblet from* ANNAS.]

CAYPHAS I will do as ye say;

Do give us wine of the best.

For be we once well wet,

6.20 The better will we rest.

ANNAS My lord, here is wine that will make you to wink;

It is liquor full delicious, my lord, if you like.

Wherefore I deem deeply a draught that ye drink,

For in this country that we know I vow is none like.

6.25 Therefore we counsel you

This cup savorly for to kiss.

[CAYPHAS, *belching.*]

CAYPHAS Come now daintily, and dress me on t' dais,˙
  And handily heap on me happing,˙
  And warn all wights˙ to be in peace,
  For I am laid late unto napping.   6.30

ANNAS My lord, with your leave,
  If it like you, I pass.

  [**CAYPHAS**, *addressing audience.*]

CAYPHAS Adieu be unto you,
  As the manner has.

  [*Exeunt* **CAYPHAS** *and* **ANNAS**. *Music* (*drums*).]

Glosses (left margin):
dais · a raised platform
happing · covers for warmth, a quilt
wights · creatures, people

7 · PETER DENIES JESUS

[*Enter into the pit a* **WOMAN**, *the* **FOUR KNIGHTS** *holding* **JESUS** *in a kind of "cart," and* **PETER**. *The* **WOMAN** *faces the* **KNIGHTS**; **PETER** *stands opposite. The remaining company forms a* **CROWD** *in the pit.*]

WOMAN Sir knights, do keep this boy so bound,   7.1
  For I will go wit what it may mean,
  Why that yon wight was following found
  Early and late, morning and even.
  He will come near, he will not let;˙   7.5
  He is a spy, I warrant, full bold.

KNIGHT 3 It seems by his semblance he'd sooner be set
  By the fervent fire, to flee from the cold.

WOMAN Yea, but ye wist˙ as well as I
  What wonders that this wight has wrought;   7.10
  And for his master's sorcery
  Full fiercely should his death be bought.

KNIGHT 1 Dame, we have him now at will
  That we have long time sought;
  If others go by us still,   7.15
  For them we have no thought.

WOMAN It were great scorn if he should 'scape,
  Without he had reason and skill;
  He looketh lurking like an ape;
  I think in haste to take him still.   7.20
  Thou caitiff, what moves thee to stand
  So stable and still in thy thought?
  Thou has wrought mickle wrong in land,
  And wonderful works hast thou wrought.

Glosses (left margin):
let · leave
wist · know

7.25   Wait now! He looks like a brock;˙

       Were he in a band bound for to bait;

       Or else like an owl on a stock,

       Full privily his prey for to wait.

  PETER Woman, thy words and thy wind do not waste.

7.30   Of his company never was I kenned.˙

       Thou has mismarked me, truly me trust;

       Wherefore of thy miss do thou mend.

  WOMAN Then hen-heart˙ avow all ye averred was amiss˙

       When ye said that yon sawterell, shall save us from sin

7.35   And gainsay˙ that that gadling God's given son is

       Who walketh the world all wights'˙˙ worship to win.

  PETER I will consent to your saws; what should I say more?

       For women are crabbed; that comes of their kind.

       But I say as I first said, I ne'er saw him e'er.

7.40   But as a friend of your fellowship shall ye me aye find.

  [**WOMAN** *leads* **MALCUS** *from the crowd to before the* **KNIGHTS** *and* **JESUS**.]

  WOMAN Say how this sawterell swiped off thine ear.

  MALCUS Yea, sirs, this sawterell swiped off my ear.

  WOMAN This lurdan lashed out and lopped off thy lug.˙

  MALCUS This lurdan lashed out and lopped off my lug.

7.45   **WOMAN** How that harlot˙ full hastily made it all whole.

  MALCUS This Jesu here hastily made it all whole.

  PETER I was never with him in work that he wrought,

       In word nor work, in will nor in deed.

       I know none that ye have hither brought,

7.50   In no court of this kith,˙ if I should right rede.˙

  [*A cock crows.*]

  JESUS Peter, Peter, thus said I ere,

       When you said you would abide with me

       In weal˙ and in woe, in sorrow and care,

       Whilst I should thrice forsaken be.

7.55   **PETER** Alas the while that I came here,

       Or e'er denied my Lord apart.

       The look of his fair face so clear

       With full sad sorrow shears my heart.

  [**PETER** *screams. Music. Exeunt* **FOUR KNIGHTS** *and* **JESUS** *from their "cart" and enter on the stage.*]

---

brock · badger

kenned · acquainted

hen-heart · coward

avow all ... was amiss · swear that all you believed was false

gainsay · deny

wights' · creatures'

lug · lobe

harlot · vagabond

kith · country

rede · reckon

weal · wealth, good fortune

8 · JESUS EXAMINED BY CAYPHAS

[Enter **Cayphas** and **Annas** on the stage.]

CAYPHAS If thou be Christ, God's son, tell it to us two.   8.1

JESUS Sir, thou sayest it thyself, and soothly I say,

fro · from   That I shall go to my father as I came fro,⸱

And dwell with him joyful in weal alway.

CAYPHAS Why, fie on thee, traitor, untrue!   8.5

The father hast thou foully defamed.

[*To audience.*]

Now need we notices new;

Himself with his saws he has shamed.

ANNAS Now needs neither witness nor counsel to call,

But take his saws as he says them in the same stead,   8.10

He slanders the Godhead and so grieves us all,

Wherefore well worthy is he to be dead.

And therefore, sir, tell him the truth.

CAYPHAS Surely, so I shall

harlot · rascal   Hearest thou not, harlot?⸱ I'll hap⸱ on thy head.   8.15

hap · heap   Answer here directly to great and to small

And reach us out rapidly some reason, I rede.

JESUS My reasons are not to rehearse

Nor they that might help me are not here now.

ANNAS Nay, lad, if ye list to make verse,   8.20

Priest prattles prettier poetry than thou.

JESUS Sir, if I say thee sooth, thou shalt not assent,

But hinder, or haste me to hang.

I preached where people were most present,

privity · secrecy   And no point in privity⸱ to old nor young.   8.25

And also in your Temple I told my intent;

Ye might have taken me then for my telling,

brands · sticks for   Much better than bring me with brands⸱ unburnt,
burning

noy · injure   Thus to noy⸱ me by night, and also for nothing.

CAYPHAS For nothing! Losel,⸱ thou liest.   8.30

Losel · ne'er-do-well   Thy words and thy works a vengeance will bring.

JESUS Sir, since thou with wrong so turnest me awry,

Go ask them that heard of my speaking.

ding · smack   **CAYPHAS** Go dress you and ding⸱ you him down,

And deafen us no more with his deeds.   8.35

[**KNIGHT 1** *stands in front of* **JESUS** *and pulls hard on the rope round his neck, dragging him with one jerk to the ground. The other* **KNIGHTS** *close round* **JESUS** *and raise their hammer, wrench, and pliers, above their heads as if to strike* **JESUS**. *They freeze in that position, forming a tableau of the "buffeting."* **CAYPHAS** *and* **ANNAS** *turn away.*]

8.36   Go, tell to Sir Pilate our plaints all plain,
And say, this lad with his lying has our laws lorn;•   **lorn** · destroyed
And say, this same day must he be slain,
Because of the Sabbath which is in the morn;

8.40   And say that we come ourselves for certain,
For to further the affair. Now fare ye before.

[*The* **KNIGHTS** *emerge from the frozen tableau, and raise* **JESUS** *from the ground. They begin to drag him away as* **ANNAS** *addresses him.*]

ANNAS Sir, your fair fellowship we commend to the fiend.

[*Exit* **ANNAS**.]

CAYPHAS Go on, now; dance forth in the devil's way.

[*Exit* **CAYPHAS**. *The* **KNIGHTS** *drag* **JESUS** *away. Music. During the music,* **JUDAS** *emerges from the crowd carrying a bag of money.*]

9 · THE REMORSE OF JUDAS

[**JUDAS**, *to audience.*]

9.1   **JUDAS** Alas, for woe that I was wrought,
Ere ever I came by kind or kin.
I ban the bones that forth me brought;
Woe worth the womb that I bred in,

9.5   So may I bid.
For I so falsely did to him
That unto me great kindness did.
The purse with his expense about I bore;
There was none trusted so well as I.

9.10   Than me he trusted no man more,
And I betrayed him traitorly
        With lies all vain.
Blameless• I sold his body   **Blameless** · although
Unto his foes for to be slain.   Jesus is blameless

9.15   To slay my sovereign assented I,
And told them the time of his taking.
Shameless• myself thus ruined I,   **Shameless** · because
So soon to assent to his slaying.   Jesus is shameless

Now wist I how he might pass that pain…

boon · gift, benefit   To look how best that boon˙ might be   9.20

[Enter PILATE *on the bridge above the stage. Enter* CAYPHAS *and* ANNAS
on the stage.]

To priests and Sir Pilate I will again,

To save him, that he might pass free.

    That were my will.

Lords, wealth and worship with you be.

PILATE What tidings, Judas, tellest thou still?   9.25

JUDAS My tidings are painful, I tell you,

Sir Pilate, and therefore I pray,

My master that I did sell you,

Good lord, let him wend his way.

CAYPHAS Nay, needs must, Judas, that we deny.   9.30

What mind or matter has moved thee thus?

JUDAS Sir, I have sinned full grievously,

Betrayed that righteous blood Jesus

    And master mine.

CAYPHAS Fair Sir, what is that to us?   9.35

The peril and the plight are thine.

Thine is the wrong, and thou has wrought it;

Thou told us full truly to take him;

And ours is the bargain, for we bought it.

Lo, we all assent for to slay him.   9.40

JUDAS Alas, that may I rue full ill,

If ye assent him for to slay.

PILATE These words that thou names nought needs it.

Thou unhanged harlot, hark what I say.

Spare of thy speaking, for nought speeds it;   9.45

Or walk out at the door, in the devil's way.

JUDAS Why, will ye then not let him pass,

And have of me again your pay?

*[*JUDAS *holds up the bag of money to* PILATE.*]*

PILATE I tell thee, traitor, that I will not.

lorn · lost   JUDAS Then am I lorn˙ this day, alas,   9.50

    Both bone and blood.

Alas the while, so may I say,

That ever I assent to spill his blood.

To save his blood see, sirs, I pray you,

[JUDAS *again holds up the bag of money to* PILATE.]

9.55   And take you there your payment whole.

    Spare for to spill him, now I pray you,

    Else brew ye me full mickle dole.˙   **dole** · grief

PILATE Now hearest thou me, Judas, thou shalt take it again;

    We will it not; what the devil art thou?

9.60   When thou sought us, thou wast full fain

    Of this money; what ails thee now

        For to repent?

[*Exit* PILATE.]

JUDAS That which you took of me, take you it there!

[JUDAS *throws down the bag of money at his feet.*]

    Therewith your mastery make you among,

9.65   And claim it you clean.

    I loathe all my life, so live I too long;

    My treacherous turn torments me with pain.

    Since so my treason I have taken unto me,

    I need ask no mercy, for none shall I get.

9.70   Therefore in haste myself shall I fordo˙ me.   **fordo** · do away with

    Alas the hard while that I ever met yet.

    To slay myself now will I speed,

    For sadly have I served too ill.

        So welaway.˙   **welaway** · an interjec-

9.75   That ever I was in wit or will.   tion of grief

    That trusty true one to betray.

    Alas, who may I move unto?

    No other counsel now I need;

    Myself in haste I shall fordo,

9.80   And take me now unto my death.

[*Exit* JUDAS *through the crowd and into audience, drawn by the figure
of* DEATH. CAYPHAS *and* ANNAS *meet in the center of the stage over
the bag of money.*]

CAYPHAS Come then now, Sir Annas, let us see what you say

    As touching this money that here we have,

    That Judas in wrath has waved away

    And cast to us crabbedly,˙ that cursed knave.˙   **crabbedly** · angrily

9.85   How say ye thereby?   **knave** · rogue

[ANNAS *picks up the bag of money.*]

ANNAS Sir, since he it slung, we shall it save.

CAYPHAS Quick, carry it to our treasury.

[*Music. Exeunt* CAYPHAS *and* ANNAS *in opposite directions. The Band sings (words and music by John Tams).*]

BAND Look up, look up,
    The lamb shall lead the way,
    Look up, look up,   9.90
    The dogs behowl the day.
    And they shall bite,
    Full bellied in their spite.
    What care have they,
    To take the lamb away.   9.95

    Look up, look up.
    The hand divides the gloom.
    Look up, look up.
    The prophet or the doom,•
    And should we die,   9.100
    On whose word can we rely.
    The truth to see,
    Death or eternity.

doom · judgment

    Look up, look up,
    The shepherd takes his place.   9.105
    Look up, look up.
    A mother hides her face.
    And when we die,
    Will there be friends to cry.
    What hope have they,   9.110
    Who turn their heads away.

[*During the song, the* FOUR KNIGHTS *enter with* JESUS, *and set him down on the steps facing the center of the stage, at the opposite end of the pit. A chair is set center stage for* PILATE.]

10 · THE TRIAL BEFORE PILATE & THE JUDGMENT OF JESUS

PILATE Speak; and excuse thee, if thou can.   10.1

mould · mortal flesh   JESUS Every man has a mouth that made is on mould•
    In weal and in woe to wield at his will
    If he govern it goodly, like as God would,

10.5   For his spiritual speech he needs not to spill;
       And, what man shall govern it ill,
       Full unhandy and ill shall he hap.
       For each tale thou talks us until
       You account shall; you cannot escape.

10.10 **PILATE** Sirs mine,
       Ye found, in faith, all his design;
       For in this lad no lies can I trap,
       Nor no point to put him to pine.

      CAYPHAS Without cause, sir, we come not, this carl° to accuse him;   **carl** · villain
10.15   That will we ye wit, as well as worthy.

      PILATE Now. I record well the right; ye will no sooner refuse him
       Till he be driven to his death and doomed to die.
       But take him to you thereby,
       And like as your law will decide,
10.20   Doom° ye his body to abide.   **Doom** · judge

    ANNAS O, Sir Pilate without any peer,
         Now nay;
       Ye wot well (no doubt can appear)
       We may not, not all of us here,
10.25   Slay no man, to you truth to say.

      PILATE Shall I doom him to death, not deserving in deed?
       But I have heard wholly why in heart ye him hate.
       He is faultless, in faith, and so God might me speed,
       I grant him my good will to gang on his gate.°   **gang on his gate** · go
                                               on his way
      [**PILATE** *rises from his chair.*]

10.30 **CAYPHAS** Not so, Sir; for well ye it wot,
       To be king he claimeth with crown.
       Who° so stoutly will step to that state,   **Who** · whoever
       You should doom, sir, to be donged° down   **donged** · struck
         And dead.

10.35 **PILATE** Sir, truly that touches to treason,
       And ere I remove he shall rue that reason,
       Ere I stalk or stir from this stead.
       Sir knights that are comely take this caitiff in keeping;
       Skelp° him with scourges and with scathes° him scorn;   **Skelp** · flay
10.40   Wrest him and wring him till for woe he is weeping,   **scathes** · epithets
       And then bring him before us as he was before.
      [**PILATE** *sits down.*]

KNIGHT 1 He may ban time that he was born;
Soon shall he be served as ye said us.

whop · strip

KNIGHT 4 Do whop* off his weeds* that are worn.

weeds · clothes

[**KNIGHT 1**, *tearing off* **JESUS**'s *robe*]

KNIGHT 1 They are torn off in a trice, take there his trashes.   10.45

bun · bound

KNIGHT 4 He is bun* fast;* now beat on with bitter brashes.*

fast · tightly

Go on; lep,* hear ye, lordings, with lashes.

brashes · attacks

[**KNIGHT 1** *pushes* **JESUS** *towards* **KNIGHT 4** *who punches him.* **KNIGHT**

lep · beat upon

3 *hits* **JESUS** *and he falls.* **KNIGHT 2** *kicks* **JESUS**.]

niggard · stingy person

KNIGHT 2 For all our annoying, this niggard* he naps.

[*The* **KNIGHTS** *lift* **JESUS** *up from the ground.*]

KNIGHT 3 We shall wake him with wind of our whips.

flaps · blows

KNIGHT 4 Now fling to this flatterer with flaps.*   10.50

[**KNIGHT 1** *gives* **JESUS** *a savage blow, then* **KNIGHT 4**, **KNIGHT 3**, *and*
KNIGHT 2 *in turn.* **JESUS** *falls again. The* **KNIGHTS** *lift him up and sit
him down on steps.*]

KNIGHT 3 Now because he a king did him call,
We will kindly him crown with a briar.

[**KNIGHT 3** *takes pincers from his belt and with them lifts a crown of
barbed wire, and holds it above the head of* **JESUS**.]

pall · black

KNIGHT 4 Yea, but first this purple and pall*
And this worthy weed shall he wear.

[**KNIGHT 2** *puts the purple robe on* **JESUS**.]

thring · press, stick

KNIGHT 1 Now thring* to him thrayley* with this thick thorn.   10.55

thrayley · violently

KNIGHT 2 Thus we teach him to temper his tales.

[*The* **WOMAN** *sings.*]

**Sheer Thursday · the
Thursday of Holy Week
(Maundy Thursday)**

WOMAN On Sheer Thursday* and all in the morning
They made a crown of thorns for our Heavenly King.
And was not that a woeful thing
And sweet Jesus they call him by name.   10.60

[**KNIGHT 1** *and* **KNIGHT 3** *hold the crown of barbed wire with pincers,
and lower it onto* **JESUS**'s *head.*]

KNIGHT 2 His brain begins for to bleed.

KNIGHT 1 Now reach him a rush or a reed
So round;
For his scepter it serves indeed.

[**KNIGHT 4** *gives* **KNIGHT 3** *a long screwdriver to put in* **JESUS**'s *hand to
serve as a scepter. Then the* **KNIGHTS** *raise* **JESUS** *to his feet and salute
him mockingly as king.* **KNIGHT 2** *kneels.*]

10.65   **KNIGHT 2** Hail, comely king, that no kingdom has kenned!

        [**KNIGHT 3** *kneels.*]

    KNIGHT 3 Hail, man unmighty wi'out means to mend!

        [**KNIGHT 4** *kneels.*]

    KNIGHT 4 Hail, lord wi'out land for to lend.

        [**KNIGHT 1** *kneels.*]

    KNIGHT 1 Hail, freak wi'out force thee to fend.˙   **fend** · defend

        [*The* **KNIGHTS** *rise.*]

    KNIGHT 3 To Sir Pilate the prince our pride will we praise.

10.70   **KNIGHT 4** Now wightly˙ let us wend on our ways.   **wightly** · bravely, lively

        [*Music. The* **KNIGHTS** *push* **JESUS** *up towards* **PILATE**. **KNIGHT 1**
        addresses **PILATE**.]

    KNIGHT 1 My lord, will ye list˙ to our lays?˙   **list** · listen

    Here this boy is you bade us go harry˙   **lays** · songs, stories

      With blows.   **harry** · torment

    We are cumbered his corse for to carry.

10.75   Many wights on him wonder and worry.

    Lo, his flesh, how its beatings it shows.

    PILATE Well, bring him before us.

        [**KNIGHT 1** *pushes* **JESUS** *so that he staggers nearer to* **PILATE**.]

                Ah, he blushes all blue.

    I suppose of his saying he'll cease evermore

    Sirs, look here on high and see; *Ecce homo*˙   ***Ecce homo*** · "behold the man" (Latin); see John 19:5

10.80   Thus bounden and beat and brought you before.

    Meseems that it serves him full sore.

                Bring forth Barabbas!

        [**PILATE** *moves closer to* **JESUS** *and begins to address the crowd.*]

    This feast is it fashion a felon to free.

    Let each man among you make motion to me

    Which churl be chastened in chains you must choose

10.85   And which prisoner pardoned by Pilate shall pass.

        [**PILATE** *takes hold of* **BARABBAS**'*s left arm and raises it.*]

      Barabbas or…

        [**PILATE** *drops* **BARABBAS**'*s arm and raises* **JESUS**'*s right arm.*]

             Jesus? Judge, all ye Jews.

    CROWD Barabbas! Barabbas! Barabbas!

    PILATE And Jesus clept˙ Christ, how crave ye, pray cry.   **clept** · called

    The prisoner shall pine as the people all please.

10.90   **CROWD** Crucify! Crucify! Crucify!

[PILATE *moves to a* BOY *with bowl of water and a towel.* PILATE *washes his hands, then dries them and turns. As he turns, the* CROWD *stops shouting.*]

PILATE Of blameless blood shall I unblemished be. 10.91
  By Mahound· this misdeed shall not mar me.
  From Barabbas his bonds now unbend;

Mahound · Mohammed; throughout medieval Europe, references to Mohammed denoted heathenism

[KNIGHTS *undo the rope binding* BARABBAS.]
  With grace let him gang his gate
    Where you will. 10.95

BARABBAS Ye worthy men goodly and great,
  God increase all your comely estate,
  For the grace ye grant me until.

[*Exit* BARABBAS.]

PILATE Hear the judgment of Jesus, all ye in this stead.
  Crucify him on a cross, and on Calvary him kill. 10.100
  I doom him today to die this same death;
  Therefore hang him on hight upon that high hill.
  And on either side him I will
  That a harlot ye hang in this haste;
  Methinks it both reason and skill 10.105

amidst · between

  That amidst,· since his malice is most,
    Ye hang him.
  Then him torment, some torture to taste.
  More words I will not now waste;
  But stay not, to death till ye bring him. 10.110

[*Music. The* KNIGHTS *lead* JESUS *off to get the cross. Exeunt* PILATE, CAYPHAS, *and* ANNAS.]

11 · THE ROAD TO CALVARY

[KNIGHT 2, KNIGHT 3, *and* KNIGHT 4 *bring on* JESUS *and the cross.* KNIGHT 1 *clears a way through the crowd for them.*]

KNIGHT 1 Make room, make room and rule now right, 11.1
  That we may with this wearied wight

Wightely · nimbly

  Wightely· wend on our way
  He has napped not in all this night,

dight · ordained

  And this day shall his death be dight;· 11.5
  Let's see who dares say nay.
  Because tomorrow we provide
  For our dear Sabbath day,
  We will nought amiss be moved.

11.10 But mirth in all that ever men may.
We have been busy all this morn
To clothe him and to crown with thorn,
As befits a folly king.
Why, wot thou not as well as I
11.15 This carl must unto Calvary
And there on t' cross be done?

[*Music.* **JESUS** *lifts the cross, and moves slowly round the pit.* **JESUS**
drops the cross, as **JOHN** *enters the pit-side, followed by* **MARY MOTHER**,
MARY MAGDALENE, *and* **MARY SALOME**.]

MARY MOTHER Alas, the time and tide!
I wot the day is come
That once was specified
11.20 By Prophet Simeon,   **Simeon ... subtily** ·
The sword of sorrow, he said, should run   see Luke 2:28–35
Through this heart subtily.·

MARY MAGDALENE Alas, this is a pitiful sight!
He that was ever lovely and light,
11.25 And lord of high and low,
How dolefully· now is he dight.·   **dolefully** · grievously
In world is none so woeful wight,   **dight** · treated
Nor so troubled to know.
They that he mended most,
11.30 In deed and word also,
Now have they full great haste
To death him for to draw.

JESUS Daughters of Jerusalem City,
See, and mourn no more for me,
11.35 But think upon this thing.
Turn home to town again,
Since ye have seen this sight;
It is my Father's will,
All that is done and dight.

11.40 **MARY SALOME** Alas, this is a cursèd case.
He that all heal· in his hand has   **heal** · health
Shall here be blameless slain.
Ah Lord, give leave to clean thy face…

[**MARY SALOME** *carries a towel to* **JESUS**. *She wipes his face, then stares*
at the towel.]

Behold! how he has shewed his grace,

main · power He that is most of main.˙ 11.45

This sign shall bear witness

Unto all people plain,

How God's Son here guiltless

Is put to peerless pain.

[KNIGHT 1 *pushes* MARY SALOME *away.*]

KNIGHT 1 Say, whereto bide ye here about, 11.50

Ye crones, with screaming and with shout?

stevenings · shouts What do these stevenings˙ here?

clout · rag KNIGHT 2 Go home, thou baldhead, with thy clout,˙

lout · worship Or, by that lord we love and lout,˙

Thou shalt ... dear · Thou shalt abide full dear.˙ 11.55
"you'll dearly regret
staying"

MARY SALOME This sign shall vengeance call

On you all that are here.

hie · get KNIGHT 3 Go, hie˙ thee hence withal,

Or ill hail come thou here.

JOHN Lady, your weeping grieves me sore. 11.60

MARY MOTHER John, help me now or nevermore,

That I to him might come.

JOHN My lady, wend we on before,

To Calvary; when we come there,

You shall say what you will. 11.65

KNIGHT 1 What a devil is this to say?

How long shall we stand still?

Go, hie you hence away,

In the devil's name, up the hill.

[JESUS *picks up the cross again and continues round the pit. Then he*
stumbles and stops.]

for-bled · badly KNIGHT 3 Methinks this boy is so for-bled,˙ 11.70
bleeding
With this load may he not be led;

He swoons, that dare I swear.

KNIGHT 1 It needs not hard to haul;

KNIGHT 2 I see here comes a carl

Shall help him forth to bear. 11.75

[*Enter* SIMON OF CYRENE *approaching the* KNIGHTS.]

essay · attempt KNIGHT 3 That shall we see one soon essay,˙

Good man, whither is thou away?

You walk as if in wrath.

SIMON Sir, I have a great journey,
11.80   That must be done on this same day
          Or else it may do scathe.·   **do scathe** · do harm

KNIGHT 1 Thou mayest with little pain
          Ease thyself and us both.

SIMON Good sirs, that would I fain,
11.85   But to dwell were I loath.

KNIGHT 2 Nay, fair sir, you shall soon be sped.
          Lo, here a lad that must be led
          For his ill deeds to die.

KNIGHT 4 And he is bruised and all for-bled,
11.90   That makes us here thus still bested.·   **bested** · outdone
          We pray thee, sir, thereby,
          That thou wilt take this tree,
          And bear it to Calvary.

SIMON I pray you, do your deed,
11.95   And let me go my way.
          And, sirs, I shall come soon again,
          To help this man with all my main,
          And even at your own will.

KNIGHT 2 What? Wouldst thou trick us so, and feign?
11.100   Let's ding the dastard down,
          If he speeds not thereto.

SIMON Sure, sir, that was not wisely wrought,
          To beat me, though I trespassed nought,
          Either in word or deed.

11.105 KNIGHT 1 Upon his back it shall be brought
          To bear it, whether he will or not.
          What the devil! Whom should we dread?
          Go, take it up. Be alive,
          And bear it with good speed.

          [SIMON *and* JESUS *look at one another.*]

11.110 SIMON It helps not here to strive;
          Bear it then must I need.
          And therefore, sirs, as ye have said...

          [SIMON *helps* JESUS *to his feet, then lifts the cross.*]

          To bear this cross I hold me glad
          Right as ye would it were.

11.115 KNIGHT 3 If any ask after us,

Call them to Calvary. 11.116

[*Music.* SIMON *circles the pit once carrying the cross, followed by the* KNIGHTS *and* JESUS. SIMON *puts down the cross and exits. The* KNIGHTS *put the cross into position facing upstage with its foot downstage.* KNIGHT 4 *takes three bricks and throws one to* KNIGHT 2 *who places it under the foot of the cross.* KNIGHT 3 *puts one of the bricks under the right arm of the cross, and* KNIGHT 4 *puts one under the left arm.*]

12 · THE CRUCIFIXION

KNIGHT 1 Sir knights, take heed and hither hie 12.1
    This fastenin' up falls to us four.
    Ye wot yourselves as well as I
    How lords and leaders of our law
    Have given doom this dolt'll⸳ die. 12.5

dolt'll · idiot will

[KNIGHT 4, *who throughout the scene is the eagerest to get on with the job, goes to the toolbags for a length of rope.*]

KNIGHT 2 Ay we heard all that afore
    But now we're come to Calvary

[KNIGHT 2 *looks at* KNIGHT 3, *who is something of the butt of the group.*]

    Muck in 'n' moan no more.

KNIGHT 3 Moaning, nay I know I'm not
    So, sirs, let all make speed. 12.10

[KNIGHT 4 *throws the end of the length of rope to the right arm of the cross.*]

KNIGHT 4 Just you work out whose job is what
    And we shall do this deed.

[KNIGHT 4 *moves to the toolbags for a second length of rope; then* KNIGHT 1 *moves to the toolbags.*]

KNIGHT 1 We must start, sirs, and that right soon
    If we shall any wages win.

[KNIGHT 2 *moves to the toolbags.*]

KNIGHT 2 He must be dead, needs must, by noon. 12.15

[KNIGHT 3 *moves to the toolbags.*]

KNIGHT 3 Then it is good time that we begin.

[KNIGHT 4, *taking the length of rope.*]

KNIGHT 4 Let's ding him down! Then he is done.
    He shall not daunt us with his din.

KNIGHT 1 T' lad needs lesson, learn him one

12.20   Wi' care to him and all his kin.

KNIGHT 2 This lad his life shall loss

    In the worst of woeful ways.

KNIGHT 3 That means, put him up on t' cross.

    [KNIGHT 1, KNIGHT 2, *and* KNIGHT 4 *stare at* KNIGHT 3.]

KNIGHT 4 'Ark˙ at what the smart lad says.   'Ark · harken

12.25 **KNIGHT 1** Then to this work us must tek˙ heed,   tek · take

    So that our working be not wrong.

KNIGHT 2 None other note to name is need

    But let us haste him for to hang.

KNIGHT 3 And I've gone for gear, good speed

12.30   Both hammers and nails large an' long.

KNIGHT 4 Then may we boldly do this deed

    Come on, let's kill this traitor strong.

KNIGHT 1 This lad's like not to be t' last

    We'll rivet to t' rough rood.˙   rood · cross

12.35 **KNIGHT 2** And we'll fasten him full fast

    And wedge this wight to t' wood.

KNIGHT 3 Since ilka˙ thing is right arrayed   ilka · each

    The wiselier now work may we.

KNIGHT 4 The cross on t' ground is goodly spread

12.40   And bored even as it ought to be.

KNIGHT 1 Look that the lad on length be laid,

    And made be tied unto this tree.

    [KNIGHT 2 *turns to the crowd and the audience beyond.*]

KNIGHT 2 For all his brag he shall be brayed:˙   brayed · crushed to
                                                              powder
    Stay stood there and you shall see.

    [KNIGHT 3, *to* JESUS.]

12.45 **KNIGHT 3** Thou cursèd cur, come forth

    Thy comfort soon shall cool.

    [KNIGHT 4, *to* JESUS.]

KNIGHT 4 Win the wages thou art worth.

    [KNIGHT 1, *to* JESUS.]

KNIGHT 1 Walk on! Now work we well!

JESUS Almighty God, my Father free

12.50   Let these matters be marked in mind

    Thou bade that I should buxom be   plight · condition

    For Adam's plight˙ must be pined.˙   pined · suffered

Here to death I do pledge me
Saving mankind that has sinned
And sovereignly beseech I thee   12.55
That they through me may favor find.
And from the fiend them fend,
So that their souls be safe,
In wealth wi'out'en end;
I care nought else to crave.   12.60

[JESUS *walks toward the cross.*]

KNIGHT 1 Hey, hark, Sir knights, for Mahound's blood!
        Of Adam's kind is all his thought.

warlock · sorcerer or demon

KNIGHT 2 This warlock* waxes worse than wode!*
        This doleful death ne dreadeth he nought.*

wode · insane

KNIGHT 3 Thou should have mind with main and mood   12.65
        Of wicked works that thou did'st do.

ne ... nought · in Middle English, a negative is formed by adding "ne" before the verb — in this case making "he dreads not"

KNIGHT 4 Had that wight had wit he would
        Have ceased off saws he swore was true.

[KNIGHT 1 *holds up the saw from the toolbag.*]

KNIGHT 1 These saws shall rue him sore
        For all his sauntering, soon.   12.70

KNIGHT 2 Ill speed them that him spare
        Till he to death be done!

[KNIGHT 3, *to* JESUS.]

belive · quickly

KNIGHT 3 Have done belive* boy and make thee boun
        And bend thy back unto this tree.

[JESUS *unfastens his purple robe and lets it fall to the ground. He lies
down on the cross and stretches out his arms in position.*]

KNIGHT 4 Behold, himself has laid him down   12.75
        In length and breadth as he should be.

KNIGHT 1 This traitor here tainted of treason
        Go fast and fetter him then, ye three;
        And since he claims a kingdom's crown
        Even as a king here hang shall he.   12.80

[KNIGHT 2 *takes* JESUS's *right hand.*]

KNIGHT 2 Now, certes, I shall not cease

or · until, unless

        Or* his right hand be fast.

[KNIGHT 3 *takes* JESUS's *left hand.*]

KNIGHT 3 The left hand then's my piece
        Let see who bears him best.

[**KNIGHT 4** *goes to* **JESUS**'*s feet.*]

12.85 **KNIGHT 4** His limbs on length shall I lead
And even unto the bore• them bring.

bore · a hole predrilled to receive the nail

[**KNIGHT 1** *goes to* **JESUS**'*s head.*]

KNIGHT 1 Unto his head I shall take heed
And with mine hand help him to hang.

KNIGHT 2 Now since we four shall do this deed

12.90 And meddle with this unthrifty• thing
Let no man spare for special speed
Till we have made ending.

unthrifty · ill-favored

KNIGHT 3 This forward may not fail
Now we are right arrayed.

12.95 **KNIGHT 4** This boy here in our bail•
Shall bide full bitter braid.•

bail · custody

braid · assault

[**KNIGHT 2** *and* **KNIGHT 3** *tie* **JESUS**'*s hands to the cross.*]

KNIGHT 1 Sir knights, say here … how work we now?

KNIGHT 2 Why sure I hope I hold this hand.

KNIGHT 3 And to the bore I have it brought

12.100 Full buxomly• withouten band•…

buxomly · obediently

band · rope

KNIGHT 1 Strike on then. Hard. For him thee bought.

[**KNIGHT 2** *holds up a large nail.*]

KNIGHT 2 Yes, here is a stub• will stiffly stand;

stub · nail

[**KNIGHT 2** *throws the nail to* **KNIGHT 3** *who catches it.*]

Through bones and sinews it shall be sought.

[**KNIGHT 3** *hammers the nail into* **JESUS**'*s left hand.* **JESUS** *cries out with pain, flinging his right arm into the air.* **KNIGHT 2** *grasps* **JESUS**'*s right arm, and stretches it along the arm of the cross to secure it.*]

This work is well, I will warrant.

[**KNIGHT 1** *crosses to examine the work.*]

12.105 **KNIGHT 1** Say, sir, how do we there?
This bargain will we win.

KNIGHT 3 It fails a foot or more
The sinews are so gone in.•

It fails … gone in · Jesus' arm has contracted so much from the trauma that it will no longer reach the bore-hole for nailing

KNIGHT 4 I think that mark amiss be bored.

12.110 **KNIGHT 2** Then must he bide in bitter bale.

KNIGHT 3 In faith it was o'er scantly scored•
That makes it foully for to fail.

it was … scored · the holes were improperly spaced

KNIGHT 1 Why crack• ye so? Fast on a cord
And tug him to, by top and tail.

crack · complain

[KNIGHT 2 *ties a rope to the wrist of* JESUS. KNIGHT 2 *and* KNIGHT 4 *haul on the rope, stretching the arm until it reaches the bore.*]

KNIGHT 3 Yea, thou command us, lightly as a lord: 12.115
    Come help to haul him, with ill hail!

KNIGHT 1 Now certes that I shall do –

snelly · swiftly   Full snelly,˙ like a snail.

[KNIGHT 1 *makes no attempt to move.* KNIGHT 3 *begins hammering a nail into* JESUS's *right hand.*]

KNIGHT 3 And I shall 'tach him to,
    Full nimbly with a nail. 12.120

heet · promise   This work will hold that dare I heet˙

fest · fastened   For now are fest˙ fast both his hands.

KNIGHT 4 Go we all four then to his feet
    So shall our space be speedily spent.

beet · improve   KNIGHT 2 Let's see what jest his bale might beet.˙ 12.125
    Thereto my back now would I bend.

[KNIGHT 4 *examines the bore at the foot of the cross.*]

unmeet · unsatisfactory KNIGHT 4 Oh! This work is all unmeet˙
    This boring must all be amend.

KNIGHT 1 Ah, peace man, for Mahoun!
    Let no man know what wonder 12.130

rug · tug   A rope shall rug˙ him down
    If all his sinews go asunder.

kindly · naturally KNIGHT 2 That cord full kindly˙ can I knit
    The comfort of this carl to cool.

KNIGHT 1 Fest on then fast that all be fit; 12.135
    It is no force how fell he feel.

[KNIGHT 2 *and* KNIGHT 4 *move to the foot of the cross and haul on the ropes to stretch* JESUS's *legs so that his feet meet the bore.*]

KNIGHT 2 Lug on ye both a little yet.

KNIGHT 3 I shall not cease, as I have zeal.

fond · try   KNIGHT 4 And I shall fond˙ him for to hit.

KNIGHT 2 Oh! Hail! 12.140

KNIGHT 4 Ho now! I hold it well.

KNIGHT 1 Have done, drive in that nail,
    So that no fault be found.

[KNIGHT 3 *hammers a nail through* JESUS's *feet.* KNIGHT 1 *moves down to help him.*]

KNIGHT 4 This working would not fail,

12.145   If four bulls were bound.

      KNIGHT 1 These cords have evil increased his pains
           Ere he were till the borings brought.

      [**KNIGHT 2** *takes a closer look at the nails.*]

      KNIGHT 2 Yea, asunder are both sinews and veins
           On ilka side, so have we sought.

12.150   **KNIGHT 3** Now all his gauds' nothing him gains;   **gauds** · tricks
           His sauntering shall with bale be bought.

      KNIGHT 4 I will go say to our sovereigns
           Of all these works how we have wrought.

      [**KNIGHT 3** *and* **KNIGHT 4** *begin to move away.*]

      KNIGHT 1 Nay, sirs, another thing

12.155   Falls first to you and me:
           They bade we should him hang
           On height that men might see.

      [**KNIGHT 3** *and* **KNIGHT 4** *stop. They look at "the height" (the stage) and
      at* **JESUS** *securely fastened to the cross.*]

      KNIGHT 2 We wot well so their words were;
           But, sir, that deed will do us dear.

12.160   **KNIGHT 1** It may not mend to moot' it more;   **moot** · discuss
           This harlot must be afraid here.

      [**KNIGHT 2** *inspects the site for the raising of the cross.*]

      KNIGHT 2 The mortise' is made fit therefore.   **mortise** · hole in which
      KNIGHT 3 Fest your fingers then, all here.   the cross is placed

      [**KNIGHT 3** *throws a rope up to* **KNIGHT 2.** **KNIGHT 4** *takes the right
      arm of cross and* **KNIGHT 3** *takes the left arm. They try to lift the cross.
      They let it down.*]

      KNIGHT 4 I ween it will never come there;

12.165   We four'll not raise it right this year.

      KNIGHT 1 Say, man, why carp'st' thou so?   **carp'st** · complain
           Thy lifting was but light.

      KNIGHT 2 He means there must be more
           To heave him up on height.

12.170   **KNIGHT 3** Now, sirs, I hope it shall not need
           More company to cart t' cross there.
           Methinks we four should do this deed.
           'Shrew' me if I my wages share.   **'Shrew** · curse

      KNIGHT 1 It must be done, wi'out'en dread.

12.175   No more! But look ye be ready,

[KNIGHT 1 *goes to the left arm of the cross*, KNIGHT 3 *to the right.*]

    And this part shall I lift and lead;   12.176

    On length he shall no longer lie.

    Therefore now make ye boun:

    Let's bear him to yon hill.

[KNIGHT 4, *going to the foot of cross.*]

KNIGHT 4 Then will I bear here down,   12.180

    And tent his toes I will.

KNIGHT 2 This cross'll come out all cock-eyed,

    This lad here's like to let it slip.

KNIGHT 3 No, sir, not I, I'm set this side,

    I'll not let timber tip.   12.185

KNIGHT 2 More lifting, and less lip.

KNIGHT 1 *Lift up*!

[KNIGHT 1, KNIGHT 3, *and* KNIGHT 4 *lift the cross unsuccessfully.*
KNIGHT 2 *hauls on the ropes.*]

KNIGHT 4   Let see!

KNIGHT 2   Oh, lift along!

KNIGHT 3 From all this harm he should him hide

    If he were God.

KNIGHT 4   The Devil him hang!

hent · suffered KNIGHT 1 For great harm have I hent:˙   12.190

    My shoulder is asunder.

shent · ruined KNIGHT 2 And shite I am near shent,˙

    So long have I borne under.

twin · separate KNIGHT 3 This cross and I in two must twin,˙

    Else breaks my back asunder soon.   12.195

KNIGHT 4 Lay down again and leave your din;

[*The* KNIGHTS *lay the cross down.*]

    This deed for us will ne'er be done.

engine · device KNIGHT 1 Say, sirs, see if some engine˙

    May help him up without delay

    For here should workers worship win   12.200

laik · play And now go laik˙ about all day.

KNIGHT 2 Workers worthier than we

    You'll find 'em few enough.

buggers me · wipes
me out KNIGHT 3 This bargain buggers me˙

    I'm proper out of puff.˙   12.205

puff · breath KNIGHT 4 So will of work never we were

I think this carl some craft° has cast.   **craft** · spell

KNIGHT 2 My burden sat me wondrous sore;
            Unto the hill I might not last.

12.210 KNIGHT 1 Lift up, and soon he shall be there;
            Therefore fest on your fingers fast.

KNIGHT 3 Oh, lift!

[*Music. The* FOUR KNIGHTS *lift the cross and carry it up center stage;*
they set it down.]

KNIGHT 1   Heave ho!

KNIGHT 4   A little more.

KNIGHT 2 Hold then!

[*Music ends.*]

KNIGHT 1   How now?

KNIGHT 2   The worst is past.

KNIGHT 3 He weighs a wicked weight.

12.215 KNIGHT 2 So may we all four say,
            Ere he was heaved on height,
            And raised in this array.

KNIGHT 4 It made me bust my bollock stones.
            So boistous° was he for to bear.   **boistous** · bulky, clumsy

12.220 KNIGHT 1 Now raise him nimbly for the nonce°   **nonce** · purpose
            And set him by this mortise here;
            And let him fall in all at once
            For certes that pain shall have no peer.

KNIGHT 3 Heave up!

KNIGHT 4   Let down! So all his bones

12.225   Asunder now on all sides tear.

[*Music.* KNIGHT 4 *climbs up a ladder to the bridge above the stage.*
KNIGHT 2 *and* KNIGHT 3 *throw up the ropes attached to the arms*
of the cross, and KNIGHT 4 *catches them.* KNIGHT 1, KNIGHT 2, *and*
KNIGHT 3 *heave the cross into an upright position.* KNIGHT 4 *grasps*
the head of the cross and keeps it steady while KNIGHT 1, KNIGHT 2,
and KNIGHT 3 *secure the cross in an upright position.* KNIGHT 4 *secures*
the head of the cross against the bridge and ties off the ropes on the rail
of the bridge. KNIGHT 1 *looks over* JESUS's *limbs.*]

KNIGHT 1 This falling was most fell.°   **fell** · cruel
            T' cross cem° down such a clout   **cem** · came
            Now may a man well tell
            Where t' Jew's least joints jut out.

KNIGHT 3 Methinketh this cross will not abide
　　Nor stand still in this mortise yet.

12.230

KNIGHT 4 Him as made mortise made it too wide,
　　That's why it waves. Young gormless get!·

gormless get · sense-
less idiot

KNIGHT 1 It shall be set on ilka side,
　　So that it shall no further flit;

12.235

　　Good wedges shall we take this tide,
　　And fast the foot, then all is fit.

[**KNIGHT 3** *runs off stage to the toolbags to fetch wedges.*]

KNIGHT 3 Here are wedges arrayed
　　For that both great and small.

KNIGHT 1 Where are our hammers laid,
　　That we should work withal?

12.240

[**KNIGHT 3** *drops the wedges and runs off stage again to fetch hammers from the toolbags. He finds them and holds them up.* **KNIGHT 1**, **KNIGHT 2**, *and* **KNIGHT 4** *hold up their own hammers, laughing.*]

KNIGHT 4 We have them here, even at our hand.

[**KNIGHT 3** *drops the hammers and moves back to the others on the stage.*]

KNIGHT 2 Give me this wedge; I shall it drive.

[**KNIGHT 2** *hammers a wedge into the base of the cross. Then the* **FOUR KNIGHTS** *all move into the pit and look up at* **JESUS**. **KNIGHT 1** *addresses him.*]

KNIGHT 1 Say, sir, how likes ye now
　　This work that we have wrought?

12.245

[**KNIGHT 4**, *to* **JESUS**.]

KNIGHT 4 We pray you, tell us how
　　You feel, or faint ye, what?

JESUS All men that walk by way or street
　　Let this sore scene sink in thy soul.
　　Behold my head, my hands, my feet,

12.250

brood · ponder

　　And brood· ye deep on my dire dole.·

dole · lot

　　If any mourning may be meet,
　　Or mischief measured unto mine.
　　My Father that all bales may beet,

Forgive … they
nought · see Luke 23:34

　　Forgive these men that do me pine.

12.255

　　What they work wot they nought;·

[**KNIGHT 1**, *to the crowd and audience beyond.*]

KNIGHT 1 Hey! Hark! He jangles like a jay.

KNIGHT 2 Methinks he patters like a pie.•   pie • magpie

KNIGHT 3 He has been doand• so all day,   doand • doing

12.260   And made great-moving of mercy.

KNIGHT 4 Is this the same that gan us say

That he was God's Son almighty?

KNIGHT 1 Therefore he feels full fell affray

And he is doomed this day to die.

[KNIGHT 2, *to* JESUS.]

12.265 KNIGHT 2 Vah! *"qui destruis templum…"*•   *qui destruis*
                                                                        templum • "you who
KNIGHT 3 Or so he said he'd do.   would destroy [this]
                                                                        temple" (Latin); see
KNIGHT 4 And sirs he said to some   John 2:19, Mark 15:29

He'd raise it up anew.

KNIGHT 1 To muster that he had no might

12.270   For all the craft that he could cast

All if he were in word so wight

For all his force now he is fast.

As Pilate doomed is done and dight;

Therefore I rede that we go rest.

12.275 KNIGHT 2 This race mun• be rehearsèd right   mun • must

Through the world both east and west.

KNIGHT 3 Yea, let him hang there still,

And make mows• on the moon.   mows • grimaces

KNIGHT 4 Then may we wend at will.

[KNIGHT 2, KNIGHT 3, *and* KNIGHT 4 *begin to walk away.* KNIGHT 1
picks up JESUS's *purple robe from the ground.*]

12.280 KNIGHT 1 Nay, good sirs, not so soon.

For certes needs another note:

This kirtle• would I of you crave.   kirtle • tunic

KNIGHT 2 Nay, nay, Sir, we will look by lot

Which of us four falls it to have.

12.285 KNIGHT 3 I rede we draw cut• for this coat.   draw cut • draw straws

[KNIGHT 4 *gets three long nails and one shorter one from the toolbag
and holds them up in his fist to the others.*]

KNIGHT 3 Lo, see how soon all sides to save.•   see how … save • so
                                                                        everyone will be content
[*Each* KNIGHT *takes a nail.* KNIGHT 3, *thinking he has won, immedi-
ately picks up the robe to walk off with it, but* KNIGHT 4 *stops him and
shows him a shorter nail.*]

KNIGHT 1 The short cut wins, that well ye wot

Whether it fall to knight or knave.

[*Meanwhile,* **KNIGHT 1**, *with his back turned to the others and facing out, has cut his nail with wire cutters so that his is the shortest. He holds up his nail and grabs the purple robe.*]

KNIGHT 1 Brothers, ye need not brawl!
This mantle is my gain.   12.290

KNIGHT 2 The gaffer° wins again.
And we get bugger all.°

gaffer · head work-
man (perhaps also
"cheater" or old man)

bugger all · nothing

[*Exeunt* **KNIGHTS**. *Song: "The Moon Shines Bright."*]

BAND The moon shines bright and the stars give a light,
In a little while it will be day.
Our Lord our God he calls upon us all,   12.295
And he bids us awake and pray.

So dear, so dear Christ loved us,
And for our sins got slain,
I'd have you to leave all your wicked, wicked ways,
And turn to the Lord again.   12.300

For the life of a man, it is but a span,
And he flourishes like a flower,
For he's here today, tomorrow he's gone,
And he's dead all in an hour.

13 · CHRIST ON THE CROSS

[*Enter* **MARY MOTHER**, **MARY MAGDALENE**, **MARY SALOME**, *and* **JOHN**, *who stands before the cross. The three* **MARYS** *kneel facing the crowd and audience. Enter* **CAYPHAS** *and* **ANNAS**. *Enter* **PILATE**.]

seignors · lords

PILATE See, seignors,° and see what I say: 13.1
Tak tent to my talking entire.
Avoid all this din here this day,
And fall to my friendship all here.
Sir Pilate, a prince without peer   13.5
My name is full fitly to call,

doomsman · judge

And doomsman° full worthy of fear
Of most gentle Jewry of all
   Am I.
Who makes oppression   13.10
Or does transgression,
By my discretion

Shall be doomed duly to die.
To die shall I doom them indeed,
13.15   Those rebels that rule them unright.
Thus loyally the law I unlap,·   **unlap** · reveal
And punish them piteously.
But of Jesus I holt· it ill hap·   **holt** · hold
That he on yon hill hang so high,   **ill hap** · bad luck
13.20   For guilt.
His blood to spill
Ye took him still;
Thus was your will,
With spitefullest speed was he spilt.
13.25 **CAYPHAS** To spill him we spake in a speed,
For falsehood he follow i'fai';·   **i'fai'** · truly
With frauds all our folk gan he feed,
And labored to learn· them his lay.·   **learn** · teach
ANNAS Sir Pilate, of peace we you pray;   **lay** · story
13.30   Our law was full like to be lorn.·   **lorn** · destroyed
He saved not our dear Sabbath day.   **saved not ... Sab-**
For that to escape were a scorn,   **bath day** · Jesus' failure
    By law.   to keep the sabbath was
PILATE Sirs, before your sight   a common complaint of
13.35   With all my might I examined him right.   the religious authorities.
And no cause in him could I know.   See Matthew 12:2–12,
ANNAS Sir Pilate, your pleasure we pray;   John 5:16–18
Take tent to your talking this tide,
And wipe you yon writing away;
13.40   It is not best that it abide.
It suits you to set it aside,   **set it aside ... to**
And set that he said in his saw,   **know** · see John 19:21
As he that was pricked up with pride,
"The Jews' King am I, comely to know,"·
13.45   Full plain.
PILATE *Quod scripsi, scripsi*·   *Quod scripsi, scripsi* ·
Yon same wrote I;   "What I have written, I
I bide thereby.   have written" (Latin).
    See John 19:22
[*Exit* **PILATE** *followed by* **CAYPHAS** *and* **ANNAS**. **MARY MOTHER**
with **MARY MAGDALENE**, **MARY SALOME** *and* **JOHN** *begin to mourn*
for **JESUS**.]

CROWD Alas!

MARY MOTHER For my sweet son I say   13.50
   Thus dolefully death thus is dight.

CROWD Alas!

MARY MOTHER For full lovely thou lay
   In my womb, this most wonderly wight.

CROWD Alas!   13.55

MARY MOTHER That I should see this sight
   Of my son so seemly to see.

CROWD Alas!

MARY MOTHER That this blossom so bright
   Untruly is tugged to this tree.   13.60

CROWD Alas!

MARY MOTHER My lord, my life
   With full grief
   Hangs as a thief.

CROWD Alas!   13.65

MARY MOTHER He did never trespass!

CROWD Alas!

MARY MOTHER Son! Thou sorrowful sight!
   Oh that me were closed in clay,
   A sword of such sorrow me smite.   13.70
   To death I were done this day.

CROWD Alas!

Heloy ... Sabatnye ·
Jesus cries out from
the cross in Aramaic; a
translation is supplied
by the interlinear English

JESUS *Heloy! Heloy!*
   My God, my God full free,
   Lama Sabatnye! ·   13.75
   Wherefore forsook thou me?

[*Music. Exeunt* MARY MOTHER, MARY MAGDALENE, MARY SALOME
and JOHN.]

Man on mould ·
mortal man

tholed · suffered

forward · plan

JESUS Man on mould, · be meek to me,
   And have thy maker in thy mind,
   And think how I have tholed· for thee,
   With peerless pains for to be pined.   13.80
   The forward· of my Father free
   Have I fulfilled, as folk may find.
   My friends that on me in faith relies
   Now from their foes I shall defend,
   And on the third day right uprise,   13.85

13.86   And so to heaven I shall ascend.
Then shall I come again,
To judge both good and ill,
To endless joy or pain;
13.90   Thus is my Father's will.

[*Music. Enter a* **MINER**, *the lamp on his helmet shining first in the face of* **JESUS**, *then, questioningly, on the faces of the audience.*]

MINER   What may these marvels signify
That here was showed so openly
    Unto our sight
This day on which that man did die
13.95   That Jesus hight?
It is a misty thing to mean;
So strange a sight was never seen.
Our princes and our priest, I ween,˙   **ween** · believe
    Are sorely scared.
13.100   At baleful bodings that have been
    I stood and stared.

All elements, both old and young,
In their manners they made mourning.
    Creatures did cry
13.105   And kenned by countenance that their king
    Indeed did die.
The sun for woe he waxed all wan.˙   **wan** · pale
The moon and stars to blench˙ began.   **blench** · to flinch or to become pale
The clods did quake, and like a man
13.110   Did make their moan
The stark stone and stiff stock
    Did grieve and groan.
Bodies like brocks out of burial burst.
Corses through t' earth's crust crept out and cursed.

13.115   To maintain truth is well worthy.
I tell you that I saw him die
And he was God's son almighty,
    That bleedeth ye before.
Yet say I so, and stand thereby
13.120   For evermore.

But since ye set nought by my saw 13.121
    I'll wend my way.
[MINER *moves off the stage into the crowd and audience beyond.*]
  God grant you grace that you may know
    The truth some day.
[*Exit* MINER. *Song: "We Sing Allelujah" (words and music: Richard Thompson).*]

BAND A man is like a rusty wheel 13.125
    On a rusty cart.
    He sings his song as he rattles along
    And then he falls apart.

    And we sing allelujah
    At the turning of the year 13.130
    And we work all day in the old-fashioned way
    Till the shining star appears.

    A man is like a bramble briar
    Covers himself with thorns
    He laughs like a clown when his fortunes are down 13.135
    And his clothes are ragged and torn.

    And we sing allelujah
    At the turning of the year
    And we work all day in the old-fashioned way
    Till the shining star appears. 13.140

    And a man is like his father
    Wishes he'd never been born,
    He longs for the time when the clock will chime,
    And he's dead for evermore.

    And we sing allelujah 13.145
    At the turning of the year
    And we work all day in the old-fashioned way
    Till the shining star appears.
[*Exeunt all. Curtain.*]

William Shakespeare

◄(1 5 6 4 – 1 6 1 6)►

If Hamlet *is not the greatest play in the world, it is almost certainly the most famous. The sources of its appeal, four centuries after its first performance, are many. It presents one of the most complex and mysterious protagonists in the history of drama. "Hamlet is the Mona Lisa of literature," T. S. Eliot observes. Yet the Prince of Denmark seems oddly familiar to us. William Hazlitt argues: "Hamlet's thoughts we seem to know as well as our own." The Prince of Denmark is alternately endearing, querulous, troubled, bold, paralyzed by doubt and depression, and – at times – decisive; a man of stunning presence, a noble lord, and a pensive philosopher with a rich interior life: "O God, I could be bounded in a nutshell and count myself a king of infinite space, were it not that I have bad dreams" (2.2). It is no wonder that popular screen actors in our time – as various as Kevin Kline, Mel Gibson, and Ethan Hawke – have coveted this role.*

Yet the play is far more than the study of one mysterious personality. It is an ensemble piece featuring several magnificent characters. Gertrude, Claudius, Ophelia, Polonius, Horatio, and Laertes are richly developed characters as well; and they do not merely talk. They act in one of the most entertaining plots ever devised. Like any popular movie-maker today, Shakespeare was willing to please the crowd. The play opens with a sensational act in which a grieving son encounters the ghost of his dead father. Scenes of conflict, passion, and confusion quickly follow: love gone awry, court intrigue, suicide, revenge, macabre encounters in a graveyard, a stabbing; and, finally, a duel and a surfeit of corpses. One might call Hamlet *an action thriller. But unlike most action thrillers, this one leads to thoughtful meditation on the meaning of life.*

Drama is given life through conflict. George Steiner argues that the greatest dramas employ at least some of the five principal "constants of conflict" found in the human condition, namely: 1 · the erotic – the confrontation of men and women; 2 · the filial – the confrontation of youth and age; 3 · the social – the confrontation of the individual with society; 4 · the ritual – the conflict between the living and the dead; and 5 · the metaphysical – the conflict between human beings and God (or the gods). Few plays attempt to incorporate all these conflicts, but Hamlet does so with gusto. Through these conflicts Shakespeare engages the central problems that bedevil the human race.

The play opens with an apparently simple question: "Who's there?" But as events unfold, this question proves anything but simple. It acquires a theological cast. "Who's there?" might be reformulated: "Are we alone in the universe?" "Whom can we trust?" "Why are we here on this earth?" "Does God exist?" And if he does, "Is this Being evil, indifferent, or benevolent?" Hamlet is a play haunted by overt and implicit questions. They are full of urgency and pain because the cultural sands have shifted. The new science and new discoveries of Early Modern Europe have cast doubt upon the old truths that once sustained Christian Europe. Tragedy is born in the West, says Albert Camus, when "the pendulum of civilization is halfway between a sacred society and society built around man." This observation aptly names the dilemma of anyone trapped on the frontier between belief and doubt: "What's a fellow to do, crawling between heaven and earth?" Hamlet asks for us all (3.1).

The play never offers settled answers, though occasional glimmers of light break through: "There is special providence in the fall of a sparrow," a calm and resolute Hamlet declares near the end (5.2). More often, though, question leads to question; yet, even in the questioning, the audience acquires sumptuous food for thought. The great concerns of life resonate through the play: love, death, faith, doubt, fate, friendship, good, evil, truth, and the nature of humanity. The play teases. It never preaches. Finally, it leaves us in wonder. Harold Childe got it right: "When the mystery of Hamlet has been solved, the mystery of human life will have been solved."

HAMLET, PRINCE OF DENMARK

DRAMATIS PERSONÆ

GHOST *of Hamlet, former King of Denmark*

KING CLAUDIUS *King of Denmark, the former King's brother*

QUEEN GERTRUDE *Queen of Denmark, widow of the former King and now wife of Claudius*

HAMLET *Prince of Denmark, son of the late King Hamlet and of Gertrude*

POLONIUS *councillor to the King*

LAERTES *his son*

OPHELIA *his daughter*

REYNALDO *his servant*

HORATIO *Hamlet's friend and fellow student*

VOLTIMAND
CORNELIUS
ROSENCRANTZ
GUILDENSTERN } *members of the Danish court*
OSRIC
A GENTLEMAN
A LORD

BERNARDO
FRANCISCO } *officers and soldiers on watch*
MARCELLUS

FORTINBRAS *Prince of Norway*

A CAPTAIN *in his army*

THREE *or* **FOUR PLAYERS** *taking the roles of* **PROLOGUE, PLAYER KING, PLAYER QUEEN,** *and* **LUCIANUS**

TWO MESSENGERS

FIRST SAILOR

TWO CLOWNS *a gravedigger and his companion*

PRIEST

FIRST AMBASSADOR *from England*

LORDS, SOLDIERS, ATTENDANTS, GUARDS, OTHER PLAYERS, FOLLOWERS OF LAERTES, *other* **SAILORS,** *another* **AMBASSADOR** *or* **AMBASSADORS FROM ENGLAND**

ACT 1, SCENE 1

[*Denmark. Elsinore Castle. A guard platform. Enter* **BERNARDO** *and* **FRANCISCO,** *two sentinels meeting.*]

1.1.1   **BERNARDO** Who's there?

FRANCISCO Nay, answer me.˙ Stand and unfold yourself.˙

BERNARDO Long live the King!

FRANCISCO Bernardo?

me · Francisco emphasizes that *he* is the sentry currently on watch

unfold yourself · reveal your identity

BERNARDO He. 1.1.5

FRANCISCO You come most carefully upon your hour.

BERNARDO 'Tis now struck twelve. Get thee to bed, Francisco.

FRANCISCO For this relief much thanks. 'Tis bitter cold,
    And I am sick at heart.

BERNARDO Have you had quiet guard? 1.1.10

FRANCISCO Not a mouse stirring

BERNARDO Well, good night.
    If you do meet Horatio and Marcellus,
rivals · partners   The rivals˙ of my watch, bid them make haste.
    [*Enter* **HORATIO** *and* **MARCELLUS**.]

FRANCISCO I think I hear them. – Stand, ho! Who is there? 1.1.15

ground · country, land **HORATIO** Friends to this ground.˙

liegemen to the **MARCELLUS** And liegemen to the Dane.˙
Dane · men sworn to
serve the Danish king **FRANCISCO** Give˙ you good night.

Give · may God give **MARCELLUS** O, farewell, honest soldier. Who hath relieved you?

FRANCISCO Bernardo hath my place. Give you good night. 1.1.20
    [*Exit* **FRANCISCO**.]

MARCELLUS Holla! Bernardo!

BERNARDO Say, what, is Horatio there?

HORATIO A piece of him.

BERNARDO Welcome, Horatio. Welcome, good Marcellus.

HORATIO What, has this thing appeared again tonight? 1.1.25

BERNARDO I have seen nothing.

fantasy · imagination **MARCELLUS** Horatio says 'tis but our fantasy,˙
    And will not let belief take hold of him
    Touching this dreaded sight twice seen of us.
along · to come along   Therefore I have entreated him along˙ 1.1.30
watch · keep watch   With us to watch˙ the minutes of this night,
during   That if again this apparition come
approve · corroborate   He may approve˙ our eyes and speak to it.

HORATIO Tush, tush, 'twill not appear.

BERNARDO   Sit down awhile,
    And let us once again assail your ears, 1.1.35
    That are so fortified against our story,
What · with what   What˙ we have two nights seen.

HORATIO   Well, sit we down
    And let us hear Bernardo speak of this.
Last ... of all · this very **BERNARDO** Last night of all,˙
last night (emphatic)

1.1.40
When yon same star that's westward from the pole*
Had made his* course t' illume* that part of heaven
Where now it burns, Marcellus and myself,
The bell then beating one –

[*Enter* GHOST.]

MARCELLUS Peace, break thee off! Look where it comes again!

1.1.45
BERNARDO In the same figure like the King that's dead.

MARCELLUS Thou art a scholar.* Speak to it, Horatio.

BERNARDO Looks 'a* not like the King? Mark it, Horatio.

HORATIO Most like. It harrows me with fear and wonder.

BERNARDO It would be spoke to.*

MARCELLUS   Speak to it, Horatio.

1.1.50
HORATIO What art thou that usurp'st* this time of night,
Together with that fair and warlike form
In which the majesty of buried Denmark*
Did sometime* march? By heaven, I charge thee, speak!

MARCELLUS It is offended.

BERNARDO   See, it stalks away.

1.1.55
HORATIO Stay! Speak, speak! I charge thee, speak!

[*Exit* GHOST.]

MARCELLUS 'Tis gone and will not answer.

BERNARDO How now, Horatio? You tremble and look pale.
Is not this something more than fantasy?
What think you on 't?*

1.1.60
HORATIO Before my God, I might not this believe
Without the sensible* and true avouch*
Of mine own eyes.

MARCELLUS   Is it not like the King?

HORATIO As thou art to thyself.
Such was the very armor he had on

1.1.65
When he the ambitious Norway* combated
So frowned he once when, in an angry parle,*
He smote the sledded* Polacks* on the ice.
'Tis strange.

MARCELLUS Thus twice before, and jump* at this dead hour,

1.1.70
With martial stalk* hath he gone by our watch.

HORATIO In what particular thought to work* I know not,
But in the gross and scope* of mine opinion
This bodes some strange eruption to our state.

---

pole · polestar, north star

his · its

illume · illuminate

a scholar · one learned enough to know how to question a ghost properly

'a · he

It ... spoke to · it was commonly believed that a ghost could not speak until spoken to

usurp'st · wrongfully takes over

buried Denmark · the buried King of Denmark

sometime · formerly

on 't · of it

sensible · confirmed by the senses

avouch · warrant, evidence

Norway · King of Norway

parle · parley

sledded · traveling on sleds

Polacks · Poles

jump · exactly

stalk · stride

to work · to collect my thoughts and try to understand this

gross and scope · general drift

MARCELLUS Good now,* sit down, and tell me, he that knows,

Why this same strict and most observant watch   1.1.75

So nightly toils* the subject* of the land,

And why such daily cast* of brazen* cannon

And foreign mart* for implements of war,

Why such impress* of shipwrights, whose sore task

Does not divide the Sunday from the week.   1.1.80

What might be toward,* that this sweaty haste

Doth make the night joint-laborer with the day?

Who is 't that can inform me?

HORATIO   That can I;

At least, the whisper goes so. Our last king,

Whose image even but now appeared to us,   1.1.85

Was, as you know, by Fortinbras of Norway,

Thereto pricked on* by a most emulate* pride,

Dared to the combat; in which our valiant Hamlet –

For so this side of our known world* esteemed him –

Did slay this Fortinbras; who by a sealed* compact   1.1.90

Well ratified by law and heraldry

Did forfeit, with his life, all those his lands

Which he stood seized* of, to the conqueror

Against* the which a moiety competent*

Was gagèd* by our king, which had returned*   1.1.95

To the inheritance* of Fortinbras

Had he been vanquisher, as, by the same cov'nant*

And carriage of the article designed,*

His fell to Hamlet. Now, sir, young Fortinbras,

Of unimprovèd mettle* hot and full   1.1.100

Hath in the skirts* of Norway here and there

Sharked up* a list of lawless resolutes*

For food and diet* to some enterprise

That hath a stomach* in 't, which is no other –

As it doth well appear unto our state –   1.1.105

But to recover of us, by strong hand

And terms compulsatory, those foresaid lands

So by his father lost. And this, I take it,

Is the main motive of our preparations,

The source of this our watch, and the chief head*   1.1.110

Of this posthaste and rummage* in the land.

Good now · an expression denoting entreaty

toils · causes to toil

subject · subjects

cast · casting

mart · buying and selling

impress · impressment, conscription

toward · in preparation

pricked on · incited

emulate · emulous, ambitious. This line refers to old Fortinbras, not the Danish King

this … world · all Europe, the Western world

sealed · certified

seized · possessed

Against · in return for

moiety competent · corresponding portion

gagèd · engaged

had returned · would have passed

inheritance · possession

cov'nant · the sealed compact of line 90

carriage…designed · carrying out of the article or clause drawn up to cover the point

unimprovèd mettle · untried, undisciplined spirits

skirts · outlying regions

Sharked up · gathered up, as a shark takes fish

resolutes · desperadoes

For food and diet · they are to serve as food (or "means,") "to some enterprise"; also they serve for rations

stomach · a spirit of daring

head · source

rummage · commotion

BERNARDO I think it be no other but e'en so.
　　Well may it sort* that this portentous figure
　　Comes armèd through our watch so like the King

1.1.115　That was and is the question* of these wars.

HORATIO A mote* it is to trouble the mind's eye.
　　The most high and palmy* state of Rome,
　　A little ere the mightiest Julius fell,
　　The graves stood tenantless, and the sheeted* dead

1.1.120　Did squeak and gibber in the Roman streets;
　　As* stars with trains* of fire and dews of blood,
　　Disasters;* in the sun; and the moist star*
　　Upon whose influence Neptune's* empire stands*
　　Was sick almost to doomsday* with eclipse

1.1.125　And even the like precurse* of feared events,
　　As harbingers* preceding still* the fates
　　And prologue to the omen* coming on,
　　Have heaven and earth together demonstrated
　　Unto our climatures* and countrymen.

　　[*Enter* **GHOST**.]

1.1.130　But soft,* behold! Lo, where it comes again!
　　I'll cross* it, though it blast* me.

　　[*The* **GHOST** *spreads his* arms.]

　　　　　　　　　　　　Stay, illusion!
　　If thou hast any sound or use of voice,
　　Speak to me!
　　If there be any good thing to be done

1.1.135　That may to thee do ease and grace to me,
　　Speak to me!
　　If thou art privy to* thy country's fate,
　　Which, happily,* foreknowing may avoid,
　　O, speak!

1.1.140　Or if thou hast uphoarded in thy life
　　Extorted treasure in the womb of earth,
　　For which, they say, you spirits oft walk in death,
　　Speak of it!

　　[*The cock crows.*]

　　　　　　　Stay and speak! – Stop it, Marcellus.

MARCELLUS Shall I strike at it with my partisan?*

1.1.145　**HORATIO** Do, if it will not stand.

---

sort · suit

question · focus of contention

mote · speck of dust

palmy · flourishing

sheeted · shrouded

As · this abrupt transition suggests that lines may have been omitted between lines 120 and 121

trains · trails

Disasters · unfavorable signs or aspects

moist star · moon, governing tides

Neptune's · god of the sea

stands · depends

sick ... doomsday · see Matthew 24:29 and Revelation 6:12

precurse · heralding, foreshadowing

harbingers · forerunners

still · continually

omen · calamitous event

climatures · regions

soft · enough, break off

cross · stand in its path, confront

blast · wither, strike with a curse

his · its

privy to · in on the secret of

happily · haply, perchance

partisan · long-handled spear

[HORATIO *and* MARCELLUS *strike at it.]*

BERNARDO 'Tis here!   1.1.146

HORATIO 'Tis here!

[*Exit* GHOST.]

MARCELLUS 'Tis gone.

We do it wrong, being so majestical,

To offer it the show of violence,   1.1.150

For it is as the air invulnerable,

And our vain blows malicious mockery.

BERNARDO It was about to speak when the cock crew.

HORATIO And then it started like a guilty thing

Upon a fearful summons. I have heard   1.1.155

trumpet · trumpeter

The cock, that is the trumpet˙ to the morn,

Doth with his lofty and shrill-sounding throat

Awake the god of day, and at his warning,

Whether in sea or fire, in earth or air,

extravagant and
erring · wandering
beyond bounds (the
words have similar
meaning)

Th' extravagant and erring˙ spirit hies˙   1.1.160

To his confine; and of the truth herein

This present object made probation.˙

hies · hastens

MARCELLUS It faded on the crowing of the cock.

Some say that ever 'gainst˙ that season comes

probation · proof

Wherein our Savior's birth is celebrated,   1.1.165

'gainst · just before

This bird of dawning singeth all night long,

And then, they say, no spirit dare stir abroad;

strike · destroy by evil
influence

The nights are wholesome, then no planets strike,˙

No fairy takes,˙ nor witch hath power to charm,

takes · bewitches

So hallowed and so gracious˙ is that time.   1.1.170

gracious · full of grace

HORATIO So have I heard and do in part believe it.

But, look, the morn in russet mantle clad

Walks o'er the dew of yon high eastward hill.

Break we our watch up, and by my advice

Let us impart what we have seen tonight   1.1.175

Unto young Hamlet; for upon my life,

This spirit, dumb to us, will speak to him.

Do you consent we shall acquaint him with it,

As needful in our loves, fitting our duty?

MARCELLUS Let's do 't, I pray, and I this morning know   1.1.180

Where we shall find him most conveniently.

[*Exeunt.*]

ACT 1, SCENE 2

[*The castle. Flourish. Enter* CLAUDIUS, KING OF DENMARK, GERTRUDE
THE QUEEN, *the Council, as*• POLONIUS *and his son* LAERTES, HAMLET,
cum aliis• *including* VOLTIMAND *and* CORNELIUS.]

1.2.1 KING Though yet of Hamlet our• dear brother's death
The memory be green, and that it us befitted
To bear our hearts in grief and our whole kingdom
To be contracted in one brow of woe,
1.2.5 Yet so far hath discretion fought with nature
That we with wisest sorrow think on him
Together with remembrance of ourselves.
Therefore our sometime• sister, now our queen,
Th' imperial jointress• to this warlike state,
1.2.10 Have we, as 'twere with a defeated joy –
With an auspicious and a dropping eye,•
With mirth in funeral and with dirge in marriage,
In equal scale weighing delight and dole•–
Taken to wife. Nor have we herein barred
1.2.15 Your better wisdoms, which have freely gone
With this affair along. For all, our thanks.
Now follows that you know• young Fortinbras,
Holding a weak supposal• of our worth,
Or thinking by our late dear brother's death
1.2.20 Our state to be disjoint and out of frame,
Co-leaguèd• with this dream of his advantage,•
He hath not failed to pester us with message
Importing• the surrender of those lands
Lost by his father, with all bonds• of law,
1.2.25 To our most valiant brother. So much for him.
Now for ourself and for this time of meeting.
Thus much the business is: we have here writ
To Norway, uncle of young Fortinbras –
Who, impotent• and bed-rid, scarcely hears
1.2.30 Of this his nephew's purpose – to suppress
His• further gait• herein, in that the levies,
The lists, and full proportions are all made
Out of his subject;• and we here dispatch
You, good Cornelius, and you, Voltimand,
1.2.35 For bearers of this greeting to old Norway,

as • such as, including

cum aliis • with others

our • my (the royal
"we"; also in the follow-
ing lines)

sometime • former

jointress • a woman
possessing property
jointly with her husband

With ... eye • with
one eye smiling and
the other weeping

dole • grief

that you know • what
you know already, that;
or, that you should be
informed as follows

weak supposal • low
estimate

Co-leaguèd with •
joined to, allied with

dream ... advan-
tage • illusory hope of
having the advantage
(his only ally is this hope)

importing • pertain-
ing to

bonds • contracts

impotent • helpless

His • Fortinbras'

gait • proceeding

in that ... subject
since the levying of troops
and supplies is drawn
entirely from the King of
Norway's own subjects

dilated · set out at length

let ... duty · let your swift obeying of orders, rather than mere words, express your dutifulness

nothing · not at all

the Dane · the Danish King

lose your voice · waste your speech

native · connected, related

instrumental · serviceable

leave and favor · kind permission

bow ... pardon · entreatingly make a deep bow, asking your permission to depart

H' ath · he has

sealed · as if sealing a legal document

hard · reluctant

Take ... hour · enjoy your time of youth

And ... will · and may your finest qualities guide the way you choose to spend your time

cousin · any kin not of the immediate family

A little ... kind · closer than an ordinary nephew (since I am stepson), and yet more separated in natural feeling (with a pun on "kind" meaning "affectionate" and "natural," "lawful")

the sun · the sunshine of the King's royal favor, (with a pun on "son")

nighted color · mourning garments of black; dark melancholy

Denmark · the King

vailèd lids · lowered eyes

Giving to you no further personal power   1.2.36
To business with the King more than the scope
Of these dilated˙ articles allow.
[*He gives a paper.*]
  Farewell, and let your haste commend your duty.˙

CORNELIUS, VOLTIMAND In that, and all things, will we show   1.2.40
  our duty.

KING We doubt it nothing.˙ Heartily farewell.
[*Exeunt* VOLTIMAND *and* CORNELIUS.]
  And now, Laertes, what's the news with you?
  You told us of some suit; what is 't, Laertes?
  You cannot speak of reason to the Dane˙
  And lose your voice.˙ What wouldst thou beg, Laertes,   1.2.45
  That shall not be my offer, not thy asking?
  The head is not more native˙ to the heart,
  The hand more instrumental˙ to the mouth,
  Than is the throne of Denmark to thy father.
  What wouldst thou have, Laertes?   1.2.50

LAERTES   My dread lord,
  Your leave and favor˙ to return to France,
  From whence though willingly I came to Denmark
  To show my duty in your coronation,
  Yet now I must confess, that duty done,
  My thoughts and wishes bend again toward France   1.2.55
  And bow them to your gracious leave and pardon.˙

KING Have you your father's leave? What says Polonius?

POLONIUS H' ath,˙ my lord, wrung from me my slow leave
  By laborsome petition, and at last
  Upon his will I sealed˙ my hard˙ consent.   1.2.60
  I do beseech you, give him leave to go.

KING Take thy fair hour,˙ Laertes. Time be thine,
  And thy best graces spend it at thy will!˙
  But now, my cousin˙ Hamlet, and my son –

HAMLET A little more than kin, and less than kind.˙   1.2.65

KING How is it that the clouds still hang on you?

HAMLET Not so, my lord. I am too much in the sun.˙

QUEEN Good Hamlet, cast thy nighted color˙ off,
  And let thine eye look like a friend on Denmark.˙
  Do not forever with thy vailèd lids˙   1.2.70

Seek for thy noble father in the dust.
Thou know'st 'tis common,° all that lives must die,
Passing through nature to eternity.
HAMLET Ay, madam, it is common.
QUEEN   If it be,
1.2.75   Why seems it so particular° with thee?
HAMLET Seems, madam? Nay, it is. I know not "seems."
'Tis not alone my inky cloak, good Mother,
Nor customary° suits of solemn black,
Nor windy suspiration° of forced breath,
1.2.80   No, nor the fruitful° river in the eye,
Nor the dejected havior° of the visage,
Together with all forms, moods,° shapes of grief,
That can denote me truly. These indeed seem,
For they are actions that a man might play.
1.2.85   But I have that within which passes show;
These but the trappings and the suits of woe.
KING 'Tis sweet and commendable in your nature, Hamlet,
To give these mourning duties to your father.
But you must know your father lost a father,
1.2.90   That father lost, lost his, and the survivor bound
In filial obligation for some term
To do obsequious° sorrow. But to persever°
In obstinate condolement° is a course
Of impious stubbornness. 'Tis unmanly grief.
1.2.95   It shows a will most incorrect to heaven,
A heart unfortified,° a mind impatient,
An understanding simple° and unschooled.
For what we know must be and is as common
As any the most vulgar thing to sense,°
1.2.100   Why should we in our peevish opposition
Take it to heart? Fie, 'tis a fault to heaven,
A fault against the dead, a fault to nature,
To reason most absurd, whose common theme
Is death of fathers, and who still° hath cried,
1.2.105   From the first corpse° till he that died today,
"This must be so." We pray you, throw to earth
This unprevailing° woe and think of us
As of a father, for let the world take note,

common · of universal occurrence (but Hamlet plays on the sense of "vulgar" in line 74)

particular · personal

customary · socially conventional; habitual with me

suspiration · sighing

fruitful · abundant

havior · expression

moods · outward expressions of feeling

obsequious · suited to obsequies or funerals

persever · persevere

condolement · sorrowing

unfortified · unfortified against adversity

simple · ignorant

As … sense · as the most ordinary experience

still · always

the first corpse · Abel's; see Genesis 4:8–12

unprevailing · unavailing, useless

You are the most immediate* to our throne,

And with no less nobility of love   1.2.110

Than that which dearest father bears his son

Do I impart toward* you. For* your intent

In going back to school* in Wittenberg,*

It is most retrograde* to our desire,

And we beseech you bend you* to remain   1.2.115

Here in the cheer and comfort of our eye,

Our chiefest courtier, cousin, and our son.

QUEEN Let not thy mother lose her prayers, Hamlet.

I pray thee, stay with us, go not to Wittenberg.

HAMLET I shall in all my best* obey you, madam.   1.2.120

KING Why, 'tis a loving and a fair reply.

Be as ourself in Denmark. Madam, come.

This gentle and unforced accord of Hamlet

Sits smiling to* my heart, in grace* whereof

No jocund* health that Denmark drinks today   1.2.125

But the great cannon to the clouds shall tell,

And the King's rouse* the heaven shall bruit again,*

Respeaking earthly thunder.* Come away.

[*Flourish. Exeunt all but* **HAMLET**.]

HAMLET O, that this too too sullied* flesh would melt,

Thaw, and resolve itself into a dew!   1.2.130

Or that the Everlasting had not fixed

His canon* 'gainst self-slaughter!* O God, God,

How weary, stale, flat, and unprofitable

Seem to me all the uses* of this world!

Fie on 't, ah fie! 'Tis an unweeded garden   1.2.135

That grows to seed. Things rank and gross in nature

Possess it merely.* That it should come to this!

But two months dead—nay, not so much, not two.

So excellent a king, that was to* this

Hyperion* to a satyr,* so loving to my mother   1.2.140

That he might not beteem* the winds of heaven

Visit her face too roughly. Heaven and earth,

Must I remember? Why, she would hang on him

As if increase of appetite had grown

By what it fed on, and yet within a month—   1.2.145

Let me not think on 't; frailty, thy name is woman!—

---

most immediate · next in succession

impart toward · bestow my affection on

For · as for

to school · to your studies

Wittenberg · famous German university founded in 1502

retrograde · contrary

bend you · incline yourself

in all my best · to the best of my ability

to · at

grace · thanksgiving

jocund · merry

rouse · drinking of a draft of liquor

bruit again · loudly echo

earthly thunder · the thunder of trumpet and kettledrum, sounded when the king drinks; see 1.4.8–12

sullied · defiled (the early quartos read "sallied"; the Folio "solid")

canon · law

self-slaughter · suicide

all the uses · the whole routine

merely · completely

to · in comparison to

Hyperion · Titan sun-god, father of Helios

satyr · a lecherous creature of classical mythology, half-human but with a goat's legs, tail, ears, and horns

beteem · allow

A little month, or ere* those shoes were old
With which she followed my poor father's body,
Like Niobe,* all tears, why she, even she –
1.2.150   O God, a beast, that wants discourse of reason,*
Would have mourned longer – married with my uncle,
My father's brother, but no more like my father
Than I to Hercules. Within a month,
Ere yet the salt of most unrighteous tears
1.2.155   Had left the flushing in her gallèd* eyes,
She married. O, most wicked speed, to post*
With such dexterity to incestuous* sheets!
It is not, nor it cannot come to good.
But break, my heart, for I must hold my tongue.

[*Enter* HORATIO, MARCELLUS, *and* BERNARDO.]

1.2.160   HORATIO   Hail to your lordship!
HAMLET   I am glad to see you well.
Horatio! – or I do forget myself.
HORATIO   The same, my lord, and your poor servant ever.
HAMLET   Sir, my good friend; I'll change that name* with you.
And what make you from* Wittenberg, Horatio?
Marcellus.
1.2.165   MARCELLUS   My good lord.
HAMLET   I am very glad to see you.

[*To* BERNARDO.]

                                         Good even, sir. –
But what in faith make you from Wittenberg?
HORATIO   A truant disposition, good my lord.
1.2.170   HAMLET   I would not hear your enemy say so,
Nor shall you do my ear that violence
To make it truster of your own report
Against yourself. I know you are no truant.
But what is your affair in Elsinore?
1.2.175   We'll teach you to drink deep ere you depart.
HORATIO   My lord, I came to see your father's funeral.
HAMLET   I prithee, do not mock me, fellow student,
I think it was to see my mother's wedding.
HORATIO   Indeed, my lord, it followed hard* upon.
1.2.180   HAMLET   Thrift, thrift, Horatio! The funeral baked meats*
Did coldly* furnish forth the marriage tables.

---

or ere · even before

Niobe · Tantalus' daughter, Queen of Thebes, who boasted that she had more sons and daughters than Leto; for this, Apollo and Artemis, children of Leto, slew her fourteen children. She was turned by Zeus into a stone that continually dropped tears

wants . . . reason · lacks the faculty of reason

gallèd · irritated, inflamed

post · hasten

incestuous · in Shakespeare's day, the marriage of a man like Claudius to his deceased brother's wife was considered incestuous

change that name · give and receive reciprocally the name of "friend" (rather than talk of "servant")

make you from · are you doing away from

hard · close

baked meats · meat pies

coldly · as cold leftovers

Would I had met my dearest foe in heaven
Or ever I had seen that day, Horatio!
My father! – Methinks I see my father.

HORATIO Where, my lord? 1.2.185

HAMLET In my mind's eye, Horatio.

HORATIO I saw him once. 'A was a goodly king.

HAMLET 'A was a man. Take him for all in all,
I shall not look upon his like again.

HORATIO My lord, I think I saw him yesternight.

HAMLET Saw? Who? 1.2.190

HORATIO My lord, the King your father.

HAMLET The King my father?

HORATIO Season your admiration for a while
With an attent ear till I may deliver,
Upon the witness of these gentlemen, 1.2.195
This marvel to you.

HAMLET For God's love, let me hear!

HORATIO Two nights together had these gentlemen,
Marcellus and Bernardo, on their watch,
In the dead waste and middle of the night,
Been thus encountered. A figure like your father, 1.2.200
Armèd at point exactly, cap-à-pie,
Appears before them, and with solemn march
Goes slow and stately by them. Thrice he walked
By their oppressed and fear-surprisèd eyes
Within his truncheon's length, whilst they, distilled 1.2.205
Almost to jelly with the act of fear,
Stand dumb and speak not to him. This to me
In dreadful secrecy impart they did,
And I with them the third night kept the watch,
Where, as they had delivered, both in time, 1.2.210
Form of the thing, each word made true and good,
The apparition comes. I knew your father,
These hands are not more like.

HAMLET But where was this?

MARCELLUS My lord, upon the platform where we watch.

HAMLET Did you not speak to it? 1.2.215

HORATIO My lord, I did,
But answer made it none. Yet once methought

Glosses: **dearest** · closest (and therefore deadliest) · **Or ever** · before · **'A** · he · **Season your admiration** · restrain your astonishment · **attent** · attentive · **dead waste** · desolate stillness · **at point** · correctly in every detail · **cap-à-pie** · from head to foot · **truncheon's** · officer's staff · **distilled** · dissolved · **act** · action, operation · **dreadful** · full of dread

It lifted up its head and did address
Itself to motion, like as it would speak;°
But even then° the morning cock crew loud,
1.2.220 And at the sound it shrunk in haste away
And vanished from our sight.

HAMLET 'Tis very strange.

HORATIO As I do live, my honored lord, 'tis true,
And we did think it writ down in our duty
To let you know of it.

1.2.225 **HAMLET** Indeed, indeed, sirs. But this troubles me.
Hold you the watch tonight?

ALL We do, my lord.

HAMLET Armed, say you?

ALL Armed, my lord.

HAMLET From top to toe?

1.2.230 **ALL** My lord, from head to foot.

HAMLET Then saw you not his face?

HORATIO O, yes, my lord, he wore his beaver° up.

HAMLET What° looked he, frowningly?

HORATIO A countenance more in sorrow than in anger.

1.2.235 **HAMLET** Pale or red?

HORATIO Nay, very pale.

HAMLET And fixed his eyes upon you?

HORATIO Most constantly.

HAMLET I would I had been there.

1.2.240 **HORATIO** It would have much amazed you.

HAMLET Very like, very like. Stayed it long?

HORATIO While one with moderate haste might tell° a hundred.

MARCELLUS, BERNARDO Longer, longer.

HORATIO Not when I saw't.

1.2.245 **HAMLET** His beard was grizzled°–no?

HORATIO It was, as I have seen it in his life,
A sable silvered.°

HAMLET I will watch tonight.
Perchance 'twill walk again.

HORATIO I warrant° it will.

HAMLET If it assume my noble father's person,
1.2.250 I'll speak to it though hell itself should gape
And bid me hold my peace. I pray you all,

---

did address ... speak · began to move as though it were about to speak

even then · at that very instant

beaver · visor on the helmet

What · how

tell · count

grizzled · gray

sable silvered · black mixed with white

warrant · assure you

If you have hitherto concealed this sight,

tenable · held

Let it be tenable° in your silence still,

And whatsoever else shall hap tonight,

Give it an understanding but no tongue.   1.2.255

I will requite your loves. So, fare you well.

Upon the platform twixt eleven and twelve

I'll visit you.

ALL   Our duty to your honor.

HAMLET Your loves, as mine to you. Farewell.

[*Exeunt all but* HAMLET.]

My father's spirit in arms! All is not well.   1.2.260

doubt · suspect

I doubt° some foul play. Would the night were come!

Till then sit still, my soul. Foul deeds will rise,

Though all the earth o'erwhelm them, to men's eyes.

[*Exit.*]

ACT 1, SCENE 3

[*Polonius' chambers. Enter* LAERTES *and* OPHELIA, *his sister.*]

LAERTES My necessaries are embarked. Farewell.   1.3.1

convoy is assistant ·
means of conveyance
are available

And, sister, as the winds give benefit

And convoy is assistant,° do not sleep

a toy in blood · a
passing amorous fancy

But let me hear from you.

OPHELIA   Do you doubt that?

primy · in its prime,
springtime

LAERTES For Hamlet, and the trifling of his favor,   1.3.5

Hold it a fashion and a toy in blood,°

Forward · precocious

A violet in the youth of primy° nature,

supliance · supply,
filler

Forward,° not permanent, sweet, not lasting,

The perfume and suppliance° of a minute –

crescent · growing,
waxing

No more.   1.3.10

thews · bodily strength

OPHELIA   No more but so?

temple · body

LAERTES   Think it no more.

For nature crescent° does not grow alone

Grows wide withal ·
grows along with it

In thews° and bulk, but as this temple° waxes

The inward service of the mind and soul

soil · blemish

Grows wide withal.° Perhaps he loves you now,

cautel · deceit

And now no soil° nor cautel° doth besmirch   1.3.15

will · desire

The virtue of his will;° but you must fear,

His greatness
weighed · if you take
into account his high
position

His greatness weighed,° his will is not his own.

For he himself is subject to his birth.

He may not, as unvalued persons do,

1.3.20 Carve° for himself, for on his choice depends
The safety and health of this whole state,
And therefore must his choice be circumscribed
Unto the voice and yielding° of that body
Whereof he is the head. Then if he says he loves you,

1.3.25 It fits your wisdom so far to believe it
As he in his particular act and place°
May give his saying deed, which is no further
Than the main voice° of Denmark goes withal.°
Then weigh what loss your honor may sustain

1.3.30 If with too credent° ear you list° his songs,
Or lose your heart, or your chaste treasure open
To his unmastered importunity.
Fear it, Ophelia, fear it, my dear sister,
And keep you in the rear of your affection,°

1.3.35 Out of the shot and danger of desire.
The chariest° maid is prodigal enough
If she unmask° her beauty to the moon.°
Virtue itself scapes not calumnious° strokes.
The canker galls° the infants of the spring

1.3.40 Too oft before their buttons° be disclosed°
And in the morn and liquid dew° of youth
Contagious blastments° are most imminent.
Be wary then; best safety lies in fear,
Youth to itself rebels,° though none else near.

1.3.45 **OPHELIA** I shall the effect of this good lesson keep
As watchman to my heart. But, good my brother,
Do not, as some ungracious° pastors do,
Show me the steep and thorny way to heaven,
Whiles like a puffed° and reckless libertine°

1.3.50 Himself the primrose path of dalliance treads,
And recks not his own rede.°
[*Enter* POLONIUS.]
LAERTES   O, fear me not.°
I stay too long. But here my father comes.
A double blessing° is a double grace;
Occasion° smiles upon a second leave.

1.3.55 **POLONIUS** Yet here, Laertes? Aboard, aboard, for shame!

Carve · choose

voice and yielding · assent, approval

in his ... place · in his particular restricted circumstances

main voice · general assent

withal · along with

credent · credulous

list · listen to

keep ... affection don't advance as far as your affection might lead you (a military metaphor)

chariest · most scrupulously modest

If she unmask · if she does no more than show her beauty

moon · symbol of chastity

calumnious · slanderous

canker galls · canker-worm destroys

buttons · buds

disclosed · opened

liquid dew · time when dew is fresh and bright

blastments · blights

Youth ... rebels · youth is inherently rebellious

ungracious · ungodly

puffed · bloated, or swollen with pride

libertine · a dissolute, immoral person

recks ... reed · heeds not his own counsel

fear me not · don't worry on my account

double blessing Laertes has already bid his father goodbye

Occasion · the goddess Occasion, or Opportunity

The wind sits in the shoulder of your sail,　　　　1.3.56
And you are stayed for. There – my blessing with thee!
And these few precepts in thy memory

Look · be sure that

Look° thou character.° Give thy thoughts no tongue,

character · inscribe

Nor any unproportioned° thought his° act.　　　　1.3.60

unproportioned ·
badly calculated,
intemperate

Be thou familiar,° but by no means vulgar.°

his · its

Those friends thou hast, and their adoption tried,°
Grapple them unto thy soul with hoops of steel,

familiar · sociable

But do not dull thy palm° with entertainment

vulgar · common

Of each new-hatched, unfledged courage.° Beware　　1.3.65

**and their adoption
tried** · and also their
suitability for adoption
as friends having been
tested

Of entrance to a quarrel, but being in,
Bear 't that° th' opposèd may beware of thee.
Give every man thy ear, but few thy voice;
Take each man's censure,° but reserve thy judgment,

dull thy palm · shake
hands so often as to make
the gesture meaningless

Costly thy habit° as thy purse can buy,　　　　1.3.70
But not expressed in fancy;° rich, not gaudy,
For the apparel oft proclaims the man,

courage · young man
of spirit

And they in France of the best rank and station
Are of a most select and generous chief in that,°

Bear 't that · manage
it so that

Neither a borrower nor a lender be,　　　　1.3.75
For loan oft loses both itself and friend,

censure · opinion,
judgment

And borrowing dulleth edge of husbandry.°

habit · clothing

This above all: to thine own self be true,
And it must follow, as the night the day,

fancy · excessive ornament, decadent fashion

Thou canst not then be false to any man.　　　　1.3.80

Are … that · are of a
most refined and well-
bred preeminence in
choosing what to wear

Farewell. My blessing season° this in thee!

LAERTES Most humbly do I take my leave, my lord.

POLONIUS The time invests° you. Go, your servants tend.°

husbandry · thrift

LAERTES Farewell, Ophelia, and remember well

season · mature

What I have said to you.　　　　1.3.85

invests · besieges,
presses upon

OPHELIA 'Tis in my memory locked,
And you yourself shall keep the key of it.

tend · attend, wait

LAERTES Farewell.

[*Exit* LAERTES.]

POLONIUS What is 't, Ophelia, he hath said to you?

OPHELIA So please you, something touching the Lord Hamlet　1.3.90

Marry · by the virgin
Mary (a mild oath)

POLONIUS Marry,° well bethought.
'Tis told me he hath very oft of late
Given private time to you, and you yourself

Have of your audience been most free and bounteous.
1.3.95 If it be so – as so 'tis put on° me,
And that in way of caution – I must tell you
You do not understand yourself so clearly
As it behooves° my daughter and your honor.
What is between you? Give me up the truth.

1.3.100 OPHELIA He hath, my lord, of late made many tenders°
Of his affection to me.

POLONIUS Affection? Pooh! You speak like a green girl,
Unsifted° in such perilous circumstance.
Do you believe his tenders, as you call them?

1.3.105 OPHELIA I do not know, my lord, what I should think.

POLONIUS Marry, I will teach you. Think yourself a baby
That you have ta'en these tenders for true pay
Which are not sterling.° Tender° yourself more dearly,
Or – not to crack the wind° of the poor phrase,
1.3.110 Running it thus – you'll tender me a fool.°

OPHELIA My lord, he hath importuned me with love
In honorable fashion.

POLONIUS Ay, fashion° you may call it. Go to,° go to.

OPHELIA And hath given countenance° to his speech, my lord
1.3.115 With almost all the holy vows of heaven.

POLONIUS Ay, springes° to catch woodcocks.° I do know,
When the blood burns, how prodigal° the soul
Lends the tongue vows. These blazes, daughter,
Giving more fight than heat, extinct in both
1.3.120 Even in their promise as it is a-making,
You must not take for fire. From this time
Be something° scanter of your maiden presence.
Set your entreatments° at a higher rate
Than a command to parle.° For Lord Hamlet,
1.3.125 Believe so much in him° that he is young,
And with a larger tether may he walk
Than may be given you. In few,° Ophelia,
Do not believe his vows, for they are brokers,°
Not of that dye° which their investments° show,
1.3.130 But mere implorators° of unholy suits,
Breathing° like sanctified and pious bawds,
The better to beguile. This is for all:°

---

put on · impressed on, told to

behooves · befits

tenders · offers

Unsifted · untried

sterling · legal currency

Tender · hold, look after, offer

crack the wind · run it until it is worn out

tender me a fool · 1 · show yourself to me as a fool; 2 · show me up as a fool; 3 · present me with a grandchild ("fool" was a term of endearment for a child)

fashion · mere form, pretense

Go to · an expression of impatience

countenance · credit, confirmation

springes · snares

woodcocks · birds easily caught, here used to connote gullibility

prodigal · prodigally

something · somewhat

entreatments · negotiations for surrender (a military term)

parle · discuss terms with the enemy. Polonius urges Ophelia not to meet and consider giving in to Hamlet merely because he requests an interview

so much in him · this much concerning him

In few · briefly

brokers · go-betweens

dye · color or sort

investments · clothes (the vows are not what they seem)

mere implorators · out-and-out solicitors

Breathing · speaking

for all · once for all, in sum

I would not, in plain terms, from this time forth

slander · abuse, misuse

moment · moment's

Come your ways · come along

shrewdly · keenly, sharply

eager · biting

lacks of · is just short of

season · time

held his wont · was accustomed

pieces · of ordnance, cannon

wake · stay awake and hold revel

takes his rouse · carouses

wassail · carousal

Rhenish · Rhine wine

The triumph ... pledge · his feat in draining the wine in a single draft

manner · custom (of drinking)

More ... observance · better neglected than followed

east and west · everywhere

taxed of · censured by

clepe · call

with swinish phrase · by calling us swine

addition · reputation

at height · outstandingly

The pith ... attribute · the essence of the reputation that others attribute to us

for · on account of

mole of nature · natural blemish in one's constitution

Have you so slander* any moment* leisure

As to give words or talk with the Lord Hamlet.   1.3.135

Look to 't, I charge you. Come your ways.*

OPHELIA I shall obey, my lord.

[*Exeunt.*]

ACT 1, SCENE 4

[*The guard platform. Enter* **HAMLET**, **HORATIO**, *and* **MARCELLUS**.]

HAMLET The air bites shrewdly;* it is very cold.   1.4.1

HORATIO It is a nipping and an eager* air.

HAMLET What hour now?

HORATIO   I think it lacks of* twelve.

MARCELLUS No, it is struck.

HORATIO   Indeed? I heard it not.

It then draws near the season*   1.4.5

Wherein the spirit held his wont* to walk.

[*A flourish of trumpets, and two pieces* go off within.*]

What does this mean, my lord?

HAMLET The King doth wake* tonight and takes his rouse,*

Keeps wassail,* and the swaggering upspring reels;

And as he drains his drafts of Rhenish* down,   1.4.10

The kettledrum and trumpet thus bray out

The triumph of his pledge.*

HORATIO   Is it a custom?

HAMLET Ay, marry, is 't,

But to my mind, though I am native here

And to the manner* born, it is a custom   1.4.15

More honored in the breach than the observance.*

This heavy-headed revel east and west*

Makes us traduced and taxed of* other nations.

They clepe* us drunkards, and with swinish phrase*

Soil our addition;* and indeed it takes   1.4.20

From our achievements, though performed at height,*

The pith and marrow of our attribute.*

So, oft it chances in particular men,

That for* some vicious mole of nature* in them,

As in their birth – wherein they are not guilty,   1.4.25

Since nature cannot choose his origin –

By their o'ergrowth of some complexion,·
Oft breaking down the pales· and forts of reason,
Or by some habit that too much o'erleavens·
1.4.30 The form of plausive· manners, that these men,
Carrying, I say, the stamp of one defect,
Being nature's livery· or fortune's star,·
His virtues else,· be they as pure as grace,
As infinite as man may undergo,·
1.4.35 Shall in the general censure· take corruption
From that particular fault. The dram of evil
Doth all the noble substance often dout
To his own scandal.·

[*Enter* GHOST.]

HORATIO   Look, my lord, it comes!

HAMLET Angels and ministers of grace· defend us!
1.4.40 Be thou a spirit of health· or goblin damned,
Bring· with thee airs from heaven or blasts from hell,
Be thy intents wicked or charitable,
Thou com'st in such a questionable· shape
That I will speak to thee. I'll call thee Hamlet,
1.4.45 King, father, royal Dane. O, answer me!
Let me not burst in ignorance, but tell
Why thy canonized· bones, hearsèd· in death,
Have burst their cerements;· why the sepulcher
Wherein we saw thee quietly inurned·
1.4.50 Hath oped his ponderous and marble jaws
To cast thee up again. What may this mean,
That thou, dead corpse, again in complete steel,·
Revisits thus the glimpses of the moon,
Making night hideous, and we fools of nature·
1.4.55 So horridly to shake our disposition·
With thoughts beyond the reaches of our souls?
Say, why is this? Wherefore? What should we do?

[*The* GHOST *beckons to* HAMLET.]

HORATIO It beckons you to go away with it,
As if it some impartment· did desire
1.4.60 To you alone.

MARCELLUS   Look with what courteous action

---

o'ergrowth … complexion · the excessive growth of a natural trait

pales · palings, fences (as of a fortification)

o'erleavens · induces a change throughout (as yeast works in dough)

plausive · pleasing

nature's livery · sign of one's servitude to nature

fortune's star · the destiny that chance brings

His virtues else · the other qualities of these men (see line 30)

may undergo · can sustain

general censure · general opinion that people have of him

The dram … scandal · the drop of evil blots out ("douts") the noble substance of the whole and brings it into disrepute

ministers of grace · messengers of God

Be thou … health · whether you are a good angel

Bring · whether you bring

questionable · inviting question

canonized · buried according to church law

hearsèd · coffined

cerements · grave clothes

inurned · entombed

complete steel · full armor

fools of nature · mere men, limited to natural knowledge

So … disposition · to distress our mental composure so violently

impartment · communication

It wafts you to a more removèd ground.   1.4.61
But do not go with it.

HORATIO   No, by no means.

HAMLET It will not speak. Then I will follow it.

HORATIO Do not, my lord!

HAMLET   Why, what should be the fear?

fee · value
I do not set my life at a pin's fee,*   1.4.65
And for my soul, what can it do to that,
Being a thing immortal as itself?
It waves me forth again. I'll follow it.

flood · sea
HORATIO What if it tempt you toward the flood,* my lord,
Or to the dreadful summit of the cliff   1.4.70

beetles o'er · over-
hangs threateningly
(like bushy eyebrows)
That beetles o'er* his* base into the sea,
And there assume some other horrible form

his · its
Which might deprive your sovereignty of reason*

deprive … reason ·
take away the rule of
reason over your mind
And draw you into madness? Think of it.
The very place puts toys of desperation,*   1.4.75

toys of desperation ·
fancies of desperate
acts (suicide)
Without more motive, into every brain
That looks so many fathoms to the sea
And hears it roar beneath.

HAMLET It wafts me still. – Go on, I'll follow thee.

MARCELLUS You shall not go, my lord.   1.4.80

[MARCELLUS *and* HORATIO *try to stop him.*]

HAMLET   Hold off your hands!

HORATIO Be ruled. You shall not go.

My fate cries out · my
destiny summons me
HAMLET   My fate cries out,*

petty · weak
And makes each petty* artery* in this body

artery · through which
the vital spirits were
thought to have been
conveyed
As hardy as the Nemean lion's* nerve.*
Still am I called. Unhand me, gentlemen.
By heaven, I'll make a ghost of him that lets* me!   1.4.85

Nemean lion's · one
of the monsters slain by
Hercules in his twelve
labors
I say, away! – Go on, I'll follow thee.

[*Exeunt* GHOST *and* HAMLET.]

HORATIO He waxes desperate with imagination.

nerve · sinew
MARCELLUS Let's follow. 'Tis not fit thus to obey him.

lets · hinders
HORATIO Have after.* To what issue* will this come?

Have after · let's go
after him
MARCELLUS Something is rotten in the state of Denmark.   1.4.90

HORATIO Heaven will direct it.*

issue · outcome
MARCELLUS   Nay, let's follow him.

it · the outcome
[*Exeunt.*]

ACT 1, SCENE 5

[*The battlements of the castle. Enter the* GHOST *and* HAMLET.]

1.5.1 HAMLET Whither wilt thou lead me? Speak. I'll go no further.

GHOST Mark me.

HAMLET   I will.

GHOST   My hour is almost come,
When I to sulfurous and tormenting flames
Must render up myself.

HAMLET   Alas, poor ghost!

1.5.5 GHOST Pity me not, but lend thy serious hearing
To what I shall unfold.

HAMLET Speak. I am bound· to hear.

GHOST So art thou to revenge, when thou shalt hear.

HAMLET What?

1.5.10 GHOST I am thy father's spirit,
Doomed for a certain term to walk the night,
And for the day confined to fast· in fires,
Till the foul crimes· done in my days of nature·
Are burnt and purged away. But that· I am forbid

1.5.15 To tell the secrets of my prison house,
I could a tale unfold whose lightest word
Would harrow up· thy soul, freeze thy young blood,
Make thy two eyes like stars start from their spheres,·
Thy knotted and combinèd locks· to part,

1.5.20 And each particular hair to stand on end
Like quills upon the fretful porcupine.
But this eternal blazon· must not be
To ears of flesh and blood. List, list, O, list!
If thou didst ever thy dear father love –

1.5.25 HAMLET O God!

GHOST Revenge his foul and most unnatural murder.

HAMLET Murder?

GHOST Murder most foul, as in the best· it is,
But this most foul, strange, and unnatural.

1.5.30 HAMLET Haste me to know 't, that I, with wings as swift
As meditation or the thoughts of love,
May sweep to my revenge.

GHOST   I find thee apt;
And duller shouldst thou be· than the fat· weed

bound · 1 · ready 2 · obligated by duty and fate. The Ghost, in line 8, answers in the second sense

fast · do penance by fasting

crimes · sins

of nature · as a mortal

But that · were it not that

harrow up · lacerate, tear

spheres · eye-sockets, here compared to the orbits or transparent revolving spheres in which, according to Ptolemaic astronomy, the heavenly bodies were fixed

knotted ... locks · hair neatly arranged and confined

eternal blazon · revelation of the secrets of eternity

in the best · even at best

shouldst thou be · you would have to be

fat · torpid, lethargic

Lethe · the river of
forgetfulness in Hades

That roots itself in ease on Lethe· wharf,
Wouldst thou not stir in this. Now, Hamlet, hear. 1.5.35

orchard · garden

'Tis given out that, sleeping in my orchard,·
A serpent stung me. So the whole ear of Denmark

forgèd process ·
falsified account

Is by a forgèd process· of my death
Rankly abused.· But know, thou noble youth,

abused · deceived

The serpent that did sting thy father's life 1.5.40
Now wears his crown.

HAMLET O, my prophetic soul! My uncle!

GHOST Ay, that incestuous, that adulterate· beast,

adulterate · adulterous

With witchcraft of his wit, with traitorous gifts·—

gifts · 1 · talents;
2 · presents

O wicked wit and gifts, that have the power 1.5.45
So to seduce!—won to his shameful lust

even with the vow ·
with the very vow

The will of my most seeming-virtuous queen.
O Hamlet, what a falling off was there!

To · compared to

From me, whose love was of that dignity

virtue, as it · as virtue

That it went hand in hand even with the vow· 1.5.50

shape of heaven ·
heavenly form

I made to her in marriage, and to decline
Upon a wretch whose natural gifts were poor

sate ... bed · cease
to find sexual pleasure
in a virtuously lawful
marriage

To· those of mine!
But virtue, as it· never will be moved,
Though lewdness court it in a shape of heaven,· 1.5.55

secure · confident,
unsuspicious

So lust, though to a radiant angel linked,
Will sate itself in a celestial bed·

hebona · a poison. The
word seems to be a
form of "ebony," though
it is thought perhaps to
be related to "henbane,"
a poison, or to "ebenus,"
"yew"

And prey on garbage.
But soft, methinks I scent the morning air.
Brief let me be. Sleeping within my orchard, 1.5.60
My custom always of the afternoon,
Upon my secure· hour thy uncle stole,

porches of my ears ·
ears as a porch or
entrance of the body

With juice of cursèd hebona· in a vial,
And in the porches of my ears· did pour

leprous distillment ·
distillation causing lep-
rosy-like disfigurement

The leprous distillment,· whose effect 1.5.65
Holds such an enmity with blood of man

posset · coagulate,
curdle

That swift as quicksilver it courses through
The natural gates and alleys of the body,

eager · sour, acid

And with a sudden vigor it doth posset·

tetter · eruption of
scabs

And curd, like eager· droppings into milk, 1.5.70
The thin and wholesome blood. So did it mine,

barked · covered with
a rough covering, like
bark on a tree

And a most instant tetter· barked· about,

Most lazar-like,˙ with vile and loathsome crust,
All my smooth body.

1.5.75 Thus was I, sleeping, by a brother's hand
Of life, of crown, of queen at once dispatched,˙
Cut off even in the blossoms of my sin,
Unhouseled,˙ disappointed,˙ unaneled,˙
No reckoning˙ made, but sent to my account
1.5.80 With all my imperfections on my head.
O, horrible! O, horrible, most horrible!
If thou hast nature˙ in thee, bear it not.
Let not the royal bed of Denmark be
A couch for luxury˙ and damnèd incest.
1.5.85 But, howsoever thou pursues this act,
Taint not thy mind nor let thy soul contrive
Against thy mother aught. Leave her to heaven
And to those thorns that in her bosom lodge,
To prick and sting her. Fare thee well at once.
1.5.90 The glowworm shows the matin˙ to be near,
And 'gins to pale his˙ uneffectual fire.
Adieu, adieu, adieu! Remember me.
[*Exit.*]

HAMLET O all you host of heaven! O earth! What else?
And shall I couple˙ hell? O, fie! Hold,˙ hold, my heart
1.5.95 And you, my sinews, grow not instant˙ old,
But bear me stiffly up. Remember thee?
Ay, thou poor ghost, whiles memory holds a seat
In this distracted globe.˙ Remember thee?
Yea, from the table˙ of my memory
1.5.100 I'll wipe away all trivial fond˙ records,
All saws˙ of books, all forms,˙ all pressures˙ past
That youth and observation copied there,
And thy commandment all alone shall live
Within the book and volume of my brain,
1.5.105 Unmixed with baser matter. Yes, by heaven!
O most pernicious woman!
O villain, villain, smiling, damnèd villain!
My tables˙– meet it is˙ I set it down
That one may smile, and smile, and be a villain.
1.5.110 At least I am sure it may be so in Denmark.

lazar-like · leper-like

dispatched · suddenly deprived

Unhouseled · without having received the Sacrament

disappointed · unready (spiritually) for the last journey

unaneled · without having received extreme unction

reckoning · settling of accounts

nature · the promptings of a son

luxury · lechery

matin · morning

his · its

couple · add

Hold · hold together

instant · instantly

globe · 1 · head; 2 · world

table · tablet, slate

fond · foolish

saws · wise sayings

forms · shapes or images copied onto the slate; general ideas

pressures · impressions stamped

tables · writing tablets

meet it is · it is fitting

[*Writing.*]

So, uncle, there you are.• Now to my word:

there you are · there, I've written that down against you

It is "Adieu, adieu! Remember me."

I have sworn 't.

[*Enter* HORATIO *and* MARCELLUS.]

HORATIO My lord, my lord!

MARCELLUS Lord Hamlet!   1.5.115

HORATIO Heavens secure him!•

secure him · keep him safe

HAMLET So be it.

MARCELLUS Hilo, ho, ho, my lord!

Hillo … come · A falconer's call to a hawk in the air. Hamlet mocks the hallooing as though it were a part of hawking

HAMLET Hillo, ho, ho, boy! Come, bird, come.•

MARCELLUS How is 't, my noble lord?   1.5.120

HORATIO What news, my lord?

HAMLET O, wonderful!

HORATIO Good my lord, tell it.

HAMLET No, you will reveal it.

HORATIO Not I, my lord, by heaven.   1.5.125

MARCELLUS Nor I, my lord.

once · ever

HAMLET How say you, then, would heart of man once• think it?
  But you'll be secret?

HORATIO, MARCELLUS Ay, by heaven, my lord.

HAMLET There's never a villain dwelling in all Denmark
  But he's an arrant• knave.   1.5.130

arrant · thoroughgoing

HORATIO There needs no ghost, my lord, come from the grave
  To tell us this.

HAMLET   Why, right, you are in the right.
  And so, without more circumstance• at all,

circumstance · ceremony, elaboration

  I hold it fit that we shake hands and part,
  You as your business and desire shall point you –   1.5.135
  For every man hath business and desire,
  Such as it is – and for my own poor part,

Saint Patrick · the keeper of Purgatory, and patron saint of all blunders and confusion

  Look you, I'll go pray.

HORATIO These are but wild and whirling words, my lord.

offense · Hamlet deliberately changes Horatio's "no offense taken" to "an offense against all decency"

HAMLET I am sorry they offend you, heartily;   1.5.140
  Yes, faith, heartily.

HORATIO   There's no offense, my lord.

HAMLET Yes, by Saint Patrick,• but there is, Horatio,

an honest ghost · a real ghost and not an evil spirit

  And much offense• too. Touching this vision here,
  It is an honest ghost,• that let me tell you.

1.5.145   For your desire to know what is between us,
       O'ermaster't as you may. And now, good friends,
       As you are friends, scholars, and soldiers,
       Give me one poor request.

HORATIO What is 't, my lord? We will.

1.5.150 **HAMLET** Never make known what you have seen tonight,

HORATIO, MARCELLUS My lord, we will not.

HAMLET Nay, but swear 't.

HORATIO In faith, my lord, not I.•

MARCELLUS Nor I, my lord, in faith.

1.5.155 **HAMLET** Upon my sword.•

    [**HAMLET** *holds out his sword.*]

MARCELLUS We have sworn, my lord, already.•

HAMLET Indeed, upon my sword, indeed.

    [*The* **GHOST**, *crying from under the stage.*]

GHOST Swear.

HAMLET Ha, ha, boy, sayst thou so? Art thou there, truepenny?•

1.5.160   Come on, you hear this fellow in the cellarage.
       Consent to swear.

HORATIO   Propose the oath, my lord.

HAMLET Never to speak of this that you have seen,
       Swear by my sword.

    [*The* **GHOST**, *from beneath.*]

GHOST Swear.

    [*They swear.*]•

1.5.165 **HAMLET** *Hic et ubique?*• Then we'll shift our ground.

    [*He moves to another spot.*]

       Come hither, gentlemen,
       And lay your hands again upon my sword.
       Swear by my sword
       Never to speak of this that you have heard.

    [*The* **GHOST**, *from beneath.*]

1.5.170 **GHOST** Swear by his sword.

    [*They swear.*]

HAMLET Well said, old mole. Canst work i' th' earth so fast?
       A worthy pioner!•– Once more remove, good friends,

    [**HAMLET** *moves again.*]

HORATIO O day and night, but this is wondrous strange!

HAMLET And therefore as a stranger• give it welcome.

In faith ... not I • swear not to tell what I have seen. Horatio is not refusing to swear

sword • the hilt in the form of a cross

We ... already • Marcellus notes that they have already sworn in faith

truepenny • honest old fellow

They swear • seemingly they swear here, and at lines 170 and 190, as they lay their hands on Hamlet's sword. Triple oaths would have particular force; these three oaths deal with what they have seen, what they have heard, and what they promise about Hamlet's "antic disposition"

Hic et ubique • "here and everywhere" (Latin)

Pioner • a foot soldier assigned to dig tunnels and excavations

as a stranger • as someone needing your hospitality

There are more things in heaven and earth, Horatio, 1.5.175
Than are dreamt of in your philosophy.*
But come;
Here, as before, never, so help you mercy,*
How strange or odd soe'er I bear myself –
As I perchance hereafter shall think meet 1.5.180
To put an antic* disposition on –
That you, at such times seeing me, never shall,
With arms encumbered* thus, or this headshake,
Or by pronouncing of some doubtful phrase
As "Well, we know," or "We could, an if* we would," 1.5.185
Or "If we list* to speak," or "There be, an if they might,"*
Or such ambiguous giving out,* to note*
That you know aught* of me – this do swear,
So grace and mercy at your most need help you.
[*The* **Ghost,** *from beneath.*]

Ghost Swear. 1.5.190

[*They swear.*]

Hamlet Rest, rest, perturbèd spirit! So, gentlemen,
With all my love I do commend me to you;*
And what so poor a man as Hamlet is
May do t' express his love and friending* to you,
God willing, shall not lack.* Let us go in together, 1.5.195
And still* your fingers on your lips, I pray.
The time* is out of joint. O cursèd spite*
That ever I was born to set it right!

[*They wait for him to leave first.*]
Nay, come, let's go together.*

[*Exeunt.*]

ACT 2, SCENE 1

[*Polonius' chambers. Enter old* **Polonius** *with his man* **Reynaldo.**]

Polonius Give him this money and these notes, Reynaldo. 2.1.1

[*He gives money and papers.*]

Reynaldo I will, my lord.

Polonius You shall do marvelous* wisely, good Reynaldo,
Before you visit him, to make inquire*
Of his behavior. 2.1.5

Reynaldo   My lord, I did intend it.

---

your philosophy · this subject called "natural philosophy" or "science" that people talk about

so help you mercy · as you hope for God's mercy when you are judged

antic · fantastic, mad

encumbered · folded

an if · if

list · wished

There … might · there are people here (we, in fact) who could tell news if we were at liberty to do so

giving out · intimation

note · draw attention to the fact

aught · something secret

do … you · entrust myself to you

friending · friendliness

lack · be lacking

still · always

The time · the state of affairs

spite · the spite of Fortune

let's go together · probably they wait for him to leave first, but he refuses this ceremoniousness

marvelous · marvelously, very

inquire · inquiry

2.1.6	**POLONIUS** Marry, well said, very well said. Look you, sir,	
	Inquire me first what Danskers° are in Paris,	Danskers · Danes
	And how, and who, what means,° and where they keep,°	what means · what wealth (they have)
	What company, at what expense; and finding	keep · dwell
2.1.10	By this encompassment° and drift° of question	encompassment · roundabout talking
	That they do know my son, come you more nearer	drift · gradual approach or course
	Than your particular demands will touch it.°	
	Take you,° as 'twere, some distant knowledge of him,	come you ... touch it · you will find out more this way than by asking pointed or direct questions ("particular demands")
	As thus, "I know his father and his friends,	
2.1.15	And in part him." Do you mark this, Reynaldo?	
	REYNALDO Ay, very well, my lord.	
	POLONIUS "And in part him, but," you may say, "not well.	Take you · assume, pretend
	But if 't be he I mean, he's very wild,	
	Addicted so and so," and there put on° him	put on · impute to
2.1.20	What forgeries° you please – marry, none so rank°	forgeries · invented tales
	As may dishonor him, take heed of that,	
	But, sir, such wanton,° wild, and usual slips	rank · gross, distasteful
	As are companions noted and most known	wanton · sportive, unrestrained
	To youth and liberty.	
2.1.25	**REYNALDO** As gaming, my lord.	
	POLONIUS Ay, or drinking, fencing, swearing,	
	Quarreling, drabbing°– you may go so far.	drabbing · whoring
	REYNALDO My lord, that would dishonor him.	
	POLONIUS Faith, no, as you may season° it in the charge.	season · temper, soften
2.1.30	You must not put another scandal on him	incontinency · habitual sexual excess
	That he is open to incontinency;°	
	That's not my meaning. But breathe his faults so quaintly°	quaintly · artfully, subtly
	That they may seem the taints of liberty,°	
	The flash and outbreak of a fiery mind,	taints of liberty · faults resulting from free living
2.1.35	A savageness in unreclaimèd blood,	
	Of general assault.°	A savageness ... assault · a wildness in untamed youth that assails all indiscriminately
	REYNALDO But, my good lord –	
	POLONIUS Wherefore should you do this?	
	REYNALDO Ay, my lord, I would know that.	
2.1.40	**POLONIUS** Marry, sir, here's my drift,	fetch of warrant · legitimate trick
	And I believe it is a fetch of warrant.°	
	You laying these slight sullies on my son,	soiled wi' the working · soiled by handling while it is being made – by involvement in the ways of the world
	As 'twere a thing a little soiled wi' the working,°	
	Mark you,	

converse · conversation

sound · sound out

Having ever · if he
has ever

prenominate
crimes · before-men-
tioned offenses

breathe · speak

closes … conse-
quence · takes you into
his confidence in some
fashion, as follows

addition · title

Your party in converse,˙ him you would sound,˙   2.1.45
Having ever˙ seen in the prenominate crimes˙
The youth you breathe˙ of guilty, be assured
He closes with you in this consequence:˙
"Good sir," or so, or "friend," or "gentleman,"
According to the phrase or the addition˙   2.1.50
Of man and country.

REYNALDO   Very good, my lord.

POLONIUS And then, sir, does 'a this – 'a does – what was I about
to say? By the Mass, I was about to say something. Where
did I leave?

REYNALDO At "closes in the consequence."   2.1.55

POLONIUS At "closes in the consequence," ay, marry.
He closes thus: "I know the gentleman,
I saw him yesterday," or "th' other day,"
Or then, or then, with such or such, "and as you say,

o'ertook in 's rouse ·
overcome by drink

falling out · quarreling

Videlicet · namely

carp · a fish

reach · capacity, ability

windlasses · circu-
itous paths – literally,
circuits made to head
off the game in hunting

assays of bias ·
attempts through
indirection (like the curv-
ing path of a bowling
ball, which is biased or
weighted to one side)

directions · the way
things really are

have · understand

b' wi' · be with

in yourself · in your
own person (as well as
by asking questions)

There was 'a gaming," "there o'ertook in 's rouse,"˙   2.1.60
"There falling out˙ at tennis," or perchance
"I saw him enter such a house of sale,"
Videlicet˙ a brothel, or so forth. See you now,
Your bait of falsehood takes this carp˙ of truth;
And thus do we of wisdom and of reach,˙   2.1.65
With windlasses;˙ and with assays of bias,˙
By indirections find directions˙ out.
So by my former lecture and advice
Shall you my son. You have˙ me, have you not?

REYNALDO My lord, I have.   2.1.70

POLONIUS   God b' wi'˙ ye; fare ye well

REYNALDO Good my lord.

POLONIUS Observe his inclination in yourself.˙

REYNALDO I shall, my lord.

POLONIUS And let him ply his music.

REYNALDO Well, my lord.   2.1.75

POLONIUS   Farewell.

[*Exit* **REYNALDO**. *Enter* **OPHELIA**.]

How now, Ophelia, what's the matter?

OPHELIA O my lord, my lord, I have been so affrighted!

POLONIUS With what, i' the name of God?

closet · private chamber

OPHELIA My lord, as I was sewing in my closet,˙

2.1.80 Lord Hamlet, with his doublet° all unbraced,°
No hat upon his head, his stockings fouled,
Ungartered, and down-gyvèd° to his ankle,
Pale as his shirt, his knees knocking each other,
And with a look so piteous in purport°
2.1.85 As if he had been loosèd out of hell
To speak of horrors – he comes before me.

POLONIUS Mad for thy love?

OPHELIA   My lord, I do not know,
But truly I do fear it.

POLONIUS   What said he?

OPHELIA He took me by the wrist and held me hard.
2.1.90 Then goes he to the length of all his arm,
And, with his other hand thus o'er his brow
He falls to such perusal of my face
As° 'a would draw it. Long stayed he so.
At last, a little shaking of mine arm
2.1.95 And thrice his head thus waving up and down,
He raised a sigh so piteous and profound
As it did seem to shatter all his bulk°
And end his being. That done, he lets me go,
And with his head over his shoulder turned
2.1.100 He seemed to find his way without his eyes,
For out o' doors he went without their helps,
And to the last bended their light on me.

POLONIUS Come, go with me. I will go seek the King.
This is the very ecstasy° of love,
2.1.105 Whose violent property° fordoes° itself
And leads the will to desperate undertakings
As oft as any passion under heaven
That does afflict our natures. I am sorry.
What, have you given him any hard words of late?

2.1.110 OPHELIA No, my good lord, but as you did command
I did repel his letters and denied
His access to me.

POLONIUS   That hath made him mad.
I am sorry that with better heed and judgment
I had not quoted° him. I feared he did but trifle
2.1.115 And meant to wrack° thee. But beshrew my jealousy!°

doublet · close-fitting jacket

unbraced · unfastened

down-gyvèd · fallen to the ankles (like gyves or fetters)

in purport · in what it expressed

As · as if (also in line 97)

bulk · body

ecstasy · madness

property · nature

fordoes · destroys

quoted · observed

wrack · ruin, seduce

beshrew my jealousy · a plague upon my suspicious nature

By heaven, it is as proper to our age
To cast beyond* ourselves in our opinions
As it is common for the younger sort
To lack discretion. Come, go we to the King.
This must be known,* which, being kept close,* might move   2.1.120
More grief to hide than hate to utter love.*
Come.
[*Exeunt.*]

ACT 2, SCENE 2

[*The Castle. Flourish. Enter* KING *and* QUEEN, ROSENCRANTZ, *and*
GUILDENSTERN *with* OTHERS.]

KING Welcome, dear Rosencrantz and Guildenstern.   2.2.1
Moreover that* we much did long to see you,
The need we have to use you did provoke
Our hasty sending. Something have you heard
Of Hamlet's transformation – so call it,   2.2.5
Sith nor* th' exterior nor the inward man
Resembles that* it was. What it should be,
More than his father's death, that thus hath put him
So much from th' understanding of himself,
I cannot dream of. I entreat you both   2.2.10
That, being of so young days* brought up with him,
And sith so neighbored to* his youth and havior,*
That you vouchsafe your rest* here in our court
Some little time, so by your companies
To draw him on to pleasures, and to gather   2.2.15
So much as from occasion* you may glean,
Whether aught to us unknown afflicts him thus
That, opened,* lies within our remedy.
QUEEN Good gentlemen, he hath much talked of you,
And sure I am two men there is not living   2.2.20
To whom he more adheres. If it will please you
To show us so much gentry* and good will
As to expend your time with us awhile
For the supply and profit of our hope,*
Your visitation shall receive such thanks   2.2.25
As fits a king's remembrance.*
ROSENCRANTZ   Both Your Majesties

---

cast beyond · overshoot, miscalculate (a metaphor from hunting)

known · made known (to the King)

close · secret

might move … love · might cause more grief (because of what Hamlet might do) by hiding the knowledge of Hamlet's strange behavior than the unpleasantness of telling it

Moreover that · besides the fact that

Sith nor · since neither

that · what

of so young days · from such early youth

And sith so neighbored to · and since you are (or, and since that time you are) intimately acquainted with

havior · demeanor

vouchsafe your rest · please to stay

occasion · opportunity

opened · being revealed

gentry · courtesy

supply … hope · aid and furtherance of what we hope for

As fits … remembrance · as would be a fitting gift from a king who rewards true service

Might, by the sovereign power you have of˙ us,   of · over

Put your dread˙ pleasures more into command   dread · inspiring awe

Than to entreaty.

GUILDENSTERN   But we both obey,

2.2.30   And here give up ourselves in the full bent˙   in the full bent · to

To lay our service freely at your feet,   the utmost degree

To be commanded.   of our capacity (an

                                         archery metaphor)

KING Thanks, Rosencrantz and gentle Guildenstern.

QUEEN Thanks, Guildenstern and gentle Rosencrantz.

2.2.35   And I beseech you instantly to visit

My too much changèd son. Go, some of you,

And bring these gentlemen where Hamlet is.

GUILDENSTERN Heavens make our presence and our practices˙   practices · doings

Pleasant and helpful to him!

QUEEN   Ay, amen!

[*Exeunt* **ROSENCRANTZ** *and* **GUILDENSTERN** *with some* **ATTENDANTS**.

Enter **POLONIUS**.]

2.2.40 **POLONIUS** Th' ambassadors from Norway, my good lord,

Are joyfully returned.

KING Thou still˙ hast been the father of good news.   still · always

POLONIUS Have I, my lord? I assure my good liege

I hold˙ my duty, as˙ I hold my soul,   hold · maintain

2.2.45   Both to my God and to my gracious king;   as · as firmly as

And I do think, or else this brain of mine

Hunts not the trail of policy˙ so sure   policy · sagacity

As it hath used to do, that I have found

The very cause of Hamlet's lunacy.

2.2.50 **KING** O, speak of that! That do I long to hear.

POLONIUS Give first admittance to th' ambassadors.

My news shall be the fruit˙ to that great feast.   fruit · dessert

KING Thyself do grace˙ to them and bring them in.   grace · honor (pun-

[*Exit* **POLONIUS**.]   ning on grace said

He tells me, my dear Gertrude, he hath found   before a feast, line 52)

2.2.55   The head and source of all your son's distemper.

QUEEN I doubt˙ it is no other but the main,˙   doubt · fear, suspect

His father's death and our o'erhasty marriage.   main · chief point,

[*Enter Ambassadors* **VOLTIMAND** *and* **CORNELIUS**, *with* **POLONIUS**.] principal concern

KING Well, we shall sift him.˙– Welcome, my good friends!   sift him · question

Say, Voltimand, what from our brother˙ Norway?   Polonius closely

                                         brother · fellow king

VOLTIMAND Most fair return of greetings and desires.° 2.2.60
  Upon our first,° he sent out to suppress
  His nephew's levies,° which to him appeared
  To be a preparation 'gainst the Polack,
  But, better looked into, he truly found
  It was against Your Highness. Whereat grieved 2.2.65
  That so his sickness, age, and impotence°
  Was falsely borne in hand,° sends out arrests°
  On Fortinbras, which he, in brief, obeys,
  Receives rebuke from Norway, and in fine°
  Makes vow before his uncle never more 2.2.70
  To give th' assay° of arms against Your Majesty.
  Whereon old Norway, overcome with joy,
  Gives him three thousand crowns in annual fee
  And his commission to employ those soldiers,
  So levied as before, against the Polack, 2.2.75
  With an entreaty, herein further shown,
  [*Giving a paper.*]
  That it might please you to give quiet pass
  Through your dominions for this enterprise
  On such regards of safety and allowance°
  As therein are set down. 2.2.80
KING   It likes° us well,
  And at our more considered° time we'll read,
  Answer, and think upon this business.
  Meantime we thank you for your well-took labor.
  Go to your rest; at night we'll feast together.
  Most welcome home! 2.2.85
  [*Exeunt* **AMBASSADORS**.]
POLONIUS   This business is well ended.
  My liege, and madam, to expostulate°
  What majesty should be, what duty is,
  Why day is day, night night, and time is time,
  Were nothing but to waste night, day, and time.
  Therefore, since brevity is the soul of wit,° 2.2.90
  And tediousness the limbs and outward flourishes,
  I will be brief. Your noble son is mad.
  Mad call I it, for, to define true madness,
  What is 't but to be nothing else but mad?

desires · good wishes
Upon our first · at our first words on the business
levies · drafting of men into military service
impotence · helplessness
borne in hand · deluded, taken advantage of
arrests · orders to desist
in fine · in conclusion
give th' assay · make trial of strength, challenge
On ... allowance · with such considerations for the safety of Denmark and permission for Fortinbras
likes · pleases
considered · suitable for deliberation
expostulate · expound, inquire into
wit · sense or judgment

2.2.95   But let that go.

QUEEN   More matter, with less art.

POLONIUS   Madam, I swear I use no art at all.
That he's mad, 'tis true; 'tis true 'tis pity,
And pity 'tis 'tis true – a foolish figure,˙   **figure** · figure of speech
But farewell it, for I will use no art.

2.2.100   Mad let us grant him, then, and now remains
That we find out the cause of this effect,
Or rather say, the cause of this defect,
For this effect defective comes by cause.˙   **For ... cause** · for this
defective behavior, this
Thus it remains, and the remainder thus.   madness, has a cause

2.2.105   Perpend.˙   **Perpend** · consider
I have a daughter – have while she is mine –
Who, in her duty and obedience, mark,
Hath given me this. Now gather and surmise.˙   **gather and surmise** ·
draw your own
[*He reads the letter.*]   conclusions
"To the celestial and my soul's

2.2.110   idol, the most beautified Ophelia"–
That's an ill phrase, a vile phrase; "beautified" is a
vile phrase. But you shall hear. Thus:
[*He reads.*]
"In her excellent white bosom,˙ these,˙ etc."   **In her ... bosom** ·
the letter is poetically
QUEEN   Came this from Hamlet to her?   addressed to her heart

2.2.115   POLONIUS   Good madam, stay˙ awhile, I will be faithful.˙   **these** · the letter
[*He reads.*]   **stay** · wait
        "Doubt˙ thou the stars are fire,   **faithful** · faithful
            Doubt that the sun doth move,   in reading the letter
            Doubt truth to be a liar,   accurately
            But never doubt I love.   **Doubt** · suspect

2.2.120   O dear Ophelia, I am ill at these numbers.˙ I have not   **ill ... numbers** · un-
skilled at writing verses
art to reckon˙ my groans. But that I love thee best, O
most best, believe it. Adieu.   **reckon** · 1 · count;
2 · number metrically,
        Thine evermore, most dear lady, whilst this   scan
                        machine˙ is to him, Hamlet."   **machine** · body

2.2.125   This in obedience hath my daughter shown me,   **more above** · moreover
And, more above,˙ hath his solicitings,   **fell out** · occurred
As they fell out˙ by˙ time, by means, and place,
All given to mine ear.˙   **by** · according to

KING   But how hath she   **given ... ear** · told
me about

Received his love?

POLONIUS   What do you think of me?

KING As of a man faithful and honorable.   2.2.130

POLONIUS I would fain* prove so. But what might you think,

When I had seen this hot love on the wing –

As I perceived it, I must tell you that,

Before my daughter told me – what might you,

Or my dear Majesty your queen here, think,   2.2.135

If I had played the desk or table book,*

Or given my heart a winking,* mute and dumb,

Or looked upon this love with idle sight?*

What might you think? No, I went round* to work,

And my young mistress thus I did bespeak:*   2.2.140

"Lord Hamlet is a prince out of thy star,*

This must not be." And then I prescripts* gave her,

That she should lock herself from his resort,*

Admit no messengers, receive no tokens.

Which done, she took the fruits of my advice;   2.2.145

And he, repellèd – a short tale to make –

Fell into a sadness, then into a fast,

Thence to a watch,* thence into a weakness,

Thence to a lightness,* and by this declension*

Into the madness wherein now he raves,   2.2.150

And all we* mourn for.

[*The* KING, *to the* QUEEN.]

KING   Do you think 'tis this?

QUEEN It may be, very like.

POLONIUS Hath there been such a time – I would fain know that –

That I have positively said "Tis so,"

When it proved otherwise?   2.2.155

KING   Not that I know.

POLONIUS Take this from this,* if this be otherwise.

If circumstances lead me, I will find

Where truth is hid, though it were hid indeed

Within the center.*

KING   How may we try* it further?

QUEEN You know sometimes he walks four hours together   2.2.160

Here in the lobby.

QUEEN   So he does indeed.

---

fain · gladly

played ... table book · remained shut up, concealing the information

given ... winking · closed the eyes of my heart to this

with idle sight · complacently or incomprehendingly

round · roundly, plainly

bespeak · address

out of thy star · above your sphere, position

prescripts · orders

his resort · his visits

watch · state of sleeplessness

lightness · lightheadedness

declension · decline, deterioration (with a pun on the grammatical sense)

all we · all of us, or, into everything that we

Take this from this · the actor probably gestures, indicating that he means his head from his shoulders, or his staff of office or chain from his hands or neck, or something similar

center · middle point of the earth (which is also the center of the Ptolemaic universe)

try · test, judge

POLONIUS At such a time I'll loose˙ my daughter to him.
 Be you and I behind an arras˙ then.
 Mark the encounter. If he love her not
2.2.165 And be not from his reason fall'n thereon,˙
 Let me be no assistant for a state,
 But keep a farm and carters.˙

KING   We will try it.

[Enter HAMLET, reading on a book.]

QUEEN But look where sadly˙ the poor wretch comes reading.

POLONIUS Away, I do beseech you both, away.
2.2.170 I'll board˙ him presently.˙ O, give me leave.˙

[Exeunt KING and QUEEN with attendants.]

 How does my good Lord Hamlet?

HAMLET Well, God-a-mercy.˙

POLONIUS Do you know me, my lord?

HAMLET Excellent well. You are a fishmonger.˙

2.2.175 POLONIUS Not I, my lord.

HAMLET Then I would you were so honest a man.

POLONIUS Honest, my lord?

HAMLET Ay, sir. To be honest, as this world goes, is to be one
 man picked out of ten thousand.

2.2.180 POLONIUS That's very true, my lord.

HAMLET For if the sun breed maggots in a dead dog, being a
 good kissing carrion˙– Have you a daughter?

POLONIUS I have, my lord.

HAMLET Let her not walk i' the sun.˙ Conception˙ is a blessing,
2.2.185 but as your daughter may conceive, friend, look to 't.

[POLONIUS, aside.]

POLONIUS How say you by that? Still harping on my daughter. Yet
 he knew me not at first; 'a˙ said I was a fishmonger. 'A is far gone.
 And truly in my youth I suffered much extremity for love, very
 near this. I'll speak to him again. – What do you read, my lord?

2.2.190 HAMLET Words, words, words.

POLONIUS What is the matter,˙ my lord?

HAMLET Between who?

POLONIUS I mean, the matter that you read, my lord.

HAMLET Slanders, sir, for the satirical rogue says here that old
2.2.195 men have gray beards, that their faces are wrinkled, their eyes
 purging˙ thick amber˙ and plum-tree gum, and that they have

loose · as one might release an animal that is being mated

arras · hanging, tapestry

thereon · on that account

carters · wagon drivers

sadly · seriously

board · accost

presently · at once

give me leave · excuse me, leave me alone (said to those he hurries offstage, including the King and Queen)

God-a-mercy · God have mercy, thank you

fishmonger · fish merchant

a good kissing carrion · a good piece of flesh for kissing, or for the sun to kiss

i' the sun · in public, with the additional implication of the sunshine of princely favors

Conception · 1 · understanding; 2 · pregnancy

'a · he

matter · substance (but Hamlet plays on the sense of "basis for a dispute")

purging · discharging

amber · resin, like the resinous "plum-tree gum"

wit · understanding

honesty · decency, decorum

old · as old

out of the air · the open air was considered dangerous for sick people

pregnant · quick-witted, full of meaning

happiness · felicity of expression

prosperously · successfully

suddenly · immediately

withal · with

old fools · old men like Polonius

indifferent · ordinary, at neither extreme of fortune or misfortune

favors · sexual favors

her privates we · 1 · we are sexually intimate with Fortune, the fickle goddess who bestows her favors indiscriminately; 2 · we are her private citizens

strumpet · prostitute (a common epithet for indiscriminate Fortune; see line 461)

a plentiful lack of wit,* together with most weak hams. All which, sir, though I most powerfully and potently believe, yet I hold it not honesty* to have it thus set down, for yourself, sir, shall grow old* as I am, if like a crab you could go backward. 2.2.200
[POLONIUS, *aside.*]

POLONIUS Though this be madness, yet there is method in 't – Will you walk out of the air,* my lord?

HAMLET Into my grave.

POLONIUS Indeed, that's out of the air.
[*Aside.*]
How pregnant* sometimes his replies are! A happiness* that 2.2.205 often madness hits on, which reason and sanity could not so prosperously* be delivered of. I will leave him and suddenly* contrive the means of meeting between him and my daughter. – My honorable lord, I will most humbly take my leave of you.

HAMLET You cannot, sir, take from me anything that I will more will- 2.2.210 ingly part withal* – except my life, except my life, except my life.
[*Enter* GUILDENSTERN *and* ROSENCRANTZ.]

POLONIUS Fare you well, my lord.

HAMLET These tedious old fools!*

POLONIUS You go to seek the Lord Hamlet. There he is.
[ROSENCRANTZ, *to* POLONIUS.]

ROSENCRANTZ God save you, sir! 2.2.215
[*Exit* POLONIUS.]

GUILDENSTERN My honored lord!

ROSENCRANTZ My most dear lord!

HAMLET My excellent good friends! How dost thou, Guildenstern? Ah, Rosencrantz! Good lads, how do you both?

ROSENCRANTZ As the indifferent* children of the earth. 2.2.220

GUILDENSTERN Happy in that we are not overhappy. On Fortune's cap we are not the very button.

HAMLET Nor the soles of her shoe?

ROSENCRANTZ Neither, my lord.

HAMLET Then you live about her waist, or in the middle of her 2.2.225 favors?*

GUILDENSTERN Faith, her privates we.*

HAMLET In the secret parts of Fortune? O, most true, she is a strumpet.* What news?

ROSENCRANTZ None, my lord, but the world's grown honest. 2.2.230

2.2.231   **HAMLET** Then is doomsday near. But your news is not true. Let me question more in particular. What have you, my good friends, deserved at the hands of Fortune that she sends you to prison hither?

2.2.235   **GUILDENSTERN** Prison, my lord?

HAMLET Denmark's a prison.

ROSENCRANTZ Then is the world one.

HAMLET A goodly one, in which there are many confines,˙ wards,˙ and dungeons, Denmark being one o' the worst.

2.2.240   **ROSENCRANTZ** We think not so, my lord.

HAMLET Why then 'tis none to you, for there is nothing either good or bad but thinking makes it so. To me it is a prison.

ROSENCRANTZ Why then, your ambition makes it one. 'Tis too narrow for your mind.

2.2.245   **HAMLET** O God, I could be bounded in a nutshell and count myself a king of infinite space, were it not that I have bad dreams.

GUILDENSTERN Which dreams indeed are ambition, for the very substance of the ambitious˙ is merely the shadow of a dream.

HAMLET A dream itself is but a shadow.

2.2.250   **ROSENCRANTZ** Truly, and I hold ambition of so airy and light a quality that it is but a shadow's shadow.

HAMLET Then are our beggars bodies,˙ and our monarchs and outstretched˙ heroes the beggars' shadows. Shall we to the court? For, by my fay,˙ I cannot reason.

2.2.255   **ROSENCRANTZ, GUILDENSTERN** We'll wait upon˙ you.

HAMLET No such matter. I will not sort˙ you with the rest of my servants, for, to speak to you like an honest man, I am most dreadfully attended.˙ But, in the beaten way˙ of friendship, what make˙ you at Elsinore?

2.2.260   **ROSENCRANTZ** To visit you, my lord, no other occasion.

HAMLET Beggar that I am, I am even poor in thanks; but I thank you, and sure, dear friends, my thanks are too dear a halfpenny.˙ Were you not sent for? Is it your own inclining? Is it a free˙ visitation? Come, come, deal justly with me. Come, come. Nay, speak.

2.2.265   **GUILDENSTERN** What should we say, my lord?

HAMLET Anything but to the purpose.˙ You were sent for, and there is a kind of confession in your looks which your modesties˙ have not craft enough to color.˙ I know the good King and Queen have sent for you.

---

confines · places of confinement

wards · cells

the very . . . ambitious · that seemingly very substantial thing that the ambitious pursue

bodies · solid substances rather than shadows (since beggars are not ambitious)

outstretched · 1 · far-reaching in their ambition; 2 · elongated as shadows

fay · faith

wait upon · accompany, attend (but Hamlet uses the phrase in the sense of providing menial service)

sort · class, categorize

dreadfully attended · waited upon in slovenly fashion

beaten way · familiar path, tried-and-true course

make · do

too dear a halfpenny · 1 · too expensive at even a halfpenny — of little worth; 2 · too expensive by a halfpenny in return for worthless kindness

free · voluntary

Anything but to the purpose · anything except a straightforward answer (said ironically)

modesties · sense of shame

color · disguise

conjure · adjure, entreat

the consonancy of our youth · our closeness in our younger days

charge · urge

even · straight, honest

of · on

hold not off · don't hold back

so ... discovery · in that way my saying it first will spare you from revealing the truth

molt no feather · not diminish in the least

brave · splendid

fretted · adorned (with fretwork, as in a vaulted ceiling)

piece of work · masterpiece

express · well-framed, exact, expressive

apprehension · power of comprehending

quintessence · the fifth essence of ancient philosophy, beyond earth, water, air, and fire, supposed to be the substance of the heavenly bodies and to be latent in all things

Lenten entertainment · meager reception (appropriate to Lent)

coted · overtook and passed by

tribute · 1 · applause; 2 · homage paid in money

of · from

foil and target · sword and shield

gratis · for nothing

humorous man · an eccentric character, dominated by one trait or "humor"

ROSENCRANTZ To what end, my lord?   2.2.270

HAMLET That you must teach me. But let me conjure˙ you, by the
rights of our fellowship, by the consonancy of our youth,˙ by
the obligation of our ever-preserved love, and by what more
dear a better proposer could charge˙ you withal, be even˙ and
direct with me whether you were sent for or no.   2.2.275

[ROSENCRANTZ, *aside to* GUILDENSTERN.]

ROSENCRANTZ What say you?

[HAMLET, *aside.*]

HAMLET Nay, then, I have an eye of˙ you. – If you love me, hold
not off.˙

GUILDENSTERN My lord, we were sent for.

HAMLET I will tell you why; so shall my anticipation prevent   2.2.280
your discovery,˙ and your secrecy to the King and Queen molt
no feather.˙ I have of late – but wherefore I know not – lost all
my mirth, forgone all custom of exercises; and indeed it goes
so heavily with my disposition that this goodly frame, the
earth, seems to me a sterile promontory; this most excellent   2.2.285
canopy, the air, look you, this brave˙ o'erhanging firmament,
this majestical roof fretted˙ with golden fire, why, it appeareth
nothing to me but a foul and pestilent congregation of vapors.
What a piece of work˙ is a man! How noble in reason, how
infinite in faculties in form and moving how express˙ and   2.2.290
admirable, in action how like an angel, in apprehension˙ how
like a god! The beauty of the world, the paragon of animals!
And yet, to me, what is this quintessence˙ of dust? Man
delights not me – no, nor woman neither, though by your
smiling you seem to say so.   2.2.295

ROSENCRANTZ My lord, there was no such stuff in my thoughts.

HAMLET Why did you laugh, then, when I said man delights
not me?

ROSENCRANTZ To think, my lord, if you delight not in man,
what Lenten entertainment˙ the players shall receive from   2.2.300
you. We coted˙ them on the way, and hither are they coming
to offer you service.

HAMLET He that plays the king shall be welcome; His Majesty
shall have tribute˙ of˙ me. The adventurous knight shall use
his foil and target,˙ the lover shall not sigh gratis,˙ the humor- 2.2.305
ous man˙ shall end his part in peace, the clown shall make

those laugh whose lungs are tickle o' the sear,° and the lady shall say her mind freely, or the blank verse shall halt° for 't. What players are they?

2.2.310 ROSENCRANTZ Even those you were wont to take such delight in, the tragedians of the city.

HAMLET How chances it they travel? Their residence,° both in reputation and profit, was better both ways.

ROSENCRANTZ I think their inhibition° comes by the means of
2.2.315 the late innovation.°

HAMLET Do they hold the same estimation they did when I was in the city? Are they so followed?

ROSENCRANTZ No, indeed are they not.

HAMLET How comes it? Do they grow rusty?

2.2.320 ROSENCRANTZ Nay, their endeavor keeps in the wonted° pace. But there is, sir, an ærie° of children, little eyases,° that cry out on the top of question° and are most tyrannically clapped for 't. These are now the fashion, and so berattle° the common stages – so they call them – that many wearing rapiers° are
2.2.325 afraid of goose quills° and dare scarce come thither.

HAMLET What, are they children? Who maintains 'em? How are they escoted?° Will they pursue the quality° no longer than they can sing?° Will they not say afterwards, if they should grow themselves to common° players – as it is most like, if
2.2.330 their means are no better – their writers do them wrong to make them exclaim against their own succession?°

ROSENCRANTZ Faith, there has been much to-do on both sides, and the nation holds it no sin to tar° them to controversy. There was for a while no money bid for argument unless the
2.2.335 poet and the player went to cuffs in the question.°

HAMLET Is 't possible?

GUILDENSTERN O, there has been much throwing about of brains.

HAMLET Do the boys carry it away?°

ROSENCRANTZ Ay, that they do, my lord – Hercules° and his
2.2.340 load too.

HAMLET It is not very strange; for my uncle is King of Denmark, and those that would make mouths° at him while my father lived give twenty, forty, fifty, a hundred ducats° apiece for his picture in little.° 'Sblood,° there is something in this more than
2.2.345 natural, if philosophy° could find it out.

---

tickle o' the sear · ready to laugh easily (a "sear" is part of a gunlock)

halt · limp

residence · remaining in their usual place

inhibition · formal prohibition (from acting plays in the city)

late innovation · the next several lines refer to the so-called "War of the Theaters" (1599–1602)

wonted · usual

ærie · nest

eyases · young hawks

cry … question · speak shrilly, dominating the controversy

berattle · berate

many wearing rapiers · men of fashion, afraid to patronize the common players for fear of being satirized by the poets

goose quills · pens of satirists

escoted · maintained

quality · profession

no longer … sing · until their voices change

common · regular, adult

succession · careers

tar · set on (as dogs)

There … question · for a time, no money was offered to playwrights unless these two groups came to blows during the play itself

carry it away · win

Hercules … load · perhaps an allusion to the Globe's sign, which featured Hercules

mouths · faces

ducats · gold coins

in little · in miniature

'Sblood · by God's (Christ's) blood

philosophy · science

appurtenance · proper accompaniment	[*A flourish of trumpets within.*]
comply · observe the formalities of courtesy	**GUILDENSTERN** There are the players. 2.2.346
garb · manner	**HAMLET** Gentlemen, you are welcome to Elsinore. Your hands,

appurtenance · proper accompaniment

comply · observe the formalities of courtesy

garb · manner

my extent · that which I extend – polite behavior

show fairly outwards · show cordiality

entertainment · a (warm) reception

north-north-west · just off true north, only partly

hawk … handsaw · perhaps playing on a mattock ("hack") and a carpenter's cutting tool, or two different kinds of birds, a raptor and a heron ("hernshaw")

swaddling clouts · cloths in which to wrap a newborn baby

Haply · perhaps

Roscius · a famous Roman actor (died 62 BC)

Buzz · an interjection used to denote stale news

scene individable · a play observing the unity of place; or perhaps one that is performed without intermission

poem unlimited · a play disregarding the unities of time and place; one that is all-inclusive

Seneca · writer of Latin tragedies

Plautus · writer of Latin comedy

law … liberty · dramatic composition both according to the rules and disregarding the rules

Jephthah … Israel · Jephthah sacrificed his daughter (see Judges 11)

passing · surpassingly

[*A flourish of trumpets within.*]

GUILDENSTERN There are the players. 2.2.346

HAMLET Gentlemen, you are welcome to Elsinore. Your hands, come then. Th' appurtenance· of welcome is fashion and ceremony. Let me comply· with you in this garb,· lest my extent· to the players, which, I tell you, must show fairly outwards,· should 2.2.350 more appear like entertainment· than yours. You are welcome. But my uncle-father and aunt-mother are deceived.

GUILDENSTERN In what, my dear lord?

HAMLET I am but mad north-north-west.· When the wind is southerly I know a hawk from a handsaw.· 2.2.355

[*Enter* POLONIUS.]

POLONIUS Well be with you, gentlemen!

HAMLET Hark you, Guildenstern, and you too; at each ear a hearer. That great baby you see there is not yet out of his swaddling clouts.·

ROSENCRANTZ Haply· he is the second time come to them, for 2.2.360 they say an old man is twice a child.

HAMLET I will prophesy he comes to tell me of the players. Mark it. – You say right, sir, o' Monday morning, 'twas then indeed.

POLONIUS My lord, I have news to tell you.

HAMLET My lord, I have news to tell you. When Roscius· was 2.2.365 an actor in Rome –

POLONIUS The actors are come hither, my lord.

HAMLET Buzz,· buzz!

POLONIUS Upon my honor –

HAMLET Then came each actor on his ass. 2.2.370

POLONIUS The best actors in the world, either for tragedy, comedy, history, pastoral, pastoral-comical, historical-pastoral, tragical-historical, tragical-comical-historical-pastoral, scene individable,· or poem unlimited.· Seneca· cannot be too heavy, nor Plautus· too light. For the law of writ and the 2.2.375 liberty,· these are the only men.

HAMLET O Jephthah, judge of Israel,· what a treasure hadst thou!

POLONIUS What a treasure had he, my lord?

HAMLET Why,

"One fair daughter, and no more, 2.2.380
The which he lovèd passing· well."

[**POLONIUS**, *aside.*]

POLONIUS Still on my daughter.

HAMLET Am I not i' the right, old Jephthah?

POLONIUS If you call me Jephthah, my lord, I have a daughter
2.2.385   that I love passing well.

HAMLET Nay, that follows not.

POLONIUS What follows then, my lord?

HAMLET Why,
        "As by lot,˙ God wot,"˙
2.2.390   and then, you know,
            "It came to pass, as most like˙ it was"–
        the first row˙ of the pious chanson˙ will show you more, for
        look where my abridgement comes.

        [*Enter the* **PLAYERS**.]

        You are welcome, masters; welcome, all. I am glad to see thee
2.2.395   well. Welcome, good friends. O, old friend! Why, thy face is
        valanced˙ since I saw thee last. Com'st thou to beard˙ me in
        Denmark? What, my young lady˙ and mistress! By 'r Lady,˙
        your ladyship is nearer to heaven than when I saw you last,
        by the altitude of a chopine.˙ Pray God your voice, like a piece
2.2.400   of uncurrrent˙ gold, be not cracked within the ring.˙ Masters,
        you are all welcome. We'll e'en to 't˙ like French falconers, fly
        at anything we see. We'll have a speech straight.˙ Come, give
        us a taste of your quality.˙ Come, a passionate speech.

FIRST PLAYER What speech, my good lord?

2.2.405 **HAMLET** I heard thee speak me a speech once, but it was never
        acted, or if it was, not above once, for the play, I remember,
        pleased not the million; 'twas caviar to the general.˙ But it
        was – as I received it, and others, whose judgments in such
        matters cried in the top of˙ mine – an excellent play, well
2.2.410   digested˙ in the scenes, set down with as much modesty˙ as
        cunning. I remember one said there were no sallets˙ in the
        lines to make the matter savory, nor no matter in the phrase
        that might indict the author of affectation, but called it an
        honest method, as wholesome as sweet, and by very much
2.2.415   more handsome than fine.˙ One speech in 't I chiefly loved:
        'twas Æneas' tale to Dido, and thereabout of it especially when
        he speaks of Priam's slaughter.˙ If it live in your memory, begin
        at this line: let me see, let me see –
            "The rugged Pyrrhus,˙ like th' Hyrcanian beast"˙–

lot · chance

wot · knows

like · likely, probable

row · stanza

chanson · ballad, song

valanced · fringed
(with a beard)

beard · confront, chal-
lenge (with obvious pun)

young lady · boy
playing women's parts

By 'r Lady · by Our Lady

chopine · thick-soled
shoe of Italian fashion

uncurrent · not pass-
able as lawful coinage

cracked … ring ·
changed to an adult
male voice, no longer
suitable for women's
roles (coins featured rings
enclosing the sovereign's
head; if the coin was
cracked within this ring,
it was unfit for currency)

e'en to 't · go at it

straight · at once

quality · professional skill

caviar to the general ·
a choice dish too elegant
for coarse tastes

cried in the top of ·
exceeded in authority

digested · arranged

modesty · moderation

sallets · spicy
improprieties

handsome than
fine · more by propor-
tion than by decoration

Æneas' tale … slaugh-
ter · story of the slaying of
Troy's king by the Greeks

Pyrrhus · a Greek hero
in the Trojan War

Hyrcanian beast ·
a tiger (see *Æneid*
4.366–367)

'Tis not so. It begins with Pyrrhus: 2.2.420

> "The rugged° Pyrrhus, he whose sable° arms,
> Black as his purpose, did the night resemble
> When he lay couchèd° in the ominous horse,
> Hath now this dread and black complexion smeared
> With heraldry more dismal.° Head to foot   2.2.425
> Now is he total gules,° horridly tricked°
> With blood of fathers, mothers, daughters, sons,
> Baked and impasted° with the parching streets,°
> That lend a tyrannous° and a damnèd light
> To their lord's° murder. Roasted in wrath and fire,   2.2.430
> And thus o'ersizèd° with coagulate gore,
> With eyes like carbuncles,° the hellish Pyrrhus
> Old grandsire Priam seeks."

So proceed you.

POLONIUS 'Fore God my lord, well spoken, with good accent   2.2.435
and good discretion.

FIRST PLAYER   "Anon he finds him

> Striking too short at Greeks. His antique° sword,
> Rebellious to his arm, lies where it falls,
> Repugnant° to command. Unequal matched,
> Pyrrhus at Priam drives, in rage strikes wide,   2.2.440
> But with the whiff and wind of his fell° sword
> Th' unnervèd° father falls. Then senseless Ilium,°
> Seeming to feel this blow, with flaming top
> Stoops to his° base, and with a hideous crash
> Takes prisoner Pyrrhus' ear. For, lo! His sword,   2.2.445
> Which was declining° on the milky° head
> Of reverend Priam, seemed i' th' air to stick.
> So as a painted° tyrant Pyrrhus stood,
> And, like a neutral to his will and matter,°
> Did nothing.   2.2.450
> But as we often see against° some storm
> A silence in the heavens, the rack° stand still
> The bold winds speechless, and the orb° below
> As hush as death, anon the dreadful thunder
> Doth rend the region,° so, after Pyrrhus' pause,   2.2.455
> A rousèd vengeance sets him new a-work,
> And never did the Cyclops' hammers° fall

Glossary (margin notes):

rugged · shaggy, savage

sable · black (for reasons of camouflage)

couchèd · concealed

dismal · ill-omened

total gules · entirely red (a heraldic term)

tricked · spotted and smeared (heraldic)

impasted · crusted, like a thick paste

with ... streets · by the parching heat of the streets (because of the fires everywhere)

tyrannous · cruel

their lord's · Priam's

o'ersized · covered as with size or glue

carbuncles · large fiery-red precious stones thought to emit their own light

antique · ancient

Repugnant · disobedient, resistant

fell · cruel

unnervèd · strengthless

senseless Ilium · inanimate citadel of Troy

his · its

declining · descending

milky · white-haired

painted · painted in a picture

like ... matter · as though suspended between his intention and its fulfillment

against · just before

rack · mass of clouds

orb · globe, earth

region · sky

Cyclops' hammers · giant armor makers in the smithy of Vulcan

On Mars's armor forged for proof eterne•
With less remorse• than Pyrrhus' bleeding sword
2.2.460   Now falls on Priam.
Out, out, thou strumpet Fortune! All you gods
In general synod• take away her power!
Break all the spokes and fellies• from her wheel,
And bowl the round nave• down the hill of heaven•
2.2.465   As low as to the fiends!"

POLONIUS This is too long.

HAMLET It shall to the barber's with your beard. – Prithee, say
   on. He's for a jig• or a tale of bawdry, or he sleeps. Say on;
   come to Hecuba.•

2.2.470 **FIRST PLAYER** "But who, ah woe! had• seen the moblèd• queen"–

HAMLET "The moblèd queen?"

POLONIUS That's good. "Moblèd queen" is good.

FIRST PLAYER "Run barefoot up and down, threat'ning the flames•
   With bisson rheum,• a clout• upon that head
2.2.475   Where late• the diadem stood, and, for a robe,
About her lank and all o'erteemèd• loins
A blanket, in the alarm of fear caught up –
Who this had seen, with tongue in venom steeped,
'Gainst Fortune's state• would treason have pronounced.•
2.2.480   But if the gods themselves did see her then
When she saw Pyrrhus make malicious sport
In mincing with his sword her husband's limbs,
The instant burst of clamor that she made,
Unless things mortal move them not at all,
2.2.485   Would have made milch• the burning eyes of heaven,•
And passion• in the gods."

POLONIUS Look whe'er• he has not turned his color and has
   tears in's eyes. Prithee, no more.

HAMLET 'Tis well; I'll have thee speak out the rest of this
2.2.490   soon. – Good my lord, will you see the players well bestowed?•
   Do you hear, let them be well used, for they are the abstract•
   and brief chronicles of the time. After your death you were
   better have a bad epitaph than their ill report while you live.

POLONIUS My lord, I will use them according to their desert.

2.2.495 **HAMLET** God's bodikin,• man, much better. Use every man after•
   his desert, and who shall scape whipping? Use them after your

---

proof eterne · eternal resistance to assault

remorse · pity

synod · assembly

fellies · pieces of wood forming the rim of a wheel

nave · hub

hill of heaven · Mount Olympus

jig · comic song and dance often given at the end of a play

Hecuba · wife of Priam

who . . . had · anyone who had (also in line 478)

moblèd · muffled

threat'ning the flames · weeping hard enough to dampen the flames

bisson rheum · blinding tears

clout · cloth

late · lately

all o'erteemèd · utterly worn out with bearing children

state · rule, managing

pronounced · proclaimed

milch · milky, moist with tears

burning eyes of heaven · heavenly bodies

passion · overpowering emotion

whe'er · whether

bestowed · lodged

abstract · summary account

God's bodikin · God's (Christ's) little body ("bodykin") – not to be confused with bodkin ("dagger")

after · according to

own honor and dignity. The less they deserve, the more merit is in your bounty. Take them in.

POLONIUS Come, sirs.

[*Exit.*]

HAMLET Follow him, friends. We'll hear a play tomorrow. 2.2.500

[*As they start to leave,* **HAMLET** *detains the* **FIRST PLAYER**.]

Dost thou hear me, old friend? Can you play *The Murder of Gonzago*?

FIRST PLAYER Ay, my lord.

HAMLET We'll ha 't* tomorrow night. You could, for a need, study* a speech of some dozen or sixteen lines which I would set down and insert in 't, could you not? 2.2.505

FIRST PLAYER Ay, my lord.

HAMLET Very well. Follow that lord, and look you mock him not.

[*Exeunt* **PLAYERS**.]

My good friends, I'll leave you till night. You are welcome to Elsinore. 2.2.510

ROSENCRANTZ Good my lord!

[*Exeunt* **ROSENCRANTZ** *and* **GUILDENSTERN**.]

HAMLET Ay, so, goodbye to you. – Now I am alone.
O, what a rogue and peasant slave am I!
Is it not monstrous that this player here,
But* in a fiction, in a dream of passion, 2.2.515
Could force his soul so to his own conceit*
That from her working* all his visage wanned,*
Tears in his eyes, distraction in his aspect,*
A broken voice, and his whole function suiting
With forms to his conceit?* And all for nothing! 2.2.520
For Hecuba!
What's Hecuba to him, or he to Hecuba,
That he should weep for her? What would he do
Had he the motive and the cue for passion
That I have? He would drown the stage with tears 2.2.525
And cleave the general ear* with horrid* speech,
Make mad the guilty and appall* the free,*
Confound the ignorant,* and amaze* indeed
The very faculties of eyes and ears. Yet I,
A dull and muddy-mettled* rascal, peak* 2.2.530
Like John-a-dreams,* unpregnant of* my cause,

---

ha't · have it

study · memorize

But · merely

force ... conceit · bring his innermost being so entirely into accord with his conception (of the role)

from her working · as a result of, or in response to, his soul's activity

wanned · grew pale

aspect · look, glance

his whole ... conceit · all his bodily powers responding with actions to suit his thought

the general ear · everyone's ear

horrid · horrible

appall · literally, make pale

free · innocent

Confound the ignorant · dumbfound those who know nothing of the crime that has been committed

amaze · stun

muddy-mettled · dull-spirited

peak · mope, pine

John-a-dreams · a sleepy, dreaming idler

unpregnant of · not quickened by

And can say nothing – no, not for a king
Upon whose property° and most dear life
A damned defeat° was made. Am I a coward?

2.2.535 Who calls me villain? Breaks my pate° across?
Plucks off my beard and blows it in my face?
Tweaks me by the nose? Gives me the lie i' the throat°
As deep as to the lungs? Who does me this?
Ha, 'swounds,° I should take it; for it cannot be

2.2.540 But I am pigeon-livered° and lack gall
To make oppression bitter,° or ere this
I should ha' fatted all the region kites°
With this slave's offal.° Bloody, bawdy villain!
Remorseless,° treacherous, lecherous, kindless° villain!

2.2.545 O, vengeance!
Why, what an ass am I! This is most brave,°
That I, the son of a dear father murdered,
Prompted to my revenge by heaven and hell,
Must like a whore unpack my heart with words

2.2.550 And fall a-cursing, like a very drab,°
A scullion!° Fie upon 't, foh! About,° my brains!
Hum, I have heard
That guilty creatures sitting at a play
Have by the very cunning° of the scene°

2.2.555 Been struck so to the soul that presently°
They have proclaimed their malefactions;
For murder though it have no tongue, will speak
With most miraculous organ. I'll have these players
Play something like the murder of my father

2.2.560 Before mine uncle. I'll observe his looks;
I'll tent° him to the quick.° If 'a do blench,°
I know my course. The spirit that I have seen
May be the devil, and the devil hath power
T' assume a pleasing shape; yea, and perhaps,

2.2.565 Out of my weakness and my melancholy,
As he is very potent with such spirits,°
Abuses° me to damn me. I'll have grounds
More relative° than this. The play's the thing
Wherein I'll catch the conscience of the King.

[*Exit.*]

---

property · the crown; also character, quality

damned defeat · damnable act of destruction

pate · head

Gives ... throat · calls me an out-and-out liar

'swounds · by his (Christ's) wounds

pigeon-livered · the pigeon or dove was popularly supposed to be mild because it secreted no gall

bitter · bitter to me

region kites · kites (birds of prey) of the air

offal · entrails

Remorseless · pitiless

kindless · unnatural

brave · fine, admirable (said ironically)

drab · whore

scullion · menial kitchen servant (apt to be foul-mouthed)

About · about it, to work

cunning · art, skill

scene · dramatic presentation

presently · at once

tent · probe

the quick · the tender part of a wound, the core

blench · quail, flinch

spirits · humors (of melancholy)

Abuses · deludes

relative · cogent, pertinent

ACT 3, SCENE 1

[*The castle. Enter* KING, QUEEN, POLONIUS, OPHELIA, ROSENCRANTZ, GUILDENSTERN, *Lords.*]

drift of conference ·
directing of conversation

KING And can you by no drift of conference˙   3.1.1
    Get from him why he puts on this confusion,
    Grating so harshly all his days of quiet
    With turbulent and dangerous lunacy?

ROSENCRANTZ He does confess he feels himself distracted,   3.1.5
    But from what cause 'a will by no means speak.

forward · willing
sounded · questioned

GUILDENSTERN Nor do we find him forward˙ to be sounded,˙
    But with a crafty madness keeps aloof
    When we would bring him on to some confession
    Of his true state.   3.1.10

QUEEN   Did he receive you well?

ROSENCRANTZ Most like a gentleman.

disposition · inclination

GUILDENSTERN But with much forcing of his disposition.˙

Niggard · stingy
question · conversation

ROSENCRANTZ Niggard˙ of question,˙ but of our demands
    Most free in his reply.

assay · try to win

QUEEN   Did you assay˙ him
    To any pastime?   3.1.15

ROSENCRANTZ Madam, it so fell out that certain players

o'erraught · overtook

    We o'erraught˙ on the way. Of these we told him,
    And there did seem in him a kind of joy
    To hear of it. They are here about the court,
    And, as I think, they have already order   3.1.20
    This night to play before him.

POLONIUS   'Tis most true,
    And he beseeched me to entreat your Majesties
    To hear and see the matter.

KING With all my heart, and it doth much content me
    To hear him so inclined.   3.1.25

edge · incitement

    Good gentlemen, give him a further edge˙
    And drive his purpose into these delights.

ROSENCRANTZ We shall, my lord.

[*Exeunt* ROSENCRANTZ *and* GUILDENSTERN.]

KING   Sweet Gertrude, leave us too,

closely · privately

    For we have closely˙ sent for Hamlet hither,
    That he, as 'twere by accident, may here   3.1.30

Affront · confront, meet

    Affront˙ Ophelia.

Her father and myself, lawful espials,˙
Will so bestow ourselves that seeing, unseen,
We may of their encounter frankly judge,
3.1.35 And gather by him, as he is behaved,
If 't be th' affliction of his love or no
That thus he suffers for.
QUEEN   I shall obey you.
And for your part, Ophelia, I do wish
That your good beauties be the happy cause
3.1.40 Of Hamlet's wildness. So shall I hope your virtues
Will bring him to his wonted˙ way again,
To both your honors.
OPHELIA   Madam, I wish it may.
[Exit QUEEN.]
POLONIUS Ophelia, walk you here. – Gracious,˙ so please you,
We will bestow˙ ourselves.
[To OPHELIA.]
                        Read on this book,
[Giving her a book.]
3.1.45 That show of such an exercise˙ may color˙
Your loneliness.˙ We are oft to blame in this –
'Tis too much proved˙ – that with devotion's visage
And pious action we do sugar o'er
The devil himself.
[The KING, aside.]
3.1.50 KING O, 'tis too true!
How smart a lash that speech doth give my conscience!
The harlot's cheek, beautied with plastering art,
Is not more ugly to˙ the thing˙ that helps it
Than is my deed to my most painted word.
3.1.55 O heavy burden!
POLONIUS I hear him coming. Let's withdraw, my lord.
[The KING and POLONIUS withdraw.˙ Enter HAMLET. OPHELIA pretends to read a book.]
HAMLET To be, or not to be, that is the question:
Whether 'tis nobler in the mind to suffer
The slings˙ and arrows of outrageous fortune,
3.1.60 Or to take arms against a sea of troubles
And by opposing end them. To die, to sleep –

espials · spies

wonted · accustomed

Gracious · Your Grace (the King)

bestow · conceal

exercise · religious exercise (the book she reads is one of devotion)

color · give a plausible appearance to

loneliness · being alone

too much proved · too often shown to be true, too often practiced

to · compared to

the thing · the cosmetic

withdraw · the King and Polonius may retire behind an arras. The stage directions specify that they "enter" again near the end of the scene

slings · missiles

No more – and by a sleep to say we end
The heartache and the thousand natural shocks
That flesh is heir to. 'Tis a consummation
Devoutly to be wished. To die, to sleep;   3.1.65
To sleep, perchance to dream. Ay, there's the rub,•
For in that sleep of death what dreams may come,
When we have shuffled• off this mortal coil,•
Must give us pause. There's the respect•
That makes calamity of so long life.•   3.1.70
For who would bear the whips and scorns of time,
Th' oppressor's wrong, the proud man's contumely,•
The pangs of disprized• love, the law's delay,
The insolence of office,• and the spurns•
That patient merit of th' unworthy takes,•   3.1.75
When he himself might his quietus• make
With a bare bodkin?• Who would fardels• bear,
To grunt and sweat under a weary life,
But that the dread of something after death,
The undiscovered country from whose bourn•   3.1.80
No traveler returns, puzzles the will,
And makes us rather bear those ills we have
Than fly to others that we know not of?
Thus conscience does make cowards of us all;
And thus the native hue• of resolution   3.1.85
Is sicklied o'er with the pale cast• of thought,
And enterprises of great pitch• and moment•
With this regard• their currents• turn awry
And lose the name of action. – Soft you• now,
The fair Ophelia. Nymph, in thy orisons•   3.1.90
Be all my sins remembered.

OPHELIA   Good my lord,
How does your honor for this many a day?

HAMLET I humbly thank you; well, well, well.

OPHELIA My lord, I have remembrances of yours,
That I have longèd long to redeliver.   3.1.95
I pray you, now receive them.

[*She offers tokens.*]

HAMLET No, not I, I never gave you aught.

OPHELIA My honored lord, you know right well you did,

---

rub · literally, an obstacle in the game of bowls

shuffled · sloughed, cast

coil · turmoil

respect · consideration

of . . . life · so long-lived, something we willingly endure for so long (also suggesting that long life is itself a calamity)

contumely · insolent abuse

disprized · unvalued

office · officialdom

spurns · insults

of th' unworthy takes · receives from unworthy persons

quietus · acquittance; here, death

a bare bodkin · a mere dagger, unsheathed

fardels · burdens

bourn · frontier, boundary

native hue · natural color, complexion

cast · tinge, shade of color

pitch · height (as of a falcon's flight)

moment · importance

regard · respect, consideration

currents · courses

Soft you · wait a minute, gently

orisons · prayers

And with them words of so sweet breath composed
As made the things more rich. Their perfume lost,
Take these again, for to the noble mind
Rich gifts wax poor when givers prove unkind.
There, my lord.

[*She offers tokens.*]

HAMLET Ha, ha! Are you honest?*

OPHELIA My lord?

HAMLET Are you fair?*

OPHELIA What means your lordship?

HAMLET That if you be honest and fair, your honesty* should admit no discourse to* your beauty.

OPHELIA Could beauty, my lord, have better commerce* than with honesty?

HAMLET Ay, truly, for the power of beauty will sooner transform honesty from what it is to a bawd than the force of honesty can translate beauty into his* likeness. This was sometime* a paradox,* but now the time* gives it proof. I did love you once.

OPHELIA Indeed, my lord, you made me believe so.

HAMLET You should not have believed me, for virtue cannot so inoculate* our old stock but we shall relish of it.* I loved you not.

OPHELIA I was the more deceived.

HAMLET Get thee to a nunnery.* Why wouldst thou be a breeder of sinners? I am myself indifferent honest,* but yet I could accuse me of such things that it were better my mother had not borne me: I am very proud, revengeful, ambitious, with more offenses at my beck* than I have thoughts to put them in, imagination to give them shape, or time to act them in. What should such fellows as I do crawling between earth and heaven? We are arrant knaves all; believe none of us. Go thy ways to a nunnery. Where's your father?

OPHELIA At home, my lord.

HAMLET Let the doors be shut upon him, that he may play the fool nowhere but in 's own house. Farewell.

OPHELIA O, help him, you sweet heavens!

HAMLET If thou dost marry, I'll give thee this plague for thy dowry: be thou as chaste as ice, as pure as snow, thou shalt not escape calumny. Get thee to a nunnery, farewell. Or, if thou wilt needs marry, marry a fool, for wise men know well

---

honest · 1 · truthful; 2 · chaste

fair · 1 · beautiful; 2 · just, honorable

your honesty · your chastity

discourse to · familiar dealings with

commerce · dealings, intercourse

his · its

sometime · formerly

a paradox · a view opposite to commonly held opinion

the time · the present age

inoculate · graft, be engrafted to

but ... it · that we do not still have about us a taste of the old stock, retain our sinfulness

nunnery · convent (with possibly an awareness that the word was also used derisively to denote a brothel)

indifferent honest · reasonably virtuous

beck · command

enough what monsters* you* make of them. To a nunnery, go,
and quickly too. Farewell.

OPHELIA Heavenly powers, restore him!

HAMLET I have heard of your paintings too, well enough. God   3.1.140
hath given you one face, and you make yourselves another. You
jig,* you amble,* and you lisp, you nickname God's creatures,*
and make your wantonness your ignorance.* Go to, I'll no
more on 't,* it hath made me mad. I say we will have no more
marriage. Those that are married already – all but one – shall   3.1.145
live. The rest shall keep as they are. To a nunnery, go.

[*Exit.*]

OPHELIA O, what a noble mind is here o'erthrown!
The courtier's, soldier's, scholar's, eye, tongue, sword,
Th' expectancy* and rose* of the fair state,
The glass of fashion and the mold of form,*   3.1.150
Th' observed of all observers,* quite, quite down!
And I, of ladies most deject and wretched,
That sucked the honey of his music* vows,
Now see that noble and most sovereign reason
Like sweet bells jangled out of tune and harsh,   3.1.155
That unmatched form and feature of blown* youth
Blasted* with ecstasy.* O, woe is me,
T' have seen what I have seen, see what I see!

[*Enter* KING *and* POLONIUS.]

KING Love? His affections* do not that way tend;
Nor what he spake, though it lacked form a little,   3.1.160
Was not like madness. There's something in his soul
O'er which his melancholy sits on brood,*
And I do doubt* the hatch and the disclose*
Will be some danger; which for to prevent,
I have in quick determination   3.1.165
Thus set it down:* he shall with speed to England
For the demand of* our neglected tribute.
Haply the seas and countries different
With variable objects* shall expel
This something-settled matter in his heart,*   3.1.170
Whereon his brains still* beating puts him thus
From fashion of himself.* What think you on 't?

POLONIUS It shall do well. But yet do I believe

---

monsters · an allusion to the horns of a cuckold

you · you women

jig · dance

amble · move coyly

you ... creatures · you give trendy names to things in place of their God given names

make ... ignorance · excuse your affectation on the grounds of pretended ignorance

on 't · of it

expectancy · hope

rose · ornament

The glass ... form · the mirror of true self-fashioning and the pattern of courtly behavior

Th' observed ... observers · the center of attention and honor in the court

music · musical, sweetly uttered

blown · blooming

Blasted · withered

ecstasy · madness

affections · emotions, feelings

sits on brood · sits like a bird on a nest, about to hatch mischief (line 169)

doubt · fear

disclose · disclosure, hatching

set it down · resolved

For ... of · to demand

variable objects · various sights and surroundings to divert him

This something ... heart · the strange matter settled in his heart

still · continually

From ... himself · out of his natural manner

The origin and commencement of his grief

3.1.175 Sprung from neglected love. – How now, Ophelia?

You need not tell us what Lord Hamlet said;

We heard it all. – My lord, do as you please,

But, if you hold it fit, after the play

Let his queen-mother° all alone entreat him

3.1.180 To show his grief. Let her be round° with him,

And I'll be placed, so please you, in the ear

Of all their conference. If she find him not,°

To England send him, or confine him where

Your wisdom best shall think.

KING   It shall be so.

3.1.185 Madness in great ones must not unwatched go.

[*Exeunt.*]

ACT 3, SCENE 2

[*The castle. Enter* **HAMLET** *and three of the* **PLAYERS**.]

3.2.1 **HAMLET** Speak the speech, I pray you, as I pronounced it to you, trippingly on the tongue. But if you mouth it as many of our players° do, I had as lief° the town crier spoke my lines. Nor do not saw the air too much with your hand, thus, but use all

3.2.5 gently; for in the very torrent, tempest, and, as I may say, whirlwind of your passion, you must acquire and beget a temperance that may give it smoothness. O, it offends me to the soul to hear a robustious° periwig-pated° fellow tear a passion to tatters, to very rags, to split the ears of the groundlings,° who for the

3.2.10 most part are capable of° nothing but inexplicable dumb shows° and noise. I would have such a fellow whipped for o'erdoing Termagant.° It out-Herods Herod.° Pray you, avoid it.

FIRST PLAYER I warrant your honor.

HAMLET Be not too tame neither, but let your own discretion be

3.2.15 your tutor. Suit the action to the word, the word to the action, with this special observance, that you o'erstep not the modesty° of nature. For anything so o'erdone is from° the purpose of playing, whose end, both at the first and now, was and is to hold as 'twere the mirror up to nature, to show virtue her feature, scorn°

3.2.20 her own image, and the very age and body of the time° his form and pressure.° Now this overdone or come tardy off,° though it makes the unskillful° laugh, cannot but make the judicious grieve,

queen-mother · queen and mother

round · blunt

find him not · fails to discover what is troubling him

our players · players nowadays

I had as lief · I would just as soon

robustious · violent, boisterous

periwig-pated · wearing a wig

groundlings · spectators who paid least and stood in the yard of the theater

capable of · able to understand

dumb shows · mimed performances, often used before Shakespeare's time to precede a play or each act

Termagant · a supposed deity of the Mohammedans, not found in any English medieval play but elsewhere portrayed as violent and blustering

Herod · a character in *The Slaughter of the Innocents* and other cycle plays. The part was played with great noise and fury

modesty · restraint, moderation

from · contrary to

scorn · something foolish and deserving of scorn

the very … time · the present state of affairs

pressure · stamp, impressed character

come tardy off · inadequately done

the unskillful · those lacking in judgment

the censure of the which one• must in your allowance• o'erweigh
a whole theater of others. O, there be players that I have seen
play, and heard others praise, and that highly, not to speak it pro- 3.2.25
fanely,• that, neither having th' accent of Christians• nor the gait
of Christian, pagan, nor man,• have so strutted and bellowed that
I have thought some of nature's journeymen• had made men and
not made them well, they imitated humanity so abominably.•

FIRST PLAYER I hope we have reformed that indifferently• with 3.2.30
us, sir.

HAMLET O, reform it altogether. And let those that play your
clowns speak no more than is set down for them; for there be
of them• that will themselves laugh, to set on some quantity
of barren• spectators to laugh too, though in the meantime 3.2.35
some necessary question of the play be then to be considered.
That's villainous, and shows a most pitiful ambition in the fool
that uses it. Go make you ready.

[*Exeunt* PLAYERS. *Enter* POLONIUS, GUILDENSTERN, *and* ROSEN-
CRANTZ.]

How now, my lord, will the King hear this piece of work?

POLONIUS And the Queen too, and that presently.• 3.2.40

HAMLET Bid the players make haste.

[*Exit* POLONIUS.]

Will you two help to hasten them?

ROSENCRANTZ Ay, my lord.

[*Exeunt they two.*]

HAMLET What ho, Horatio!

[*Enter* HORATIO.]

HORATIO Here, sweet lord, at your service.

HAMLET Horatio, thou art e'en as just a man 3.2.45
As e'er my conversation coped withal.•

HORATIO O, my dear lord –

HAMLET Nay, do not think I flatter,
For what advancement may I hope from thee
That no revenue hast but thy good spirits
To feed and clothe thee? Why should the poor be flattered? 3.2.50
No, let the candied• tongue lick absurd pomp,
And crook the pregnant• hinges of the knee
Where thrift• may follow fawning. Dost thou hear?
Since my dear soul was mistress of her choice

---

the censure ... one · the judgment of even one of whom

your allowance · your scale of values

not ... profanely · Hamlet anticipates his idea in lines 26–27 that some men were not made by God at all

Christians · ordinary decent folk

nor man · nor any human being at all

journeymen · laborers who are not yet masters in their trade

abominably · Shakespeare's usual spelling, "abhominably," suggests a literal though etymologically incorrect meaning, "removed from human nature"

indifferently · tolerably

of them · some among them

barren · of wit

presently · at once

my ... withal · my dealings encountered

candied · sugared, flattering

pregnant · compliant

thrift · profit

3.2.55   And could of men distinguish her election,*

Sh' hath sealed thee* for herself, for thou hast been

As one, in suffering all, that suffers nothing,

A man that Fortune's buffets and rewards

Hast ta'en with equal thanks; and blest are those

3.2.60   Whose blood* and judgment are so well commeddled*

That they are not a pipe for Fortune's finger

To sound what stop* she please, Give me that man

That is not passion's slave, and I will wear him

In my heart's core, ay, in my heart of heart,

3.2.65   As I do thee. – Something too much of this. –

There is a play tonight before the King.

One scene of it comes near the circumstance

Which I have told thee of my father's death.

I prithee, when thou seest that act afoot,

3.2.70   Even with the very comment of thy soul*

Observe my uncle. If his occulted* guilt

Do not itself unkennel* in one speech,

It is a damnèd ghost that we have seen,

And my imaginations are as foul

3.2.75   As Vulcan's stithy.* Give him heedful note,

For I mine eyes will rivet to his face,

And after we will both our judgments join

In censure of his seeming.*

HORATIO   Well, my lord.

If 'a steal aught* the whilst this play is playing

3.2.80   And scape detecting, I will pay the theft.

[*Flourish. Enter trumpets and kettledrums,* **KING**, **QUEEN**, **POLONIUS**, **OPHELIA**, **ROSENCRANTZ**, **GUILDENSTERN**, *and other* **LORDS**, *with* **GUARDS** *carrying torches.*]

HAMLET They are coming to the play. I must be idle.* Get you a place.

[*The* **KING**, **QUEEN**, *and* **COURTIERS** *sit.*]

KING How fares our cousin* Hamlet?

HAMLET Excellent, i' faith, of the chameleon's dish:* I eat the air,

3.2.85   promise-crammed. You cannot feed capons* so.

KING I have nothing with* this answer, Hamlet. These words are not mine.*

HAMLET No, nor mine now.*

---

could … election · could make distinguishing choices among persons

sealed thee · literally, as one would seal a legal document to mark possession

blood · passion

commeddled · commingled

stop · hole in a wind instrument for controlling the sound

very … soul · your most penetrating observation and consideration

occulted · hidden

unkennel · as one would say of a fox driven from its lair

stithy · smithy, place of "stiths" (anvils)

censure of his seeming · judgment of his appearance or behavior

If 'a steal aught · if he gets away with anything

idle · 1 · unoccupied; 2 · mad

cousin · close relative

chameleon's dish · chameleons were supposed to feed on air. Hamlet deliberately misinterprets the King's "fares" as "feeds." By his phrase "eat the air," he also plays on the idea of feeding himself with the promise of succession, of being the "heir"

capons · roosters castrated and crammed with feed to make them succulent

have … with · make nothing of, or gain nothing from

are not mine · do not respond to what I asked

nor mine now · words spoken are proverbially no longer the speaker's

brute · the Latin meaning of *brutus*, "stupid," was often used punningly with the name Brutus

part · 1 · deed; 2 · role

calf · fool

stay upon · await

metal · substance that is attractive, magnetic, but with suggestion also of mettle, "disposition"

country matters · sexual intercourse (making a bawdy pun on the first syllable of "country")

Nothing · the figure zero or "naught," suggesting the female sexual anatomy. Thing not infrequently has a bawdy connotation of male or female anatomy, and the reference here could be male.

only jig maker · very best composer of jigs, pointless merriment. Hamlet replies sardonically to Ophelia's observation that he is merry by saying, "If you're looking for someone who is *really* merry, you've come to the right person"

within 's · within this (these)

suit of sables · garments trimmed with the fur of the sable and hence suited for a wealthy person, not a mourner (but with a pun on sable, "black," ironically suggesting mourning once again)

suffer ... on · undergo oblivion

For ... forgot · verse of a song. The hobbyhorse was a character resembling a horse and rider, appearing in the morris dance. This song laments the disappearance of such customs under the Puritans

[*To* POLONIUS.]

My lord, you played once i' th' university, you say?

POLONIUS That did I, my lord, and was accounted a good actor. 3.2.90

HAMLET What did you enact?

POLONIUS I did enact Julius Cæsar. I was killed i' the Capitol; Brutus killed me.

HAMLET It was a brute° part° of him to kill so capital a calf° there. – Be the players ready? 3.2.95

ROSENCRANTZ Ay, my lord. They stay upon° your patience.

QUEEN Come hither, my dear Hamlet, sit by me.

HAMLET No, good Mother, here's metal° more attractive.

[POLONIUS, *to the* KING.]

POLONIUS O, ho, do you mark that?

HAMLET Lady, shall I be in your lap? 3.2.100

[*Lying down at* OPHELIA's *feet.*]

OPHELIA No, my lord.

HAMLET I mean, my head upon your lap?

OPHELIA Ay, my lord.

HAMLET Do you think I meant country matters?°

OPHELIA I think nothing, my lord. 3.2.105

HAMLET That's a fair thought to lie between maids' legs.

OPHELIA What is, my lord?

HAMLET Nothing.°

OPHELIA You are merry, my lord.

HAMLET Who, I? 3.2.110

OPHELIA Ay, my lord.

HAMLET O God, your only jig maker.° What should a man do but be merry? For look you how cheerfully my mother looks, and my father died within 's° two hours.

OPHELIA Nay, 'tis twice two months, my lord. 3.2.115

HAMLET So long? Nay then, let the devil wear black, for I'll have a suit of sables.° O heavens! Die two months ago, and not forgotten yet? Then there's hope a great man's memory may outlive his life half a year. But, by 'r Lady, 'a must build churches, then, or else shall 'a suffer not thinking on,° with the hobbyhorse, 3.2.120 whose epitaph is "For O, for O, the hobbyhorse is forgot."°

[*The trumpets sound. The dumb show follows: enter a* KING *and a* QUEEN *very lovingly, the* QUEEN *embracing him, and he her. She kneels, and makes a show of protestation unto him. He takes her up, and declines his*

head upon her neck. He lies him down upon a bank of flowers. She, seeing
him asleep, leaves him. Anon comes in another MAN, *takes off his crown,*
kisses it, pours poison in the sleeper's ears, and leaves him. The QUEEN
returns, finds the KING *dead, makes passionate action. The* POISONER
with some THREE *or* FOUR *come in again, seem to condole with her. The*
dead body is carried away. The POISONER *woos the* QUEEN *with gifts; she*
seems harsh awhile, but in the end accepts his love. Exeunt PLAYERS.]

OPHELIA What means this, my lord?

HAMLET Marry, this' miching mallico;• it means mischief.

OPHELIA Belike• this show imports the argument• of the play.

[*Enter* PROLOGUE.]

3.2.125 HAMLET We shall know by this fellow. The players cannot
keep counsel;• they'll tell all.

OPHELIA Will 'a tell us what this show meant?

HAMLET Ay, or any show that you will show him. Be not you•
ashamed to show, he'll not shame to tell you what it means.

3.2.130 OPHELIA You are naught,• you are naught. I'll mark the play.

PROLOGUE For us, and for our tragedy,
Here stooping• to your clemency,
We beg your hearing patiently.

[*Exit.*]

HAMLET Is this a prologue, or the posy of a ring?•

3.2.135 OPHELIA 'Tis brief, my lord.

HAMLET As woman's love.

[*Enter* TWO PLAYERS *as* KING *and* QUEEN.]

PLAYER KING Full thirty times hath Phoebus' cart• gone round
Neptune's salt wash• and Tellus'• orbèd ground,
And thirty dozen moons with borrowed• sheen

3.2.140 About the world have times twelve thirties been,
Since love our hearts and Hymen• did our hands
Unite commutual• in most sacred bands.•

PLAYER QUEEN So many journeys may the sun and moon
Make us again count o'er ere love be done!

3.2.145 But, woe is me, you are so sick of late,
So, far from cheer and from your former state,
That I distrust• you. Yet, though I distrust,
Discomfort• you, my lord, it nothing• must.
For women's fear and love hold quantity,•

3.2.150 In neither aught, or in extremity.•

---

this' miching mallico · this is sneaking mischief

Belike · probably

argument · plot

counsel · secret

Be not you · provided you are not

naught · indecent. Ophelia is reacting to Hamlet's pointed remarks about not being ashamed to show all

stooping · bowing

posy of a ring · brief motto in verse inscribed in a ring

Phoebus' cart · the sun-god's chariot, making its yearly cycle

salt wash · the sea

Tellus · goddess of the earth, of the "orbèd ground"

borrowed · reflected

Hymen · god of matrimony

commutual · mutually

bands · bond

distrust · am anxious about

Discomfort · distress

nothing · not all

hold quantity · keep proportion with one another

In neither … extremity · women fear and love either too little or too much but the two, fear and love, are equal in either case

Now, what my love is, proof· hath made you know,   3.2.151
And as my love is sized,· my fear is so.
Where love is great, the littlest doubts are fear,
Where little fears grow great, great love grows there.

PLAYER KING Faith, I must leave thee, love, and shortly too;   3.2.155
My operant powers· their functions leave to do.·
And thou shalt live in this fair world behind,·
Honored, beloved; and haply one as kind
For husband shalt thou –

PLAYER QUEEN   O, confound the rest!
Such love must needs be treason in my breast.   3.2.160
In second husband let me be accurst!
None· wed the second but who· killed the first.

HAMLET Wormwood,· Wormwood.

PLAYER QUEEN The instances· that second marriage move·
Are base respects of thrift,· but none of love.   3.2.165
A second time I kill my husband dead
When second husband kisses me in bed.

PLAYER KING I do believe you think what now you speak,
But what we do determine oft we break.
Purpose is but the slave to memory,·   3.2.170
Of violent birth, but poor validity,·
Which· now, like fruit unripe, sticks on the tree,
But fall unshaken when they mellow be.
Most necessary 'tis that we forget
To pay ourselves what to ourselves is debt.·   3.2.175
What to ourselves in passion we propose,
The passion ending, doth the purpose lose.
The violence of either grief or joy
Their own enactures· with themselves destroy.
Where joy most revels, grief doth most lament,   3.2.180
Grief joys, joy grieves, on slender accident.·
This world is not for aye,· nor 'tis not strange
That even our loves should with our fortunes change;
For 'tis a question left us yet to prove,
Whether love lead fortune, or else fortune love.   3.2.185
The great man down,· you mark his favorite flies;
The poor advanced makes friends of enemies.·
And hitherto· doth love on fortune tend;·

Glossary (left margin):

proof · experience

sized · in size

operant powers · vital functions

leave to do · cease to perform

behind · after I have gone

None · let no woman

but who · except the one who

Wormwood · how bitter (literally, a bitter-tasting plant)

instances · motives

move · motivate

base ... thrift · ignoble considerations of material prosperity

Purpose ... memory · our good intentions are subject to forgetfulness

validity · strength, durability

Which · purpose

Most ... debt · it's inevitable that in time we forget the obligations we have imposed on ourselves

enactures · fulfillments

Where ... accident · the capacity for extreme joy and grief go together, and often one extreme is instantly changed into its opposite on the slightest provocation

aye · ever

down · fallen in fortune

The poor ... enemies · when one of humble station is promoted, you see his enemies suddenly becoming his friends

hitherto · up to this point in the argument, or, to this extent

tend · attend

For who not needs˙ shall never lack a friend,
3.2.190 And who in want˙ a hollow friend doth try˙
Directly seasons him˙ his enemy.
But, orderly to end where I begun,
Our wills and fates do so contrary run˙
That our devices still˙ are overthrown;
3.2.195 Our thoughts are ours, their ends˙ none of our own.
So think thou wilt no second husband wed,
But die thy thoughts when thy first lord is dead.
PLAYER QUEEN Nor˙ earth to me give food, nor heaven light,
Sport and repose lock from me day and night,˙
3.2.200 To desperation turn my trust and hope,
An anchor's cheer˙ in prison be my scope!˙
Each opposite that blanks the face of joy
Meet what I would have web and it destroy!˙
Both here and hence˙ pursue me lasting strife
3.2.205 If, once a widow, ever I be wife!
HAMLET If she should break it now!
PLAYER KING 'Tis deeply sworn. Sweet, leave me here awhile;
My spirits˙ grow dull, and fain I would beguile
The tedious day with sleep.
PLAYER QUEEN   Sleep rock thy brain,
3.2.210 And never come mischance between us twain!
[*He sleeps. Exit* PLAYER QUEEN.]
HAMLET Madam, how like you this play?
QUEEN The lady doth protest too much, methinks.
HAMLET O, but she'll keep her word.
KING Have you heard the argument?˙ Is there no offense in 't?
3.2.215 HAMLET No, no, they do but jest,˙ poison in jest. No offense˙
i' the world.
KING What do you call the play?
HAMLET *The Mousetrap.* Marry, how? Tropically.˙ This play is
the image of a murder done in Vienna. Gonzago is the Duke's
3.2.220 name, his wife, Baptista. You shall see anon. 'Tis a knavish
piece of work, but what of that? Your Majesty, and we that
have free˙ souls, it touches us not. Let the galled jade˙ wince,
our withers˙ are unwrung.˙
[*Enter* LUCIANUS.]
This is one Lucianus, nephew to the King.

who not needs · he who is not in need (of wealth)

who in want · he who, being in need

try · test (his generosity)

seasons him · ripens him into

Our ... run · what we want and what we get go so contrarily

devices still · intentions continually

ends · results

Nor · let neither

Sport ... night · may day deny me its pastimes and night its repose

anchor's cheer · anchorite's or hermit's fare

my scope · the extent of my happiness

Each ... destroy · may every adverse thing that causes the face of joy to turn pale ("blanks") meet and destroy everything that I desire to see prosper

hence · in the life hereafter

spirits · vital spirits

argument · plot

offense ... offense · cause for objection ... actual injury, crime

jest · make believe

Tropically · figuratively

Duke's · King's

free · guiltless

galled jade · horse whose hide is rubbed by saddle or harness

withers · the part between the horse's shoulder blades

unwrung · not rubbed sore

chorus · in Elizabethan plays, the forthcoming action was often explained by an actor known as the "chorus"; at a puppet show, the actor who spoke the dialogue was known as an "interpreter," as indicated by the lines following

puppets dallying · with suggestion of sexual play, continued in "keen" (sexually aroused), "groaning" (moaning in pregnancy), and "edge" (sexual desire or impetuosity)

keen · sharp, bitter

Still … worse · always bettering what other people say, but at the same time more offensive

mis-take · take false-heartedly and cheat on

Confederate season · the time and occasion conspiring

Hecate's ban · the curse of Hecate, the goddess of witchcraft

false fire · the discharge of a gun loaded with powder but no shot

Why … weep · allusion to the popular belief that a wounded deer retires to weep and die

ungallèd · unafflicted

this · the play

feathers · allusion to the plumes that Elizabethan actors wore

turn Turk with · turn renegade against

Provincial roses · rosettes of ribbon

razed · with ornamental slashing

fellowship…players · partnership in a theatrical company

Damon · the friend of Pythias, as Horatio is friend of Hamlet

OPHELIA You are as good as a chorus,˙ my lord. 3.2.225

HAMLET I could interpret between you and your love, if I could see the puppets dallying.˙

OPHELIA You are keen,˙ my lord, you are keen.

HAMLET It would cost you a groaning to take off mine edge.

OPHELIA Still better, and worse.˙ 3.2.230

HAMLET So you mis-take˙ your husbands. Begin, murderer, leave thy damnable faces and begin. Come, the croaking raven doth bellow for revenge.

LUCIANUS Thoughts black, hands apt, drugs fit, and time agreeing, Confederate season,˙ else no creature seeing, 3.2.235
Thou mixture rank, of midnight weeds collected,
With Hecate's ban˙ thrice blasted, thrice infected,
Thy natural magic and dire property
On wholesome life usurp immediately.

[*He pours the poison into the sleeper's ear.*]

HAMLET 'A poisons him i' the garden for his estate. His name's 3.2.240
Gonzago. The story is extant, and written in very choice Italian. You shall see anon how the murderer gets the love of Gonzago's wife.

[KING CLAUDIUS *rises.*]

OPHELIA The King rises.

HAMLET What, frighted with false fire?˙ 3.2.245

QUEEN How fares my lord?

POLONIUS Give o'er the play.

KING Give me some light. Away!

POLONIUS Lights, lights, lights!

[*Exeunt all but* HAMLET *and* HORATIO.]

HAMLET "Why, let the strucken deer go weep,˙ 3.2.250
The hart ungallèd˙ play.
For some must watch while some must sleep;
Thus runs the world away."
Would not this,˙ sir, and a forest of feathers˙ – if the rest of my fortunes turn Turk with˙ me – with two Provincial roses˙ on 3.2.255
my razed˙ shoes, get me a fellowship in a cry of players?˙

HORATIO Half a share.

HAMLET A whole one, I.
"For thou dost know, O Damon˙ dear,
This realm dismantled was 3.2.260

3.2.261   Of Jove himself, and now reigns here
                A very, very – pajock."*

HORATIO You might have rhymed.

HAMLET O good Horatio, I'll take the ghost's word for a thou-
3.2.265   sand pound. Didst perceive?

HORATIO Very well, my lord.

HAMLET Upon the talk of the poisoning?

HORATIO I did very well note him.

    [*Enter* ROSENCRANTZ *and Guildenstern.*]

HAMLET Aha! Come, some music! Come, the recorders.*
3.2.270   "For if the King like not the comedy,
        Why then, belike, he likes it not, perdy."*
    Come, some music.

GUILDENSTERN Good my lord, vouchsafe me a word with you.

HAMLET Sir, a whole history.

3.2.275 **GUILDENSTERN** The King, sir –

HAMLET Ay, sir, what of him?

GUILDENSTERN Is in his retirement* marvelous distempered.*

HAMLET With drink, sir?

GUILDENSTERN No, my lord, with choler.*

3.2.280 **HAMLET** Your wisdom should show itself more richer to signify
    this to the doctor, for me to put him to his purgation* would
    perhaps plunge him into more choler.

GUILDENSTERN Good my lord, put your discourse into some
    frame* and start* not so wildly from my affair.

3.2.285 **HAMLET** I am tame, sir. Pronounce.

GUILDENSTERN The Queen, your mother, in most great affliction
    of spirit, hath sent me to you.

HAMLET You are welcome.

GUILDENSTERN Nay, good my lord, this courtesy is not of the
3.2.290   right breed.* If it shall please you to make me a wholesome
    answer, I will do your mother's commandment; if not, your
    pardon* and my return shall be the end of my business.

HAMLET Sir, I cannot.

ROSENCRANTZ What, my lord?

3.2.295 **HAMLET** Make you a wholesome answer; my wit's diseased. But,
    sir, such answer as I can make, you shall command, or rather,
    as you say, my mother. Therefore no more, but to the matter.
    My mother, you say –

This realm … pajock · love, representing divine authority and justice, has abandoned this realm to its own devices, leaving in his stead only, a peacock or vain pretender to virtue (though the rhyme-word expected in place of pajock or "peacock" suggests that the realm is now ruled over by an "ass")

recorders · wind instruments of the flute kind

perdy · a corruption of the French *par dieu*, "by God"

retirement · withdrawal to his chambers

distempered · out of humor (but Hamlet deliberately plays on the wider application to any illness of mind or body, as in lines 308–309, especially drunkenness.)

choler · anger (but Hamlet takes the word in its more basic humoral sense of "bilious disorder")

purgation · Hamlet hints at something going beyond medical treatment to bloodletting and the extraction of confession

frame · order

start · shy or jump away (like a horse; the opposite of "tame" in line 284)

breed · 1 · kind; 2 · breeding, manners

pardon · permission to depart

ROSENCRANTZ Then thus she says: your behavior hath struck her into amazement and admiration.• 3.2.300

admiration · bewilderment

HAMLET O wonderful son, that can so stonish a mother! But is there no sequel at the heels of this mother's admiration? Impart.

closet · private chamber

ROSENCRANTZ She desires to speak with you in her closet• ere you go to bed.

HAMLET We shall obey, were she ten times our mother. Have you any further trade with us? 3.2.305

ROSENCRANTZ My lord, you once did love me.

pickers and stealers · hands (so called from the catechism, "to keep my hands from picking and stealing")

HAMLET And do still, by these pickers and stealers.•

liberty · being freed from distemper, line 336; but perhaps with a veiled threat as well

ROSENCRANTZ Good my lord, what is your cause of distemper? You do surely bar the door upon your own liberty• if you deny• your griefs to your friend. 3.2.310

HAMLET Sir, I lack advancement.

deny · refuse to share

ROSENCRANTZ How can that be, when you have the voice of the King himself for your succession in Denmark?

"While ... grows" · the rest of the proverb: "the silly horse starves"; Hamlet may not live long enough to succeed to the kingdom

HAMLET Ay, sir, but "While the grass grows"•– the proverb is something• musty. 3.2.315

[*Enter the* **PLAYERS**• *with recorders.*]

O, the recorders. Let me see one.

something · somewhat

[**HAMLET** *takes a recorder.*]

Players · actors

To withdraw• with you: why do you go about to recover the wind• of me, as if you would drive me into a toil?

withdraw · speak privately

GUILDENSTERN O, my lord, if my duty be too bold, my love is too unmannerly:• 3.2.320

recover the wind · get to the windward side (thus driving the game into the toil, or "net")

HAMLET I do not well understand that.• Will you play upon this pipe?

if ... unmannerly · if I am using an unmannerly boldness, it is my love that occasions it

GUILDENSTERN My lord, I cannot.

HAMLET I pray you. 3.2.325

GUILDENSTERN Believe me, I cannot.

HAMLET I do beseech you.

I do not ... that · I don't understand how genuine love can be unmannerly

GUILDENSTERN I know no touch of it, my lord.

HAMLET It is as easy as lying. Govern these ventages• with your fingers and thumb, give it breath with your mouth, and it will discourse most eloquent music. Look you, these are the stops. 3.2.330

ventages · fingerholes or stops (line 359) of the recorder

GUILDENSTERN But these cannot I command to any utterance of harmony. I have not the skill.

HAMLET Why, look you now, how unworthy a thing you make of me! You would play upon me, you would seem to know my 3.2.335

3.2.336 stops, you would pluck out the heart of my mystery, you would sound° me from my lowest note to the top of my compass,° and there is much music, excellent voice, in this little organ,° yet cannot you make it speak. 'Sblood, do you think I am easier
3.2.340 to be played on than a pipe? Call me what instrument you will, though you can fret° me, you cannot play upon me.

[*Enter* POLONIUS.]

God bless you, sir!

POLONIUS My lord, the Queen would speak with you, and presently.°

3.2.345 HAMLET Do you see yonder cloud that's almost in shape of a camel?

POLONIUS By the Mass and 'tis, like a camel indeed.

HAMLET Methinks it is like a weasel.

POLONIUS It is backed like a weasel.

HAMLET Or like a whale.

3.2.350 POLONIUS Very like a whale.

HAMLET Then I will come to my mother by and by.°

[*Aside.*]

They fool me° to the top of my bent.° – I will come by and by.

POLONIUS I will say so.

[*Exit.*]

HAMLET "By and by" is easily said. Leave me, friends.

[*Exeunt all but* HAMLET.]

3.2.355 'Tis now the very witching time° of night,
When churchyards yawn and hell itself breathes out
Contagion to this world. Now could I drink hot blood
And do such bitter business as the day
Would quake to look on. Soft, now to my mother.
3.2.360 O heart, lose not thy nature!° Let not ever
The soul of Nero° enter this firm bosom.
Let me be cruel, not unnatural;
I will speak daggers to her, but use none.
My tongue and soul in this be hypocrites:
3.2.365 How in my words soever° she be shent,°
To give them seals° never my soul consent!

[*Exit.*]

ACT 3, SCENE 3

[*The castle. Enter* KING, ROSENCRANTZ, *and* GUILDENSTERN.]

---

sound · 1 · fathom; 2 · produce sound in

compass · range (of voice)

organ · musical instrument

fret · irritate (with a quibble on "fret," meaning the piece of wood, gut, or metal that regulates the fingering on an instrument)

presently · at once

by and by · quite soon

fool me · trifle with me, humor my fooling

top of my bent · limit of my ability or endurance (literally, the extent to which a bow may be bent)

witching time · time when spells are cast and evil is abroad

nature · natural feeling

Nero · murderer of his mother, Agrippina

How ... soever · however much by my words

shent · rebuked

give them seals · confirm them with deeds

KING I like him* not, nor stands it safe with us   3.3.1
   To let his madness range. Therefore prepare you.
   I your commission will forthwith dispatch,*
   And he to England shall along with you.
   The terms of our estate* may not endure   3.3.5
   Hazard so near 's as doth hourly grow
   Out of his brows.*

GUILDENSTERN   We will ourselves provide.
   Most holy and religious fear* it is
   To keep those many many bodies safe
   That live and feed upon Your Majesty.   3.3.10

ROSENCRANTZ The single and peculiar* life is bound
   With all the strength and armor of the mind
   To keep itself from noyance,* but much more
   That spirit upon whose weal depends and rests
   The lives of many. The cess* of majesty   3.3.15
   Dies not alone, but like a gulf* doth draw
   What's near it with it; or it is a massy* wheel
   Fixed on the summit of the highest mount,
   To whose huge spokes ten thousand lesser things
   Are mortised* and adjoined, which, when it falls,*   3.3.20
   Each small annexment, petty consequence,*
   Attends* the boisterous ruin. Never alone
   Did the King sigh, but with a general groan.

KING Arm* you, I pray you, to this speedy voyage,
   For we will fetters put about this fear,   3.3.25
   Which now goes too free-footed.

ROSENCRANTZ   We will haste us.
[*Exeunt gentlemen* **ROSENCRANTZ** *and* **GUILDENSTERN**. *Enter* **POLONIUS**.]

POLONIUS My lord, he's going to his mother's closet.
   Behind the arras* I'll convey myself
   To hear the process.* I'll warrant she'll tax him home,*
   And, as you said – and wisely was it said –   3.3.30
   'Tis meet* that some more audience than a mother,
   Since nature makes them partial, should o'erhear
   The speech, of vantage.* Fare you well, my liege.
   I'll call upon you ere you go to bed
   And tell you what I know.   3.3.35

him · his behavior
dispatch · prepare, cause to be drawn up
terms of our estate · circumstances of my royal position
Out of his brows · from his brain, in the form of plots and threats
religious fear · sacred concern
single and peculiar · individual and private
noyance · harm
cess · decease, cessation
gulf · whirlpool
massy · massive
mortised · fastened (as with a fitted joint)
when it falls · when it descends, like the wheel of Fortune, bringing a king down with it
Each…consequence · every hanger-on and unimportant person or thing connected with the King
Attends · participates in
Arm · prepare
arras · screen of tapestry placed around the walls of household apartments. On the Elizabethan stage, the arras was presumably over a door or discovery space in the tiring-house facade
process · proceedings
tax him home · reprove him severely
meet · fitting
of vantage · from an advantageous place, or, in addition

3.3.35	**KING** Thanks, dear my lord.	

[*Exit* POLONIUS.]

O, my offense is rank! It smells to heaven.
It hath the primal eldest curse˙ upon 't,
A brother's murder. Pray can I not,
Though inclination be as sharp as will;˙

3.3.40 My stronger guilt defeats my strong intent,
And like a man to double business bound˙
I stand in pause where I shall first begin,
And both neglect. What if this cursèd hand
Were thicker than itself with brother's blood,

3.3.45 Is there not rain enough in the sweet heavens
To wash it white as snow? Whereto serves mercy
But to confront the visage of offense?˙
And what's in prayer but this twofold force,
To be forestallèd˙ ere we come to fall,

3.3.50 Or pardoned being down? Then I'll look up.
My fault is past. But O, what form of prayer
Can serve my turn? "Forgive me my foul murder"?
That cannot be, since I am still possessed
Of those effects for which I did the murder:

3.3.55 My crown, mine own ambition, and my queen.
May one be pardoned and retain th' offense?˙
In the corrupted currents˙ of this world
Offense's gilded hand˙ may shove by˙ justice,
And oft 'tis seen the wicked prize˙ itself

3.3.60 Buys out the law. But 'tis not so above.
There˙ is no shuffling,˙ there the action lies˙
In his˙ true nature, and we ourselves compelled,
Even to the teeth and forehead˙ of our faults,
To give in˙ evidence. What then? What rests?˙

3.3.65 Try what repentance can. What can it not?
Yet what can it, when one cannot repent?
O wretched state, O bosom black as death,
O limèd˙ soul that, struggling to be free,
Art more engaged!˙ Help, angels! Make assay.˙

3.3.70 Bow, stubborn knees, and heart with strings of steel,
Be soft as sinews of the newborn babe!
All may be well.

---

the primal eldest curse · the curse of Cain the first murderer; he killed his brother Abel. See Genesis 4

Though ... will · though my desire is as strong as my determination

bound · 1 · destined; 2 · obliged (the King wants to repent and still enjoy what he has gained)

Whereto ... offense · what function does mercy serve other than to meet sin face to face?

forestallèd · prevented (from sinning)

th' offense · the thing for which one offended

currents · courses

gilded hand · hand offering gold as a bribe

shove by · thrust aside

wicked prize · prize won by wickedness

There · in heaven

shuffling · escape by trickery

the action lies · the accusation is made manifest (a legal metaphor)

his · its

to the teeth and forehead · face to face, concealing nothing

give in · provide

rests · remains

limèd · caught as with birdlime, a sticky substance used to ensnare birds

engaged · entangled

assay · trial (said to himself)

[He kneels. Enter HAMLET.*]*

HAMLET Now might I do it pat,* now 'a is a-praying;

And now I'll do 't.

[He draws his sword.]

And so 'a goes to heaven,

And so am I revenged. That would be scanned:*   3.3.75

A villain kills my father, and for that,

I, his sole son, do this same villain send

To heaven.

Why, this is hire and salary, not revenge.

'A took my father grossly, full of bread,*   3.3.80

With all his crimes broad blown,* as flush* as May;

And how his audit* stands who knows save* heaven?

But in our circumstance and course of thought*

'Tis heavy with him. And am I then revenged,

To take him in the purging of his soul,   3.3.85

When he is fit and seasoned* for his passage?

No!

Up, sword, and know thou a more horrid hent.*

[He puts up his sword.]

When he is drunk asleep, or in his rage,*

Or in th' incestuous pleasure of his bed,   3.3.90

At game,* a-swearing, or about some act

That has no relish* of salvation in 't –

Then trip him, that his heels may kick at heaven,

And that his soul may be as damned and black

As hell, whereto it goes. My mother stays.*   3.3.95

This physic* but prolongs thy sickly days.

[Exit.]

KING My words fly up, my thoughts remain below.

Words without thoughts never to heaven go.

[Exit.]

ACT 3, SCENE 4

[The Queen's private chamber. Enter QUEEN GERTRUDE *and* POLONIUS.*]*

POLONIUS 'A will come straight. Look you lay home* to him.   3.4.1

Tell him his pranks have been too broad* to bear with,

And that Your Grace hath screened and stood between

Much heat* and him. I'll shroud* me even here.

---

pat · opportunely

would be scanned · needs to be looked into, or, would be interpreted as follows

grossly, full of bread · enjoying his worldly pleasures rather than fasting (see Ezekiel 16:49)

crimes broad blown · sins in full bloom

flush · vigorous

audit · account

save · except for

in … thought · as we see it from our mortal perspective

seasoned · matured, readied

know … hent · await to be grasped by me on a more horrid occasion

drunk … rage · dead drunk, or in a fit of sexual passion

game · gambling

relish · trace, savor

stays · awaits (me)

physic · purging (by prayer), or, Hamlet's postponement of the killing

lay home · thrust to the heart, reprove him soundly

broad · unrestrained

Much heat · the King's anger

shroud · conceal (with ironic fitness to Polonius' imminent death. The word is only in the First Quarto; the Second Quarto and the Folio read "silence")

3.4.5 Pray you, be round* with him.

[HAMLET, *calling from within.*]

HAMLET Mother, Mother, Mother!

QUEEN I'll warrant you, fear me not.

Withdraw, I hear him coming.

[POLONIUS *hides behind the arras. Enter* HAMLET.]

HAMLET Now, Mother, what's the matter?

3.4.10 QUEEN Hamlet, thou hast thy father* much offended.

HAMLET Mother, you have my father much offended.

QUEEN Come, come, you answer with an idle* tongue.

HAMLET Go, go, you question with a wicked tongue.

QUEEN Why, how now, Hamlet?

HAMLET What's the matter now?

3.4.15 QUEEN Have you forgot me?*

HAMLET No, by the rood,* not so:

You are the Queen, your husband's brother's wife,

And – would it were not so! – you are my mother.

QUEEN Nay, then, I'll set those to you that can speak.*

HAMLET Come, come, and sit you down; you shall not budge.

3.4.20 You go not till I set you up a glass

Where you may see the inmost part of you.

QUEEN What wilt thou do? Thou wilt not murder me?

Help, ho!

[POLONIUS, *calling from behind the arras.*]

POLONIUS What ho! Help!

[HAMLET, *drawing.*]

3.4.25 HAMLET How now? A rat? Dead for a ducat,* dead!

[HAMLET *thrusts his rapier through the arras. Polonius calls from behind the arras.*]

POLONIUS O, I am slain!

[*He falls and dies.*]

QUEEN O me, what hast thou done?

HAMLET Nay, I know not. Is it the King?

QUEEN O, what a rash and bloody deed is this!

HAMLET A bloody deed – almost as bad, good Mother,

3.4.30 As kill a king, and marry with his brother.

QUEEN As kill a king!

HAMLET Ay, lady, it was my word.

[*He parts the arras and discovers* POLONIUS.]

---

round · blunt

thy father · your stepfather, Claudius

idle · foolish

forgot me · forgotten that I am your mother

rood · cross of Christ

speak · speak to someone so rude

Dead for a ducat · I bet a ducat he's dead; or, a ducat is his life's fee busy · nosey

damnèd custom ·
habitual wickedness

brazed · brazened,
hardened

proof · armor

sense · feeling

sets a blister · brands
as a harlot

contraction · the
marriage contract

sweet religion makes ·
makes marriage vows

rhapsody · senseless
string

Heaven's face ... act ·
heaven's face blushes
at this solid world
compounded of the
various elements, with
sorrowful face as though
the day of doom were
near, and is sick with
horror at the deed
(Gertrude's marriage)

index · table of
contents, prelude or
preface

counterfeit present-
ment · portrayed
representation

Hyperion's · the
sun-god's

front · brow

Mars · god of war

station · manner of
standing

Mercury · winged
messenger of the gods

New-lighted · newly
alighted

set his seal · affix his
approval

ear · ear of grain

Blasting · blighting

leave · cease

Thou wretched, rash, intruding fool, farewell!
I took thee for thy better. Take thy fortune.
Thou find'st to be too busy* is some danger. –
Leave wringing of your hands. Peace, sit you down,   3.4.35
And let me wring your heart, for so I shall,
If it be made of penetrable stuff,
If damnèd custom* have not brazed* it so
That it be proof* and bulwark against sense.*

QUEEN What have I done, that thou dar'st wag thy tongue   3.4.40
In noise so rude against me?

HAMLET   Such an act
That blurs the grace and blush of modesty,
Calls virtue hypocrite, takes off the rose
From the fair forehead of an innocent love
And sets a blister* there, makes marriage vows   3.4.45
As false as dicers' oaths. O, such a deed
As from the body of contraction* plucks
The very soul, and sweet religion makes*
A rhapsody* of words. Heaven's face does glow
O'er this solidity and compound mass   3.4.50
With tristful visage, as against the doom,
Is thought-sick at the act.*

QUEEN   Ay me, what act,
That roars so loud and thunders in the index?*
[HAMLET, *showing her two likenesses.*]

HAMLET Look here upon this picture, and on this,
The counterfeit presentment* of two brothers.   3.4.55
See what a grace was seated on this brow:
Hyperion's* curls, the front* of Jove himself,
An eye like Mars* to threaten and command,
A station* like the herald Mercury*
New-lighted* on a heaven-kissing hill –   3.4.60
A combination and a form indeed
Where every god did seem to set his seal*
To give the world assurance of a man.
This was your husband. Look you now what follows:
Here is your husband, like a mildewed ear,*   3.4.65
Blasting* his wholesome brother. Have you eyes?
Could you on this fair mountain leave* to feed

And batten* on this moor?* Ha, have you eyes?
You cannot call it love, for at your age
3.4.70 The heyday* in the blood is tame, it's humble,
And waits upon the judgment, and what judgment
Would step from this to this? Sense,* sure, you have,
Else could you not have motion, but sure that sense
Is apoplexed,* for madness would not err,
3.4.75 Nor sense to ecstasy was ne'er so thralled,
But it reserved some quantity of choice
To serve in such a difference.* What devil was 't
That thus hath cozened* you at hoodman-blind?*
Eyes without feeling, feeling without sight,
3.4.80 Ears without hands or eyes, smelling sans* all,
Or but a sickly part of one true sense
Could not so mope.* O shame, where is thy blush?
Rebellious hell,
If thou canst mutine* in a matron's bones,
3.4.85 To flaming youth let virtue be as wax
And melt in her own fire. Proclaim no shame
When the compulsive ardor gives the charge,
Since frost itself as actively doth burn,
And reason panders will.*
3.4.90 QUEEN O Hamlet, speak no more!
Thou turn'st mine eyes into my very soul,
And there I see such black and grainèd* spots
As will not leave their tinct.*
HAMLET   Nay, but to live
In the rank sweat of an enseamèd* bed,
3.4.95 Stewed* in corruption, honeying and making love
Over the nasty sty!
QUEEN O, speak to me no more!
These words like daggers enter in my ears.
No more, sweet Hamlet!
HAMLET   A murderer and a villain,
3.4.100 A slave that is not twentieth part the tithe*
Of your precedent lord,* a vice* of kings,
A cutpurse of the empire and the rule,
That from a shelf the precious diadem stole
And put it in his pocket!

---

batten · gorge

moor · barren or marshy ground (suggesting also "dark-skinned")

heyday · excitement

Sense · perception through the five senses

apoplexed · paralyzed. Hamlet explains that without such a paralysis of will, even deranged states of mind would be able to make this obvious choice

To … difference · to help in making a choice between two such men

cozened · cheated

hoodman-blind · blindman's buff (Hamlet says the devil must have pushed Claudius toward Gertrude while she was blindfolded)

sans · without

mope · be dazed, act aimlessly

mutine · incite mutiny

Proclaim … will · call it no shameful business when the ardor of youth commits lechery, since the frost of advanced age burns with as active a fire of lust and reason perverts itself by fomenting lust rather than restraining it

grainèd · dyed indelibly

leave their tinct · surrender their color

enseamèd · saturated in the grease and filth of passionate lovemaking

Stewed · soaked, bathed (with a suggestion of "stew," brothel)

tithe · tenth part

precedent lord · former husband

vice · buffoon, a reference to the Vice of the morality plays

QUEEN No more!   3.4.105

[*Enter* GHOST *in his nightgown.*]

shreds and patches · motley, the traditional costume of the clown or fool

HAMLET A king of shreds and patches˙–
 Save me, and hover o'er me with your wings,
 You heavenly guards! What would your gracious figure?

QUEEN Alas, he's mad!

HAMLET Do you not come your tardy son to chide,   3.4.110

lapsed · delaying

 That, lapsed˙ in time and passion, lets go by

important · importunate, urgent

 Th' important˙ acting of your dread command?
 O, say!

GHOST Do not forget. This visitation
 Is but to whet thy almost blunted purpose.   3.4.115

amazement · distraction

 But look, amazement˙ on thy mother sits.
 O, step between her and her fighting soul!

Conceit · imagination

 Conceit˙ in weakest bodies strongest works.
 Speak to her, Hamlet.

HAMLET   How is it with you, lady?

incorporal · immaterial

QUEEN Alas, how is 't with you,   3.4.120
 That you do bend your eye on vacancy,

as ... th' alarm · like soldiers called out of sleep by an alarum

 And with th' incorporal˙ air do hold discourse?
 Forth at your eyes your spirits wildly peep,
 And, as the sleeping soldiers in th' alarm,˙

bedded · laid flat

 Your bedded˙ hair, like life in excrements,˙   3.4.125

like life in excrements · as though hair, an outgrowth of the body, had a life of its own. Hair was thought to be lifeless because it lacks sensation, and so its standing on end would be unnatural and ominous

 Start up and stand on end. O gentle son,
 Upon the heat and flame of thy distemper˙
 Sprinkle cool patience. Whereon do you look?

HAMLET On him, on him! Look you how pale he glares!

distemper · disorder

 His form and cause conjoined,˙ preaching to stones,   3.4.130

His ... conjoined · his appearance joined to his cause for speaking

 Would make them capable.˙– Do not look upon me,
 Lest with this piteous action you convert

capable · receptive

 My stern effects.˙ Then what I have to do

convert ... effects · divert me from my stern duty

 Will want true color – tears perchance for blood.˙

QUEEN To whom do you speak this?   3.4.135

want ... blood · lack plausibility so that (with a play on the normal sense of color) I shall shed colorless tears instead of blood

HAMLET Do you see nothing there?

QUEEN Nothing at all, yet all that is I see.

HAMLET Nor did you nothing hear?

QUEEN No, nothing but ourselves.

habit · clothes

HAMLET Why, look you there, look how it steals away!   3.4.140

as · as when

 My father, in his habit˙ as˙ he lived!

Look where he goes even now out at the portal!

[*Exit* GHOST.]

QUEEN This is the very° coinage of your brain.

This bodiless creation ecstasy

3.4.145   Is very cunning in.°

HAMLET Ecstasy?

My pulse as yours doth temperately keep time,

And makes as healthful music. It is not madness

That I have uttered. Bring me to the test,

3.4.150   And I the matter will reword,° which madness

Would gambol° from. Mother, for love of grace,

Lay not that flattering unction° to your soul

That not your trespass but my madness speaks.

It will but skin° and film the ulcerous place,

3.4.155   Whiles rank corruption, mining° all within,

Infects unseen. Confess yourself to heaven,

Repent what's past, avoid what is to come,

And do not spread the compost° on the weeds

To make them ranker. Forgive me this my virtue;°

3.4.160   For in the fatness° of these pursy° times

Virtue itself of vice must pardon beg,

Yea, curb° and woo for leave° to do him good.

QUEEN O Hamlet, thou hast cleft my heart in twain.

HAMLET O, throw away the worser part of it,

3.4.165   And live the purer with the other half.

Good night. But go not to my uncle's bed;

Assume a virtue, if you have it not.

That monster, custom, who all sense doth eat,°

Of habits devil,° is angel yet in this,

3.4.170   That to the use of actions fair and good

He likewise gives a frock or livery°

That aptly° is put on. Refrain tonight,

And that shall lend a kind of easiness

To the next abstinence; the next more easy;

3.4.175   For use° almost can change the stamp of nature,°

And either°... the devil, or throw him out

With wondrous potency. Once more, good night;

And when you are desirous to be blest,

I'll blessing beg of you.° For this same lord,

---

very · mere

This ... cunning in · madness is skillful in creating this kind of hallucination

reword · repeat word for word

gambol · skip away

unction · ointment

skin · grow a skin for

mining · working under the surface

compost · manure

this my virtue · my virtuous talk in reproving you

fatness · grossness

pursy · flabby, out of shape

curb · bow, bend the knee

leave · permission

who ... eat · which consumes all proper or natural feeling, all sensibility

Of habits devil · devil-like in prompting evil habits

livery · an outer appearance, a customary garb (and hence a predisposition easily assumed in time of stress)

aptly · readily

use · habit

the stamp of nature · our inborn traits

And either · defective line, usually emended by inserting the word "master" after either, following the Fourth Quarto and early editors

when ... you · when you are ready to be penitent and seek God's blessing, I will ask your blessing as a dutiful son should

their scourge and
minister · agent of
heavenly retribution.
Hamlet also suggests
that he himself will suffer
punishment in the process

bestow · stow, dispose of

This · the killing of
Polonius

behind · to come

Pinch wanton · leave
his love pinches on your
cheeks, branding you as
wanton

reechy · dirty, filthy

paddling · fingering
amorously

ravel ... out · disclose

in craft · by cunning

good · said sarcastically
(like the following lines)

paddock · toad

gib · tomcat

dear concernings ·
important affairs

sense and secrecy ·
secrecy that common
sense requires

Unpeg the basket ·
open the cage, let out
the secret

try conclusions · test
the outcome (in which
the ape apparently
enters a cage from which
birds have been released
and then tries to fly out
of the cage as they have
done, falling to its death)

down · in the fall; utterly

enginer · maker of
military contrivances

Hoist with · blown up by

petard · an explosive
used to make a breach

't shall ... will · unless
luck is against me, I will

mines · tunnels used in
warfare to undermine the
enemy's emplacements;
Hamlet will countermine
by going under their mines

[*Pointing to* POLONIUS.]

I do repent; but heaven hath pleased it so   3.4.180
To punish me with this, and this with me,
That I must be their scourge and minister.·
I will bestow· him, and will answer well
The death I gave him. So, again, good night.
I must be cruel only to be kind.   3.4.185
This· bad begins, and worse remains behind.·
One word more, good lady.

QUEEN   What shall I do?

HAMLET Not this by no means that I bid you do:
Let the bloat king tempt you again to bed,
Pinch wanton· on your cheek, call you his mouse,   3.4.190
And let him, for a pair of reechy· kisses,
Or paddling· in your neck with his damned fingers,
Make you to ravel all this matter out·
That I essentially am not in madness,
But mad in craft.· 'Twere good· you let him know,   3.4.195
For who that's but a queen, fair, sober, wise,
Would from a paddock,· from a bat, a gib,·
Such dear concernings· hide? Who would do so?
No, in despite of sense and secrecy,·
Unpeg the basket· on the house's top,   3.4.200
Let the birds fly, and like the famous ape,
To try conclusions,· in the basket creep
And break your own neck down.·

QUEEN Be thou assured, if words be made of breath,
And breath of life, I have no life to breathe   3.4.205
What thou hast said to me.

HAMLET I must to England. You know that?

QUEEN   Alack,
I had forgot. 'Tis so concluded on.

HAMLET There's letters sealed, and my two schoolfellows,
Whom I will trust as I will adders fanged,   3.4.210
They bear the mandate; they must sweep my way
And marshal me to knavery. Let it work.
For 'tis the sport to have the enginer·
Hoist with· his own petard,· and 't shall go hard
But I will· delve one yard below their mines·   3.4.215

And blow them at the moon. O, 'tis most sweet
When in one line* two crafts* directly meet.
This man shall set me packing.*
I'll lug the guts into the neighbor room.
3.4.220 Mother, good night indeed. This counselor
Is now most still, most secret, and most grave,
Who was in life a foolish prating knave. –
Come, sir, to draw toward an end* with you.–
Good night, Mother.

[*Exeunt separately*, **HAMLET** *dragging off* **POLONIUS**.]

ACT 4, SCENE 1

[*Enter* **KING** *and* **QUEEN**,* *with* **ROSENCRANTZ** *and* **GUILDENSTERN**.]

4.1.1 KING There's matter* in these sighs, these profound heaves.*
You must translate; 'tis fit we understand them.
Where is your son?

QUEEN Bestow this place on us a little while.

[*Exeunt* **ROSENCRANTZ** *and* **GUILDENSTERN**.]

4.1.5 Ah, mine own lord, what have I seen tonight!

KING What, Gertrude? How does Hamlet?

QUEEN Mad as the sea and wind when both contend
Which is the mightier. In his lawless fit,
Behind the arras hearing something stir,
4.1.10 Whips out his rapier, cries, "A rat, a rat!"
And in this brainish apprehension* kills
The unseen good old man.

KING   O heavy* deed!
It had been so with us,* had we been there.
His liberty is full of threats to all –
4.1.15 To you yourself, to us, to everyone.
Alas, how shall this bloody deed be answered?*
It will be laid to us, whose providence*
Should have kept short,* restrained, and out of haunt*
This mad young man. But so much was our love,
4.1.20 We would not understand what was most fit,
But, like the owner of a foul disease,
To keep it from divulging,* let it feed
Even on the pith of life. Where is he gone?

QUEEN To draw apart the body he hath killed,

---

in one line · mines and countermines on a collision course, or the countermines directly below the mines

crafts · acts of guile, plots

set me packing · set me to making schemes, and set me to lugging (him), and, also, send me off in a hurry

draw ... end · finish up (with a pun on draw, "pull")

Enter ... Queen · some editors argue that Gertrude never exits in 3.4 and that the scene is continuous here, as suggested in the Folio, but the Second Quarto marks an entrance for her and at line 35, Claudius speaks of Gertrude's closet as though it were elsewhere. A short time has elapsed, during which the King has become aware of her highly wrought emotional state

matter · significance

heaves · heavy sighs

brainish apprehension · headstrong conception

heavy · grievous

us · me (the royal "we," also in line 15)

answered · explained

providence · foresight

short · on a short tether

out of haunt · secluded

divulging · becoming evident

ore · vein of gold

mineral · mine

O'er whom his very madness, like some ore° 4.1.25
Among a mineral° of metals base,
Shows itself pure: 'a weeps for what is done.
KING O Gertrude, come away!
The sun no sooner shall the mountains touch
But we will ship him hence, and this vile deed 4.1.30
We must with all our majesty and skill

countenance · put the best face on

Both countenance° and excuse. – Ho, Guildenstern!
[*Enter* ROSENCRANTZ *and* GUILDENSTERN.]
Friends both, go join you with some further aid.
Hamlet in madness hath Polonius slain,
And from his mother's closet hath he dragged him. 4.1.35
Go seek him out, speak fair, and bring the body
Into the chapel. I pray you, haste in this.
[*Exeunt* ROSENCRANTZ *and* GUILDENSTERN.]
Come, Gertrude, we'll call up our wisest friends
And let them know both what we mean to do

And … done · a defective line; conjectures as to the missing words include "So haply, slander" (Capell and others); "For, haply, slander" (Theobald and others); and "So envious slander" (Jenkins)

diameter · extent from side to side

As level · with as direct aim

his blank · its target at point-blank range

woundless · invulnerable

And what's untimely done............° 4.1.40
Whose whisper o'er the world's diameter,°
As level° as the cannon to his blank,°
Transports his poisoned shot, may miss our name
And hit the woundless° air. O, come away!
My soul is full of discord and dismay. 4.1.45
[*Exeunt.*]

ACT 4, SCENE 2

[*The castle. Enter* HAMLET.]
HAMLET Safely stowed. 4.2.1
[ROSENCRANTZ *and* GUILDENSTERN, *calling from within.*]
ROSENCRANTZ, GUILDENSTERN Hamlet! Lord Hamlet!
HAMLET But soft, what noise? Who calls on Hamlet? O, here
they come.
[*Enter* ROSENCRANTZ *and* GUILDENSTERN.]
ROSENCRANTZ What have you done, my lord, with the dead body? 4.2.5
HAMLET Compounded it with dust, whereto 'tis kin.
ROSENCRANTZ Tell us where 'tis, that we may take it thence
And bear it to the chapel.
HAMLET Do not believe it.
ROSENCRANTZ Believe what? 4.2.10

4.2.11 **HAMLET** That I can keep your counsel and not mine own.• Besides, to be demanded of• a sponge, what replication• should be made by the son of a king?

ROSENCRANTZ Take you me for a sponge, my lord?

4.2.15 **HAMLET** Ay, sir, that soaks up the King's countenance,• his rewards, his authorities.• But such officers do the King best service in the end. He keeps them, like an ape, an apple, in the corner of his jaw, first mouthed to be last swallowed. When he needs what you have gleaned, it is but squeezing you, and,

4.2.20 sponge, you shall be dry again.

ROSENCRANTZ I understand you not, my lord.

HAMLET I am glad of it. A knavish speech sleeps in• a foolish ear.

ROSENCRANTZ My lord, you must tell us where the body is and go with us to the King.

4.2.25 **HAMLET** The body is with the King, but the King is not with the body.• The King is a thing –

GUILDENSTERN A thing, my lord?

HAMLET Of nothing.• Bring me to him. Hide fox, and all after!•

[*Exeunt running.*]

ACT 4, SCENE 3

[*The castle. Enter* **KING** *and two or three.*]

4.3.1 **KING** I have sent to seek him, and to find the body.
How dangerous is it that this man goes loose!
Yet must not we put the strong law on him.
He's loved of• the distracted• multitude,

4.3.5 Who like not in their judgment, but their eyes,
And where 'tis so, th' offender's scourge• is weighed,•
But never the offense. To bear all smooth and even,•
This sudden sending him away must seem
Deliberate pause.• Diseases desperate grown

4.3.10 By desperate appliance• are relieved,
Or not at all.

[*Enter* **ROSENCRANTZ**, **GUILDENSTERN**, *and all the rest.*]
How now, what hath befall'n?

ROSENCRANTZ Where the dead body is bestowed, my lord,
We cannot get from him.

KING   But where is he?

ROSENCRANTZ Without, my lord; guarded, to know your pleasure.

That . . . own · that I can follow your advice (by telling where the body is) and still keep my own secret

demanded of · questioned by

replication · reply

countenance · favor

authorities · delegated power, influence

sleeps in · has no meaning to

The . . . body · perhaps alludes to the legal commonplace of "the king's two bodies," which drew a distinction between the sacred office of kingship and the particular mortal who possessed it at any given time. Hence, although Claudius' body is necessarily a part of him, true kingship is not contained in it. Similarly, Claudius will have Polonius' body when it is found, but there is no kingship in this business either

Of nothing · 1 · of no account; 2 · lacking the essence of kingship

Hide . . . after · an old signal cry in the game of hide-and-seek, suggesting that Hamlet now runs away from them

of · by

distracted · fickle, unstable

scourge · punishment (literally, blow with a whip)

weighed · sympathetically considered

To bear' . . . even · to manage the business in an unprovocative way

Deliberate pause · carefully considered action

appliance · remedies

KING Bring him before us.   4.3.15

ROSENCRANTZ   Ho! Bring in the lord.

[*They enter with* **HAMLET**.]

KING Now, Hamlet, where's Polonius?

HAMLET At supper.

KING At supper? Where?

HAMLET Not where he eats, but where 'a is eaten. A certain convocation of politic worms· are e'en· at him. Your worm· is your only   4.3.20
emperor for diet.· We fat all creatures else to fat us, and we fat
ourselves for maggots. Your fat king and your lean beggar is but
variable service·– two dishes, but to one table. That's the end.

KING Alas, alas!

HAMLET A man may fish with the worm that hath eat· of a king,   4.3.25
and eat of the fish that hath fed of that worm.

KING What dost thou mean by this?

HAMLET Nothing but to show you how a king may go a progress·
through the guts of a beggar.

KING Where is Polonius?   4.3.30

HAMLET In heaven. Send thitherto see. If your messenger find
him not there, seek him i' th' other place yourself. But if indeed
you find him not within this month, you shall nose him as
you go up the stairs into the lobby.

[*The* **KING**, *to some* **ATTENDANTS**.]

KING Go seek him there.   4.3.35

HAMLET 'A will stay till you come.

[*Exeunt* **ATTENDANTS**.]

KING Hamlet, this deed, for thine especial safety –
Which we do tender,· as we dearly· grieve
For that which thou hast done – must send thee hence
With fiery quickness. Therefore prepare thyself.   4.3.40
The bark· is ready, and the wind at help,
Th' associates tend,· and everything is bent·
For England.

HAMLET For England!

KING Ay, Hamlet.   4.3.45

HAMLET Good.

KING So is it, if thou knew'st our purposes.

HAMLET I see a cherub· that sees them. But come, for England!
Farewell, dear mother.

---

politic worms · crafty worms (suited to a master spy like Polonius)

e'en · even now

Your worm · your average worm (compare "your fat king" and "your lean beggar" in line 22)

diet · food, eating (with a punning reference to the Diet of Worms, a famous convocation held in 1521)

variable service · different courses of a single meal

eat · eaten (pronounced "et")

progress · royal journey of state

tender · regard, hold dear

dearly · intensely

bark · sailing vessel

tend · wait

bent · in readiness

cherub · cherubim are angels of knowledge. Hamlet hints that both he and heaven are onto Claudius' tricks

4.3.50   **KING** Thy loving father, Hamlet.

        HAMLET My mother. Father and mother is man and wife, man
          and wife is one flesh, and so, my mother. Come, for England!
        [*Exit.*]

        KING Follow him at foot,˙ tempt him with speed aboard.   **at foot** · close behind,
          Delay it not. I'll have him hence tonight.   at heel

4.3.55   Away! For everything is sealed and done

          That else leans on˙ th' affair. Pray you, make haste.   **leans on** · bears upon,
        [*Exeunt all but the* **KING**.]   is related to

          And, England,˙ if my love thou hold'st at aught˙–   **England** · King of
          As my great power thereof may give thee sense,˙   England

          Since yet thy cicatrice˙ looks raw and red   **at aught** · at any value

4.3.60   After the Danish sword, and thy free awe˙   **As ... sense** · for so

          Pays homage to us – thou mayst not coldly set˙   my great power may
          Our sovereign process,˙ which imports at full,˙   give you a just apprecia-
          By letters congruing˙ to that effect,   tion of the importance
          The present˙ death of Hamlet. Do it, England,   of valuing my love

4.3.65   For like the hectic˙ in my blood he rages,   **cicatrice** · scar

          And thou must cure me. Till I know 'tis done,   **free awe** · voluntary
          Howe'er my haps,˙ my joys were ne'er begun.   show of respect
        [*Exit.*]

                                                       coldly set · regard with
                                                       indifference

ACT 4, SCENE 4

        [*The coast of Denmark. Enter* **FORTINBRAS** *with his* **ARMY** *over the stage.*]   **process** · command

                                                        imports at full · con-
4.4.1   **FORTINBRAS** Go, Captain, from me greet the Danish king.   veys specific directions for

          Tell him that by his license˙ Fortinbras   **congruing** · agreeing

          Craves the conveyance of˙ a promised march   **present** · immediate

          Over his kingdom. You know the rendezvous.   **hectic** · persistent fever

4.4.5   If that His Majesty would aught with us,   **haps** · fortunes

          We shall express our duty˙ in his eye;˙   **license** · permission

          And let him know so.   **the conveyance of** ·

        CAPTAIN I will do 't, my lord.   escort during

        FORTINBRAS Go softly˙ on.   **duty** · respect

        [*Exeunt all but the* **CAPTAIN**. *Enter* **HAMLET**, **ROSENCRANTZ**,   **eye** · presence
        GUILDENSTERN, *etc.*]

                                                        softly · slowly,
4.4.10   **HAMLET** Good Sir, whose powers˙ are these?   circumspectly

        CAPTAIN They are of Norway, Sir.

        HAMLET How purposed, Sir, I pray you?   **powers** · forces

        CAPTAIN Against some part of Poland.

HAMLET Who commands them, Sir?

CAPTAIN The nephew to old Norway, Fortinbras. 4.4.15

main · main part

HAMLET Goes it against the main· of Poland, Sir,
Or for some frontier?

addition · exaggeration

CAPTAIN Truly to speak, and with no addition,·
We go to gain a little patch of ground
That hath in it no profit but the name. 4.4.20

To pay · pay for a yearly rental of

To pay· five ducats, five, I would not farm it;·
Nor will it yield to Norway or the Pole

farm it · take a lease of it

A ranker· rate, should it be sold in fee.·

ranker · higher

HAMLET Why, then the Polack never will defend it.

in fee · fee simple, outright

CAPTAIN Yes, it is already garrisoned. 4.4.25

debate … straw · settle this trifling matter

HAMLET Two thousand souls and twenty thousand ducats
Will not debate the question of this straw.·
This is th' impostume· of much wealth and peace,

impostume · abscess

That inward breaks, and shows no cause without
Why the man dies. I humbly thank you, sir. 4.4.30

CAPTAIN God b' wi' you, Sir.

[*Exit.*]

inform against · denounce, betray; take shape

ROSENCRANTZ   Will 't please you go, my lord?

HAMLET I'll be with you straight. Go a little before.

[*Exeunt all except* **HAMLET**.]

market of · profit of, compensation for

How all occasions do inform against· me
And spur my dull revenge! What is a man,

discourse · power of reasoning

If his chief good and market of· his time 4.4.35
Be but to sleep and feed? A beast, no more.

Looking before and after · able to review past events and anticipate the future

Sure he that made us with such large discourse,·
Looking before and after,· gave us not
That capability and godlike reason

fust · grow moldy

To fust· in us unused. Now, whether it be 4.4.40

oblivion · forgetfulness

Bestial oblivion,· or some craven· scruple

craven · cowardly

Of thinking too precisely· on th' event·–

precisely · scrupulously

A thought which, quartered, hath but one part wisdom

event · outcome

And ever three parts coward – I do not know

Sith · since

Why yet I live to say "This thing's to do," 4.4.45

gross · obvious

Sith· I have cause, and will, and strength, and means

charge · expense

To do 't. Examples gross· as earth exhort me:
Witness this army of such mass and charge,·

delicate and tender · of fine and youthful qualities

Led by a delicate and tender· prince,

4.4.50 Whose spirit with divine ambition puffed
Makes mouths˙ at the invisible event,˙
Exposing what is mortal and unsure
To all that fortune, death, and danger dare,
Even for an eggshell. Rightly to be great
4.4.55 Is not to stir without great argument,
But greatly to find quarrel in a straw
When honor's at the stake.˙ How stand I, then,
That have a father killed, a mother stained,
Excitements of˙ my reason and my blood,
4.4.60 And let all sleep, while to my shame I see
The imminent death of twenty thousand men
That for a fantasy˙ and trick˙ of fame
Go to their graves like beds, fight for a plot˙
Whereon the numbers cannot try the cause,˙
4.4.65 Which is not tomb enough and continent˙
To hide the slain? O, from this time forth
My thoughts be bloody or be nothing worth!
[*Exit.*]

ACT 4, SCENE 5

[*The castle. Enter* HORATIO, QUEEN GERTRUDE, *and a* GENTLEMAN.]
4.5.1 QUEEN I will not speak with her.
GENTLEMAN   She is importunate,
Indeed distract.˙ Her mood will needs be pitied.
QUEEN What would she have?
GENTLEMAN She speaks much of her father, says she hears
4.5.5 There's tricks i' the world, and hems,˙ and beats her heart,˙
Spurns enviously at straws,˙ speaks things in doubt˙
That carry but half sense. Her speech is nothing,
Yet the unshapèd use˙ of it doth move
The hearers to collection;˙ they yawn˙ at it,
4.5.10 And botch˙ the words up fit to their own thoughts,
Which, as her winks and nods and gestures yield˙ them,
Indeed would make one think there might be thought,˙
Though nothing sure, yet much unhappily.˙
HORATIO 'Twere good she were spoken with, for she may strew
4.5.15 Dangerous conjectures in ill-breeding˙ minds.
QUEEN Let her come in.

Makes mouths ·
makes scornful faces

invisible event ·
unforeseeable outcome

Rightly … stake ·
true greatness does
not normally consist of
rushing into action over
some trivial provocation;
however, when one's
honor is involved, even
a trifling insult requires
that one respond greatly

at the stake · a metaphor from gambling or
bear-baiting

Excitements of ·
promptings by

fantasy · fanciful
caprice, illusion

trick · trifle, deceit

plot · plot of ground

Whereon…cause ·
on which there is insuffi-
cient room for the soldiers
needed to engage in a
military contest

continent · receptacle

distract · distracted

hems · makes "hmm"
sounds

heart · breast

Spurns … straws ·
kicks spitefully, takes
offense at trifles

in doubt · obscurely

unshapèd use ·
incoherent manner

collection · inference,
a guess at some sort of
meaning

yawn · gape, wonder;
grasp

botch · patch

yield · deliver, represent

thought · intended

unhappily · unpleasantly
near the truth, shrewdly

ill-breeding · prone
to suspect the worst
and to make mischief

[*Exit* GENTLEMAN. *The* QUEEN, *aside.*]

    To my sick soul, as sin's true nature is,

    Each toy• seems prologue to some great amiss.•

    So full of artless jealousy is guilt,

    It spills itself in fearing to be spilt.•   4.5.20

[*Enter* OPHELIA,• *distracted.*]

OPHELIA Where is the beauteous majesty of Denmark?

QUEEN How now, Ophelia?

[OPHELIA *sings.*]

OPHELIA "How should I your true love know

      From another one?

    By his cockle hat• and staff,   4.5.25

      And his sandal shoon."•

QUEEN Alas, sweet lady, what imports this song?

OPHELIA Say you? Nay, pray you, mark.

[*Singing.*]

      "He is dead and gone, lady,

        He is dead and gone;   4.5.30

      At his head a grass-green turf,

        At his heels a stone."

    O, ho!

QUEEN Nay, but Ophelia –

OPHELIA Pray you, mark.   4.5.35

[*Singing.*]

      "White his shroud as the mountain snow"–

[*Enter* KING.]

QUEEN Alas, look here, my lord.

[OPHELIA, *singing.*]

OPHELIA "Larded• with sweet flowers;

      Which bewept to the ground did not go

      With true-love showers."•   4.5.40

KING How do you, pretty lady?

OPHELIA Well, God 'ild• you! They say the owl• was a baker's daughter. Lord, we know what we are, but know not what we may be. God be at your table!

KING Conceit• upon her father.   4.5.45

OPHELIA Pray let's have no words of this; but when they ask you what it means, say you this:

[*Singing.*]

Margin glosses:

toy · trifle

amiss · calamity

So … spilt · guilt is so full of suspicion that it unskillfully betrays itself in fearing betrayal

Enter Ophelia · in the First Quarto, Ophelia enters, "playing on a lute, and her hair down, singing"

cockle hat · hat with cockleshell stuck in it as a sign that the wearer had been a pilgrim to the shrine of Saint James of Compostella in Spain

shoon · shoes

Larded · decorated

showers · tears

God 'ild · God yield or reward

owl · refers to a legend about a baker's daughter who was turned into an owl for being ungenerous when Jesus begged a loaf of bread

Conceit · brooding

"Tomorrow is Saint Valentine's day,
4.5.50   All in the morning betime,˙   **betime** · early
And I a maid at your window,
        To be your Valentine.
Then up he rose, and donned his clothes,
        And dupped˙ the chamber door,   **dupped** · did up,
4.5.55   Let in the maid, that out a maid   opened
        Never departed more."

KING Pretty Ophelia –

OPHELIA Indeed, la, without an oath, I'll make an end on 't:
[*Singing.*]
        "By Gis˙ and by Saint Charity,   **Gis** · Jesus
4.5.60   Alack, and fie for shame!
Young men will do 't, if they come to 't;
        By Cock,˙ they are to blame.   **Cock** · a perversion of
Quoth she, 'Before you tumbled me,   "God" in oaths; here also
        You promised me to wed.'"   with a quibble on the
                                                                        slang word for penis
4.5.65   He answers:
[*Singing.*]
        "'So would I ha' done, by yonder sun,
        An˙ thou hadst not come to my bed.'"   **An** · if

KING How long hath she been thus?

OPHELIA I hope all will be well. We must be patient, but I
4.5.70   cannot choose but weep to think they would lay him i' the
cold ground. My brother shall know of it. And so I thank you
for your good counsel. Come, my coach! Good night, ladies,
good night, sweet ladies, good night, good night.
[*Exit. The* **KING,** *to* **HORATIO**.]

KING Follow her close. Give her good watch, I pray you.
[*Exit* **HORATIO**.]
4.5.75   O, this is the poison of deep grief; it springs
All from her father's death – and now behold!
O Gertrude, Gertrude,
When sorrows come, they come not single spies,˙   **spies** · scouts sent in
But in battalions. First, her father slain;   advance of the main force
4.5.80   Next, your son gone, and he most violent author   **remove** · removal
Of his own just remove;˙ the people muddied,˙
Thick and unwholesome in their thoughts and whispers   **muddied** · stirred up,
For good Polonius' death – and we have done but greenly,˙   confused

hugger-mugger · secret haste

as much containing · as full of serious matter

feeds ... clouds · feeds his resentment or shocked grievance, holds himself inscrutable and aloof amid all this rumor

wants · lacks

buzzers · gossipers, informers

necessity · the need to invent some plausible explanation

of matter beggared · unprovided with facts

Will nothing ... ear · will not hesitate to accuse my (royal) person in everybody's ears

murdering piece · cannon loaded so as to scatter its shot

Gives ... death · kills me over and over

Attend · guard me

Switzers · Swiss guards, mercenaries

overpeering of his list · overflowing its shore, boundary

flats · flatlands near shore

impetuous · violent (perhaps also with the meaning of "impiteous" ["impitious," Q2], "pitiless")

head · insurrection

as · as if

The ratifiers ... word · antiquity (or tradition) and custom ought to confirm ("ratify") and underprop our every word or promise

Caps · the caps are thrown in the air

counter · a hunting term meaning to follow the trail in a direction opposite to that which the game has taken

In hugger-mugger* to inter him; poor Ophelia
Divided from herself and her fair judgment,   4.5.85
Without the which we are pictures or mere beasts.,
Last, and as much containing* as all these,
Her brother is in secret come from France,
Feeds on this wonder, keeps himself in clouds,*
And wants* not buzzers* to infect his ear   4.5.90
With pestilent speeches of his father's death,
Wherein necessity,* of matter beggared,*
Will nothing stick our person to arraign
In ear and ear.* O my dear Gertrude, this,
Like to a murdering piece,* in many places   4.5.95
Gives me superfluous death.*
[*A noise within.*]
QUEEN Alack, what noise is this?
KING Attend!*
Where is my Switzers?* Let them guard the door.
[*Enter a* MESSENGER.]
What is the matter?   4.5.100
MESSENGER   Save yourself, my lord!
The ocean, overpeering of his list,*
Eats not the flats* with more impetuous* haste
Than young Laertes, in a riotous head,*
O'erbears your officers. The rabble call him lord,
And, as* the world were now but to begin,   4.5.105
Antiquity forgot, custom not known,
The ratifiers and props of every word,*
They cry, "Choose we! Laertes shall be king!"
Caps,* hands, and tongues applaud it to the clouds,
"Laertes shall be king, Laertes king!"   4.5.110
QUEEN How cheerfully on the false trail they cry!
[*A noise within.*]
O, this is counter,* you false Danish dogs!
[*Enter* LAERTES *with others.*]
KING The doors are broke.
LAERTES Where is this King? – Sirs, stand you all without.
ALL No, let's come in.   4.5.115
LAERTES I pray you, give me leave.
ALL We will, we will.

LAERTES I thank you. Keep the door.

[*Exeunt followers.*]

O thou vile king,

Give me my father!

[*The* QUEEN, *restraining him.*]

QUEEN Calmly, good Laertes.

LAERTES That drop of blood that's calm proclaims me bastard,

Cries cuckold to my father, brands the harlot

Even here, between• the chaste unsmirchèd brow

Of my true mother.

KING What is the cause, Laertes,

That thy rebellion looks so giantlike?

Let him go, Gertrude. Do not fear our• person.

There's such divinity doth hedge• a king

That treason can but peep to what it would,•

Acts little of his will.• Tell me, Laertes,

Why thou art thus incensed. Let him go, Gertrude.

Speak, man.

LAERTES Where is my father?

KING Dead.

QUEEN But not by him.

KING Let him demand his fill.

LAERTES How came he dead? I'll not be juggled with.•

To hell, allegiance! Vows, to the blackest devil!

Conscience and grace, to the profoundest pit!

I dare damnation. To this point I stand,•

That both the worlds I give to negligence,•

Let come what comes, only I'll be revenged

Most throughly• for my father.

KING Who shall stay you?

LAERTES My will, not all the world's.•

And for• my means, I'll husband them so well

They shall go far with little.

KING Good Laertes,

If you desire to know the certainty

Of your dear father, is 't writ in your revenge

That, swoopstake,• you will draw both friend and foe,

Winner and loser?

LAERTES None but his enemies.

between · in the middle of

fear our · fear for my

hedge · protect, as with a surrounding barrier

can ... would · can only peep furtively, as through a barrier, at what it would intend

Acts ... will · (but) performs little of what it intends

juggled with · cheated, deceived

To ... stand · I am resolved in this

both ... negligence · both this world and the next are of no consequence to me

throughly · thoroughly

My will ... world's · I'll stop ("stay") when my will is accomplished, not for anyone else's

for · as for

swoopstake · indiscriminately (literally, taking all stakes on the gambling table at once. "Draw" is also a gambling term, meaning "take from")

KING Will you know them, then?

LAERTES To his good friends thus wide I'll open my arms,
    And like the kind life-rendering pelican·   4.5.150
    Repast· them with my blood.

KING   Why, now you speak
    Like a good child and a true gentleman.
    That I am guiltless of your father's death,
    And am most sensibly· in grief for it,
    It shall as level· to your judgment 'pear   4.5.155
    As day does to your eye.
    A noise within.

LAERTES How now, what noise is that?
    [Enter OPHELIA.]

KING   Let her come in.

LAERTES O heat, dry up my brains! Tears seven times salt
    Burn out the sense and virtue· of mine eye!   4.5.160
    By heaven, thy madness shall be paid with weight·
    Till our scale turn the beam.· O rose of May!
    Dear maid, kind sister, sweet Ophelia!
    O heavens, is 't possible a young maid's wits
    Should be as mortal as an old man's life?   4.5.165
    Nature is fine in· love, and where 'tis fine
    It sends some precious instance· of itself
    After the thing it loves.·
    [OPHELIA, singing.]

OPHELIA "They bore him barefaced on the bier,
          Hey non nonny, nonny, hey nonny,   4.5.170
            And in his grave rained many a tear –"
    Fare you well, my dove!

LAERTES Hadst thou thy wits and didst persuade· revenge,
    It could not move thus.

OPHELIA You must sing "A-down a-down," and "call him a-down-   4.5.175
    a."· O, how the wheel· becomes it! It is the false steward· that
    stole his master's daughter.

LAERTES This nothing's more than matter.·

OPHELIA There's rosemary,· that's for remembrance; pray you,
    love, remember. And there is pansies;· that's for thoughts.   4.5.180

LAERTES A document· in madness, thoughts and remembrance
    fitted.

Glossary (margin notes):

pelican · refers to the belief that the female pelican fed its young with its own blood

Repast · feed

sensibly · feelingly

level · plain

virtue · faculty, power

paid with weight · repaid, avenged equally or more

beam · crossbar of a balance

fine in · refined by

instance · token

After … loves · into the grave, along with Polonius

persuade · argue cogently for

You must sing "A-down … a-down-a" · Ophelia assigns the singing of refrains, like her own "Hey non nonny," to others present

wheel · spinning wheel as accompaniment to the song, or refrain

false steward · the story is unknown

This … matter · this seeming nonsense is more eloquent than sane utterance

rosemary · used as a symbol of remembrance both at weddings and at funerals

pansies · emblems of love and courtship; perhaps from French *pensées*, "thoughts"

document · instruction, lesson

OPHELIA There's fennel• for you, and columbines.• There's rue•
for you, and here's some for me; we may call it herb of grace o'
4.5.185 Sundays. You must wear your rue with a difference.• There's
a daisy.• I would give you some violets,• but they withered all
when my father died. They say 'a made a good end –
[*Singing.*]
"For bonny sweet Robin is all my joy."

LAERTES Thought• and affliction, passion,• hell itself,
4.5.190 She turns to favor• and to prettiness.
[**OPHELIA**, *singing.*]

OPHELIA "And will 'a not come again?
And will 'a not come again?
No, no, he is dead.
Go to thy deathbed,
4.5.195 He never will come again.

"His beard was as white as snow,
All flaxen was his poll.•
He is gone, he is gone,
And we cast away moan.
4.5.200 God ha' mercy on his soul!"
And of all Christian souls, I pray God. God b' wi' you.
[*Exit, followed by* **QUEEN GERTRUDE**.]

LAERTES Do you see this, O God?

KING Laertes, I must commune with your grief,
Or you deny me right. Go but apart,
4.5.205 Make choice of whom• your wisest friends you will,
And they shall hear and judge twixt you and me.
If by direct or by collateral hand•
They find us touched,• we will our kingdom give,
Our crown, our life, and all that we call ours
4.5.210 To you in satisfaction; but if not,
Be you content to lend your patience to us,
And we shall jointly labor with your soul
To give it due content.

LAERTES   Let this be so.
His means of death, his obscure funeral –
4.5.215 No trophy,• sword, nor hatchment• o'er his bones,
No noble rite, nor formal ostentation•–

---

fennel • emblem of flattery

columbines • emblems of unchastity or ingratitude

rue • emblem of repentance – a signification that is evident in its popular name, "herb of grace"

with a difference • a device used in heraldry to distinguish one family from another on the coat of arms, here suggesting that Ophelia and the others have different causes of sorrow and repentance; perhaps with a play on rue in the sense of "ruth," "pity"

daisy • emblem of dissembling, faithlessness

violets • emblems of faithfulness

Thought • melancholy

passion • suffering

favor • grace, beauty

poll • head

whom • whichever of

collateral hand • indirect agency

us touched • me implicated

trophy • memorial

hatchment • tablet displaying the armorial bearings of a deceased person

ostentation • ceremony

Cry to be heard, as 'twere from heaven to earth

That · so that

That· I must call 't in question.·

call 't in question · demand an explanation

KING   So you shall,

And where th' offense is, let the great ax fall.

I pray you, go with me.   4.5.220

[*Exeunt.*]

ACT 4, SCENE 6

[*The castle. Enter* **HORATIO** *and others.*]

HORATIO What are they that would speak with me?   4.6.1

GENTLEMAN Seafaring men, sir. They say they have
letters for you.

HORATIO Let them come in.

[*Exit* **GENTLEMAN**.]

I do not know from what part of the world   4.6.5

I should be greeted, if not from Lord Hamlet.

[*Enter* **SAILORS**.]

FIRST SAILOR God bless you, Sir.

HORATIO Let him bless thee too.

an't · if it

FIRST SAILOR 'A shall, Sir, an 't· please him. There's a letter for

th' ambassador · evidently Hamlet. The sailor is being circumspect

you, sir – it came from th' ambassador· that was bound for   4.6.10
England – if your name be Horatio, as I am let to know it is.

[*He gives a letter.* **HORATIO** *reads.*]

overlooked · looked over

HORATIO "Horatio, when thou shalt have overlooked· this, give

means · means of access

these fellows some means· to the King; they have letters for
him. Ere we were two days old at sea, a pirate of very war-

appointment · equipage

like appointment· gave us chase. Finding ourselves too slow   4.6.15
of sail, we put on a compelled valor, and in the grapple I
boarded them. On the instant they got clear of our ship, so
I alone became their prisoner. They have dealt with me like

thieves of mercy · merciful thieves

thieves of mercy,· but they knew what they did: I am to do a
good turn for them. Let the King have the letters I have sent,   4.6.20

repair · come

and repair· thou to me with as much speed as thou wouldest
fly death. I have words to speak in thine ear will make thee
dumb, yet are they much too light for the bore· of the matter.

bore · caliber, importance

These good fellows will bring thee where I am. Rosencrantz
and Guildenstern hold their course for England. Of them I   4.6.25
have much to tell thee. Farewell.

He that thou knowest thine, Hamlet."

Come, I will give you way° for these your letters,
And do 't the speedier that you may direct me
4.6.30   To him from whom you brought them.
[*Exeunt.*]

ACT 4, SCENE 7

[*The castle. Enter* KING *and* LAERTES.]

4.7.1   KING Now must your conscience my acquittance seal,°
And you must put me in your heart for friend,
Sith° you have heard, and with a knowing ear,
That he which hath your noble father slain
4.7.5   Pursued my life.
LAERTES   It well appears. But tell me
Why you proceeded not against these feats°
So crimeful and so capital° in nature,
As by your safety, greatness, wisdom, all things else,
You mainly° were stirred up.
4.7.10   KING O, for two special reasons,
Which may to you perhaps seem much unsinewed.°
But yet to me they're strong. The Queen his mother
Lives almost by his looks, and for myself —
My virtue or my plague, be it either which —
4.7.15   She is so conjunctive° to my life and soul
That, as the star moves not but in his° sphere,°
I could not but by her. The other motive
Why to a public count° I might not go
Is the great love the general gender° bear him,
4.7.20   Who, dipping all his faults in their affection,
Work° like the spring° that turneth wood to stone,
Convert his gyves° to graces, so that my arrows,
Too slightly timbered° for so loud° a wind,
Would have reverted° to my bow again
4.7.25   But not where I had aimed them.
LAERTES And so have I a noble father lost,
A sister driven into desperate terms,°
Whose worth, if praises may go back° again,
Stood challenger on mount° of all the age
4.7.30   For her perfections. But my revenge will come.
KING Break not your sleeps for that. You must not think

---

way · means of access

my acquittance seal · confirm or acknowledge my innocence

Sith · since

feats · acts

capital · punishable by death

mainly · greatly

unsinewed · weak

conjunctive · closely united (an astronomical metaphor)

his · its

sphere · one of the hollow spheres in which, according to Ptolemaic astronomy, the planets were supposed to move

count · account, reckoning indictment

general gender · common people

Work · operate, act

spring · a spring with such a concentration of lime that it coats a piece of wood with limestone, in effect gilding and petrifying it

gyves · fetters (which, gilded by the people's praise, would look like badges of honor)

slightly timbered · light

loud · suggesting public outcry on Hamlet's behalf

reverted · returned

terms · state, condition

go back · recall what she was

on mount · set up on high

That we are made of stuff so flat and dull
That we can let our beard be shook with danger
And think it pastime. You shortly shall hear more.
I loved your father, and we love ourself;
And that, I hope, will teach you to imagine –

4.7.35

[*Enter a* MESSENGER *with letters.*]

How now? What news?

MESSENGER   Letters, my lord, from Hamlet:
This to Your Majesty, this to the Queen.

[*He gives letters.*]

KING From Hamlet? Who brought them?

MESSENGER Sailors, my lord, they say. I saw them not.
They were given me by Claudio. He received them
Of him that brought them.

4.7.40

KING   Laertes, you shall hear them. –
Leave us.

[*Exit* MESSENGER. *He reads.*]

"High and mighty, you shall know I am set naked• on your
kingdom. Tomorrow shall I beg leave to see your kingly eyes,
when I shall, first asking your pardon,• thereunto recount the
occasion of my sudden and more strange return.

4.7.45

Hamlet."

What should this mean? Are all the rest come back?
Or is it some abuse,• and no such thing?•

4.7.50

LAERTES Know you the hand?

KING   'Tis Hamlet's character.• "Naked!"
And in a postscript here he says "alone."
Can you devise• me?

LAERTES I am lost in it, my lord. But let him come.
It warms the very sickness in my heart
That I shall live and tell him to his teeth,
"Thus didst thou."•

4.7.55

KING   If it be so, Laertes –
As how should it be so? How otherwise?•–
Will you be ruled by me?

LAERTES   Ay, my lord,
So• you will not o'errule me to a peace.

KING To thine own peace. If he be now returned,
As checking at• his voyage, and that• he means

4.7.60

naked · destitute, unarmed, without following
pardon · permission

abuse · deceit
no such thing · not what it appears
character · handwriting
devise · explain to
Thus didst thou · here's for what you did to my father
As ... otherwise · how can this (Hamlet's return) be true? Yet how otherwise than true (since we have the evidence of his letter)?
So · provided that
checking at · turning aside from (like a falcon leaving the quarry to fly at a chance bird)
that · if

No more to undertake it, I will work him
To an exploit, now ripe in my device,°

4.7.65 Under the which he shall not choose but fall;
And for his death no wind of blame shall breathe,
But even his mother shall uncharge the practice°
And call it accident.

LAERTES   My lord, I will be ruled,
The rather if you could devise it so

4.7.70 That I might be the organ.°

KING   It falls right.
You have been talked of since your travel much,
And that in Hamlet's hearing, for a quality
Wherein they say you shine. Your sum of parts°
Did not together pluck such envy from him

4.7.75 As did that one, and that, in my regard,
Of the unworthiest siege.°

LAERTES What part is that, my lord?

KING A very ribbon in the cap of youth,
Yet needful too, for youth no less becomes°

4.7.80 The light and careless livery that it wears
Than settled age his sables° and his weeds°
Importing health and graveness.° Two months since
Here was a gentleman of Normandy.
I have seen myself, and served against, the French,

4.7.85 And they can well° on horseback, but this gallant
Had witchcraft in 't; he grew unto his seat,
And to such wondrous doing brought his horse
As had he been incorpsed and demi-natured°
With the brave beast. So far he topped° my thought

4.7.90 That I in forgery° of shapes and tricks
Come short of what he did.

LAERTES   A Norman was 't?

KING A Norman.

LAERTES Upon my life, Lamord.

KING   The very same.

LAERTES I know him well. He is the brooch° indeed

4.7.95 And gem of all the nation.

KING He made confession° of you,
And gave you such a masterly report

device · devising, invention

uncharge the practice · acquit the stratagem of being a plot

organ · agent, instrument

Your … parts · all your other virtues

unworthiest siege · least important rank

no less becomes · is no less suited by

his sables · its rich robes furred with sable

weeds · garments

Importing … graveness · signifying a concern for health and dignified prosperity; also, giving an impression of comfortable prosperity

can well · are skilled

As … demi-natured · as if he had been of one body and nearly of one nature (like the centaur)

topped · surpassed

forgery · imagining

brooch · ornament

confession · testimonial, admission of superiority

For ... defense · with respect to your skill and practice with your weapon

escrimers · fencers

sudden · immediate

play · fence

begun by time · created by the right circumstance and hence subject to change

passages of proof · actual instances that prove it

qualifies · weakens, moderates

snuff · the charred part of a candlewick

nothing ... still · nothing remains at a constant level of perfection

pleurisy · excess, plethora (literally, a chest inflammation)

in ... much · of its own excess

As ... accidents · as there are tongues to dissuade, hands to prevent, and chance events to intervene

spendthrift sigh · an allusion to the belief that sighs draw blood from the heart

hurts by easing · costs the heart blood and wastes precious opportunity even while it affords emotional relief

quick o' th' ulcer · heart of the matter

sanctuarize · protect from punishment. (alludes to the right of sanctuary with which certain religious places were invested)

Will you do this · if you wish to do this

put on those · shall arrange for some to

For art and exercise in your defense,˙
And for your rapier most especial,
That he cried out 'twould be a sight indeed   4.7.100
If one could match you. Th' escrimers˙ of their nation,
He swore, had neither motion, guard, nor eye
If you opposed them. Sir, this report of his
Did Hamlet so envenom with his envy
That he could nothing do but wish and beg   4.7.105
Your sudden˙ coming o'er, to play˙ with you.
Now, out of this—

LAERTES   What out of this, my lord?

KING Laertes, was your father dear to you?
Or are you like the painting of a sorrow,
A face without a heart?   4.7.110

LAERTES   Why ask you this?

KING Not that I think you did not love your father,
But that I know love is begun by time,˙
And that I see, in passages of proof,˙
Time qualifies˙ the spark and fire of it.
There lives within the very flame of love   4.7.115
A kind of wick or snuff˙ that will abate it,
And nothing is at a like goodness still,˙
For goodness, growing to a pleurisy,˙
Dies in his own too much.˙ That we would do,
We should do when we would; for this "would" changes   4.7.120
And hath abatements and delays as many
As there are tongues, are hands, are accidents,˙
And then this "should" is like a spendthrift sigh,˙
That hurts by easing.˙ But, to the quick o' th' ulcer:˙
Hamlet comes back. What would you undertake   4.7.125
To show yourself in deed your father's son
More than in words?

LAERTES   To cut his throat i' the church.

KING No place, indeed, should murder sanctuarize;˙
Revenge should have no bounds. But good Laertes
Will you do this,˙ keep close within your chamber.   4.7.130
Hamlet returned shall know you are come home.
We'll put on those˙ shall praise your excellence
And set a double varnish on the fame

The Frenchman gave you, bring you in fine* together,

4.7.135 And wager on your heads. He, being remiss,*

Most generous,* and free from all contriving,

Will not peruse the foils, so that with ease,

Or with a little shuffling, you may choose

A sword unbated,* and in a pass of practice*

4.7.140 Requite him for your father.

LAERTES   I will do 't,

And for that purpose I'll anoint my sword.

I bought an unction* of a mountebank*

So mortal that, but dip a knife in it,

Where it draws blood no cataplasm* so rare,

4.7.145 Collected from all simples* that have virtue*

Under the moon,* can save the thing from death

That is but scratched withal. I'll touch my point

With this contagion, that if I gall* him slightly,

It may be death.

KING   Let's further think of this,

4.7.150 Weigh what convenience both of time and means

May fit us to our shape.* If this should fail,

And that our drift look through our bad performance,*

'Twere better not assayed. Therefore this project

Should have a back or second, that might hold

4.7.155 If this did blast in proof.* Soft, let me see.

We'll make a solemn wager on your cunnings*—

I ha 't!

When in your motion you are hot and dry—

As* make your bouts more violent to that end—

4.7.160 And that he calls for drink, I'll have prepared him

A chalice for the nonce,* whereon but sipping,

If he by chance escape your venomed stuck,*

Our purpose may hold there.

[*A cry within.*]

                              But stay, what noise?

[*Enter* QUEEN.]

QUEEN One woe doth tread upon another's heel.

4.7.165 So fast they follow. Your sister's drowned, Laertes.

LAERTES Drowned! O, where?

QUEEN There is a willow grows askant* the brook,

---

in fine · finally

remiss · negligently unsuspicious

generous · noble-minded

unbated · not blunted, having no button

pass of practice · treacherous thrust

unction · ointment

mountebank · quack doctor

cataplasm · plaster or poultice

simples · herbs

virtue · potency

Under the moon · anywhere (with reference perhaps to the belief that herbs gathered at night had a special power)

gall · graze, wound

shape · part we propose to act

drift ... performance · intention should be made visible by our bungling

blast in proof · burst in the test (like a cannon)

cunnings · respective skills

As · and you should

nonce · occasion

stuck · thrust (from *stoccado*, a fencing term)

askant · aslant

That shows his hoar leaves• in the glassy stream; —
Therewith fantastic garlands did she make
Of crowflowers, nettles, daisies, and long purples,•   4.7.170
That liberal• shepherds give a grosser name,•
But our cold• maids do dead men's fingers call them.
There on the pendent• boughs her crownet• weeds
Clamb'ring to hang, an envious sliver• broke,
When down her weedy• trophies and herself   4.7.175
Fell in the weeping brook. Her clothes spread wide,
And mermaidlike awhile they bore her up,
Which time she chanted snatches of old lauds,•
As one incapable of• her own distress,
Or like a creature native and endued•   4.7.180
Unto that element. But long it could not be
Till that her garments, heavy with their drink,
Pulled the poor wretch from her melodious lay
To muddy death.

LAERTES   Alas, then she is drowned?

QUEEN Drowned, drowned.   4.7.185

LAERTES Too much of water hast thou, poor Ophelia,
And therefore I forbid my tears. But yet
It is our trick;• nature her custom holds,
Let shame say what it will.

[*He weeps.*]
                              When these are gone,
The woman will be out.• Adieu, my lord.   4.7.190
I have a speech of fire that fain would blaze,
But that this folly douts• it.

[*Exit.*]

KING   Let's follow, Gertrude.
How much I had to do to calm his rage!
Now fear I this will give it start again;
Therefore let's follow.   4.7.195

[*Exeunt.*]

ACT 5, SCENE 1

[*A churchyard. Enter* TWO CLOWNS• *with spades and mattocks.*]

FIRST CLOWN Is she to be buried in Christian burial, when she   5.1.1
willfully seeks her own salvation?•

---

hoar leaves · white or gray undersides of the leaves

long purples · early purple orchids

liberal · free-spoken

a grosser name · the testicle-resembling tubers of the orchid, which also in some cases resemble dead men's fingers, have earned various slang names like "dogstones" and "cullions"

cold · chaste

pendent · overhanging

crownet · made into a chaplet or coronet

envious sliver · malicious branch

weedy · of plants

lauds · hymns

incapable of · lacking capacity to apprehend

endued · adapted by nature

It is our trick · weeping is our natural way (when sad)

When ... out · when my tears are all shed, the woman in me will be expended, satisfied

douts · extinguishes (the Second Quarto reads "drowns")

Clowns · rustics

salvation · a blunder for "damnation," or perhaps a suggestion that Ophelia was taking her own shortcut to heaven

SECOND CLOWN I tell thee she is; therefore make her grave straight.°
The crowner° hath sat on her,° and finds it Christian burial.

5.1.5 **FIRST CLOWN** How can that be, unless she drowned herself in
her own defense?

SECOND CLOWN Why, 'tis found so.°

FIRST CLOWN It must be *se offendendo*,° it cannot be else. For
here lies the point: if I drown myself wittingly, it argues an
5.1.10 act, and an act hath three branches – it is to act, to do, and to
perform. Argal,° she drowned herself wittingly.

SECOND CLOWN Nay, but hear you, goodman° delver –

FIRST CLOWN Give me leave. Here lies the water, good. Here
stands the man; good. If the man go to this water and drown
5.1.15 himself, it is, will he, nill he,° he goes, mark you that. But if the
water come to him and drown him, he drowns not himself. Argal,
he that is not guilty of his own death shortens not his own life.

SECOND CLOWN But is this law?

FIRST CLOWN Ay, marry, is 't – crowner's quest° law.

5.1.20 **SECOND CLOWN** Will you ha' the truth on 't? If this had not
been a gentlewoman, she should have been buried out o'
Christian burial.

FIRST CLOWN Why, there thou sayst.° And the more pity that
great folk should have countenance° in this world to drown or
5.1.25 hang themselves, more than their even-Christian.° Come, my
spade. There is no ancient° gentlemen but gardeners, ditchers,
and grave makers. They hold up° Adam's profession.

SECOND CLOWN Was he a gentleman?

FIRST CLOWN 'A was the first that ever bore arms.°

5.1.30 **SECOND CLOWN** Why, he had none.

FIRST CLOWN What, art a heathen? How dost thou understand
the Scripture? The Scripture says Adam digged. Could he
dig without arms?° I'll put another question to thee. If thou
answerest me not to the purpose, confess thyself°–

5.1.35 **SECOND CLOWN** Go to.

FIRST CLOWN What is he that builds stronger than either the
mason, the shipwright, or the carpenter?

SECOND CLOWN The gallows maker, for that frame° outlives a
thousand tenants.

5.1.40 **FIRST CLOWN** I like thy wit well, in good faith. The gallows
does well. But how does it well? It does well° to those that

---

straight · straightway,
immediately (but
with a pun on strait,
"narrow")

crowner · coroner

sat on her · conducted
an inquest on her case

finds it gives his official
verdict that her means of
death was consistent with

found so · determined
so in the coroner's verdict

se offendendo · a comic
mistake for *se defendendo*,
a term used in verdicts of
justifiable homicide

Argal · corruption of
ergo, "therefore" (Latin)

goodman · an honor-
ific title often used with
the name of a profession
or craft

will he, nill he ·
whether he will or no,
willy-nilly

quest · inquest

there thou sayst ·
that's right

countenance · privilege

even-Christian ·
fellow Christians

ancient · going back
to ancient times

hold up · maintain

bore arms · to be
entitled to bear a coat of
arms would make Adam
a gentleman, but as one
who bore a spade, our
common ancestor was
an ordinary delver in
the earth

arms · the arms of
the body

confess thyself · the
saying continues "and
be hanged"

frame · 1 · gallows;
2 · structure

does well · 1 · is an
apt answer; 2 · does a
good turn

do ill. Now thou dost ill to say the gallows is built stronger than the church. Argal, the gallows may do well to thee. To 't again, come.

SECOND CLOWN "Who builds stronger than a mason, a ship- 5.1.45 wright, or a carpenter?"

FIRST CLOWN Ay, tell me that, and unyoke.•

SECOND CLOWN Marry, now I can tell.

FIRST CLOWN To 't.

SECOND CLOWN Mass,• I cannot tell. 5.1.50

[*Enter* HAMLET *and* HORATIO *at a distance.*]

FIRST CLOWN Cudgel thy brains no more about it, for your dull ass will not mend his pace with beating; and when you are asked this question next, say "a grave maker." The houses he makes lasts till doomsday. Go get thee in and fetch me a stoup• of liquor. 5.1.55

[*Exit* SECOND CLOWN. FIRST CLOWN *digs, singing.*]
     "In youth, when I did love, did love,•
          Methought it was very sweet,
     To contract – O – the time for – a – my behove,•
          O, methought there – a – was nothing – a – meet."•

HAMLET Has this fellow no feeling of his business, 'a• sings in 5.1.60 grave-making?

HORATIO Custom hath made it in him a property of easiness.•

HAMLET 'Tis e'en so. The hand of little employment hath the daintier sense.•

[**FIRST CLOWN**, *singing.*]

FIRST CLOWN "But age with his stealing steps 5.1.65
          Hath clawed me in his clutch,
     And hath shipped me into the land,•
          As if I had never been such."

[*He throws up a skull.*]

HAMLET That skull had a tongue in it and could sing once. How the knave jowls• it to the ground, as if 'twere Cain's jawbone, 5.1.70 that did the first murder! This might be the pate of a politician,• which this ass now o'erreaches,• one that would circumvent God, might it not?

HORATIO It might, my lord.

HAMLET Or of a courtier, which could say, "Good morrow, sweet 5.1.75 lord! How dost thou, sweet lord?" This might be my Lord

---

unyoke · after this great effort, you may unharness the team of your wits

Mass · by the Mass

stoup · two-quart measure

In . . . love · this and the two following stanzas, with nonsensical variations, are from a poem attributed to Lord Vaux and printed in Tottel's *Miscellany*, 1557. The "O" and "a" (for "ah") seemingly are the grunts of the digger

To contract . . . behove · to shorten the time for my own advantage (perhaps he means to prolong it)

meet · suitable, more suitable

'a · that he

property of easiness · something he can do easily and indifferently

daintier sense · more delicate sense of feeling

into the land · toward my grave (?) (but note the lack of rhyme in steps, land)

jowls · dashes (with a pun on jowl, "jawbone")

politician · schemer, plotter

o'erreaches · circumvents, gets the better of (with a quibble on the literal sense)

Such-a-one, that praised my Lord Such-a-one's horse when
'a meant to beg it, might it not?

HORATIO Ay, my lord.

5.1.80 **HAMLET** Why, e'en so, and now my Lady Worm's, chapless,· and
knocked about the mazard· with a sexton's spade. Here's fine
revolution,· an· we had the trick· to see 't. Did these bones
cost no more the breeding, but· to play at loggets· with them?
Mine ache to think on 't.

[**FIRST CLOWN**, *singing*.]

5.1.85 **FIRST CLOWN** "A pickax and a spade, a spade,
For and· a shrouding sheet,
O, a pit of clay for to be made
For such a guest is meet."

[*He throws up another skull*.]

HAMLET There's another. Why may not that be the skull of
5.1.90 a lawyer? Where be his quiddities· now, his quillities,· his
cases, his tenures,· and his tricks? Why does he suffer this
mad knave now to knock him about the sconce· with a dirty
shovel, and will not tell him of his action of battery?· Hum,
this fellow might be in 's time a great buyer of land, with his
5.1.95 statutes, his recognizances,· his fines, his double vouchers,·
his recoveries.· Is this the fine· of his fines and the recovery
of his recoveries, to have his fine pate· full of fine dirt? Will
his vouchers vouch him no more of his purchases, and double
ones too, than the length and breadth of a pair of indentures?·
5.1.100 The very conveyances· of his lands will scarcely lie in this box,·
and must th' inheritor· himself have no more, ha?

HORATIO Not a jot more, my lord.

HAMLET Is not parchment made of sheepskins?

HORATIO Ay, my lord, and of calves' skins too.

5.1.105 **HAMLET** They are sheep and calves which seek out assurance in
that.· I will speak to this fellow. – Whose grave's this, sirrah?·

FIRST CLOWN Mine, sir.

[*Sings*.]

"O, pit of clay for to be made
For such a guest is meet."

5.1.110 **HAMLET** I think it be thine, indeed, for thou liest in 't.

FIRST CLOWN You lie out on 't, Sir, and therefore 'tis not yours.
For my part, I do not lie in 't, yet it is mine.

---

chapless · having no
lower jaw

mazard · head (liter-
ally, a drinking vessel)

revolution · turn of
Fortune's wheel, change

an · if

trick · knack

cost ... but · involve so
little expense and care in
upbringing that we may

loggets · game involving pieces of hard wood
shaped bowling pins

For and · and moreover

quiddities · quibbles
(from Latin *quid*, "a thing")

quillities · verbal nice-
ties, subtle distinctions

tenures · the holding
of a piece of property
or office

sconce · head

action of battery ·
lawsuit about physical
assault

**statutes, recogni-
zances** · legal documents
guaranteeing a debt

fines ... recoveries ·
ways of converting
entailed estates into
"fee simple" or freehold

double vouchers ·
guarantees of the legality
of a title to real estate
signed by two signatories

fine · end

fine pate · elegant head

pair of indentures ·
legal document drawn
up on a single sheet
and then cut apart on a
zigzag line like teeth

conveyances · deeds

box · 1 · deed box; 2 · coffin

inheritor · owner

assurance in that ·
safety in legal parchments

sirrah · a form of
address to inferiors

HAMLET Thou dost lie in 't, to be in 't and say it is thine. 'Tis for the dead, not for the quick;* therefore thou liest.

FIRST CLOWN 'Tis a quick lie, sir; 'twill away again from me to you. 5.1.115

HAMLET What man dost thou dig it for?

FIRST CLOWN For no man, sir.

HAMLET What woman, then?

FIRST CLOWN For none, neither.

HAMLET Who is to be buried in 't? 5.1.120

FIRST CLOWN One that was a woman, sir, but, rest her soul, she's dead.

HAMLET How absolute* the knave is! We must speak by the card,* or equivocation* will undo us. By the Lord, Horatio, this three years I have took* note of it: the age is grown so picked* that 5.1.125 the toe of the peasant comes so near the heel of the courtier, he galls his kibe.*– How long hast thou been grave maker?

FIRST CLOWN Of all the days i' the year, I came to 't that day that our last king Hamlet overcame Fortinbras.

HAMLET How long is that since? 5.1.130

FIRST CLOWN Cannot you tell that? Every fool can tell that. It was that very day that young Hamlet was born – he that is mad and sent into England.

HAMLET Ay, marry, why was he sent into England?

FIRST CLOWN Why, because 'a was mad. 'A shall recover his wits 5.1.135 there, or if 'a do not, 'tis no great matter there.

HAMLET Why?

FIRST CLOWN 'Twill not be seen in him there. There the men are as mad as he.

HAMLET How came he mad? 5.1.140

FIRST CLOWN Very strangely, they say.

HAMLET How strangely?

FIRST CLOWN Faith, e'en with losing his wits.

HAMLET Upon what ground?*

FIRST CLOWN Why, here in Denmark. I have been sexton here, 5.1.145 man and boy, thirty years.

HAMLET How long will a man lie i' th' earth ere he rot?

FIRST CLOWN Faith, if 'a be not rotten before 'a die – as we have many pocky* corpses nowadays, that will scarce hold the laying in*– 'a will last you* some eight year or nine year. 5.1.150 A tanner will last you nine year.

Glossary (left margin):

absolute · strict, precise

by the card · with precision (literally, by the mariner's compass-card, on which the points of the compass were marked)

equivocation · ambiguity in the use of terms

took · taken

picked · refined fastidious

galls his kibe · chafes the courtier's chilblain

ground · cause (but, in the next line, the gravedigger takes the word in the sense of "land," "country")

pocky · rotten, diseased (literally, with the "pox," or syphilis)

hold the laying in · hold together long enough to be interred

last you · last (you is used colloquially here and in the following lines)

HAMLET Why he more than another?

FIRST CLOWN Why, sir, his hide is so tanned with his trade that 'a will keep out water a great while, and your water is a sore° decayer of your whoreson° dead body.

sore · terrible, great

whoreson · vile, scurvy

5.1.155

[*He picks up a skull.*]

Here's a skull now hath lien you° i' th' earth three-and-twenty years.

lien you · lain (see the note at line 147)

HAMLET Whose was it?

FIRST CLOWN A whoreson mad fellow's it was. Whose do you think it was?

5.1.160

HAMLET Nay, I know not.

FIRST CLOWN A pestilence on him for a mad rogue! 'A poured a flagon of Rhenish° on my head once. This same skull, Sir, was, Sir, Yorick's skull, the King's jester.

Rhenish · Rhine wine

5.1.165

HAMLET This?

FIRST CLOWN E'en that.

HAMLET Let me see.

[*He takes the skull.*]

Alas, poor Yorick! I knew him, Horatio, a fellow of infinite jest, of most excellent fancy. He hath bore° me on his back a thousand times, and now how abhorred in my imagination it is! My gorge rises° at it. Here hung those lips that I have kissed I know not how oft. Where be your gibes now? Your gambols, your songs, your flashes of merriment that were wont° to set the table on a roar? Not one now, to mock your own grinning?° Quite chopfallen?° Now get you to my lady's chamber and tell her, let her paint an inch thick, to this favor° she must come. Make her laugh at that. Prithee, Horatio, tell me one thing.

bore · borne

My gorge rises · I feel nauseated

were wont · used

mock your own grinning · mock at the way your skull seems to be grinning (just as you used to mock at yourself and those who grinned at you)

5.1.170

5.1.175

HORATIO What's that, my lord?

5.1.180

HAMLET Dost thou think Alexander looked o' this fashion i' th' earth?

chopfallen · 1 · lacking the lower jaw; 2 · dejected

favor · aspect, appearance

HORATIO E'en so.

HAMLET And smelt so? Pah!

[*He throws down the skull.*]

HORATIO E'en so, my lord.

5.1.185

HAMLET To what base uses we may return, Horatio! Why may not imagination trace the noble dust of Alexander till 'a find it stopping a bunghole?°

bunghole · hole for filling or emptying a cask

HORATIO 'Twere to consider too curiously* to consider so.

HAMLET No, faith, not a jot, but to follow him thither with mod-
esty* enough, and likelihood to lead it. As thus: Alexander died, 5.1.190
Alexander was buried, Alexander returneth to dust, the dust is
earth, of earth we make loam,* and why of that loam whereto
he was converted might they not stop a beer barrel?
Imperious* Cæsar, dead and turned to clay,
Might stop a hole to keep the wind away. 5.1.195
O, that that earth which kept the world in awe
Should patch a wall t' expel the winter's flaw!*

[*Enter* KING, QUEEN, LAERTES, *and the corpse of* OPHELIA, *in procession, with* PRIEST, LORDS, *etc.*]

But soft,* but soft awhile! Here comes the King,
The Queen, the courtiers. Who is this they follow?
And with such maimèd* rites? This doth betoken 5.1.200
The corpse they follow did with desperate hand
Fordo* its own life. 'Twas of some estate.*
Couch we* awhile and mark.

[HAMLET *and* HORATIO *conceal themselves.* OPHELIA*'s body is taken
to the grave.*]

LAERTES What ceremony else?

[HAMLET, *to* HORATIO.]

HAMLET That is Laertes, a very noble youth. Mark. 5.1.205

LAERTES What ceremony else?

PRIEST Her obsequies have been as far enlarged
As we have warranty.* Her death was doubtful,
And but that great command o'ersways the order*
She should in ground unsanctified been lodged* 5.1.210
Till the last trumpet. For* charitable prayers,
Shards,* flints, and pebbles should be thrown on her.
Yet here she is allowed her virgin crants,*
Her maiden strewments,* and the bringing home
Of bell and burial.* 5.1.215

LAERTES Must there no more be done?

PRIEST   No more be done.
We should profane the service of the dead
To sing a requiem and such rest* to her
As to peace-parted souls.*

LAERTES   Lay her i' th' earth,

Marginal glosses:

curiously · minutely

modesty · plausible moderation

loam · mortar consisting chiefly of moistened clay and straw

Imperious · imperial

flaw · gust of wind

soft · wait, be careful

maimèd · mutilated, incomplete

Fordo · destroy

estate · rank

Couch we · let's hide, lie low

warranty · ecclesiastical authority

great . . . order · orders from on high overrule the prescribed procedures

She should . . . lodged · she should have been buried in unsanctified ground

For · in place of

Shards · broken bits of pottery

crants · garlands betokening maidenhood

strewments · flowers strewn on a coffin

bringing . . . burial · laying the body to rest to the sound of the bell

such rest · to pray for such rest

peace-parted souls · those who have died at peace with God

5.1.220
And from her fair and unpolluted flesh
May violets˙ spring! I tell thee, churlish priest,
A ministering angel shall my sister be
When thou liest howling.˙

[HAMLET, *to* HORATIO.]

HAMLET   What, the fair Ophelia!

[*The* QUEEN, *scattering flowers.*]

QUEEN Sweets to the sweet! Farewell.

5.1.225
I hoped thou shouldst have been my Hamlet's wife.
I thought thy bride-bed to have decked, sweet maid,
And not t' have strewed thy grave.

LAERTES   O, treble woe
Fall ten times treble on that cursèd head
Whose wicked deed thy most ingenious sense˙

5.1.230
Deprived thee of! Hold off the earth awhile,
Till I have caught her once more in mine arms.

[*He leaps into the grave and embraces* OPHELIA.]

Now pile your dust upon the quick and dead,
Till of this flat a mountain you have made

5.1.235
T' o'ertop old Pelion or the skyish head
Of blue Olympus.˙

[HAMLET, *coming forward.*]

HAMLET   What is he whose grief
Bears such an emphasis,˙ whose phrase of sorrow
Conjures the wandering stars˙ and makes them stand
Like wonder-wounded˙ hearers? This is I,

5.1.240
Hamlet the Dane.˙

[LAERTES, *grappling with him.*˙]

LAERTES   The devil take thy soul!

HAMLET Thou pray'st not well.
I prithee, take thy fingers from my throat,
For though I am not splenitive˙ and rash,
Yet have I in me something dangerous,

5.1.245
Which let thy wisdom fear. Hold off thy hand.

KING Pluck them asunder.

QUEEN Hamlet, Hamlet!

ALL Gentlemen!

HORATIO Good my lord, be quiet.

[HAMLET *and* LAERTES *are parted.*]

violets · see 4.5.186 and note

howling · in hell

ingenious sense · a mind that is quick, alert, of fine qualities

Pelion ... Olympus · sacred mountains in the north of Thessaly; see also Ossa, below, at line 286

emphasis · rhetorical and florid emphasis ("phrase" has a similar rhetorical connotation)

wandering stars · planets

wonder-wounded · struck with amazement

the Dane · this title normally signifies the King; see 1.1.17 and note

grappling with him · the testimony of the First Quarto that "Hamlet leaps in after Laertes" and the "Elegy on Burbage" ("Oft have I seen him leap into the grave") seem to indicate one way in which this fight was staged; however, the difficulty of fitting two contenders and Ophelia's body into a confined space (probably the trapdoor) suggests to many editors the alternative – that Laertes jumps out of the grave to attack Hamlet

splenitive · quick-tempered

wag · move (a fluttering eyelid is a conventional sign of life)

forbear him · leave him alone

'Swounds · by His (Christ's) wounds

Woo't · wilt thou

eisel · vinegar

crocodile · crocodiles were tough and dangerous, and were supposed to shed hypocritical tears

quick · alive

his pate · its head, top

burning zone · zone in the celestial sphere containing the sun's orbit, between the tropics of Cancer and Capricorn

Ossa · another mountain in Thessaly. In their war against the Olympian gods, the giants attempted to heap Ossa on Pelion to scale Olympus

an · if

mouth · rant

mere · utter

golden couplets · two baby pigeons, covered with yellow down

disclosed · hatched

Let … day · 1 · even Hercules couldn't stop Laertes' theatrical rant; 2 · I, too, will have my turn; despite any blustering attempts at interference, every person will sooner or later do what he or she must do

in · by recalling

present push · immediate test

living · lasting (for Laertes' private understanding, Claudius also hints that Hamlet's death will serve as such a monument)

hour of quiet · time free of conflict

HAMLET Why, I will fight with him upon this theme 5.1.250
    Until my eyelids will no longer wag.˙
QUEEN O my son, what theme?
HAMLET I loved Ophelia. Forty thousand brothers
    Could not with all their quantity of love
    Make up my sum. What wilt thou do for her? 5.1.255
KING O, he is mad, Laertes.
QUEEN For love of God, forbear him.˙
HAMLET 'Swounds,˙ show me what thou'lt do.
    Woo't˙ weep? Woo't fight? Woo't fast? Woo't tear thyself?
    Woo't drink up eisel?˙ Eat a crocodile?˙ 5.1.260
    I'll do 't. Dost come here to whine?
    To outface me with leaping in her grave?
    Be buried quick˙ with her, and so will I.
    And if thou prate of mountains, let them throw
    Millions of acres on us, till our ground, 5.1.265
    Singeing his pate˙ against the burning zone,˙
    Make Ossa˙ like a wart! Nay, an˙ thou'lt mouth,˙
    I'll rant as well as thou.
QUEEN   This is mere˙ madness,
    And thus awhile the fit will work on him;
    Anon, as patient as the female dove 5.1.270
    When that her golden couplets˙ are disclosed,˙
    His silence will sit drooping.
HAMLET   Hear you, sir.
    What is the reason that you use me thus?
    I loved you ever. But it is no matter.
    Let Hercules himself do what he may, 5.1.275
    The cat will mew, and dog will have his day.˙
    [*Exit* HAMLET.]
KING I pray thee, good Horatio, wait upon him.
    [*Exit* HORATIO. *To* LAERTES.]
    Strengthen your patience in˙ our last night's speech;
    We'll put the matter to the present push.˙–
    Good Gertrude, set some watch over your son. – 5.1.280
    This grave shall have a living˙ monument.
    An hour of quiet˙ shortly shall we see;
    Till then, in patience our proceeding be.
    [*Exeunt.*]

ACT 5, SCENE 2

[*The castle. Enter* HAMLET *and* HORATIO.]

HAMLET So much for this, sir, now shall you see the other.°
5.2.1

You do remember all the circumstance?

HORATIO Remember it, my lord!

HAMLET Sir, in my heart there was a kind of fighting

5.2.5 That would not let me sleep. Methought I lay

Worse than the mutines° in the bilboes.° Rashly,°

And praised be rashness for it — let us know°

Our indiscretion° sometimes serves us well

When our deep plots do pall,° and that should learn° us

5.2.10 There's a divinity that shapes our ends,

Rough-hew° them how we will —

HORATIO   That is most certain.

HAMLET Up from my cabin,

My sea-gown° scarfed° about me, in the dark

Groped I to find out them,° had my desire,

5.2.15 Fingered° their packet, and in fine° withdrew

To mine own room again, making so bold,

My fears forgetting manners, to unseal

Their grand commission; where I found, Horatio —

Ah, royal knavery! — an exact command,

5.2.20 Larded° with many several° sorts of reasons

Importing° Denmark's health and England's too,

With, ho! such bugs° and goblins in my life,°

That on the supervise,° no leisure bated,°

No, not to stay° the grinding of the ax,

5.2.25 My head should be struck off.

HORATIO   Is 't possible?

[HAMLET, *giving Horatio a document.*]

HAMLET Here's the commission. Read it at more leisure.

But wilt thou hear now how I did proceed?

HORATIO I beseech you.

HAMLET Being thus benetted round with villainies —

5.2.30 Ere I could make a prologue to my brains,

They had begun the play° — I sat me down,

Devised a new commission, Wrote it fair.°

I once did hold it, as our statists° do,

A baseness° to write fair, and labored much

---

see the other · hear the other news

mutines · mutineers

bilboes · shackles

Rashly · on impulse (this adverb goes with lines 12 ff)

know · acknowledge

indiscretion · lack of foresight and judgment (not an indiscreet act)

pall · fail, falter, go stale

learn · teach

Rough-hew · shape roughly

sea-gown · seaman's coat

scarfed · loosely wrapped

them · Rosencrantz and Guildenstern

Fingered · pilfered, pinched

in fine · finally, in conclusion

Larded · garnished

several · different

Importing · relating to

bugs · bugbears, hobgoblins

in my life · to be feared if I were allowed to live

supervise · reading

leisure bated · delay allowed

stay · await

Ere ... play · before I could consciously turn my brain to the matter, it had started working on a plan

fair · in a clear hand

statists · statesmen

baseness · lower-class trait

How to forget that learning, but, sir, now 5.2.35
It did me yeoman's° service. Wilt thou know
Th' effect° of what I wrote?

HORATIO   Ay, good my lord.

HAMLET An earnest conjuration° from the King,
As England was his faithful tributary,
As love between them like the palm° might flourish, 5.2.40
As peace should still° her wheaten garland° wear
And stand a comma° 'tween their amities,
And many suchlike "as"es° of great charge,°
That on the view and knowing of these contents,
Without debatement further more or less, 5.2.45
He should those bearers put to sudden death,
Not shriving time° allowed.

HORATIO   How was this sealed?

HAMLET Why, even in that was heaven ordinant.°
I had my father's signet° in my purse,
Which was the model of that Danish seal; 5.2.50
Folded the writ° up in the form of th' other,
Subscribed° it, gave 't th' impression,° placed it safely,
The changeling° never known. Now, the next day
Was our sea fight, and what to this was sequent°
Thou knowest already. 5.2.55

HORATIO So Guildenstern and Rosencrantz go to 't.

HAMLET Why, man, they did make love to this employment.
They are not near my conscience. Their defeat°
Does by their own insinuation° grow.
'Tis dangerous when the baser nature comes 5.2.60
Between the pass° and fell° incensèd points
Of mighty opposites.°

HORATIO   Why, what a king is this!

HAMLET Does it not, think thee, stand me now upon°—
He that hath killed my king and whored my mother,
Popped in between th' election° and my hopes, 5.2.65
Thrown out his angle° for my proper° life,
And with such cozenage°—is 't not perfect conscience
To quit° him with this arm? And is 't not to be damned
To let this canker° of our nature come
In° further evil? 5.2.70

---

yeoman's · substantial, faithful, loyal

effect · purport

conjuration · entreaty

palm · an image of health; see Psalm 92:12

still · always

wheaten garland · symbolic of peace and plenty

comma · indicating continuity, link

"as"es · 1 · the "whereases" of a formal document; 2 · asses

charge · 1 · import; 2 · burden (appropriate to asses)

shriving time · time for confession and absolution

ordinant · directing

signet · small seal

writ · writing

Subscribed · signed (with forged signature)

impression · with a wax seal

changeling · substituted letter

was sequent · followed

defeat · destruction

insinuation · intrusive intervention, sticking their noses in my business

pass · thrust

fell · fierce

opposites · antagonists

stand me now upon · become incumbent on me now

election · the Danish monarch was "elected" by a small number of high-ranking electors

angle · fishhook

proper · very

cozenage · trickery

quit · requite, pay back

canker · ulcer

come In · grow into

5.2.71   **HORATIO** It must be shortly known to him from England
      What is the issue of the business there.

  HAMLET It will be short. The interim is mine,
      And a man's life's no more than to say "one."*

5.2.75   But I am very sorry, good Horatio,
      That to Laertes I forgot myself,
      For by the image of my cause I see
      The portraiture of his. I'll court his favors.
      But, sure, the bravery* of his grief did put me

5.2.80   Into a tow'ring passion.

  HORATIO   Peace, who comes here?

  [*Enter a Courtier,* **OSRIC**.]

  OSRIC Your lordship is right welcome back to Denmark.

  HAMLET I humbly thank you, sir.

  [*To* **HORATIO**.]

              Dost know this water fly?

  HORATIO No, my good lord.

  HAMLET Thy state is the more gracious, for 'tis a vice to know
5.2.85   him. He hath much land, and fertile. Let a beast be lord of
      beasts, and his crib* shall stand at the King's mess.* 'Tis a
      chuff,* but, as I say, spacious in the possession of dirt.

  OSRIC Sweet lord, if your lordship were at leisure, I should
      impart a thing to you from His Majesty.

5.2.90   **HAMLET** I will receive it, sir, with all diligence of spirit. Put your
      bonnet* to his* right use; 'tis for the head.

  OSRIC I thank your lordship, it is very hot.

  HAMLET No, believe me, 'tis very cold. The wind is northerly.

  OSRIC It is indifferent* cold, my lord, indeed.

5.2.95   **HAMLET** But yet methinks it is very sultry and hot for my
      complexion.*

  OSRIC Exceedingly, my lord. It is very sultry, as 'twere – I cannot
      tell how. My lord, His Majesty bade me signify to you that 'a
      has laid a great wager on your head. Sir, this is the matter –

5.2.100   **HAMLET** I beseech you, remember.

  [**HAMLET** *moves him to put on his hat.*]

  OSRIC Nay, good my lord; for my ease,* in good faith. Sir, here is
      newly come to court Laertes – believe me, an absolute* gentle-
      man, full of most excellent differences,* of very soft society*
      and great showing.* Indeed, to speak feelingly* of him, he is

---

a man's ... "one" · one's whole life occupies such a short time, only as long as it takes to count to 1

bravery · bravado

Let a beast ... mess · if a man, no matter how beastlike, is as rich in livestock and possessions as Osric, he may eat at the King's table

crib · manger

chuff · boor, churl. The Second Quarto spelling, "chough," is a variant spelling that also suggests the meaning here of "chattering jackdaw"

bonnet · any kind of cap or hat

his · its

indifferent · somewhat

complexion · temperament

for my ease · a conventional reply declining the invitation to put his hat back on

absolute · perfect

differences · special qualities

soft society · agreeable manners

great showing · distinguished appearance

feelingly · with just perception

the card or calendar of gentry, for you shall find in him the   5.2.105
continent of what part a gentleman would see.

HAMLET Sir, his definement suffers no perdition in you, though
I know to divide him inventorially would dozy th' arithmetic
of memory, and yet but yaw neither in respect of his quick
sail. But, in the verity of extolment, I take him to be a soul of   5.2.110
great article, and his infusion of such dearth and rareness as,
to make true diction of him, his semblable is his mirror and
who else would trace him his umbrage, nothing more.

OSRIC Your lordship speaks most infallibly of him.

HAMLET The concernancy, sir? Why do we wrap the gentleman   5.2.115
in our more rawer breath?

OSRIC Sir?

HORATIO Is 't not possible to understand in another tongue?
You will do 't, sir, really.

HAMLET What imports the nomination of this gentleman?   5.2.120

OSRIC Of Laertes?

[**HORATIO**, *to* **HAMLET**.]

HORATIO His purse is empty already; all 's golden words are spent.

HAMLET Of him, Sir.

OSRIC I know you are not ignorant –

HAMLET I would you did, Sir. Yet in faith if you did, it would not   5.2.125
much approve me. Well, Sir?

OSRIC You are not ignorant of what excellence Laertes, is –

HAMLET I dare not confess that, lest I should compare with him
in excellence. But to know a man well were to know himself.

OSRIC I mean, sir, for his weapon; but in the imputation laid   5.2.130
on him by them, in his meed he's unfellowed.

HAMLET What's his weapon?

OSRIC Rapier and dagger.

HAMLET That's two of his weapons – but well.

OSRIC The King, sir, hath wagered with him six Barbary horses,   5.2.135
against the which he has impawned, as I take it, six French
rapiers and poniards, with their assigns, as girdle, hangers,
and so. Three of the carriages, in faith, are very dear to fancy,
very responsive to the hilts, most delicate carriages, and of
very liberal conceit.   5.2.140

HAMLET What call you the carriages?

[**HORATIO**, *to* **HAMLET**.]

Glossary (margin):

card · chart, map
calendar · guide
gentry · good breeding
continent · qualities
definement · definition. Hamlet proceeds to mock Osric by throwing his lofty diction back at him
perdition · diminution
divide … inventorially · enumerate his graces
dozy · dizzy
yaw · swing unsteadily off course (said of a ship)
neither · for all that
in … extolment · in true praise (of him)
of great article · one with a large inventory
infusion · essence
semblable · likeness
umbrage · shadow
concernancy · import
rawer breath · unrefined speech
to understand … tongue · Horatio twits Osric for not understanding the kind of flowery speech he himself uses
You will do 't · you can if you try
nomination · naming
But … himself · To know another person well, one must know oneself
imputation · reputation
meed · merit
unfellowed · unmatched
but well · never mind
impawned · wagered
poniards · daggers
assigns · appurtenances
hangers · straps on which the sword hung
carriages · an affected way of saying "hangers"
responsive · matching
liberal conceit · elaborate design

HORATIO I knew you must be edified by the margent° ere you
had done.

OSRIC The carriages, sir, are the hangers.

5.2.145 **HAMLET** The phrase would be more germane to the matter
if we could carry a cannon by our sides; I would it might
be hangers till then. But, on: six Barbary horses against six
French swords, their assigns, and three liberal-conceited carriages; that's the French bet against the Danish. Why is this
5.2.150 impawned, as you call it?

OSRIC The King, sir, hath laid,° sir, that in a dozen passes°
between yourself and him, he shall not exceed you three hits.
He hath laid on twelve for nine, and it would come to immediate trial, if your lordship would vouchsafe the answer.°

5.2.155 **HAMLET** How if I answer no?

OSRIC I mean, my lord, the opposition of your person in trial.

HAMLET Sir, I will walk here in the hall. If it please His Majesty, it
is the breathing time° of day with me. Let the foils be brought,
the gentleman willing, and the King hold his purpose, I will
5.2.160 win for him an I can; if not, I will gain nothing but my shame
and the odd hits.

OSRIC Shall I deliver you° so?

HAMLET To this effect, sir – after what flourish your nature will.

OSRIC I commend° my duty to your lordship.

5.2.165 **HAMLET** Yours, yours.

[*Exit* OSRIC.]

'A does well to commend it himself, there are no tongues else
for 's turn.°

HORATIO This lapwing° runs away with the shell on his head.

HAMLET 'A did comply with his dug° before 'a sucked it. Thus has
5.2.170 he – and many more of the same breed that I know the drossy°
age dotes on – only got the tune° of the time and, out of an habit
of encounter,° a kind of yeasty° collection,° which carries them
through and through the most fanned and winnowed opinions;°
and do but blow them to their trial, the bubbles are out.°

[*Enter a* LORD.]

5.2.175 **LORD** My lord, His Majesty commended him to you by young
Osric, who brings back to him that you attend him in the hall.
He sends to know if your pleasure hold to play with Laertes,
or that° you will take longer time.

---

margent · margin, place for explanatory notes

laid · wagered

passes · bouts. The details of the bet are hard to decipher

vouchsafe the answer · be so good as to accept the challenge. Hamlet deliberately takes the phrase in its literal sense of replying

breathing time · exercise period

deliver you · report what you say

commend · commit to your favor (a conventional salutation, but Hamlet wryly uses a more literal meaning –"recommend," "praise" – in line 166)

for 's turn · for his purposes, to do it for him

lapwing · youthful forwardness; also, a bird thought to run about with its head in the shell when newly hatched (a seeming reference to Osric's hat)

comply … dug · observe ceremonious formality toward his nurse's or mother's teat

drossy · laden with impurities, frivolous

tune · temper, mood

an habit of encounter · a demeanor in courtly conversation

yeasty · frothy

collection · collection of current phrases

carries … opinions · sustains them through the scrutiny of those with refined opinions like grain separated from its chaff

blow … out · merely blow on them and their bubbles burst

that · if

HAMLET I am constant to my purposes; they follow the King's
pleasure. If his fitness speaks, mine is ready,* now or when- 5.2.180
soever, provided I be so able as now.

LORD The King and Queen and all are coming down.

HAMLET In happy time.*

LORD The Queen desires you to use some gentle entertainment*
to Laertes before you fall to play. 5.2.185

HAMLET She well instructs me.

[*Exit* LORD.]

HORATIO You will lose, my lord.

HAMLET I do not think so. Since he went into France, I have
been in continual practice; I shall win at the odds. But thou
wouldst not think how ill all's here about my heart; but it is 5.2.190
no matter.

HORATIO Nay, good my lord –

HAMLET It is but foolery, but it is such a kind of gaingiving* as
would perhaps trouble a woman.

HORATIO If your mind dislike anything, obey it. I will 5.2.195
forestall their repair* hither and say you are not fit.

HAMLET Not a whit, we defy augury. There is special providence
in the fall of a sparrow. If it be now, 'tis not to come; if it be
not to come, it will be now; if it be not now; yet it will come.
The readiness is all. Since no man of aught he leaves knows, 5.2.200
what is 't to leave betimes? Let be.*

[*A table prepared. Enter trumpets, drums, and* OFFICERS *with cushions;*
KING, QUEEN, OSRIC *and all the state; foils, daggers, and wine borne
in; and enter* LAERTES.]

KING Come, Hamlet, come and take this hand from me.

[*The* KING *puts* LAERTES' *hand into* HAMLET'S. HAMLET, *to* LAERTES.]

HAMLET Give me your pardon, sir. I have done you wrong,
But pardon 't as you are a gentleman.
This presence* knows, 5.2.205
And you must needs have heard, how I am punished*
With a sore distraction. What I have done
That might your nature, honor, and exception*
Roughly awake, I here proclaim was madness.
Was 't Hamlet wronged Laertes? Never Hamlet. 5.2.210
If Hamlet from himself be ta'en away,
And when he's not himself does wrong Laertes,

Marginal glosses:

If ... ready · if he declares his readiness, my convenience waits on his

In happy time · a phrase of courtesy indicating that the time is convenient

entertainment · greeting

gaingiving · misgiving

repair · coming

Since ... Let be · since no one has knowledge of what he is leaving behind, what does an early death matter after all? Enough; don't struggle against it

presence · royal assembly

punished · afflicted

exception · disapproval

Then Hamlet does it not, Hamlet denies it.
Who does it, then? His madness. If 't be so,
Hamlet is of the faction° that is wronged;

faction · party

5.2.215

His madness is poor Hamlet's enemy.
Sir, in this audience
Let my disclaiming from a purposed evil
Free me so far in your most generous thoughts
That I have° shot my arrow o'er the house

That I have · as if I had

5.2.220

And hurt my brother.

LAERTES   I am satisfied in nature,°
Whose motive° in this case should stir me most
To my revenge. But in my terms of honor
I stand aloof, and will no reconcilement
Till by some elder masters of known honor
I have a voice° and precedent of peace°
To keep my name ungored.° But till that time
I do receive your offered love like love,
And will not wrong it.

in nature · as to my personal feelings

motive · prompting

5.2.225

voice · authoritative pronouncement

of peace · for reconciliation

name ungored · reputation unwounded

HAMLET   I embrace it freely,
And will this brother's wager frankly° play. –
Give us the foils. Come on.

LAERTES   Come, one for me.

HAMLET I'll be your foil,° Laertes. In mine ignorance
Your skill shall, like a star i' the darkest night,
Stick fiery off° indeed.

frankly · without ill feeling or the burden of rancor

foil · thin metal background which sets a jewel off (with pun on the blunted rapier for fencing)

stick fiery off · stand out brilliantly

5.2.230

LAERTES   You mock me, sir.

5.2.235 HAMLET No, by this hand.

KING Give them the foils, young Osric. Cousin Hamlet,
You know the wager?

HAMLET   Very well, my lord.
Your Grace has laid the odds o'° the weaker side.

laid the odds o' · bet on, backed

KING I do not fear it; I have seen you both.
But since he is bettered,° we have therefore odds.

is bettered · has improved, is the odds-on favorite. Laertes' handicap is the "three hits" specified in line 153

5.2.240

LAERTES This is too heavy. Let me see another.

[He exchanges his foil for another.]

HAMLET This likes me° well. These foils have all a length?

likes me · pleases me

[They prepare to play.]

OSRIC Ay, my good lord.

KING Set me the stoups of wine upon that table.

If Hamlet give the first or second hit,   5.2.245

Or ... exchange · or requites Laertes in the third bout for having won the first two

Or quit in answer of the third exchange,*
Let all the battlements their ordnance fire.
The King shall drink to Hamlet's better breath,*

better breath · improved vigor

And in the cup an union* shall he throw
Richer than that which four successive kings   5.2.250

union · pearl, so called, according to Pliny's Natural History 9, because pearls are unique, never identical

In Denmark's crown have worn. Give me the cups,
And let the kettle* to the trumpet speak,
The trumpet to the cannoneer without,

kettle · kettledrum

The cannons to the heavens, the heaven to earth,
"Now the King drinks to Hamlet." Come, begin.   5.2.255
[*Trumpets the while.*]
And you, the judges, bear a wary eye.

HAMLET Come on, sir.

LAERTES Come, my lord.
[*They play.* **HAMLET** *scores a hit.*]

HAMLET One.

LAERTES No.   5.2.260

HAMLET Judgment.

OSRIC   A hit, a very palpable hit.
[*Drum, trumpets, and shot. Flourish. A piece goes off.*]

LAERTES Well, again.

KING Stay, give me drink. Hamlet, this pearl is thine.
[*He drinks, and throws a pearl in* **HAMLET**'s *cup.*]
Here's to thy health. Give him the cup.

HAMLET I'll play this bout first. Set it by awhile.   5.2.265
Come.
[*They play.*]
Another hit; what say you?

LAERTES A touch, a touch, I do confess 't.

KING Our son shall win.

fat · not physically fit, out of training

QUEEN   He's fat* and scant of breath.
Here, Hamlet, take my napkin,* rub thy brows.   5.2.270

napkin · handkerchief

carouses · drinks a toast

The Queen carouses* to thy fortune, Hamlet.

HAMLET Good madam!

KING Gertrude, do not drink.

QUEEN I will, my lord, I pray you pardon me.
[*She drinks; the* **KING**, *aside.*]

KING It is the poisoned cup. It is too late.   5.2.275

.2.276 HAMLET I dare not drink yet, madam; by and by.

QUEEN Come, let me wipe thy face.

[LAERTES, *to the* KING.]

LAERTES My lord, I'll hit him now.

KING   I do not think 't.

[LAERTES, *aside.*]

LAERTES And yet it is almost against my conscience.

HAMLET Come, for the third, Laertes. You do but dally.

.2.280 I pray you, pass° with your best violence;   **pass** · thrust

I am afeard you make a wanton of me.°   **make … me** · treat
                                                                      me like a spoiled child,
LAERTES Say you so? Come on.   trifle with me

[*They play.*]

OSRIC Nothing neither way.

LAERTES Have at you now!

[LAERTES *wounds* HAMLET, *then, in scuffling, they change rapiers,*° *and*   **in scuffling … rapi-**
HAMLET *wounds* LAERTES.]   **ers** · This stage direction
                                                                                occurs in the Folio.
KING   Part them! They are incensed.   According to a wide-
                                                                                spread stage tradition,
.2.285 HAMLET Nay, come, again.   Hamlet receives a scratch,
                                                                                realizes that Laertes'
[*The* QUEEN *falls.*]   sword is unblunted, and
                                                                                accordingly forces an
OSRIC   Look to the Queen there, ho!   exchange

HORATIO They bleed on both sides. How is it, my lord?

OSRIC How is 't, Laertes?

LAERTES Why, as a woodcock° to mine own springe,° Osric;   **woodcock** · a bird, a
                                                                      type of stupidity, or as
I am justly killed with mine own treachery.   a decoy

.2.290 HAMLET How does the Queen?   **springe** · trap, snare

KING   She swoons to see them bleed.

QUEEN No, no, the drink, the drink – O my dear Hamlet –

The drink, the drink! I am poisoned.

[*She dies.*]

HAMLET O villainy! Ho, let the door be locked!

Treachery! Seek it out.

[LAERTES *falls. Exit* OSRIC.]

.2.295 LAERTES It is here, Hamlet. Hamlet, thou art slain.

No med'cine in the world can do thee good;

In thee there is not half an hour's life.

The treacherous instrument is in thy hand,

Unbated° and envenomed. The foul practice°   **Unbated** · not blunted
                                                                      with a button
.2.300 Hath turned itself on me. Lo, here I lie,

Never to rise again. Thy mother's poisoned.   **practice** · plot

I can no more. The King, the King's to blame.

HAMLET The point envenomed too? Then, venom, to thy work.

[*He stabs the* **KING**.]

ALL Treason! Treason!

KING O, yet defend me, friends! I am but hurt.   5.2.30�|

[**HAMLET**, *forcing the* **KING** *to drink*.]

HAMLET Here, thou incestuous, murderous, damnèd Dane,

union · pearl (see line 270), with grim puns on the word's other meanings: marriage, shared death

Drink off this potion. Is thy union* here?

Follow my mother.

[*The* **KING** *dies*.]

LAERTES   He is justly served.

tempered · mixed

It is a poison tempered* by himself.

Exchange forgiveness with me, noble Hamlet.   5.2.31⁰

Mine and my father's death come not upon thee,

Nor thine on me!

[*He dies*.]

HAMLET Heaven make thee free of it! I follow thee.

I am dead, Horatio. Wretched Queen, adieu!

chance · mischance

You that look pale and tremble at this chance,*   5.2.31⁵

mutes · silent observers (literally, actors with nonspeaking parts)

That are but mutes* or audience to this act,

Had I but time — as this fell* sergeant,* Death,

fell · cruel

Is strict* in his arrest* — O, I could tell you —

sergeant · sheriff's officer

But let it be. Horatio, I am dead;

strict · 1 · severely just; 2 · unavoidable

Thou livest. Report me and my cause aright   5.2.32⁰

To the unsatisfied.

arrest · 1 · taking into custody; 2 · stopping my speech

HORATIO   Never believe it.

I am more an antique Roman* than a Dane.

antique Roman · suicide was considered an honorable choice for many Romans as an alternative to a dishonorable life

Here's yet some liquor left.

[*He attempts to drink from the poisoned cup.* **HAMLET** *prevents him*.]

HAMLET   As thou'rt a man,

Give me the cup! Let go! By heaven, I'll ha 't.

O God, Horatio, what a wounded name,   5.2.32⁵

Things standing thus unknown, shall I leave behind me!

If thou didst ever hold me in thy heart,

Absent thee from felicity awhile,

And in this harsh world draw thy breath in pain

To tell my story.   5.2.33⁰

[*A march afar off and a volley within*.]

                What warlike noise is this?

[*Enter* OSRIC.]

OSRIC Young Fortinbras, with conquest come from Poland,
  To th' ambassadors of England gives
  This warlike volley.

HAMLET   O, I die, Horatio!
  The potent poison quite o'ercrows° my spirit.

5.2.335 I cannot live to hear the news from England,
  But I do prophesy th' election lights
  On Fortinbras. He has my dying voice.°
  So tell him, with th' occurrents° more and less
  Which have solicited°– the rest is silence.

  [*He dies.*]

5.2.340 HORATIO Now cracks a noble heart. Good night, sweet prince,
  And flights of angels sing thee to thy rest!

  [*March within.*]

  Why does the drum come hither?

  [*Enter* FORTINBRAS, *with the* ENGLISH AMBASSADORS *with drum,*
  colors, and ATTENDANTS.]

FORTINBRAS Where is this sight?

HORATIO   What is it you would see?
  If aught of woe or wonder, cease your search.

5.2.345 FORTINBRAS This quarry° cries on havoc.° O proud Death,
  What feast° is toward° in thine eternal cell,
  That thou so many princes at a shot
  So bloodily hast struck?

FIRST AMBASSADOR   The sight is dismal,
  And our affairs from England come too late.

5.2.350 The ears are senseless that should give us hearing,
  To tell him his commandment is fulfilled,
  That Rosencrantz and Guildenstern are dead.
  Where should we have our thanks?

HORATIO   Not from his° mouth,
  Had it th' ability of life to thank you.

5.2.355 He never gave commandment for their death.
  But since, so jump° upon this bloody question,°
  You from the Polack wars, and you from England,
  Are here arrived, give order that these bodies
  High on a stage° be placèd to the view,

5.2.360 And let me speak to th' yet unknowing world

---

o'ercrows · triumphs over, like the winner in a cockfight

voice · vote

occurrents · events, incidents

solicited · moved, urged. Hamlet doesn't finish saying what the events have prompted – presumably, his acts of vengeance, or his reporting of those events to Fortinbras

quarry · heap of dead

cries on havoc · proclaims a general slaughter

feast · Death feasting on those who have fallen

toward · in preparation

his · Claudius'

jump · precisely, immediately

question · dispute, affair

stage · platform

How these things came about. So shall you hear 5.2.361
Of carnal, bloody, and unnatural acts,
Of accidental judgments,* casual* slaughters,
Of deaths put on* by cunning and forced cause,*
And, in this upshot, purposes mistook 5.2.365
Fall'n on th' inventors' heads. All this can I
Truly deliver.

FORTINBRAS   Let us haste to hear it,
And call the noblest to the audience.
For me, with sorrow I embrace my fortune.
I have some rights of memory* in this kingdom, 5.2.370
Which now to claim my vantage* doth invite me.

HORATIO Of that I shall have also cause to speak,
And from his mouth whose voice will draw on more.*
But let this same be presently* performed,
Even while men's minds are wild, lest more mischance 5.2.375
On* plots and errors happen.

FORTINBRAS   Let four captains
Bear Hamlet, like a soldier, to the stage,
For he was likely, had he been put on,*
To have proved most royal; and for his passage,*
The soldiers' music and the rite of war 5.2.380
Speak* loudly for him.
Take up the bodies. Such a sight as this
Becomes the field,* but here shows much amiss.
Go bid the soldiers shoot.

[*Exeunt marching, bearing off the dead bodies; a peal of ordnance is shot off.*]

judgments · retributions

casual · occurring by chance

put on · instigated

forced cause · contrivance

of memory · traditional, remembered, unforgotten

vantage · favorable opportunity

voice ... more · vote will influence still others

presently · immediately

On · on the basis of, on top of

put on · invested in royal office and so put to the test

passage · the passage from life to death

Speak · let them speak

Becomes the field · suits the field of battle

Horton Foote

⁂ 1916 – ⁂

Winner of the Pulitzer Prize for Drama for The Young Man From
Atlanta *as well as two Academy Awards for the screenplays of* To Kill
a Mockingbird *and* Tender Mercies, *Horton Foote is an important
American voice in both theater and film. Foote started out as an actor
and then began writing play scripts in an attempt to create roles for
himself. Soon he realized that his future lay in writing for the theater.
Wharton, Texas, where he was born, provided the model for the fictional town of Harrison, Texas, which has been the setting for many of
Foote's plays. The playwright has noted that though he lived for years
in New York and founded an acting company, he never felt free to
choose New York as the setting for his plays. Indeed, he believed that
the setting of his plays had already been decided by his birth. The sense
of rural home and belonging figure importantly in Foote's plays and
screenplays, as do the familiar struggles of family life. In his temperate
way, he explores the mystery of why some individuals can survive
tragedies while others are shattered by them. During his fifty years
of writing, sometimes his themes have enjoyed great success, while at
other times they have been out of favor. Horton Foote is distinguished
not merely for his remarkable scripts and numerous awards, but for
the admiration of directors, actors, and younger playwrights, who
respect his tenacity, his generosity, and his moral vision.*

*During his year in residence at New York's Signature Theatre
from 1994–1995, Horton Foote produced three new plays, one of
which was* Talking Pictures. *The play was critically acclaimed by
Kate Blackburn as*

> *jewel-like in its setting and performance. A Horton Foote
> script demands (but ever so gently) a staging that illumi-
> nates our least obtrusive realizations, insists on a romance
> with the ordinary. This is archetypal Horton Foote – quiet,
> dutiful, understated but never dull.*

In fact, because of its focus on rural settings, its exploration of the family, and the way it documents small, revealing moments, Horton Foote's work has been compared to the plays of Chekhov, in which for periods of time nothing seems to be happening.

And yet it is worth considering how many life-changing events occur during the two acts of Talking Pictures. *Against the apparently hum-drum backdrop of Katie Bell and Vesta's sisterly squabbling, we watch as Myra discovers that her beloved son Pete has chosen not to live with her, but instead to spend his time with his father. Myra suffers a visit from her former husband, entertains a marriage proposal, meets the estranged wife of the man who has proposed to her, and discovers that she has lost her job as a pianist in a silent film theatre because talking pictures have come to town. With quiet courage she faces these catastrophic events and makes illuminating decisions, which lead to the comic ending. Foote paints the whole community of characters in the play with a careful brush. For most of them, the action of the play involves a journey. Even the quibbling teenage Katie Bell develops, from her friendship with the young evangelist, Estaquio, a longing to broaden her horizons: "I bet I get to Mexico one day," she announces at the end of the play.*

It can be said of Foote's plays that much of what is important happens in the interstices, in the silence between words and sentences. All theatre scripts are, of course, recipes for a stage production and so all theatre scripts gain immensely from being performed – both seen and heard. A script as subtle as Talking Pictures *particularly demands some kind of production, at least to be read aloud, even if informally.*

TALKING PICTURES

COMPANY OF CHARACTERS

KATIE BELL JACKSON *16, daughter of Mr. and Mrs. Jackson*

VESTA JACKSON *18, daughter of Mr. and Mrs. Jackson*

MYRA TOLLIVER *34, a divorcée, boarder in the Jackson home and Pete's mother*

MR. JACKSON *45, a sad, soft-spoken railroad engineer*

MRS. JACKSON *mother of Katie Bell and Vesta, very involved in the Missionary Society*

WILLIS *estranged husband of Gladys, suitor to Myra*

ESTAQUIO TREVINO *17, a Mexican, son of a Baptist preacher*
PETE *14, son of Myra and Gerard*
GLADYS *estranged wife of Willis, whom she has abandoned*
ASHENBACK *Gladys' boyfriend*
GERARD ANDERSON *Myra's ex-husband, father of Pete, and currently married to Jackie Kate*

ACT 1, SCENE 1

[*The scene shows a living room, bedroom, porch, and a portion of the yard of the Jackson house in Harrison, Texas, in 1929. It has very small rooms, a small parlour and yard.* KATIE BELL JACKSON *is reading a book in the living room. Her sister,* VESTA *is eating popcorn.*]

1.1.1 KATIE BELL Sister, come give me some popcorn.

VESTA No. Go out in the kitchen and get your own.

KATIE BELL Selfish!

VESTA Selfish, yourself.

[MYRA TOLLIVER *comes into the house looking down at a run in her stockings.*]

1.1.5 What's the matter?

MYRA I've got a run in my stocking. Brand new, too.

[MYRA *goes into her room and takes off the stocking.*]

KATIE BELL How was the picture show this afternoon?

MYRA Pretty fair.

[VESTA, *calling to* MYRA.]

VESTA Was it hot walking from town?

1.1.10 MYRA Yes. And dusty.

[KATIE BELL, *calling to* MYRA.]

KATIE BELL Who was in that picture show?

MYRA Bessie Love.

[MYRA *has changed stockings and begins to darn the damaged one.* KATIE BELL *and* VESTA *go into* MYRA'*s room.*]

VESTA Who?

MYRA Bessie Love. What are you reading, Katie Bell?

1.1.15 KATIE BELL Ben Hur.

MYRA Oh, that was a wonderful movie.

KATIE BELL It looks like it. There are scenes from the movie in the book. Were you playing the piano for the picture show when you saw it?

1.1.20 MYRA Yes, I was.

KATIE BELL Ramón Navarro was in the movie, wasn't he? 1.1.21

MYRA Yes, and Frances X. Bushman.

KATIE BELL Was the movie like the book?

MYRA I don't know. I never read the book.

KATIE BELL Is Ramón Navarro very handsome? 1.1.25

MYRA I think so.

VESTA He's a Mexican.

KATIE BELL No, he's not.

VESTA Yes, he is too.

KATIE BELL Is he, Miss Myra? 1.1.30

MYRA Yes, he is. And he's very worried, I read.

KATIE BELL Why?

MYRA What will happen to his career when the movies are all talkies.

KATIE BELL Why does that worry him? 1.1.35

VESTA Because he talks Mexican, goose. Once people hear him talk Mexican they'll all know he's not American.

KATIE BELL Can't he learn to speak English? I saw a Mexican boy up town the other day and I asked him his name and he said it was Estaquio Trevino and he spoke English just as 1.1.40 plain as anybody.

VESTA Katie Bell Jackson, were you talking to a Mexican? Mama would have a fit if she knew.

KATIE BELL I wasn't talking to him. I just asked him his name.

VESTA You mean you walked right up to a strange Mexican and 1.1.45 asked him his name?

KATIE BELL No, I didn't go right up to anybody. Sally Meyers and I were walking down the street and he came up to us and asked us if there were any other Mexicans here and Sally said yes, there were some across the track and I said yes that was 1.1.50 true and he said enough to start a church?

VESTA Enough to start a church?

KATIE BELL That's what he said.

VESTA Why did he say that?

KATIE BELL I don't know. I didn't ask him and then he asked us 1.1.55 our name and we told him.

VESTA You told him? You told a Mexican boy your name?

KATIE BELL Yes.

VESTA Sister, I am shocked. Then what happened?...

1.1.60   KATIE BELL And then we asked him his name, and a colored boy
         walked by and he asked if there were many colored people
         here and I said as many as there are white, and Sally said she
         thought more, and then we bid him goodbye and walked on.
         [MYRA *leaves her room and goes to the piano in the living room and starts*
         to look over sheet music. VESTA *and* KATIE BELL *follow after her.*]
         VESTA Myra, Mama says in exchange for part of your rent you
1.1.65   are going to give Katie Bell and me music lessons –
         MYRA Yes.
         VESTA Mama says after I learn to play the piano, I can take organ
         lessons so I can play for the church on Sunday.
         [KATIE BELL *makes a face.*]
         Why are you making a face?
1.1.70   KATIE BELL Because I don't ever want to play an organ in
         church or anywhere. I want to play the piano for picture
         shows like Myra.
         VESTA I'd like to hear you tell Mama that.
         KATIE BELL I'm not about to tell Mama that.
         [MYRA *going back to her room with sheet music and calling out to the*
         girls. KATIE BELL *and* VESTA *remain in the living room.*]
1.1.75   MYRA Well, honey, don't ever think about playing piano in pic-
         ture shows. Those days are about over, I fear. I think the Queen
         here is about one of the last of the silent theaters. Mr. Santos
         says he will keep it that way as long as he can, as he doesn't care
         for the talkies, but I don't think he can hold out much longer.
1.1.80   The theaters in El Campo, Bay City and Richmond have all
         gone talkie, and I hear Eagle Lake and Columbus are about to.
         Why, I read the other day in some movie magazine or other
         where they may stop making silent pictures all together.
         KATIE BELL Miss Myra has seen a talking picture. She saw it in
1.1.85   Houston when she took Pete in to stay with his Daddy. I wish
         I could see a talking picture.
         VESTA Well, you're never going to get to so just get over wishing
         that. You've never seen a silent movie.
         KATIE BELL Well, neither have you –. Anyway, Miss Myra tells
1.1.90   me the stories of all the movies she sees and she tells them
         so wonderfully I feel like I've seen them.
         VESTA Does Mama know she tells you the stories of all those
         pictures?

KATIE BELL No.

VESTA Well, I bet she would have a fit if she knew. 1.1.95

[*A pause.*]

Did she tell you the story of that talking picture she saw in Houston?

KATIE BELL Yes. She did.

VESTA Was it a love story?

[KATIE BELL *and* VESTA *go back into* MYRA'*s room.*] 1.1.100

KATIE BELL Miss Myra, was that talking picture you saw in Houston a love story?

MYRA No, not really. Well, now I don't know. It was a love story, I suppose, but an unconventional one. It was the story of the love of a father for his son. 1.1.105

VESTA What was the name of it?

MYRA *The Singing Fool.*ᐧ

KATIE BELL Would you tell the story to Vesta? She's never heard you tell the story of a picture show and I told her…

MYRA You tell the story to Vesta – 1.1.110

KATIE BELL Oh, I can't.

MYRA Sure, you can. Tell it like I told it to you.

KATIE BELL I can't remember it all.

MYRA Sure you can.

KATIE BELL I remember there was this man and he was a famous singer and he was married. Is that right? 1.1.115

MYRA Yes, that's right.

KATIE BELL And they had a little boy and he loved his little boy very much, but then he and his wife were separated and one night when he was to sing his little boy got sick and died. But he had to go on stage and sing anyway, even though his heart was breaking. 1.1.120

VESTA That's sad.

KATIE BELL Of course, it's sad. Miss Myra said everybody in the picture show was crying. Didn't you? 1.1.125

MYRA Yes.

VESTA Were you crying?

MYRA Oh, yes. Like a baby.

KATIE BELL Sing that song for Vesta.

[MYRA, *singing (song: Ray Henderson, Lew Brown, B. G. DeSylva)*] 1.1.130

MYRA "Friends may forsake us

The Singing Fool · a popular "part-talkie" movie starring Al Jolson (1928)

Let them all forsake us
I still have you, Sonny Boy.
You came from heaven

1.1.135 And I know your worth,
You made a heaven for me right here on earth.
But the angels they got lonely
And they took you because they were lonely
Now I'm lonely, too, Sonny Boy."

1.1.140 VESTA Did the little boy die?

MYRA Yes.

KATIE BELL And the father had to go and sing that song even
though his heart was breaking.

VESTA Oh, that's so sad. It's like the story Brother Meyers told
1.1.145 in church the other night about this poor widow who had no
money and no job.

KATIE BELL Didn't she have a husband?

VESTA No, goose. Didn't you hear me say she was a widow?
Widows don't have husbands. If you're a widow your husband
1.1.150 is dead. And if you're a grass widow your husband is alive and
you're divorced. Myra is a grass widow.

KATIE BELL Are you?

MYRA Yes.

[VESTA *goes into the living room.* KATIE BELL *follows her.*]

KATIE BELL What did that woman's husband die of?

1.1.155 VESTA What woman?

KATIE BELL The one Brother Meyers told you about.

VESTA Good heavens, I don't know that. Ask Brother Meyers.

KATIE BELL Is that the whole story?

VESTA No, there's more to it.

1.1.160 KATIE BELL Well, what's the rest of it?

VESTA Well, she was desperate because she had starving children
and everything...

KATIE BELL And what happened?

VESTA Well, if you'll be quiet for five minutes I'll tell you.

1.1.165 KATIE BELL I know what happened. She prayed to God and he
saved them.

VESTA How did you know that?

KATIE BELL Because that's what always happens when Brother
Meyers tells a story.

[VESTA, *calling to* MYRA.]

VESTA What was the name of that talking picture you saw? 1.1.170

MYRA *The Singing Fool.*

[MR. JACKSON *comes in wearing overalls, carrying a lunch pail.*]

MR. JACKSON Hello.

VESTA Hello, Daddy.

KATIE BELL Hello, Daddy.

[MYRA, *calling from her room.*]

MYRA Hello, Mr. Jackson. 1.1.175

[KATIE BELL, *calling to* MYRA.]

KATIE BELL Daddy got bumped.

[MYRA, *calling from her room.*]

MYRA I know, I heard, I'm so sorry.

MR. JACKSON Well, it's not the end of the world. I still have a job.

VESTA Who bumped you Daddy?

MR. JACKSON Someone with more seniority than I have that 1.1.180
wanted my job here.

KATIE BELL Now Daddy's going to have to bump somebody – We're going over to Cuero on his day off to look it
over and if he likes it, he'll bump the man that works there,
and we'll all go live in Cuero. When are we going to Cuero, 1.1.185
Daddy, if we go?

MR. JACKSON Well, we have to try and sell our house, see if we
can't find a place to live there.

[KATIE BELL, *calling to* MYRA.]

KATIE BELL Have you ever been to Cuero, Miss Myra?

[MYRA, *calling from her room.*]

MYRA Yes, I've played in the picture house there. 1.1.190

[KATIE BELL, *calling to* MYRA.]

KATIE BELL Is it a nice town?

[MYRA, *calling from her room.*]

MYRA I think so.

[VESTA, *calling to* MYRA.]

VESTA As nice as here?

[MYRA, *calling from her room.*]

MYRA I like it here better –

VESTA Oh, Daddy, if we move to Cuero in six weeks I better 1.1.195
start my piano lessons with Myra right away, if she's going
to teach me.

MR. JACKSON Well, that's up to you and your Mama.

[VESTA, *calling to* MYRA.]

VESTA Can you start teaching me right away?

[MYRA, *calling from her room.*]

1.1.200 MYRA Why, yes, I don't see why not.

VESTA Oh, grand.

MR. JACKSON Where is your Mama?

VESTA She's at the Missionary Society.

MR. JACKSON I'm going across the road to work in my garden
1.1.205 while it's still light.

[*He starts out – he pauses. He goes to the door of* MYRA's *room.*]

Your boy coming here today, Myra?

MYRA Yes, I'm waiting for him now.

MR. JACKSON How long has he been in Houston?

MYRA Two weeks.

1.1.210 MR. JACKSON Two weeks? Doesn't seem possible. Staying with
his father?

MYRA Yes.

MR. JACKSON Is he married again?

MYRA Yes.

1.1.215 MR. JACKSON Does he have any other children?

MYRA Yes, two. Both boys.

MR. JACKSON Where did you come from Myra?

MYRA I was born and raised in Nacogdoches.

MR. JACKSON Oh yes. I remember now. Mrs. Jackson told me
1.1.220 that. I used to have a run through Nacogdoches.

MYRA Did you?

MR. JACKSON That was the run I had before I came to
Harrison.

[MRS. JACKSON *enters the living room through the front door.*]

MRS. JACKSON Well, Daddy, you beat me home.

1.1.225 MR. JACKSON Yes, I did. How was the Missionary Society?

MRS. JACKSON Oh, I tell you the sorrow in this world. You don't
know when you are blessed. Mrs. Davis was with us today telling us about the missionaries among the leper colonies. Oh, the
tales of those lepers are harrowing. Brother Meyers is going to
1.1.230 preach a whole sermon about the lepers on Sunday, he says.

MR. JACKSON I thought Mrs. Davis was a Presbyterian.

MRS. JACKSON She is.

MR. JACKSON Then why was she at the Methodist Missionary Society?

MRS. JACKSON To get us all interested in the leper work. She says it's interdenominational. Brother Meyers agrees. He prayed so beautifully about it. I just love to hear Brother Meyers pray – Well, I'd better get supper started. 1.1.235

MR. JACKSON And I'm going out to my garden.

[MR. JACKSON *exits.* MRS. JACKSON *goes to the door to* MYRA'S *room.*]

MRS. JACKSON Your boy not home yet, Myra? 1.1.240

MYRA No, I'm expecting him any second now.

VESTA Mama, may I start my piano lessons right away with Myra? Daddy says we may be moving to Cuero pretty soon.

MRS. JACKSON We'll discuss that later.

[MRS. JACKSON *starts out.*] 1.1.245

VESTA I'll help you, Mama.

[MRS. JACKSON *and* VESTA *leave.* KATIE BELL *goes into* MYRA'S *room.*]

KATIE BELL If I tell you a secret will you swear not to tell anybody?

MYRA Yes, I swear.

KATIE BELL Two years ago when I was in El Campo visiting Sarah Lundy we slipped into the picture show over there. We saw Clara Bow in *Rough House Rosie*. Did you see that? 1.1.250

MYRA Yes, I did.

KATIE BELL How many picture shows have you seen?

MYRA Oh, hundreds –

KATIE BELL How long have you been playing the piano at picture shows? 1.1.255

MYRA Let's see. About eleven years.

KATIE BELL What made you come here?

MYRA Because they were looking for someone to play the piano at the Queen. 1.1.260

KATIE BELL What was the best picture show you ever saw?

[MYRA *goes into the living room and to the piano. She takes more sheet music.* KATIE BELL *follows her.*]

MYRA Oh, heavens … I'll have to think about that.

KATIE BELL Who is your favorite actor?

MYRA I'll have to think about that, too.

[*A pause.*]

I think *Romona* with Dolores Del Río was one of my favorite pictures. 1.1.265

KATIE BELL She's Mexican, too, isn't she?

MYRA Yes—

KATIE BELL Are there any other Mexican movie stars?

1.1.270 **MYRA** Yes. Lupe Velez, Antonio Moreno.

KATIE BELL They're movie stars?

MYRA Yes.

[**MYRA** *goes back into her room. She gets her purse, gloves and hat.* **KATIE BELL** *follows.*]

KATIE BELL How do you get to be a movie star?

MYRA Oh, I don't know.

1.1.275 **KATIE BELL** Are there only Mexican and American movie stars?

MYRA No. There are Russian and German and Italian and English and Polish—

KATIE BELL Movie stars?

MYRA Yes.

1.1.280 **KATIE BELL** How much money does a movie star make?

MYRA Depends on the movie star.

[**MYRA** *has her hat and gloves on. She goes again into the living room.* **KATIE BELL** *follows.*]

KATIE BELL They're all rich aren't they?

MYRA Pretty rich. Richer than I am certainly.

[**MRS. JACKSON** *enters.*]

MRS. JACKSON Katie Bell, come in and help your sister, please.

[**MRS. JACKSON** *and* **KATIE BELL** *exit for the kitchen.* **MYRA** *goes outside to the porch, sits on the steps.* **WILLIS** *enters.*]

1.1.285 **WILLIS** Hi—

MYRA Hello.

WILLIS Pete home yet?

MYRA No. How was work?

WILLIS Hot. I'm tired. Laying bricks in the hot sun is not my
1.1.290 idea of a classy job.

[*A pause.*]

Well, beggars can't be choosers.

MYRA Is your room over the garage hot?

WILLIS Like an oven. How is your room?

MYRA It gets pretty hot.

1.1.295 **WILLIS** A little breeze now.

MYRA Yes.

WILLIS How about a date Sunday night after the picture show?

MYRA Don't you have to get up early Monday morning?

WILLIS Five o'clock. Same as usual.

MYRA Willis, you'll be dead if we go on having dates at night   1.1.300
and your having to get up for work so early. Anyway, where
can we go at ten o'clock at night, but the ice cream parlour
and it closes at eleven and they just sigh when we come in at
ten as if to say I hope you won't loiter.

WILLIS When else can I see you? You work at the picture show   1.1.305
every afternoon and every night, seven days a week. I wanted
a date tonight, but you said you thought you should come
back since it was Pete's first night home.

[**KATIE BELL** *comes to the door.*]

KATIE BELL Phone, Myra –

MYRA Excuse me –   1.1.310

[**MYRA** *goes into the house.* **KATIE BELL** *comes outside.*]

KATIE BELL Did you ever see a talking picture?

WILLIS I saw one in Houston that was partly talking.

KATIE BELL How do they get those pictures to talk?

WILLIS Beats me.

KATIE BELL Are you a Baptist?   1.1.315

WILLIS Born and bred.

KATIE BELL Someone said you were. We're Methodists. Myra is
Methodist, too. Can Baptists and Methodists marry?

WILLIS They can if they want to.

KATIE BELL Vesta was about to date a Baptist boy, but Mama   1.1.320
discouraged it. She says mixed marriages are not a very good
idea. It's very confusing to the children. With the father going
to one church and the mother to another. Now my father
doesn't go to any church and that worries my mother considerable. Of course, like Mama says, he is the best man that   1.1.325
ever walked this earth, but still.

[*A pause.*]

Do you think people that attend picture shows are going to
Hell?

WILLIS No, I don't.

KATIE BELL I don't either. Brother Meyers says if they go on   1.1.330
weekdays they are liable to go and if they go on Sundays they
are bound to. I certainly don't think Myra is going to Hell,
do you?

WILLIS No.

1.1.335 **KATIE BELL** Anyway, she has to go. It's her job.

[**MYRA** *comes back out.*]

Willis says you're not going to Hell if you go to the picture shows.

MYRA I wasn't worried. Thank you anyway, Willis, for telling me. That was Pete's Daddy on the phone. He said Pete wanted to
1.1.340 know if he could stay another day – I said, yes. Well, it's time for me to go to work. See you all later.

[**MYRA** *exits.*]

KATIE BELL She had been crying. Couldn't you tell?

WILLIS No.

KATIE BELL Well, she had. I can tell. She cries all the time, too, in
1.1.345 her room when Pete isn't there. I guess she doesn't think we can hear her, but we can. Papa says she's worried over losing her job at the picture show. He says she has lots to worry her, says it's hard having to raise a boy by herself. I think she's pretty, don't you?

WILLIS Yes, I do.

[**MRS. JACKSON** *comes to the door.*]

1.1.350 **MRS. JACKSON** Katie Bell, come here, please.

KATIE BELL Yes, Ma'am.

[**KATIE BELL** *goes to her mother.*]

MRS. JACKSON What's all this about some little boy dying at the picture show? Vesta's all upset about it.

KATIE BELL He didn't die at the picture show, Mama. He died
1.1.355 in the picture show.

MRS. JACKSON Oh, is that how it was. I thought some little boy died at the picture show here.

KATIE BELL No, he died in a picture show in Houston.

MRS. JACKSON It seems to me you are awfully interested in
1.1.360 picture shows all of a sudden.

KATIE BELL No, Ma'am. Just interested in the stories, Mama.

[*A pause.*]

Mama –

MRS. JACKSON What?

KATIE BELL Do you think that people that go to picture shows
1.1.365 will go to Hell, especially if they go on Sundays?

MRS. JACKSON No, I don't. Not that I would go myself and I don't want you or your sister ever going.

[*A pause.*]

I went to a tent show once.

KATIE BELL You did?

MRS. JACKSON Yes, and a medicine show, too. I didn't care too   1.1.370
much for either of them, but I don't think I'm going to Hell,
because I went. That's just Brother Meyers talking. He's a good
man, but extreme in his views. How are you, Willis?

WILLIS Pretty fair, thank you.

MRS. JACKSON Hot enough for you?   1.1.375

WILLIS Oh, yes.

[*He starts out.*]

See you all later.

[**WILLIS** *exits.*]

KATIE BELL Mama?

MRS. JACKSON Yes.

KATIE BELL I think he is courting Miss Myra, don't you?   1.1.380

MRS. JACKSON It seems. He's over here a lot.

KATIE BELL I think he's nice, don't you?

MRS. JACKSON Yes, I do. And I think Myra is nice, too.

KATIE BELL Pete isn't coming home today.

MRS. JACKSON Oh.   1.1.385

KATIE BELL When she came out to tell us that I think she'd
been crying.

MRS. JACKSON She's very emotional. I think it's seeing all those
picture shows.

KATIE BELL Papa says it's not, he says –

[**MRS. JACKSON**, *interrupting.*]

MRS. JACKSON I know what he says, but your Papa isn't the final   1.1.390
authority on everything. Just think how hearing the story
of one of those picture shows upset your sister, what if you
watched as many as she does – why I think you'd be upset all
the time.

KATIE BELL Mama, do you know any Mexicans?   1.1.395

MRS. JACKSON Good Lord, no. Why would I know any
Mexicans? You're the strangest child I ever saw. Never know
what you're going to worry me with next. Moving picture
shows and now Mexicans.

[**MRS. JACKSON** *goes into the house.* **KATIE BELL** *follows as the light
fades.*]

ACT 1, SCENE 2

[*The lights are brought up – it is later that evening.* WILLIS *is sitting on the Jackson steps.* KATIE BELL *and* VESTA *enter in the living room.* KATIE BELL *turns on the radio. She gets classical music.* MYRA *comes into the yard.*]

1.2.1 WILLIS Good evening.

MYRA Sh. Mr. Jackson's asleep. He goes to bed by eight-thirty or nine. He's up at four. He takes his train at five.

WILLIS I know. There are lights on in the house though.

1.2.5 MYRA That's the girls in the living room listening to the radio

WILLIS They let them listen to the radio, but not go to the picture show?

MYRA They can only listen to programs of classical music. Jessica Dragonette, *The Firestone Hour*, Lawrence Tibbett. Once Mrs.

1.2.10 Jackson caught Katie Bell listening to Rudy Vallee and she threatened to throw the radio out the window.

WILLIS The Joplins have a radio. They invited me over the other night to listen to a boxing match.

MYRA Did you go?

1.2.15 WILLIS Oh, yes.

MYRA Why aren't you in bed asleep?

WILLIS It's very close in my room tonight.

MYRA You should have a fan.

WILLIS I know, I'm going to get one. Do you have a fan?

1.2.20 MYRA No.

WILLIS I bet your room is hot too?

MYRA Terrible.

WILLIS I'd say let's walk back to town and get some ice cream but I think the drug store would be closed by the time we

1.2.25 got there.

MYRA Yes, it would. Anyway, I'm too tired tonight to walk another step.

WILLIS Why were you so late getting home tonight?

MYRA Sue Jessie had to leave early because of some kind of

1.2.30 going on at the Eastern Star,* so I told her I would total up the ticket sales for her. She sells the tickets, you see, and she's always worrying she'll come out short. Anyway, it took me longer than I thought to get it all straight so Sue Jessie

the Eastern Star · a women's organization affiliated with the secret fraternal society of Freemasons

wouldn't have a breakdown when she comes tomorrow. And then I went for a walk. 1.2.35

WILLIS By yourself?

MYRA Yes, sir –

WILLIS Myra, don't be walking around by yourself this time of night.

[*Inside,* **KATIE BELL** *changes the radio station to dance music.*]

It's not safe.

VESTA Katie Bell Jackson, what are you doing? That's dance music! Mama would have a fit if she knew you were listening to dance music! Turn that off and come to bed! 1.2.40

[**KATIE BELL** *turns off the radio. She and* **VESTA** *exit.*]

WILLIS Myra –

MYRA What?

WILLIS Were you crying today? 1.2.45

MYRA When?

WILLIS Right after you talked to your husband.

MYRA My ex-husband. I was crying.

[*A pause.*]

My ex-husband can be so insensitive sometimes. After I gave my permission for Pete to stay he said right out that Pete didn't want to live with me any longer. He said he wanted to stay in Houston with him and his wife and his boys all the time. 1.2.50

WILLIS What is his name?

MYRA Whose?

WILLIS Your ex-husband's? 1.2.55

MYRA Gerard. Gerard Anderson. His new wife's name is Jacqueline Kate. They call her Jackie Kate.

WILLIS Would you let Pete live permanently in Houston?

MYRA No, he's just making the whole thing up to get at me. I said to him why don't you leave me alone, stop tormenting me. The courts have given Pete to me except for two weeks in the summertime. He said, it wasn't his doing, Pete doesn't want to come back, well, I said, put Pete on the phone and let him tell me that. He's in the pool swimming, he says, in our swimming pool. Do you have even a public swimming pool in Harrison, he said? No, I said we don't, we do have the river which Pete is not allowed to go in because of snakes, alligators, and suckholes. That's what you think, he says. He goes into that river all the time, sneaking, he said, while you're busy playing the piano at the picture 1.2.60 1.2.65

1.2.70   show. Well, listen, I said, that's the way I put a roof over our head and food on the table by playing at the picture show. Then he said, in a very sarcastic way, I hear you may lose your job at the picture show to the talking pictures. How are you going to support a fourteen-year-old boy if that happens, he said, don't

1.2.75   you worry about me, I said, I'll get a job. I always have. And I have, too. When we divorced I didn't have a dime and he was working in construction then and barely making anything and so I knew I couldn't count on him for any kind of support, and I didn't want to take anything from him even if I could – And

1.2.80   so it was up to me to always take care of Pete and myself from then on. Oh, he sent Pete five dollars at Christmas and on his birthday, but that's all. He'd been drinking, you know.

WILLIS Does he drink?

MYRA He sure does, all the time these days.

1.2.85   **WILLIS** I don't drink.

MYRA I know you don't.

WILLIS My Daddy drank something fierce. The sight of him cured me once and for all. Is that why you left him because he drank?

1.2.90   **MYRA** No, he didn't drink then.

WILLIS Why did you separate?

MYRA Oh, Lord. I don't know really. I've asked myself that a million times, to tell you the truth. We started going together back in High School.

1.2.95   **WILLIS** Nacogdoches?

MYRA Yes.

[*A pause.*]

I guess you might say we just outgrew each other. My Daddy said if I left him he'd never speak to me again and he didn't until the day he died and then he just barely nodded to me

1.2.100   when I went into his room. But Gerard and I thought it was the best thing to do at the time. A year after the divorce he came over where I was living with Pete and asked me to marry him again. But by then I had my first job at a picture show and was supporting myself and Pete.

[*A pause.*]

1.2.105   Gerard's a contractor now. He's a rich man, he tells me, and Pete says he thinks he is. He has a car and a truck and a swimming pool and a two story house and a new wife and two more sons—

[*A pause.*]

Of course, I've never regretted leaving him. He wasn't mean to me, he never hit me or yelled at me—but he never stayed home except to eat and sleep. I don't think he was running around with other women and he wasn't drinking then, but he just never stayed home. I had Pete the first year we were married, and he'd say, come on and bring the baby, where to, I'd say, the domino parlour or the pool hall? I can't bring a baby to a domino parlour or a pool hall, I'd tell him. Do you mind if I go, he'd say, no, I would always say, go on, I don't mind. I got lonesome, of course.

[*A pause. She sings half to herself ("Sonny Boy").*]

"When there are gray skies. I don't mind the gray skies."

WILLIS I hope to be rich one day.

MYRA Well, I hope you are for your sake. If that's what you want. And if it brings you happiness—

[*She sings again to herself.*]

"The angels, they grew lonely"—

WILLIS What's that song? I never heard it before.

MYRA It's a song they sang in that picture show I saw in Houston.

WILLIS Was it a talking picture?

MYRA Yes.

WILLIS What was it called?

MYRA *The Singing Fool*, with Al Jolson.

WILLIS Oh, yes. I saw him *in The Jazz Singer.*˙ Did you see that?

MYRA No.

WILLIS That wasn't all talking. That was part talking and part silent. He sang "Mammy" in that one. He wore black face when he sang it.

MYRA He wore black face in this one, too.

WILLIS When he sang?

MYRA Yes.

WILLIS I wonder why he does that?

MYRA I don't know.

WILLIS You've been here a year, Myra?

MYRA Yes, and before that Flatonia and before that—

WILLIS Were you always playing the piano in picture shows?

The Jazz Singer · the first talking picture (1927)

1.2.110

1.2.115

1.2.120

1.2.125

1.2.130

1.2.135

1.2.140

MYRA Yes.

WILLIS Did you ever think of marrying again?

1.2.145 **MYRA** Once. A man in Lufkin, Harold Menefee. I almost married him, but Pete didn't like him and I don't think he liked Pete, though he swore he did and I was afraid he might not be good to Pete after we married, so I said no.

WILLIS I like Pete.

1.2.150 **MYRA** I'm glad.

WILLIS Does he like me?

MYRA I don't know, I've never asked him.

WILLIS We played catch together the night before he went to visit his Daddy.

1.2.155 **MYRA** I know you did.

WILLIS I bought a glove just so I could play with him – I want to play with him a lot when he gets back. My youngest brother is sixteen and I play catch a lot with him when I go back home.

MYRA It's not easy, you know living in a rented room in some-
1.2.160 body else's house with a fourteen-year-old boy. I dream some day of having my own house with a room for myself and a room for Pete.

[*A pause.*]

It's a pretty night, isn't it?

WILLIS Yes.

[*A pause.*]

1.2.165 I had some good news tonight.

MYRA What?

WILLIS Mr. Charlie called me into his house tonight after supper and he said his business had improved a lot and that he was very pleased with my work and that he has had contracts for
1.2.170 four more houses and I could count on steady work and a raise in pay. I told him that was certainly good news because I was trying to make some plans of my own, what kind of plans he asked, and I said, personal plans.

[*A pause.*]

I don't know what you think about me exactly, but I think
1.2.175 you're a mighty fine person. I have my eye on a small lot and now that I know I'll have a steady job and a raise in pay I can see my way clear on making an offer on the lot and if I can get it at a price I can afford, I could start building a house.

Mr. Charlie said he would help me every Sunday after church. It would be a small house, of course, and it wouldn't have a swimming pool. Anyway, like I said, I don't know what you think about me, but I think highly of you.

[*A pause.*]

Of course, I don't know if you remembered my telling you I was married before, too.

MYRA Yes, I remember you telling me that.

WILLIS We had no children, my wife left me for another man two years after we were married. That hurt a lot, of course, because I won't lie to you, I was sure crazy about her. And I thought the sun rose and set on her. And I swore to myself at the time I would never marry again, it shook me up so. That was five years ago, of course, and I only think of Gladys once in a while now, like when she sends me a postcard from New Orleans or Galveston – we're still married because I could never get the money together for a divorce, but now –

[**MYRA**, *interrupting.*]

MYRA What's your wife's name?

WILLIS Gladys.

MYRA Gladys what?

WILLIS Gladys Mayfield was her girlhood name, then Gladys Toome when she married me –

MYRA Is it Ashenback now?

WILLIS Well, that's the name of the man she left me for.

MYRA Well, I never.

WILLIS That's if they're still together and they were last I heard –

MYRA I got a postcard from her a week ago –

WILLIS You did? Do you know her?

MYRA Never heard of her before in my life.

WILLIS What did the postcard say?

MYRA "Keep away from my husband. I warn you. Gladys Ashenback." I said to Pete this must be a crazy woman. I don't know anybody named Gladys Ashenback.

WILLIS Well, I'll be switched.

MYRA So will you please tell her for me the next time you see her I'm not interested in her husband.

WILLIS Maybe she meant me – You see, like I said, we've never divorced.

1.2.180

1.2.185

1.2.190

1.2.195

1.2.200

1.2.205

1.2.210

1.2.215

1.2.216 **MYRA** Well, then, maybe she did.

WILLIS Well, she can just send all the postcards she wants, she will never get me back –

[*A pause.*]

I've told you what I think about you, Myra. What do you think
1.2.220 about me?

MYRA I think you're very nice, too, Willis.

WILLIS If I get a divorce now, would you ever consider marrying me?

MYRA I might.

1.2.225 **WILLIS** Would I have to get my house built first? I know a nice two bedroom apartment over at Mrs. Carver –

MYRA Well, Willis –

WILLIS Marry me, Myra, please. Please marry me. I'm very lonesome, Myra. I know I'm a Baptist and you're a Methodist, but
1.2.230 I'll join the Methodist church if you wanted me to.

MYRA Oh, I don't care about that at all, Willis. But I think you have to get a divorce first and then we'll talk of marriage – and, of course, I'll have to see how Pete feels about my marrying.

[**MRS. JACKSON** *comes out of the house.*]

MRS. JACKSON Oh, excuse me, Myra. I didn't realize you had
1.2.235 company. Hello, Willis.

WILLIS Hello, Mrs. Jackson.

MRS. JACKSON Mr. Jackson is snoring so it woke me up. Did you hear him snoring?

MYRA No.

1.2.240 **WILLIS** I didn't either.

MRS. JACKSON I'm surprised, he was snoring loud enough, I thought, to wake the dead – listen.

[*A pause; we can hear snoring.*]

I swear, Gabriel won't need a trumpet on resurrection morning, I tell him, they'll just have to get you to snore.

[*A pause.*]

1.2.245 It's so warm in the house – cool out here.

[*A pause.*]

What time is it?

WILLIS Eleven.

MRS. JACKSON Is it? I'll be dead tomorrow. You're a Baptist, Willis?

WILLIS Yes.   1.2.250

MRS. JACKSON We're all Methodists in this house. Except Mr.
Jackson, I'm sorry to say. He belongs to no church; of course, he's
the finest man I know – good and steady, no bad habits. Myra?

MYRA Yes, Ma'am.

MRS. JACKSON I have to speak with you about the girls' piano les-   1.2.255
sons. I know we talked of their studying with you in exchange
for part of your rent, but with all the expenses facing us in
moving after Mr. Jackson bumps another man, we can't afford
to give up even part of the rent. I hope you don't mind and
you haven't counted too much on it.   1.2.260

MYRA That's all right. I understand.

MRS. JACKSON Vesta's very disappointed and upset. She had her
heart set on studying with you.

[*A pause.*]

Oh, I almost forgot to tell you there is a note for you by the
phone, Myra. It's from Pete. He said to tell you he's spending   1.2.265
the rest of the summer in Houston. He'll go to summer school
there if he can.

[*A pause.*]

MYRA Well, I'm going to say good night.

MRS. JACKSON Good night.

WILLIS Good night.   1.2.270

[MYRA *goes into her room.*]

MRS. JACKSON She's a very nice person. We often hear her crying
in her room at night these last two weeks, but she's nice. That
worries Mr. Jackson so. I think she gets upset from watching
all those picture shows. A lot of them are sad, you know. Mr.
Jackson says it is not picture shows worrying her, he says it's   1.2.275
having to raise a boy alone on little money and now having to
worry about maybe losing her job at the picture show. That's
why we were all hoping Pete would come home soon – he's
company for her. He's a nice boy –

WILLIS Yes, he is.   1.2.280

MRS. JACKSON Well, I think I'm going to bed and try to get to
sleep. Good night.

[MRS. JACKSON *goes into the house.*]

WILLIS Good night.

[WILLIS *starts out of the yard as the light fades.*]

ACT 1, SCENE 3

[*The lights are brought up. It is the next day.* Vesta *is sitting on the porch doing her nails; her hair is in curlers.* Estaquio Trevino *comes into the yard.*]

1.3.1   Estaquio *Buenos días.*

Vesta What did you say?

Estaquio *Buenos días.* Good day – *Buenos días.* That's Spanish for good day.

1.3.5   Vesta Well, you couldn't prove it by me.

Estaquio *Buenas noches* is good night. Don't you study Spanish in school?

Vesta No.

Estaquio I would think you would study Spanish being so
1.3.10   close to Mexico and all. Texas used to belong to Mexico. It was called *Tejas* then.

Vesta Any fool knows that.

Estaquio I just a met a colored boy who didn't. He said I was making the whole thing up. I'm a preacher's son.

1.3.15   Vesta My foot –

Estaquio I certainly am. We came here hoping to start a church. A Spanish-speaking church. We hoped with the Mexicans in New Gulf and the Mexicans here there would be some inter-est. But we got discouraged very soon. There are plenty of
1.3.20   Mexicans in New Gulf, but they are all Catholic.

Vesta I thought all Mexicans were Catholic.

Estaquio No. Definitely not. There are plenty of Mexican Baptists, and we're spreading the word. Do you have a sister?

Vesta Yes. What's it to you?

1.3.25   Estaquio And her name is Katie Bell.

Vesta Why?

Estaquio I've come to tell her goodbye.

Vesta How do you know my sister?

Estaquio We exchanged greetings downtown the other day.

[Katie Bell *comes in.*]

1.3.30   Hello.

Katie Bell Hello.

[Vesta *goes into the house.*]

What are you doing here?

ESTAQUIO I've come to say goodbye. I'm going back to Mexico.

KATIE BELL Oh, well. Goodbye.

ESTAQUIO And I've come to invite you to visit me in Mexico one day.

1.3.35

KATIE BELL Thank you, but I wouldn't dare go there.

ESTAQUIO Why?

KATIE BELL It's too far away and besides, I wouldn't know a word anybody was saying.

1.3.40

ESTAQUIO You could learn to speak Spanish –

KATIE BELL I guess I could. I almost took it in school. I took Latin instead because Vesta did. Did you and your Papa get your church started?

ESTAQUIO No.

1.3.45

KATIE BELL I didn't ask the other day what kind of church it was.

ESTAQUIO Baptist.

KATIE BELL We are all Methodists.

ESTAQUIO Are you? We Baptists believe in total immersion and we have no crosses in our church –

1.3.50

KATIE BELL Is that so?

ESTAQUIO I hope to be a preacher one day –

KATIE BELL Baptist?

ESTAQUIO Certainly – Jesus was a Baptist, you know –

KATIE BELL Was he?

1.3.55

ESTAQUIO Yes.

KATIE BELL I never knew that. When you preach are you going to preach in English or Spanish?

ESTAQUIO In Spanish. *Jehová es mi pastor, nada me faltará.*

KATIE BELL What does that mean?

1.3.60

ESTAQUIO The Lord is my Shepherd, I shall not want.

KATIE BELL Oh, go on –

[PETE *comes into the yard. He has a suitcase.*]

PETE Hello, Katie Bell.

KATIE BELL Hi.

PETE Is my Mom here?

1.3.65

KATIE BELL She's still at the picture show.

[PETE *takes his suitcase into his room.*]

His Mom and Daddy are divorced. She's a grass widow. Do you know what that means?

ESTAQUIO No.

[PETE *comes out to them.*]

1.3.70 PETE I'm going to find my Mom.

KATIE BELL Bye Pete.

[PETE *goes.*]

Well, if you're a widow your husband is dead, but if you're a grass widow he's still alive.

ESTAQUIO My Papa may let me start preaching soon. I'm prac-

1.3.75 ticing now. My first sermon is going to be about sin. That's a terrible thing you know, sin is.

KATIE BELL Yes, I expect so –

ESTAQUIO Sin makes you drink and makes you gamble and go wrong. I wrestle with the devil all the time.

1.3.80 KATIE BELL Do you?

ESTAQUIO All the time. I talk rough to him. I tell him to go away and leave me alone. The devil got hold of my Mama, you know.

KATIE BELL Did he?

1.3.85 ESTAQUIO Oh, yes. Got hold of her and wouldn't let her go. My Papa prayed and I prayed but he won out. She ran off and left Papa and me. She hated church. Hated the Bible. Hated hymns. Hated Jesus. That was just the devil making her say that. We don't know where Mama is. We saw her on the street one day

1.3.90 in Mexico City, but when we went up to her she said she didn't even know who we were. She told us to go away and mind our own business. But we didn't listen to her. We stayed right there beside her on the street corner praying, and then we went on. She never was a true Baptist, Papa said. Not in her heart. She

1.3.95 used to slip off and go to confession all the time. I'm going to pray. Bow your head. *Dios, dame valor para testificar a esta muchacha y su familia la palabra de Dios. Y que sean bendecidos. También por medio de tu bendición, ellos logren sus metas. Te pido SEÑOR, que con ternura ella se fije en mí.* AMÉN. Don't I pray good? Papa

1.3.100 taught me to do that. What does your Papa do?

KATIE BELL He's an engineer. He's been bumped.

ESTAQUIO What does that mean?

KATIE BELL It means when you work for the railroad when someone who has more seniority than you do wants your

1.3.105 job they can have it.

ESTAQUIO Is he out of a job?

Dios ... en mí · "God, give me courage to witness God's word to this girl and her family. And let them be won over. Also through your blessing, let them achieve their goals. I ask, Lord, that she look on me with kindness" (Spanish)

KATIE BELL No, but now he has to bump someone and take their job.

ESTAQUIO Maybe he'll bump someone in Mexico.

KATIE BELL Oh, I don't think so.   1.3.110

[MRS. JACKSON *comes out on the porch followed by* VESTA.]

MRS. JACKSON Come in the house now, Katie Bell.

KATIE BELL He's a preacher's son.

MRS. JACKSON Who is?

KATIE BELL That boy there. He and his Daddy came here to start a Mexican Baptist church.   1.3.115

MRS. JACKSON What kind of a Baptist church?

KATIE BELL Mexican. They do everything in Mexican. Preach and all.

[*She turns to* ESTAQUIO.]

Is your Bible in Mexican, too?

ESTAQUIO Yes.   1.3.120

MRS. JACKSON Why, I never heard of such a thing.

VESTA We have colored Methodist and Baptist churches – how many, Mama?

MRS. JACKSON Oh, Lord. More than I can count.

KATIE BELL Say to her what you said to me.   1.3.125

ESTAQUIO *Jehová es mi pastor, nada me faltará.*

KATIE BELL You know what that says?

VESTA No, and you don't either.

KATIE BELL I do, too. "The Lord is my Shepherd and I shall not want –"   1.3.130

MRS. JACKSON Is that so? Mercy. Why, that's remarkable.

[ESTAQUIO *begins to sing "Rock of Ages."*]

ESTAQUIO *"Roca de la eternidad,*
    fuiste abierta tú por mí,
    sé mi escondedero fiel,   1.3.135
    sólo encuentro paz en ti,
    rico, limpio manantial,
    en el cual lavado fui." •

[MR. JACKSON *comes in.*]

MRS. JACKSON Daddy, that was "Rock of Ages" in Mexican.

MR. JACKSON Is that so? I thought I recognized the tune. You   1.3.140
from Mexico?

ESTAQUIO Yes.

Roca … fui · Spanish version of the English hymn written by Augustus Toplady (1776)

MRS. JACKSON His Daddy is a preacher.

ESTAQUIO There are plenty of Mexicans across the tracks over there.
1.3.145   They told my Daddy they're going to start a Mexican school.

MRS. JACKSON Is that so? Have you heard that, Daddy?

MR. JACKSON No.

MRS. JACKSON We have a nice white school here, of course, and a colored school and now we'll have a Mexican school. Well –

1.3.150   **MR. JACKSON** I wonder if there are any Mexican Methodists –

[MYRA *and* PETE *come in.*]

Well, look who's home. When did you get here?

MYRA He came in on the four o'clock bus. He wanted to take the train, Mr. Jackson, but it would have gotten him home too late.

MR. JACKSON Oh, don't worry about hurting my feelings. I don't
1.3.155   own the railroads. I just work for them.

MRS. JACKSON But I worry a lot about it, Daddy. Now more people seem to me ride the bus – what'll happen to the trains if everybody starts riding the bus?

MR. JACKSON I don't know. I got enough to worry about without
1.3.160   worrying about that.

[MR. JACKSON *goes inside.*]

MRS. JACKSON He does worry about it. He worries about it all the time. Only he says one day we could wake up and find there are no trains at all. But that's foolishness, of course. There will always be trains.

1.3.165   **KATIE BELL** Myra, Estaquio is Mexican. Estaquio, Myra plays the piano at the picture show and she says that Ramón Navarro, Lupe Veléz, Antonio Moreno and Dolores Del Río are Mexican. Do you know them?

ESTAQUIO Oh, yes. Very well. They're all Baptists.

1.3.170   **MRS. JACKSON** Is that so?

ESTAQUIO Just like Jesus.

MRS. JACKSON Oh –

ESTAQUIO Well, so very nice to have met you all.

[ESTAQUIO *leaves.*]

KATIE BELL Was there a good crowd at the picture show this
1.3.175   afternoon?

MYRA Pretty fair.

KATIE BELL Is it still the Bessie Love picture?

MYRA No. Colleen Moore.

KATIE BELL She has one brown eye and one blue eye.

MYRA That's what they say.   1.3.180

MRS. JACKSON How do you know that, Katie Bell?

KATIE BELL Someone told me.

VESTA No one told you anything. You got it out of movie magazines. When she's down at the drug store she slips those movie
magazines and reads them.   1.3.185

KATIE BELL I do not.

VESTA You do too.

[WILLIS comes in.]

WILLIS Well, look who's home. Get your glove and let's play a
game of catch.

PETE I don't want to play catch –   1.3.190

[PETE goes inside the house.]

MYRA He's mad because he had to come home. Well, he'll get
over it.

[MYRA goes inside.]

VESTA His Daddy has a swimming pool in Houston, I guess he
misses that –

[MRS. JACKSON goes into the house.]

KATIE BELL Did you know Jesus was a Baptist?   1.3.195

VESTA That's a big lie – who told you that?

KATIE BELL That Mexican boy.

VESTA My foot. That's a big lie.

[Calling into the house.]

Mama, was Jesus a Baptist?

[MRS. JACKSON comes out on the porch.]

MRS. JACKSON What?   1.3.200

VESTA You heard that Mexican boy tell her Jesus was a Baptist.
Was he?

MRS. JACKSON Well, that don't make it so –

VESTA What was he, Mama?

MRS. JACKSON What was who?   1.3.205

VESTA Jesus – was he a Methodist?

MRS. JACKSON Well, now. I'm not sure – he could have been, of
course. I don't know if it says in the Bible, do you Willis?

WILLIS What?

MRS. JACKSON What denomination Jesus was.   1.3.210

WILLIS I don't believe so. He was born a Jew.

1.3.212   **VESTA** Well, he's certainly not any Mexican Baptist. I know that. Tell that to your Mexican friend next time you see him —

[**VESTA** *goes into the house.*]

WILLIS I'm going to wash up.

[**WILLIS** *goes.* **MRS. JACKSON** *and* **KATIE BELL** *go inside as the lights fade.*]

ACT 1, SCENE 4

[*The lights are brought up in the bedroom* **MYRA** *and* **PETE** *share.* **PETE** *is there with his glove and baseball. He is angrily throwing the ball into the glove over and over.* **MYRA** *comes in. She gets a newspaper and tries to read, ignoring the noise of the ball as it hits the glove.*]

1.4.1   **MYRA** If you want to do that, Son, go outside.

PETE I don't want to go outside.

MYRA Let's both go outside, it's cooler out there.

PETE I don't want to go outside.

1.4.5   **MYRA** Come on.

PETE How many times do I have to tell you, Lady, I don't want to go outside.

MYRA All right, then.

[*A pause.*]

Daddy told me you'd been swimming in the river here.

[**PETE** *doesn't answer. He continues to smack the ball into the glove.*]

1.4.10   Did you hear my question, Pete?

PETE I heard it.

MYRA Is what your Daddy said true?

PETE I guess so.

MYRA You guess? Don't you know? Did you go swimming in

1.4.15   that river?

PETE Yes.

[**PETE** *stops throwing the ball into his glove.*]

MYRA How many times?

PETE Six or seven.

MYRA Pete, I told you not to do that, you promised me you

1.4.20   wouldn't.

PETE What do you expect me to do — just sit around here in this room and rot?

MYRA I don't want you to go into a river that's dangerous and that has suckholes and alligators and poisonous snakes and

1.4.25   where you could be drowned —

PETE A lot of boys go in the river.   1.4.26

MYRA I don't care what a lot of boys do. I don't want you to go.

[*A pause.*]

You hear me?

[*A pause.*]

Pete?

PETE What.   1.4.30

MYRA How do you like Willis?

PETE He's O. K.

MYRA He likes you.

PETE So?

MYRA He likes you a lot.   1.4.35

[PETE *goes back to the ball and glove.*]

Put the ball down, Son, it's making me very nervous.

[PETE *does so.*]

Pete...

PETE Yes?

MYRA He's asked me to marry him when he gets a divorce from
his wife.   1.4.40

[*A pause.*]

How would you feel about that?

[PETE *shrugs his shoulders, but says nothing.*]

I told him I couldn't say I'd marry him until I talked it over with
you first, I told him I couldn't marry anyone you didn't like.

[*A pause.*]

Do you like him?

[*Again* PETE *shrugs his shoulders.*]

Maybe if you could get to know him better you would get to   1.4.45
like him.

[*A pause.*]

Pete, I'm at my wits end, Son. I promised you we would never
move again and I am going to keep my promise if it's humanly
possible, but I don't know what I'll do if the picture show goes
talkie, but if I married Willis we would live on here, he has   1.4.50
money to buy a lot and build a house where you can have
your own room. He's a nice man, Son, kind, he doesn't drink,
he works hard and could support us –

[*A pause.*]

PETE Mama?

1.4.55 **MYRA** Yes, Son.

PETE I feel terrible about this, Mama –

MYRA What about, Son?

PETE What I'm about to tell you.

MYRA What is it, Son?

1.4.60 **PETE** Well, you go ahead and marry Willis, if you want to, Mama,
but I don't want to live here anymore –

MYRA You don't?

PETE No.

MYRA Well, that makes everything different, then.

1.4.65 **PETE** Mama?

MYRA Yes, Son.

PETE This sure is hard for me to say, because it's not that I don't
love you, because I do, but I don't want to live here with you
anymore, Mama, or any place –

1.4.70 **MYRA** Now that's just your Daddy poisoning your mind. He
has no right to –

PETE It's not Daddy, Mama. It's me. I almost ran off just now and
hitchhiked back to Houston without saying anything, but I
just couldn't do that, Mama. So please let me go back.

1.4.75 **MYRA** When?

PETE Tomorrow.

MYRA Tomorrow?

PETE Yes, Ma'am.

[*A pause.*]

You see, Mama, there's nothing for me to do here –

1.4.80 **MYRA** I know that.

PETE Dad said he will teach me to drive his truck and I can start
to work for him in my spare time. They have a swimming pool
and a car and a nice house and he's married to a nice lady.

MYRA Is she?

1.4.85 **PETE** Oh, very nice and I like my brothers. We all have a lot of
fun together.

[*A pause.* **MYRA** *cries.*]

Mama, please don't cry. I don't mean to make you cry.

[*A pause.* **MYRA** *wipes her eyes.*]

MYRA I know that. If I let you go will you come and spend your
holidays with me?

1.4.90 **PETE** Sure. Are you gonna marry Willis?

MYRA I don't know.

PETE Dad said the other night he hoped you would get married again. He said you sure couldn't make a living any longer playing the picture shows.

MYRA When do you want to leave, Son?

PETE Tomorrow.

MYRA Tomorrow?

PETE Yes, Ma'am, if you don't mind. Dad is driving everybody to Colorado for a two week vacation and they all want me to go with them.

MYRA What about summer school?

PETE I'll catch up next summer.

MYRA Pete.

PETE Please, Mama. I want to go.

MYRA All right, then.

[MYRA *looks at her wristwatch.*]

I have to go to work. Here's some money. Go on uptown and get something to eat later on.

PETE Yes, Ma'am.

MYRA I'll see you later, Son.

PETE All right.

MYRA And when you go to Houston tomorrow take the train instead of the bus; it would please Mr. Jackson.

PETE I don't have to take either, Dad is coming for me.

MYRA Oh. Bye, Son.

[MYRA *leaves him.*]

PETE Mama.

[MYRA *goes out of her room, into the living room, and outside.* PETE *takes his glove and baseball and follows her. When he gets to the yard he stops.*]

MYRA So long –

PETE So long –

[MYRA *continues.* PETE *throws the ball up in the air and catches it as the lights fade.*]

ACT 1, SCENE 5

[*The lights are brought up. It is an hour later.* PETE *is still in the yard.* KATIE BELL *comes to the door.*]

KATIE BELL Mama says if you'd like to have supper with us there's plenty.

PETE Thanks, I'd like to.

KATIE BELL We'll eat in about a half hour.

1.5.5 **PETE** Thanks.

[**KATIE BELL** *goes as* **WILLIS** *comes over with his glove.*]

WILLIS Feel like a game of catch now?

PETE Sure.

WILLIS Gotta break in my new glove. Where'd you get yours?

PETE From my Daddy.

[*They start to play catch.* **GLADYS** *comes in.*]

1.5.10 **GLADYS** Well, Willis –

[**WILLIS** *looks up.*]

Aren't you going to say hello?

WILLIS Hello.

GLADYS How have you been?

WILLIS All right. How have you been, Gladys?

1.5.15 **GLADYS** Tolerable. Who's your friend?

WILLIS He's Pete.

PETE Hello.

GLADYS You're Myra's boy, aren't you?

PETE Yes, Ma'am.

1.5.20 **GLADYS** I just bought a ticket to the picture show so I could get
a look at her, but it was too dark in there and her back was
turned so I couldn't see a thing. She plays the piano nicely
though. Where do you live, Willis?

WILLIS Up there over that garage.

1.5.25 **GLADYS** Are you working?

WILLIS Yes.

GLADYS I'm miserable, Willis. Just miserable.

WILLIS I'm sorry to hear that, Gladys.

GLADYS Has Ashenback been around here?

1.5.30 **WILLIS** Not that I know of.

GLADYS Well, I'm warning you. He's liable to come with a gun,
too. He's very jealous-hearted, he's very jealous of you ever
since I told him I made a mistake in leaving you. I walked up
to your girlfriend at the picture show, tapped her on the back

1.5.35 and told her her game was up. She didn't even turn around
and look at me if she heard me. She didn't miss a note on that
piano. I'm very tired, Willis. I've come a long way. Aren't you
going to invite me up to your room?

WILLIS It's just a small room, Gladys.

GLADYS I don't care how small it is. Nothing could be smaller   1.5.40
than the room we had when we first married. Do you remem-
ber that room, Willis?

WILLIS Yes.

GLADYS A regular closet. Ashenback is a four-flusher, Willis.
He talks big but it never comes to nothing.   1.5.45

WILLIS Is that so?

GLADYS Oh, my God, Willis. I made a mistake running off with him.

WILLIS Did you?

GLADYS Yes, I did. You know what he's doing now? He's a vendor
for cigarette machines. That's how I heard about you and Myra.   1.5.50
He said he looked you up the last time he was in Harrison and
you proceeded to tell him about your girlfriend, Myra.

WILLIS He never looked me up.

GLADYS Ashenback is such a liar. He's lied since the first day I met
him. Told me the first time I met him that he had a bank account   1.5.55
of a hundred thousand dollars. And I believed him, too. And that's
not the only lie of his I believed. We'd be here all night if I told you
all the lies Ashenback has told me since we were together.

[ASHENBACK *comes in.*]

Ashenback, you are the biggest liar God ever made. Willis   1.5.60
never told you nothing about a girlfriend. Did you, Willis?

WILLIS No.

ASHENBACK Never mind about that. His having a girlfriend
wasn't a lie, was it? You don't always tell the truth yourself – you told me you were going to visit your Mama and
when I called your Mama to see if you had gotten there, she   1.5.65
said she hadn't heard a word from you in a month. But I wasn't
born yesterday, I figured exactly where you had gone.

[*He draws a gun.*]

Keep away from Gladys, Mister.

WILLIS Are you crazy? I don't know what you are talking about.
This is the first time I've seen Gladys in I don't know when.   1.5.70

GLADYS Willis, don't let him intimidate you, he's all bluff.

[KATIE BELL *appears.*]

KATIE BELL Supper, Pete.

PETE I'll be along in a minute.

KATIE BELL Who's your company?

1.5.75   **GLADYS** I'm Willis' wife.

KATIE BELL How do you do?

ASHENBACK Come on home, Gladys. Don't cause me to commit murder.

GLADYS You're all bluff.

1.5.80   **ASHENBACK** Am I?

GLADYS You sure are.

[MRS. JACKSON *comes out.*]

MRS. JACKSON Children, supper's on the table and getting cold. Who are these nice people, Willis?

GLADYS I'm Willis' wife —

1.5.85   [ESTAQUIO *comes in with a Bible.*]

ESTAQUIO Evening, everybody.

[ESTAQUIO *goes to* KATIE BELL *and* MRS. JACKSON.]

I have brought you a Spanish Bible.

MRS. JACKSON Isn't that nice. I called Brother Meyers and told him about "Rock of Ages" being sung in Spanish. He was thrilled. He says there are Methodist Mexicans.

1.5.90   **ESTAQUIO** Yes, Ma'am. Glad to hear it.

[VESTA *comes out.*]

VESTA Mama, the food is getting stone cold.

[VESTA *sees* ESTAQUIO.]

MRS. JACKSON Vesta, the Mexican boy brought us a Spanish Bible.

ESTAQUIO Estaquio.

1.5.95   **MRS. JACKSON** E s t —

ESTAQUIO Estaquio.

[MRS. JACKSON, *slowly.*]

MRS. JACKSON Estaquio. Would you read something to us from the Bible?

ESTAQUIO Sure.

1.5.100   [ESTAQUIO *takes the Bible.*]

VESTA Mama, our supper is getting cold.

MRS. JACKSON Be quiet, Vesta, this is a chance of a lifetime.

ASHENBACK Well, I'm not standing around here listening to any Mexican read the Bible. Come on Gladys.

[ASHENBACK *grabs her.* GLADYS *pulls away.*]

GLADYS I don't love you anymore. Leave me alone.

1.5.105   **ASHENBACK** Gladys —

GLADYS I don't love you and I never have. I love Willis and I   1.5.106
always have and he loves me and I'm leaving you and going
back to him.

WILLIS Now look here —

ASHENBACK Do you mean that, Gladys? Do you really mean   1.5.110
you don't love me?

GLADYS From the bottom of my heart, I mean that. You and
Willis fight it out. I'm going up to his room.

[GLADYS *walks out.*]

ASHENBACK Gladys, wait. Please. Don't leave me. I'll kill myself
if you do.   1.5.115

[*He runs after her.*]

MRS. JACKSON They're very upset, aren't they?

ESTAQUIO Shall I read some —

MRS. JACKSON If you will.

[ESTAQUIO, *reading in Spanish.*]

ESTAQUIO *En el principio creó Dios los cielos y la tierra. Y la
tierra estaba desordenada y vacía, y las tinieblas estaban*   1.5.120
sobre la faz del abismo, y el Espíritu de Dios se movía sobre
la faz de las aguas.

MRS. JACKSON Isn't that interesting. What does all that mean?

ESTAQUIO That's the first few verses of Genesis.

MRS. JACKSON Is that right?   1.5.125

[ESTAQUIO, *reading.*]

ESTAQUIO In the beginning God created the heaven and the
earth. *En el principio creó Dios los cielos y la tierra.* And the
earth was without form and void. *Y la tierra estaba desorde-*
nada y vacía. And darkness was upon the face of the deep. *Y*
las tinieblas estaban sobre la faz del abismo. And the spirit   1.5.130
moved upon the face of the waters. *Y el Espíritu de Dios se*
movía sobre la faz de las aguas.

MRS. JACKSON Spirit of God? Do you know any other hymns
in Spanish?

ESTAQUIO Oh, yes.   1.5.135

MRS. JACKSON "Blessed Assurance?"

ESTAQUIO Oh, yes.

MRS. JACKSON Would you sing that, please?

VESTA Mama —

MRS. JACKSON Oh, Vesta —   1.5.140

[ESTAQUIO, *singing.*]

1.5.141 ESTAQUIO *"En Jesucristo, mártir de paz,*
En horas negras de tempestad,
Grato consuelo felicidad,
Nuevo aliento al corazón.

1.5.145 *Gloria, cantemos al redentor,*
Que por nosotros quiso morir."•

[*A gun is fired offstage. A woman screams.* GLADYS *runs in.*]

GLADYS Oh, Willis. Come quick. Ashenback has shot himself.
Somebody call a doctor.

[VESTA *and* KATIE BELL *scream.* WILLIS *goes running off to get to*
ASHENBACK.]

MRS. JACKSON Now keep calm girls.

[*To Gladys.*]

1.5.150 I'll call a doctor.

GLADYS Thank you.

[MRS. JACKSON *goes into the house.* GLADYS *goes off as the lights fade.*]

"En Jesucristo …
morir" · "In Jesus
Christ, martyr of
peace,/In the black
hours of the tempest,/
There is sweet comfort
and happiness,/New
life for the heart./Glory,
sing to the Savior,/Who
was willing to die for
our sins" (Spanish)

ACT 2, SCENE 1

[*The lights are brought up. It is later that night.* MYRA *sits on the steps.*
MRS. JACKSON *comes out in her robe.*]

2.1.1 MRS. JACKSON Willis and Pete not back from the hospital yet?

MYRA No.

MRS. JACKSON Oh, my heavens. I almost died myself when I
heard that gun go off. Do you know what Mr. Ashenback's

2.1.5 religious affiliation is?

MYRA No.

MRS. JACKSON I don't either, but I called Brother Meyers to stand
by in case he's a Methodist and he's needed. Brother Meyers
said he would go right over to the hospital in case he wanted

2.1.10 someone to pray for him.

[KATIE BELL *and* VESTA *come out.*]

Why in the world aren't you girls in bed asleep?

VESTA Who can sleep with all that has been going on?

KATIE BELL Where's that Bible Estaquio left, Mama?

MRS. JACKSON In my room.

2.1.15 VESTA I hope he doesn't make a practice of coming by here.

KATIE BELL How is he going to make a practice of coming by
here if he is leaving for Mexico in the morning?

[PETE *and* WILLIS *come in.*]

WILLIS He's going to live.

PETE He just shot his foot is all.   2.1.20

MRS. JACKSON That's a relief.

VESTA That can be dangerous – Cal Burton shot his foot to keep
from going into the Army –

MRS. JACKSON Sister –

VESTA Well, he did. Everybody knows that and he developed   2.1.25
gangrene and they had to amputate his leg. He had to use a
wooden leg which swells when you get it wet and when he went
to college and was taking a bath in his fraternity house, one of
his fraternity brothers, a practical joker, used to come into the
bathroom and say it's Saturday night and you're supposed to   2.1.30
wash all over and throw that wooden leg in the tub with him.

MRS. JACKSON Sister, –

VESTA It's the truth, Mama, Thomas told me so.

MRS. JACKSON Well, don't be talking about such unladylike
things, it's not refined.   2.1.35

PETE I'm going to bed, good night.

[PETE *starts in.*]

MRS. JACKSON In all the excitement you never did get your
supper did you, Son?

PETE No, Ma'am.

MRS. JACKSON There's some cold chicken in the ice box.   2.1.40

PETE Thank you.

MRS. JACKSON I hear you're leaving in the morning, Son?

PETE Yes, Ma'am.

MRS. JACKSON We'll sure miss you.

PETE Yes, Ma'am.   2.1.45

VESTA Who do you look more like? Your Daddy or your Mama?

PETE I don't know.

[PETE *exits.*]

VESTA Miss Myra. Who does he look more like? You or your
ex-husband?

MYRA I don't know, Vesta. I'm not a good judge of things like that. 2.1.50

KATIE BELL Myra, tell her the story of that talking picture you
saw in Houston with that colored man –

MYRA He wasn't colored, honey. He just put on black face when
he sings –

2.1.55   **KATIE BELL** Why does he do that?

MYRA I don't know.

KATIE BELL Anyway, tell her the story.

MRS. JACKSON You better not start. We might get Vesta all upset again.

2.1.60   **KATIE BELL** Let her go in the house if it upsets her.

VESTA You go in the house. I'm not about to go into the house.

KATIE BELL Will it upset you if she sings the song?

VESTA No.

KATIE BELL Sing the song to Mama, Myra, that the man sang
2.1.65   in the picture show after his son died.

MRS. JACKSON Was this a little colored boy?

KATIE BELL No, Mama.

MRS. JACKSON Oh, I thought you said the man was colored.

MYRA No, Ma'am. He is a white man, but he puts on black face
2.1.70   when he sings.

MRS. JACKSON I wonder why he does that.

KATIE BELL Nobody knows that, Mama, didn't you just hear
Myra? Will you sing it for us, Myra?

MYRA I'm sorry, honey. I just don't feel like singing now.

[**MYRA** *goes into the house.*]

2.1.75   **KATIE BELL** Mama, if I tell you something will you not get mad
at me?

MRS. JACKSON Depends on what it is.

KATIE BELL No. I'm not going to tell you.

MRS. JACKSON Tell me. I won't get mad.

2.1.80   **KATIE BELL** No matter what it is?

MRS. JACKSON No.

KATIE BELL Swear.

MRS. JACKSON No, I won't swear. I promise, but I won't swear.
What kind of language is that?

2.1.85   **KATIE BELL** I went to a picture show once.

MRS. JACKSON When?

KATIE BELL Two years ago when I was visiting in El Campo.

VESTA What did you see?

KATIE BELL Clara Bow in *Rough House Rosie*.

2.1.90   **VESTA** No, you didn't. You're just telling Mama that to get
attention.

KATIE BELL I did too. Are you mad at me, Mama?

MRS. JACKSON No, not as long as you don't ever go again.

KATIE BELL My conscience hurt me something terrible.

MRS. JACKSON Of course, it did. Mine did, too, when I went to   2.1.95
the medicine show and the tent show. Did you ask God to
forgive you?

KATIE BELL Yes, Ma'am. Every night for a month.

VESTA Oh, rot.

KATIE BELL I did, too.   2.1.100

VESTA You don't even say your prayers at night.

KATIE BELL I do, too.

VESTA You do not. I hear you snoring as soon as the lights are
turned off.

[GLADYS comes in.]

GLADYS Willis?   2.1.105

WILLIS Yes?

GLADYS One of the nice doctors from the hospital drove me
over here. I got me a room at the hotel but I left my suitcase
here. I said you could drive me over to the hotel.

WILLIS All right.   2.1.110

MRS. JACKSON How's your husband?

GLADYS He's not my husband. An ex-boyfriend.

VESTA Is he going to lose his foot?

GLADYS No, I don't think so. You know what he said to me, Willis, just
before I left? He said he loved me as much as he did his God.   2.1.115

MRS. JACKSON What is his religious affiliation?

GLADYS Good Lord, Lady, I don't know. We never discussed
religion.

MRS. JACKSON Our Methodist minister, Brother Meyers, went
over to see him in case he wanted prayer.   2.1.120

GLADYS And you know what else he said to me, Willis? He said
I love you too much to stand in the way of your happiness. I
want you to do what you want. Tell Willis he has my blessing.
Wasn't that sweet? Of course, like I told Ashenback, I said,
Willis may not want me back.   2.1.125

WILLIS Gladys?

GLADYS Yes?

WILLIS I don't want you back.

GLADYS You don't?

WILLIS No. I want a divorce now. I am going to marry someone else.   2.1.130

2.1.131   **GLADYS** Myra?

WILLIS If she'll have me.

GLADYS Oh, I thought so. What a sneak she is. Moving next door to you taking advantage of you because you're lonely and miss-

2.1.135   ing me. Didn't you tell me when I left you you would never get over it? Never look at another woman as long as you lived!

WILLIS Yes, I did, but —

GLADYS Don't give me any buts, please. You men are all alike. Philanderers…

2.1.140   **MRS. JACKSON** Vesta, you and Katie Bell come on in the house now.

[MRS. JACKSON, KATIE BELL, *and* VESTA *go in.*]

GLADYS I have no money, I'm tired and I want to go to the hotel, but I have no money.

WILLIS Here's fifteen dollars —

GLADYS I can't walk into town with my suitcase.

2.1.145   **WILLIS** Come on, I'll take you.

[WILLIS *picks up the suitcase. He and* GLADYS *start out.* MRS. JACKSON *comes to the door and watches.* VESTA *and* KATIE BELL *join her at the door.*]

VESTA She's gone.

KATIE BELL And I hope she never comes back —

[MRS. JACKSON, KATIE BELL, *and* VESTA *come outside.*]

VESTA Now, what do you think is going to happen Mama?

MRS. JACKSON About what?

2.1.150   **VESTA** You know.

[VESTA *points to* MYRA's *room.*]

MRS. JACKSON Sh. Myra's in her room. She might hear you.

[*Calling to* MYRA.]

   Myra —

[MYRA, *calling from her room.*]

MYRA Yes.

[MRS. JACKSON, *calling to* MYRA.]

MRS. JACKSON Come on out and visit with us.

[MYRA *comes outside.*]

2.1.155   **KATIE BELL** Where's Pete?

MYRA He's gone to bed.

MRS. JACKSON I hope I'll get to meet Pete's father when he comes for him in the morning. It seems every time he comes here to see Pete, I'm gone.

VESTA Who taught you to play the piano, Myra?   2.1.160

MYRA A nice lady back in Nacogdoches, Miss Eppie Daughty.

VESTA Was she strict? Did she make you practice?

MYRA Yes she did.

　[*A pause.*]

　Did Willis leave with his wife?

MRS. JACKSON Yes. He took her to the hotel.   2.1.165

VESTA Did you know he was married?

MRS. JACKSON Vesta!

MYRA Yes I knew it. He told me when I first met him.

MRS. JACKSON We'll miss Pete. He's been a lot of company.

KATIE BELL I finished *Ben Hur* – I'm starting *The Four Horsemen*   2.1.170
　now. It says in the book it was a movie with Rudolph Valentino.
　Did you see that movie?

MYRA Yes, I did.

KATIE BELL Did you play for it?

MYRA No, I hadn't begun to play the movie houses then.   2.1.175
　[ASHENBACK *comes in. His foot's bandaged.*]

ASHENBACK Ladies. Do you know where Gladys went to?

MRS. JACKSON She went to the Riverside Hotel, I think.

ASHENBACK Thank you. I want to apologize for the scene I
　caused. Jealousy is a terrible thing and I'm infected with it.
　I can tell by your kind faces you've never been infected by   2.1.180
　jealousy. You should thank your Maker for that blessing.
　[MR. JACKSON *comes out.*]

MR. JACKSON How do you do? I'm Ray Jackson.

ASHENBACK Delbert Ashenback.

MR. JACKSON You the fellow shot his foot?

ASHENBACK Yes.   2.1.185

MR. JACKSON Mama was telling me about it. You're lucky to be
　alive. Well, I hope you have that out of your system now.

ASHENBACK I hope so.

MR. JACKSON You certainly got everything fired up in this house.
　I'm usually asleep way before this, but I haven't been able to   2.1.190
　sleep. What doctor treated your foot, Vails or White?

ASHENBACK White.

MR. JACKSON Then your foot is going to be all right. Not that
　Dr. Vails isn't a perfectly competent doctor, but I have great
　faith in Doctor White.   2.1.195

2.1.196   **ASHENBACK** Does Willis live up there over the garage?

MR. JACKSON Yes, he does.

MRS. JACKSON He's not there now, he drove that lady to the hotel.

ASHENBACK I see, when you see him tell him I'm sorry for all
2.1.200   the trouble I caused him.

    [*He starts out.*]

MR. JACKSON Will you be getting a room at the hotel too?

ASHENBACK No, I'm driving on home tonight, alone.

MR. JACKSON I see.

    [**ASHENBACK** *goes.*]

    I'm turning in. I think I'll sleep now. You coming, Mama?
2.1.205   **MRS. JACKSON** I think so.

    [**MR. JACKSON** *goes into the house.*]

    Come on girls.

VESTA Let us stay up a little longer, Mama.

KATIE BELL Please Mama.

MRS. JACKSON Will you get up in the morning the minute I
2.1.210   call you?

VESTA Yes we will.

MRS. JACKSON Well, all right. This once. But don't ever think
    I'm going to let you do it again.

    [**MRS. JACKSON** *goes in.*]

KATIE BELL The time I went to Sister Pate's slumber party we
2.1.215   stayed up until two. Some of the girls didn't go to sleep at all.
    But I couldn't stay awake after two. Rudolph Valentino died
    with appendicitis, didn't he?

MYRA Yes.

KATIE BELL There were headlines in all the Houston papers
2.1.220   when he died, weren't there?

MYRA Yes.

VESTA Was he a Mexican?

MYRA No, Italian.

KATIE BELL He was 31 when he died. On the anniversary of his
2.1.225   death, there appeared at his grave a mysterious lady with a
    long black veil. She told the reporters, she's coming back every
    year. Some say it's Pola Negri. Who do you think it is?

MYRA I don't know.

KATIE BELL Guess.

2.1.230   **MYRA** I just don't know – Wouldn't do me any good to guess –

[WILLIS *comes in.*]   2.1.231

VESTA The man that shot his foot was here looking for you. He
 said he was sorry for all that had happened.

WILLIS Where is he now?

VESTA He said he was going back to his home.   2.1.235

KATIE BELL Without that lady.

VESTA I'm going to bed. You better come too, Katie Bell.

[VESTA *and* KATIE BELL *go in.*]

WILLIS I'm really sorry for all that happened.

MYRA I know you are.   2.1.240

WILLIS I hope the Jacksons won't think any the less of me. I'll
 apologize to them tomorrow. I told Gladys I wanted a divorce
 so I could marry you. She said she'll fight me in every court
 in the land to keep me from getting a divorce. I said go ahead
 I don't care how long it takes I'm getting a divorce so I can   2.1.245
 marry Myra, if she'll have me.

[PETE *comes outside.*]

MYRA I thought you were asleep.

PETE I'm too excited to sleep.

WILLIS You're journey proud Pete.

PETE I guess. Have you ever been to Colorado, Willis?   2.1.250

WILLIS No.

MYRA Ever since you've told me about Colorado I've been thinking about my Mama. She always said there were two places
 she wanted to go before she died – Colorado and California.
 Colorado in the summer time and California in the winter.   2.1.255

WILLIS Did she ever get there?

MYRA No, she never got out of Nacogdoches.

[*A pause.*]

 I'm tired. I think I'm ready for bed. I bet I'll sleep sound tonight.
 Goodnight, Willis.

WILLIS Goodnight.   2.1.260

MYRA You better come to bed too, Son.

PETE I can't get to sleep Mama, I'm too excited.

MYRA You'll get to sleep – come on.

PETE All right, goodnight.

[PETE *goes into the house.* MYRA *starts in.*]

WILLIS Myra, what was your Mama's name? I never heard you say.   2.1.265

MYRA Corinne.

WILLIS Corinne?

MYRA Yes, like Corinne Griffith, the movie star. My Mama died when I was sixteen.

2.1.270 **WILLIS** Is Myra the name of a movie star?

MYRA Not that I ever heard of.

WILLIS I don't think Willis is either.

MYRA No, I don't believe so. There is a Wallace, a Wallace Berry, and there was a Wallace Reed.

2.1.275 **WILLIS** He's dead?

MYRA Yes. He died a dope fiend.

WILLIS My mother's name was Lena.

MYRA That's the name of a movie star – Lena Basquette.

WILLIS Is that so? I never heard of her. Myra, I'm really sorry
2.1.280 for what happened.

MYRA I know you are.

WILLIS And I am going to get a divorce. I am –

[**PETE** *comes out.*]

PETE Mama – I thought you were going to bed?

MYRA I'm on my way.

2.1.285 **WILLIS** Well, goodnight.

MYRA Goodnight.

[**WILLIS** *leaves.* **MYRA** *and* **PETE** *enter their room.*]

Warm in our room?

PETE Like an oven.

MYRA Well, you'll be out of it soon. It's cool in Colorado. You
2.1.290 sleep under blankets at night I'm told.

[*She turns the lamp off as the lights fade.*]

ACT 2, SCENE 2

[*The lights are brought up – it is the next day. In* **MYRA***'s room.* **PETE***'s
bag is packed and waiting to be put into his father's car.* **PETE** *is in front
of the house with his glove and ball. The* **JACKSONS***, dressed for a trip,
come into the living room.* **MRS. JACKSON** *knocks on* **MYRA***'s door.*]

2.2.1 **MRS. JACKSON** Myra –

[**MYRA** *comes to the door.*]

MYRA Yes?

MRS. JACKSON We're leaving for the day, Myra. We won't be back until late tonight.

2.2.5 **MYRA** You're going to look over Cuero?

MRS. JACKSON Yes, to see if we like it.   2.2.6

VESTA I think it's terrible of the railroad pulling something like this. Daddy has been an engineer for twenty-five years.

MR. JACKSON That's the system, Sister. I knew it when I started with the railroad. Seniority is everything. I always knew every   2.2.10 time I went to a town I could be bumped and my job taken by someone who had been longer with the railroad. Mama knew that when she married me. I bumped somebody to get here.

MRS. JACKSON Only because you were bumped by somebody in the last town we lived in.   2.2.15

MR. JACKSON And I can be bumped again, I guess, if someone with seniority wants my job there. Mama wants me to quit the railroad, but like I explained to her I've given twenty-five years of my life working there, I have benefits. Not every place gives you benefits.   2.2.20

MRS. JACKSON That's true. He has a pension when he retires.

[KATIE BELL, *crying.*]

KATIE BELL I don't want to leave Harrison. All my friends are here. Sally Doris said I could live with her until I finished school.

[MR. JACKSON *exits.*]

VESTA Oh, that would be just fine. Sally Doris! You'd be ruined forever living here with her.   2.2.25

KATIE BELL Shut up, Vesta.

VESTA Shut up, yourself You'd be sneaking out to the picture show all the time just like you did in El Campo.

KATIE BELL Vesta, you are mean. I told Mama I was sorry I did that.   2.2.30

MRS. JACKSON Yes, she did, Vesta –

KATIE BELL Can I stay on here, Mama?

MRS. JACKSON No, you can't do that. We have to be together as a family.

[MRS. JACKSON, KATIE BELL, *and* VESTA *go out to* PETE *in the yard.*]

Pete, I expect you'll be gone by the time we get back. So we   2.2.35 want to say goodbye to you.

PETE Goodbye.

VESTA When's your Daddy coming for you?

PETE He was supposed to be here at twelve o'clock.

VESTA It's two now.   2.2.40

PETE I know that.

VESTA Maybe he's not coming today.

PETE No, he's coming. We're all going to Colorado tomorrow on a two week vacation.

2.2.45 **VESTA** That's up in the mountains. Have you ever been on a mountain?

PETE No, have you?

VESTA No, and I don't care to. Laurie LaBelle and her family drove out to Colorado and when they got there they took one

2.2.50 look at those mountains standing up ahead and they scared them so, the very thought of taking a car up them things, that they turned right around and came home. Her Mama said, "no mountains for me. I was born where it was flat and I intend to die where it's flat."

2.2.55 **KATIE BELL** I'd like to see the mountains. I'm going to take Spanish in school next year so I can visit Mexico one day.

VESTA Is she, Mama?

MRS. JACKSON If she wants to.

[**MRS. JACKSON** *goes back into the living room.* **VESTA** *and* **KATIE BELL** *follow.*]

VESTA Are you going to let her go to Mexico?

2.2.60 **MRS. JACKSON** Well, that's a long way down the road. We'll see about that when the time comes.

VESTA If she goes to Mexico, are you going to let her see that Mexican Baptist man preach?

MRS. JACKSON No, if she goes to Mexico or anywhere, she'll go

2.2.65 to the Methodist church just like she does here.

[**MR. JACKSON** *enters.*]

KATIE BELL What if they don't have a Methodist church in Mexico? Can't I go to the Baptist church then?

MRS. JACKSON We'll talk about that when the time comes.

MR. JACKSON I'll talk about that right now. No child of mine

2.2.70 is going to Mexico to be carried off by bandits and white slavers.

KATIE BELL Papa.

MR. JACKSON No and that settles that.

[**MR. JACKSON** *exits.*]

MRS. JACKSON Well, let's don't stand here arguing about Mexico.

2.2.75 Let's go if we're going. Goodbye, Pete.

PETE Goodbye.

[OTHERS *call out "Goodbye, Pete," "Have a good time in Colorado," etc.*
MYRA *sits in a chair.*]

PETE I wonder where Daddy is, Mama?

MYRA I don't know, Son. Something delayed him, I'm sure. He'll
be along. Now I've packed your suitcase with paper, pencils,
stamps, and envelopes. I want you to be sure to write me as   2.2.80
soon as you get to Colorado. I'll be anxious to hear.

[*The phone rings.* PETE *goes to answer it.* MYRA *goes into the house and
to the piano. She plays a Chopin étude.* PETE *comes back.*]

Was that your Daddy?

PETE No. His wife.

[*A pause.*]

The trip's off.

[MYRA *stops playing.*]

MYRA Why?   2.2.85

PETE He's on a drunk and they had a fight and she says she won't
go any place with him now or ever. She's mad.

MYRA Oh, I expect she'll calm down. They'll probably call you
tomorrow and say they're coming for you.

PETE No, Mama I don't think so. She asked me if he had invited   2.2.90
me to live with them and I said yes he had, and she said she
can't have me living there. That she has two boys of her own
to see to. She said Daddy is always saying things he shouldn't
and putting his foot in it.

MYRA I thought she knew you were going there to live?   2.2.95

PETE I thought so, too, but I guess she didn't.

MYRA I'm awfully sorry.

PETE That's O. K. I'll go and unpack my clothes.

MYRA I'll unpack them.

[PETE *goes out.* MYRA *goes into their room and begins to unpack the
clothes.* ESTAQUIO *comes in.*]

ESTAQUIO Hi.   2.2.100

PETE Hi.

ESTAQUIO Is Katie Bell in?

PETE No, she's gone for the day.

ESTAQUIO Oh, well give her this will you?

[ESTAQUIO *hands* PETE *a sheet of paper.*]

Tell her my Papa has decided not to go back to Mexico. He will   2.2.105
stay and do missionary work trying to convert the Mexican

Catholics to Baptists. He is preaching his first sermon this Sunday. All are invited, you too.

PETE Thank you.

2.2.110 **ESTAQUIO** Do you speak Spanish?

PETE No.

ESTAQUIO Then you probably won't enjoy it. It will be in Spanish. Tell Katie Bell I will be going to the Mexican school here next year.

2.2.115 **PETE** All right.

ESTAQUIO Are you a Baptist?

PETE No, Methodist.

ESTAQUIO Explain to me about the Methodists.

PETE What do you want to know about them?

2.2.120 **ESTAQUIO** Their creed, what exactly do they believe?

PETE Oh, I don't know a whole lot about things like that.

ESTAQUIO Do you go to church?

PETE Not too often, Christmas, Easter…

ESTAQUIO Then how do you know you're a Methodist?

2.2.125 **PETE** Because my mother told me I was. John Wesley was Methodist. I remember hearing that.

ESTAQUIO Who is John Wesley?

PETE I don't know exactly. I just remember hearing he was a famous Methodist.

[*A very drunk man comes in. He is* **GERARD ANDERSON**, *Pete's father.*]

2.2.130 **GERARD** Pete?

PETE Yessir.

GERARD Who is your Mexican friend?

ESTAQUIO Estaquio. Estaquio Trevino.

GERARD Run on. I have to discuss personal matters with my son.

[**ESTAQUIO** *leaves.*]

2.2.135 Did that old witch I'm married to call you?

PETE Yessir.

GERARD The Colorado trip is off because of that old witch. I said, all right. We won't go to Colorado, and I'm going to see my boy and tell him why. Tell him I'm married to the meanest

2.2.140 white woman God ever created. Nag, nag, nag, all the time. Where's Myra?

PETE She's inside.

[**PETE** *goes to the door and calls.*]

Mama, Daddy is here.

GERARD How is your Mama?

PETE She's all right.   2.2.145

GERARD Has the picture show here gone talkie yet?

PETE No.

GERARD It will. My God. I've told and told her. There's no future
in picture shows. Where are your suitcases, I've come to take
you to Houston.   2.2.150

PETE Well, I don't know. Your wife says I can't come.

GERARD Did she? Well, hell, she'll get over that. Well, maybe I
better not take you back today while she's still on the warpath.

[**MYRA** *comes out.*]

MYRA Hello, Gerard.

GERARD Hello, Myra. How are you today?   2.2.155

MYRA Pretty well.

GERARD I'm in trouble myself. I tied one on last night and Jackie
Kate pitched a fit. Called our trip to Colorado off. Did Pete
tell you that?

MYRA Yes.   2.2.160

GERARD Well, hell, who was that Mexican boy I just saw here?

MYRA He's a Baptist preacher's son.

PETE A Mexican Baptist preacher.

GERARD Well, hell, I don't care whose son he is. I don't want my
boy associating with Mexicans. That's one reason I'm deter-   2.2.165
mined to have him live with me so I can teach him right from
wrong. If they put in talking pictures here, what are you going
to do? Look for another playing for silent pictures?

MYRA I don't know.

GERARD Give it all up. God Almighty – where are picture shows   2.2.170
going to get you? I have a truck, a car, a beautiful house in
a lovely part of Houston, a swimming pool, a wife and two
lovely children and I didn't get that playing in no picture show.
I got it by being practical in a practical world.

[*A pause. He sways. He sits on the steps.*]

Excuse me. I'm drunk. I'm very drunk. I beg your pardon. I   2.2.175
have lots of troubles. I have to lie down for a while.

MYRA Take him into our room, Pete. He can lie down on
your bed.

[**MYRA** *goes into the living room.*]

PETE Come on, Daddy.

[**PETE** *takes* **GERARD** *into the house and into the bedroom and helps him onto the bed.* **WILLIS** *comes in with his glove.* **PETE** *comes out.*]

2.2.180   **WILLIS** I thought you were going to Houston today?

PETE No, sir, not now. Our plans have changed.

WILLIS I see. Who do you think is going to win the pennant in the Dixie League this year?

PETE I don't know. Who do you think?

2.2.185   **WILLIS** I think it is going to be a toss-up between Atlanta and Houston.

PETE Did you ever see Houston play?

WILLIS Yes.

PETE Who did you see them play?

2.2.190   **WILLIS** Atlanta.

PETE Who won?

WILLIS Atlanta. Want to play a game of catch?

PETE I don't mind.

[*They begin their game.*]

My Daddy is in there.

2.2.195   **WILLIS** Is he?

PETE Under the weather. That's why we're not going on our trip to Colorado.

[**MYRA** *comes out.*]

MYRA Pete, your father's wanted on the phone, see if you can rouse him.

2.2.200   **PETE** Yes 'm.

[**PETE** *goes inside and into the bedroom and begins to try to rouse his father.*]

WILLIS Hello, Myra.

MYRA Hello, Willis.

WILLIS Been warm today. A little cooler now.

MYRA Yes.

[*A pause.*]

2.2.205   Don't tell Pete, because I don't want to worry him. But Mr. Santos called me up this morning and said they decided they are not going to hold out any longer. They're going to put in a sound system right away.

WILLIS I'm sorry, what will you do now?

2.2.210   **MYRA** I don't know. I want to try to find a job here.

[PETE *has awakened* GERARD *and begins to lead him out to the phone.*]

WILLIS Don't despair – I learned that from my Mama. She used to say no matter how bad things look, Willis, we musn't despair. My Mama was a blessed woman. She had more than her share of troubles, God knows, but she never despaired. Never, never – as God is my witness she never despaired.   2.2.211

          2.2.215

[PETE *comes out.*]

MYRA Did you rouse him?

PETE Yes, Ma'am. Who wanted to talk to him?

MYRA His wife. She sounded very agitated.

WILLIS I'm moving out tonight. I'm staying with a friend I work with. Gladys is moving into my room. She spent the fifteen dollars I loaned her on clothes. The hotel won't let her stay on and I can't pay her bills there.   2.2.220

[GERARD *enters.*]

GERARD Myra, I went to see that talking picture *The Singing Fool* because you recommended it. I thought it was awful. I don't go to the motion pictures to be depressed. I like happy picture shows. Pete, who is your friend?   2.2.225

PETE This is Willis. Willis, this is my Dad.

WILLIS How do you do?

[*They shake hands.*]

GERARD I have to go back to Houston or there'll be no living with her whatsoever – she's on a real tear now. Accusing me now of being unfaithful with you, Myra. I guess the trip is really off now, Son.   2.2.230

PETE Yessir.

GERARD And I guess, too, I spoke too soon about your living with us. She said I had dreamed the whole thing up. I thought you liked the boy, I said. I do like him, she said, he's nice and polite, but our boys get jealous when I pay attention to him. She's just making all that up, of course, they are not jealous of anybody, she just changed her mind because she knew I wanted you there. Well, she may change her mind again.   2.2.235

          2.2.240

[*A pause. To* MYRA.]

I know you don't want my advice, but you're still an attractive woman. You should get married and have somebody take care of you. You're not getting any younger, you know.

[*To* WILLIS.]

Did you see that picture *The Singing Fool*?

2.2.245 WILLIS No, I sure didn't.

GERARD Don't waste your money. Unless you like being depressed. What was that song he sang after his boy died?

MYRA "Sonny Boy."

GERARD Oh, yes. How did it go?

2.2.250 MYRA I don't remember.

GERARD Jackie Kate said there ought to be a law against having picture shows like that that did nothing but get you upset and depressed.

[GLADYS *comes in. She carries a suitcase.*]

GLADYS I thought you were coming for me in your car?

2.2.255 WILLIS I said after supper, Gladys.

GLADYS After whose supper – I ate mine an hour ago, not that I had much. A tuna fish sandwich and a Coke was all I could afford.

GERARD How do you do? I'm Gerard Anderson. I'm Pete's

2.2.260 father.

GLADYS I'm Willis' wife. In name only it seems. He's smitten with somebody else.

GERARD Well, those things happen, unfortunately.

GLADYS Unfortunately. You still want a divorce, Willis?

2.2.265 WILLIS Yes.

GLADYS Well, you give me a thousand dollars and I'll give you one.

WILLIS I can't do that, Gladys. You know I can't afford that kind of money.

GLADYS You can't?

2.2.270 WILLIS No way in the world.

GLADYS Hell, I knew that before I asked you. What can you afford?

WILLIS Let me think about it?

GERARD Well, I'm going to have to go, folks. I have a long ride

2.2.275 ahead of me.

GLADYS Where are you going?

GERARD Houston.

GLADYS Houston, oh, you lucky thing. Do you live there?

GERARD Yes, I do. I have a fine new brick house and swimming

2.2.280 pool. Right in a lovely section of Houston.

GLADYS Oh, you lucky thing. How much can you afford,   2.2.281
Willis?

WILLIS I'm thinking.

GLADYS Seven-fifty.

WILLIS Well...   2.2.285

GLADYS Five hundred, two-fifty –

WILLIS I could afford a hundred –

GERARD Well, I'll be seeing you, goodbye now.

[*To* GLADYS.]

If you get to Houston look me up. Gerard Anderson, I'm in
the phone book.   2.2.290

GLADYS Oh, I will.

GERARD So long everybody.

PETE Goodbye, Papa.

GERARD So long, Son.

[GERARD *leaves.*]

GLADYS When can you get me the hundred dollars, Willis?   2.2.295

WILLIS By the end of next week –

GLADYS All right. You sure you can't make it a hundred and
fifty?

WILLIS No, I can't, Gladys.

GLADYS All right, will you take my suitcase up to your room   2.2.300
for me?

WILLIS I will.

GLADYS Where are you staying?

WILLIS With a friend.

[WILLIS *goes out.* GLADYS *follows after him.*]

PETE If the Jacksons move and sell their house, where will we   2.2.305
live, Mama?

MYRA We'll find some place.

PETE Mama –

MYRA Yes, Son.

PETE What if you can't get a job?   2.2.310

MYRA I'll find something.

PETE Mama –

MYRA Yes, Son.

PETE I'm scared.

MYRA You musn't be, Son, we're going to be all right.   2.2.315

[*She holds him.*]

2.2.316   You're awfully disappointed about your Daddy, aren't you?

PETE Well. I knew it wouldn't work out. Nothing ever does.

MYRA Don't say that, Son.

PETE Does it?

2.2.320   **MYRA** Sometimes –

PETE What –

MYRA Well –

PETE What –

MYRA Some things have worked out.

2.2.325   **PETE** Name me one.

[**WILLIS** *comes in.*]

WILLIS I'll be staying here tonight after all. Mr. Joplin loaned me twenty-five dollars to give Gladys on that hundred I promised her. She doesn't want to stay here. She wants to take the bus on into Houston. She says she wants to start divorce proceed-
2.2.330   ings in the morning. Well, I said, Gladys, I don't know if I can afford to give you your hundred dollars and start divorce proceedings at that same time. I may have to wait on that and save a little more money. Don't wait, she said, get the divorce first. You can pay me later.

[**GLADYS** *appears.*]

2.2.335   **GLADYS** Let's go.

WILLIS All right.

GLADYS So long, you all.

[**GLADYS** *goes out –* **WILLIS** *follows as the lights fade.*]

ACT 2, SCENE 3

[*The lights are brought up; it is a week later.* **KATIE BELL** *is in the house sitting on the couch. She has the paper* **ESTAQUIO** *left. It is "Rock of Ages" in Spanish. She is trying to learn the words.* **VESTA** *comes in and sits beside her.*]

2.3.1   **VESTA** Is that a letter?

KATIE BELL No.

VESTA What is it?

KATIE BELL I'm not going to tell you.

2.3.5   **VESTA** Why?

KATIE BELL Because I don't want to.

VESTA Let me see it.

KATIE BELL No.

[VESTA *tries to grab it out of* KATIE BELL's *hand.* KATIE BELL *goes out to the yard.* VESTA *goes offstage to the kitchen.* MYRA *enters and is addressed by* KATIE BELL.]

You've been looking for a job?

MYRA Yes. 2.3.10

KATIE BELL Any luck?

MYRA No, not yet.

KATIE BELL We've had some good news.

MYRA What's that?

KATIE BELL The man that bumped Daddy to get his job, has 2.3.15
changed his mind and he wants to stay where he is and so
we can stay on here.

MYRA Oh, that is wonderful, Katie Bell. I am so happy for you.

[VESTA *and* MRS. JACKSON *come out.*]

MRS. JACKSON Did Katie Bell tell you our news?

MYRA Yes, she did. I'm very happy for you. 2.3.20

VESTA And now Mama says I can take music lessons from you
if you stay on here.

MYRA That's nice. I would like that.

VESTA Are you going to stay on?

MYRA If I can find work. I've no luck so far. 2.3.25

VESTA When may I start my lessons?

MYRA As soon as you want.

VESTA Oh, grand.

KATIE BELL Are you going to the opening of the talking pictures
tonight? 2.3.30

MYRA Yes, Willis is taking me.

KATIE BELL I bet it will seem funny going there and not playing
the piano.

MYRA I expect it will.

MRS. JACKSON What will happen if you don't find a job here? 2.3.35

MYRA Then I will have to look for a job somewhere else.

[PETE *comes in with books.*]

KATIE BELL How is school?

[PETE *starts for his room.*]

PETE It's all right. I'm only taking one course. I wouldn't have to
take that, if we hadn't had to change schools so many times.

[MYRA *follows* PETE *into the living room.*]

MYRA It'll be behind you soon. 2.3.40

2.3.41 **PETE** Did you find a job?

MYRA No, not today –

KATIE BELL We don't have to leave. Papa is not bumped any longer.

2.3.45 **PETE** That's good.

[**MYRA** *goes out to the porch.* **PETE** *goes into his room.*]

VESTA Could I have a lesson on the piano now?

MYRA All right. Come on.

MRS. JACKSON We'd better make some business arrangements first – will you still be willing to teach in exchange for part of

2.3.50 your room rent?

MYRA Yes. Thank you.

MRS. JACKSON May Katie Bell and I watch the lessons?

MYRA Oh, yes.

[**VESTA** *and* **MYRA** *go into the house and to the piano.*]

KATIE BELL Mama, do you know what this is?

[**MRS. JACKSON** *looks at the paper.*]

2.3.55 **MRS. JACKSON** It doesn't look like anything I've ever seen.

KATIE BELL It's "Rock of Ages" in Spanish. Estaquio gave me the words and I'm learning to sing it. Want to hear me?

[**KATIE BELL** *starts to sing.* **VESTA** *calls from the living room.*]

VESTA Mama, are you coming?

[**MRS. JACKSON**, *to* **KATIE BELL**.]

MRS. JACKSON Maybe later.

[**MRS. JACKSON** *goes inside.* **KATIE BELL** *sits in the yard.*]

2.3.60 **VESTA** I am so nervous.

MYRA Now, don't be nervous. Now, you sit on the piano stool and I'll stand beside you. We'll start with some scales – now – let me explain the keyboard – This is middle C.

[**WILLIS** *comes in.*]

WILLIS Hi.

2.3.65 **KATIE BELL** Hi, Myra is giving Vesta a music lesson.

WILLIS I hear –

KATIE BELL And I'm learning to sing "Rock of Ages" in Spanish. We don't have to leave Harrison after all.

WILLIS You don't?

2.3.70 **KATIE BELL** No.

WILLIS Well, that's good news.

[**GLADYS** *and* **GERARD** *enter.*]

GLADYS Hey there, Willis.

GERARD Hello, Willis. Remember me?

WILLIS Sure. How are you?

[**PETE** *comes out of his room to his father.*]

GERARD Hi, Son.   2.3.75

PETE Hi.

GERARD I have some news for you. Jackie Kate and I have decided to split up. And I've fallen in love with this lady here. You remember her, don't you?

PETE Yessir.   2.3.80

GERARD We're on our way to Mexico to get our divorces so we can marry. I just wanted to stop by and give you the news myself.

GLADYS And it won't cost you a cent, Willis. Gerard's paying for the whole thing.   2.3.85

GERARD Every penny.

GLADYS The minute I laid eyes on him in this yard I knew we were made for each other. He said he felt the same way.

GERARD Yes I did.

GLADYS It was love at first sight.   2.3.90

GERARD Yes it was.

GLADYS Just like in the movies.

GERARD Just like in the movies I like.

KATIE BELL What kind of movies do you like?

GERARD Happy ones.   2.3.95

GLADYS That's the kind I like too.

KATIE BELL What's your favorite one?

GLADYS Oh I don't know. I like them all, as long as they have a happy ending.

GERARD Tell your Mama to come out.   2.3.100

[**PETE** *goes into his mother at the piano.*]

GLADYS I called him the minute I got into Houston and he was all alone because his wife had gone off and left him.

GERARD Took the boys, too. Said she was going to her Mama's in Louisiana and was never coming back.

GLADYS And she meant it, too. When he called her and told her   2.3.105
about wanting a divorce, she said go ahead and get it and see if she cared – so –

[**MYRA** *comes outside with* **PETE**.]

GERARD Myra, I took Gladys to see that picture show you told me and Jackie Kate to go see and she didn't like it any more than we did.

2.3.110

GLADYS Oh, no I couldn't stand it.

GERARD Gladys says she doesn't think talking pictures will last, but I think she's wrong about that.

GLADYS You do?

2.3.115 **GERARD** Yes, I do.

GLADYS Well, I just bet I am then, if you say so – Miss Myra, did you hear our news? We are going to Mexico so Gerard can divorce Jackie Kate and I can divorce Willis. Then we're going to Mexico City to be married. Isn't that just thrilling?

2.3.120 **GERARD** Of course I'm having to give Jackie Kate everything I've got except my truck to get her consent. She gets the house, the car, the swimming pool.

[**MRS. JACKSON** *and* **VESTA** *come out.*]

Well, folks, we're going to have to be on our way.

[*He goes to* **PETE**.]

So long, Son. I'll send you a postcard from Mexico.

[*He and* **GLADYS** *start out.*]

2.3.125 So long, everybody.

GLADYS So long –

[**GLADYS** *and* **GERARD** *leave.*]

MRS. JACKSON Now, who are they? I know I've seen them before but I can't place them.

WILLIS That's my wife and Myra's ex-husband and they're going

2.3.130 to Mexico to get a divorce so they can get married.

MRS. JACKSON Why are they going to Mexico?

WILLIS Because you can get a divorce there right away.

MRS. JACKSON Oh.

[*A train whistle blows.*]

VESTA That's Papa's train right on time. He'll be here before we

2.3.135 know it. Papa loves trains. He's said he loved them ever since he was a boy.

MRS. JACKSON No wonder. He grew up in Palestine.* All the Texas trains used to come through there. The L and N, the Southern Pacific, the Katy. He told me all he wanted ever to

2.3.140 do in this world was to work for the railroad. He was working for the L and N when I first met him.

Palestine · a town in East Texas

KATIE BELL And he's never had a wreck.

MRS. JACKSON No thank heavens. And I pray he never will.

[ESTAQUIO *comes in.*]

Why, Vesta, there's that little Mexican preacher boy. Good
afternoon, Son.   2.3.145

ESTAQUIO Good afternoon –

MRS. JACKSON Why, you're all out of breath.

ESTAQUIO Yes Ma'am.

MRS. JACKSON How's the church coming along?

ESTAQUIO Not too well – thank you Ma'am. Nobody came.   2.3.150

MRS. JACKSON Oh.

ESTAQUIO So my Papa says we have to go back to Mexico. We're
taking the bus to the border now.

MRS. JACKSON Oh, I'm sorry to hear that.

KATIE BELL I'm trying to learn "Rock of Ages" in Spanish. It's not   2.3.155
easy. Would you like to hear me sing what I have learned?

ESTAQUIO I don't have time. Our bus is leaving. If you ever get
to Mexico, please look me up.

KATIE BELL Where in Mexico?

ESTAQUIO I don't know yet. I'll send you a postcard.   2.3.160

[ESTAQUIO *leaves.*]

MRS. JACKSON Goodbye, Son.

[ESTAQUIO, *calling from offstage.*]

ESTAQUIO Goodbye.

KATIE BELL So long. Everybody's going to Mexico. I wish I
could go.

VESTA You'll never get to Mexico, so you can just put that out   2.3.165
of your head –

MRS. JACKSON Willis, did you ever hear that young man sing
"Rock of Ages" in Spanish?

WILLIS No.

MRS. JACKSON It was something. Wasn't it girls?   2.3.170

[*She starts to sing "Rock of Ages."*]

I'd better get supper started.

[*She goes offstage into the kitchen.*]

WILLIS Want to play catch, Pete?

PETE After I finish studying –

[PETE *starts for the house.* MYRA *goes to him.*]

MYRA Pete.

2.3.175 PETE I'm all right.

[*A pause.*]

I guess I'm going to have a new step Mama.

MYRA I guess so.

PETE Maybe I'll try to find me a job here after school.

[PETE *goes into the house.*]

KATIE BELL Are you all still going to the picture show tonight?

2.3.180 WILLIS I think so –

KATIE BELL Will you tell me the story tomorrow, Myra?

MYRA Yes, I will.

KATIE BELL I went by the picture show this afternoon. They
were trying out the sound inside and you could hear it as
2.3.185 you went by.

[MR. JACKSON *comes in. He seems very dejected.*]

VESTA Papa, what is it? You look upset

MR. JACKSON Where's your Mother?

VESTA Inside – what is it, Papa?

MR. JACKSON That fool engineer has changed his mind again
2.3.190 and I'm being bumped after all.

VESTA Oh, Papa –

[MR. JACKSON *goes in;* VESTA *and* KATIE BELL *follow after him.*]

MYRA Oh, isn't that too bad?

WILLIS Well, maybe that engineer will change his mind again.

MYRA I hope he does.

2.3.195 WILLIS I hope Gerard and Gladys don't change their minds, and
if they don't I'm going to be free next week to ask you to marry
me. Will you marry me?

MYRA Yes I will.

[KATIE BELL *comes out of the house.*]

How did your Mother take the news?

2.3.200 KATIE BELL She was upset at first, but she's all right.

[*A pause.*]

Myra, one of my friends said she saw *Peter Pan* with an actress
named Betty Bronson. Did you see that?

MYRA Yes.

KATIE BELL And she said she has never heard of Betty Bronson
2.3.205 since. And she wondered whatever became of her. And I told
her I would ask you as you know all about the movies and
movie stars.

MYRA Well, I'm sorry I don't know.

[KATIE BELL *begins trying to sing half to herself in Spanish "Rock of Ages." She finds the words difficult.*]

WILLIS Is that Spanish?

KATIE BELL Yes. "Rock of Ages." 2.3.210

[KATIE BELL *continues singing half to herself, then pauses.*]

Would you ever like to go to Mexico?

WILLIS Oh, I don't know.

[MYRA, *calling to* PETE.]

MYRA When you finish your studying, come sit with us, Son. It's cooler out here.

KATIE BELL How far is it to Mexico? 2.3.215

WILLIS Depending on where you're going.

[KATIE BELL *continues singing.* PETE *comes out and sits.*]

MYRA Get your studying done?

PETE I've got a little bit more.

[WILLIS, *calling to* KATIE BELL.]

WILLIS That's Spanish, Pete.

PETE I know. 2.3.220

KATIE BELL The name of the picture tonight is *Wonder* with Richard Barthelmes, Lila Lee, and Betty Compson.

MYRA I know.

[KATIE BELL *goes back to learning the words of "Rock of Ages."*]

PETE I'm going to go downtown and get something to eat.

MYRA Do you have any money? 2.3.225

PETE Yes.

[PETE *leaves.*]

MYRA Well, I'd better get ready for tonight.

WILLIS I had too.

[*They leave.* KATIE BELL *continues to learn the words for a beat.*]

KATIE BELL I bet I get to Mexico one day.

[*She continues the song as the lights fade.*]

Selected Themes

OTHERNESS & ETHICS

ENVIRONMENT, NATURE, & SACRAMENTALISM

NONFICTION

FICTION

POETRY

EPIPHANY, DISCOVERY, & IDENTITY

NONFICTION

THE MYSTERY OF EVIL & THE SEARCH FOR GOD

DRAMA

Permissions

743

DARRYL L. TIPPENS is Provost and Professor of English at Pepperdine University, where he teaches courses in medieval and early modern literature. Before coming to Pepperdine University in 2001, he taught at Abilene Christian University for many years, where he was James W. Culp Professor of English literature. Dr. Tippens earned the MA and PhD in English literature at Louisiana State University. He has published scholarly articles on Shakespeare, Milton, the Bible as literature, literary theory, and the works of Walter McDonald. He has published numerous essays on religion, spirituality, popular culture, and film. He is associate editor of *Explorations in Renaissance Culture*.

✦ ✦ ✦

JEANNE MURRAY WALKER is Professor of English at The University of Delaware, where she teaches courses in the English Renaissance, as well as script and poetry writing. Her PhD is from The University of Pennsylvania. She travels widely to do readings and teach workshops at universities and writing conferences. For twenty years she served as Poetry Editor for *Christianity and Literature* and she currently sits on the Board of *Shenandoah*. The author of six books of poetry, including *Coming Into History* and *A Deed To the Light*, she also writes essays and scripts for the theatre. Among honors for her work, she holds an NEA Fellowship in the Arts and a Pew Fellowship, and her poetry has appeared on busses and trains with *Poetry in Motion*.

✦ ✦ ✦

STEPHEN WEATHERS is Associate Professor of English at Abilene Christian University. Having earned the PhD at Florida State University in 1999, he currently teaches a broad range of courses in American, British, and World literatures. His creative writing has appeared in a number of literary journals including the *Concho River Review*, *Image: A Journal of the Arts & Religion*, and *American Short Fiction*, and it has garnered prizes in competition.